T0181999

Lecture Notes of the Institute for Computer Sciences, Social Informatics and Telecommunications Engineering 508

The LNICST series publishes ICST's conferences, symposia and workshops.
LNICST reports state-of-the-art results in areas related to the scope of the Institute.
The type of material published includes

- Proceedings (published in time for the respective event)
- Other edited monographs (such as project reports or invited volumes)

LNICST topics span the following areas:

- General Computer Science
- E-Economy
- E-Medicine
- Knowledge Management
- Multimedia
- Operations, Management and Policy
- Social Informatics
- Systems

Sanjay Goel · Pavel Gladyshev ·
Akatyev Nikolay · George Markowsky ·
Daryl Johnson
Editors

Digital Forensics and Cyber Crime

13th EAI International Conference, ICDF2C 2022
Boston, MA, November 16–18, 2022
Proceedings

 Springer

Editors
Sanjay Goel
University at Albany
Albany, NY, USA

Akatyev Nikolay
Horangi Cyber Security
Singapore, Singapore

Daryl Johnson
Rochester Institute of Technology
Rochester, NY, USA

Pavel Gladyshev
University College Dublin
Dublin, Ireland

George Markowsky
Missouri University of Science
and Technology
Rolla, MO, USA

ISSN 1867-8211 ISSN 1867-822X (electronic)
Lecture Notes of the Institute for Computer Sciences, Social Informatics
and Telecommunications Engineering
ISBN 978-3-031-36573-7 ISBN 978-3-031-36574-4 (eBook)
https://doi.org/10.1007/978-3-031-36574-4

© ICST Institute for Computer Sciences, Social Informatics and Telecommunications Engineering 2023

This Springer imprint is published by the registered company Springer Nature Switzerland AG
The registered company address is: Gewerbestrasse 11, 6330 Cham, Switzerland

Preface

We are delighted to introduce the proceedings of the 13th edition of the European Alliance for Innovation (EAI) International Conference on Digital Forensics and Cyber Crime (ICDF2C). This conference brought together researchers and practitioners around the world who are developing and using digital forensic technologies and techniques for a variety of applications in criminal investigations, incident response and broader information security. In line with last year's edition, the focus of ICDF2C 2022 was on various applications of digital evidence and forensics beyond "traditional" cyber-crime investigations and litigation.

The technical program of ICDF2C 2021 consisted of 28 full papers presented over three days at the main conference track. Aside from the high-quality technical paper presentations, the technical program also featured a keynote speech and two technical workshops. The keynote speech was given by Lee Sult, co-founder of Horangi Cyber Security. The two workshops organized were Password Cracking and Rainbow Tables by George Markowsky, and Secret Powers of Yara by Vitaly Kamluk, the head of Kaspersky APAC Threat Research Team.

Coordination with EAI was essential for the success of the conference. We sincerely appreciate their constant support and guidance. We are grateful to Conference Manager Radka Vasileiadis, Managing Editor Patrícia Gabajová, and all the authors who submitted their papers to the ICDF2C 2021 conference.

Pavel Gladyshev
Sanjay Goel
Nikolay Akatyev
George Markowsky
Daryl Johnson

Organization

Steering Committee

Imrich Chlamtac   University of Trento, Italy
Sanjay Goel   University at Albany, SUNY, USA

Organizing Committee

General Chair

Sanjay Goel   University at Albany, SUNY, USA

General Co-chair

Pavel Gladyshev   University College Dublin, Ireland

TPC Chair and Co-chairs

Nikolay Akatyev   Horangi Cyber Security, Singapore
Daryl Johnson   Rochester Institute of Technology, State University of New York, USA
George Markowsky   Missouri University of Science & Technology, USA

Sponsorship and Exhibit Chair

Nikolay Akatyev   Horangi Cyber Security, Singapore

Local Chair

Sanjay Goel   University at Albany, SUNY, USA

Workshops Chair

Paulo Roberto Nunes de Souza   Federal University of Espírito Santo, Brazil

Publications Chair

Xiaoyu Du   University College Dublin, Ireland

Web Chair

Pavel Gladyshev   University College Dublin, Ireland

Technical Program Committee

Ahmed Hamza	Rochester Institute of Technology, USA
Anca Delia Jurcut	University College Dublin, Ireland
Anthony Cheuk Tung Lai	VX Research Limited, China
Ding Wang	Nankai University, China
Daryl Johnson	Rochester Institute of Technology, State University of New York, USA
Fahim Khan	University of Tokyo, Japan
Farkhund Iqbal	Zayed University, UAE
Francis Newbonyi	University College Dublin, Ireland
Glenn Dardick	Longwood University, USA
George Markowsky	Missouri University of Science & Technology, USA
John Sheppard	Waterford Institute of Technology, Ireland
M. P. Gupta	Indian Institute of Technology Delhi, India
Vivienne Mee	VMGroup, Ireland
Mengjun Xie	University of Tennessee at Chattanooga, USA
Nhien An Le Khac	University College Dublin, Ireland
Nickkisha Farrell	Concordia University of Edmonton, Canada
Nikolay Akatyev	Horangi Cyber Security, Singapore
Omid Mirzaei	Elastic, USA
Pavel Gladyshev	University College Dublin, Ireland
Pavol Zavarsky	Concordia University College of Alberta, Canada
Pradeep Atrey	University at Albany, SUNY, USA
Prakash G.	Amrita Vishwa Vidyapeetham University, India
Sai Mounika Errapotu	University of Texas at El Paso, USA
Seungjoo Kim	Korea University, South Korea
Shaikh Akib Shahriyar	Rochester Institute of Technology, USA
Spiridon Bakiras	Hamad Bin Khalifa University, Qatar
Stig Mjolsnes	NTNU, Norway
Umit Karabiyik	Purdue University, USA
Vinod Bhattathiripad	G J Software Forensics, India

Xianzhi Wang   University of Technology Sydney, Australia
Xiaochun Cheng   Middlesex University London, UK
Xiaoyu Du   University College Dublin, Ireland

Contents

Privacy and Security

Image Forensics

Image-to-Image Translation Generative Adversarial Networks for Video Source Camera Falsification

Maryna Veksler[1](✉), Clara Caspard[2], and Kemal Akkaya[1]

[1] Florida International University, Miami, FL 33174, USA
{mveks001,kakkaya}@fiu.edu
[2] Pomona College, Claremont, CA 91711, USA
cfcb2020@mymail.pomona.edu

Abstract. The emerging usage of multimedia devices led to a burst in criminal cases where digital forensics investigations are needed. This necessitate development of accurate digital forensic techniques which require not only the confirmation of the data integrity but also the verification of its origin source. To this end, machine and/or deep learning techniques are widely being employed within forensics tools. Nevertheless, while these techniques became an efficient tool for the forensic investigators, they also provided the attackers with novel methods for the data and source falsification. In this paper, we propose a simple and effective anti-forensics attack that uses generative adversarial networks (GANs) to compromise the video's camera source traces. In our approach, we adopt the popular image-to-image translation GANs to fool the existing algorithms for video source camera identification. Our experimental results demonstrate that the proposed attack can be implemented to successfully compromise the existing forensic methods with 100% probability for non-flat videos while producing the high quality content. The results indicate the need for attack-prone video source camera identification forensics approaches.

Keywords: Generative Adversarial Networks (GANs) · Multimedia forensics · Video Source Identification · Machine learning

1 Introduction

The rapid increase of Internet of Things (IoT) technologies triggered a massive impact on the digital forensics field due to the heavy involvement of such devices in crime science applications. Specifically, the popularity of multimedia content generated by various IoT devices such as phones, body cameras, drones, vehicles, etc. for information sharing and storage caused the forensics investigators to develop techniques that will enable thorough data validation and analysis [10]. At the same time, the improvements in machine learning (ML) and artificial

© ICST Institute for Computer Sciences, Social Informatics and Telecommunications Engineering 2023
Published by Springer Nature Switzerland AG 2023. All Rights Reserved
S. Goel et al. (Eds.): ICDF2C 2022, LNICST 508, pp. 3–18, 2023.
https://doi.org/10.1007/978-3-031-36574-4_1

intelligence (AI) algorithms provided criminals with sophisticated tools for media content alteration and forgeries [12, 22, 30].

One example use case where forgeries can be employed is multimedia forensics where one of the major problems is the identification of the source camera to validate the data origin. Given that identifying a video emerging from a specific device belonging to a victim or suspect might be crucial for the digital forensics investigation, it is vital to identify the source camera with high precision. Researchers developed numerous techniques aimed to determine the model of the camera devices used for image and video recording, based on the noiseprints introduced by the source camera. Proven to be unique, the camera noiseprints are the result of insignificant manufacturing defects present on camera lenses and can be extracted using statistical analysis [6, 15] and deep learning (DL) [32] approaches.

These techniques, however, can be compromised by the attacker deploying various anti-forensics techniques [13, 21, 24, 29] to disrupt the camera identification process. Thus, researchers and investigators require a comprehensive knowledge of anti-forensics to understand the weaknesses of the existing methods and incorporate the appropriate protection mechanisms [5, 27, 38].

One approach to fool video source camera identification techniques is to deploy a DL framework called *generative adversarial network* (GAN) to generate data that mimics camera-specific noise. GANs have become popular within the last several years with many applications [1–3, 36]. In the context of video source camera identification, criminals might aim to generate fake videos as if these are coming from the phone camera of a specific victim. However, the existing GANs for source camera falsification mostly target images omitting the video content, as the latter requires complex processing of various elements (e.g., sequence of the video frames, bit-rate, and audio stream). Moreover, despite the wide variety of the video GANs [4] (i.e., generating fake videos based on the given input conditions), there is no demonstration of the GAN used to falsify video source camera origin.

In this paper, we explore the effectiveness of using GANs for the source camera origin falsification and the resistance of the existing video source camera identification (VSI) techniques against fake data. Specifically, we select a pre-trained video source camera identification framework proposed in [32] as a forensic classifier. Our choice of the VSI network is justified by its high accuracy compared to the other existing methods. Due to the complexity of the video streams, and the fact that most of the VSI approaches are applied to the patches extracted from the video frames, we apply the GANs on the patches directly. Therefore, we demonstrate that the adversary may fool the VSI networks by manipulating the selected patch data and does not require generating realistic video footage. Furthermore, we adopt the popular open-source image-to-image translation GANs to implement video source falsification techniques. Thus, we indicate that the video source falsification attack can be implemented given limited resources. Specifically, we select CycleGAN to generate fake data for two distinct video source cameras and then use the trained networks to generate the falsified video data for both devices.

We conducted a series of experiments to (1) assess the ability of GANs to trick the video source identification framework and (2) identify the performance of the VSI network in adversarial settings. The results demonstrate that Cycle-GAN can successfully fool the video source camera classifier with 66% and 100% probability for video content of any and non-flat types respectively. Moreover, the generated data preserves the original content, indicating that the accuracy of the selected VSI network is not affected by the objects present in the video.

The rest of the paper is organized as follows. First, we present the review of related work in Sect. 2. In Sect. 3 we provide the background on implemented video source camera identification model and GAN architecture, followed by the description of our methodology in Sect. 4. In Sect. 5, we describe the experimental results and summarize the key outcomes. Finally, we present the conclusions and highlight some future work in Sect. 6.

2   Related Work

The applications of multimedia GANs widely vary from improving the quality of scientific datasets [3] and entertainment development [1] to protecting users' privacy [36], and can be used to compromise forensics analysis of the data, such as source camera identification [7] and facial recognition [33]. These networks can be used to compromise the forensic analysis of the data.

General Applications of Multimedia GANs. The existing video GANs can be grouped into three distinct categories based on their architecture. The first type of video GANs uses recurrent neural networks (RNN) architectures to analyze time-series data and produce the final video via temporal correlations [34]. Tulyakov et al. [31] designed a Motion Content GAN that derives the fake video by mapping random vector sequences to the video frames sequences, where each random vector consists of content and motion parts. The second category of video GANs is referred to as progressive video GANs which generate frames first, and then another generator is used to convert frames into the video [14,23]. Finally, video GANs with two-stream architecture analyze different aspects of video and its frames. The video GAN developed in [35], contains two independent generator streams for background and foreground content. The results of these generators are then combined via a motion pathway mask to produce a short video.

Forensics Applications for Multimedia GANs. In the multimedia forensics field, the GANs can be used to disrupt the data analysis or to impose the modified data as authentic. In [25], the authors developed a BDC-GAN for bi-directional conversion between computer-generated and natural images, which allows bypassing the majority of existing forensic detectors. Zou et al. [38] applied GANs, which improves the image quality while staying undetected by the methods of contrast enhancement detection.

The recent work attempt to use GANs as a means to disrupt the forensics approaches for multimedia source camera detection. However, it primarily targets the image data omitting complex video content. Chen et al. [8] designed an image source falsification GAN based on the Convolution Neural Network (CNN) architecture. In [9], the authors introduce a new component into the traditional GAN architecture, called the embedding network. This network is used to extract the camera noiseprint feature vector, that provides feedback to the generator based on the loss between falsified and real source camera images.

Difference from Existing Work. Unlike previous works, we focus on video forgeries that target video source camera identification frameworks. Therefore, our main aim is to replicate the insignificant noise traces unique to the camera device rather than the video contents. We develop a simple GAN attack on the VSI forensics techniques that can be implemented at a low resource and effort cost. We further transferred the video source camera falsification problem to the image level by applying the GAN directly to the patches extracted from the video frames. To the best of our knowledge, it is the first work to implement GAN-based anti-forensics video source camera falsification.

3   Background

In this section, we provide details about video source camera identification and the structure of GANs.

3.1   Video Source Camera Identification Network

Video source camera identification helps us identify the genuine source of an existing video among various cameras as shown in Fig. 1. The majority of the recent approaches use DL-based Convolutional Neural Networks (CNN) to extract the device-specific noiseprint across the set of videos [11, 18, 26, 32]. Before being analyzed by CNN networks, the video data is processed such that the video intra-coded or I-frames are extracted and often split into patches of smaller size. For our implementation, we selected a recent video source camera identification approach developed in [32] as a benchmark since it is proven to achieve higher classification accuracy compared to other systems. The proposed network consists of four independent CNNs, where each extracts noiseprint from one of four non-overlapping quadrants of the video I-frames.

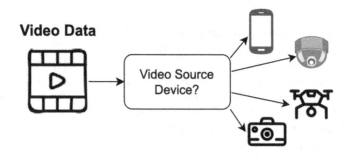

Fig. 1. Diagram illustrating video source camera identification process.

The video source camera is identified as follows. First, 15 I-frames are extracted from the video under the investigation, followed by dividing each frame into four non-overlapping patches of 128×128 size. Next, homogeneous patches are selected from each quadrant based on the standard deviation of the quadrant data. This techniques allows to determine the patches that may contain camera specific noise, while excluding the patches with needless amount of foreground content. Then, 4 pre-trained CNNs are used to identify the patches from different quadrant of the same video frame. The final stage of the ensemble CNNs utilizes average voting to aggregate the base learner CNN predictions for quadrant patches, followed by the majority voting to obtain video source camera prediction. The average voting produce the ensemble output vector representing the camera source prediction for the frame. After collecting the ensemble prediction for all video frames, the majority voting technique is applied to determine the video source camera label.

3.2   Generative Adversarial Networks (GANs)

First proposed in 2014 [17], generative adversarial networks (GANs) established a new category of DL algorithms. The capability to generate a realistic and highly accurate data from various domains such as text, images, video, and statistical measurements, triggered the wide adaptation of GANs in the industry and academia. Compared to other generative algorithms, GANs provides an efficient way to train the generator using a game theory principles, two-player zero-sum minimax game. Specifically, the GAN consists of two sub-models, referred to as a generator model trained to generate a new data and a discriminator model used to classify the data as either real or fake. These sub-models are set against each other with a simple goal to outperform the opponent. At the same time, the gain and loss are exactly balanced between the generator and discriminator, attempting to reach the total of zero utilization. The analogy of the process can be drawn by comparing the generator model to a counterfeiter who tries to create fake banking checks while the discriminator model is the authorities trying to accurately pick out those counterfeit checks.

Based on the unsupervised learning algorithm, GANs do not require a labeled or pre-processed dataset to generalize the data. Rather, the network attempts to devise the new samples by interpreting the feedback from the discriminator. The GANs are trained by taking any random type of input and generating a new data similar to the real samples provided to the discriminator.

The architecture of GAN sub-models is highly flexible and depends solely on the input data type. Moreover, the discriminator can be represented by any type of the classifier suited for the data type produced by the generator. Therefore, multimedia GANs usually implement CNN networks as a generative sub-model. On the other hand, the generator architecture is generally either that of the neural network (NN) or the CNN depending on the complexity of the task. However, most of the multimedia GANs employ the CNN architecture to either generate synthetic samples from a random noise or translate data from one domain to another. Figure 2 illustrates the generic architecture of an image GAN.

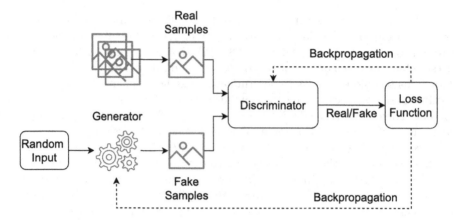

Fig. 2. General setup for GANs architecture and training.

4   Methodology

The goal of our work is to explore the viability of an anti-forensic attack against the video source camera identification method. Therefore, we define three primary objectives as follows:

- The GAN content should disrupt the accuracy of the video source camera identification framework;
- The GAN generator should mimic a specific video source camera noiseprint;
- The GAN data should look realistic and contain no visible artifacts of modifications.

To this end, we propose implementing the image-to-image translation GAN for video source camera falsification via applying the network to the patches extracted from the video frames as detailed below.

4.1   Selecting GAN Network

When selecting the optimal GAN architecture, we focused on the networks that can be easily implemented and do not require extensive knowledge of the video source camera identification framework. Moreover, since most of the existing video source camera identification mechanisms, including the one described in Sect. 3, often operate on video frames' patches of the sizes between 128×128 and 512×512, the GAN should be oriented toward generating smaller-sized images.

We examined various types of GAN architectures such as conditional GAN (CGAN) [16], progressive GAN [20], and image-to-image translation [19]. First, we rejected the CGAN architectures, as our objectives were not concerned with labels-based targeted image generation. Next, we eliminated progressive GANs since their primary goal is the generation of high-resolution images and the progressive GAN requires a large amount of computational power. Therefore, it contradicts two of our goals; minimizing the complexity of the architecture and producing fake images with lower resolution.

As a result, we decided to pick the image-to-image translation (I2IT) GAN approach as the backbone of our method. Specifically, we selected the CycleGAN [37] architecture since, unlike traditional I2IT GANs, it does not require the pre-determined pairing of the images from the opposite domains. Rather, the image pairs are detected automatically, which significantly reduces the pre-processing time. Thus, we can train the network on the limited data set with the indirectly correlating samples. Moreover, as CycleGAN is designed to operate on images with size 128 × 128 pixels in either three-channel (RGB) or gray-scale domains, its architecture does not require significant modifications when used for video source camera falsification.

4.2   GAN Architecture

CycleGAN consists of two generators and two discriminators sub-models. It accepts as an input a pair of images from two different domains, A and B, and transforms them into the data of the opposite domain. Figure 3 illustrates the architectural overview of both networks. Specifically, *generator AB* accepts the samples from Domain A and translates them into the Domain B. Next, *discriminator B* is used to classify the real and newly generated fake samples of the Domain B. At the same time, *generator BA* converts samples from Domain B to Domain A, with subsequent *discriminator A* as a classifier.

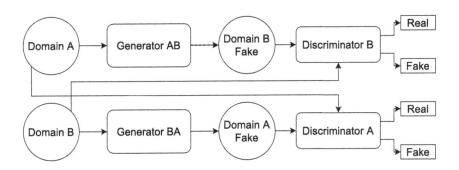

Fig. 3. Overview of the CycleGAN Architecture.

Generator. The inner architecture of the CycleGAN generator is given in Fig. 4. It consists of two phases down-sampling and up-sampling. First, the original image is downsampled by applying four convolutional layers with a stride 2 (i.e., the filters are advancing by the step of two pixels). After each convolutional layers, we apply LeakyReLU activation Ⓐ followed by the Instance Normalization Ⓝ. We select Instance Normalization instead of Batch Normalization, as it allows us to normalize each sample independently instead of generalizing across multiple samples.

During the up-sampling process, the output of the previous layer passes through the *Up Sampling Block*, which consists of the simple UpSampling2D layer followed by the convolutional and instance normalization layers. Then the output of the *Up Sampling Block* is concatenated with the output of the corresponding downsampling convolutional layer. As a result, the generators produce an image of the same size as the Input layer.

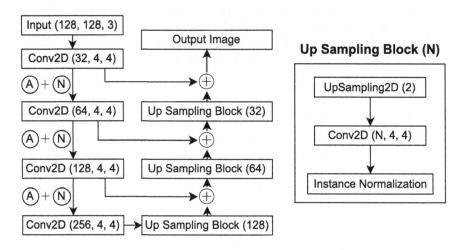

Fig. 4. CycleGAN Generator Architecture.

Discriminator. We select a simple discriminator architecture that consists of an input layer of the size $3 \times 128 \times 128$, four consecutive residual blocks, and an output layer. Each of the residual blocks contains a 2D Convolution layer, followed by LeakyReLU activation, and instance normalization. The first convolutional layer applies 64 filters of kernel size 4×4, while each consecutive convolution doubles the filter size. The design of the discriminator is driven by (1) a low number of convolutional layers to increase processing time and (2) high accuracy for images classification.

Loss Function. We used two types of loss functions, adversarial and cycle consistency. The adversarial loss is calculated using the mean square error (MSE) function and reflects the generators' attempts to successfully "fool" the discriminators. On the other hand, the cycle consistency, calculated as a mean absolute error (MAE) value, not only reflects the likelyhood of the generated data to be of the given domain but also asses the probability of the generators' input and output images to look the same. The CycleGAN uses a single cycle consistency loss to assess the performance of both generators. During the training process, the main objective of the GAN generators is to minimize the cycle-consistency loss.

5   Evaluation Results

We implemented the CycleGAN using Python scripting language to evaluate its effectiveness for video source camera falsification. Specifically, we selected the framework proposed in [32] as a benchmark for video source camera identification (VSI) and tested our hypothesis for the video content of two distinct phone models. During the experiments, we assessed the efficacy of the proposed approach based on:

- the requirements and limitations of the approach;
- the presence of the artifacts in the GAN generated data;
- the ability of the GAN-generated content to disrupt the functionality of the VSI framework and mimic specific video camera noise prints;
- the performance of the VSI network.

5.1   Dataset

We used the open-source VISION dataset [28] designed for multimedia forensics investigations to obtain the videos for our work. Specifically, we selected three phones of distinct models - Huawei P9, Apple iPhone 6, and Samsung Galaxy S5. For each device, we picked three types of videos containing flat, indoor, and outdoor scene content.

For each content type, we selected natively recorded videos and their corresponding WhatsApp and YouTube processed versions. This totaled to nine distinct video types per device. Therefore, for each device we selected 19 native videos, such that each video has its corresponding WhatsApp and YouTube version, resulting in a total of 57 videos per phone model. This collection of data provided us with adequately varied media content to train and test both GAN and VSI models. To train our GAN and VSI models, we split the dataset into training and test sets with a ratio of 70:30. As a result, we ended up with 18 test videos per device. To further prepare the dataset, we split each video into I-frames, subsequently divided into four non-overlapping quadrants. From each quadrant, we extracted 128×128 pixels patches, so that each video in our dataset was reduced to a series of a few thousand patches of images belonging to a certain area of the full frame at one specific moment of the video. Figure 5 demonstrates a complete process of video decomposition into the patches.

5.2   Experiments

Requirements and Limitations: We simplify the complex video generation problem by applying the transformation for video frame patches directly to implement the CycleGAN for video source camera falsification. To successfully train CycleGAN for falsification of the particular video camera source, the adversary should have access to the data from both the original and target devices. Nonetheless, if the main goal is to simply hide the fingerprints of the video camera source origin, the adversary only needs access to the original video and the

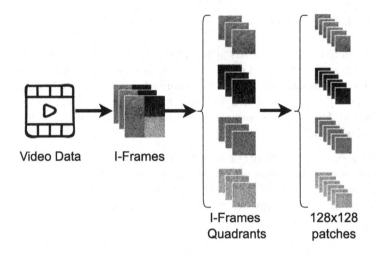

Fig. 5. Decomposition of the videos into 128×128 patches.

data from a set of random devices. In this case, the CycleGAN generators will change the trace of the source camera by overlapping them with information from other devices.

System Setup: The setup of our experiment consisted of two phases. First, we reproduced the ensemble CNNs framework [32] as a baseline for VSI process. We trained the network to classify three distinct devices and achieved the accuracy of 95.6% for patch level classification, resulting in all test videos to be classified correctly.

Next, we trained our GANs. We designed four independent CycleGANs corresponding to the data obtained from the four non-overlapping video frame quadrants. Unlike for VSI framework, we trained GANs using only Apple iPhone 6 and Samsung Galaxy S5 data, which corresponded to Domain A and Domain B. As a result, each GAN produced 2 distinct generators for Apple-to-Samsung and Samsung-to-Apple patch conversion. Figure 6 illustrates the flow of our experimental setup to impose the video data originating from an Apple device as belonging to the Samsung.

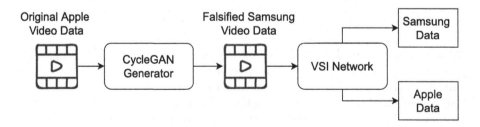

Fig. 6. The flow of the experimental setup for the video source camera falsification.

We used an Adam optimizer for the CycleGAN discriminators and generators with a learning rate set to 2e−4 and the exponential decay rate of 0.5. We conducted multiple rounds of experiments to determine the optimal settings for both networks that allow to achieve high network stability while minimizing the network training time. According to our tests, the network reaches the optimal performance with a batch size of 1 used to train the model for 15 epochs.

While we used a test dataset to evaluate the accuracy of the video source camera identification framework, the same test data was used as an input to the trained CycleGAN generators. This approach ensured that the generated video data have remains unknown to the source camera identification framework during the training stage. From each GAN architecture, we obtained a generator trained to translate Apple data into Samsung data, and a generator with the opposite function. Therefore, we trained eight CycleGAN generators in total.

Experimental Results: We conducted a total of two experiments. First, we used Samsung-to-Apple (S2A) generators to test the VSI network's ability to correctly classify CycleGAN-modified Samsung video data. Table 1 indicates the percentage of the videos classified as originating from one of the three devices. The results indicate that the VSI network successfully identified all of the fake video data as belonging to the correct origin device - Samsung Galaxy S5. Therefore, the S2A CycleGAN generator failed to fool the VSI network.

Table 1. The results of the VSI network for the data generated using the S2A Cycle-GAN generator (i.e., actual video data source is Samsung, fake video is generated as if this is from Apple), indicate the percentage of the videos identified originating from a given device.

	Huawei	Apple	Samsung
Flat videos	0.0%	**0.0%**	*100.00%*
Indoor videos	0.0%	**0.0%**	*100.00%*
Outdoor videos	0.0%	**0.0%**	*100.00%*

For the second experiment, we generated a new batch of video data using the Apple-to-Samsung (A2S) generator. The results of the VSI classification for the CycleGAN data are represented in Table 2. Unlike in the first experiment, the A2S generator achieved high success in imposing indoor and outdoor types of Apple video content as originating from the Samsung device. At the same time, VSI system was able to correctly identify the origin device for faked data containing flat scenes.

Artifacts Indicating the GAN Processing: One of the most important features of the GAN network when applied as an anti-forensics technique is its ability to hide the presence of artificial modification. Figure 7 illustrates video patches generated by CycleGAN generators. When analyzing the visible modification traces present, the video patches produced by both SA and AS generators

Table 2. The results of the VSI network for the data generated using the A2S Cycle-GAN generator (i.e., actual video data source is Apple, fake video is generated as if this is from Samsung), indicate the percentage of the videos identified originating from a given device

	Huawei	Apple	Samsung
Flat videos	0.0%	*100.00%*	**0.0%**
Indoor videos	0.0%	*0.0%*	**100.00%**
Outdoor videos	0.0%	*0.0%*	**100.00%**

have a pixelization noise. Nonetheless, the CycleGAN was able to mostly preserve the content of the original data. The main visual artifact which give away the manipulation appearance of intensified red and green pixelized lines as a content overlay.

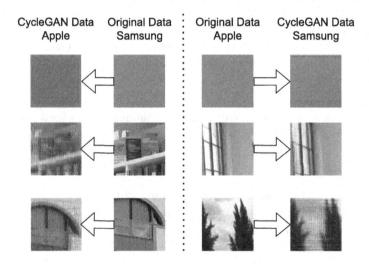

Fig. 7. The example of patches generated by CycleGAN for three types of video data based on the content - flat (top), indoor (middle), and outdoor(bottom). Left side: video patches produced by SA generator. Right side: video patches produced by AS generator.

CycleGAN Performance: Our experiments demonstrated that CycleGAN architectures can be successfully applied as an anti-forensics approach for video source camera identification. However, the results vary depending on the type of the original device and its content. While trained together using the same amount of training data and same setup, two generators exhibit very different results. Specifically, the SA generators failed to fool or partially disrupt the VSI network classification accuracy. On the contrary, the AS generator was able to successfully falsify the video source camera for the videos containing indoor and outdoor content. Analyzing the realisticity of the data, CycleGAN generators successfully produced patches closely reflecting the original content. However, the resulting fake data contained noise artifacts which present a strong evidence to claim data manipulation. While these traces can be recognized during the manual analysis, it does not seem to influence the performance of VSI network specifically. Moreover, as a patch represents a smaller part of the video frame, it will not be recognized by a human eye easily.

VSI Network Performance: According to our analysis, the VSI network accuracy was partially affected by the proposed video source camera falsification attack. The network appears to recognize the original traces of the Samsung device better than the Apple device. Since for both cases, the content of fake data was close to the original with the visible noise artifacts present, we conclude that the network (1) does not consider the video content during the identification process and focuses on the source device fingerprints and (2) artificial noises do not have a direct impact on the system classification ability. Consequently, the outcome of this research indicates that a detailed analysis of the factors causing a given VSI network to recognize the traces of one source device better than the other is needed.

6   Conclusion and Future Work

In this work, we implemented the CycleGAN as the anti-forensics video source falsification technique and evaluated the resistance of the VSI ensemble CNNs framework against the adversarial attacks. Our results indicate that CycleGAN can be successfully applied to falsify the traces of video source device with the probability of 100% for the videos containing indoor or outdoor content. We also identify that CycleGAN generators do not have the same probability for the successful video source camera falsification, caused either by (1) flaws in the GAN or (2) VSI network inability to recognize the fingerprints of the video source camera with the equal precision. At the same time, our experiments indicate that the tested ensemble CNNs do not consider the visual video content when determining the video camera origin, while also is not disturbed by artificial noises.

For future work, we will focus on improving the performance of the GAN generators, via modifying the GAN architecture such that the content does not contain visible artifacts. Furthermore, we will explore the approaches to produce the complete video sequence with modified video source camera noiseprints. Finally, we will conduct an extensive analysis to identify the causes of the unequal performance of VSI and GAN networks for different device models.

Acknowledgements. Research was sponsored by the Army Research Office and was accomplished under Grant Number W911NF-21-1-0264. The views and conclusions contained in this document are those of the authors and should not be interpreted as representing the official policies, either expressed or implied, of the Army Research

Office or the U.S. Government. The U.S. Government is authorized to reproduce and distribute reprints for Government purposes notwithstanding any copyright notation herein.

References

1. Auto-painter: cartoon image generation from sketch by using conditional Wasserstein generative adversarial networks. Neurocomputing **311**, 78–87 (2018). https://doi.org/10.1016/j.neucom.2018.05.045
2. GANs for medical image analysis. Artif. Intell. Med. **109**, 101938 (2020). https://doi.org/10.1016/j.artmed.2020.101938
3. Super-resolution using GANs for medical imaging. Proc. Comput. Sci. **173**, 28–35 (2020). https://doi.org/10.1016/j.procs.2020.06.005. International Conference on Smart Sustainable Intelligent Computing and Applications Under ICITETM 2020
4. Aldausari, N., Sowmya, A., Marcus, N., Mohammadi, G.: Video generative adversarial networks: a review. ACM Comput. Surv. **55**(2), 1–25 (2022)
5. Barni, M., Chen, Z., Tondi, B.: Adversary-aware, data-driven detection of double JPEG compression: how to make counter-forensics harder. In: 2016 IEEE International Workshop on Information Forensics and Security (WIFS), pp. 1–6 (2016). https://doi.org/10.1109/WIFS.2016.7823902
6. Chen, C., Stamm, M.: Robust camera model identification using demosaicing residual features. Multimed. Tools Appl. **80**, 1–29 (2021). https://doi.org/10.1007/s11042-020-09011-4
7. Chen, C., Zhao, X., Stamm, M.C.: MISLGAN: an anti-forensic camera model falsification framework using a generative adversarial network. In: 2018 25th IEEE International Conference on Image Processing (ICIP), pp. 535–539 (2018). https://doi.org/10.1109/ICIP.2018.8451503
8. Chen, C., Zhao, X., Stamm, M.C.: Generative adversarial attacks against deep-learning-based camera model identification. IEEE Trans. Inf. Forensics Secur. **PP**, 1 (2019). https://doi.org/10.1109/TIFS.2019.2945198
9. Cozzolino, D., Thies, J., Rössler, A., Nießner, M., Verdoliva, L.: SpoC: spoofing camera fingerprints (2019)
10. Cozzolino, D., Verdoliva, L.: Multimedia forensics before the deep learning era. In: Rathgeb, C., Tolosana, R., Vera-Rodriguez, R., Busch, C. (eds.) Handbook of Digital Face Manipulation and Detection. ACVPR, pp. 45–67. Springer, Cham (2022). https://doi.org/10.1007/978-3-030-87664-7_3
11. Dal Cortivo, D., Mandelli, S., Bestagini, P., Tubaro, S.: CNN-based multi-modal camera model identification on video sequences. J. Imag. **7**(8), 135 (2021)
12. Damiani, J.: A voice deepfake was used to scam a CEO out of $243,000 (2019). https://www.forbes.com/sites/jessedamiani/2019/09/03/a-voice-deepfake-was-used-to-scam-a-ceo-out-of-243000/?sh=34e8298a2241
13. Das, T.K.: Anti-forensics of JPEG compression detection schemes using approximation of DCT coefficients. Multimed. Tools Appl. **77**(24), 31835–31854 (2018)
14. Duan, B., Wang, W., Tang, H., Latapie, H., Yan, Y.: Cascade attention guided residue learning GAN for cross-modal translation (2019)
15. Flor, E., Aygun, R., Mercan, S., Akkaya, K.: PRNU-based source camera identification for multimedia forensics. In: 2021 IEEE 22nd International Conference on Information Reuse and Integration for Data Science (IRI), pp. 168–175 (2021). https://doi.org/10.1109/IRI51335.2021.00029

16. Gauthier, J.: Conditional generative adversarial nets for convolutional face generation (2015)
17. Goodfellow, I., et al.: Generative adversarial nets. Advances in Neural Information Processing Systems, vol. 27 (2014)
18. Hosler, B., et al.: A video camera model identification system using deep learning and fusion. In: ICASSP 2019 - 2019 IEEE International Conference on Acoustics, Speech and Signal Processing (ICASSP), pp. 8271–8275 (2019). https://doi.org/10.1109/ICASSP.2019.8682608
19. Jeong, S., Lee, J., Sohn, K.: Multi-domain unsupervised image-to-image translation with appearance adaptive convolution (2022)
20. Karras, T., Aila, T., Laine, S., Lehtinen, J.: Progressive growing of GANs for improved quality, stability, and variation (2017)
21. Kirchner, M., Bohme, R.: Hiding traces of resampling in digital images. IEEE Trans. Inf. Forensics Secur. 3(4), 582–592 (2008)
22. Korshunova, I., Shi, W., Dambre, J., Theis, L.: Fast face-swap using convolutional neural networks (2016)
23. Li, Y., Min, M.R., Shen, D., Carlson, D., Carin, L.: Video generation from text. In: Proceedings of the Thirty-Second AAAI Conference on Artificial Intelligence and Thirtieth Innovative Applications of Artificial Intelligence Conference and Eighth AAAI Symposium on Educational Advances in Artificial Intelligence, AAAI 2018/IAAI 2018/EAAI 2018. AAAI Press (2018)
24. Mayer, O., Stamm, M.C.: Countering anti-forensics of lateral chromatic aberration. Association for Computing Machinery, New York, NY, USA (2017)
25. Peng, F., Yin, L., Long, M.: BDC-GAN: bidirectional conversion between computer-generated and natural facial images for anti-forensics. IEEE Trans. Circ. Syst. Video Technol. 32, 1 (2022). https://doi.org/10.1109/TCSVT.2022.3177238
26. Rong, D., Wang, Y., Sun, Q.: Video source forensics for IoT devices based on convolutional neural networks. Open J. Internet Things (OJIOT) 7(1), 23–31 (2021)
27. Sharma, S., Ravi, H., Subramanyam, A., Emmanuel, S.: Anti-forensics of median filtering and contrast enhancement. J. Vis. Commun. Image Represent. 66(C), 102682 (2020)
28. Shullani, D., Fontani, M., Iuliani, M., Alshaya, O., Piva, A.: Vision: a video and image dataset for source identification. EURASIP J. Inf. Secur. 2017, 15 (2017). https://doi.org/10.1186/s13635-017-0067-2
29. Stamm, M.C., Lin, W.S., Liu, K.J.R.: Temporal forensics and anti-forensics for motion compensated video. IEEE Trans. Inf. Forensics Secur. 7(4), 1315–1329 (2012). https://doi.org/10.1109/TIFS.2012.2205568
30. Thies, J., Zollhöfer, M., Stamminger, M., Theobalt, C., Nießner, M.: Face2Face: real-time face capture and reenactment of RGB videos, vol. 62, no. 1 (2018)
31. Tulyakov, S., Liu, M.Y., Yang, X., Kautz, J.: MoCoGAN: decomposing motion and content for video generation (2017)
32. Veksler, M., Aygun, R., Akkaya, K., Iyengar, S.: Video origin camera identification using ensemble CNNs of positional patches. In: 2022 IEEE 5th International Conference on Multimedia Information Processing and Retrieval (IEEE MIPR) (2022). (in Press)
33. Venkatesh, S., Zhang, H., Ramachandra, R., Raja, K., Damer, N., Busch, C.: Can GAN generated morphs threaten face recognition systems equally as landmark based morphs? - vulnerability and detection (2020)
34. Villegas, R., Yang, J., Hong, S., Lin, X., Lee, H.: Decomposing motion and content for natural video sequence prediction. ArXiv abs/1706.08033 (2017)

35. Vondrick, C., Pirsiavash, H., Torralba, A.: Generating videos with scene dynamics. In: NIPS 2016, pp. 613–621. Curran Associates Inc., Red Hook, NY, USA (2016)

36. Yu, J., Xue, H., Liu, B., Wang, Y., Zhu, S., Ding, M.: GAN-based differential private image privacy protection framework for the internet of multimedia things. Sensors **21**(1), 58 (2021)

37. Zhu, J.Y., Park, T., Isola, P., Efros, A.A.: Unpaired image-to-image translation using cycle-consistent adversarial networks. In: 2017 IEEE International Conference on Computer Vision (ICCV), pp. 2242–2251 (2017). https://doi.org/10.1109/ICCV.2017.244

38. Zou, H., Yang, P., Ni, R., Zhao, Y., Zhou, N.: Anti-forensics of image contrast enhancement based on generative adversarial network (2021)

Towards Efficient On-Site CSAM Triage by Clustering Images from a Source Point of View

Samantha Klier$^{(\boxtimes)}$ and Harald Baier

Research Institute CODE, University of the Bundeswehr Munich,
Neubiberg, Germany
{samantha.klier,harald.baier}@unibw.de
https://www.unibw.de/digfor

Abstract. In digital forensics the Computer Forensics Field Triage Process Model (CFFTPM) addresses use cases, where an immediate on-site processing of digital evidence is necessary to impede ongoing severe criminal offences like child abuse, abduction or extortion. For instance in case of Child Sexual Abuse Material (CSAM) an instant in situ digital forensics investigation of seized devices may reveal digital traces to identify incriminated pictures produced by the suspect himself. In order to protect the victims from further violation the fast and reliable identification of such self produced CSAM files is of utmost importance, however, it is a non-trivial task. In this paper we propose an efficient and effective clustering method as part of the CFFTPM to identify self-produced incriminated images on-site. Our concept extends the classical hash-based identification of chargeable data and makes use of image metadata to cluster pictures according to their source. We successfully evaluate our approach on base of a publicly available image data set and show that our clustering even works in the presence of anti-forensics measures.

Keywords: Digital Forensics · Triage · CSAM · Clustering · EXIF · UMAP

1 Introduction

Crimes related to CSAM exhibit different levels of offences. For instance the study of Bouhours and Broadhurst [1] reveals that 11.5% of offenders possessing CSAM and 18.4% of offenders distributing CSAM engage in the production of CSAM, too. Furthermore, Bissias et al. [2] provide a survey of law enforcement information and state that 9.5% of offenders arrested for the distribution of CSAM over P2P networks offended children sexually offline. Additionally, the study of Gewirtz-Meydan et al. [3] states that 93% of CSAM production victims are family members or acquaintances of the offender. The systematical review of Cale et al. [4] synthesises empirical studies from the past decade investigating CSAM production and distribution. A key result of their review is a crucial overlap between child sexual abuse on the one hand and the production of CSAM on

© ICST Institute for Computer Sciences, Social Informatics and Telecommunications Engineering 2023
Published by Springer Nature Switzerland AG 2023. All Rights Reserved
S. Goel et al. (Eds.): ICDF2C 2022, LNICST 508, pp. 19–33, 2023.
https://doi.org/10.1007/978-3-031-36574-4_2

the other. Hence missing evidence of CSAM production during a digital forensic investigation leads to an ongoing physical abuse of involved children with a non-negligible probability.

The fast detection of CSAM production in order to protect children in the suspect's sphere of influence from (further) sexual abuse is hence an important issue. As a consequence applying triage to CSAM investigations needs further attention. In digital forensics the CFFTPM due to Rogers et al. [5] addresses use cases, where an immediate on-site processing of digital evidence is essential. In case of CSAM an instant inspection of seized devices may reveal digital traces to identify incriminated pictures produced by the suspect himself and hence gives a pointer to a still ongoing physical abuse. However, the fast identification of self-produced CSAM is an important, yet difficult issue in a digital forensic investigation.

While this problem is well-known in the digital forensic community there is no lightweight technical solution provided. Already back in 2009 Casey et al. [6] state that to concentrate during investigations on the actual instances of CSAM is not sufficient anymore. Actually Casey et al. [6] advice to concentrate on CSAM that has been "knowingly possessed" and to mitigate the risk of missing vital evidence by training investigators and relativizing by the risk delayed investigations impose. A lightweight technical support for the investigator, however, is still missing.

To sum up the instant identification of self-produced CSAM among acquired CSAM must become more prominent during a CSAM investigation. In this paper we propose a lightweight, clustering-based approach using metadata of the images under examination (IUE) to identify yet unknown, self-produced CSAM. The approach is efficient and hence lightweight in the sense that it can easily be applied to seized material on-site as it runs on common hardware (with respect to computing and storage power) and utilises computationally cheap extractable metadata.

Based on the extracted metadata we provide a pair-wise similarity score used to build the clusters. As a consequence the clustering does not comprise a learning phase and effectively separates files on base of their metadata with respect to the source of the files (i.e. the device used to produce the pictures). The clustering outcome results in a high-dimensional data problem. In order to provide a visualisation of a given picture data set in form of a 2-dimensional graph we make use of the well-known and open-source library UMAP [7].

We successfully evaluate our approach using the publicly available database The Forchheim Image Database (FOIDB) due to Hadwiger et al. [8]. The evaluated approach offers a visualisation of the IUE to an investigator in the field which takes the source of an image into account. Hence we show the suitability of our concept to reduce the risk of missing evidence of actual child abuse when triage is applied to a CSAM case.

The rest of the paper is organised as follows. In Sect. 2 we introduce foundations of our approach, that is the CFFTPM, picture metadata, and clustering using UMAP. Then we present related work to our approach in Sect. 3 followed by the presentation of our concept and our prototypical implementation in Sect. 4. In Sect. 5 we provide experimental results using the FOIDB to prepare the actual evaluation of our approach in Sect. 6 in terms of the classical errors false-positive and false-negative, respectively. We conclude our paper in Sect. 7 and point to future work.

2 Foundations

We present in this section the foundations necessary to follow our approach. After introducing the CFFTPM in Sect. 2.1, we explain in Sect. 2.2 the relevant picture metadata used in our concept. We close our foundation presentation with a short introduction of the UMAP library in Sect. 2.3.

2.1 Computer Forensics Field Triage Process Model

The aim of the CFFTPM due to Rogers et al. [5] is to provide an on-site or field approach for circumstances where a traditional digital forensics approach is not suitable (e.g. the transportation to a lab and the search of the entire system takes too long in the respective case). This includes circumstances where children are at risk of being sexually abused. The CFFTPM foci are to:

1. Find usable evidence immediately;
2. Identify victims at acute risk;
3. Guide the ongoing investigation;
4. Identify potential charges;
5. Accurately assess the offender's danger to society; and
6. Protect the integrity of the evidence for further analysis.

We concentrate on the triage phase of the CFFTPM, which is defined as: "A process in which things are ranked in terms of importance or priority. Essentially, those items, pieces of evidence or potential containers of evidence that are the most important or the most volatile need to be dealt with first."

For our purposes the child pornography section of the CFFTPM is of special importance as [5] states: "The highest priority should obviously be given to actual instances of child pornography on the drive." Consequently, we provide guidance in our approach how CSAM or activities to acquire/distribute CSAM can be detected efficiently and effectively.

2.2 Metadata

The classic definition of metadata is "data about data" [9]. Metadata can be classified by their purpose in the categories: descriptive metadata (e.g. comments, thumbnails), preservation metadata (e.g. hash sums), rights metadata, structural metadata (e.g. directory) and for our purposes most importantly technical metadata [9]. Most digital cameras save numerous technical metadata in their images based on the Exchangeable Image File Format (EXIF) [10] as part of a JPEG File Interchange Format (JFIF) [11] file. The EXIF standard defines numerous tags that point to the source of an image explicitly (e.g. *Make, Model*) or implicitly (e.g. *Compression, Image Width*).

However, JFIF and EXIF enable digital camera manufacturers to define customized tags while the storage of technical metadata is not even limited to EXIF, naming Extensible Metadata Platform (XMP) [12] as an alternative. Therefore, the metadata that can actually be derived from an image is elusive. Nonetheless it is stored and does not need to be calculated, just retrieved and is consequently computationally cheap.

2.3   Clustering with UMAP

A classic approach for the visualisation of high-dimensional data is Multidimensional scaling (MDS) [13] which is based on a pair-wise similarity score. MDS has a time complexity of $\mathcal{O}(n^3)$, where n is the number of elements in the data set. This cubic run time dependency makes MDS unsuitable for real life IUE.

The state-of-the-art competitor for the visualisation of high-dimensional data at the moment is UMAP [7]. Its empirical run time efficiency is by far the best of the applicable approaches. UMAP offers visualisation of high dimensional data by calculating similarity scores in the high-dimensional space, initialising a low-dimensional graph and resembling the clusters of the high-dimensional space in the low-dimensional graph. UMAP achieves this by calculating similarity scores in the low-dimensional space based on a t-distribution trying to maximise respectively minimise the similarity score in the low-dimensional space depending on the affiliation of the points to a cluster in the high-dimensional space.

UMAP offers the calculation of similarity scores in the high-dimensional space based on a custom metric, but it operates exclusively on the data type `float`, which is not sufficient for our purposes as metadata includes additional data types like e.g. strings. Therefore, we precompute the high-dimensional similarity scores and only facilitate UMAPs capabilities of embedding the data into the low-dimensional space for visualisation.

3   Related Work

In the first part of this section we discuss related work that has facilitated metadata of images to deduce the source of an image in the past. The second part of this section discusses state-of-the-art approaches to the Source Camera Identification (SCI) or Source Model Identification (SMI) problem based on image processing techniques.

Using metadata, primarily EXIF, to deduce the source camera of an image and correlating the finding with cameras used by a suspect is a established procedure [14,15] used by investigators and is well supported by common forensic tools. Investigators can filter or correlate images by certain EXIF tags (like model, make or serial number). However, this approach is not sufficient as it fails if these tags are not set (e.g. deleted by EXIF remover tools), have been tampered or are not significant (e.g. for common smartphone models). Therefore, a view on metadata besides EXIF has been used for image authentication and identification of the source model in traditional cameras by Kee et al. [16]. This approach is also useful for smartphones as shown by Mullan et al. [17] although it will identify the software stack rather than the smartphone model that captured the image.

Image processing techniques have been applied with success to the SCI or SMI problem in the past. Most attention has been drawn to approaches based on sensor pattern noise [18–21] which is unique per camera. SCI has been proposed based on lens radial distortion [22], as well. These approaches are computationally expensive and even the efficient approach of Bernacki [23] needs about 45 s per image to calculate a fingerprint based on sensor pattern noise on up to date hardware.

Both classes of proposed approaches expect an investigator to put remarkable effort into the preparation of a image set for classification. For example, an investigator needs to prepare a labeled image set for training or has to elaborate EXIF tags of interest. This is knowledge is hard to gain and probably incomprehensive anyways which leads to an open set problem as identified by Gloe [24]. Lorch et al. [25] proposes to reject images from cameras which are not part of the prepared set in order prevent silent failure, at least. Hence, these approaches allow an investigator to support or refute a hypothesis about the source camera/model of certain images but do not enable an investigator to form such an hypothesis on a real life image set in the first place.

4   Clustering Concept and Its Prototype

We first present in Sect. 4.1 the theoretical foundations of our approach followed by the technical details of our prototypical proof of concept in Sect. 4.2.

4.1   Clustering Concept

An investigator at a crime scene is working on a set of IUE. We model this by the set P consisting of n picture files as input, i.e. $P = \{P_1, P_2, \ldots, P_n\}$. The investigator's goal is to assign a picture (i.e. an element of P) to the respective source, that is the corresponding camera or smartphone. We model the set of sources by the set of cameras $C = \{C_1, C_2, \ldots, C_i\}$ supposedly used by the suspect. We remark that our clustering approach solely expects the set P as input.

Let $P_i \in P$ be a picture file and M_i its extracted metadata, that is the set of metadata elements is $M = \{M_1, M_2, \ldots, M_n\}$. We model the metadata element $M_i \in M$ as an array of length l, where each entry of the array M_i is a field-value pair. The set of all metadata fields F available from the IUE is defined as

$$F = \{f|(f, v) \in \cup M\} = \{f_1, f_2, \ldots, f_l\}$$

Hence our representation of a metadata element M_i is

$$M_i = ((f_1, v_{i_1}), (f_2, v_{i_2}), \ldots, (f_l, v_{i_l}))$$

where possibly values of a metadata element is empty due to the missing field in the corresponding picture file P_i. Actually we denote by $|M_i|$ the number of fields present in the metadata set element M_i.

We next define our similarity function, which we call s and which expects two metadata set elements as input. The goal of the similarity function is to enable a clustering based on the evaluation of the metadata entries. More precisely let $M_x, M_y \in M$ be two metadata arrays of the picture files $P_x, P_y \in P$, respectively. In order to define the similarity function $s(M_x, M_y)$, we first need two additional parameters:

1. First the *agreement* is the number of identical field-value pairs contained in both M_x and M_y, that is it is equal to the number of field-value pairs in the intersection of M_x and M_y. We denote the agreement by agr and define it as

$$agr(M_x, M_y) = |M_x \cap M_y|. \tag{1}$$

Please note that this requires the presence of a field and an identical field value in both metadata arrays to score for the agreement. The agreement serves to measure the match between both metadata arrays as an absolute number.

2. Second the *specificity* denoted by $spec$ is the minimum of the two numbers of field-value pairs present in M_x or M_y, i.e.

$$spec(M_x, M_y) = \min(|M_x|, |M_y|). \tag{2}$$

The specificity serves to normalise the absolute agreement in our similarity score. The reason is that in case of only few fields set in a metadata array, the absolute agreement may be low, however, the relative one may be high. Actually we are interested in the second one as our practical results show.

The similarity of M_x, M_y is essentially the normalised agreement of M_x and M_y, i.e. $s(M_x, M_y) = {agr(M_x, M_y)}/{spec(M_x, M_y)}$ and thus a real number in the range $[0, 1]$. However, we also want to be robust against anti-forensic measures which are usually characterized by deleting metadata from an image which metadata in turn appears as a sub-array of other images from the same source. In real life this metadata sub-array might show some deviation (e.g. comments added), hence, we introduce a heuristic threshold of 2%

$$s(M_x, M_y) = \begin{cases} 1, & \text{if } |M_x \setminus M_y| < 0.02 \cdot |F| \text{ or } |M_y \setminus M_x| < 0.02 \cdot |F| \\ {agr}/{spec}, & \text{else} \end{cases} \tag{3}$$

To separate clusters, we introduce the pair-wise dissimilarity based on the similarity function in the obvious way, i.e. $diss(M_x, M_y) = 1 - s(M_x, M_y)$. Finally we organise the dissimilarity scores in an $(n \times n)$-matrix D, where the element in the x-th row and y-th column of D is equal to $diss(M_x, M_y)$, i.e.

$$D = D_{1 \leq x \leq n, 1 \leq y \leq n} \qquad D_{x,y} = 1 - s(M_x, M_y). \tag{4}$$

For instance the matrix element $D_{5,3}$ holds the dissimilarity metric of image P_5 to image P_3. Furthermore all diagonal elements $D_{i,i} = 0$.

Finally the dissimilarity matrix D is passed to UMAP in order to find a 2-dimensional visualisable embedding of P represented by its corresponding set of metadata.

4.2 Proof of Concept

This section provides an overview of our proof of concept[1]. It consists of the following components. First as IUE data set our approach is applied to FOIDB [8], an image database designed for ranking forensic approaches to the SCI problem. FOIDB offers 143 scenes taken by 27 smartphone cameras (that is for each scene all cameras were used under the same condition). All pictures of the FOIDB are available as saved by the camera (referred to as *original*) as well as post-processed by Facebook, Instagram, Telegram, Twitter and WhatsApp. The FOIDB includes indoor and outdoor scenes, day and night, close-up and distant, and natural and man-made scenes. The FOIDB is suitable for our proof of concept, because the original images contain untampered metadata as saved by the camera. Another advantage of the FOIDB is the wide variety of models included and the possibility to expand our approach to images post-processed by social media applications in the future.

Second the metadata of the IUE has been extracted into a CSV file with ExifTool 12.42[2] in binary mode. Exiftool does not only extract EXIF metadata from a plethora of manufacturers, as the name suggests, but also other metadata as XMP, ICC profiles, information about the encoding process and many more. ExifTool has been chosen as it is well-established in the digital forensic community, very comprehensive, yields machine processable outputs and could be easily used in the field.

Third our approach is implemented in Python 3.10 with pandas 1.4.2 and numpy 1.12.5. The visualisation is generated with bokeh 2.4.3. Furthermore we make use of UMAP as available in the Python package umap-learn 0.5.3[3] for the clustering. UMAP is being initialised as

```
UMAP(n_neighbors = 100, metric = 'precomputed', random_state = 42).
```

n_neighbors indicates how much nearest neighbors UMAP should expect, this value is usually set to a value in the range from 15 to 100. As we expect that

---

[1] The used metadata and source code is available at
https://cloud.digfor.code.unibw-muenchen.de/index.php/s/xq2jtbqpEnTdNEZ
[2] https://exiftool.org/
[3] https://pypi.org/project/umap-learn/

many images origin from one camera we have set the value accordingly. As we pass the matrix D with precomputed distances to UMAP we force UMAP not to calculate the distances between the given data with its built-in mechanism by setting `metric` to `precomputed`. Setting the `random_state` to a constant value results in a fixed initialisation and consequently repeatable results.

Finally the metadata containing CSV file is loaded via pandas and is being preprocessed as follows:

1. The field *Directory* is being dismissed, as the directory structure of the FOIDB would leak the belonging of a picture to a certain camera.
2. The fields *FileAccessDate*, *FileInodeChangeDate*, *FileModifyDate*, *FileName*, *FilePermissions*, *CreateDate*, *DateTimeOriginal* and *ModifyDate* are dismissed because of similar reasons.
3. The values of all *Width* and *Height* fields are swapped if *Width* > *Height*

5   Experimental Results

We apply our prototype as described in Sect. 4.2 on the image set FOIDB. The experiments in this section are conducted on an ordinary laptop (HP EliteBook G3, 16 GiB RAM, i7-7500U@2.70 GHz) with a runtime of less than 150 s for the 3,851 images in the FOIDB serving as IUE. The ordinary runtime environment simulates the lightweight on-site infrastructure of a digital forensic investigator. The metadata has been preprocessed as described in Sect. 4.2, which took us less than 45 s on our commodity hardware.

The experimental results have been computed in terms of the common classification metrics:

FN Images from one device in different clusters (false negatives).
FP Images of different devices in one cluster (false positives).

We now present our two experimental settings. First Sect. 5.1 shows the successful clustering of the original images of the FOIDB. Then in Sect. 5.2 we show that we can reliably cluster even in case of anti-forensic measures.

5.1   Clustering the Original FOIDB Images

In the first experiment we applied our approach on all original images of the FOIDB in order to explore the general capability for clustering the images from a source point of view.

Two figures have been generated for the achieved clustering. Figure 1 shows the achieved clustering as perceived by an investigator. While Fig. 2 shows the same clustering, with colored data points indicating their true belonging to a certain device and circled[4] clusters, for evaluation purposes.

As shown in Fig. 2 three devices are affected by an error of type *FN* and three clusters with a total of six devices are affected by *FP*. Eighteen devices have been clustered correctly.

---

[4] Circle size is arbitrary.

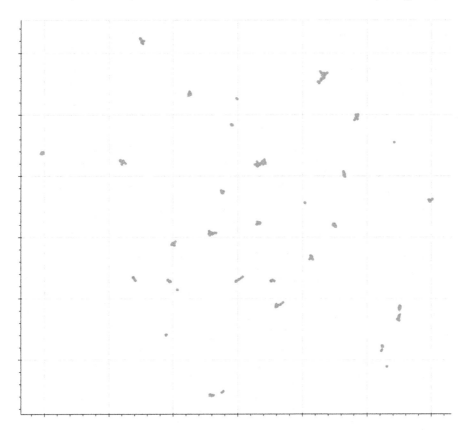

Fig. 1. Visualization of the FOIDB original images as perceived by an investigator. (Color figure online)

5.2   Clustering FOIDB After Anti-forensic Actions

The second experiment we conducted aimed at exploring the capabilities of our clustering approach in the presence of anti-forensic actions on the images of FOIDB. From all original images of the FOIDB we defined the images *0140* and *0142*, of every device as incriminated. We removed the EXIF metadata from these incriminated images via ExifTool. Therefore, the IUE did not contain the untampered versions of the incriminated images and, therefore, depicts the worst case for a metadata based approach when a suspect deletes metadata and is not in the possession of the corresponding original image. In this case the popular approach to look for *Make* or *Model* in the EXIF metadata would fail completely. Again, two figures have been generated for the achieved clustering. Figure 3 shows the clustering as perceived by an investigator, incriminated images are marked with an asterisk.

Figure 4 shows the same clustering for evaluation purposes. As shown in Fig. 4 three devices are affected by an error of type *FN* and three clusters with a total of fourteen devices are affected by an error of type *FP*.

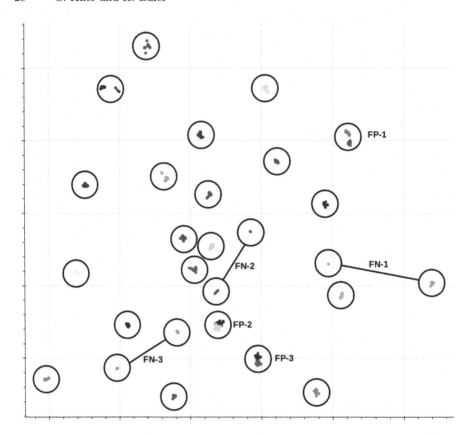

Fig. 2. Visualization of the FOIDB original images for evaluation. (Color figure online)

6   Evaluation

Errors of type *FN* impose the risk to miss evidence of CSAM production, while errors of type *FP* impose the risk of false accusations and reduce the efficiency of the approach. The risk of *FN* is realized when incriminated images, which have been produced by the suspect, are separated from images pointing to the suspect and in turn are deferred for analysis later on or even dismissed. Errors of type *FP* are less severe as long as an investigator keeps in mind that this approach does not prove anything.

Evaluation of FN Errors in Fig. 2: The two distinct clusters of *FN-1* originate from a *Google Nexus 5* (device 21). The metadata of these images differ in fact considerably which is dedicated to the *HDR+* mode some images have been taken with.

The two distinct clusters of *FN-2* originate from a *BQ Aquaris X* (device 22) and have considerably different metadata for an unknown reason.

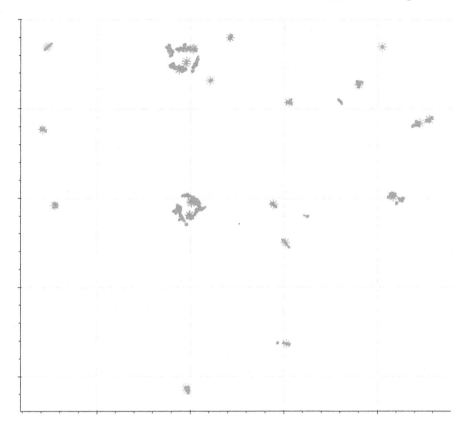

Fig. 3. Clustering after removing EXIF metadata of certain images (marked with asterisk) as perceived by an investigator.

The two distinct clusters of *FN-3* originate from a *Sony Xperia E5* (device 13). The images of this device have little metadata set, and even few changes due to two different scene capture types lead to different clusters.

Evaluation of FP Errors in Fig. 2: The two sub clusters of *FP-1* originate from an *Apple iPhone 7* (device 17) and an *Apple iPhone 8+* (device 19). These *iPhones* took the images while operating on different software versions, however, sharing many equal field-value pairs, specially those related to the ICC profile.

The cluster of *FP-2* originate from a *LG G6* (device 06) and *LG G3* (device 04). The images of the *LG G6* hold considerably more metadata than those of the *LG G3*. Whereas the metadata of some images of the *LG G3* are recognized as sub sets of images originating from the *LG G6* which tempts our approach to cluster them very close together.

The cluster of *FP-3* originate from two different *Huawei P9lite* (device 23 and 25) devices of the same model. The metadata differs only slightly due to different software versions of the two devices.

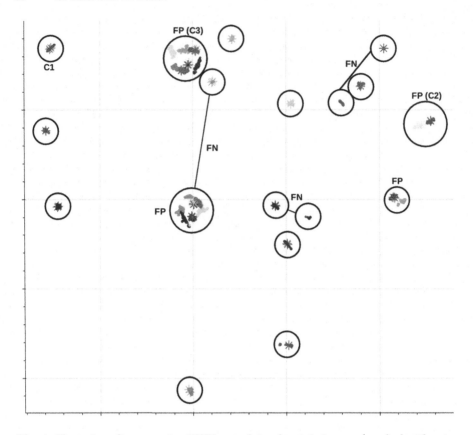

Fig. 4. Clustering after removing EXIF metadata of certain images (marked with asterisk) for evaluation.

The FOIDB also includes images of two *Samsung Galaxy A6* (device 15 and 16, red and yellow data points) devices. Those have been clustered far apart due to considerable deviation of the metadata stemming from different software versions.

Evaluation of Cluster C1 in Fig. 4: The cluster *C1* is clearly distinct from other clusters and contains every image originating from the *Samsung Galaxy S4* (device 18) including the incriminated images with removed EXIF metadata and therefore depicts a perfect outcome.

Evaluation of C2 in Fig. 4: The cluster *C2* is clearly distinct from other clusters and contains every image originating from the two *Samsung Galaxy A6* devices (device 15 and 16) including the incriminated images with removed EXIF metadata. The two devices of the same model are distinguishable inside the cluster and the incriminated images have been clustered to the correct device. In this experiment the two devices of the *Samsung Galaxy A6* can be distinguished by the *MCCData* (Samsung specific) field which is set by device 16 but not by device 15.

Evaluation of C3 in Fig. 4: The cluster *C3* contains images of six devices and is showing a ring of sub-clusters formed around some incriminated images in the middle (Fig. 5 shows a zoomed view on *C3*). The metadata of the incriminated images in the middle is a subset of the metadata of the surrounding images and therefore glues these more or less unrelated clusters together. The surrounding clusters which form the ring also show some overlap between the devices because of the same reason. Even though this clusters is affected by an error of type *P2* this is helpful, as an investigator is instantly confronted with those images that have undergone anti forensic actions and gets a clue of possible sources of these images without facing a false classification. In this case it might be useful to redo the clustering after handling the incriminated images in the middle separately (e.g. with one of the approaches mentioned in Sect. 3).

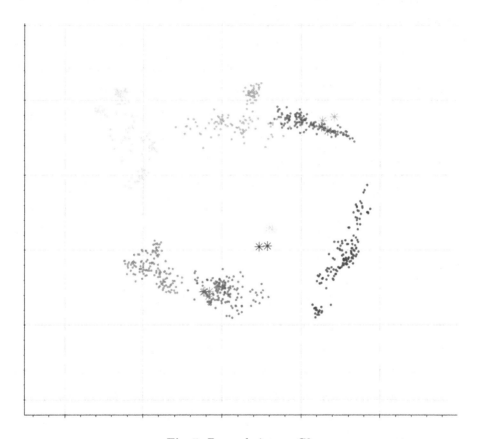

Fig. 5. Zoomed view on C3.

Hence, our approach works as expected and confirms the findings of Mullan et al. [17] that the metadata of images taken by smartphones is highly depending on the software stack. However, we expect this approach to be helpful in a triage situation though it is limited in its capabilities by design.

7   Conclusion and Future Work

Our first approach to a metadata based clustering with the aim to quickly identify the production of CSAM is promising. Even in the presence of anti forensic actions every incriminated image is in a cluster with other images from its originating device and a maximum number of six out of 27 devices per incriminated image are suggested in less than five minutes, with no special preparatory work of an investigator required.

Right now, the approach does not take full advantage of the information that is buried in the metadata and might yield better results when applying some fuzzy equality to certain field-value pairs (e.g. file size, file name). At the moment the extracted metadata is not curated which makes the approach lightweight but leads to unintentionally weighing information that is represented in the metadata more than once (e.g. several fields for resolution). The runtime could be reduced by exchanging the pair-wise calculation ($\mathcal{O}(n^2)$) of similarities with a nearest neighbor approximation algorithm.

More experiments with other databases, including those with classical digital cameras, should be conducted to verify the results. Furthermore, the aspect of software stack needs further research. This aspect will likely enforce images that have been shared via social media etc. to be clustered together which could be an advantage but will need cautious interpretation of an investigator. Particularly, our approach does not technically prove anything and does not facilitate any information that is concealed to a human investigator. However, it relieves the mental load on a human investigator by reducing the dimensionality of the problem and reducing the amount of images that need to be reviewed. Our approach could also lead to an improvement of privacy aspects if personal images are only reviewed if they are related to CSAM.

References

1. Bouhours, B., Broadhurst, R.: On-line child sex offenders: Report on a sample of peer to peer offenders arrested between July 2010–June 2011 (2011). SSRN 2174815
2. Bissias, G., et al.: Characterization of contact offenders and child exploitation material trafficking on five peer-to-peer networks. Child Abuse Neglect **52**, 185–199 (2016)
3. Gewirtz-Meydan, A., Walsh, W., Wolak, J., Finkelhor, D.: The complex experience of child pornography survivors. Child Abuse Neglect **80**, 238–248 (2018)
4. Cale, J., Holt, T., Leclerc, B., Singh, S., Drew, J.: Crime commission processes in child sexual abuse material production and distribution: a systematic review. Trends Issues Crime Crim. Justice **617**, 1–22 (2021)
5. Rogers, M.K., Goldman, J., Mislan, R., Wedge, T., Debrota, S.: Computer forensics field triage process model. J. Digit. Forensics Secur. Law **1**(2), 2 (2006)
6. Casey, E., Ferraro, M., Nguyen, L.: Investigation delayed is justice denied: proposals for expediting forensic examinations of digital evidence. J. Forensic Sci. **54**(6), 1353–1364 (2009)
7. McInnes, L., Healy, J., Melville, J.: UMAP: uniform manifold approximation and projection for dimension reduction. arXiv preprint arXiv:1802.03426 (2018)

8. Hadwiger, B., Riess, C.: The Forchheim image database for camera identification in the wild. In: Del Bimbo, A., et al. (eds.) ICPR 2021. LNCS, vol. 12666, pp. 500–515. Springer, Cham (2021). https://doi.org/10.1007/978-3-030-68780-9_40

9. Riley, J.: Understanding metadata, vol. 23. National Information Standards Organization, Washington DC, United States (2017). http://www.niso.org/publications/press/UnderstandingMetadata.pdf

10. Exchangeable image file format for digital still cameras: Exif version 2.32. Standard, Camera & Imaging Products Association (2019)

11. JPEG file interchange format (JFIF), version 1.02. Standard, International Organization for Standardization, May 2013 (2013)

12. Graphic technology—Extensible metadata platform (XMP) specification—Part 1: data model, serialization and core properties. Standard, International Organization for Standardization, February 2012 (2012)

13. Kruskal, J.B.: Multidimensional scaling by optimizing goodness of fit to a nonmetric hypothesis. Psychometrika **29**(1), 1–27 (1964)

14. Sorrell, M.J.: Digital camera source identification through JPEG quantisation. In: Multimedia Forensics and Security, pp. 291–313. IGI Global (2009)

15. Orozco, A.S., González, D.A., Corripio, J.R., Villalba, L.G., Hernandez-Castro, J.: Techniques for source camera identification. In: Proceedings of the 6th International Conference on Information Technology, pp. 1–9 (2013)

16. Kee, E., Johnson, M.K., Farid, H.: Digital image authentication from JPEG headers. IEEE Trans. Inf. Forensics Secur. **6**(3), 1066–1075 (2011)

17. Mullan, P., Riess, C., Freiling, F.: Forensic source identification using JPEG image headers: the case of smartphones. Digit. Investig. **28**, S68–S76 (2019)

18. Lukas, J., Fridrich, J., Goljan, M.: Digital camera identification from sensor pattern noise. IEEE Trans. Inf. Forensics Secur. **1**(2), 205–214 (2006)

19. Thai, T.H., Retraint, F., Cogranne, R.: Camera model identification based on the generalized noise model in natural images. Digit. Signal Process. **48**, 285–297 (2016)

20. Freire-Obregón, D., Narducci, F., Barra, S., Castrillón-Santana, M.: Deep learning for source camera identification on mobile devices. Pattern Recognit. Lett. **126**, 86–91 (2019). Robustness, Security and Regulation Aspects in Current Biometric Systems

21. Bharathiraja, S., Rajesh Kanna, B., Hariharan, M.: A deep learning framework for image authentication: an automatic source camera identification Deep-Net. Arab. J. Sci. Eng. **48**, 1–13 (2022)

22. Choi, K.S., Lam, E.Y., Wong, K.K.Y.: Automatic source camera identification using the intrinsic lens radial distortion. Opt. Express **14**, 11551–11565 (2006)

23. Bernacki, J.: Digital camera identification by fingerprint's compact representation. Multimed. Tools Appl. **81**, 1–34 (2022)

24. Gloe, T.: Feature-based forensic camera model identification. In: Shi, Y.Q., Katzenbeisser, S. (eds.) Transactions on Data Hiding and Multimedia Security VIII. LNCS, vol. 7228, pp. 42–62. Springer, Heidelberg (2012). https://doi.org/10.1007/978-3-642-31971-6_3

25. Lorch, B., Schirrmacher, F., Maier, A., Riess, C.: Reliable camera model identification using sparse Gaussian processes. IEEE Signal Process. Lett. **28**, 912–916 (2021)

Can Image Watermarking Efficiently Protect Deep-Learning-Based Image Classifiers? – A Preliminary Security Analysis of an IP-Protecting Method

Jia-Hui Xie, Di Wu, Bo-Hao Zhang, Hai Su, and Huan Yang[✉]

School of Software, South China Normal University, Foshan 528225, Guangdong,
People's Republic of China
{20192005204,20192005368,20192005249,suhai,huan.yang}@m.scnu.edu.cn

Abstract. Being widely adopted by an increasingly rich array of classification tasks in different industries, image classifiers based on deep neural networks (DNNs) have successfully helped boost business efficiency and reduce costs. To protect the intellectual property (IP) of DNN classifiers, a blind-watermarking-based technique that opens "backdoors" through image steganography has been proposed. However, it is yet to explore whether this approach can effectively protect DNN models under practical settings where malicious attacks may be launched against it. In this paper, we study the feasibility and effectiveness of this previously proposed blind-watermarking-based DNN classifier protection technique from the security perspective (Our code is available at https://github.com/ByGary/Security-of-IP-Protection-Frameworks.). We first show that, IP protection offered by the original algorithm, when trained with 256×256 images, can easily be evaded due to obvious visibility issue. Adapting the original approach by replacing its steganalyzer with watermark extraction algorithm and revising the overall training strategy, we are able to mitigate the visibility issue. Furthermore, we evaluate our improved approaches under three simple yet practical attacks, i.e., evasion attacks, spoofing attacks, and robustness attacks. Our evaluation results reveal that further security enhancements are indispensable for the practical applications of the examined blind-watermarking-based DNN image classifier protection scheme, providing a set of guidelines and precautions to facilitate improved protection of intellectual property of DNN classifiers.

Keywords: Blind watermarking · Intellectual property protection · Image steganography · Watermark extraction · Steganalysis · Evasion attacks · Spoofing attacks · Robustness attacks

1 Introduction

As deep-learning-based image classification techniques continue to make exciting progress in miscellaneous application domains, ranging from medical image

S. Goel et al. (Eds.): ICDF2C 2022, LNICST 508, pp. 34–57, 2023.
https://doi.org/10.1007/978-3-031-36574-4_3

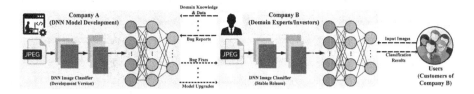

Fig. 1. A business case for DNN image classifiers where the right to use (also known as possession [15]) and ownership must be carefully distinguished.

recognition [11,12] to COVID-19 prevention [26], abuses of the copyrights of trained deep neural network (DNN) image classifiers have become a major concern hindering their widespread adoption [9,19]. With the growing complexity of DNN image classifiers (e.g., in terms of model size and architectural complexity [16]), time and computational resources dedicated to the training and fine-tuning of DNN models have been increasing rapidly. Consequently, copyright infringement targeting DNN image classifiers will result in an ever-growing loss to their legal owners, necessitating the development of techniques that protect the intellectual property (IP) of these classifiers.

In many practical applications of DNN image classifiers, drawing a distinction between the right to use (sometimes termed possession) and ownership is inevitable. Figure 1 depicts a business case [15] where two companies A and B, one specialized in the design and implementation of DNN models while the other serving as a domain expert, work collaboratively to develop a DNN image classifier for profit. Company A may choose to lease its newly developed DNN image classifier to Company B under some contract clearly specifying the terms and scope of use. For instance, Company A may require that the model should only be used by Company B and should never be transferred to other companies without its explicit consent. Company B, while serving its customers for profit with the leased model, will report bugs to Company A, share newly acquired domain knowledge, and/or get feature/model upgrades from Company A. Oftentimes, Company A, as the developer (and ownership holder) of the DNN image classifier, may be unaware of the fact that his/her model, shipped and/or deployed without proper protection, can get stolen by adversaries through exploiting various mechanisms, such as electromagnetic side channel attacks [6] and model extraction attacks [10]. It is also possible that a certain malicious insider at Company B secretly shares the DNN image classifier with other companies, which violates the terms of use set by Company A. Without proper protection mechanisms in place, it is hard for Company A to detect/prove such violations, which will result in not only a loss to Company A but also a discouraging business atmosphere for other companies specialized in DNN model development.

To protect the copyrights of DNN image classifiers, an IP protection technique based on blind image watermarking is proposed in [19], which opens "backdoors" in the DNN image classifiers and enables model owners to externally verify their ownership. For instance, Company A in Fig. 2 can leverage this technique to train a DNN image classifier and then ship it to Company B. When a certain company

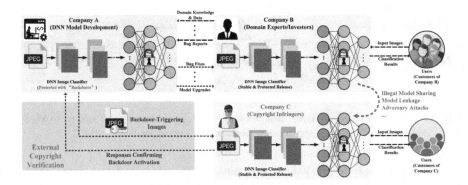

Fig. 2. External ownership/copyright verification enabled by image-watermarking-based techniques (e.g., ACSAC19 [19]) for DNN image classifiers.

other than Company B is suspected of illegally exploiting the DNN image classifier, Company A may externally verify whether an unmodified version of the model is being abused by sending image classification requests that can trigger the "backdoors" and verifying whether the embedded "backdoors" are indeed activated. However, this technique has not been thoroughly studied from the security perspective in practical context. The original version of this technique [19] will be called "ACSAC19" throughout this paper. In this paper, we re-examine the performance of ACSAC19, an end-to-end IP protection technique proposed in [19] and propose necessary enhancements to mitigate ACSAC19's visibility issue so that the external ownership verification operations can better evade the scrutiny of infringers. Furthermore, security analyses are conducted on our enhanced blind-watermarking-based IP protection techniques for DNN image classifiers, revealing the applicability and practicality issues of this DNN IP protection paradigm. The contributions of this paper can be summarized as follows:

- *Evaluation of a blind-watermarking-based IP protection technique (i.e., ACSAC19 [19]) for DNN image classifiers on a more practically-sized image dataset.* In contrast to the experiments conducted in [19] mainly on the CIFAR-10 dataset [18] consisting of tiny (32×32) images, we further evaluate ACSAC19 on the mini-ImageNet dataset [21,30] consisting of more realistic 256×256 images. Our results show that the ACSAC19 approach [19] does not perform well in terms of invisibility on Mini-ImageNet, which may lead to evasion attacks that can easily be launched by infringers (e.g., through visual inspection).
- *Proposal of two enhanced versions of ACSAC19 that mitigate (in)visibility issue on mini-ImageNet.* Two enhanced versions of ACSAC19, namely end-to-end model with watermark extraction (termed "E2E-Extraction" approach throughout this paper) and two-phase host model fine-tuning (called "Two-Phase" approach throughout this paper), are proposed and evaluated. Our evaluation results show that the enhanced versions can mitigate the visibility issue, making it more practical for DNN image classifiers to adopt blind-image-watermarking-based IP protection techniques such as ACSAC19 [19].

– *A preliminary security analysis of blind-watermarking-based IP protection for DNN image classifiers based on our enhanced versions of ACSAC19.* Assuming that attackers may be able to gain access to miscellaneous sensitive information in the blind-watermarking-based IP protection process, we study whether our enhanced IP protection techniques, i.e., E2E-Extraction and Two-Phase approaches, are vulnerable to evasion attacks, spoofing attacks, and robustness attacks. Our analyses identify critical information that must be kept secret from adversaries and generate useful guidelines on how the blind-watermarking-based IP protection paradigm, such as ACSAC19 and our enhanced versions, should be utilized in practical applications to protect the copyrights of DNN image classifiers.

2   Related Work

2.1   Protecting Deep Neural Network (DNN) Models from Copyright Infringements

As the business value of deep neural network (DNN) models continues to be substantiated by various successful applications ranging from medical image recognition [11,12] to COVID-19 prevention [26], concerns on abuses of licensed DNN models have become a major issue, which not only undermines the business model of the artificial intelligence (AI) industry but discourages technological innovations as well [15]. To protect the copyrights of DNN models, intellectual property (IP) protection techniques have been proposed in recent years [35] for DNN models of different forms and objectives. For instance, the blind-watermarking-based IP protection method proposed in [19] is designed for DNN image classifiers. For DNN models that generate images as outputs (e.g., for tasks such as image segmentation), an IP protection framework utilizing watermarks encrypted by secret keys is proposed in [31]. To protect speech-to-text deep recurrent neural network models, a watermarking approach based on adversarial examples is devised in [24] to facilitate external verification of model ownership in a black-box manner. In [37], different types of watermarks are compared in the context of blind-watermarking-based DNN model protection. Recently, deep watermarking technique is applied to protect low-level image processing tasks (e.g., DNN backbones that automatically extract image features) against student-teacher learning [38]. In addition to IP protection through embedding watermarks into the data samples, other mechanisms, such as fingerprinting the classification boundaries of DNN models [8], embedding serial numbers to prevent unauthorized uses of models [29], deliberately rearranging DNN model's weights chaotically [20], and quantifying the similarities between victim and surrogate models [9], have been devised.

As IP protection methods for DNN models continue to improve and proliferate, security properties of these methods and possible attacks on them begin to draw the attention of both AI and security research communities. In [3], removal attacks on black-box backdoor watermarks protecting DNN model copyrights are

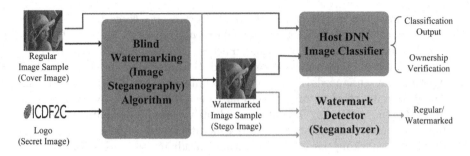

Fig. 3. The original end-to-end blind-watermarking-based IP protection method for DNN image classifiers proposed in [19]. Note that this technique is termed "ACSAC19" throughout this paper.

reported, and successful watermark removal attacks on CIFAR-10 are demonstrated while maintaining sufficient host task performance (e.g., above 80% on CIFAR-10). Among recent studies on the security of blind-watermarking-based IP protection, ambiguity attacks, in which an adversary forges counterfeit watermarked images to undermine the reliability of the external ownership verification results, have shown to be a major issue. It is found in [13] that ambiguity attacks pose serious threats to existing DNN watermarking methods, and an enhanced watermarking strategy is proposed, which enables the protected models to reject counterfeit watermarked images. Meanwhile, the IP protection of generative adversarial networks (GANs) with possible presence of ambiguity attacks is also studied in [23].

Although blind-watermarking-based IP protection is recently studied extensively by the AI and security research communities, we observe that many of the existing results (e.g., [3,13,19,23,27,37]) are primarily obtained using the CIFAR-10 dataset [18], which contains 32 × 32 images that seem to be overly small for both whole-image steganography and realistic image classification applications. It is hence necessary to further evaluate the performance of IP protection techniques for DNN models on datasets with more realistically sized images.

In this paper, we focus our attention on the IP protection of DNN image classifiers using the ACSAC19 method [19] in practical contexts from the security perspective. Figure 3 presents the ACSAC19 method originally proposed in [19]. In the ACSAC19 method, whole-image steganography, which embeds secret images into cover images as blind watermarks, is leveraged to generate stego images (also known as "trigger" images) that will be presented to the host DNN image classifier to verify ownership. During the end-to-end training process of the ACSAC19 approach, the steganalyzer detects whether images presented to the host model contain blind watermarks or not, interacting with the steganography module to ensure invisibility of the watermarks. The host DNN is the target model to be protected, and ACSAC19's end-to-end method trains the host DNN in such a way that it will generate correct classification outputs for regular images and produce ownership verification outputs for the stego images. In ACSAC19, the ownership verification outputs are random numbers associated with individual stego images. Note that both the host DNN image classifier and the steganalyzer interact with the blind watermarking module throughout the end-to-end training process, which strives to generate stego images that can evade the scrutiny of the steganalyzer while being correctly recognized by the host DNN image classifier as "trigger" images. Although satisfactory IP protection performance is achieved on CIFAR-10, we note that the ACSAC19 approach has not been thoroughly examined in practical settings from the security perspective.

2.2 Whole-Image Steganography and Steganalysis

Whole-image steganography [28] refers to the process of hiding a secret image into a cover image so that it is visually hard to tell whether an arbitrary image is a stego image (i.e., image containing a blind watermark) or not. In contrast to conventional message steganography algorithms based on the least-significant-bit (LSB) approach [22], whole-image steganography naturally requires a larger information hiding capacity, and deep-learning-based approaches typically outperform conventional methods. In [4,5], a set of convolutional neural networks (CNNs) are combined into an end-to-end model to achieve large capacity information hiding required by whole-image steganography. In [25], a CNN-based encoder-decoder network is designed to embed secret images as blind watermarks into cover images. Recently, HiNet [17] leverages invertible neural network (INN) architecture, discrete wavelet transform (DWT), and inverse DWT (IDWT) to construct a whole-image steganography model that outperforms peer models in terms of secret image recovery. We note that deep-learning-based whole-image steganography algorithms typically offer a pair of models, one for hiding the secret images and the other for extracting them.

In contrast to blind-watermarking-based IP protection for DNN models, deep-learning-based steganography algorithms (e.g., [4,17,25]) are all evaluated on realistic image datasets such as ImageNet. To facilitate practical applications of existing IP protection techniques in production systems based on DNN image classifiers, it is necessary to re-examine their feasibility and performance on realistic datasets with images of reasonable sizes. Furthermore, it has been well understood that it is generally hard for image steganography to balance among invisibility, security, information hiding capacity, and robustness [4,28]. Therefore, it is also important to further evaluate existing blind-watermarking-based IP protection techniques from the perspective of steganography algorithm performance.

The security of a steganography algorithm refers to how hard it is to detect that a certain secret image is embedded, and the detector is known as a steganalysis algorithm (or a steganalyzer). Proposed in [34] and evaluated in [33], XuNet consists of a group of CNNs and can effectively tell whether some secret is hidden in a given image. In [36], the YeNet steganalyzer is proposed to directly learn hierarchical representations of images using CNNs. In addition, to thoroughly examine "noise residuals" where secret information may be embedded, SRNet [7] is proposed to construct deep residual network and detect previously suppressed stego signals. In [32], a CNN-based steganalyzer for content-adaptive image steganography in the spatial domain is proposed. We note that the various

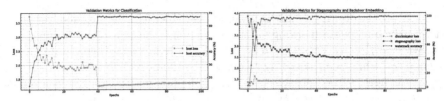

(a) Host DNN image classifier (ResNet-18) performance.   (b) Performance of steganography and steganalysis algorithms.

Fig. 4. End-to-end training of the original ACSAC19 method [19]. Note that all the performance results are obtained on the validation set throughout training and that the host model is ResNet-18.

steganalyzers developed by the security research community may be exploited by adversaries to deter model owners from externally verifying their ownership. Hence, it is important to investigate whether such tools can be exploited and to what extent existing blind-watermarking-based IP protection approaches based on image steganography can be jeopardized.

3   Enhancing a Blind-Watermarking-Based IP Protection Technique (ACSAC19) for DNN Image Classifiers

3.1   Re-examining the Original End-to-End Blind-Watermarking Method (ACSAC19) for DNN Image Classifier Protection

In this section, we re-examine the steganography performance of the ACSAC19 approach [19] on the mini-ImageNet dataset [21,30]. We use the authors' implementation [39]. The host model to be protected is ResNet-18 [14], which is also used in the evaluation of ACSAC19 in [19].

Experiment Settings. To evaluate ACSAC on a more practically sized image dataset, we construct the mini-ImageNet dataset without downsizing the images using an open-source tool [21]. The resultant min-ImageNet dataset includes $60,000$ 256×256 images, evenly drawn from 100 classes (i.e., 600 images per class in our 256×256 image dataset). We perform a $8 : 1 : 1$ split on the dataset, with 80% of that images dedicated to training, 10% for validation, and the remaining 10% for testing. We note that the same dataset split will be applied to other experiments throughout this paper.

We closely follow the ACSAC19 training process outlined in [19] and implemented in [39]. Figure 4 depicts the training process and shows that all three modules of ACSAC19, namely the host model, the steganography algorithm, and the steganalyzer, are trained until convergence. At the end of the training process, the accuracy of the ownership verification task for the host model settles above 92% on the testing set, while the performance of ResNet-18 (i.e., the image classification task) does not obviously deteriorate. Although this result is consistent with those reported in [19], we observe that ACSAC19 does not visually perform well on

Carrier/
Cover
Images

Stego
Images

Fig. 5. Visual defects generated by the ACSAC19 approach [19] on the mini-ImageNet dataset. Note that secret images (i.e., watermarks) are randomly selected from mini-ImageNet.

mini-ImageNet: Fig. 5 includes a set of cover images and the corresponding stego images generated by ACSAC19 trained on mini-ImageNet. Despite the deployment of a steganalyzer to enhance steganography invisibility, the steganography module of ACSAC19 trained on mini-ImageNet does not perform well in terms of (in)visibility. All stego images in Fig. 5 contain obvious visual defects. Take the leftmost image pair in Fig. 5 as an example. The facial part of the male singer in the cover image does not include obvious defects, whereas the corresponding part in the stego image contains evident defects that may alert an image inspector (e.g., the copyright infringer). Such a visibility issue significantly undermines ACSAC19's main objective of blind-watermarking-based IP protection, i.e., external ownership verification: Let us consider the ACSAC19 approach illustrated in Fig. 3. If the stego images generated by the blind-watermarking algorithm, which have been properly learned by the host DNN during end-to-end training, can easily be visually discerned from regular image samples, external ownership verification relying on the outputs of the protected host DNN becomes infeasible. When the model owner presents the stego images generated by ACSAC19, the copyright infringers can easily pick them out through visual inspection, leading to the failure of external ownership verification. Therefore, for the ACSAC19 approach to be useful in realistic image classification applications with images larger than those in CIFAR-10, our results suggest that further enhancements to it are required to at least mitigate this issue of watermark detectability.

3.2 Enhancing a Blind-Watermarking-Based IP Protection Technique (ACSAC19) for DNN Image Classifiers

To address the detectability issue of the ACSAC19 method [19], we propose two alternative approaches, i.e., an enhanced end-to-end with watermark extraction (called the "E2E-Extraction" method) and a two-phase host fine-tuning approach (termed the "Two-Phase" method).

End-to-End Blind-Watermarking IP Protection with Secret Image Extraction. One of our enhancements still leverages the end-to-end training

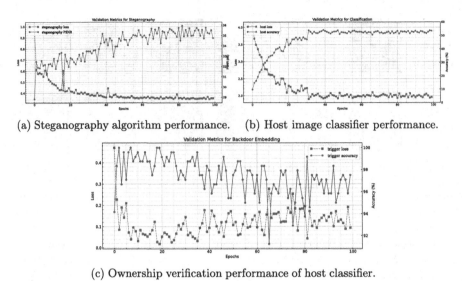

(a) Steganography algorithm performance.   (b) Host image classifier performance.

(c) Ownership verification performance of host classifier.

Fig. 6. End-to-end training of the proposed E2E-Extraction IP protection approach. Note that all the performance results are obtained on the validation set throughout training and that the host model is ResNet-18.

method presented in [19] and illustrated in Fig. 3 but replaces the pair of steganography algorithm and steganalyzer with the a pair of steganography algorithm and the corresponding secret image extraction algorithm. We call this enhanced version of ACSAC19 the E2E-Extraction approach. Note that the end-to-end training strategy as well as loss function in E2E-Extraction remain the same as ACSAC19 [39].

The rationale behind the E2E-Extraction approach is that the steganalysis in ACSAC19, which gives a binary output about whether some secret is hidden in a given image, may converge much earlier than the steganography algorithm, leading to (in)visibility/detectability issue. The steganography algorithm must strive to achieve two goals: On the one hand, it must not hide the secret images too well. Otherwise, the host model may not be able to associate the stego images with ownership verification labels. On the other hand, it should hide the secret images well enough so that the steganalyzer is not able to recognize them with high probability. ACSAC19 was able to achieve such a balance on CIFAR-10, but it fails to do so on more practically sized datasets, such as mini-ImageNet. This is substantiated by Fig. 4b, which shows that the steganalyzer (i.e., the discriminator) is able to converge after the first few epochs. During these epochs, Fig. 4b shows that all three modules of ACSAC19, i.e., the steganography algorithm, the host DNN image classifier, and the steganalyzer, actively interact with each other. However, as the steganalyzer converges, the loss function design of ACSAC19 does not demand it to further interact with the other two modules. As shown in both Fig. 4a and b, the steganography algorithm and the host model further interact toward convergence till around the 40th epoch, and the

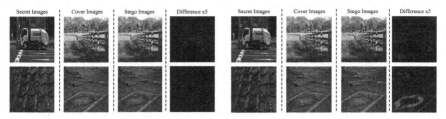

(a) Sample images used and generated by E2E-Extraction.

(b) Sample images used and generated by Two-Phase approach.

Fig. 7. Sample secret, cover, and stego images of the E2E-Extraction and Two-Phase approaches. Note that the "Difference x5" image, which is often used to help quickly detect blind watermarks, is generated by taking the difference between the cover and the stego images and then multiplying the results by 5.

steganalyzer does not effectively participate in this process after the first few epochs. As a result, the steganalyzer hardly provides further useful feedback to the steganography algorithm, which leads to visibility issue (see Fig. 5).

Unlike the steganalyzer of ACSAC19 which is designed to function as a pair with the steganography algorithm in ACSAC19, existing watermark (or secret image) extraction algorithms, on the other hand, have been trained together with the corresponding steganography algorithms as pairs in prior work (e.g., [4,5,17,25]. Since the ACSAC19 approach employs the steganalyzer with the steganography algorithm to form an generative adversarial subnetwork [19], our E2E-Extraction approach essentially pushes the adversarial training idea further by letting a more specialized model capable of extracting the embedded secrets interact with the steganography module.

To evaluate the performance of our proposed E2E-Extraction technique, we choose the pair of steganography and watermark extraction algorithms proposed in [25] and follow the end-to-end training procedures outlined in [38]. The settings of our experiment are the same as those described in Sect. 3.1. Figure 6 summarizes the performance of the three components (i.e., the steganography module, the host DNN image classifier, and the stego image extractor) in our E2E-Extraction technique on the validation set throughout the training process. As shown in Fig. 6c, stego images (i.e., "backdoor" images embedded into the host model through end-to-end training) can effectively "trigger" ownership verification outputs at the host model, achieving satisfactory verification accuracy (i.e., "trigger accuracy" in Fig. 6c). It can be observed that all three components are able to converge and achieve satisfactory performance at the end of the training process and that the ownership verification accuracy stays above 95% most of the time. Compared to the ACSAC19 approach, both the steganography algorithm (see Fig. 6a) and the host model (see Fig. 6b and c) interact with the other modules more actively (and thus more fluctuations), leading to improved visual quality of the stego images.

Figure 7a shows two group of images used and generated by the steganography algorithm we use in E2E-Extraction training. It can be observed that the stego

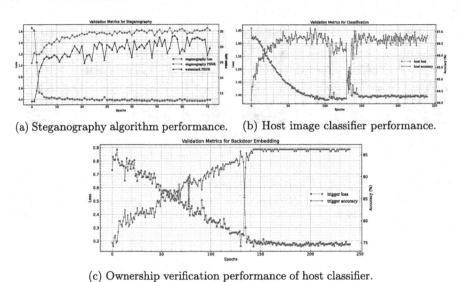

(a) Steganography algorithm performance.   (b) Host image classifier performance.

(c) Ownership verification performance of host classifier.

Fig. 8. Performance of the proposed Two-Phase IP protection approach. Note that all the performance results are obtained on the validation set throughout the respective training phases.

images indeed have better visual quality. In contrast to the ACSAC19 approach [19,39] trained on mini-ImageNet, our proposed enhancement effectively mitigates the issue of watermark detectability and are hence better-suited for protecting copyrights of DNN image classifiers. However, it should be noted that visual defects still exist and that a careful inspector (or a copyright infringer exploiting the widely used "different×5" approach) might still be able to identify images sent by the model owner for the purpose of external ownership verification.

Two-Phase Approach with Host Image Classifier Fine-Tuning. The other enhanced IP protection technique we propose is constructed as follows: First, the host DNN image classifier is trained separately to ensure that it offers satisfactory performance on its main task (i.e., image classification). Meanwhile, we choose a pair of steganography algorithm and secret image extraction algorithm, which can be regarded as our proposed alternatives to the steganography and steganalysis algorithms in ACSAC19 (see Fig. 3). Next, a set of images are randomly selected from the mini-ImageNet dataset to form the cover image set and secret image set. The steganography algorithm and the corresponding watermark extraction algorithm are then trained together using the cover and secret image sets. Using the trained steganography algorithm, we generate a third image set, which is the stego image set. Finally, we mix the stego image set with the training set of the host model and fine-tune the host model in such a way that, in addition to generating correct classification outputs for regular images, stego images will be recognized and proper ownership verification outputs will be generated. This approach is call Two-Phase approach because it virtually involves two phases, namely the preparation phase and the host fine-tuning phase. In the preparation phase, the host model as well as the pair of steganography and watermark extraction algorithms are trained separately. In the host fine-tuning phase, we further train the host model with the stego images (i.e., host model "backdoor" images) to enable external ownership verification while maintaining its performance on the main task.

To evaluate the performance of our proposed Two-Phase approach, we use the same experiment settings as described in Sect. 3.1. The steganography and watermark extraction algorithm pair remains to be the one proposed in [25] and the host classifier is still ResNet-18. Figure 8 summarizes the performance results of the major components of our Two-Phase method: As shown in Fig. 8a, the trained steganography and stego image extraction algorithms perform satisfactorily well. Since the watermark extractor achieves stego image extraction performance (i.e., "watermark PSNR" in Fig. 8a) of more than 26 dB (the extracted watermark images have acceptably good visual quality as reported in [25] at this PSNR level), it can be leveraged to further prove ownership of the host model: After external ownership verification is successfully conducted (i.e., the queried host model generates the expected ownership verification outputs), the model owner can further extract the blind watermarks to prove ownership, possibly in front of a jury or notary. We also note that the host model performance on the main task (i.e., image classification) reported throughout this paper (e.g., see Figs. 6b and 8b) is reasonable according to [1, 2]. Note that the Two-Phase approach trains the steganography algorithm and the watermark extraction algorithm as a pair in the preparation phase, whereas the host model is independently trained during this phase. As shown in Fig. 8a, the peak signal-to-noise ratios (PSNR) for both the steganography algorithm and the watermark extractor are sufficiently high after about 70 epochs. However, since the host model does not interact with the pair of steganography algorithm and watermark extractor during the preparation phase, it host model fine-tuning task requires more epochs because the steganography algorithm and the watermark extractor are able to collaboratively train each other to an extent that can be challenging for the host model. In fact, the Two-Phase approach requires careful selection of hyperparameters such as learning rate, which leads to a longer model development cycle.

Figure 7b shows the images used and generated by the steganography algorithm we use in the Two-Phase training process. It can be observed that, though

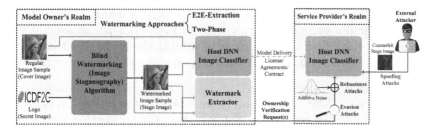

Fig. 9. The overall scheme for a preliminary security analysis of our enhanced blind-watermarking-based IP protection techniques of DNN image classifiers.

the colors of the stego images are slightly distorted, both stego image samples have better visual quality. In contrast to the ACSAC19 approach [19,39], our two-phase approach can also alleviate the issue of watermark detectability, making it more suitable for the protection of DNN classifier copyrights. It should be noted that, in practical applications of IP protection of DNN image classifiers, the original cover images may not be presented to the host model at all, so the copyright infringers will not be able to tell whether the stego images contain obvious color distortion. In fact, if the copyright infringers do not have access to the cover images, it will also be hard for them to conduct the "difference×5" operation.

4   A Preliminary Security Analysis of Our Enhanced Blind-Watermarking-Based IP Protection Techniques for DNN Image Classifiers

To facilitate applications of blind-watermarking-based IP protection in practical image classification systems, further analysis of its security performance on realistic image datasets (e.g., mini-ImageNet) is of urgent necessity. We consider the application scenarios illustrated in Fig. 9: The model owner leverages some blind-watermarking-based IP protection technique (e.g., E2E-Extraction or Two-Phase approach introduced in Sect. 3) to protect his/her newly developed DNN image classifier. The classifier is then delivered to a service provider, who agrees to utilize it within the constraints specified by a certain license or contract. However, it is possible that a certain insider may purposely leak the model, and the service provider himself/herself may also violate the license/contract terms and abuse the model (e.g., providing services to a competitor of the model owner). When the model owner becomes aware of a potential violation of the license/contract terms, he/she can pretend to be a customer requesting (illegal) model service from the service provider. Leveraging the stego images generated during the training process that opens "backdoors" to the host model through blind watermarking, the model owner can externally verify model ownership, allowing him/her to take further actions and protect his/her copyright.

Attacks on Blind-Watermarking-Based IP Protection. However, to ensure the effectiveness and reliability of the blind-watermarking-based IP protection paradigm, we note that its security properties under various attacks, should be carefully examined. As depicted in Fig. 9, our preliminary analysis proposes that the following three types of attacks should be considered when the security of blind-watermarking-based IP protection of DNN image classifiers is examined:

- *Evasion attacks.* This attack may be launched by the service provider who abuses the protected host model. Suppose that visual inspection and/or a steganalyzer may be employed by the service provider to examine every image samples passed to his/her copy of the host model. If a stego image is identified, the service provider can simply reject the corresponding request and do not pass the detected stego image to the host model. In this way, external owner-ship verification must be repeated for multiple times and may eventually fail if the attacker's steganalyzer is strong enough.

- *Spoofing attacks.* This attack is similar to the ambiguity attack described in Sect. 2.1 and is realized by an external attacker sending counterfeit stego images to the user's copy of the host model for ownership verification. The counterfeit stego images are produced by the attacker. Evidently, the more is learned about the steganography algorithm employed by the model devel-oper, the better the counterfeit stego images can be. This attack may be launched to serve one of the following purposes: On the one hand, if the attack succeeds in falsely claiming ownership of the user's copy of the host model, he/she may gain illegal financial benefits. On the other hand, even if the attack is detected, possibly via other measures such as verifying the identity of the attacker, the reliability of the external ownership verification enabled by blind-watermarking-based IP protection is undermined.
- *Robustness attacks.* Steganography algorithms are susceptible to robustness attacks [28]. For instance, the watermark extractor may fail if the stego images are severely distorted during transmission. Consequently, IP protection based on blind image watermarking should also be evaluated against robustness attacks: The service provider who abuses the host model may choose to add noise or distort all the images sent to his/her copy of the host model, in hope that such image manipulations will cause the steganography system to fail while exploiting the typically better robustness of the main task of the host model.

Assumptions on Attacker's Capabilities. In addition to the types of possi-ble attacks that may be launched in practical settings, our preliminary security analysis also takes the attacker's capabilities into account:

- *Naive external attackers.* A naive attacker external to the model owner's realm (see Fig. 9) does not have access to much detail about how the blind-watermarking-based IP protection mechanism is constructed and trained. We assume that such an attacker may be able to learn about the fact that a certain blind watermarking technique is adopted to protect the intellectual property of the host DNN image classifier he/she obtains. However, such an attacker does not know the exact steganography algorithm employed by the model owner.
- *Sophisticated external attackers.* A sophisticated attacker external to the model owner's realm (see Fig. 9) may conduct reconnaissance and eventu-ally learn about certain information on the design and training strategy of the blind-watermarking-based IP protection method. For instance, it is likely that such an attacker is able to find out the name of the steganography algo-rithm utilized by the model owner in IP-protecting training of the host model. It is also likely that such an attacker is able to get hold of a subset of the secret images used by the model owner (e.g., by analyzing external ownership verification requests previously issues by the model owner). However, it is

generally hard for such an external attacker to gain access to the weights of the trained steganography algorithm.

– *Malicious insiders.* An insider, or a sophisticated attacker assisted by an malicious insider within the model owner's realm (see Fig. 9), may be able to obtain the trained version of the steganography algorithm and the watermark extractor. For steganography algorithms, it is also possible to obtain their weights by obtaining the dataset used in the training process [28].

In the remainder of this paper, we will conduct our preliminary security analysis and examine the security performance of E2E-Extraction and Two-Phase approaches, which will both help AI practitioners better assess the applicability of blind-watermarking-based IP protection and reveal how existing IP protection techniques may be further improved.

5   Launching Evasion Attacks on Blind-Watermarking-Based Image Classifier Protection Techniques

Assuming that a copyright infringer will at least visually inspect the images submitted to his/her copy of the host model, We evaluate the security performance of our proposed E2E-Extraction and Two-Phase techniques, which have been shown to exhibit satisfactory invisibility performance. We choose two steganography algorithms and their corresponding stego image extraction algorithms proposed in [4,25] to implement our E2E-Extraction and Two-Phase IP protection mechanisms. In the remainder of this paper, the steganography algorithm in [25] is called the "Encoder-Decoder" (En2D) model in our experiments, while the steganography algorithm in [4] is called "GglNet".

Observing the fact that our Two-Phase approach generates stego images with better invisibility, we first study its security performance under evasion attacks. Our experiments are conducted as follows: First, we set the learning rate for the En2D model to 10^{-3} and the batch size to 30. Four random seeds,

Table 1. Security performance of the proposed Two-Phase approach under evasion attacks launched by naive and sophisticated external attackers. The higher the detection/evasion rate, the easier it is for an attacker to evade external ownership verification.

Attacker Type	Steganalyzer	Attacker Steganography Algorithm	Model Owner Steganography Algorithm	Detection/Evasion Rate			
				Without Dataset Overlaps		With Dataset Overlaps	
				Designed	Actual	Designed	Actual
Naïve External Attackers	SRNet	GglNet	En2D-2022	86.30%	58.83%	85.55%	56.12%
		En2D-2022	GglNet	81.00%	47.08%	82.45%	49.29%
	YeNet	GglNet	En2D-2022	77.65%	34.42%	76.5%	40.38%
		En2D-2022	GglNet	91.15%	28.12%	87.60%	44.33%
Sophisticated External Attackers	SRNet	En2D-1211	En2D-2022	83.00%	49.54%	84.70%	48.83%
		En2D-204	En2D-2022	99.70%	47.88%	86.45%	49.67%
		En2D-109	En2D-2022	67.85%	50.83%	67.05%	52.88%
	YeNet	En2D-1211	En2D-2022	91.75%	46.29%	92.05%	53.46%
		En2D-204	En2D-2022	91.30%	44.96%	90.50%	51.25%
		En2D-109	En2D-2022	72.90%	67.92%	75.85%	76.67%

i.e., $2022, 1211, 204$ and 109, are chosen to train four different versions of the En2D steganography algorithm until convergence, and we name them En2D-2022, En2D-1211, En2D-204, and En2D-109, respectively. As for GglNet, we set its learning rate to 10^{-4} and the batch size to 20. A random seed of 2022 is chosen. For both steganography algorithms, we use the widely-used mean-squared-error (MSE) loss function and the Adam optimizer. The stego image extractors are trained in pairs with the corresponding steganography algorithms. The host model (i.e., ResNet-18) is also optimized for its main task at this phase. Next, we complete the host model fine-tuning step for ownership verification using the stego images generated by different steganography algorithms. To launch evasion attacks, we choose two deep-learning-based steganalyzers, i.e., SRNet [7] and YeNet [36]. To simulate different assumptions on attacker's capabilities, we separately train new steganography models and leverage them to generate datasets for the steganalyzers, which are trained in three different manners:

- *Independently training a steganography algorithm with or without coincidental dataset overlaps.* In this case, we assume that evasion attacks are launched by a naive external attacker, who does not know the exact steganography algorithm used in the IP-protecting training process. In our experiments, such attacks are simulated by evasion attacks implemented with steganography algorithms different from the one used by the model owner. We note, however, since our images are drawn from the publicly available mini-ImageNet dataset, we also consider the scenarios where a small portion ($<5\%$) of the images randomly selected by the attacker coincides with the secret and cover images selected by the model owner.
- *Training the same steganography algorithm without sharing any model weights and/or parameters.* In this case, we assume that evasion attacks are launched by sophisticated external attackers. In our experiments, such attacks are simulated by evasion attacks implemented using the same steganography algorithm as the model owner, but with a different random seed (and hence different model weights at convergence).
- *Training the same steganography algorithms with the same data sets.* In this case, evasion attacks are launched by a malicious insider. In our experiments, we train the steganalyzers using exactly the same datasets (i.e., cover, secret, and stego image sets) as the model owner.

Table 2. Security performance (detection/evasion rates) of the proposed E2E-Extraction and Two-Phase methods under evasion attacks launched by malicious insiders. The higher the detection/evasion rate, the easier it is for an attacker to evade external ownership verification.

Steganalyzer	Attacker Steganography Algorithm	Model Owner Steganography Algorithm	E2E-Extraction	Two-Phase Approach
SRNet	En2D-2022	En2D-2022	100%	97.44%
YeNet	En2D-2022	En2D-2022	100%	89.31%

Table 1 summarizes the security performance of our Two-Phase technique under evasion attacks launched by external attackers. Note that the "designed" column reports the steganalyzers' performance of detecting stego images on the testing sets prepared by the attackers. However, since external attackers are not able to learn about internal details of the steganography algorithms used by the model owner, the actual detection is significantly lower. Table 1 suggests that an external attacker can launch evasion attacks to raise the barrier to external ownership verification: Even for the naive attacker launching evasion attacks with En2D-2022 and YeNet, the model owner must, with a non-negligible probability, prepare more watermarked images to successfully claim copyrights. However, the number of stego images for external ownership verification is fixed once the Two-Phase approach completes training. Even though it is still possible to utilize the steganography algorithm in the Two-Phase approach to generate new stego images, we note that these newly generated images have not been presented to the host image classifier for fine-tuning and the chance of failure to verify ownership is higher with these stego images.

Since coincidental overlaps are rare in practical applications (where the model owner may not disclose his/her private secret and cover image sets at all), we can also observe that coincidental overlaps of secret and cover image sets do not help much in boosting the detection rate in an evasion attack. This also suggests that knowledge about the internals of the steganography algorithm employed by the model owner can only be derived from the stego image set (an observation in consistence with the results and discussion in [28, 33, 34, 36]), which should be kept secret by the model owner. It should also be noted that the actual detection rate achieved by the sophisticated external attackers is above 44%. If such an attacker colludes with other compromised service providers using the same host model to collect stego images sent by the model owner, evasion attacks will help these adversaries exhaust the stego image set more quickly. Security performance of the E2E-Extraction approach under evasion attacks launched by external attackers exhibits characteristics similar to those of the Two-Phase method. We will report detailed results in a separate technical report due to space constraints.

We then examine the security performance of both enhanced methods under evasion attacks launched by a malicious insider. Table 2 summarizes our

Table 3. Security performance (success rates of external ownership verification) of the proposed E2E-Extraction and Two-Phase methods under spoofing attacks (Orange: attacks launched by an insider; Blue: attacks launched by naive external attackers; White: attacks launched by sophisticated external attackers.).

IP Protection Framework	Owner's / Attacker's	En2D-109	En2D-204	En2D-1211	En2D-2022	GglNet
Two-Phase	En2D-109	99.6667%	1.3333%	99.6667%	99.7500%	2.5417%
	En2D-204	3.0833%	99.2083%	3.2917%	3.7083%	47.7500%
	En2D-1211	98.6250%	4.6667%	99.2917%	99.4167%	0.5833%
	En2D-2022	98.1667%	5.6667%	98.7500%	99.3333%	0.5000%
	GglNet	2.3333%	59.6250%	2.2917%	2.2917%	88.5417%
E2E-Extraction	En2D-2022 (JPG)	0.4167%	7.4167%	0.4167%	0.4583%	2.3750%
	En2D-2022 (MAT)	0.6667%	14.9583%	0.8333%	0.5417%	7.2083%

evaluation results and shows that it is possible for a malicious insider to evade most ownership verification attempts of the model owner. Therefore, in addition to securing the one-to-one correspondence between secret image and model owner [13,35], it is also necessary to ensure that success rate of evasion attacks should be kept reasonably low. Special care must be taken to protect steganography algorithms (especially the model weights) trained with the E2E-Extraction or Two-Phase approach from insider attackers, which can help prevent significant loss to the model owner and keep the IP protection mechanism reliable.

6   Launching Spoofing Attacks on Blind-Watermarking-Based Image Classifier Protection Techniques

As revealed in Sect. 5 and in [13], the host DNN image classifier in our E2E-Extraction and Two-Phase approaches are trained to recognize stego images prepared and presented by the model owner. In the experiments in Sect. 5, we have also trained the host model on the ownership verification task while maintaining their performance on the main task. To evaluate the security performance of our proposed enhancements to ACSAC19 under spoofing attacks, we train multiple steganography algorithms independently from the blind-watermarking-based IP protection training process.

Table 3 presents the rates at which counterfeit stego images generated by an attacker are confused by the host DNN model with genuine stego images generated by the model owner. The values with a blue background are obtained under attacks initiated by a naive external attacker. Although the spoofing attack may opportunistically succeed, it is in general hard for a naive attacker to train a steganography algorithm with output stego images that are easily confused with those prepared by the model owner.

The values marked with an orange background are obtained under the assumption that the attacks are launched by a malicious insider. We note that, although such attacks can easily succeed, the resources required to collect a sufficiently large portion (e.g., >90%) of the model owner's stego image set can be prohibitively expensive. The values in Table 3 with a white background are obtained assuming that spoofing attacks are launched by a sophisticated external attacker. Obviously, it is possible that a malicious insider or a sophisticated external attacker can compromise the Two-Phase approach (e.g., the external attacker can train multiple steganography algorithms and see whether one of them can give a relatively high success rate of ownership verification). Hence, even a sophisticated external attacker, who is outside the model owner's realm, may be able to falsely claim model ownership and/or undermine the credibility of blind-watermarking-based IP protection.

Moreover, we note that an attacker can invest further on a particular steganography algorithm to opportunistically boost the success rate of spoofing attacks. Take the En2D models as an example. If the sophisticated attacker is able to confirm that some version of the En2D model is used by the model owner during IP-protecting training, then he/she can train a series of En2D models and try to

Fig. 10. Spoofing attacks launched by an external attacker who is able to obtain a subset of the model owner's secret images. Note that En2D-1211 is employed by the model owner, and the attacker attempts to launch spoofing attacks with En2D-109 and En2D204.

find out the combination of model versions offering high success rate for spoofing attacks. Such knowledge can be reused to attack multiple host models protected by the Two-Phase or E2E-Extraction approach. As shown in Table 3, the attacker do not need to find the exact version of the En2D model (or obtain the stego image set used by the model owner). If En2D-109 is employed by the model owner, the attacker implementing En2D-1211 or En2D-2022 will be able to successfully launch spoofing attacks. Therefore, in practical applications of our enhanced versions of ACSAC19, it is necessary for the model owner to conduct similar experiments in advance and verify that the steganography algorithm he/she chooses offers a sufficiently high degree of security under possible spoofing attacks.

Finally, Fig. 10 depicts how an external attacker with access to a subset of the model owner's secret images may be able to work out a plan to falsely claim model ownership. As shown in this figure, the attacker may not get a high success rate if he/she starts with En2D-204. However, if the attacker is patient enough to try multiple random seeds, it is possible that he eventually finds En2D-109, which is good enough for the purpose of spoofing attacks. Due to space constraints, further visual results will be reported in a separate technical report.

7   Launching Robustness Attacks on Blind-Watermarking-Based Image Classifier Protection Techniques

In practical applications of DNN image classifiers, additive noise may be introduced during transmission. Evidently, additive noise will impact not only the ownership verification task but the main task of the host model as well. In this paper, we launch robustness attacks on our proposed E2E-Extraction and Two-Phase techniques while ensuring the that performance of the main task does not obviously deteriorate. We choose to examine such a configuration because

Table 4. Performance (success rates) of the ownership verification task of the proposed E2E-Extraction and Two-Phase approaches under robustness attacks.

IP Protection Framework	Steganography-Host Pair	Gaussian Noise	Salt & Pepper Noise	Noiseless
Two-Phase Approach	En2D-109-ResNet18	84.8750%	96.7083%	99.6667%
	En2D-204-ResNet18	87.9167%	98.6250%	99.2083%
	En2D-1211-ResNet18	85.4583%	98.5417%	99.2917%
	En2D-2022-ResNet18	93.2500%	98.9167%	99.3333%
	GglNet-ResNet18	70.9167%	85.2917%	88.5417%
E2E-Extraction	En2D-2022-ResNet18	80.0417%	83.2917%	87.6667%

in practical settings, the attacker (i.e., the copyright infringer abusing the protected host DNN image classifier) would like to launch robustness attacks both to invalidate external ownership verification tests issued by the model owner and to utilize the host DNN classifier for profit.

In our experiments examining the impacts of robustness attacks, we assume that robustness attacks are launched by a naive external attacker. Although malicious insiders or sophisticated external attackers may also exploit robustness attacks, our assumption is reasonable because robustness attacks present a relatively low technical barrier: The attacker does not need to be an expert on whole-image steganography, so it is more practical for a naive external attackers to first consider such attacks.

Table 5 shows that both Gaussian noise (with a mean of 30, a standard deviation of 15 for 8-bit pixels) and salt & pepper noise (with 1, 200 points per image) will slightly deteriorate the performance of the main task. Meanwhile, as shown in Table 4, Gaussian noise is able to further deteriorate host model performance on the ownership verification tasks.

Based on these observations, we argue that for more sophisticated host models (e.g., ResNet-101), more noise can be added to all the input images to the host model by the external attackers (because the host model will have more representative power than the steganography module, and thus more likely to remain robust). To enforce blind-watermarking-based IP protection, the impacts of robustness attackers must be properly addressed in further enhancements.

Table 5. Performance (classification accuracy) of the main task of the proposed E2E-Extraction and Two-Phase approaches under robustness attacks.

IP Protection Framework	Steganography-Host Pair	Gaussian Noise	Salt & Pepper Noise	Noiseless
Two-Phase Approach	En2D-109-ResNet18	64.8667%	61.9833%	68.9167%
	En2D-204-ResNet18	64.2333%	61.4167%	68.0333%
	En2D-1211-ResNet18	64.9000%	61.7667%	68.8833%
	En2D-2022-ResNet18	63.3167%	60.8000%	67.2167%
	GglNet-ResNet18	63.1000%	59.4667%	66.7000%
E2D-Extraction	En2D-2022-ResNet18	45.7833%	45.1167%	50.5667%

In addition, a combination of robustness attack and evasion attack (see Fig. 9) may exhaust the stego images prepared for ownership verification, significantly undermining the practicality and applicability of the blind-watermarking-based IP protection paradigm. To address this issue, it may be necessary to investigate a blind-watermarking-based IP protection technique that works equally well on new stego images generated by the model owner after the host model is trained, watermarked and shipped.

8   Conclusion and Future Work

In this paper, we re-examine the performance of blind-watermarking-based IP protection for DNN image classifiers on the more practical mini-ImageNet dataset and propose two enhanced IP protection techniques, which are evaluated from the security perspective. We find that existing blind-watermarking-based IP protection is still susceptible to various attacks, and the benefits of external ownership verification may be undermined or exploited. As our future work, we will further examine possible defenses against the attacks reported in this paper and further evaluate our proposed techniques in production systems.

Acknowledgments. This work is supported by the Guangdong Provincial Foundation for Basic and Applied Basic Research Grant No. 2021A1515110673 from the Department of Science and Technology of Guangdong Province, P.R. China. Any opinions, findings, conclusions, or recommendations expressed in this publication are those of the author(s) and do not necessarily reflect the view of the funding agency.

References

1. ImageNet Classification. https://pjreddie.com/darknet/imagenet/
2. Models and Pre-Trained Weights – Torchvision 0.12 Documentations (2017). https://pytorch.org/vision/stable/models.html
3. Aiken, W., Kim, H., Woo, S., Ryoo, J.: Neural network laundering: removing blackbox backdoor watermarks from deep neural networks. Comput. Secur. **106**, 102277 (2021). https://doi.org/10.1016/j.cose.2021.102277
4. Baluja, S.: Hiding images in plain sight: deep steganography. In: Proceedings of the 31st International Conference on Neural Information Processing Systems, NIPS 2017, pp. 2066–2076. Curran Associates Inc., Red Hook, NY, USA (2017)
5. Baluja, S.: Hiding images within images. IEEE Trans. Pattern Anal. Mach. Intell. **42**(7), 1685–1697 (2020). https://doi.org/10.1109/TPAMI.2019.2901877
6. Batina, L., Bhasin, S., Jap, D., Picek, S.: CSI NN: reverse engineering of neural network architectures through electromagnetic side channel. In: 28th USENIX Security Symposium (USENIX Security 2019), pp. 515–532. USENIX Association, Santa Clara, CA (2019). https://www.usenix.org/conference/usenixsecurity19/presentation/batina
7. Boroumand, M., Chen, M., Fridrich, J.: Deep residual network for steganalysis of digital images. IEEE Trans. Inf. Forensics Secur. **14**(5), 1181–1193 (2019). https://doi.org/10.1109/TIFS.2018.2871749

8. Cao, X., Jia, J., Gong, N.Z.: IPGuard: protecting intellectual property of deep neural networks via fingerprinting the classification boundary. In: Proceedings of the 2021 ACM Asia Conference on Computer and Communications Security, ASIA CCS 2021, pp. 14–25. Association for Computing Machinery, New York, NY, USA (2021). https://doi.org/10.1145/3433210.3437526

9. Chen, J., et al.: Copy, Right? A testing framework for copyright protection of deep learning models. cs.CR abs/2112.05588 (2021). https://doi.org/10.48550/ARXIV.2112.05588

10. Chen, K., Guo, S., Zhang, T., Xie, X., Liu, Y.: Stealing deep reinforcement learning models for fun and profit. In: Proceedings of the 2021 ACM Asia Conference on Computer and Communications Security, ASIA CCS 2021, pp. 307–319. Association for Computing Machinery, New York, NY, USA (2021). https://doi.org/10.1145/3433210.3453090

11. Chen, X., et al.: Recent advances and clinical applications of deep learning in medical image analysis. Med. Image Anal. 102444 (2022). (in Press). https://doi.org/10.1016/j.media.2022.102444

12. Cheng, J., et al.: ResGANet: residual group attention network for medical image classification and segmentation. Med. Image Anal. **76**, 102313 (2022). https://doi.org/10.1016/j.media.2021.102313

13. Fan, L., Ng, K.W., Chan, C.S., Yang, Q.: DeepIP: deep neural network intellectual property protection with passports. IEEE Trans. Pattern Anal. Mach. Intell. **44**, 1 (2021). https://doi.org/10.1109/TPAMI.2021.3088846

14. He, K., Zhang, X., Ren, S., Sun, J.: Deep residual learning for image recognition. In: Proceedings of the IEEE Conference on Computer Vision and Pattern Recognition (CVPR) (2016)

15. Hilty, R., Hoffmann, J., Scheuerer, S.: Intellectual property justification for artificial intelligence. Artif. Intell. Intellect. Property (2021). https://doi.org/10.1093/oso/9780198870944.003.0004

16. Hu, X., Chu, L., Pei, J., Liu, W., Bian, J.: Model complexity of deep learning: a survey. Knowl. Inf. Syst. **63**(10), 2585–2619 (2021). https://doi.org/10.1007/s10115-021-01605-0

17. Jing, J., Deng, X., Xu, M., Wang, J., Guan, Z.: HiNet: deep image hiding by invertible network. In: Proceedings of the IEEE/CVF International Conference on Computer Vision (ICCV), pp. 4733–4742 (2021)

18. Krizhevsky, A.: Learning multiple layers of features from tiny images. Technical report (2009)

19. Li, Z., Hu, C., Zhang, Y., Guo, S.: How to prove your model belongs to you: a blind-watermark based framework to protect intellectual property of DNN. In: Proceedings of the 35th Annual Computer Security Applications Conference, ACSAC 2019, pp. 126–137 (2019). https://doi.org/10.1145/3359789.3359801

20. Lin, N., Chen, X., Lu, H., Li, X.: Chaotic weights: a novel approach to protect intellectual property of deep neural networks. IEEE Trans. Comput. Aided Des. Integr. Circuits Syst. **40**(7), 1327–1339 (2021). https://doi.org/10.1109/TCAD.2020.3018403

21. Liu, Y.: Tools for mini-ImageNet Dataset (2020). https://github.com/yaoyao-liu/mini-imagenet-tools

22. Luo, W., Huang, F., Huang, J.: Edge adaptive image steganography based on LSB matching revisited. IEEE Trans. Inf. Forensics Secur. **5**(2), 201–214 (2010). https://doi.org/10.1109/TIFS.2010.2041812

23. Ong, D.S., Chan, C.S., Ng, K.W., Fan, L., Yang, Q.: Protecting intellectual property of generative adversarial networks from ambiguity attacks. In: Proceedings of the IEEE/CVF Conference on Computer Vision and Pattern Recognition (CVPR), pp. 3630–3639 (2021)

24. Rathi, P., Bhadauria, S., Rathi, S.: Watermarking of deep recurrent neural network using adversarial examples to protect intellectual property. Appl. Artif. Intell. **36**(1), 2008613 (2022). https://doi.org/10.1080/08839514.2021.2008613

25. ur Rehman, A., Rahim, R., Nadeem, S., ul Hussain, S.: End-to-end trained CNN encoder-decoder networks for image steganography. In: Leal-Taixé, L., Roth, S. (eds.) ECCV 2018. LNCS, vol. 11132, pp. 723–729. Springer, Cham (2019). https://doi.org/10.1007/978-3-030-11018-5_64

26. Rokhana, R., Herulambang, W., Indraswari, R.: Multi-class image classification based on MobileNetV2 for detecting the proper use of face mask. In: 2021 International Electronics Symposium (IES), pp. 636–641 (2021). https://doi.org/10.1109/IES53407.2021.9594022

27. Rouhani, B.D., Chen, H., Koushanfar, F.: DeepSigns: a generic watermarking framework for protecting the ownership of deep learning models. Cryptology ePrint Archive, Paper 2018/311 (2018). https://eprint.iacr.org/2018/311

28. Subramanian, N., Elharrouss, O., Al-Maadeed, S., Bouridane, A.: Image steganography: a review of the recent advances. IEEE Access **9**, 23409–23423 (2021). https://doi.org/10.1109/ACCESS.2021.3053998

29. Tang, R., Du, M., Hu, X.: Deep serial number: computational watermarking for DNN intellectual property protection. CoRR abs/2011.08960 (2020). https://arxiv.org/abs/2011.08960

30. Vinyals, O., Blundell, C., Lillicrap, T., Kavukcuoglu, K., Wierstra, D.: Matching networks for one shot learning. In: Proceedings of the 30th International Conference on Neural Information Processing Systems, NIPS 2016, pp. 3637–3645. Curran Associates Inc., Red Hook, NY, USA (2016). https://dl.acm.org/doi/10.5555/3157382.3157504

31. Wu, H., Liu, G., Yao, Y., Zhang, X.: Watermarking neural networks with watermarked images. IEEE Trans. Circuits Syst. Video Technol. **31**(7), 2591–2601 (2021). https://doi.org/10.1109/TCSVT.2020.3030671

32. Xiang, Z., Sang, J., Zhang, Q., Cai, B., Xia, X., Wu, W.: A new convolutional neural network-based steganalysis method for content-adaptive image steganography in the spatial domain. IEEE Access **8**, 47013–47020 (2020). https://doi.org/10.1109/ACCESS.2020.2978110

33. Xu, G., Wu, H.Z., Shi, Y.Q.: Ensemble of CNNs for steganalysis: an empirical study. In: Proceedings of the 4th ACM Workshop on Information Hiding and Multimedia Security, IH&MMSec 2016, pp. 103–107. Association for Computing Machinery, New York, NY, USA (2016). https://doi.org/10.1145/2909827.2930798

34. Xu, G., Wu, H.Z., Shi, Y.Q.: Structural design of convolutional neural networks for steganalysis. IEEE Signal Process. Lett. **23**(5), 708–712 (2016). https://doi.org/10.1109/LSP.2016.2548421

35. Xue, M., Zhang, Y., Wang, J., Liu, W.: Intellectual property protection for deep learning models: taxonomy, methods, attacks, and evaluations. IEEE Trans. Artif. Intell. **1**(01), 1–1 (2022). https://doi.org/10.1109/TAI.2021.3133824

36. Ye, J., Ni, J., Yi, Y.: Deep learning hierarchical representations for image steganalysis. IEEE Trans. Inf. Forensics Secur. **12**(11), 2545–2557 (2017). https://doi.org/10.1109/TIFS.2017.2710946

37. Zhang, J., et al.: Protecting intellectual property of deep neural networks with watermarking. In: Proceedings of the 2018 on Asia Conference on Computer and Communications Security, ASIACCS 2018, pp. 159–172. Association for Computing Machinery, New York, NY, USA (2018). https://doi.org/10.1145/3196494.3196550

38. Zhang, J., et al.: Deep model intellectual property protection via deep watermarking. IEEE Trans. Pattern Anal. Mach. Intell. **44**, 1 (2021). https://doi.org/10.1109/TPAMI.2021.3064850

39. Zheng, L.: How to prove your model belongs to you: a blind-watermark based framework to protect intellectual property of DNN (2021). https://github.com/zhenglisec/Blind-Watermark-for-DNN

Forensic Analysis and Artifact Detection

Digital Forensics Tool Evaluation on Deleted Files

Miloš Stanković[(✉)] and Tahir M. Khan

Purdue University, West Lafayette 47906, USA
{mstankovic,tmkhan}@purdue.edu

Abstract. In a world where data is deleted every millisecond, whether on purpose or unintentionally, the question is whether deleted digital files still exist or if they are simply invisible to us on digital devices. Over the years, researchers have answered the question, but the rapid development of technologies and software makes the topic relevant. The global pandemic (coronavirus disease 2019) affected the physical and cyber worlds. Cyber attacks and data breaches have increased by over 400%. During these attacks, data is frequently deleted, mismanaged, or overwritten, making it difficult for users and digital investigators to recover and trace. Commercial tools that analyze deleted files are often expensive, and the unknown factor of free tools has always been a concern. In this paper, we evaluated two digital forensics tools, Magnet AXIOM, a commercial tool, and Autopsy, a free digital forensics tool, to partially bridge the gap for this era. We also used a differential analysis approach to investigate the persistence of deleted files. Moreover, for the best evaluation of the tools, we created files of various types and activities that mimic the daily usage of an average user on a Windows 11 operating system. The activities are divided into phases based on the processes that will most likely overwrite the deleted files. We also discussed the findings of these phases and presented the recommendations and challenges faced during the research process.

Keywords: Computer Forensics · Digital Forensics · Magnet AXIOM Suite · Autopsy · Microsoft Windows 11 · Deleted Files

1 Introduction

Digital crimes have been on the rise for years and certainly, the last two of the global pandemic created further complications. According to [1] article, Crowd-Strike, a cybersecurity company, reported a 400% increase in threats during 2019 and 2020, with four out of five coming from cybercriminals in 2020 alone. Forbes [2], noted how the year 2020 had surpassed all records regarding data breaches. On average, researchers, [3] recognized a cost increase of a data breach by $0.77 million in the last few years. Moreover, on average, a data breach costs an organization around $3.29 million [3]. Industry specialists [4] estimate the cost of downtime per minute for a small company, medium company, and large

S. Goel et al. (Eds.): ICDF2C 2022, LNICST 508, pp. 61–83, 2023.
https://doi.org/10.1007/978-3-031-36574-4_4

company is $8,000, $74,000, and $11,600, respectively. Losing valuable time and data is not only costly but time-consuming as well. On average, it is shown, ransomware causes 16.2 days of downtime [4]. Fast and guided recovery from a cyber incident is paramount.

Besides understanding the nature of the threats and the systems they affect, it is crucial to understand the capabilities of the data recovery tools used to mitigate cyber incidents. Rapid technology development forced companies to adapt and diversify in order to keep up with the ever-growing market. The need for digital forensics recovery tools led companies to develop their proprietary products. The products have been costly, forcing software developers to create alternative solutions. Often these products have different results when tested against the same situation. The question, which one is better and is there a difference, looms within the digital forensics community. Previous research [5–7] has shown some evaluation of the tools; however, there has not been updated literature found on the topic.

This research aims to address the lack of literature on evaluating free and commercial recovery tools in digital forensics. The study will evaluate two tools, one commercial, and one free tool on a spinning hard drive utilizing newly released Microsoft Windows 11. Microsoft Windows is one of the most utilized Operating Systems and according to Microsoft [8] there is 1.3 billion users of Windows 10. Microsoft Windows 11 is the next step for the users and that is why this research has chosen Microsoft Windows 11. Despite the increased presence of solid state drives, spinning hard drives are still widely used and should not be forgotten when it comes to digital forensics analysis. According to [9], in 2020 there has been sold approximately 350 million spinning hard drives and 320 million solid state drives. Most of the tools have the capabilities of analyzing solid state and spinning hard drives today. The chosen commercial tool is Magnet AXIOM Process and Examine, created by Magnet Forensics [10]. Magnet Forensics is being used by many law enforcement offices and it was nominated as DFIR Commercial Tool of the Year in July of 2021 [11]. The free tool of choice for the research is Autopsy [12] and has been one of the best open source platforms for digital forensic investigators for years. Autopsy was approved by the National Institute of Standards and Technology (NIST) in 2012 and supporting Windows runtime environment. Finally, we used differential analysis approach to ensure the validity of our analysis [13].

Contributions of this research include:

- Detailed analysis of deleted files from Windows 11 OS and their persistence in multiple stages.
- Providing a detailed evaluation of the two tools used for the experiment.
- Comparison of the different stages of deleted files and their persistence utilizing differential analysis.

The rest of the document is structured as follows, Sect. 2 discusses the related work pertaining to the problem pointed out in the paper. Section 3, discusses the methodology and the design of the experiment. Section 4, discusses the results and the analysis of the experiment. Lastly, Sect. 5, presents the conclusion and the future works.

2   Related Work

The difference between free and commercially available tools for digital forensics has been debated for years. Free tools have been closing the gap in recent years but is that gap close enough to switch to the free tool? In the research [7], five tools were assessed under the same conditions to evaluate the outcome of the recovered files. The tools included in the study were, EnCase, FTK, Recuva, R-Studio, and Stellar Phoenix. The EnCase and FTK were commercial tools, where the other three tools were data recovery tools but did not classify as digital forensics tools [7]. The tools were picked based on popularity at the time of the paper. The experimental method included a machine with a Windows operating system and installation of previously selected applications as well as data population. The research [7] showed that neither tool had the same recovered data, and no tool recovered all the files.

In the research, [5] two popular filesystems New Technology File System (NTFS) and File Allocation Table 32 (FAT32) were examined. The end goal was to verify against predetermined files, forensically discovered files that had been deleted and recovered to examine the success of the file system. The process consisted of four phases, assess, acquire, analyze and report. The three sections used to organize hard drives included information, file storage, and basic data [5]. In order to prove the recoverability of the two different filessystems (FAT32 and NTFS), the files were deleted first and wiped afterward. Upon imaging process, FTK was used for analysis. The results of the experiment [5] showed that the deleted files using Evidence Emulator (EE) could not be recovered forensically. The EE at the time of the experiment was used to wipe all of the data from the storage devices.

Actions performed after the files have been deleted greatly impact the process of recovering deleted items. In the paper [13], a differential analysis approach was utilised to evaluate the persistence of deleted files and better understand the process of deletion. Similarly in [14], factors affecting deleted files were identified. The studies have compared the images taken before the files were deleted, after they were deleted as well as after some actions performed on the system. Images of the hard disks were compared and the conclusions were drawn. Throughout the process a prototype of the software was developed to aid the analysis. The developed software allows for parsing the DFXML file form the NTFS system [15]. The full code is available at the GitHub page (https://github.com/AllisonShen/security_mft). As the conclusion the study has shown the way of comparing different stages of the deleted files and their reminiscence.

Unauthorized access to computer systems has been a problem for years. Recent research [16], conducted an experiment from a data recovery perspective utilizing Windows and Unix platforms. The researchers wanted to utilize multiple methodologies on deleted data. The paper [16], pointed out a four-step process of acquiring digital evidence. The first step is the acquisition of the evidence. Next, authentication of the evidence is necessary to ensure the integrity of the data. The third step is to analyze gathered data. Lastly, evaluation of the information and if the evidence can be used in court. Later in the paper, researchers explained the differences between Windows and Unix systems and showed the locations where the evidence is most likely to be. Tools used to recover data from Windows OS were, Drivespy, Encase, and Ilook. The Sleuth Kit and The Coroner's Tool Kit were used in Unix OS. Basics overview of computer forensics methods and tools was presented in the paper [16], and explaining an overview of the tools used.

The variety of digital evidence has increased, never the less, it still can be sorted into five different categories according to [6] paper. Out of the five categories, the main three related to this research include image/video like files, system files, and document files. Increased storage is gained through hard drives, which are comprised of programs to store data and an operating system. The research [6] designates six levels to organize the files. The structure of levels numbered 0 through 5 is as follows:

- regular files
- temporary files
- deleted files
- retained data blocks
- vendor hidden blocks
- overwritten data

The experiment [6] was conducted on different hard drive technologies and file structures. Various tools were applied to recover data on such structures as photographs and videos. These tools, when compared, were found to be able to recover the data to a certain extent. The results showed Encase performing the best compared to Autopsy, OSForensics, and Recuva. The difference was almost 90% between Autopsy and Encase in found files, although Autopsy had 70% of data usability after restoration. As a conclusion of the study [6] the researchers noted Encase was the tool best suited for recovering data and reliability of use, followed by Autopsy.

On the other hand, in the paper [17] researchers investigated connections within computer forensics and recovering of the data. Additionally, research [17] investigated applications of anti-forensics and computer forensics. Anti-forensics technology was divided into three main categories, data hiding, data erasure, and encrypted data [17]. The most common tool for data hiding is Runefs, manipulating data to be stored as bad blocks. Data erasure is the most effective anti-forensics strategy by attempting to remove evidence. Encrypted data is not hidden but unknown to a user, potentially containing malicious code. The research [17] also divided computer forensics technology into two levels, hardware and software forensics tools. Hardware forensics tools utilize disk reading, firmware restoration, and hardware substitution [17]. Software forensics tools vary based on the data in need of recovery. The researchers concluded that data recovery is an important link in the crime-solving process due to the increased number of cybercrimes.

A survey paper [18] examined ten database extraction tools that were selected based on recency and the ability to support different platforms. Supporting different platforms was important in order to reach a wide area of users. The researchers could not evaluate tools on the same sample database due to the differences of each tool and their execution. Regardless of the different formats of the data used for the tools, the results were valid. The tools from the experiment [18] provided various uses, including verification and data extraction.

Computer forensics and mobile forensics have been becoming more coherent, with platforms sharing similar hardware and software specifications. In the paper [19], a comparison of android forensics was utilized for retrieving file systems. The methodology used in this study consisted of six stages. The stages included the evidence intake phase, identification phase, preparation phase, isolation phase, processing phase, verification phase, and documentation/reporting phase. The outcome showed the method of AccessData FTK Imager and dd Image Evidence Tree, file carving utilizing Autopsy produced the most results [19]. Moreover, the researchers recommended EaseUS Data Recovery Wizard Free for recovering deleted files.

3   Methodology

The goal of this study was to compare two tools and analyze their findings based on the different stages of the files being deleted. The files were carefully created for this experiment based on average user habits. For example, files were placed in the downloads and documents folder where the user is most likely to store them. Each folder contained multiple files and multiple types of files varying in size. After the deletion process, various activities were performed, such as web browsing, downloading of the files, watching videos, and many more. The process presented multiple stages of the user's activity, giving the researchers multiple points for the examination. The operating system of choice was a newly released Microsoft Windows 11 installed on a spinning hard drive.

The experimental design of the study follows the four-step methodology presented below.

3.1   Environment Preparation

The first step of the experiment was choosing the equipment for the study. The environment consisted of one laptop (Dell Latitude 5591) with two separate hard drives. The first hard drive (HDD) was the one being examined, and the second solid-state drive (SSD) was the one containing the examination software. The hard drives were altered in the laptop based on the need and were never in the laptop at the same time. This is to ensure no cross-contamination of the data. The solid-state drive containing the necessary software did not need any additional setup, where the HDD (Hitachi 100 GB) had to be wiped, and the new Microsoft Windows 11 required installation. Since the HDD was not a new unit, a complete wipe was performed. This step was completed utilizing Ultimate Boot CD (Version5.3.8) [20] and Darik's Boot and Nuke (2.3.0) [21] software. The wipe method used the 'DoD Short' option with three rounds of wiping. Upon wiping, the next step was to install Windows 11 Pro and update.

Once the drivers and operating system was up to date, the updates and driver updates were paused for a month, so there would not be any additional traffic interfering. In addition to the pausing updates, a modified script [22] was run to stop any unnecessary services. The last step before transferring the files to the laptop was to open the Microsoft Edge browser and set it up. The default setup was followed. The specifications of the Hitachi HDD that is being examined is presented in Table 1.

Table 1. Hitachi Hard Drive Information

Manufacturer	HITACHI
Serial Number	MPCZN7Y0HGP1ML
Model Number	HTS721010G9SA00
Capacity	100 GB
Date of Creation	January 2007
RPM	7200
P/N	0A27318
MLC	DA1373
CHS	16383/16/63
F/W	C10H

3.2   Data Creation

In order to control the environment as best as possible, 24 separate files were created with three different categories text, images, and videos. Each category consisted of eight files, four that were placed in the documents folder and four for the downloads folder. The naming scheme was followed by the folder placement, type of the file, and file number. For example, image three that was placed in the downloads folder was named *downloads_ image_ 3.jpg*.

The text files had four different sizes starting with around 1 KB, 1 MB, 100 MB, and 500 MB. This strategy ensured the range of multiple text files. Since the files were created by the researchers manually and the custom text was in each of the files, the exact sizes (e.g., 100 MB, or 500 MB) were not possible to achieve. Nevertheless, the sizes are close to the ones referenced. The first text file had 30 lines of the following text *documents_file1_ column_ A_ row_ 1* except where the row number would increase for the each row added. The reason for allocating columns and rows in the text files was so if a partial recreation of the file was possible, the researchers would know exactly what part of the file was recovered.

Just like the text files, the four images created for the study were of different sizes. Since the size of the photos is harder to predict, a different approach was used. For the creation of the photos, the Nikon D5200 D-SLR camera with various modes created different size images. The first and the smallest images in both documents and downloads folder were taken using 'BASIC' image quality and 'Small' image size equaling to around 430 KB. The second image settings were 'NORM' image quality and 'Medium' image size adding to around 3.5 MB for each folder. The third image had 'FINE' and 'Large' settings for the image quality and the image size, respectively equaling to around 8.1 MB. Lastly, the fourth image, 'RAW' image quality, and 'Large' image size adding up to around 25 MB. The content of the photo was the name of the photo with a white background. For example, the second photo placed in the downloads folder (*downloads_ image_ 2.jpg*) had the content showing *downloads image 2*. All of the photos were shot in the same environment, from the same place, and the mode of the pictures was set to auto.

Lastly, the videos were taken with the same camera (Nikon D5200) following the same naming scheme as the photos, except having video instead of an image. The process of creating the videos differed from creating the photos. The quality settings of each video was the same; movie quality set to 'high', and frame size/frame rate set to '1920 × 1080 and 60'. The microphone was set to auto sensitivity, and the automatic focus was left on. Background audio was generic beeping noise which was the same for all videos. To differentiate the sizes of the videos the first video was 5 s long, the second was the 60 s, the third was 300 s, and the last video was 600 s long, equaling to sizes of around 15 MB, 164 MB, 817 MB, and 1.5 GB respectively.

Presented in Table 2 are all of the created files for this experiment. For the full MD5 and SHA256 values of the files created, please reference the A. Appendix, Tables 6 and 5.

3.3   Data Population and Collection

Data population and the data collection for this experiment was conducted in five different phases. Each of the phases was built upon the previous and linked together to complete the study. After each phase, an image of the Hitachi HDD was captured.

Consequent to the creation of the files, the researchers placed Hitachi HDD into the laptop, powered it on, and copied the files in the already predesignated folders (documents and downloads). Once the files were copied, the laptop was powered off, and the HDD was pulled out from the laptop. Meanwhile, the SSD with the examination software was put back on the laptop. In order to create an image of the Hitachi HDD, a write blocker presented in Fig. 1 was used. This was to eliminate any potential writing to the HDD. Software utilized to create the RAW (dd) image of the physical device (Hitachi HDD) was AccessData's FTK Imager (Version 4.2.1.4) [23]. The created image was named *image_ 01_ BI*, BI abbreviating the base image. The base image was used as the reference to the other images and in checking hash values of the files.

The second phase of the data population and collection consisted of reinstalling the Hitachi HDD and powering on the laptop. In this phase of the experiment, all the files previously copied (total of 24) were deleted from the

Table 2. Created Files for the Examination

File Name	Size
documents_file_1.txt	1011 bytes (1,011 bytes)
documents_file_2.txt	1.04 MB (1,098,892 bytes)
documents_file_3.txt	106 MB (111,666,573 bytes)
documents_file_4.txt	528 MB (554,332,869 bytes)
documents_image_1.JPG	431 KB (442,055 bytes)
documents_image_2.JPG	3.37 MB (3,537,995 bytes)
documents_image_3.JPG	7.95 MB (8,346,930 bytes)
documents_image_4.NEF	24.7 MB (25,959,999 bytes)
documents_video_1.MOV	14.7 MB (15,432,643 bytes)
documents_video_2.MOV	159 MB (166,766,872 bytes)
documents_video_3.MOV	793 MB (832,085,550 bytes)
documents_video_4.MOV	1.54 GB (1,662,377,424 bytes)
downloads_file_1.txt	1009 bytes (1,009 bytes)
downloads_file_2.txt	1.04 MB (1,098,892 bytes)
downloads_file_3.txt	106 MB (111,666,573 bytes)
downloads_file_4.txt	528 MB (554,332,869 bytes)
downloads_image_1.JPG	434 KB (444,917 bytes)
downloads_image_2.JPG	3.42 MB (3,596,578 bytes)
downloads_image_3.JPG	7.97 MB (8,358,210 bytes)
downloads_image_4.NEF	24.4 MB (25,648,008 bytes)
downloads_video_1.MOV	14.7 MB (15,420,553 bytes)
downloads_video_2.MOV	160 MB (168,357,406 bytes)
downloads_video_3.MOV	798 MB (837,483,431 bytes)
downloads_video_4.MOV	1.54 GB (1,662,532,158 bytes)

laptop (SHIFT + Del), and the laptop was powered off. The second image of the HDD was taken, again using a write blocker and FTK Imager. The name of the image was *image_02_AD*, referring to after the delete process.

In the third phase, the laptop was powered on, and the laptop was left idling for 60 min (±3 min). The idling process did not involve any user interaction besides powering on and off the laptop and opening the task manager to monitor the 'up time' of the machine. After an hour, the laptop was powered off, and the HDD was extracted once more. The third image was taken from the extracted HDD using the same methods as before. The image was named *image_03_ADI*, abbreviating after delete and idling period.

The fourth image followed the same procedure for installing the HDD and powering on the laptop. The purpose of this phase was to create an image of the HDD after an hour of browsing the internet, mimicking the everyday activity of a user. For the browsing activity, the researchers have chosen not to use

Fig. 1. Write Blocker with HDD Attached

more than five tabs at the time, with one of the tabs dedicated to the timer on YouTube.com, showing the time spent on browsing. The browser used for this activity was Microsoft Edge (Version 90.0.818.66). The rest of the tabs were used for searching news and articles on stocks, technology, science, etc. For the full browsing history, please refer to the B. Appendix. When the 60 min (±3 min) mark elapsed, the laptop was turned off, and the same procedure for imaging the HDD was repeated. The name of the fourth image was *image_04_ADW*, W standing for the web.

Lastly, the fifth activity of the last phase was to download a file that is larger than 10% of the entire size of the HDD. In this case, the file needed to be over 10 GB. In order to download a known file, the researchers have created and uploaded the file to Microsoft's OneDrive using a different computer. The name of the file was *download_file_test.zip* and the size was 10.4 GB. For the last time the HDD was extracted from the laptop for the imaging process. The same procedure was followed as in the previous steps for obtaining the image.

3.4 Data Processing and Analysis

Data processing for this experiment started when the five images were taken. Since the images were in the RAW (dd) format, it allowed both examining software to use the files. The machine used for the examination was the same laptop used for the experiment, except the hard drives were swapped. Instead of Hitachi HDD, which was pulled out of the laptop after the fifth image, the SSD with examination software was installed back in the laptop. The specifications of the laptop with the examination software are as follow:

- Processor: Intel(R) Core(TM) i7-8850H CPU @ 2.60 GHz 2.59 GHz
- RAM: 16.0 GB
- Graphics Card: NVIDIA GeForce MX130

– Integrated Graphics: Inte(R) UHD Graphics 630
– Examination SSD: NVMe CA3-8D512-Q11 NV
– BaseBoard: Dell Inc. 0DVVG1 A00
– Operating System: Windows 10 Pro (Version: 21H1, OS Build: 19043.1348)

Magnet Forensics Suite [10], more specifically Magnet AXIOM Process (v5.6.0.26839) and Magnet AXIOM Examine (v5.6.0.26839) was the commercial tools of choice for the project. The examination of the RAW (dd) images followed the same procedure for all five of the images captured and involved both tools. The first tool, the Magnet AXIOM Process, was used to acquire the evidence. For the examination all of the artifacts were selected except the memory, which was grayed out and not allowed to be selected. An additional step was taken before the acquisition process started, a custom keyword search. The custom keyword search included all 24 file names without their extensions (e.g.,*documents_ image_ 1*). This added an additional layer of search. Once the acquiring process was finished, Magnet AXIOM Examine was used to analyze the cases.

The procedure followed for creating the case in Autopsy (version 4.19.1) was very similar to Magnet AXIOM Process, except some of the features of the Autopsy were turned off. The ingests that were not included were Email Parser, Encryption Detection, Virtual Machine Extractor, Android Analyzer (aLEAPP), DJI Drone Analyzer, Plaso, iOS Analyzer (iLEAPP), Android Analyzer. It is important to note that the custom keyword search list was created for the Autopsy with the names of all 24 files created for the experiment.

The analysis process involved two stages in five different phases. The first stage was analyzing five different cases utilizing Magnet AXIOM Examine. The second phase involved the same process, just using Autopsy. In addition, cases from the same RAW (dd) image were compared with both Magnet AXIOM and Autopsy. This process ensured the best evaluation of the tools and eliminated any potential bias since two different tools were used. Given that there was nothing deleted on the first image, both applications should produce the same results giving it a good starting point for the rest of the analysis. In the last phase of the analysis, the five different images were observed using the methods from [13,14] showing the persistence of files throughout different stages of the research.

4   Discussion of the Results and Analysis

Reading the literature and observing that there was not a lot of updated documentation on evaluating digital forensics tools gave us an idea to do just that. Part of the reason for this gap could be the releasing of the frequent updates for the tools. This section discusses the experimental results and analyzes the findings. The first part of this section discusses the reasoning of the experiment, and the second part takes a look into the results organized by the RAW (dd) images taken of the Hitachi HDD.

The five different stages selected for the analysis of the project were chosen based on the daily use of an average user. The usage included file transfer, file delete, not performing any tasks for an hour after the delete, an additional hour of web search after the delete and the idle, and lastly, a large file download. The progression of the activities goes from basic to where comprehensive writing was introduced to the hard drive.

4.1 First Image - Base Image

During the analysis of the first image, the 24 files previously created were just transferred onto the laptop, and the laptop was turned off shortly after. The files were copied from the USB into two folders, documents and downloads. Once the cases were created, it was expected for the files to be present. As this image was referenced as the base image, the researchers wanted to observe how the programs processed the RAW (dd) image and be able to compare the images in the future. As it can be seen in Fig. 2, the files were found and located in the dedicated folders utilizing Magnet AXIOM Examine.

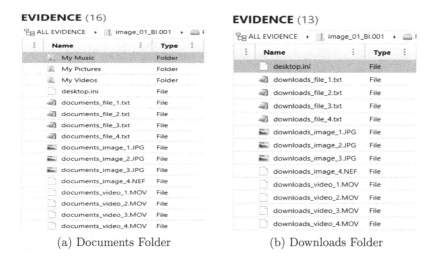

(a) Documents Folder   (b) Downloads Folder

Fig. 2. Base Image - Magnet AXIOM

All file sizes matched when compared to the initial files. Additionally, the MD5 hash values of the files matched as well, except for the *documents_file_4.txt, documents_video_3.MOV, documents_video_3.MOV* and *downloads_file_4.txt, downloads_video_3.MOV, downloads_video_4.MOV* in the downloads folder. Magnet AXIOM for these files was not able to calculate the hash values.

For the analysis in the Autopsy, the process did not change compared to the Magnet AXIOM, and also the results did not differ greatly. All files were in the designated folders and the sizes matched to the original sizes of the files. Unlike Magnet AXIOM, all of the hash values were matching and showing. Despite the hash values being correct for the files, Autopsy flagged *documents_video_3.MOV, documents_video_4.MOV, downloads_video_3.MOV, downloads_video_4.MOV* with the message, 'Hash an unlikely notable analysis result score'. Figure 3 shows the files found by Autopsy.

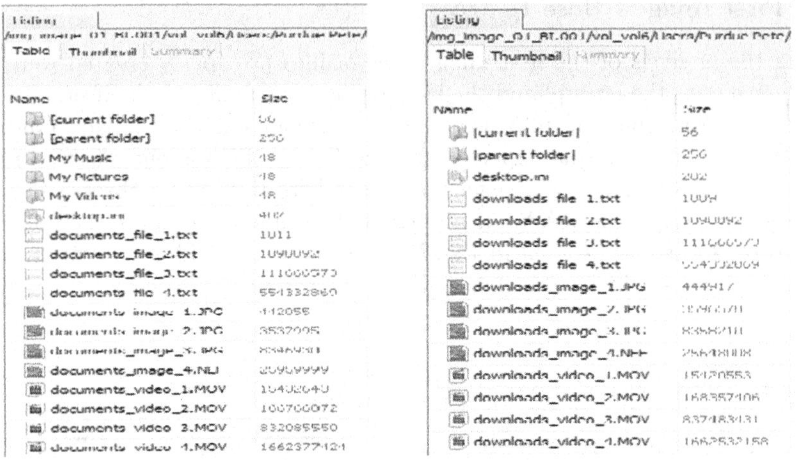

(a) Documents Folder   (b) Downloads Folder

Fig. 3. Base Image - Autopsy

4.2   Second Image - After Delete

The analysis of the second image took place after all 24 files previously transferred were deleted using 'SHIFT + Delete' method and turning off the laptop. The process consisted of the same procedures as analyzing the first image. As it can be seen in Fig. 4, the results show *documents_image_1*, and *downloads_image_1* are missing from the list.

The files that were not missing are marked as deleted. The contents of those files were the same as in the first image except for the (*documents_file_1, downloads_file_1*). This is also confirmed by hash values not matching compared to the base image. The files where the hash values matched were able to display the contents without any issues. The two text files missing, additional information about them was found in *$LogFile Analysis* and *$UsnJrnl*. The analysis was performed by utilizing a previously created keyword search. The messages presented by Magnet AXIOM in the update sequence number journal ($UsnJrnl) of the related files were:

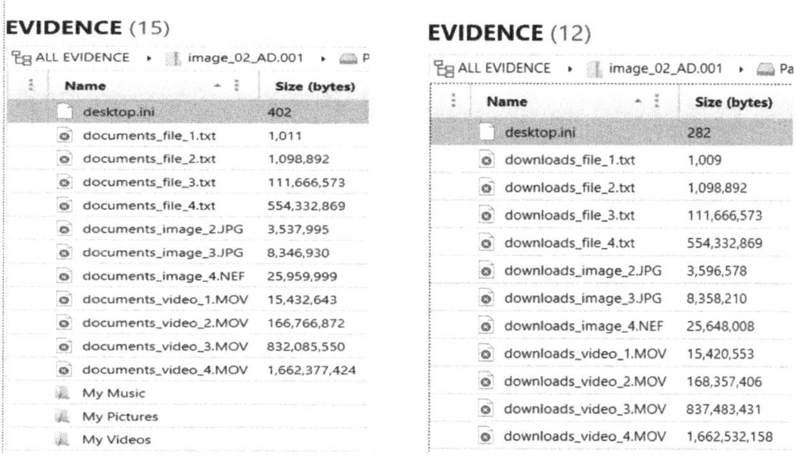

EVIDENCE (15)

ALL EVIDENCE › image_02_AD.001 › P

Name ▲	Size (bytes)
desktop.ini	402
documents_file_1.txt	1,011
documents_file_2.txt	1,098,892
documents_file_3.txt	111,666,573
documents_file_4.txt	554,332,869
documents_image_2.JPG	3,537,995
documents_image_3.JPG	8,346,930
documents_image_4.NEF	25,959,999
documents_video_1.MOV	15,432,643
documents_video_2.MOV	166,766,872
documents_video_3.MOV	832,085,550
documents_video_4.MOV	1,662,377,424
My Music	
My Pictures	
My Videos	

(a) Documents Folder

EVIDENCE (12)

ALL EVIDENCE › image_02_AD.001 › Pa

Name ▲	Size (bytes)
desktop.ini	282
downloads_file_1.txt	1,009
downloads_file_2.txt	1,098,892
downloads_file_3.txt	111,666,573
downloads_file_4.txt	554,332,869
downloads_image_2.JPG	3,596,578
downloads_image_3.JPG	8,358,210
downloads_image_4.NEF	25,648,008
downloads_video_1.MOV	15,420,553
downloads_video_2.MOV	168,357,406
downloads_video_3.MOV	837,483,431
downloads_video_4.MOV	1,662,532,158

(b) Downloads Folder

Fig. 4. After Delete - Magnet AXIOM

- The data in the file or directory is overwritten.
- The file or directory is extended (added to).
- The file or directory is created for the first time.
- A user has either changed one or more files or directory attributes (for example, the read-only, hidden, system, archive, or sparse attribute), or one or more time stamps.
- The file or directory is closed.

For the files that were not showing, the only locations where the names of the files (*documents_ image_ 1, downloads_ image_ 1*) were found are the same locations as for the *documents_ file_ 1, downloads_ file_ 1*, giving the same reason as previously stated.

The analysis utilizing Autopsy shows a different results but not by much. Like Magnet AXIOM tools, Autopsy could not show the (*documents_ image_ 1, downloads_ image_ 1*) files in the original folder as seen in Fig. 5. Moreover, hash values of the *documents_ file_ 1, downloads_ file_ 1* did not match also and the text files were unreadable. Keyword search for the two files showed presence showed in Table 3.

Traces of the two files (*documents_ image_ 1, downloads_ image_ 1*) that were not appearing in the initial folders were found in *$LogFile* and *$UsnJrnl:$J*. Lastly, compared to the base image only *images_ 2, images_ 3*, and *images_ 4* did not have the flag 'Hash an unlikely notable analysis result score' given by Autopsy.

4.3 Third Image - After Delete and Idle

After the process of creating the second image using FTK Imager, the third phase consisted of powering on the laptop and letting it idle for 60 min (±3 min) and

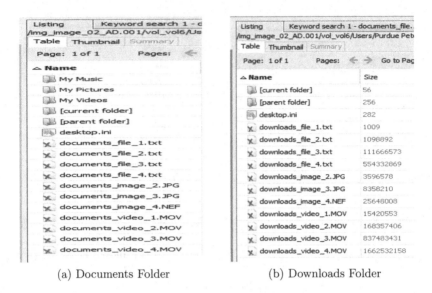

(a) Documents Folder   (b) Downloads Folder

Fig. 5. After Delete - Autopsy

turning the laptop off before taking the third image. Upon opening the created case in Magnet AXIOM and navigating to the designated folders (Documents and Downloads), there were no files showing. Keyword search showed the only traces of the file names were in *$LogFile Analysis* and *$UsnJrnl*. Reasons for the files shown are the same as in the previous analysis of the second image, right after the delete.

The autopsy showed similar results to Magnet AXIOM, where the files did not show in either of the folders, and the traces were only found in *$LogFile*, *$MFT* and *$UsnJrnl:$J*.

4.4   Fourth Image - After Delete and Web Browsing

The fourth image was after the files were deleted, the idle of the laptop for an hour, and an additional hour of web browsing. Following the process and case creation, Magnet AXIOM was not able to recognize any files in the designated folders of the deleted files. The only location where the keyword search was able to find a match was in *$UsnJrnl*. The keyword search found all 24 file names, and the messages presented by Magnet AXIOM in the update sequence number journal ($UsnJrnl) of the related files showed the same reasons as before.

The report from the Autopsy and the keyword search shows the traces of all 24 files in *$UsnJrnl:$J*. In the *MpWppTracing-20211119-195058-00000003-ffffff.bin* are found traces of the *documents_file_1.txt*. Lastly in the *$MFT file*, keyword search found *downloads_video_4.MOV* and *downloads_file_1.txt* but no other information was able to be presented.

Table 3. Keyword Search

Name	Location
MpWppTracing-20211119-195058-00000003-ffffffff.bin	/img_image_02_AD.001/vol_vol6/ProgramData/Microsoft/Windows Defender/Support/MpWppTracing-20211119-195058-00000003-ffffffff.bin
U snJrnl :J	/img_image_02_AD.001/vol_vol6/Extend/U snJrnl : $J
$LogFile	/img_image_02_AD.001/vol_vol6/$LogFile
$MFT	/img_image_02_AD.001/vol_vol6/$MFT
documents_file_1.txt	/img_image_02_AD.001/vol_vol6/Users/******Pete/Documents/documents_file_1.txt
documents_file_1.txt-slack	/img_image_02_AD.001/vol_vol6/Users/******Pete/Documents/documents_file_1.txt-slack
U snJrnl :J	/img_image_02_AD.001/vol_vol6/Extend/U snJrnl : $J
downloads_file_1.txt	/img_image_02_AD.001/vol_vol6/Users/******Pete/Downloads/downloads_file_1.txt
downloads_file_1.txt-slack	/img_image_02_AD.001/vol_vol6/Users/******Pete/Downloads/downloads_file_1.txt-slack
$LogFile	/img_image_02_AD.001/vol_vol6/$LogFile
$MFT	/img_image_02_AD.001/vol_vol6/$MFT

4.5   Fifth Image - After Delete and Download

In the last image we wanted to download a large file that was over 10% of the whole size of the disk. In our case that was a file over 10 GB in size. Upon the download of the file, the laptop was turned off and the RAW (dd) image was taken. Magnet AXIOM once more was not able to show the deleted files and the only place where the traces of the files were found are in *$UsnJrnl*. Same as in the step four, the keyword search was able to find all 24 names in the *$UsnJrnl*. Autopsy showed the traces only in *$UsnJrnl:$J* for all 24 files.

4.6   Persistence of Deleted Files

For the last test we wanted to ensure that the results we got from both, commercial and free software were accurate and no data was overlooked. This is often seen due to the software limitations which can cause issues when the evidence is presented in courts or just resolved with the newer updates. The Table 4 shows the persistence of all files throughout five images utilising persistence of deleted files script. Additionally, the table shows the percentage of the files left after each of the five actions. Magnet AXIOM Process and Autopsy were able to see files right after they have been deleted (image 2) with the exceptions of *documents_ image_ 1.JPG* and *downloads_ image_ 1.JPG*. Magnet AXIOM Process and Autopsy were not able to decipher any usable files in images 3, 4, and 5. On the other hand, persistence analysis script for some of the files was not able to recognise any persistence left (e.g., *documents_ file_ 1*) while showing lot more persistence on other files such as *documents_ file_ 4*. Note that for both *documents_ image_ 1.JPG* and *downloads_ image_ 1.JPG* files were not created. It is suspected that the proprietary software was not able to pick it up for an unknown reason to the researchers.

Table 4. Persistence of Deleted Files after Each Image

Name of the file	Base Image (image 1)	After Delete (image 2)	After Delete and Idle (image 3)	After Delete and Web Browsing (image 4)	After Delete and Download (image 5)
documents_file_1	100%	0%	0%	0%	0%
documents_file_2	100%	100%	100%	0%	0%
documents_file_3	100%	100%	100%	30%	0%
documents_file_4	100%	100%	100%	100%	0%
documents_image_1	100%	unknown	unknown	unknown	unknown
documents_image_2	100%	100%	100%	0%	0%
documents_image_3	100%	100%	100%	0%	0%
documents_image_4	100%	100%	100%	80%	0%
documents_video_1	100%	100%	100%	100%	0%
documents_video_2	100%	100%	100%	0%	0%
documents_video_3	100%	100%	100%	100%	0%
documents_video_4	100%	100%	100%	100%	0%
downloads_file_1	100%	0%	0%	0%	0%
downloads_file_2	100%	100%	100%	0%	0%
downloads_file_3	100%	100%	100%	80%	0%
downloads_file_4	100%	100%	100%	100%	0%
downloads_image_1	100%	unknown	unknown	unknown	unknown
downloads_image_2	100%	100%	100%	0%	0%
downloads_image_3	100%	100%	100%	1–5%	0%
downloads_image_4	100%	100%	100%	100%	0%
downloads_video_1	100%	100%	100%	0%	0%
downloads_video_2	100%	100%	100%	100%	0%
downloads_video_3	100%	100%	100%	100%	0%
downloads_video_4	100%	100%	100%	100%	0%

5   Conclusion and Future Works

The main goal of this paper was to study and evaluate two different tools for digital forensics investigators on the deleted files. One commercial and one free tool was evaluated on Windows 11 Pro operating system utilizing a spinning hard drive. This analysis and evaluation included five different scenarios, each of which gave the experiment different steps after the files were deleted.

In this experiment both tools performed equally well with some minor differences. Acquisition time of Magnet AXIOM Process was significantly less compared to Autopsy. The acquisition process of the RAW (dd) image utilizing

Magnet AXIOM Process on average took 55 min, and using Autopsy with multiple injests unchecked took on average around 5 h. Moreover, Magnet AXIOM Examine showed more reasons for the possibilities of the files being deleted. Despite the difference of the software no different information was found once compared. Both software solutions were able to recognize the deleted files in the second image and were not able to see it in the rest of the experiment. A possible explanation for the lack of evidence given the nature of NTFS structure could be due to the two programs used in the study are not able to read the remnants of deleted files. In contrast the persistence analysis throughout all files on all images has shown that deleted files mostly survived until the third image.

Continuation of this project will follow, analysis of the *$MFT* files and *$UsnJrnl* files on all images to understand the metadata. Moreover, adding more tools to be examined for both commercial and open source. Some of the questions that can also be answered during the future works are how does the poweroff preserve the files, probabilities of the smaller size files being preserved longer. Finally, in the future works is to utilize different methods of data storage and different file structures and types. The approach will allow for greater data set for the future use, aiding digital forensics investigators and digital forensics enthusiasts.

A   Appendix - Hash Values of the Created Files

Table 5. SHA256 Values of the Files

File Name	SHA256
documents_file_1.txt	D1BEA1EA1FE26B7D550CC7E6C5295C3A41AE98EADE9D837B9FEDF0ADBD79CFB2
documents_file_2.txt	F6E5BEEEB604AC2701356BD46DBF34F367D83651F9AFB25E0F503EA5239D609B
documents_file_3.txt	D9ECBB1E43031E588FD5C75B551F0BE1277BAACB93EF10C5267DCCF4A90BD511
documents_file_4.txt	3714966D123BC9832342BDA5D84250FE73C8F0E142338658753146207B7AA866
documents_image_1.JPG	B42CECE6F5E6280A07012358DAF88A7FE42D3A0E574CCD9384A8BB0E043170D5
documents_image_2.JPG	6B26FB548EDE7F9E06C1619CEE9CD273914A2FCE491671C1C542AD794FA35C5E
documents_image_3.JPG	3E4AA3C286B74C6DF4EDBE2AF4D5D44F358ACE938B7CA87C2D1C993817AED583
documents_image_4.NEF	0929F4747218CE984CB51ACA22A22C0C06DD7DE335761A38DEC80C6AEEFAB4F4
documents_video_1.MOV	347471C37D0358B93055A8B459AE17E29ACEBCC11EA051EDB0EE52DE79187A28
documents_video_2.MOV	8B853A3FEB09D1D53971649BBAC10621AC4C8564D9AD0D243E7C700D1ECB0D5B
documents_video_3.MOV	4434D6FC562E459EF527B396FFCF23DFB7644678BC319B29F5075CC36A5CC64C
documents_video_4.MOV	586DEF420099C97A0D3A1E39CD0A3BA54421033EFD8094E12974D4556B837E09
downloads_file_1.txt	9F1D88A8AC810659C6B0560AD35E4DB7ACDBB19B8AA1B2645165D3190D2BE636
downloads_file_2.txt	8AA0DCA4B1EC2AE16371F8046422B202E842EA0E386541FD86E384052DB0F29C
downloads_file_3.txt	7C27BA8A3AC7CA54C6ECCC8C11B330C13CAF824C21E7D47A767FEDB862F4102B
downloads_file_4.txt	8380874C6EEFAFC9016D4F6D980B27586814320C273005B81CBF5478FC92588C
downloads_image_1.JPG	7B04459AADEEFCC0BE4EFD35AA11ACD8282970C401022AB8BF16C3976DFC6131
downloads_image_2.JPG	92213B800D5A9D5793523DC1DD5DFFF86FC497774F216E8AE5935BA0FCEF0332
downloads_image_3.JPG	409D62F6DECB10B496986C769A1056A3FA0E6E8760CE14400BE0C8C6D3419086
downloads_image_4.NEF	AFA4C90D1C08F20687AA6C20B30F626E41FF5C06C81D0624A231A2966DCBAAC3
downloads_video_1.MOV	038F6C8793893936129C2C41768E9B86F93CB9BE97B23032BD84D67F189B973E
downloads_video_2.MOV	6EC3E100E72B45242A26D899B93C104CA818227000BB784304405267B51E0F08
downloads_video_3.MOV	32FA70ADF0FAC8EF6DEBC22032184E8C5CB19C121837E777A011D93C552B0EEA
downloads_video_4.MOV	F44CCAC646A5C685444BDA79816F6A2D71A6BBE80744B5BF3979FF2683115A8A

Table 6. MD5 Values of the Files

File Name	MD5 Value
documents_file_1.txt	18E9B2B48C85038F40FF56FAB92CCFE7
documents_file_2.txt	A6C813724F90A6DEDC9E90CC85420692
documents_file_3.txt	8012575698CC73C2271CBEAF1509E53D
documents_file_4.txt	91A699C84D1FB777CF8770BFBF0C0CA5
documents_image_1.JPG	4E71D99F41DED0496B4A662E130A640B
documents_image_2.JPG	F2DD9996CE24B8D018F1EC2CB908517F
documents_image_3.JPG	8D678D9168016CB1DF0D78CF5401DA08
documents_image_4.NEF	6EFDD9F736F595B66D24D041C39DA13A
documents_video_1.MOV	FE8AE4FB0B41BBDA2C660C4A8718F8AF
documents_video_2.MOV	7B8B826B20DEB6213EF56E7ADAF39B10
documents_video_3.MOV	EAB8A5C9692449EAEA6357BDF26AED84
documents_video_4.MOV	40A034E5602103161551A812C6FDBF4A
downloads_file_1.txt	C2565A04AE5846A1B240AF64FDCB083F
downloads_file_2.txt	CD2390F4531F00BC4C46AEFA544004B9
downloads_file_3.txt	981D64297FCD6E48011DD0BCA9445A64
downloads_file_4.txt	E95A2322DF03855B609A3375586EB13F
downloads_image_1.JPG	9B41B370F3F68661E02392E175089223
downloads_image_2.JPG	82481249AA00504C36021C1A2179AB92
downloads_image_3.JPG	9F6512743155F1D639D94E40EC9E65B2
downloads_image_4.NEF	11C865193ECBB083A9D576D218E66156
downloads_video_1.MOV	25000B37CA3619D0307BDA2563323D4B
downloads_video_2.MOV	FB38471A126C94ED04B7D122F9D8B7E4
downloads_video_3.MOV	C0930EA581932DB24DAB957E3F9882F9
downloads_video_4.MOV	188A26DA51F8C9A499E71E7E2CE4C56D

B   Appendix - Microsoft Edge Browsing History

The items below are listed in the chronological order by browsing activity. The format follows **Title | Time (UTC+0) | URL**.

1. YouTube | 11/21/2021 17:15 | http://www.youtube.com/
2. YouTube | 11/21/2021 17:16 | https://www.youtube.com/
3. 60 min timer - YouTube | 11/21/2021 17:16 | https://www.youtube.com/results?search_query=60+minute+timer
4. 60 min video - YouTube | 11/21/2021 17:16 | https://www.youtube.com/results?search_query=60+minute+video

5. AUTUMN 60 min TIMER, no music #60minutetimer - YouTube |
   11/21/2021 17:16 | https://www.youtube.com/watch?v=QRjSongCKkM
6. stocks - Bing | 11/21/2021 17:16 | https://www.bing.com/search?q=stocks&
   cvid=86ab3c620a934928aa8e1e67a2efb5a3&aqs=edge.0.0l9.2100j0j1&
   pglt=2083&FORM=ANNTA1&PC=U531
7. Google | 11/21/2021 17:17 | https://www.google.com/
8. news - Google Search | 11/21/2021 17:17 | https://www.google.com/search?
   q=news&source=hp&ei=K3-aYfH7KNbVtAabjYugAg&iflsig=ALs-wAMA
   AAAAYZqNO6Vlx2uhjMZ4JLj8S5Z7fNhmRNql&ved=0ahUKEwixveD3-q
   n0AhXWKs0KHZvGAiQQ4dUDCAk&uact=5&oq=news&gs_lcp=Cgdnd3
   Mtd2l6EAMyCwgAEIAEELEDEIMBMgsIABCABBCxAxCDATIICAAQg
   AQQsQMyBQgAEIAEMgUILhCABDIICC4QgAQQsQMyBQgAELEDMgg
   IABCxAxCDATIFCAAQgAQyBQgAELEDOg4IABCPARDqAhCMAxDlA
   joOCC4QjwEQ6gIQjAMQ5QI6CwguEIAEELEDEIMBOg4ILhCABBCxAx
   DHARDRAzoOCC4QgAQQsQMQxwEQowI6EQguEIAEELEDEIMBEMc
   BENEDOgsILhCABBDHARCvAVC8CFjlDWDGD2gBcAB4AIABeogB1
   QKSAQMzLjGYAQCgAQGwAQo&sclient=gws-wiz
9. Google News | 11/21/2021 17:18 | https://news.google.com/
10. Google News | 11/21/2021 17:18 | https://news.google.com/topstories?
    hl=en-US&gl=US&ceid=US:en
11. Google News - Technology - Latest | 11/21/2021 17:18 | https://news.
    google.com/topics/CAAqJggKIiBDQkFTRWdvSUwyMHZNRGRqTVhZ
    U0FtVnVHZ0pWVXlnQVAB?hl=en-US\&gl=US\&ceid=US\%3Aen
12. Ferrari Introduces the Daytona SP3, an 828-HP Tribute to the '60s - auto-
    evolution | 11/21/2021 17:19:16 | https://news.google.com/articles/CAIiE
    OKi16f4Pv4pSWm8Q5nkEQIqMwgEKioIACIQFloNoavzTzBvP2PfEiuO2
    yoUCAoiEBZaDaGr808wbz9j3xIrjtswx-StBw?hl=en-US&gl=US&ceid=US
    %3Aen
13. Ferrari Introduces the Daytona SP3, an 828-HP Tribute to the '60s -
    autoevolution | 11/21/2021 17:19:16 | https://www.autoevolution.com/
    news/ferrari-introduces-the-daytona-sp3-an-828-hp-tribute-to-the-60s-174
    687.html
14. https://www.bing.com/search?q=krebs+on+security&cvid=4b58f3d343ac
    4148bb07f3270f3c769a\&aqs=edge..69i57.4000j0j1\&pglt=2083\&FORM=
    ANNTA1\&PC=U531 | 11/21/2021 17:21:22 | https://www.bing.com/sea
    rch?q=krebs+on+security\&cvid=4b58f3d343ac4148bb07f3270f3c769a\&aqs
    =edge..69i57.4000j0j1\&pglt=2083\&FORM=ANNTA1\&PC=U531
15. n/a | 11/21/2021 17:21:22 | https://www.bing.com/newtabredir?url=https
    %3A%2F%2Fkrebsonsecurity.com%2F
16. Krebs on Security – In-depth security news and investigation | 11/21/2021
    17:21:23 | https://krebsonsecurity.com/

17. Can You Jailbreak Your iPhone Running iOS 15 to iOS 15.1? Everything You Need to Know | 11/21/2021 17:31:44 | https://news.google.com/articles/CBMiamh0dHBzOi8vd2NjZnRlY2guY29tL2Nhbi15b3UtamFpbGJyZWFrLXlvdXItaXBob25lLXJ1bm5pbmctaW9zLTE1LXRvLWlvcy0xNS0xLWV2ZXJ5dGhpbmcteW91LW5lZWQtdG8ta25vdy_SAW5odHRwczovL3djY2Z0ZWNoLmNvbS9jYW4teW91LWphaWxicmVhay15b3VyLWlwaG9uZS1ydW5uaW5nLWlvcy0xNS10by1pb3MtMTUtMS1ldmVyeXRoaW5nLXlvdS1uZWVkLXRvLWtub3cvYW1wLw?hl=en-US&gl=US&ceid=US%3Aen

18. Can You Jailbreak Your iPhone Running iOS 15 to iOS 15.1? Everything You Need to Know | 11/21/2021 17:31:44 | https://wccftech.com/can-you-jailbreak-your-iphone-running-ios-15-to-ios-15-1-everything-you-need-to-know/

19. 6 incredible Apple deals on Amazon ahead of Black Friday | 11/21/2021 17:35:07 | https://news.google.com/articles/CAIiECDYkClfUpv1m44PIS2Shw4qFQgEKg0IACoGCAow9ckFMIBVMJCfBA?hl=en-US\&gl=US\&ceid=US\%3Aen

20. 6 incredible Apple deals on Amazon ahead of Black Friday | 11/21/2021 17:35:07 | https://appleinsider.com/articles/21/11/20/6-epic-apple-deals-on-amazon-599-m1-mac-mini-99-apple-pencil-2-189-airpods-with-magsafe-more

21. Google News - World - Latest | 11/21/2021 17:36:01 | https://news.google.com/topics/CAAqJggKIiBDQkFTRWdvSUwyMHZNRGx1YlY4U0FtVVnVHZ0pWVXlnQVAB?hl=en-US\&gl=US\&ceid=US\%3Aen

22. Google News - Sports - Latest | 11/21/2021 17:36:25 | https://news.google.com/topics/CAAqJggKIiBDQkFTRWdvSUwyMHZNRFp1ZEdvU0FtVnVHZ0pWVXlnQVAB?hl=en-US\&gl=US\&ceid=US\%3Aen

23. Google News - Science - Latest | 11/21/2021 17:36:45 | https://news.google.com/topics/CAAqJggKIiBDQkFTRWdvSUwyMHZNRFp0Y1RjU0FtVnVHZ0pWVXlnQVAB?hl=en-US\&gl=US\&ceid=US\%3Aen

24. NASA's DART Mission To Crash a Spacecraft Into an Asteroid Is Set To Launch – Watch It Live | 11/21/2021 17:36:56 | https://news.google.com/articles/CBMicmh0dHBzOi8vc2NpdGVjaGRhaWx5LmNvbS9uYXNhcy1kYXJ0LW1pc3Npb24tdG8tY3Jhc2gtYS1zcGFjZWNyYWZ0LWludG8tYW4tYXN0ZXJvaWQtaXMtc2V0LXRvLWxhdW5jaC13YXRjaC1pdC1saXZlL9IBdmh0dHBzOi8vc2NpdGVjaGRhaWx5LmNvbS9uYXNhcy1kYXJ0LW1pc3Npb24tdG8tY3Jhc2gtYS1zcGFjZWNyYWZ0LWludG8tYW4tYXN0ZXJvaWQtaXMtc2V0LXRvLWxhdW5jaC13YXRjaC1pdC1saXZlL2FtcC88?hl=en-US&gl=US&ceid=US%3Aen

25. NASA's DART Mission To Crash a Spacecraft Into an Asteroid Is Set To Launch – Watch It Live | 11/21/2021 17:36:57 | https://scitechdaily.com/nasas-dart-mission-to-crash-a-spacecraft-into-an-asteroid-is-set-to-launch-watch-it-live/

26. https://www.bing.com/search?q=zdnet&cvid=e5e4121259b54fefb3b3bd6ec
d0daac1\&aqs=edge.0.0l9.1355j0j4\&FORM=ANAB01\&PC=U531 | 11/
21/2021 17:39:11 | https://www.bing.com/search?q=zdnet&cvid=e5e412
1259b54fefb3b3bd6ecd0daac1\&aqs=edge.0.0l9.1355j0j4\&FORM=ANAB
01\&PC=U531
27. n/a | 11/21/2021 17:39:11 | `https://www.bing.com/newtabredir?url=`
`https%3%2F%2Fwww.zdnet.com%2F`
28. Technology News, Analysis, Comments and Product Reviews for IT Profes-
sionals ZDNet | 11/21/2021 17:39:11 | https://www.zdnet.com/
29. FBI warning: This zero-day VPN software flaw was exploited by APT hack-
ers | ZDNet | 11/21/2021 17:39:45 | https://www.zdnet.com/article/fbi-
warning-this-zero-day-vpn-software-flaw-was-exploited-by-apt-hackers/
30. Nylas | Universal Email API | 11/21/2021 17:40:39 | https://www.nylas.
com/products/email-api/?gclid=EAIaIQobChMIx8jSg4Cq9AIVi8D2Ah1X_
gKBEAEYASAAEgJFSvD_BwE
31. Palo Alto Networks raises FY22 revenue guidance | ZDNet | 11/21/2021
17:41:08 | https://www.zdnet.com/article/palo-alto-networks-raises-fy22-
revenue-guidance/
32. Dark web crooks are now teaching courses on how to build botnets | ZDNet
| 11/21/2021 17:41:56 | https://www.zdnet.com/article/college-for-cyber-
criminals-dark-web-crooks-are-teaching-courses-on-how-to-build-botnets/
33. Security | ZDNet | 11/21/2021 17:48:01 | https://www.zdnet.com/topic/
security/
34. Cloud security firm Lacework secures $1.3 billion in new funding round
| ZDNet | 11/21/2021 17:48:07 | https://www.zdnet.com/article/cloud-
security-firm-lacework-secures-1-3-billion-in-series-d-funding-round/
35. n/a | 11/21/2021 17:52:43 | https://www.bing.com/newtabredir?url=http
%3A%2F%2Fwww.foxnews.com%2F
36. Fox News - Breaking News Updates | Latest News Headlines | Photos &
News Videos | 11/21/2021 17:52:43 | https://www.foxnews.com/
37. Fox News - Breaking News Updates | Latest News Headlines | Photos &
News Videos | 11/21/2021 17:52:43 | http://www.foxnews.com/
38. NBC News - Breaking News & Top Stories - Latest World, US & Local News
| NBC News | 11/21/2021 17:54:13 | https://www.nbcnews.com/
39. n/a | 11/21/2021 17:54:13 | https://www.bing.com/newtabredir?url=https
%3A%2F%2Fwww.nbcnews.com%2F
40. n/a | 11/21/2021 17:57:27 | https://www.bing.com/newtabredir?url=https
%3A%2F%2Fwww.cnn.com%2F
41. CNN - Breaking News, Latest News and Videos | 11/21/2021 17:57:27 |
https://www.cnn.com/
42. n/a | 11/21/2021 18:00:33 | https://www.bing.com/newtabredir?url=https
%3A%2F%2Fabcnews.go.com%2F
43. ABC News – Breaking News, Latest News, Headlines & Videos - ABC News
| 11/21/2021 18:00:34 | https://abcnews.go.com/

44. https://www.bing.com/search?q=news&cvid=5b6fa467060a443d88ffe7369 05bde5c\&aqs=edge..69i57j0l4j69i60l4.1971j0j4\&FORM=ANAB01\&P C=U531 | 11/21/2021 18:07:12 | https://www.bing.com/search?q=news& cvid=5b6fa467060a443d88ffe736905bde5c\&aqs=edge..69i57j0l4j69i60l4.1 971j0j4\&FORM=ANAB01\&PC=U531
45. n/a | 11/21/2021 18:07:12 | https://www.bing.com/newtabredir?url=https %3A%2F%2Fnypost.com%2Fnews%2F
46. New York Post – Breaking News, Latest US & World Headlines | 11/21/2021 18:07:12 | https://nypost.com/news/
47. n/a | 11/21/2021 18:08:27 | https://www.bing.com/newtabredir?url=%3A %2F%2Fmoney.cnn.com%2Fdata%2Fmarkets%2F
48. Stock Market Data - Dow Jones, Nasdaq, S&P 500 - CNNMoney | 11/21/2021 18:11:48 | https://money.cnn.com/data/markets/
49. https://www.bing.com/search?q=stock&qs=n&form=QBRE&sp=-1& pq=stock&sc=8-5&sk=&cvid=5209CCE60D7448CB9FB5488184E0944B | 11/21/2021 18:12:50 | https://www.bing.com/search?q=stock&qs=n& form=QBRE\&sp=-1\&pq=stock\&sc=8-5\&sk=\&cvid=5209CCE60D7448 CB9FB5488184E0944B
50. Stock Market Data with Stock Price Feeds | Nasdaq | 11/21/2021 18:12:50 | https://www.nasdaq.com/market-activity/stocks
51. n/a | 11/21/2021 18:12:50 | https://www.bing.com/newtabredir?url=https %3A%2F%2Fwww.nasdaq.com%2Fmarket-activity%2Fstocks

References

1. Riley, T.: The cybersecurity 202: Cybercrime skyrocketed as workplaces went virtual in 2020, new report finds, February 2021 (2021)
2. Brooks, C.: Alarming cybersecurity stats: what you need to know for 2021. Forbes, March 2021 (2021)
3. Staff, D.: Data breach costs: calculating the losses for security and it pros, February 2021 (2021)
4. Gill, M.: 10 shocking data loss and disaster recovery statistics, August 2021 (2021)
5. Nabity, P., Brett, L.: Recovering deleted and wiped files: a digital forensic comparison of FAT32 and NTFS file systems using evidence eliminator, no. 2007, pp. 1–10 (2009)
6. Lazaridis, I., Arampatzis, T., Pouros, S.: Evaluation of digital forensics tools on data recovery and analysis. In: The Third International Conference on Computer Science, Computer Engineering, and Social Media (CSCESM2016), p. 67 (2016)
7. Buchanan-Wollaston, J., Storer, T., Glisson, W.: Comparison of the Data Recovery Function of Forensic Tools, pp. 331–347 (2017). To cite this version: HAL Id: hal-01460614
8. Microsoft by the numbers windows devices. https://news.microsoft.com/ bythenumbers/en/windowsdevices. Accessed Oct 2021
9. Alsop, T.: Shipments of hard and solid state disk (HDD/SSD) drives worldwide from 2015 to 2021, March 2020 (2020)
10. Magnet forensics. https://support.magnetforensics.com/s/. Accessed Oct 2021
11. Another set of amazing wins at the 2021 forensic 4:cast awards! Magnet Forensics Blog (2021)

12. Autopsy. https://www.autopsy.com/. Accessed Oct 2021
13. Jones, J.H., Khan, T.M.: A method and implementation for the empirical study of deleted file persistence in digital devices and media. In: 2017 IEEE 7th Annual Computing and Communication Workshop and Conference (CCWC), pp. 1–7 (2017)
14. Khan, T.M.: Identifying factors affecting deleted file persistence through empirical study and analysis. Ph.D. thesis. George Mason University (2017)
15. AllisonShen. security_mft (2021). https://github.com/
16. Aggarwal, K., Garg, S.K.: Computer forensics: data recovery perspective over Windows and Unix, vol. 6, no. 8, pp. 6–8 (2021)
17. Duan, R., Zhang, X.: Research on computer forensics technology based on data recovery. J. Phys.: Conf. Ser. **1648**(3), 032025 (2020)
18. Cankaya, E.C., Kupka, B.: A survey of digital forensics tools for database extraction. In: FTC 2016 - Proceedings of Future Technologies Conference, December, pp. 1014–1019 (2017)
19. Al-Sabaawi, A., Foo, E.: A comparison study of Android mobile forensics for retrieving files system. Ernest Foo Int. J. Comput. Sci. Secur. (IJCSS) **13**, 2019–148 (2019)
20. Ultimate boot CD [software]. https://www.ultimatebootcd.com/. Accessed Oct 2021
21. DBAN, hard drive eraser & data clearing utility. [software]. DBAN Hard Drive Eraser & Data Clearing Utility. https://dban.org/. Accessed Oct 2021
22. Robertson, A.: [Software], September 2018. https://gist.github.com/alirobe/ 7f3b34ad89a159e6daa1file-reclaimwindows10-ps1. Accessed Oct 2021
23. Ftk imager. [software]. https://accessdata.com/. Accessed Oct 2021

Forensic Analysis of Webex on the iOS Platform

Jiaxuan Zhou and Umit Karabiyik[(✉)]

Purdue University, West Lafayette, IN 47907, USA
{zhou757,umit}@purdue.edu

Abstract. An increasing number of companies have adopted online telecommunication software for their office software pack, and Webex was one of the popular choices. With the surging usage of online telecommunication software, online meeting exploitation and disruptions cases also increased. However, there is limited research performed on online telecommunication software from the forensics perspective, and most are focused on Skype. Also, even though the iPhone's market share outperforms Android in the United States, the iOS system is under-researched. This paper fills the gap by performing a forensic analysis of Webex on the iOS platform, elucidating the structure of Webex in the iOS system, and displaying pertinent artifacts. The findings show that retrieving critical information in plain text from the application is possible. We retrieved data such as the username, phone number, device type, meeting session start time, meeting session attendee ID, etc. Also, we compared the evidence left from two types of accounts, basic and enterprise. The result shows that an enterprise account leaves more user data on the phone, a basic account keeps more device data. We used three tools, Cellebrite, Axiom, and DB Browser for SQLite, to validate the results. The result of the three tools all align.

Keywords: Mobile Forensics · Webex · Digital Forensics · iOS Forensics

1 Introduction

With the continuation of the COVID-19 pandemic, many organizations use a hybrid work model, which allows the employee to work from home most of the time. When employees stay at home, they rely on online telecommunication tools to attend meetings and communicate with their colleagues. Thus, teleconferencing applications became essential software for work. With the increase in the use of teleconferencing applications, the number of malicious attacks against teleconferencing applications also increased in the United States. FBI received multiple reports on the use of online meeting rooms and disruptions [19].

The idea of identifying forensically valuable data from video conferencing applications is not new. Studies began more than a decade ago, but most of

© ICST Institute for Computer Sciences, Social Informatics and Telecommunications Engineering 2023
Published by Springer Nature Switzerland AG 2023. All Rights Reserved
S. Goel et al. (Eds.): ICDF2C 2022, LNICST 508, pp. 84–96, 2023.
https://doi.org/10.1007/978-3-031-36574-4_5

the work focused on the Skype application [15]. Some research has been done on other popular software, such as Microsoft Teams and Zoom [10], but most studies are limited to covering only the Android and Windows platforms. However, in real life, there are many mobile applications and software on the market. The combination of mobile and software would decide where and how the evidence is preserved. Therefore, to help forensic practitioners deal with this issue, researchers should expand the scope from both the platform and the software perspectives.

This research paper fills the gap in forensic analysis for video conferencing software by investigating the digital evidence produced by the Webex application on the iOS platform. This information would help forensic practitioners solve an investigation involving the Webex application. Specifically, this research determines data discovered on iOS smartphones, such as installation data, user data, location information, contact database, and attachment files. This research is broken down into three phases. The first phase is the configuration of the device and the population of data. The mobile device used in this research is an iPhone 7 with iOS 14.4.1. The data population followed the Mobile Device Data Population Setup Guide published by NIST [16]. The second phase is acquisition. Cellebrite UFED 4PC with version 7.30.1.165 was used to acquire data from the iOS device. The final phase examined the images created using Magnet AXIOM Examine and Cellebrite Physical Analyzer. Both forensic analysis software are widely adopted in the digital forensics community. SQLite databases were verified using DB Browser for SQLite with version 3.12.1.

The rest of this paper is structured as follows. Section 2 discusses related work conducted for the Voice over Internet Protocol (VoIP) application from the forensic perspective. Section 3 details the acquisition and analysis techniques of this study. Section 4 presents the analysis findings and compares the result with other VoIP applications. Finally, Sect. 5 concludes the comments and future work.

2   Literature Review

Research related to the analysis of VoIP applications on iOS is precious for case investigation due to the time restriction nature. Therefore, we present the current literature on forensic analysis of VoIP applications.

Levinson et al. in [12] mentioned that the analysis of third-party applications could be difficult for forensic investigators if no prior study has been conducted. There is no standard that all companies need to follow when developing applications; therefore, how data are stored varies from application to application. Every application stores general information, such as username or email, but developers have the flexibility to decide the format and location. Previous work can provide guidance to law enforcement when investigating cases involving VoIP applications.

Although vendors store a lot of information on the server, cooperation could be tricky [11]. For example, the Tango software saves user personally identifiable information and non-personal identifiable information. However, Tango's

Privacy Policy gives the company immense flexibility for investigation cooperation. Furthermore, Tango does not share the retention period of stored data; the needed data can be deleted from the company side [11].

A Voice Over IP application is software that is installed on a computer or mobile device that can make a voice or video call over the Internet [7]. Webex belongs to the category of VoIP applications. Early work mainly focused on Skype, because it was one of the few VoIP software at the time. Later, researchers expanded the scope to Webex [9], Zoom [15], Microsoft Teams [10], Viber [20], and Tango [11].

Simon and Slay in [21] conducted an early research on VoIP. In 2006 VoIP was a novel technology that was not prevalent. So long ago, they wrote that VoIP's rise would bring a challenge to law enforcement. Unlike traditional phone calls, VoIP applications have strong encryption to control message and voice payload. This characteristic could make VoIP applications abused by criminals to communicate illegal activities. They defined the categories of retrievable data, which influenced many future researches.

Le-Khac et al. [11] analyzed the Tango application on iOS and Android devices. They were enlightened by Simon and Slay's work and defined the category of potential artifacts. Their paper [11] compared the artifacts available after three different extraction methods applied to the iOS device: logical extraction, file system extraction, and manual file system extraction. The result shows that the logical extraction contains no related data, the file system extraction has some data left, and the manual file system extraction retains most of the data. The research finding aligns with the study of [20].

In [9], Khalid et al. performed network analysis, memory analysis, and disk space analysis of the Webex application on the Windows operating system. The authors found that memory forensics provides ample amount of information; especially some encrypted artifacts on the static disk are plain text in memory. The username, email address, personal room number, and video address of the user were found. Even chat messages communicated and media shared were found with timestamps. Disk space analysis found that most databases are encrypted, but they found some artifacts in plain text, including profile photos, meeting metadata, and location information. The network artifacts offer information regarding client-server communication.

Mahr et al. in [15] analyzed the primary disk, memory, and network of the Zoom application on various operating systems such as Android, iOS, Windows, and macOS. They found that critical information could be retrieved from the device, such as chat messages, contact lists, exchanged media, and user profiles. Different devices show minor differences in terms of artifacts left. The research found that Zoom creates separate folders for every logged-in user. If no user logs in, then the *Zoommetting* and *Zoomus* databases are used to store information. Furthermore, Mahr et al. [15] warned that the Zoom company continues to patch vulnerabilities; when they started the research, they stopped updating. However, it is interesting that the Windows system automatically starts the update every time Zoom is initiated.

In [17], Nisticò et al. analyzed and compared thirteen real-time communication applications from the perspective of the network, which includes Skype, Google Meet, Microsoft Teams, Webex, and other communication applications. Webex employs normal RTP to stream media for network protocol and employs STUN to establish sessions. This shows similarities with Skype and Microsoft Teams. Webex does not provide peer-to-peer communication. Although peer-to-peer communication keeps communication latency low, the security level is also low. As an enterprise solution, Webex weighs security over speed. Their solution offers customers the option to install dedicated appliances.

Carpene in [3] approached the iTunes backup method to extract data from the mobile device and detailed the attainable data from the device. Skype and Facebook were included as two examples of application analysis. The author explained that *info.plist* is forensically valuable. It contains metadata on installed applications and can be used to check the list of applications that have been installed on the device. They found that the Skype folder is located under the *Library/Application Support* path. The data left behind includes limited contacts, limited call history, and limited chat history.

Sgaras et al. examined and analyzed four VoIP applications (WhatsApp, Skype, Viber, and Tango) for both Android and iOS in [20]. They concluded that the logical extraction of iOS does not produce any explicit data related to the four applications. However, with the extraction of the file system, they successfully recovered the installation data, traffic data, content data, user profile data, and contact database. The authors argue that manual file system analysis is still necessary even after the file system extraction, and it is highly possible that more valuable artifacts remain. In their research, they found more information on the four applications after manual analysis. Another contribution of the paper is the definition of the taxonomy of target artifacts; the purpose is to guild future forensic researches. They created eight categories of artifacts: installation data, traffic data, content data, user profile data, user authentication data, contact database, attachments, and location data.

There is several research done on Android phones, however, there is limited research done on iOS devices [1]. The original iOS device lacked many security features at first, so it was relatively easier to obtain forensic data from the devices [2]. However, with newer versions, iOS added additional security features in the software to prevent such data extractions along with the hardware to enable extra encryption of data. Such updates are a feature that disables USB data traffic if the phone has been locked for an hour [6]. Another update is the feature that the data on iOS can completely delete the data on the device if the password was incorrectly entered 10 times [13]. These security features make digital forensics harder to do on iOS devices [2].

The study in [18] performed research on iOS devices. The authors did a wide scale analysis of applications on Android and iOS devices and cross-validated the result using commercial and open source forensic software. More than 30 applications were analyzed. Popular choices of telecommunication application covered are Skype, Zoom, Houseparty, and Viber. The authors found that iOS takes a snapshot for all applications that were moved to the background before. Snapshots are saved under the path `<AppUUID>/Library/SplashBoard/Snapshots/sceneID:<AppPackage>`. Also, among all applications, most have relevant artifacts left behind in the `/private/var/mobile/Containers` folder.

3   Methodology

This study for the Webex Meet application is broken down into three stages: data population, data extraction, and data analysis. Data population and data extraction followed the National Institute of Standards and Technology (NIST) guidelines [16], a guidebook published on mobile device forensics. The mobile device that was used in this research is an iPhone 7 running iOS 14.4.1.

The data population phase aims to simulate real life scenario and mimic real user behaviors. This phase is crucial because it determines what could be found later in the analysis phase. The iPhone 7 was jailbroken in the data extraction phase. This will ensure that researchers can access the full file system and maximize the amount of data that can be found.

Image acquisition was performed with Cellebrite UFED 4PC version 7.30.1.165 because it is known for its efficiency in data extraction and is widely accepted in the mobile forensics community [8]. As for the workstation, an HP ENVY laptop running Microsoft Windows 10 Home 64-bit Build 19042 with 32 GB RAM and an Intel(R) Core(TM) i7-10750H processor was used for extraction and analysis.

3.1   Data Population

This stage focuses on simulating real user behaviors and populating data in the mobile phone device. First, we reset the mobile device to factory settings. Then, a proton email was signed up and the proton email account was used to register a new iCloud account. The Webex Meet application was then downloaded from the Apple Store. Two types of Webex accounts were used: basic and enterprise. The new proton email address was used to register for a new Webex basic account, and an email with our institution's domain was used for the enterprise account. Lastly, we started to mimic user interactions. The user behaviors stimulated are the following:

- Add contact
- Delete contact
- Host meeting
- Attend meeting
- Record meeting
- Schedule meeting and tag other attendee(s)
- Send text messages, images, website URLs, and videos via chat
- Add profile picture
- Post question in Q&A board during meeting session

– Answer question in Q&A board during meeting session
– Share picture during meeting session
– Add annotation during meeting session
– Log in to Google Drive during meeting session
– Draw in white board during meeting session

3.2 Data Extraction

In this stage, the main objective is to acquire the phone image. We conducted an advanced logical acquisition that combines logical and file system extractions [4]. Cellebrite also took the role of jailbreaking the iPhone device, jailbreaking allows full access to the file system and extract the maximum amount of data.

3.3 Data Analysis

In this phase, we examined the acquired image and searched for artifacts. We examined the image using two forensic tools: Cellebrite Physical Analyzer with version 7.42.0.50 and Magnet Axiom Examine with version 4.9.1. For the database files in the image, we used DB Browser SQLite with version 3.12.1.

We first used the Cellebrite Physical Analyzer for analysis, mainly through the file system feature. Cellebrite is a popular tool that supports data extraction on various devices. Cellebrite does not proprietary the image, which allows investigators and researchers to have the freedom to load the image created by Cellebrite into many different forensic analysis tools [14]. The UFED extension image file was successfully loaded into the AXIOM Process for case generation. After the case was generated, AXIOM Examine was launched to analyze the image. Most artifacts found by both software were identical. Some files with *db* extension files could not be properly loaded. These database files were later loaded into the DB Browser SQLite for cross-validation.

4 Results and Findings

This section presents the findings of the study and explains the findings in detail. A summary of the findings is organized in Table 1, and all screenshots are presented subsequently in the rest of this section. The artifacts tell a story about the interactions the device had with Webex before, and practitioners could use the pieces found to complete the story of the case.

To analyze Webex, we first need to understand how the iOS device stores Webex data locally. The application status database records the file path for application source and application data, the path to the database is `/private/var/mobile/Library/FrontBoard/applicationState.db`. In the directory of application source, it contains application bundle such as libraries and icons. These information has little forensic value. The path of application data is `/containers/Bundle/Application/<Webexfolder>`, which is the main directory that Webex used to store user generated data. Besides the two paths provided by the applicationState.db, the path `/mobile/Containers/Shared/<Webex>` also contains forensically valuable data of Webex.

Table 1. List of Behaviors and Recovered Artifacts

Behavior	Artifacts Recovered
Add contact	No
Delete contact	No
Host meeting	Yes
Attend meeting	Yes
Record meeting	No
Schedule meeting and tag other attendee(s)	Yes
Send text messages, images, website URLs, and videos via chat	No
Add profile picture	Yes
Post question in Q&A board during meeting session	No
Answer question in Q&A board during meeting session	No
Share picture during meeting session	No
Add annotation during meeting session	Partial
Log in to Google Drive during meeting session	No
Draw in white board during meeting session	Partial

4.1 Application Information

Identifying the target application in the device is essential in the initial stages, as these findings lead to the subsequent investigation. That is why the path `/private/var/mobile/Library/ApplicationSupport/com.apple.remotemanagementd/RMAdminStore-Local.sqlite` was searched. This database contains application usage information such as the installed application name, start time, and total active time. Investigators could use this database and its information to determine whether the target application is installed, how long the target application was used, what time the target application was used, etc.

4.2 User Data

User information was recovered from the path `/private/var/mobile/Containers/Data/Application/72DAA48E-576A-427B-9BB3-DEC25487AFEC/SystemData/com.apple.SafariViewService/Library/WebKit/WebsiteData/https\_cart.webex.com\_0.localstorage-wal`. The file recorded the user's timezone as shown in Fig. 1. The location of the user could be narrowed down using the timezone information. Additionally, this file also records the Internet provider and the ASN information. Both information can be used to estimate which region the user is in.

The path `/private/var/mobile/Containers/Data/Application/72DAA48E-576A-427B-9BB3-DEC25487AFEC/Library/Caches/Datas/Avatars` contains the avatars of the users that were uploaded. Each user has its own encrypted folder. Inside the folder, the avatar has 5 copies in different sizes.

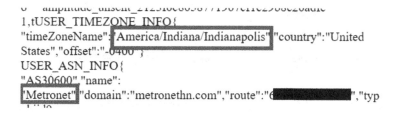

Fig. 1. Recovered timezone and ASN of an account

As Webex defines itself as a product for business meetings, security was an important factor when the application was developed [5]. The company can limit the sign-in request to Webex to accounts only from a predefined list of domains. The sign-in request from other domains can be blocked. Information about the predefined domain list could be found in `/private/var/mobile/Containers/Data/Application/72DAA48E-576A-427B-9BB3-DEC25487AFEC/Library/Caches/com.apple.WebKit.Networking/HSTS.plist`. The basic account has a domain name of "idbroker-b-us.webex.com" and the institution account had a domain of "purdue-student.webex.com" as shown in Fig. 2.

> ◢ idbroker-b-us.webex.com : dict = {
>   HSTS Host : boolean = True
>   Expiry : real = 688044659.895857
>   Create Time : real = 656508659.895859
>
> ◢ ████-student.webex.com : dict = {
>   Include Subdomains : boolean = True
>   Create Time : real = 657065466.447291
>   Expiry : real = 688601466.447284
>   HSTS Host : boolean = True

Fig. 2. List of account domains recovered

Many of the user information for the institution account is located in the path `/var/mobile/Containers/Data/Application/72DAA48E-576A-427B-9BB3-DEC25487AFEC/Library/Caches/com.webex.meeting/Cache.db`. Using the information saved in this database, a professional profile can be drawn, as it contains many user information. In the *cfurl_cache_receiver* table of the database, many valuable information about the account owner's were found. The details of the account user information, as well as the employer information, are saved inside. The data are of the form of a JSON object, as shown in Fig. 3.

It is worth noting that the employer's name is displayed here. This name is the name of the account owner registered in the company. An experiment

```
"id":1,"name":"▬▬▬▬▬","title":""}],
"adp_data":{},"num_direct_reports":0,"phone_numbers":null,
    "first_name":"▬▬▬▬","picture":null,"direct_reports":null,"photo_sizes":[],
    "last_name":"▬▬","manager":null},"external_url_info":{},
    "first_name":"▬▬▬▬","last_name":"▬▬","name":"▬▬▬▬▬▬",
    "professional_summary":{
        "employment":[
            {"id":"4ff6e4a72c8ff26df0162335cf1bc567-i",
                "normalized_employer_name":"▬▬▬▬▬▬",
                "director":false,
                "employer_name":"▬▬▬▬▬▬",
                "trusted_end_month":false,"title":"",
                "officer":false,"org_private":true,
                "location":"(1000.000000,1000.000000)",
                "current":true,
                "company_logo":"https://accompani.s3.amazonaws.com/images/companie
```

Fig. 3. Information recovered about enterprise account

was conducted to see if the real name can be deleted. The display name of the institution account in Webex was changed. However, the real name of the account still remained there. The basic account recorded more information about the device on which the Webex was installed compared to the institution account. The type of device, device name, device model and system version were recorded in the database as shown in Fig. 4.

4.3 Meeting Data

The list of all previous meetings was stored in the file path /private/ var/mobile/Containers/Data/Application/72DAA48E-576A-427B-9BB3- DEC25487AFEC/Library/Caches/com.webex.meeting/Cache.db-wal. For each meeting, the start time, local IP address, user type, attendeeID, and browser type could be found on the device as shown in Fig. 5. An interesting finding was that using the institution account, hosted meetings were recorded on the phone as call events. The file In the file /private/var/mobile/Containers/ Shared/AppGroup/049A2701-EE6F-48E2-A24E-67B69C93FA93/Library/ Caches/Logs/current_log.txt provides some details about the initial setup of the video call, such as if the video was enabled when the video initiated, and when the video was turned on. An example of metadata for video initialization is shown in Fig. 6.

As for scheduled meetings, the Webex application interacted with the Calendar application and wrote down the scheduled meeting as a calendar event. The calendar event contains the start time, end time, meeting URL, attendees, and timezone of the scheduled meeting as shown in Fig. 7.

4.4 Interactions During Meeting Session

Few data about the interactions inside the meeting room was left in the device. No plain text of the conversation was found on the QA board. However, we were able to find that a data-proven annotation and a whiteboard were used during the meeting session. In the file /private/var/mobile/Containers/Shared/

{"url":"https://wdm-r.wbx2.com/wdm/api/v1/devices/254da7e0-5344-
    "webSocketUrl":"wss://mercury-connection-partition0-r.wbx2.c
    "deviceType":"WEBEX_IPHONE",
    "name":"Jane's iPhone",
    "model":"iPhone 7",
    "localizedModel":"iPhone",
    "systemName":"Webex@iOS",
    "systemVersion":"iOS(13.7)/Webex(41.10.1)",
    "capabilities":{"groupCallSupported":false,
        "localNotificationSupported":false,
        "deleteNotificationSupported":false,
        "sdpSupported":true,
        "isBackgroundCapable":false,
        "isNseFilterEnabled":false,
        "isApnsMissedCallPushSupported":false},
        "creationTime":"2021-10-26T09:05:19.373Z",
        "modificationTime":"2021-10-26T09:05:19.373Z",
        "deviceSettings":{},"deviceSettingsString":"{}",
            "showSupportText":false,
            "reportingSiteUrl":"",
            "reportingSiteDesc":"",
            "customerCompanyName":"Self Signup 20210920-2424",

Fig. 4. Information recovered about basic account

pd":"WebEx","v":{"extVal":{"appversio
n":"41.10.1"},"label":"first time","e
vent":"Connected Meeting","category":
"App"},"ver":"2.1.8"},{"t":"Info","ts
":"2021-10-26T08:08:21.950-0400","tid
":"952D3137-E85A-4684-AD3C-D4A6D5DB50
04_0_656942900","pd":"WebEx","v":{"ex
tVal":{"meetNumber":"1725308711","mee
tType":"MC","CMRVersion":"0","CMRFlag
":true,"userType":"host","nodeID":"16
781313","confID":"209233521448853622"
,"appversion":"41.10.1","SignInFlag":
true,"joinType":"return user","GID":"
551774567","siteID":"868262","siteNam
e":"https:\/\/   -student.webex.co
m\/   -student","attendeeID":"7572
73","TrainVersion":"41.10.7.14","PMRF
lag":true},"userID":"584986127","cate
gory":"Conference","version":"Webex\/

Fig. 5. Various recovered metadata for video meeting

AppGroup/049A2701-EE6F-48E2-A24E-67B69C93FA93/Library/Caches/Logs
/current_log.txt, the Webex logs were recorded. The log message was written when the annotation function, shown in Fig. 8, or the whiteboard function
was enabled (see Fig. 9).

```
true
2021-10-26T09:25:53.584Z <Detail> [0x10ccd9840]
VideoStreamContentViewController.swift:720
updateVideoLayerIfNecessary():stream [local]: canRender = true, hasVideo
= true isVideoAdded = nil|
2021-10-26T09:25:53.584Z <Detail> [0x10ccd9840]
VideoStreamContentViewController.swift:726
```

Fig. 6. Various recovered metadata for video initialization

Summary	Meeting
Start Date/Time	10/27/2021 11:30:00 PM
End Date/Time	10/28/2021 12:30:00 AM
Notes	Join Cisco Webex meeting https://meet154.webex.com/m/cad5093e-fd99-496d-9bb7-d0fd652a698f Join by Video system sip:25540765144@meet154.webex.com Join using Microsoft Skype for Business sip:25540765144.meet154@lync.webex.com
Calendar	Home
Attendees	Jane Doe (mailto:janedoecnit55700@protonmail.com), Jane Doe (mailto:janedoecnit55700@protonmail.com), ████████ (mailto:████████)
Timezone	America/Indiana/Indianapolis

Fig. 7. Recovered scheduled meeting invitation

```
webex-assistant-skills:true
userapps-data-migration-enabled:true
dev-portal-search:true
ios-board-annotation-shared-screen:true
web-pmr-contact-card:true
ios-cobranding-enabled-v2:true
mobile-cucm-callforward-enabled:true
```

Fig. 8. Recovered log data for annotation

```
mobile-cucm-callforward-enabled:true
ios-us-auto-retry-sso-failure:true
desktop-whiteboard-snapshot-format-pdf:true
analytics-traffic-analysis-feature:true
atlas-control-hub-refresh-notification--spark-
atlas-react-control-hub-lite--not-now-zoons-us
```

Fig. 9. Recovered log data for whiteboard

5   Conclusion and Future Work

With the continuity of the COVID pandemic, videoconferencing software became an integral part of people's lives and is used as a basic tool by everyone from kids to seniors. Webex is one of the video conferencing software which is favored by educational institutions. However, to the best of our knowledge, no published paper has focused on the forensic analysis of Webex on mobile platforms. This research fills the gap by conducting a forensic analysis of the Webex software on the iOS platform. The identified artifacts could assist practitioners when performing investigation. The results indicate that much user-related information, meeting information, and software information could be retrieved. The institution account contains additional professional information, such as title, phone number, name, and employer. The basic account contains additional device-related information, such as the device type, device name, and device model. However, not all previous operations could be discovered. For events such as recorded meetings, QA board interaction, video call chats, and video call media sharing, no data were found locally.

Future extensions of this work could include other platforms of Webex, including Android, Windows, and MacOS. Another direction could be conducting an investigation of the memory and network. This may provide additional valuable artifacts. Furthermore, a comparison of different versions of Webex is worth looking into. With rapid patching and update, the structure and evidence presented in this paper may be different from other Webex versions.

References

1. Azfar, A., Choo, K.-K.R., Liu, L.: Android mobile VoIP apps: a survey and examination of their security and privacy. Electron. Commer. Res. **16**(1), 73–111 (2015). https://doi.org/10.1007/s10660-015-9208-1
2. Bullock, D., Aliyu, A., Maglaras, L., Ferrag, M.A.: Security and privacy challenges in the field of iOS device forensics (2020). https://doi.org/10.3934/ms.2019.x.xxx
3. Carpene, C.: Looking to iPhone backup files for evidence extraction (2011)
4. Cellebrite: Supporting new extraction methods and devices (2019)
5. Center, W.H.: Configure a list of allowed domains to access WebEx while on your corporate network (2021)
6. Edge, C., Trouton, R.: The Evolution of Apple Device Management, pp. 1–54 (2020). https://doi.org/10.1007/978-1-4842-5388-5_1
7. Goode, B.: Voice over internet protocol (VoIP). Proc. IEEE **90**(9), 1495–1517 (2002). https://doi.org/10.1109/JPROC.2002.802005
8. Hutchinson, S., Shantaram, N., Karabiyik, U.: Forensic analysis of dating applications on Android and iOS devices. In: 2020 IEEE 19th International Conference on Trust, Security and Privacy in Computing and Communications (TrustCom), pp. 836–847 (2020). https://doi.org/10.1109/TrustCom50675.2020.00113
9. Khalid, Z., Iqbal, F., Kamoun, F., Hussain, M., Khan, L.A.: Forensic analysis of the Cisco WebEx application. In: 2021 5th Cyber Security in Networking Conference (CSNet), pp. 90–97 (2021). https://doi.org/10.1109/CSNet52717.2021.9614647

10. Kim, Y., Kwon, T.: On artifact analysis for user behaviors in collaboration tools-using differential forensics for distinct operating environments. J. Korea Inst. Inf. Secur. Cryptol. **31**(3), 353–363 (2021)
11. Le-Khac, N.A., Sgaras, C., Kechadi, T.: Forensic acquisition and analysis of Tango VoIP (2014)
12. Levinson, A., Stackpole, B., Johnson, D.: Third party application forensics on apple mobile devices. In: 2011 44th Hawaii International Conference on System Sciences, pp. 1–9 (2011). https://doi.org/10.1109/HICSS.2011.440
13. Lutes, K.D.: Challenges in mobile phone forensics (2008)
14. Magnet: Loading cellebrite images into magnet axiom (2021). https://www.magnetforensics.com/blog/loading-cellebrite-images-into-magnet-axiom/
15. Mahr, A., Cichon, M., Mateo, S., Grajeda, C., Baggili, I.: Zooming into the pandemic! A forensic analysis of the zoom application. Forensic Sci. Int.: Digit. Investig. **36**, 301107 (2021). https://doi.org/10.1016/j.fsidi.2021.301107
16. NIST: Mobile device data population setup guide (2016). https://www.nist.gov/itl/ssd/software-quality-group/computer-forensics-tool-testing-program-cftt/cftt-technical/mobile
17. Nisticò, A., Markudova, D., Trevisan, M., Meo, M., Carofiglio, G.: A comparative study of RTC applications. In: 2020 IEEE International Symposium on Multimedia (ISM), pp. 1–8 (2020). https://doi.org/10.1109/ISM.2020.00007
18. Salamh, F.E., Mirza, M.M., Hutchinson, S., Yoon, Y.H., Karabiyik, U.: What's on the horizon? An in-depth forensic analysis of android and iOS applications. IEEE Access **9**, 99421–99454 (2021). https://doi.org/10.1109/ACCESS.2021.3095562
19. Secara, I.A.: Zoombombing - the end-to-end fallacy. Netw. Secur. **2020**(8), 13–17 (2020). https://doi.org/10.1016/S1353-4858(20)30094-5
20. Sgaras, C., Kechadi, T., Le-Khac, N.A.: Forensics acquisition and analysis of instant messaging and VoIP applications (2014). https://doi.org/10.1007/978-3-319-20125-2_16
21. Simon, M., Slay, J.: Recovery of skype application activity data from physical memory. In: 2010 International Conference on Availability, Reliability and Security, pp. 283–288 (2010). https://doi.org/10.1109/ARES.2010.73

Watch Your WeChat Wallet: Digital Forensics Approach on WeChat Payments on Android

Jiaxuan Zhou and Umit Karabiyik[✉]

Purdue University, West Lafayette, IN 47907, USA
{zhou757,umit}@purdue.edu

Abstract. WeChat is one of the most popular instant messaging applications in the world. In 2021, WeChat had 1.24 billion active users. Its users call it 'super app' due to its various functions, and they particularly enjoy the payment feature for both personal and business purposes. Criminals abused the platforms to facilitate illegal activities such as bank fraud. Previous research on WeChat focused mostly on the messaging function of the WeChat app, but it has rarely been considered as a wallet or payment app. The payment feature on WeChat can provide crucial evidence, especially for scam cases. Therefore, this research intends to fill the gap by performing a forensic analysis of the WeChat payment function on Android devices. This research has five stages: device preparation, data population, data extraction, analysis, and reporting. In this research, five activities were examined: registering a credit card in the account, sending and receiving money with contact, performing money transactions with the corporate account, making payment through the *Service portal*, and requesting the complete payment history from the official Weixin Pay account. The result shows that money transactions between contacts and money transactions through *Service portal* can be fully recovered. Partial information can be retrieved when users register for credit cards or purchase official account services. However, no data on payment history could be recovered from the official Weixin Pay account. Magnet Axiom Process and Examine tools were used for image extraction and artifact analysis.

Keywords: Digital Forensics · Mobile Forensics · Android Forensics · WeChat Forensics

1 Introduction

WeChat is one of the most popular applications in the world. As of 2021, there are 1.24 billion users of WeChat [4]. Wechat started as an instant messaging mobile app but later developed as a multi-purpose app. Many people call it the "super app" because it is an application for everything. Besides the basic messaging functions, it also supports online payment, mini-games, news aggregation,

S. Goel et al. (Eds.): ICDF2C 2022, LNICST 508, pp. 97–110, 2023.
https://doi.org/10.1007/978-3-031-36574-4_6

and much more. People register their credit cards in this app and make money transactions daily for both personal and business use. Especially in China, from tuition payments to restaurant checks, WeChat Pay is in every nook and corner of the country. In 2021, there were 251 billion US dollar transactions in WeChat [7]. Criminals had their eyes on this application due to the convenient money transaction feature. The traditional phone scam requires criminals to lead the victim through a full process of bank transactions. However, with WeChat, they only need to lure the victim to do a few clicks on the phone. To link criminals with the case, authorities need digital evidence such as money transaction records.

Most of the research done on WeChat so far views it mostly as an instant messaging application. Previous studies include pertinent artifacts on the device [9,13], network analysis [5], and volatile memory analysis [17]. However, few studies have been done on WeChat as a wallet application. The research carried out by Yan et al. [14] analyzed the network traffic of the fund transaction function. Transaction-related artifacts could be extremely valuable to law enforcement when investigating a WeChat-related case. When a transaction is complete, WeChat leaves a transaction record message in the chat. This chat history can give law enforcement insight into why the transaction happened, who was involved in the transaction, and when the transaction occurred.

This research fills the gap by focusing on forensic analysis of WeChat as a wallet on an Android device, identifying pertinent artifacts, and discussing privacy and security concerns. This research is broken down into four phases. The first phase is the device preparation step. The Android mobile device that was used is a Google Pixel 5a. The smartphone was rooted using TWRP and Magisk. The second phase is the data population phase. This phase was abide by the Mobile Device Data Population Setup Guide published by the National Institute of Standards and Technology (NIST [1]). The third phase is data acquisition, a physical acquisition was performed. In the fourth phase, we analyzed the image using Magnet Axiom Examine and Magnet Axiom Examine was used for artifact analysis. The last phase was to report the findings. All forensic analysis tools were chosen because they are widely adopted in the digital forensic community.

2 Literature Review

To understand the current research that has been done on WeChat, this section included research related to WeChat analysis methodologies, WeChat analysis in Android, WeChat analysis in payment features, and WeChat database decryption methodologies. It is also worth noting that WeChat continuously updates the app. These updates sometimes add new features or patch bugs, which can cause changes in the security mechanism or data storage structure. Therefore, papers earlier than 2015 are not included.

2.1 WeChat Payment Feature Analysis

WeChat did not specify in their retention policy about payment information, such as payment transaction and card information. Log data and chat data were addressed. Log data has relatively long retention period, the data can stays maximum of three months [2]. Chat data stays in the internal server for maximum three hours before deletion. Under all conditions, the message is permanently deleted from internal server within 72 h after the message sent [2].

Red packet and fund transfer are basic models for the WeChat payment feature. Users can make transactions with other contacts in a conversation. Until the time of this study, there is only one paper published about the payment function. Yan et al. [14] performed a network analysis of the traffic pattern generated by red pocket and fund transfer. The result shows the traffic of red pocket and fund transfer can be differentiated from plain text and pictures. However, the research did do any analysis of the artifacts that could be on the devices.

2.2   WeChat Analysis on Android

There was a study by Sihombing, Fajar, and Utama [10] that did a systematic review of digital forensic research on instant messaging apps. The study restated that extracting data from the backup feature does not work on smartphones with Android versions later than 6.0. The authors suggested taking advantage of analytical tools such as Apktool or dex2jar.

Azfar, Choo, and Liu [3] proposed a two-dimensional taxonomy of the forensic artifacts of communication apps. The taxonomy is summarized after analyzing thirty popular Android communication apps. The generated files and data are stored in /data/data/com.tencent.mm. Some user picture remnants are stored in the /sdcard/tencent/MicroMsg folder. The main database of WeChat is MicroMsg.db, this database contains 73 tables inside. The taxonomy is composed of four groups: users and contact information, timestamps, exchanged messages, and others. The users and contact information group contains all user identifiable information and the contacts information. The timestamps are a group that identifies the specific time of communication. The messages exchanged identify artifacts exchanged during chat sessions, including text, multimedia, or group communication. The other category collects all artifacts that cannot fit into the three other groups mentioned above. Examples include databases, voice call duration, and group chat member lists.

Wu et al. [13] examined two basic features of WeChat: messenger and post. The study emphasized that root privilege is necessary. The directory com.tencent.mm contains critical data related to messages and posts. Without root privilege, the directory cannot be accessed. The study tested the Android emulator to check whether it can retrieve forensic artifacts or not. The study used two emulator tools and both showed identical results to those for smartphones. There was another important question that was discussed in the paper. Some researchers mentioned that, for Android versions older than 6.0, the 'backup' command provided by Android Debug Bridge (ADB) no longer works. An alternative proposed was to downgrade WeChat to version 6.0. However, the researchers argued that downgrading can cause inconsistency. In their paper, nine files were modified and three files were removed. Although core database files such as EnMicroMsg.db were successfully extracted, researchers advised processing this method with caution.

The research done by Silla [11] used logical acquisition tools to locate and recover artifacts related to instant messaging applications, specifically WeChat data in the internal memory of an Android smartphone. The study focused on partial activities on WeChat. Partial activities include text messages, audio, videos, images, GPS locations, and downloaded documents. The authors also discussed the effectiveness of two logical extraction techniques, ADB and MPE+. The two tools cannot completely extract artifacts. The database files could not be extracted. As a sequence, the shared conversation, the contact list, and user information were not discovered. Therefore, the author claimed that file system extraction is necessary.

Menahil et al. [6] analyzed five social networking apps on Android, WeChat included the five. The scope of populated data was the account profile, friends, status, exchanged messages, video calls, and posts. Many artifacts were found in Tencent directory. In the path com.tencent/media/0/MicroMsg, the images, videos, and audios transferred during chat sessions were stored there. Account information was stored in the shared preference folder, such as the username and phone number. The capability of three forensic tools (Axiom, XRY, and Autopsy) was also evaluated. The research followed the NIST standards for smartphone analysis tools, and the result showed that Axiom is ranked first.

Wu et al. [12] proposed a new approach to analyze remote WeChat data on Android. WeChat relies heavily on local storage. However, there are many third parties that create mini services on WeChat. When users access the third-party service, the data is stored on the remote server of the third party. Wu et al. [12] proposed using the ADB shell command to obtain the WeChat data on the computer and then load the data onto the virtual machine of Android. After WeChat runs successfully on the virtual machine, researchers can start to operate the application and request data from remote servers.

Park et al. in [8] performed an analysis of WeChat on Windows and Android platforms. The populated artifacts include the five categories: user information, chatting room, chatting, posting, and app usage. The result shows that the Android device can retrieve more artifacts than the Windows device. The authors analyzed the location card and real location sharing functions on both devices. The capabilities of the two devices are different. Only the mobile device can send location cards and join real-time location sharing. The Windows device can only receive location cards. For both devices, all populated location data was recovered. In the Android device, the location data was located in the EnMicroMsg.db, and the MSG0.db file stores the location data in Windows.

2.3   WeChat Database Decryption

Zhang et al. in [16] conducted a forensic analysis of the WeChat application. The paper identified the location of databases and the recovery of voice and deleted messages. It also analyzed what encryption the WeChat database uses, as well as analyzing how to decrypt the database.

3   Methodology

The objective of this study is to identify payment-related artifacts from the WeChat application on Android phone. The methodology consists of five stages: device preparation, data creation, image acquisition, image analysis, and reporting. The test and examination process is consistent with the guidelines of the National Institute of Standards and Technology (NIST). The workflow is shown in the diagram 1.

Fig. 1. Workflow for WeChat analysis on Android

3.1   Test Environment and Requirements

To make sure the experiment could be conducted, a set of hardware and software was prepared in advance. The list is shown below:

- Google Pixel 5a with Android 11
- USB cable
- Workstation with Windows 10, Intel i7, 64 bit
- WeChat application with version 8.0.18
- TWRP barbet application
- Minimal ADB and Fastboot with version 1.4.3
- Magisk application with version 21.0
- Magisk Manager application with version 8.0.2
- Root checker application with version 6.5.0
- DB Browser for SQLCipher tool with version 4.4.0
- DB browser for SQLite tool with version 3.12.1
- Magnet Axiom Process tool with version 4.9.1
- Magnet Axiom Examine tool with version 4.9.1

3.2   Device Preparation

The Pixel 5a was rooted in this stage to maximize artifacts that can be retrieved in the analysis stage. The smartphone was set to developer mode and connected to a Windows workstation. On the workstation, the Minimal ADB and Fastboot tool was initiated, and the command `fastboot flashing unlock` was entered to unlock the bootloader of the smartphone. The TWRP software installed the custom firmware on the smartphone by entering the command `fastboot boot twrp.img`, and the device entered the custom recovery mode. Then, the Magisk app was installed on the smartphone. It is worth noting that the Magisk app is not available in the Google Play store, the setting must allow third-party download. In recovery mode, the Magisk file was installed and the smartphone was restarted. Later, the root checker app verified that the Android device was successfully rooted.

3.3   Data Creation

In this first stage, our goal was to create a real-life scenario and to perform a list of real user activities. We reset the phone to manufacture mode and downloaded the WeChat app from the Google Play Store. Then we created a new WeChat account on the phone and then started to populate the data. Real users usually make personal transactions when they discuss an event with other contacts, such as visiting a restaurant or going shopping, the transaction renders as a chat message in a chat room. We mimic real users, populated text messages of an event, and the transaction. Next, we paid to a corporate account. WeChat has many third-party corporate accounts providing paid services such as psychological evaluation. Once the transaction is complete, the user received a receipt from the WeChat Pay account (WeChat payment management account). Besides virtual services, the WeChat platform is a universal payment platform for offline activities. In the Services module, WeChat provides offline activity assistance that covers all aspects of life, such as booking movie tickets, paying utility bills, scheduling taxis, and more. We also made a payment for an offline activity in the *Services* module as well. The WeChat Pay account records all user transactions on the WeChat platform. We requested bill histories from this account. In summary, we focused on the following five activities:

1. Register a credit card to the account
2. Send and receive money with friend
3. Send money to corporate account
4. Use the Services function and purchase movie ticket
5. Request full payment history from the Weixin Pay account

3.4   Data Acquisition

We want to acquire the maximum amount of information from the device so that we can understand how much information is left on the phone locally using the WeChat app. We performed a full image acquisition of the phone in Magnet Axiom Process, having root access guarantees Magnet Axiom Process that the full image acquisition was successful.

3.5   Forensic Analysis

In the analysis stage, we processed the image in Axiom Examine and analyzed the artifacts using both the auto-carved artifacts and the manually carved artifacts of the file system. In addition, we took a close look at the database that stores messages. An enormous amount of chat messages are stored inside that database file, which is a gold mine for forensic investigators. However, the database was encrypted, we needed to crack the database file. Zhang and Yin [15] declare that manual decryption of the WeChat database file is possible, as long as we obtain the WeChat database file, the uin value, and the IMEI serial number. The MD5 value of the IMEI serial number and the uin value are the decryption key. However, this method does not apply to all phones.

4   Results

This section presents the findings of the study and explains the findings in detail. A summary of the findings is organized in Table 2. Due to the nature that it is a communication app originally developed by a Chinese company, some carved files contain Chinese characters. Before diving into the details, an analysis of the file structure was performed. The full path and the primary artifacts are listed in Table 1.

Table 1. List of Behaviors and Recovered Artifacts

Artifact Path	Artifact Description
\data\data\com.tencent.mm\MicroMsg\ ab84a9f6209480113c856a38b719582e\EnMicroMsg.db	The database stores message information
\data\data\com.tencent.mm\MicroMsg\mmslot\ webcached\	Stores articles posted by followed official account
data\data\com.tencent.mm\MicroMsg\ ab84a9f6209480113c856a38b719582e\TextStatus.db	A database stores status information
\data\data\com.tencent.mm\MicroMsg\ ab84a9f6209480113c856a38b719582e\SnsMicroMsg.db	Stores moment post information
\data\data\com.tencent.mm\files\mmkv\	Stores memory synced data
\data\data\com.tencent.mm\MicroMsg\ ab84a9f6209480113c856a38b719582e\avatar\	Stores contact avatars
\data\data\com.tencent.mm\cache\ ab84a9f6209480113c856a38b719582e\finder\avatar\	Stores creator avatars of viewed videos
\data\data\com.tencent.mm\cache\ ab84a9f6209480113c856a38b719582e\finder\image\	Stores image clips of viewed videos

4.1   Registered Credit Card

Two credit cards were registered in the WeChat account. When the cards were registered, additional personally identifiable information was required, such as legal name, gender, passport number, etc. Among these data, only part of the credit card information was found: bank type and card tail (last four

Table 2. List of Behaviors and Recovered Artifacts

Behavior	Artifacts Recovered
Registered Credit Card	Partial
Money transfer between friends	Yes
Red packet sent between friends	Yes
Official account service receipt	Yes
Official account service details	No
Third party service receipt	Yes
Third party service details	Yes

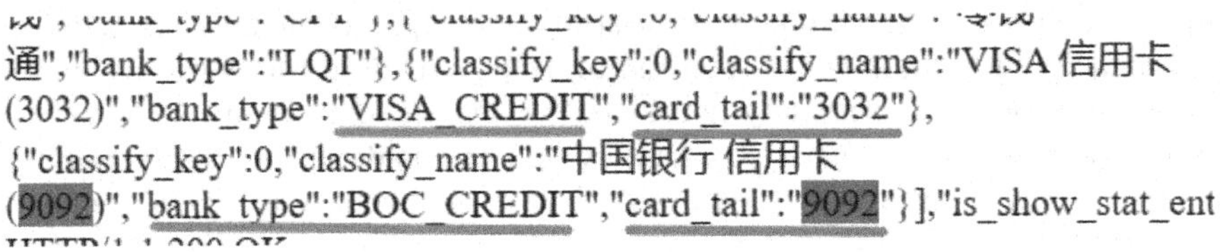

区" , bank_type : 信用卡 "},{ classify_key :0, classify_name : 交通
通","bank_type":"LQT"},{"classify_key":0,"classify_name":"VISA 信用卡
(3032)","bank_type":"VISA_CREDIT","card_tail":"3032"},
{"classify_key":0,"classify_name":"中国银行 信用卡
(9092)","bank_type":"BOC_CREDIT","card_tail":"9092"}],"is_show_stat_ent
HTTP/1.1 200 OK

Fig. 2. Information of credit cards

digits of the card number). The carved information is shown in Fig. 2. This
data is located in the path \data\data\com.tencent.mm\cache\Default\HTTP
Cache\0c45d524731a6b5f_0. No personally identifiable information was found.

4.2   Money Transaction with Friends

The money transaction between friends can take two forms: red pocket and
money transfer. The two forms of monetary transactions were captured in the
EnMicroMsg.db database file, under the path \data\data\com.tencent.mm\
MicroMsg\9d8d3de00f8797d8e2f4d 83d76640a5d".

For money transfer, the sent time, the received time, the amount, the sender
and the receiver username were retrieved as shown in Fig. 3. The money transfer
remained in uncollected status for two hours and WeChat automatically generated a reminder message in the chat room to remind the uncollected transaction.
This screenshot of the autogenerated reminder message is shown in Fig. 4.

The red packet is shown in Fig. 5, the sent time, received time, and memo
were able to be retrieved in the EnMicroMsg.db database file as well. However,
the text does not include the transaction amount.

4.3   Money Transaction with Corporate Account

A corporate account was followed that specializes in entertainment personality tests. The account offers paid services. To access a test, a description article was first viewed. At the bottom of the page, the "one-click

wxid_sfw7zu6tvkgz22

4/18/2022 1:36:14 PM

```
<msg>
<appmsg appid="" sdkver="">
<title><![CDATA[微信转账]]></title>
<des><![CDATA[收到转账1.00元。如需收钱，请点此升级至最新版本]]></des>
<action></action>
<type>2000</type>
<content><![CDATA[]]></content>
<url><![CDATA[https://support.weixin.qq.com/cgi-bin/mmsupport-
bin/readtemplate?
t=page/common_page__upgrade&text=text001&btn_text=btn_text_0]]>
</url>
<thumburl><![CDATA[https://support.weixin.qq.com/cgi-bin/mmsupport-
bin/readtemplate?
t=page/common_page__upgrade&text=text001&btn_text=btn_text_0]]>
</thumburl>
<lowurl></lowurl>
<extinfo>
</extinfo>
<wcpayinfo>
<paysubtype>1</paysubtype>
<feedesc><![CDATA[¥1.00]]></feedesc>
<transcationid><![CDATA[1000050001220418000573125559551157320]]>
</transcationid>
<transferid><![CDATA[1000050001202204180318032458678]]>
</transferid>
<invalidtime><![CDATA[1650375373]]></invalidtime>
<begintransfertime><![CDATA[1650288973]]></begintransfertime>
<effectivedate><![CDATA[1]]></effectivedate>
<pay_memo><![CDATA[]]></pay_memo>
<receiver_username><![CDATA[wxid_i9r5y1bilod122]]>
</receiver_username>
<payer_username><![CDATA[]]></payer_username>
```

Fig. 3. Message of monetary transfer

purchase" button was clicked to complete the purchase. On the path \data\data\com.tencent.mm\MicroMsg\mmslot\webcached\900\0\1833744_ content_matched___biz:MzU3MTkxNTExMg==-mid:2247491051-idx:4-,   the article was found. The recovered metadata are the corporate account nickname, the title of the article, and the description of the article as shown in Fig. 6. The article was written in Chinese, and the metadata stayed in Chinese characters. It did not provide an English translation, but all viewed articles are cached in the same folder.

The corresponding payment receipt was also found on the path \data\ data\com.tencent.mm\MicroMsg\9d8d3de00f8797d8e2f4d83d76640a5d\ EnMicroMsg.db. The WeChat pay account automatically generates a message to the user with timestamp and amount (see Fig. 7).

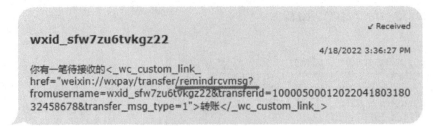

Fig. 4. Reminder message of transfer waiting

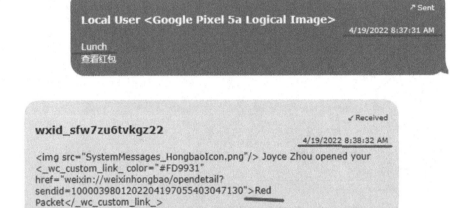

Fig. 5. Messages exchanges of red packet (Color figure online)

4.4 Money Transaction with Services Function

The service used was a movie ticket vendor and a movie ticket was ordered. The Service Notification account, an official WeChat account in charge of third-party service messages, was sending information to the user. The conversation was located in the EnMicroMsg.db database file as shown in Fig. 8. The notification message contains the timestamp, movie name, movie time, seat information, and movie theater. However, all information was delivered in Chinese and no corresponding English translations were found. It is also worth noting that the timestamp is a few seconds later than the exact time at which the payment transaction took place.

Another message was received from the WeChat Pay account, shown in Fig. 9. This message is a digital payment receipt with the timestamp, the amount paid, and the last 4 digits of the credit card used.

user_name : "gh_9d50d6ebd9f7"

nick_name : "壹心理精选"

round_head_img : "http://mmbiz.qpic.cn/mmbiz_png/E1ibfkxSw4icjloBl

title : "天才在左，疯子在右，你的潜意识里，藏着怎样的天才人格？"

desc : "普通人如何发掘自己的隐藏天赋？"

content_noencode : "<section data-role="outer" label="Powered by 13
gTC-light;color: rgb(48, 107, 182);"><strong><span style="font-family: (
n-left: 15px;margin-right: 15px;">
</p><p style="letter-spacing: '
t-size: 15px;letter-spacing: 1px;font-family: Optima-Regular, PingFangTC

create_time : "2022-04-14 18:59"

Fig. 6. Metadata of corporate article

gh_3dfda90e39d6

4/19/2022 12:22:15 PM

付款金额¥19.90
支付方式零钱
收单机构财付通支付科技有限公司

Fig. 7. Receipt message of the corporate service

notifymessage

✓ Received

4/19/2022 1:17:56 PM

影片名称:神奇动物:邓布利多之谜
放映时间:04-21 19:30
座位信息:特选座(IMAX) 8排19座
影院影厅:CGV影城 (万象城IMAX店) IM...
取票信息:验证码:55961962

Fig. 8. Notification of third party service

✓ Received

gh_3dfda90e39d6

4/19/2022 1:17:15 PM

付款金额¥48.00
优惠共优惠¥10.00
支付方式中国银行信用卡(9092)
收单机构财付通支付科技有限公司

Fig. 9. WeChat Payment account notification

✓ Received

gh_3dfda90e39d6

4/19/2022 12:22:15 PM

付款金额¥19.90
支付方式零钱
收单机构财付通支付科技有限公司

✓ Received

gh_3dfda90e39d6

4/19/2022 1:17:15 PM

付款金额¥48.00
优惠共优惠¥10.00
支付方式中国银行信用卡(9092)
收单机构财付通支付科技有限公司

)ETAILS

RTIFACT INFORMATION

Sender Username   **gh_3dfda90e39d6**

Sender Nickname   微信支付   WeChat Pay

Fig. 10. WeChat Payment account notification

4.5   Full Transaction History

The full transaction history was requested in the WeChat Pay account. The history displays all money transactions with personal and business accounts. It was attempted to retrieve the full transaction history of the WeChat Pay account. However, we were unable to find them. Only receipt messages were retrieved. Although it may seem similar, the full transaction history and receipt messages are different. Full transaction history composed of all monetary transactions that happened in this account. WeChat Pay account has receipt messages for all business-purpose payments in the `EnMicroMsg.db` database file as shown in Fig. 10.

5   Conclusion and Future Work

WeChat app is one of the most popular instant messaging apps in the world, and the company aims to build the app as a multi-purpose platform. The payment feature was launched and loved by the Chinese community due to its easy and real-time operation. Unfortunately, the two features also became the reason scammers pay attention to the app. Furthermore, WeChat does not provide a detailed explanation of its features and updates. It is extremely difficult for beginners to understand the scope of the app and the available functions. Moreover, because it is a product of a Chinese company, much of the information is written in only Chinese. These reasons set a high bar for investigators when a case involves WeChat. This study fills the gap by performing an analysis of the WeChat payment feature on Android. The structure of the data and the identified artifacts can help investigators better locate forensic artifacts from the Android device. The results show that `EnMicroMsg.db` is a critical file that contains a large number of payment transaction records and payment receipts. For personal payment transactions, the red packet and the money transfer can be differentiated. The red packet option contains the keyword "red packet". The money transfer option has its transfer id and the transfer amount. Both options can retrieve the sent time, received time, sender username, and receiver username. For corporate service, the viewed articles were able to be retrieved with the payment receipt. For the third-party service, two pieces of evidence were able to be found, service details and the receipt. The service details, including time, event and location, were able to be found. The receipt contains the amount paid, the timestamp and the last four digits of the card. Although the full payment history could not be found, the list of business purpose payments history was found with the amount and timestamp.

Future extensions of this study can test other WeChat platforms, such as Windows, MacOS, and the iPhone. Another direction can be the cloud analysis, which may provide additional information such as third-party services and mini programs. Some data are only stored on the third-party server. In addition, other features such as floating articles, channels, and shaking are worth looking at. These features could reflect the location, interest, and social interactions of the user. This information can offer valuable forensic artifacts to investigators.

References

1. Mobile devices (2017). https://www.nist.gov/itl/ssd/software-quality-group/computer-forensics-tool-testing-program-cftt/cftt-technical/mobile
2. WeChat privacy policy (2022). https://www.wechat.com/en/privacy_policy.html
3. Azfar, A., Choo, K.K.R., Liu, L.: An Android communication app forensic taxonomy. J. Forensic Sci. **61** (2016). https://doi.org/10.1111/1556-4029.13164
4. Iqbal, M.: WeChat revenue and usage statistics. Business of Apps (2022). https://www.businessofapps.com/data/wechat-statistics/

5. Kao, D.Y., Wang, T.C., Tsai, F.C.: Forensic artifacts of network traffic on WeChat calls. In: 2020 22nd International Conference on Advanced Communication Technology (ICACT), pp. 262–267 (2020). https://doi.org/10.23919/ICACT48636.2020.9061437
6. Menahil, A., Iqbal, W., Iftikhar, M., Shahid, W., ul Hassan, K., Rubab, S.: Forensic analysis of social networking applications on an Android smartphone. Wirel. Commun. Mob. Comput. **2021**, 1–36 (2021). https://doi.org/10.1155/2021/5567592
7. Nancy: The WeChat scams sweeping Asia. HackerNews (2019). https://myhackernews.com/blog/the-wechat-scams-sweeping-asia/
8. Park, E., Kim, S., Kim, J.: Analysis of WeChat Messenger on Windows and Android platforms. In: Digital Forensics Research, vol. 14, pp. 205–220 (2020)
9. Rathi, K., Karabiyik, U., Aderibigbe, T., Chi, H.: Forensic analysis of encrypted instant messaging applications on Android. In: 2018 6th International Symposium on Digital Forensic and Security (ISDFS), pp. 1–6 (2018). https://doi.org/10.1109/ISDFS.2018.8355344
10. Sihombing, H.C., Fajar, A.N., Utama, D.N.: Instant messaging as information goldmines to digital forensic: a systematic review. In: 2018 International Conference on Information Management and Technology (ICIMTech), pp. 235–240 (2018). https://doi.org/10.1109/ICIMTech.2018.8528089
11. Silla, C.: WeChat forensic artifacts: Android phone extraction and analysis (2015)
12. Wu, S., Sun, W., Liu, X., Zhang, Y.: Forensics on Twitter and WeChat using a customised Android emulator. In: 2018 IEEE 4th International Conference on Computer and Communications (ICCC), pp. 602–608 (2018). https://doi.org/10.1109/CompComm.2018.8781056
13. Wu, S., Zhang, Y., Wang, X., Xiong, X., Du, L.: Forensic analysis of WeChat on Android smartphones. Digit. Invest. **21** (2017). https://doi.org/10.1016/j.diin.2016.11.002
14. Yan, F., et al.: Identifying WeChat red packets and fund transfers via analyzing encrypted network traffic. In: 2018 17th IEEE International Conference on Trust, Security and Privacy in Computing and Communications/12th IEEE International Conference on Big Data Science and Engineering (TrustCom/BigDataSE), pp. 1426–1432 (2018). https://doi.org/10.1109/TrustCom/BigDataSE.2018.00198
15. Zhang, C., Yin, J.: Research on security mechanism and forensics of SQLite database. In: Sun, X., Zhang, X., Xia, Z., Bertino, E. (eds.) ICAIS 2021. CCIS, vol. 1423, pp. 614–629. Springer, Cham (2021). https://doi.org/10.1007/978-3-030-78618-2_51
16. Zhang, L., Yu, F., Ji, Q.: The forensic analysis of WeChat message. In: 2016 Sixth International Conference on Instrumentation Measurement, Computer, Communication and Control (IMCCC), pp. 500–503 (2016). https://doi.org/10.1109/IMCCC.2016.24
17. Zhou, F., Yang, Y., Ding, Z., Sun, G.: Dump and analysis of Android volatile memory on WeChat. In: 2015 IEEE International Conference on Communications (ICC), pp. 7151–7156 (2015). https://doi.org/10.1109/ICC.2015.7249467

Crypto Wallet Artifact Detection on Android Devices Using Advanced Machine Learning Techniques

Abhishek Bhattarai$^{(\boxtimes)}$, Maryna Veksler, Hadi Sahin, Ahmet Kurt, and Kemal Akkaya

Electrical and Computer Engineering Department, Florida International University, Miami, FL 33174, USA

{abhat031,mveks001,asahi004,akurt005,kakkaya}@fiu.edu

Abstract. As cryptocurrencies started to be used frequently as an alternative to regular cash and credit card payments, the wallet solutions/apps that facilitate their use also became increasingly popular. This also intensified the involvement of these cryptowallet apps in criminal activities such as ransom requests, money laundering, and transactions on dark markets. From a digital forensics point of view, it is crucial to have tools and reliable approaches to detect these wallets on the machines/devices and extract their artifacts. However, in many cases forensic investigators need to reach these file artifacts quickly with minimal manual intervention due to time and resource constraints. Therefore, in this paper, we present a comprehensive framework that incorporates various machine learning approaches to enable fast and automated extraction/triage of crypto related artifacts on Android devices. Specifically, our method can detect which cryptowallets exist on the device, their artifacts (i.e., database/log files), the crypto related pictures and web browsing data. For each type of data, we offer a specific machine learning technique such as Support Vector Machine, Logistic Regression and Neural Networks to detect and classify these files. Our evaluation results show very high accuracy detecting the file artifacts with respect to alternative tools.

Keywords: Crypto wallet · Cryptocurrency artifacts · Triage · Forensics · Machine learning · Android devices

1 Introduction

The adoption of the cryptocurrency has been expanding in the last decade. Bitcoin [27], originally introduced in 2009, has proposed a cash like payment system that relied on digital elements and cryptography but also have the characteristics of physical cash. The convenience of performing financial transactions in

---

M. Veksler, H. Sahin and A. Kurt—These authors contributed equally.

© ICST Institute for Computer Sciences, Social Informatics and Telecommunications Engineering 2023
Published by Springer Nature Switzerland AG 2023. All Rights Reserved
S. Goel et al. (Eds.): ICDF2C 2022, LNICST 508, pp. 111–132, 2023.
https://doi.org/10.1007/978-3-031-36574-4_7

a decentralized, secure, and peer-to-peer manner made cryptocurrencies popular and a preferable way over traditional payment methods. With this, multiple cryptocurrencies have also been introduced with various features and market capitalization such as Ethereum [33] and Monero [30].

The cryptocurrencies are held in *cryptocurrency wallet* applications and can be used in financial transactions with the associated *private key* of the wallet. Wallets can communicate with the underlying blockchain software allowing users to send and receive cryptocurrencies with ease. Crypto wallets generate different types of the supporting files within the device of the deployment, called artifacts, that include log files, databases, mnemonic files. In this work, we focus on mobile Android devices, as it leads the current market share with 71.85% worldwide [23].

The convenience for using the cryptocurrencies and lack of oversight made them attractive for criminal activities such as money laundering, drug trade and tax evasions. Therefore, the artifacts acquired from wallet applications are crucial in digital forensics investigations. Specifically, recovered data is useful to trace illegal money flows and recovery of stolen money. Wallet applications generally record transaction history on the device storage which may include cryptocurrency wallet addresses, timestamps, sent and received transaction amounts. The most critical artifacts include *private key*, *mnemonic*, and *seed files*. The law enforcement uses the obtained data in the attempts to unlock the wallet and access the funds.

Thus, the accurate retrieval of wallet's artifacts is crucial. However, the current approaches lack generalization, while tools such as Cellebrite require thorough manual analysis of the extracted data. Moreover, the various types of data within the phone may significantly contribute to the investigation. For example, the screenshots and notes may contain seed phrases, while browsing activity reveals the suspect's intentions.

In this paper, we propose an automated tool for the detection of crypto wallets and crypto artifacts. Moreover, we design a tool for the investigators to analyze extracted data efficiently. Proposed framework consists of 3 components, (1) dynamic detection of crypto wallet applications using machine learning (ML) classifiers, (2) image analysis to identify the presence of crypto related information using deep learning (DL) techniques, and (3) image analysis to identify the presence of crypto related information using deep learning (DL) techniques.

The results indicate that our crypto wallet detection method outperforms Cellebrite Crypto Tracer solution with the accuracy of 100%. We also achieve 98% accuracy for crypto related images classification. We demonstrate that our browsing activity analysis is robust across various browsers, unlike Cellebrite, and allows to accurately identify all crypto related artifacts, including history, bookmarks, and cache.

The rest of this paper is organized as follows. First, we discuss the related work in Sect. 2. In Sect. 3, we present our automated framework for crypto wallet mobile forensics and describe its components. We provide the implementation details and evaluation results in Sect. 4. Finally, we conclude the paper in Sect. 5.

2   Related Work

The majority of the works targeting crypto wallet forensics heavily rely on Cellebrite [1] software. Being the most popular digital forensics tool, it allows to extract all artifacts present within the device using Cellebrite UFED and Physical Analyzer suits. Moreover, Cellebrite "CryptoCurrency Analyzer" interface specifically focuses on identifying crypto wallet application. However, we determined that this software is not dynamic and cannot detect recently released applications. Specifically, Cellebrite successfully detected "Trust Wallet", but not "CryptoWallet PRO: Earn Crypto" applications. Despite Cellebrite's ability to extract all of the artifacts present within the phone, it fails to identify and filter out newly added crypto-related data, thus requiring a significant manual effort.

In [26], the authors used Cellebrite to analyze Bitcoin, Litecoin, and Darkcoin artifacts on both Android and iOS mobile devices. They focuses on the application installation and deletion dates, and preformed crypto transactions. As a results, five folders containing the artifacts were extracted and analyzed. Chang et al. in [6] conducted a more detailed analysis of cryptocurrency related information (e.i., transactions, timestamps, emails, and browser cookies). Moreover, the authors used Ciphertrace software [2] to examine the extracted data. They demonstrated the structural differences in the crypto wallet artifacts. However, their analysis was limited to two coins, Bitcoin and Dogecoin, and three wallets, Coinomi, Atomic, and Coinbase.

The authors in [21] focused on detecting wallet artifacts for Exodus and Electrum applications within Linux operating system. This work point out the weaknesses of data protection and tools for exploring wallet structure and its artifacts. As a result, the authors proposed a command line interface (CLI) tool for the evidence analysis.

The categorization of the cryptocurrency application in a phone accelerates the forensic investigation. This can be achieved by analyzing each application's description to understand its functionality.

Qiang Xu et al. [34] presented a framework that automate categorization of health and fitness applications gathered from Apple's apps and Google's play stores. The applications were first classified into two broad categories, paid and free, and then further sub-classified into 11 categories using supervised learning.

In [15] authors proposed a game apps classifier using the Latent Semantic Indexing. They classify various genres of games applications in the Apple App Store using support vector machine (SVM) classifier with a mean accuracy of 77%. [10] focuses on categorization of mobile apps into more focused categories based on their functionalities. The author categorized 600 Apple App store application from Education, Health and Fitness, and Medical categories. This paper demonstrates that metadata such as installs and ratings does not necessarily improve classification, but information from the title and the description of the application can increase accuracy.

Text categorization method allows to extract information from the text and assign it to the specific predefined categories based on the content (e.i. spam and genuine emails; rain, humid, and sunny). In digital forensics, natural language processing (NLP) text categorization is widely used to understand the context of the collected evidence [31]. It allows to reduce the manual workload required to manually analyze thousands of text artifacts present on the device.

One of the most popular and effective NLP approaches is Term Frequency-Inverse Document Frequency (TF-IDF) [16]. Dzisevic et al. [9] employs three information retrieval methods on both large and small datasets: plain TF-IDF, modified TD-IDF with LSA (Latent Semantic Analysis) and Linear Discriminant Analysis (LDA). The paper concludes that on both datasets, plain TF-IDF achieve similar accuracy with the other two methods.

3   Framework for Cryptocurrency Wallet Application Analysis

In this section we provide an overview of the proposed automated triage framework for crypto wallet forensics.

3.1   Overview

Figure 1 illustrates the main components of our system - android file system, image, and browser activities. First, we examine the android file system to classify installed crypto wallet applications and extract relevant data such as transaction history, mnemonic codes, and seed phrases. Next, we analyze the images on the device to identify those containing important crypto data (e.i, screenshots of QR codes and photos of seed phrases). Finally, we extract relevant history, bookmarks, cookies, and cache files from the browser activity. We use Cellebrite UFED software to extract the data from Android phones. Specifically, we select Qualcom Live extraction as recommended for the devices using Qualcomm mobile platform.

3.2   Android File System Analysis

The android file system analysis is the first component of our framework. Figure 2 illustrates the steps of the algorithm for crypto wallet applications detection.

First, we identify the Google Play Store ID for each application installed within the device. The names of the folders located in /data/data folder corresponds the application IDs.

We use FuzzyWuzzy string matching Python library package to calculate the differences of the given sequence of strings [7]. We compare discovered applications against those in the local database, which contains the list of the application IDs previously labeled as crypto wallet apps (①). The maintenance of the local database allows to optimize classification and prevent the algorithm from analyzing the same application twice. Subsequently, we identify the application not present in the database for the further categorization analysis (②).

For each unidentified application, we search for its information in the Google Play Store. We use the application ID to obtain the app description using Google-Play-Scraper library [17] (③).

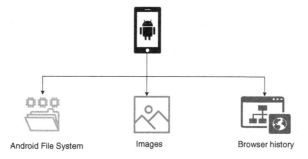

Fig. 1. Components of cryptowallet artifacts that will be analyzed under our proposed framework.

Next, we apply *keyword filtering* (④) using FuzzyWuzzy module in the extracted description text. We pre-compiled the list of keywords (i.e., crypto, coin, bitcoin, etc.) based on the existing crypto wallet applications in Google Play; and added the functionality to expand it as required. The keyword search allows to clean the data before passing it to the our classifier. Thus, we filter out the non-crypto applications such as Facebook to reduce the processing time of the model and increase the classifier's accuracy. All of the filtered-out applications are added to the local database and marked as "0" (i.e., Not Crypto wallet).

For the application that pass *keyword filtering* stage, we apply *preprocessing techniques* (⑤) to reduce the various noises present in the applications' descriptions. The unreadable format, special characters, parentheses, white spaces, brackets, punctuation, digits, and emoticons noises are removed, and the text is converted to lowercase character. We then tokenize the text by splitting the corpus of words using the tokenizer class of Natural Language Toolkit (NLTK). To reduce the dimensionality, we remove the stop words that do carry no significance, such as a, an, but, before. Finally, each word is reduced to its root form and plural or tense forms are removed. For example, made is converted to make.

As ML classifier model is not able to accurately process the resulting application description text, we apply *feature extraction* technique (⑥). We use TF-IDF [16] to extract the significant words from the original text. We maintain the vocabulary created based on the local database, which contains Term Frequency (TF) and Inverse Document Frequency (IDF) and values for each term calculated using Eqs. 1 and 2.

$$TF(t, d) = \frac{\text{Number of each } t \text{ in } d}{\text{Total number of } t \text{ in } d} \tag{1}$$

$$IDF(t) = \log(\frac{\text{Number of total } d}{\text{Numbers of } d \text{ containing } t}) \tag{2}$$

If t is the term and d is the document, then TF-IDF score is calculated as:

$$TF\text{-}IDF \text{ score} = TF * IDF \tag{3}$$

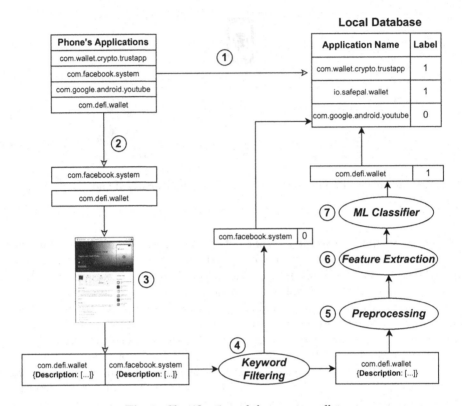

Fig. 2. Classification of the crypto wallet

Finally, we feed the extracted features to *ML classifier* ((7)). As a result, the model predicts the application as belonging to one of three categories - Crypto exchange, Crypto portfolio, and Crypto wallet. Crypto exchange denotes the applications that provides platform for the exchange or trading of crypto coins. Crypto portfolio category is for applications that manages the crypto assets or cryptocurrency profile. Crypto wallet category is for the applications that store the private keys of users and helps sending and receiving digital currency. While our main focus is crypto wallets, we added two specific categories to provide our model with an ability to learn more specific semantic features extracted from apps' descriptions. Based on the classifier output for the description, the application is marked as "1" (Crypto wallet) or "0", before being added to the local database.

3.3   Detecting Crypto Related Images

We use a combination of ML and fuzzy search methods to locate and extract crypto related information from images. Our approach is the first to offer a comprehensive image analysis for cryptocurrencies by integrating image filtering, optical character recognition, handwritten text recognition, text extraction and fuzzy search. Figure 3 provides the overview of our algorithm.

First, we filter out graphics used by mobile applications for the user interface (UI), namely the icons. Mostly located in the application folder, they are of PNG format and characterized by small resolution and size. Next, using Neural Networks (NNs) we classify the images into three categories; images with no text, images with printed-text and images with handwritten-text. We then use optical character recognition (OCR) engine to extract text information from images with printed text. We employ Handwritten Text Recognition (HTR) model using Convolutional Neural Networks (CNNs) and Recurrent Neural Networks (RNNs) to extract text information from images with handwritten-text. Finally, we implement fuzzy search to locate crypto related information and wallet recovery seeds from the extracted texts.

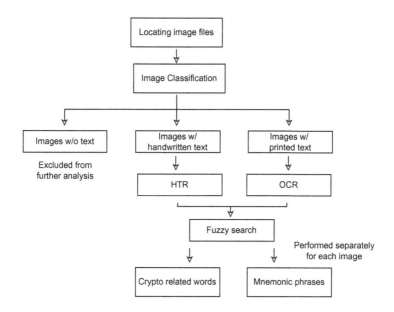

Fig. 3. Steps of image analysis

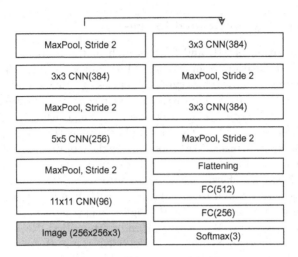

Fig. 4. Model schematics for image classification

Text/Non-Text Image Classification. Our Neural Network architecture, displayed in Fig. 4, implements a modified version of AlexNet [22].[1] Our model includes five CNN modules each followed by a maximum pooling (MaxPool) layer, and three fully connected layers (FC). Using the model we classify images into images with no text, images with printed-text and images with handwritten-text. We remove images with no text from further analyses.

Handwriting Recognition. Before running a handwriting recognition model (HTR), we use text-line and word detection/segmentation techniques to delineate lines and then words in the images. These word segments are then saved as separate images and fed to the trained model for prediction. The segmentation technique focuses on spatial distances between dark/black pixels and puts the connected components into bounding boxes [13]. Although most of the state of the art HTR models use them, it should be noted they are open to error as handwriting style and orientation could change significantly across individuals and images. There are studies which calculate line and word segmentation dynamically and incorporate them into their ML models (See [29,32]). However, they can be computationally expensive as they analyze the whole page rather than word segments [35].

We adapted the model created by [18]. The model architecture is displayed in Fig. 5. It includes two CNN models followed by maximum pooling layer, a fully connected layer, and two bidirectional Long Short-Term Memory (LSTM) layers with 25% dropouts. The model employs Connectionist Temporal Classification (CTC) loss function. CTC is extensively used in sequence labelling for speech

---

[1] AlexNet has won ImageNet Large Scale Visual Recognition Challenge (ILSVRC) in 2012, and since then has been extensively employed in visual recognition and classification tasks.

and handwriting recognition as it reduces the need for presegmentation of the input and postprocessing [12].

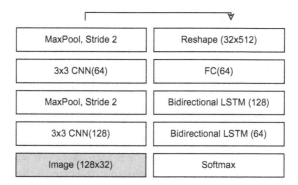

Fig. 5. Model schematics for handwriting recognition

3.4   Detecting Crypto Related Browser History

Web browser activity is an important component of the phones' forensic analysis. Visited websites, search history, and bookmarks can be used to build a detailed profile of user's interests. However, the existing research heavily relies on the manual inspection of the web browser files. Moreover, the investigators are often required to target a specific Web browser, one at a time, resulting in large time effort. Therefore, we propose using a triage approach which aims to recover web browser artifacts that unveil crypto-related activities.

In the analysis, we focused on recovering and identifying the following forensics artifacts: web history, bookmarks, user credentials, cookies, and cache. Web history of the Internet browsers information is generally stored in SQLite format and contains timestamps, urls, search terms, and downloads information. It reveals the interest of the subject and indicates all visited crypto-related websites if any. Similarly, session data can be used to restore users web activity, as it contains a record about open tabs and visited websites.

Bookmarks and user credentials provide more insight into recurring web browsing activity. Moreover, the credentials information allows to pinpoint the suspect's identity and/or aliases if any. The browser cookies are used to store information such as user preferences, session information, and personal information, thus, being an additional source for digital profiling of a suspect. Finally, the cache stores images, strings, and scripting data of the visited websites, which is normally used to accelerate the time required for the website loading. Therefore, cache contains the information to support and extend the browsing history evidence.

In our approach, we focus on the most popular Android web browser applications, Chrome, Opera, Mozilla Firefox, and Samsung Internet. On Android system, the web browsing artifacts are located in the web browsers' applications folders shown in Table 1. However, the structure of the stored information is not constant across various applications, and varies in the folder hierarchy and file types.

Table 1. The data folders of popular web browsers application and user data.

Web Browser	Folder Name
Mozila Firefox	/data/data/org.mozilla.firefox
Samsung Internet	/data/data/com.sec.android.app.sbrowser
Opera Browser	/data/data/com.opera.browser
Google Chrome	/data/data/com.android.chrome

For example, the files containing the browsing history are generally located inside *"Default/History"* folder, while the other artifacts are widely spread out among the browsers data folders. At the same time, the type of the files storing relevant artifacts varies highly from SQLite database to binary formats. For example, the Bookmarks for the Google Chrome browsers are stored as a JSON dictionary, while Samsung Internet stores this information in SQLite database file.

In this work, we designed an automated tool to read and analyze Android browser applications' files using the string-searching algorithm. It operates by traversing all files within the web browser's directory and then applying the search to identify and extract the information relevant for the investigation. We define a starting vector of the cryptocurrency terms consisting of the 3 categories: (1) names of the websites for cryptocurrency exchanges; (2) names and abbreviations of the most popular cryptocurrencies; and (3) frequently used cryptocurrency glossary. The first category contains the list of 50 most used cryptocurrency applications based on the scores derived from the traffic and trading volumes.[2] Similarly, we select 50 cryptocurrencies based on the highest exchanged volume[3]. Finally, we use publicly available cryptocurrency glossaries to complement our string vector by the terms that indirectly indicate the connection to crypto wallets [8,14]. The match cases for each Android browser are then extracted and presented to the investigator as illustrated by Table 2.

Table 2. Results of crypto related web artifacts discovered using the automated triage approach

Data Type	Data	File Location
URLs	http://crypto.com, crypto.com, The Best Place to Buy, Sell, and Pay with Cryptocurrency	/app_sbrowser/Default/History
Cookies	crypto.com, /price	/app_sbrowser/Default/Cookies
Bookmarks	https://www.coinbase.com, Coinbase - Buy and Sell Bitcoin, Ethereum, and more with trust	/databases/SBrowser.db

---

[2] https://coinmarketcap.com/rankings/exchanges/.
[3] https://coinmarketcap.com/all/views/all/.

4   Evaluation

In this section, we present the details of out implementation and evaluation of our proposed framework. First, we describe the phone data setup and extraction. Then, we analyze each component separately and compare it against Cellebrite.

4.1   Data Extraction

For the experiments, we select three different Android phones: Samsung Galaxy Note 10+, Xiaomi Mi 10T 5G, and Google Pixel 5a. For each phone, we installed six cryptocurrency applications from different categories (i.e., Crypto Wallet, Crypto Portfolio/Tracker, and Crypto Exchange) listed in Table 3. In our evaluation we included the most popular applications according to Google Play Download stats (e.g., Trust (10M+), Crypto Tracker (1M+), Binance (50M+)), and the most recently added (e.g., D-Wallet, Moni, KoinBasket).

To test framework components for crypto related images detection, we took multiple pictures of handwritten seed files. Finally, we browsed cryptocurrency websites using Google Chrome, Android Browser, Opera, and Firefox applications. Table 4 lists a full list of the crypto related artifacts created on the phone of the interest. Once we generated the realistic data on each device, we used Cellebrite UFED Qualcomm Live to extract phone data.

Table 3. Summary of crypto applications installed on the devices of the interest

Wallet	Portfolio/Tracker	Exchange
Trust	Crypto Tracker	Binance
Coinbase Wallet	HODL Real-Time Crypto Tracker	FTX
Exodus	Hodler	KuCoin
Crypto.com — DeFi Wallet	CoinFolio	WazirX
CryptoWallet PRO: Earn Crypto	Coin Portfolio	CoinDCX
D-Wallet	Moni	KoinBasket

Table 4. Summary of the crypto related artifacts present on the phone.

Bookmarks	Visited Websites	Searches
freewallet.org	freewallet.org	cryptowallets online
nerdwallet.com	coinbase.com	set up anonymous cryptowallet
coinbase.com	cryptowallet.com	untraceable online crypto transactions
	nerdwallet.com	
	binance.com	

4.2   Crypto Wallet Application Analysis Results

Creation of Dataset for Crypto Wallet Apps and Training: We trained
our application ML classifier using manually created dataset. First, we downloaded a Google Play Store dataset of 2.3 million+ application from Kaggle.com
[28]. Then, we reduced the original dataset to finance genre only and then applied
Python script to select applications that include the following keywords, *crypto,
bitcoin, blockchain, coins,* and *cryptocurrency.* The final dataset included more
than 4000 cryptocurrency applications. These applications were then labeled
manually into predefined categories based on the information provided in their
descriptions. Initially, we identified 12 categories ranging from crypto wallet to
banking but later reduced it to three.

As a result, we removed the application that completely irrelevant to the
crypto wallets and categorize the rest as crypto wallet, crypto portfolio and
crypto exchange. After reviewing the categories, we merged portfolio and tracker
apps into one category - crypto portfolio. Our final dataset consisted of 720
applications with the following sample distribution, 281 wallets, 231 portfolios,
and 209 exchanges.

Training ML Classifiers: We applied TF-IDF feature selection approach to
prepare the dataset for the model training. Thus, for each word in the applications descriptions we obtained TF-IDF score using Eq. 3 such that the higher
score indicated more significance of a word in a given text. Next, we established
the feature vectors comprising of the TF-IDF values. We split the obtained
dataset in train and test sets in 80/20 relation. To determine the best performing ML Classifier, we tested four classifiers Random Forest (RF), Support Vector
Machine (SVM), Naive Bayes (NB), and LogisticRegresssion (LogReg). We then
tunned maximum and minimum thresholds, unit normalization, and n-grams
boundary parameters for TF-IDF as follows **min_df** (0.5), **max_df** (3), **norm**
('l1'), **ngram_range** ((1, 3)). We trained each ML model using 5 cross-validation
folds (K-folds).

Performance Results: Table 5 illustrate the results for 2 best performing ML
classifiers: SVM and LogReg. We selected, precision, recall, and F1 score metrics
to determine the optimal algorithm. Since our main focus is on crypto wallets, we
focus on analyzing the performance of ML algorithm for this category exclusively.
Table 5 illustrates the results for our models, where **precision** indicates the
number of positive class that actually belongs to positive class, **recall** means
ratio of true positive class correctly predicted to the total positive class, and
F1 score is a weighted average of both (e.i., F1 score interprets the overall
performance of the classifier).

The results demonstrate that both SVM and LogReg algorithms allows to
achieve the recall of 93%. It indicates that both models identified majority of
crypto wallet applications. However, SVM slightly outperforms LogReg for precision metrics, indicating that the former algorithm produces less false positive
results. We use F-1 score to asses the overall performance of the model as 85%
contributed to the relatively high percentage of false positives (22%). In con-

Table 5. Classification results of classifiers models for Crypto Wallets.

	SVM			LogReg		
	Precision	*Recall*	*F1 Score*	*Precision*	*Recall*	*F1 Score*
Crypto Wallet	**0.78**	*0.93*	**0.85**	0.76	*0.93*	0.84

clusion, we identify SVM as an optimal model. We attribute the low precision of ML algorithms to the fact that exchanges functionality is similar to crypto wallets. Particularly, both applications allow to store, receive, and send crypto, which leads to a similar description semantics.

End-to-End Evaluation of Crypto Wallet Categorization Component: We proceeded to test the performance of our algorithm for Android file system analysis. First, we identified the IDs of all applications present on the phone. As a results of description extraction and keyword filtering, we obtained 18 distinct application IDs. Next, we applied ML classifier preceded by text preprocessing and feature extraction.

We were able to classify all applications listed in Table 3 with the F1 score of 100%. Specifically, we identified six wallets, Trust, Coinbase, Exodus, DeFi, CryptoWallet PRO, and D-Wallet (Table 6).

Table 6. Classification results for the applications installed on the test phones.

	Precision	*Recall*	*F1 Score*
Wallet	1.00	1.00	1.00
Portfolio	1.00	1.00	1.00
Exchange	1.00	1.00	1.00
Accuracy			1.00

All applications discovered by our algorithm were added to the local database, such that apps filtered out by keyword search, crypto exchanges, and crypto portfolios were marked as non-crypto, while crypto wallets marked as crypto related. Therefore, the investigators can save a significant amount of time if any of the identified applications will appear on the Android devices in the future.

Comparison with Cellebrite: We compared our approach to the Cellebrite tool. Based on the experiments, we determined that Cellebrite did not recognize *CryptoWallet PRO: Earn Crypto* and *D-Wallet : Crypto Wallet* application installed on the phone. Thus, we concluded that Cellebrite is not robust against apps newly added to the Google Play Store. At the same time, our framework successfully classified both crypto wallets.

4.3 Crypto Related Image Analysis Results

Text/Non-text Image Classification Setup: We implemented our Neural Network Analysis in TensorFlow [3]. We trained the model on the training set for 50 epochs with Adam optimizer [19] and the default learning rate (α) of 0.001. We employed 9080 colored images which were resized to 256×256 pixels. We kept the original aspect ratio and padded the images if needed. The data were split into train and test sets with a ratio of 90% and 10%. We use several data resources to diversify the training set. Below is the list of the data resources:

 i. Non-text image data: 1000 images from ImageNet database [9] and 3002 from Flickr30k dataset [36].
 ii. Printed-text image data: 322 images from Old Books dataset [5] and 2997 web screenshots data [4].
 iii. handwritten-text image data: 1042 images from IAM dataset [25] and 687 from GNHK dataset [24].
 iv. 15 screenshot images created on the examined phones.

We run the model on the test set. It was able to classify the images into three categories with 98.57% accuracy.

Handwriting Recognition Setup: We used Adam optimizer [19] with the default learning rate of 0.001. The model was trained on 96,456 grayscale images for 50 epochs. The data were divided into train, validation and test sets with 90%, 5% and 5% ratios. Images were padded to have a uniform size of 128×32. We used Levenstein edit distance to measure the accuracy of our predictions. This metric compares the real and predicted labels and measures the amount of changes needed to transform the predictions into true labels [20]. Our metric takes the average value of the edit distances. The mean edit distance for our model was 17.36.

After extracting the text information, we pre-processed it for fuzzy search analysis. We removed the white spaces and single character strings, and convert the text to lower case characters. We also created a spelling-corrected version of the text. We run fuzzy search analyses with crypto wallet related keywords on both versions of the text. The keywords include the following terms: *crypto, currency, wallet, bitcoin, coin, chain, btc, stake, nft,* and *token.* The first five words of the list are commonly used in descriptions of wallet related applications as found in earlier sections.

In addition, we run fuzzy search on a list of mnemonic phrases. Specifically we used BIP39 mnemonic phrases used by Bitcoin.[4] This list includes 2048 standard words; each of these phrases correspond to a number and a combination of these, 12-word phrases, includes all information needed to recover bitcoin wallet. Our goal is to detect whether a phone includes these mnemonic phrases, recovery seeds, in the image files.

Performance Results: We created 15 images which include 6 images with handwritten text, 5 images of phone screenshots with printed-text and 4 images with

---

[4] https://github.com/bitcoin/bips/blob/master/bip-0039/english.txt.

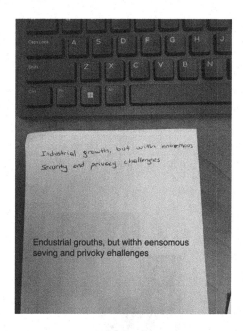

Fig. 6. Image with handwritten text. Extracted text information is included at the bottom of the image.

no text. The handwritten-text images included both the paper the text is written on and the background, as they may appear in the wild (see Fig. 6). The printed text images include various screenshots of the phone menus, crypto-wallet transactions, and QR codes of wallet transactions. These sample images were located in /data/* folder.

Text/non-text classification Neural Network model successfully predicted the categories of these 15 images with 100% accuracy. Figure 7 presents the confusion matrix from the results.

Then, we run handwriting recognition model on six handwriting images. Figure 6 displays one of the images with extracted text information at the bottom. As seen from the figure, handwriting recognition may not reliably recognize all words. Therefore, depending on the number of handwritten images, forensic analysts may choose to examine them manually if they found some traces of crypto currency activities in the phone.

Next, we run OCR machine on printed text images. Then, we run fuzzy search on extracted text. We run the analysis with maximum Levenshtein edit distance of one, meaning that we looked at the words that differ from the keywords by one or less alteration. Table 7 presents the crypto-wallet related words extracted from the images. Out of ten keywords our images contained seven crypto currency related words. Our results successfully extracted all these keywords.

We also measured our performance with two commonly used metrics; Recall and Precision rates [11]. Table 8 presents the results. OCR method were able to

Table 7. Results of crypto related word search from images

	No Spelling Check	w/ Spelling Check
bitcoin	'bitcoin'	'bitcoin'
wallet	'wallet'	'wallet'
btc	'btc', 'bitc', 'tc'	'btc', 'bitc', 'tc'
coin	'coin', 'coln', 'coun', 'con'	'coin', 'coln', 'coun', 'con'
chain	'chain'	'chain'
nft	'nft', 'nt', 'net', 'ft', 'nbt'	'nft', 'nt', 'net', 'ft', 'nbt'
token	'token'	'token'

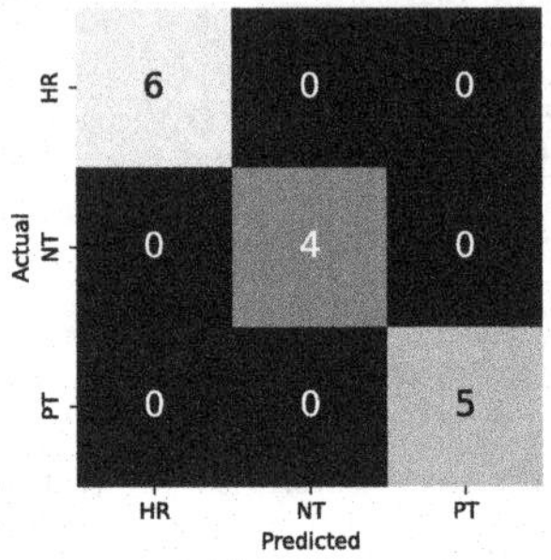

Fig. 7. Results from image classification. PT, NT, HR denote printed text image, non-text image, and handwritten image respectively.

extract printed text with around 90% Recall and Precision rates. HTR method was relatively less successful, Recall and Precision rates were around 65%. But, even at these levels we can comfortably argue whether a phone image includes wallet artifacts or not.

Table 8. Results from search for crypto related words

	# of words	Recall	Precision
Handwritten image 1	12	1.00	0.71
Handwritten image 2	16	0.98	0.64
Handwritten image 3	12	1.00	0.61
Handwritten image 4	9	1.00	0.78
Handwritten image 5	8	0.97	0.75
Handwritten image 6	12	1.00	0.69
Screenshot image 1	12	0.92	0.92
Screenshot image 2	14	0.98	0.98
Screenshot image 3	25	1.00	1.00
Screenshot image 4	10	0.89	0.89
Screenshot image 5	30	0.93	0.93

Table 9 presents results from fuzzy search analysis on mnemonic phrases. We measure success with a modified version of Recall rate. Mnemonic phrases are standard English words. A long text may contain several of them even though the text does not include a recovery seed. Therefore, we penalize the *recall* rate if the text is long. As Eq. 4 shows, we multiply recall rate with a weight which decreases as the number of recognized mnemonic phrases move away from 12.

$$P = \frac{m}{\text{\# of mnemonic phrases}} \times w \tag{4}$$

$$w = \begin{cases} \exp \frac{\eta - 12}{\eta}, & \eta \leq 12 \\ \exp \frac{13 - \eta}{\eta}, & \eta > 12 \end{cases}$$

where m is the number of extracted mnemonic phrases, w is the weight and η is the total number of extracted words.

Table 9. Results from search for mnemonic phrases

	Includes Mnemonic Phrases	Recall	Requires consideration
Handwritten image 1	True	75.0%	Yes
Handwritten image 2	False	28.4%	No
Handwritten image 3	True	73.6%	Yes
Handwritten image 4	False	26.4%	No
Handwritten image 5	False	39.2%	No
Handwritten image 6	True	70.8%	Yes
Screenshot image 1	False	30.9%	No
Screenshot image 2	False	36.1%	No
Screenshot image 3	False	19.8%	No
Screenshot image 4	False	41.4%	No
Screenshot image 5	False	0.09%	No

In our sample, only three of the images, *Handwritten image 1, 3 and 6* included a recovery seed. We were able to predict them with over 70%. The results show low Recall rates for the images which do not include the phrases, as expected. However, as discussed earlier the list of mnemonic phrases include ordinary words. If we have a longer text, it is possible to get false positives. Therefore, forensic analysts are advised to look closely at cases that have 50% and higher recall rates.

4.4 Browser History Analysis Results

In order to demonstrate the effectiveness of out approach, We evaluated the performance of the tool based on the (1) detection accuracy for crypto artifacts (i.e., the ability to identify all previously created crypto artifacts), (2) robustness across various browsers (i.e., the ability to extract crypto data from each of the targeted browser), and (3) and time consumption.

First, we analyzed the tool's effectiveness to identify crypto related data. We identified three file types, SQLite database, JSON dictionary, and other. However, due to the large diversity of the file types containing the browsing activity, we identified two stand alone categories as SQLite database and JSON dictionary, while classifying the other types as the plain text. Table 10 contains the summary of all discovered files for each browser filtered by the type.

Table 10. Summary of all discovered files containing the traces of crypto-related activities for the corresponding web browser.

Browser	SQLite Databases	JSON dictionaries	Plain Text
Google Chrome	7	3	745
Samsung Internet	8	2	486
Firefox	12	4	411
Opera	6	0	417

Table 11 lists a summary of the crypto-related forensic evidence extracted for each browser. While not illustrated, the tool also provides the location for each forensics data type, which generally corresponds to a single file per type, except for cache data. The locations for cache data are located in the "/cache/" folder found in the home path of the Android browser applications. However, the type of recovered data varies across the browser applications. For example, Quota Manager data is only applicable for Google Chrome and Samsung Internet applications, while Opera and Firefox apps store the automatically provided browsing suggestions.

Table 11. Summary of the discovered forensics evidence

	Google Chrome	Firefox	Opera	Samsung Internet
History	31	20	20	26
Bookmarks	1	1	1	2
Cookies	42	18	21	32
Favicons	38		N/A	25
Recent Tabs	2	0	0	1
Cache	650	152	310	344
Top Sites	2	1	1	2
Login Data	2	1	1	N/A
Network Persistent State	10	9	7	5
QuotaManager	2	N/A	2	1
Suggestions	N/A	1	9	N/A

To further demonstrate the effectiveness of our approach, we compared it with the Cellebrite analysis. Table 12 illustrates the amount of the artifacts detected by both Cellebrite and our approach based on the initial list of the artifacts in Table 4. Specifically, Cellebrite analysis did not recover the data for freewallet.org and binance.com. Moreover, the Cellebrite analysis did not contain any artifacts from Firefox browser, while only discovering a limited history for the Opera browser. On the contrary, our approach allowed to recover all crypto-related artifacts for each of the four browsers under the investigation. Therefore, our approach outperforms the Cellebrite for the browser history analysis of the crypto related artifacts in the detection accuracy and robustness across all browsers. Finally, when comparing the processing time, our approach finished analyzing the browser artifacts within 10 s compared to the Cellebrite processing the data for approximately 7 min.

Table 12. Amount of recovered crypto-related artifacts discovered by Cellebrite and our approach.

	Cellebrite	Our Approach
Bookmarks	66%	100%
Visited Websites	60%	100%
Searches	100%	100%

Table 13 illustrates the summary of all artifacts detected by our approach. Therefore, our approach was able to successfully identify all visited crypto currency websites and bookmarked pages, recover the Google search information, and partially reveal personal user data for each web browser. Moreover, the cookies and cache data provide a significant evidences to the users activity for each of the crypto-related websites. Also, while revealing the presence of the credentials data for the Firefox, our tool did not recover encrypted login credentials, but only the website it was used for, coinbase.com.

According to our evaluation, our approach for web browser activity provides comprehensive summary of all the artifacts related to the cryptocurrency investigation. Moreover, we were able to robustly extract all manually created artifacts listed in Table 4 for each Android web browser application. The majority of the important crypto activity traces were listed in the format provided in Table 2 allowing us to quickly identify visited websites, bookmarks, and account data. The automated extraction of the data and its further categorization resulted in significant reduction of time and effort required for forensics analysis of the web browsers.

Table 13. Results of crypto related web artifacts discovered using the automated triage approach

	Google Chrome	Samsung Internet	Opera	Firefox
Visited Websites	✓	✓	✓	✓
Google Searches	✓	✓	✓	✓
Bookmarks	✓	✓	✓	✓
Cookies	✓	✓	✓	✓
Cache	✓	✓	✓	✓
Credentials	✓	✓	✓	X

5   Conclusion

In this paper, we designed and developed an automated triage framework for Crypto Wallet mobile forensics for Android operating system. We implemented an algorithm to identify crypto wallet applications present on the phone, by leveraging SVM classifier for the contextual analysis of the app's descriptions. We used combination of NNs, CNNs, and LTSMs networks to identify the images containing crypto wallet seed phrases and crypto related information. Our framework also discovered the online traces of crypto activity containing crypto related credentials and browsing history, which allows to support the suspects' intentions and interests.

We evaluated our framework on the data extracted from 3 distinct phones. Our validation result indicate that the framework can successfully classify the crypto wallet applications with the accuracy of 93%. However, in the real-life scenario the proposed approach identified all crypto wallets present on the phones with the precision of 100%. We demonstrated that proposed framework succeeds in identifying images containing handwritten seed phrases with the threshold for the image weight of 70%. Finally, we were able to recover complete crypto related browsing activity. We also established that our tool outperforms Cellebrite for the crypto wallet apps identification and analysis of browsing activity.

For the future work, we will focus on expanding our framework to analyze specific crypto wallet artifacts such as transaction IDs, timestamps, seed files, and keys. We will expand the crypto related image recognition analysis to include the analysis of transaction QR codes and improve the recognition of seed phrases.

Acknowledgement. This work is supported by US National Science Foundation under the grant # 1739805.

References

1. Cellebrite. https://cellebrite.com/en/home/
2. Ciphertrace. https://ciphertrace.com/

3. Abadi, M., et al.: TensorFlow: a system for large-scale machine learning. In: 12th USENIX Symposium on Operating Systems Design and Implementation (OSDI 2016), pp. 265–283 (2016)
4. Aydos, F.: Webscreenshots (2020). https://www.kaggle.com/datasets/aydosphd/webscreenshots
5. Barcha, P.: Old books dataset (2017). https://github.com/PedroBarcha/old-books-dataset
6. Chang, E., Darcy, P., Choo, K.K.R., Le-Khac, N.A.: Forensic artefact discovery and attribution from Android cryptocurrency wallet applications. arXiv preprint arXiv:2205.14611 (2022)
7. Cohen, A.: FuzzyWuzzy (2020). https://pypi.org/project/fuzzywuzzy/
8. CoinMarketCap: Crypto glossary (2022). https://coinmarketcap.com/alexandria/glossary
9. Dzisevič, R., Šešok, D.: Text classification using different feature extraction approaches. In: 2019 Open Conference of Electrical, Electronic and Information Sciences (eStream), pp. 1–4. IEEE (2019)
10. Ebrahimi, F., Tushev, M., Mahmoud, A.: Classifying mobile applications using word embeddings. ACM Trans. Softw. Eng. Methodol. (TOSEM) **31**(2), 1–30 (2021)
11. Faustina Joan, S., Valli, S.: A survey on text information extraction from born-digital and scene text images. Proc. Natl. Acad. Sci. India Sect. A: Phys. Sci. **89**(1), 77–101 (2019)
12. Graves, A.: Connectionist temporal classification. In: Graves, A. (ed.) Supervised Sequence Labelling with Recurrent Neural Networks, pp. 61–93. Springer, Heidelberg (2012). https://doi.org/10.1007/978-3-642-24797-2_7
13. Ha, J., Haralick, R.M., Phillips, I.T.: Document page decomposition by the bounding-box project. In: Proceedings of 3rd International Conference on Document Analysis and Recognition, vol. 2, pp. 1119–1122. IEEE (1995)
14. Hooson, M.: Cryptocurrency glossary of terms & acronyms (2022). https://www.forbes.com/advisor/investing/cryptocurrency/crypto-glossary/
15. Horppu, I., Nikander, A., Buyukcan, E., Mäkiniemi, J., Sorkhei, A., Ayala-Gómez, F.: Automatic classification of games using support vector machine. arXiv preprint arXiv:2105.05674 (2021)
16. Joachims, T.: A probabilistic analysis of the rocchio algorithm with TFIDF for text categorization. Carnegie-mellon univ pittsburgh pa dept of computer science (1996)
17. JoMingyu: Google-Play-Scraper (2022). https://pypi.org/project/google-play-scraper/
18. Keras Team: Handwriting recognition (2022). https://github.com/keras-team/keras-io/blob/master/examples/vision/handwriting_recognition.py
19. Kingma, D.P., Ba, J.: Adam: a method for stochastic optimization. arXiv preprint arXiv:1412.6980 (2014)
20. Konstantinidis, S.: Computing the Levenshtein distance of a regular language. In: IEEE Information Theory Workshop, pp. 4-pp. IEEE (2005)
21. Kovalcik, T.: Digital forensics of cryptocurrency wallets. Master's thesis, Halmstad University, School of Information Technology (2022)
22. Krizhevsky, A., Sutskever, I., Hinton, G.E.: ImageNet classification with deep convolutional neural networks. In: Advances in Neural Information Processing Systems, vol. 25 (2012)

23. Laricchia, F.: Global mobile OS market share 2012–2022 (2022). https://www.statista.com/statistics/272698/global-market-share-held-by-mobile-operating-systems-since-2009/
24. Lee, A.W.C., Chung, J., Lee, M.: GNHK: a dataset for English handwriting in the wild. In: Lladós, J., Lopresti, D., Uchida, S. (eds.) ICDAR 2021. LNCS, vol. 12824, pp. 399–412. Springer, Cham (2021). https://doi.org/10.1007/978-3-030-86337-1_27
25. Marti, U.V., Bunke, H.: The IAM-database: an English sentence database for offline handwriting recognition. Int. J. Doc. Anal. Recogn. 5(1), 39–46 (2002)
26. Montanez, A.: Investigation of cryptocurrency wallets on iOS and Android mobile devices for potential forensic artifacts. Marshall University Research Project (2014)
27. Nakamoto, S.: Bitcoin: a peer-to-peer electronic cash system (2008). https://bitcoin.org/bitcoin.pdf
28. Prakash, G., Koshy, J.: Google play store apps (2021). https://www.kaggle.com/datasets/gauthamp10/google-playstore-apps
29. Singh, S.S., Karayev, S.: Full page handwriting recognition via image to sequence extraction. In: Lladós, J., Lopresti, D., Uchida, S. (eds.) ICDAR 2021. LNCS, vol. 12823, pp. 55–69. Springer, Cham (2021). https://doi.org/10.1007/978-3-030-86334-0_4
30. The Monero Project: Monero - secure, private, untraceable (2022). https://www.getmonero.org/
31. Ukwen, D.O., Karabatak, M.: Review of NLP-based systems in digital forensics and cybersecurity. In: 2021 9th International Symposium on Digital Forensics and Security (ISDFS), pp. 1–9, Elazig, Turkey (2021). https://doi.org/10.1109/ISDFS52919.2021.9486354
32. Wigington, C., Tensmeyer, C., Davis, B., Barrett, W., Price, B., Cohen, S.: Start, follow, read: end-to-end full-page handwriting recognition. In: Proceedings of the European Conference on Computer Vision (ECCV), pp. 367–383 (2018)
33. Wood, G.: Ethereum: a secure decentralised generalised transaction ledger (2014). https://github.com/ethereum/yellowpaper
34. Xu, Q., Ibrahim, G., Zheng, R., Archer, N.: Toward automated categorization of mobile health and fitness applications. In: Proceedings of the 4th ACM MobiHoc Workshop on Pervasive Wireless Healthcare, pp. 49–54 (2014)
35. Ye, Q., Doermann, D.: Text detection and recognition in imagery: a survey. IEEE Trans. Pattern Anal. Mach. Intell. 37(7), 1480–1500 (2014)
36. Young, P., Lai, A., Hodosh, M., Hockenmaier, J.: From image descriptions to visual denotations: new similarity metrics for semantic inference over event descriptions. Trans. Assoc. Comput. Linguist. 2, 67–78 (2014)

Spread Spectrum Analysis

CSCD: A Cyber Security Community Detection Scheme on Online Social Networks

Yutong Zeng[1], Honghao Yu[1], Tiejun Wu[2], Yong Chen[1], Xing Lan[2], and Cheng Huang[1(✉)]

[1] School of Cyber Science and Engineering, Sichuan University, Chengdu, China
opcodesec@gmail.com
[2] NSFOCUS Technologies Group Co., Ltd., Beijing, China

Abstract. Online social networks (OSNs) are playing a crucial role in daily life, cyber security guys such as hackers, cyber criminals, and researchers also like to communication and publish opinions. Their discussions and relations can provide unprecedented opportunities for researcher to develop better insights about those accounts' activities in communities, which could be helpful for different purposes like cyber threat intelligent hunting and attack attribution. In this paper, we propose a scheme for cyber security community detection named CSCD on OSNs. We present a social relevance analysis method by building an ego network from one seed account. Through multidimensional analysis, features organized into four categories are taken into consideration and a recognition model is used to detect security-related accounts. Then we construct the social network, consisting of detected accounts, and propound a pruning strategy to remove weak relationships between accounts on the basis of edge features. An unsupervised overlapping community detection model is applied to unearthing potential communities. To evaluate our proposed scheme, we utilize Twitter as the platform to construct datasets. The recognition model achieves an accuracy up to 95.1%, and the community detection model obtains the best performance comparing to other former algorithms.

Keywords: online social network · community detection · cyber security · social network analysis

1 Introduction

Online social networks, where users can share information on different topics, follow any other people unidirectionally and keep track of the hottest trends, have exploded in popularity over the past few years. At the same time, there are lots of security researchers and hackers active on OSNs. OSNs have been utilized as a new platform to conduct malicious behaviors, including spreading malware

© ICST Institute for Computer Sciences, Social Informatics and Telecommunications Engineering 2023
Published by Springer Nature Switzerland AG 2023. All Rights Reserved
S. Goel et al. (Eds.): ICDF2C 2022, LNICST 508, pp. 135–150, 2023.
https://doi.org/10.1007/978-3-031-36574-4_8

[1], phishing [6], spamming [20,22], social engineering attack [7], and vulnerability disclosure [2,9]. As a consequence, OSNs have been preferred subjects to many security-related studies among researchers. To extract valuable information from OSNs, monitoring security-related accounts may provide a good solution. Comparing to relying on security-related keywords to identify vulnerabilities in posted content, keeping tabs on accounts such as security experts can indicate new security threats claimed to be unknown before. Therefore, how to detect such accounts automatically in a large scale has been a research hotspot.

In terms of Twitter, there have been a few recently published studies on detecting security-related accounts such as spammers, hackers or security researchers. Many methods have been proposed to combat the increasing number of these malicious accounts [20,22] in order to curb the risks brought by them. Meanwhile, some cyber security professionals, who are active users on OSNs, are spreading hacker tutorials, exchanging knowledge, providing their own insights on security incidents and etc. Monitoring these accounts has proven to be a good source of information for many purposes.

However, most current researches pay attention to detecting security-related accounts on OSNs individually rather than discovering security groups by a community-based approach, or analyzing properties within related communities. We lack basic insights into the characteristics of cyber security ecosystem on OSNs.

In this study, we propose CSCD, a scheme for cyber security community detection, and conduct an empirical study of discovered community. In summary, our contributions are as follows:

- We design a recognition model to differentiate security-related accounts from unrelated ones through extracting features from accounts' profile, behavior, time sequence of posts and content, reaching an accuracy rate of 95.1%.
- We propose a pruning strategy to construct the social network using edge features including the relevance of interaction, and the similarity of content, friends and followers, with the aim of removing the weak relationship between accounts.
- We put forward a three-staged security-related community detection scheme on OSNs, which can identify overlapping cyber security communities automatically starting from one seed account. We also present the application, evaluation of CSCD, and a case study of predicted community on Twitter.

The rest of the paper is organized as follows. Section 2 provides related work. Research goal is presented in Sect. 3. Section 4 details the methodology and different stages in CSCD. Subsequently, our results are described in Sect. 5. We conclude this paper and provide an outlook for future work in Sect. 6.

2   Related Work

2.1   Security-Related Account Recognition on OSNs

With the rapid growth of OSNs, there has been a tremendous rise in the number of malicious activities, which has been an urgent task to develop an efficient detection system that can identify security-related accounts, such as spammers, compromised accounts, hackers and etc. Ellaky et al. [8] divided malicious accounts into four categories: Cloned account, Sock Puppets account [21], Sybil account [19] and Bot account [20]. However, most studies focus on the detection of malicious account. There has been few researches on the automated detection of hackers, security researchers or cyber criminals, who can provide security insights and do not engage in malicious activities directly. Aslan et al. [3] proposed the first fully automated classifier for such accounts. Though their best-performing model reached an accuracy rate of 97%, the dataset in their study was relatively small, which only contains 424 accounts. Mahaini et al. [12] presented a more mature detection framework with a systematic dataset construction method and a richer set of features to group security accounts into different categories on the basis of the study by Aslan et al. The detection of such accounts is also the focus of our study.

2.2 Security-Related Community Detection on OSNs

Community detection is a growing field of interest in the area of social network applications. Yang et al. [16] proposed the most common definition of community which is a subset of vertices that are densely connected between them and sparsely with the other nodes of the network. Chakrabo et al. [5] underlined that community detection is approached through two phases: unveiling the community structure from the network and evaluating the goodness of the result through several measure metrics. Community detection algorithms have been used in the discovery of security-related sub-communities. Lingam et al. [11] created a weighted signed Twitter network graph focused on behavioral similarity and confidence values as weighted edges. They proposed two algorithms, where the former recognized social botnet communities with malicious behavioral similarities, while the latter reconstructed and detected social botnet communities more accurately in presence of many forms of malicious behaviors. Results of their experiments demonstrated the validity of their algorithms than previous work.

In summary, most previous studies have focused on the detection of malicious accounts. There are relatively few studies on the detection of security-related communities on social networks. For community detection in this area, most studies only considered topological information without nodes' content or simply adopted cluster algorithms according to the similarity of nodes without the relationship on social networks.

3 Research Goal

We decide to conduct an experiment about how to detect cyber security community and provide an empirical analysis on how cyber security accounts are assembled and active on OSNs, considering the lack of past studies investigating connections in cyber security community and activities of inner accounts. To specify our work, we set some separate RQs for our study:

- **RQ1**: Can we propose a scheme which helps us detect cyber security community efficiently?
- **RQ2**: Can we study the social structure of these inner accounts on the basis of the data on OSNs?
- **RQ3**: What topics can we extract from the communication of these account on OSNs?
- **RQ4**: Can we identify key accounts in each sub-community?

For **RQ1**, which is also the basis of our work, we explain how we construct CSCD and how we get such accounts belonging to the specific field in the next section. To study **RQ2**, we use unsupervised overlapping method to identify communities established on the constructed network of collected accounts. Then we figure out social structures of these sub-communities. With the purpose of solving **RQ3**, natural language processing (NLP) is applied to analyzing behavior of accounts in sub-communities. For **RQ4**, we use PageRank algorithm in order to indicate key accounts in communities.

4 Methodology

4.1 Overview of Proposed Scheme

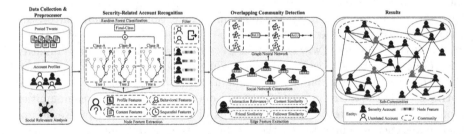

Fig. 1. The framework of proposed scheme named CSCD

Figure 1 presents the methodology adopted to achieve cyber security community detection. In this section, detailed description for each component of CSCD will be provided in following sections. A seed account is required to conduct our data collection at the beginning of CSCD. After selecting some accounts which are influential on security-related fields, we can extend other accounts by social relevance analysis. This collection method will bring in a number of accounts as well as relationships between accounts, especially after iteration. It is obvious that security accounts will also interact with unrelated account such as their family members, friends or celebrities. To remove such unrelated accounts from the dataset collected in previous step, we extract features in four categories to distinguish security accounts from unrelated ones. In addition, edge features in four categories are taken into consideration during the course of social network construction. To solve the problem that community detection needs to deal with rich non-Euclidean graph data, we adopt GNN since the rapid development of GNN in graph mining technology.

4.2 Data Collection and Pre-processing

Data Collection. The first step of our approach is data collection. There are many varied accounts active on online social networks while security-related accounts only account for a small proportion, so we need to design a method to make sure we can collect security-related accounts as efficiently as possible. Twitter is selected as the platform to illustrate our scheme design. By utilizing the social relevance and homogeneity between accounts, we can find a great number of similar accounts. Therefore, we manually select some accounts which are influential and active in the field on Twitter as seed accounts based on below searching rules:

- Searching for accounts with a number of followers, which also engaged in hot issues and events related to cyber security.
- Searching for accounts belonging to renowned security companies or agencies.
- Searching for security topics and collecting accounts which engaged in these discussions and posted amount of content with good quality.

After selecting seed accounts manually, the crawler will collect their profile data and tweets data. Profile data, including an account's friends, followers, created time and description, is the basic information. Tweets data, consisting of tweet text and an account's interactive records, can reveal topics the user interested in and accounts it interacted with. Then we extract interactive accounts through records such as mention, favorite, reply, quote and retweet in tweets data. These interactive accounts, together with friends and followers of the seed account, form the ego network of the seed after deduplication. Also, for each extended account, our crawler will collect its profile data and tweets.

Pre-processing. We apply pre-processing techniques for each tweet before tweets are available to our model. We translate all tweet texts into English to facilitate the subsequent study. There is a problem that the content of retweets crawled through Twitter API is incomplete. Therefore, we need to restore the content of retweets. Links, usernames, emojis and punctuations in tweets are removed by regular expressions. After that, tweets are tokenized and lowercased, with lemmatization applied to each word in order to represent the inflected forms of a word as a single word. In the end, stopwords are deleted.

4.3 Security-Related Account Recognition

In this section, we propose a node feature extraction strategy from four categories. Since the aim of the proposed framework is to improve the security community detection performance, node features are available to the recognition model to narrow the collected Twitter data.

Table 1. Node features in four categories

Feature	#No	Description	Feature	#No	Description
Profile Features			**Content Features**		
Screen Name	#01	The number of alphabetic characters in screen name		#14	Lexical diversity
	#02	The number of numeric characters in screen name	Readability & Difficulty	#15	Flesch-Kincaid score
	#03	The number of capitalization in screen name		#16	SMOG index
Social Information	#04	The number of friends		#17	Prototypical words
	#05	The number of followers	Keywords Score	#18	Weirdness score
	#06	The ratio of friends and followers		#19	TF-IDF
Account Settings	#07	The presence of location	**Behavioral Features**		
	#08	The presence of URL		#20	The number of posted tweets
Sequential Features				#21	The average number of hashtags
	#09	The average interval between tweets	Tweeting Habits	#22	The average number of URLs
	#10	The standard deviation between tweets intervals		#23	The average number of mentions
Time Sequence	#11	The fraction of tweets posted in recent week		#24	The average number of replies
	#12	The minimum interval between tweets	Source Diversity	#25	The distinct sources of tweets
	#13	The maximum interval between tweets			

Node Feature Extraction. Referring to the previous study in security-related accounts detection [3], which has proven to be effective, 25 features organized into four categories are summarized in Table 1.

Profile Features. Profile features are extracted from accounts' profile provided by Twitter, including ID, username, created time, description, followers, friends, statuses count, location and website URL. These profiles are set up by their owners to leave an impression on others, so we extract features to encode the information conveyed by users.

Behavioral Features. After posting a tweet, the account's timeline can display the source of the tweet and whether the tweet is retweeted from another account. At the same time, user can interact with others on posted tweets by commenting, mentioning, retweeting, replying, quoting and favoriting. Therefore, there are six different behavioral features extracted in this study, where the first five features present the user's tweeting habits while the last one reflects the user's equipment using habits. We use Margalef's index to calculate the source diversity of tweets, which is expressed by the following formula:

$$\gamma_{SD} = \frac{m_S - 1}{\ln K} \tag{1}$$

where K is the statuses count and m_s is the number of distinct sources in tweets.

Content Features. Six metrics of features including lexical diversity, Flesch-Kincaid grade level score, SMOG (Simple Measure of Gobbledygook) index, and probability of some keywords extracted through three different techniques (prototypical words [15], weirdness score [10] and TF-IDF), are based on the content of tweets. The lexical diversity is a measure of how many different words appear in a document. The Flesch-Kincaid grade level and SMOG index, which measure the text difficulty through sentence and word length, are popular readability formulas. Keywords from above three keywords extraction techniques is helpful to identify security-related accounts from normal ones. An account u is assigned a score for each keyword kw in the collection which is computed as follows:

$$kw\_score(kw, u) = \frac{|kw|}{\sum_{w \in W_u} |w|} \qquad (2)$$

where $|kw|$ is the number of times that the keyword kw is issued by account u, and W_u is the set of all words issued by u.

Sequential Features. Sequential features are extracted from time sequence of accounts' posted tweets. These features depend on the interval of accounts' tweet time (in seconds) and the fraction of tweets belonging to the recent week (out of all tweets), presenting how active accounts are on Twitter.

Account Recognition Model. We pick the Random Forest as our recognition model, which has received increasing attention due to the outstanding classification results in many fields. The Random Forest yields reliable classification results using predictions derived from an ensemble of decision trees [4].

4.4 Overlapping Community Detection

Social Network Construction. Most of the existing literature on OSNs conduct community detection on graphs established on following relationships, but following relationships may do not accurately reflect associations between accounts. We propose a construction method to remove weak relationships existing between accounts from multiple dimensions. We consider social relationships and model OSN as an undirected graph $G = (V, E)$, where each node in V corresponds to an account in the network, and each edge in E corresponds to a bilateral undirected social relationship based on following and friendship. Then we introduce edge features to provide a more detailed description of the edge relationships from four categories.

Interaction Relevance. On OSNs, accounts can interact with each other by various methods as we mention above. These behaviors can reflect the strength of association between accounts, which can be reckoned as the strength of the edge. We adopt the number of interaction behaviors between accounts as the interaction feature IR.

Content Similarity. We extract the feature considering the phenomenon of homogeneity, which refers to the tendency of interconnected accounts on OSNs to be similar. Therefore, content similarity feature based on accounts' tweets are captured by means of NLP. We choose some feature words to present the content of an account using the mutual information(MI). The mutual information of two words is calculated as follows:

$$MI(w_i, w_j) = \frac{f(w_i, w_j)}{f(w_i) + f(w_j) - f(w_i, w_j)} \qquad (3)$$

where $f(w_i, w_j)$ is the simultaneous occurrence frequency of w_i and w_j in one tweet. $f(w_i)$ is the frequency of w_i appearing in tweets. Each word gets a score

ws which is calculated by TF-IDF. An account's content can be presented as a set of words: $WS = \{w_1 : ws_1, w_2 : ws_2, ..., w_n : ws_n\}$. The content similarity between two accounts is calculated by cosine similarity algorithm, expressed as follows:

$$CS(v_i, v_j) = \frac{WS_{v_i} \cdot WS_{v_j}}{\|WS_{v_i}\| \cdot \|WS_{v_j}\|} \tag{4}$$

Friend and Follower Similarity. Twitter allows bidirectional social relationships between accounts through following, which forms a network around the account. By studying the similarity of friends and followers between two accounts, we are able to understand the overlap between accounts in terms of social structure. The follower and friends similarity are computed as follows:

$$Fo(r)Sim(v_i, v_j) = \frac{\left| Fo(r)List_{v_i} \cap Fo(r)List_{v_j} \right|}{\left| Fo(r)List_{v_i} \cup Fo(r)List_{v_j} \right|} \tag{5}$$

We construct a relationship between accounts on the basis of these edge features extracted from above four dimensions. We remove edges that do not satisfy one of the following conditions: (1)*whether there is interaction between accounts, i.e., IR > 0;* (2)*whether the content between the accounts is similar and overlap is existing in friends or followers to some extent, i.e., CS > 0 and (FoSim > 0 or FrSim > 0).* Under above conditions, edges which proved the existing of relationships between accounts are retained, and by contrast edges maintaining weak relationships are removed. These limitations guarantee the strong connection between accounts.

Overlapping Community Detection Model. It is intuitive to be aware that each account can belong to multiple communities, whose number is potentially unlimited. However, it is of great difficulty to classify an account into a literal community and confirm the number of communities in the network explicitly because of the lack of ground truth. Confronted with above problems, we divide the whole network into different communities depending on combining connections and similarities between accounts. Referring to the approach proposed by Shchur et al. [17] to detect overlapping communities, we fuse the power of GNN with the Bernoulli-Posson probabilistic model. The structure of our model is illustrated below.

Given the undirected Graph G and the matrix of node features X, A is the adjacency matrix and $F \in \mathbb{R}_{\geq 0}^{N \times C}$ is the affiliation matrix, where C is the number of communities and N is the number of nodes. For our model architecture, the same as mentioned in [17], deeper models didn't lead to better results, so we just adopt a 2-layer Graph Convolutional Network(GCN) to receive parameters:

$$F := GCN_\theta(A, X) = ReLU(\widehat{A}ReLU(\widehat{A}XW)W) \tag{6}$$

where $\widehat{A} = \widetilde{D}^{-1/2}\widetilde{A}\widetilde{D}^{-1/2}$ is the normalized adjacency matrix, $\widetilde{A} = A + I_N$ is the adjacency matrix with self loops, and $\widetilde{D}_{ii} = \sum_j \widetilde{A}_{ij}$ is the diagonal degree matrix of $\widetilde{A}$.

The negative log-likelihood of the Bernoulli-Poisson is optimized in the model in order to avoid the problem that the real-world sparse graph makes a large contribution to the loss. The balanced model is expressed as follows:

$$\mathcal{L}(F) = -\mathbb{E}_{(u,v)\sim P_E}\left[\log(1 - exp(-F_u F_v{}^{\mathrm{T}}))\right] + \mathbb{E}_{(u,v)\sim P_N}\left[-F_u F_v{}^{\mathrm{T}}\right] \quad (7)$$

where P_E and P_N denote uniform distributions over edges and non-edge, respectively.

To get the optimal affiliation matrix, the neural network parameter $\theta^\star$ is used to minimize the balanced negative log-likelihood:

$$\theta^\star = \underset{\theta}{argmin}\,\mathcal{L}(GNN_\theta(A, X)) \quad (8)$$

We can get the result of predicted communities through the obtained community affiliation matrix F.

5   Evaluation and Case Study

5.1   Experiment Design

We designed several experiments and conducted a case study to validate our methodology and answer RQs set before on Twitter. We began with a group of seed accounts to assess our account extension strategy. To evaluate features we extracted above, we compared the results over different baseline models. The community detection model was compared with other overlapping community detection algorithms over ground-truth datasets. The intuition that combining the graph with nodes' content leads to better results was verified by measuring the goodness of metrics. Besides, the result of community detection was shown by the means of visualized adjacency matrix to prove the validity of the overlapping community detection. Above processes responded to **RQ1** and **RQ2**. With the purpose of examining that CSCD truly detected security-related communities and solved **RQ3** and **RQ4**, an empirical study was provided to take deep insights on a sample community.

In order to evaluate the performance of the unsupervised community detection algorithm, we adopted the following metrics to measure the results of our experiments: Normalized Mutual Information, Modularity, Conductance, Density, and Clustering Coefficient. The first metric NMI [14] was used for evaluating model performance on ground-truth datasets, while the other four were applied to testify our intuition on Twitter dataset. Except for the Modularity, we calculated other three metrics for each predicted community and averaged the value.

We used a Modularity calculation method for overlapping community proposed by Shen et al. [18]. Conductance measures the fraction of total edge volume that points outside the community, expressed by the following formula:

$$Conductance = \frac{\sum_{u\in C,v\notin C} A_{uv}}{\sum_{u\in C,v\in C,v\neq u} A_{uv} + \sum_{u\in C,v\notin C} A_{uv}} \quad (9)$$

Density is built on the intuition that good communities are well connected, which is calculated as follows:

$$Density(C) = \frac{2|E|}{|V|(|V|-1)} \tag{10}$$

Clustering coefficient, which is based on the premise that communities are manifestations of locally inhomogeneous distributions of edges for the reason that nodes with common neighbors are more likely to be connected with each other, defined by the following formula:

$$ClustCoef(C) = \frac{1}{|V|} \sum_{i,k_i>1} \frac{2t}{k_i(k_i-1)} \tag{11}$$

where t_i is the difference between the number of edge connections in the egocentric network to which the node belongs and the degree of the node.

5.2   Dataset

We firstly selected 10 seed accounts manually, which belong to hackers or security researchers, as the initial crawl task. All crawling tasks are iterated only once, i.e., only the extended accounts of the seed are crawled. This eventually resulted in a collection of 30,469 Twitter accounts, where accounts extended from each seed ranged from 482 to 5439. There were 10,467,239 tweets obtained from collected accounts under the limitation that only 600 latest tweets were crawled.

After collecting accounts data, we needed to create a labeled dataset as a ground truth dataset in order to train the recognition model. We selected randomly 5,138 active accounts, and all the selected accounts were manually labeled by cyber security experts. After inspecting the description and posted tweets of each account, we obtained 4,058 security-related accounts and 1,080 unrelated ones. To validate of our community detection model, we chose Facebook datasets with ground truth provided by Mcauley et al. [13].

5.3   Experiment and Results

Account Recognition. We extracted 574 node features where 552 features were words generated from top 200 words in three keywords techniques after deduplication. Supervised learning was used in order to detect the security-related accounts. Table 2 compares the measure metrics over different baseline machine learning models. We finally chose the Random Forest as a part of CSCD because of its performance, obtaining an accuracy rate of 95.1%. Comparing to previous work [12], though we had a better performance in our experiments, the results we obtained were based on different datasets.

Table 2. Account recognition performance comparison over different models

	ACC	FPR	Precision	Recall	F-measure	MCC	AUC
SVM	0.491	0.062	0.938	0.099	0.178	0.190	0.545
LogisticRegression	0.622	0.013	0.987	0.331	0.495	0.413	0.663
DecisionTree	0.802	0.028	0.971	0.666	0.791	0.654	0.821
GradientBoosting	0.928	0.011	0.989	0.880	0.932	0.862	0.934
RandomForest	0.951	0.002	0.997	0.915	0.955	0.906	0.956

Community Detection. We used a dataset with 5,439 accounts extended from one seed account and four ground-truth datasets in our experiment. After detecting accounts in the extended dataset through our trained security-related recognition model, we retained 3,193 accounts and removed other unrelated accounts. We firstly constructed a graph with 65,062 edges. After removing some weak association, we retained 64,970 edges in our constructed social network.

Table 3. Community detection performance comparison over different methods

	Nodes	Edges	SNMF(%)	NNSED(%)	DANMF(%)	BigCLAM(%)	GNN(%)
Dataset I	66	2145	25.9	28.0	27.8	13.2	**42.2**
Dataset II	159	12561	19.3	33.4	41.1	32.0	**52.0**
Dataset III	227	25651	10.4	14.5	19.4	7.5	**35.8**
Dataset IV	755	284635	16.1	10.2	20.9	4.1	**43.8**

Table 4. Metrics comparisons of community detection over different inputs

	Modularity	AvgCond	AvgDens	AvgClustCoef
A	0.1942	0.3628	5.835×10^{-2}	1.634×10^{-3}
X	0.2166	0.2975	4.001×10^{-2}	6.901×10^{-4}
$A + X$	**0.2216**	**0.3855**	$\mathbf{6.077 \times 10^{-2}}$	$\mathbf{1.827 \times 10^{-3}}$

Table 3 showed how well different algorithms recover the ground-truth communities, and our model obtained the best performance competing against other methods. We also tried to use the adjacency matrix A, node features X and a combination of both A and X as input, respectively. After several attempts with different candidate values, the community number was set to seven. We measured the results under different inputs, shown in Table 4. We got a better result when we used $A + X$ as the input. Figure 2 shows the visualized adjacency matrix where the lines and columns are nodes of the whole graph after community division with the input of $A + X$. We excluded nodes that did not belong to any community in the figure. The cell at the intersection of the line

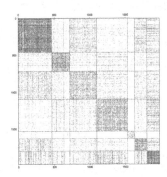

Fig. 2. Visualized adjacency matrix   **Fig. 3.** The structure and key accounts of the sample community

and column is displayed using a contrasted color. Blocks on the diagonal where nodes are densely connected represent a community. We have detected cyber security communities and presented the social structure of these inner accounts through CSCD, which well answered the **RQ1** and **RQ2**.

5.4   Case Study of a Sample Sub-Community

In this subsection, we took a sample sub-community which we found above to make an empirical study on it in order to make our predicted communities more convincing. This sub-community contained 253 accounts.

Key Accounts. There is a group of active accounts which are pivotal in the community such as opinion leaders. Although they are part of the community, for the reason that these individuals have special skills, knowledge or other characteristics, they are able to have some influence on others. We utilized the PageRank algorithm to tap into key accounts in the selected sub-community. Figure 3 shows the identified key accounts and the topological structure of the community. After inspecting these accounts manually, most of these accounts were security researchers or hackers with high impact in this community.

Hashtag Analysis. Hashtag, which is a collection of characters preceded by the (#) symbol, intends to organize a discussion for a particular event. Users can join the discussion of a specific topic through hashtags which they are interested in and express their opinions on. We extracted the top trendy hashtags and excluded some meaningless hashtags from the content of the sub-community, shown dynamically in Fig. 4. We can know the property of the community and

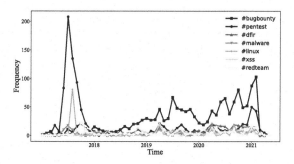

Fig. 4. Hashtags evolution over time

Table 5. Top topics words in extracted topics

Topic	Words
Daily Life	time support nice job awesome live love week fun happy read talk community wait
Vulnerability Mining	file xss cve txt bypass api target rce php injection ssrf ip bug bounty http
Pentest	windows security linux enroll team malware privilege tool penetration vulnerability
Vulnerability Mining	cyber fuzzing tickets team facebook labs free join session software read channel
Web	web google xss application exploit data dns bug post log4j bounty cve blog resources
Penetest	suite tool alert burp cve bug javascript bounty payload server src bypass poc

topics which they were interested in at different times through analyzing the evolution of hashtags.

Topic Analysis. In this part, we concentrated on analyzing topics that security-related communities usually talked about. We applied the LDA-based topic modeling algorithm to analyze the corpus of the whole sub-community. LDA regards a document as a bag of words and assume k topics spread across all m documents in a corpus. We used the timeline of an account as a document and need to adjust the k manually to get the best performance. After several attempts and optimizing by coherence, we set the k of our model to 6. Table 5 shows the extracted topics of the selected community.

We can acknowledge that this community consist of web security enthusiasts according to the above analysis. They focus on the vulnerability mining and penetration test. As we can see from Fig. 2, the community excavated from the network has been proved to be equipped with intensive connections inside. The topic analysis goes a step further, showing a uniformity of community content. We can have a comprehensive understanding of other communities with the similar analysis method, which solved the **RQ3** and **RQ4**.

6   Conclusion and Future Work

6.1   Conclusion

In summary, we demonstrated the efficiency of our account extension method in the experiment, which extended a large scale dataset containing significant quantities of security-related accounts through social relevance analysis. We trained and compared the recognition model over the features extracted from four categories. Our results showed that the Random Forest is the machine learning model with the best performance, reaching an accuracy rate of 95.1%. Besides, the recognition model helped us narrow the scope of subsequent community detection. An edge construction strategy was propounded to remove weak edges by analyzing relationships between accounts through multiple dimensions. To solve existing problems that an account can belong to multiple communities, we adopted an unsupervised overlapping community detection model. We proposed CSCD combining the content with the graph structure. Additionally, an empirical study was provided on the ecosystem of the security-related community.

6.2   Future Work

We acknowledge that our collected data only accounts for a small proportion of the whole OSN, but it can be solved through multiple iterations. The influential or key accounts in communities may be a good entry of a new iteration. There are also some problem existing in our community detection model. The challenge of unknown number of communities hasn't been solved well. Many community detection algorithms still need to define the number of communities manually, which also exists in our study. The model doesn't consider the strength of edges between accounts so we didn't use a weighted network. CSCD can be applied to community detection on other specific groups or other online social network platforms as well. Besides, the content of detected communities can be a good data source for cyber threat intelligence.

Acknowledgment. This research is funded by the National Key Research and Development Program of China (No. 2021YFB3100500), CCF-NSFOCUS KunPeng Research Fund (No. 202105).

References

1. Ab Razak, M.F., Anuar, N.B., Salleh, R., Firdaus, A.: The rise of "malware": bibliometric analysis of malware study. J. Netw. Comput. Appl. **75**, 58–76 (2016)
2. Alves, F., Bettini, A., Ferreira, P.M., Bessani, A.: Processing tweets for cybersecurity threat awareness. Inf. Syst. **95**, 101586 (2021)

3. Aslan, Ç.B., Sağlam, R.B., Li, S.: Automatic detection of cyber security related accounts on online social networks: Twitter as an example. In: Proceedings of the 9th International Conference on Social Media and Society, pp. 236–240 (2018)
4. Breiman, L.: Random forests. Mach. Learn. **45**(1), 5–32 (2001)
5. Chakraborty, T., Dalmia, A., Mukherjee, A., Ganguly, N.: Metrics for community analysis: a survey. ACM Comput. Surv. (CSUR) **50**(4), 1–37 (2017)
6. Djaballah, K.A., Boukhalfa, K., Ghalem, Z., Boukerma, O.: A new approach for the detection and analysis of phishing in social networks: the case of Twitter. In: 2020 Seventh International Conference on Social Networks Analysis, Management and Security (SNAMS), pp. 1–8. IEEE (2020)
7. Egele, M., Stringhini, G., Kruegel, C., Vigna, G.: Towards detecting compromised accounts on social networks. IEEE Trans. Dependable Secure Comput. **14**(4), 447–460 (2015)
8. Ellaky, Z., Benabbou, F., Ouahabi, S., Sael, N.: A survey of spam bots detection in online social networks. In: 2021 International Conference on Digital Age & Technological Advances for Sustainable Development (ICDATA), pp. 58–65. IEEE (2021)
9. Huang, S.Y., Ban, T.: Monitoring social media for vulnerability-threat prediction and topic analysis. In: 2020 IEEE 19th International Conference on Trust, Security and Privacy in Computing and Communications (TrustCom), pp. 1771–1776 (2020)
10. Lau, R.Y., Xia, Y., Ye, Y.: A probabilistic generative model for mining cybercriminal networks from online social media. IEEE Comput. Intell. Mag. **9**(1), 31–43 (2014)
11. Lingam, G., Rout, R.R., Somayajulu, D.V., Das, S.K.: Social botnet community detection: a novel approach based on behavioral similarity in Twitter network using deep learning. In: Proceedings of the 15th ACM Asia Conference on Computer and Communications Security, pp. 708–718 (2020)
12. Mahaini, M.I., Li, S.: Detecting cyber security related twitter accounts and different sub-groups: a multi-classifier approach. In: Proceedings of the 2021 IEEE/ACM International Conference on Advances in Social Networks Analysis and Mining, pp. 599–606 (2021)
13. Mcauley, J., Leskovec, J.: Discovering social circles in ego networks. ACM Trans. Knowl. Discov. Data (TKDD) **8**(1), 1–28 (2014)
14. McDaid, A.F., Greene, D., Hurley, N.: Normalized mutual information to evaluate overlapping community finding algorithms. arXiv preprint arXiv:1110.2515 (2011)
15. Pennacchiotti, M., Popescu, A.M.: Democrats, republicans and starbucks afficionados: user classification in Twitter. In: Proceedings of the 17th ACM SIGKDD International Conference on Knowledge Discovery and Data Mining, pp. 430–438 (2011)
16. Radicchi, F., Castellano, C., Cecconi, F., Loreto, V., Parisi, D.: Defining and identifying communities in networks. Proc. Natl. Acad. Sci. **101**(9), 2658–2663 (2004)
17. Shchur, O., Günnemann, S.: Overlapping community detection with graph neural networks. In: Deep Learning on Graphs Workshop, KDD (2019)
18. Shen, H., Cheng, X., Cai, K., Hu, M.B.: Detect overlapping and hierarchical community structure in networks. Physica A **388**(8), 1706–1712 (2009)
19. Wang, B., Jia, J., Zhang, L., Gong, N.Z.: Structure-based sybil detection in social networks via local rule-based propagation. IEEE Trans. Netw. Sci. Eng. **6**(3), 523–537 (2018)
20. Wu, Y., Lian, D., Xu, Y., Wu, L., Chen, E.: Graph convolutional networks with Markov random field reasoning for social spammer detection. In: Proceedings of the AAAI Conference on Artificial Intelligence, vol. 34, pp. 1054–1061 (2020)

21. Yamak, Z., Saunier, J., Vercouter, L.: Sockscatch: automatic detection and grouping of sockpuppets in social media. Knowl.-Based Syst. **149**, 124–142 (2018)
22. Zhang, Y., Zhang, H., Yuan, X., Tzeng, N.F.: TweetScore: scoring tweets via social attribute relationships for twitter spammer detection. In: Proceedings of the 2019 ACM Asia Conference on Computer and Communications Security, pp. 379–390 (2019)

Shedding Light on Monopoly: Temporal Analysis of Drug Trades

Daniel Dolejška[✉][ID], Vladimír Veselý[ID], Jan Pluskal[ID],
and Michal Koutenský[ID]

Faculty of Information Technology, Brno University of Technology, Božetěchova 1/2,
Brno, Czech Republic
{dolejska,veselyv,ipluskal,koutenmi}@fit.vut.cz
https://fit.vut.cz/

Abstract. Dark marketplaces pioneered a new way to monetise illicit goods. A unique combination of technologies (such as overlay networks, end-to-end encryption, and cryptocurrencies) guarantees anonymity for dark marketplace users (including operators, vendors, and buyers).

We have developed a tool for monitoring and investigating dark marketplaces (namely, collecting and processing evidence directly from their websites), which we used for real-time detection of various illicit activities.

This paper presents a well-described and structured dataset that contains high-frequency web-scraped information from Monopoly Market (one of the most popular dark marketplaces in 2021). The evaluation demonstrates how high-resolution temporal analysis can reveal mission-critical information about the frequency of trades, vendor activities, and the drug market.

Keywords: dark market · drug trade · illegal trade · purchase detection · temporal data set · market analytics · web scraping · dataset · crypto · cryptocurrency · dark marketplace · cryptomarket

1 Introduction

The dark web offers users a high level of anonymity, resulting in a digital environment that encourages nefarious activities by design. That goes hand in hand with increased interest from cybersecurity researchers and law enforcement agencies (LEAs), who are the primary audience for this paper. While the first group is investigating the dark web because they want to, the second group is doing the same thing because they need to. Especially LEAs in charge of countering cybercrimes, preventing the distribution of child sexual abuse materials, and fighting illegal trades with drugs and firearms are also focused on dark marketplaces.

1.1 Motivation

Dark marketplaces are analogous to e-commerce shopping malls from the surface web. Vendors offer their products to potential buyers through listings that

S. Goel et al. (Eds.): ICDF2C 2022, LNICST 508, pp. 151–168, 2023.
https://doi.org/10.1007/978-3-031-36574-4_9

contain product descriptions, prices, and delivery options. Buyers give the score and provide reputation comments to vendors based on their customer experience (e.g., quality of products, duration of delivery). Dark marketplace operators resolve disputes (e.g., via escrow) and receive fees from each trade.

LEAs target dark-market vendors (usually for distributing illegal commodities) and operators (usually for trafficking and money laundering). We, cybersecurity researchers, cannot credibly comment on LEA methods and approaches. Nevertheless, we assume that: a) the vendor's investigation pursues to uncover individual(s); b) the operator's investigation attempts to discover a server hosting a dark marketplace. Any successful investigation most probably involves the application of open source intelligence (OSINT, as an enabler for the Alpha Bay case [16]), human intelligence (HUMINT, its importance was shown during the Silk Road case [17]), and interception of delivery chains [9].

Our work is inspired by previous attempts to conduct a similar long-term monitoring of dark marketplaces such as [14,19], or [18]. These works have also been used by LEAs as an essential source of information when investigating criminal activities [11]. The difference between our approach and the works mentioned above is that we use up-to-date programmatic tools (enabling us to overcome particular limitations encountered by our predecessors), which allows us to web-scrape more data at a higher frequency, resulting in more granular and detailed analytical output.

1.2   Problem Statement

The conditions and circumstances regarding datasets on dark marketplaces pose a challenge that limits their general availability. The existence of such markets is very ephemeral compared to the surface web, which means that much more work needs to be done to discover and monitor them. Marketplaces appear, disappear, and reappear at various points in time at multiple locations on the dark web.

In addition, these markets are designed to be hidden and resilient and, as a result, employ numerous mechanisms to make accessing them more complex than their surface web counterparts. Their technology stack (depicted in Fig. 1) includes the following:

- *overlay network* (e.g., Tor, I2P), which provides network layer anonymity, IP traffic encryption, and covert hosting services;
- *end-to-end encryption* for communication (such as PGP for emails/files, 7z/RAR file archives) on the application layer and above it;
- *cryptocurrency* (e.g., Bitcoin, Monero, Litecoin) as a fast, decentralised, and trustless carrier of value;

Fig. 1. Darkmarket Technology Stack. This figure shows a visualisation of the technology stack used.

- *anti-crawling protection*, such as URL rotation or CAPTCHA [1] verifications, to hinder any kind of automated web processing workflow.

Although technical challenges can always be overcome, another aspect needs to be considered, which refers to the nature of the data collected. As dark markets are commonly used for illicit activities, information on them is of great interest to LEAs. Public disclosure of which data are being collected or what is possible to collect, using which methods can be viewed as undesirable and in direct opposition to the goals of LEAs, as it gives up an essential operational intelligence advantage. Therefore, data are often kept private to maximise their usability.

Commercial companies[1] focus on indexing and archiving dark web content. Such companies apply OSINT tools to scrape content from dark web pages periodically. Collecting dark web content may yield a Big Data problem. Due to that, these companies collect mainly textual data and provide full-text search capabilities within their products. However, textual form, which usually lacks temporal and contextual data, is insufficient for the primary audience of this paper. More intelligence is needed (including pictures, spotted differences, correlated blockchain events, etc.) to successfully understand the operation of a dark marketplace, which takes into account all involved actors (i.e., operators, vendors, buyers).

Therefore, we aim to explore new methods to investigate and analyse dark marketplaces.

1.3   Selection of Monopoly Market

In 2021, we thoroughly analysed trending dark marketplaces to select a good candidate for our web scraping platform prototype. Among the most notable features of Monopoly Market were:

- *accountless* website access, product browsing, and shopping (which would maintain our anonymity not associated with any account when browsing the site);
- completely *walletless* (to avoid exit scams), which mandates *direct deals* between users (i.e., the dark marketplace does not provide its users with a custodial cryptocurrency wallet. Hence, cryptocurrency transfers between users are visible on the blockchain);
- only *single-product orders* are possible;

---

[1] On the one hand, we purposely do not want to mention the name of any company or product. On the other hand, we want to provide at least some leads for the reader interested in getting more information. Therefore, we advise checking out participants of commercial cybersecurity conferences for LEAs such as ISS World, Milipol, or Security and Policing.

- relatively *simple CAPTCHA* prompts when accessing the website (unlike hard-to-overcome "community-driven" aliveness check called EndGame: Onion Service DDOS Prevention Front System[2]);
- link distribution network (LDN) always provides a reliable point through which to get the most up-to-date marketplace address;
- leveraging Bitcoin as a primary cryptocurrency (compared to these dark marketplaces, which prefer cryptocurrency with built-in obfuscation techniques such as Monero, Zcash, or Dash).

However, the features listed above were not only appealing to users of Monopoly Market. They are also precious to any third party interested in automated monitoring of websites that use them. The account-less feature for website access, the use of reasonably simple CAPTCHA challenges, and a presence of a dedicated LDN have allowed more straightforward automation of the entire web-scraping process. Furthermore, the features and content structure of Monopoly Market aligned well with our intention to correlate the detected trades with comparable transactions on the Bitcoin blockchain.

Monopoly Market[3] was one of the e-commerce-based marketplaces (see Sect. 2.1 for details on classification). The launch of this website was announced [5] in August 2019. Monopoly Market became particularly popular in 2021.

This applies especially after the publication of White House Market (WHM) retirement announcement [6]. WHM was one of the largest and most popular marketplaces at that time with 326,570 active user accounts [6] and more than 45,000 advertised product listings [2]. Monopoly Market has been explicitly mentioned in the announcement as a viable alternative for active WHM users [6]. However, that was just a few weeks before Monopoly Market went dark itself [7,8] in late December 2021.

1.4 Contribution

The outcomes of this paper are intended for anyone who is (hopefully just) researching the dark web. Our results may also interest LEA representatives investigating generally dark marketplaces (not only Monopoly Market). This paper has two main ambitions:

1. to provide the research community with a dataset containing real-life information collected not only during a one-time run but periodically (approximately one year) from a single dark marketplace (i.e., Monopoly Market);
2. to demonstrate how such a dataset (enhanced with temporal dimension) can reveal mission-critical information about dark marketplace operation and activities of its users.

---

[2] Publicly available source code can be found on this GitHub repository https://github.com/onionltd/EndGame.

[3] Review available at https://darknetlive.com/markets/monopoly-market/.

The paper is structured as follows. Section 2 outlines currently available datasets targeting dark marketplaces and briefly elaborates on dark marketplace typology and monetising models. Section 3 thoroughly describes a) the syntax and semantics of the data within the dataset; b) their relations; and c) their quality with respect to the collection process. Section 4 selects a relevant subset of purchase detection data and illustrates its temporal dimension together with its analysis. Section 5 concludes the paper with some provocative findings and indicates the next steps in the publication of our research.

2   State of the Art

Dark marketplaces may seem like emerging technologies, but their history, in various forms, spans the roots of the Internet. At least in the time when the Internet generally became available for the masses to use. These markets have not always been hidden behind overlay networks, but in the beginning, they have been a part of the surface web on IRC, web forums, regular e-commerce sites and others. [20].

The driving force behind the dark web/darknet/hidden web/cryptonet, call it as you like, may be traced back to like-minded people as Tim May, the author of "Crypto Anarchist Manifesto" [12]. Rereading it with hindsight, we believe you agree that his prediction matches the current state two decades later. This work predicts that illicit activities will be conducted over anonymisation networks using cryptographical principles and that trust between the transacting parties will be based on their reputation.

The most popular, one of the first dark markets as we know them today, was the Silk Road marketplace, launched by Ross Ulbricht in 2011 and operated until 2013. Detailed analysis provided by Christin [4] explains his investigation methodology and crawling approach (each run on average 14 h) focused on the details of the items sold and the collection and analysis of the vendor rating (customer feedback). Christin and Soska update the dataset [14] with data from 16 different marketplaces over more than two years (2013- 2015). With the help of Tai, Soska and Christin created the resulting dataset [15] as a combination of multiple sources covering eight years (2011–2018), 12 marketplace websites, and 996 snapshots.

A very unorthodox dataset was created by Buskirk et al. [18], who manually (in opposition to automated crawling) collected almost 1150 weekly snapshots of a total of 39 active cryptomarkets during October 2013-November 2015. Manual collection allowed visual verification and filtration of misleading data obtained during market downtime. The extraction of structured data was done manually using Excel and macros.

The most notable dataset is Darknet Market Archives (DNM) [3], which is a collection of 89 marketplaces and more than 37 forums, totalling about 1.6 TB of publicly available data. These data were scraped mainly between 2013 and 2015, with some older entries (2011–2012), at daily or weekly intervals. The content is categorised first by source and then by the date on which it was obtained.

The data format varies; some of it is in the "raw" form of HTML/CSS and accompanying media files, but the dataset also includes processed structured CSV files. Despite its age, it remains a popular and comprehensive dataset and was used by the scientific literature as recently as 2022.

A more recent effort is the AZSecure dataset [10]. Compared to DMA, it is much more focused on its vision. The AZSecure dataset is mainly interested in cybersecurity threats and contains both marketplaces and communication channels such as forums and IRC channels. This dataset contains information from 12 dark markets gathered between 2016 and 2018, with roughly half of all listings belonging to the Dream Market. It is not stated how often the scraping was performed. The dataset itself contains only structured information about the sellers and listings collected.

2.1 Typology of Dark Marketplaces

How the marketplaces are presented may differ. Online forums were regularly used by people to create posts in moderated categories when they needed to buy or sell something. E-shops will be user-friendly and guide the user through the shopping experience, including payment and delivery information [13].

Dark marketplaces in the form of community forums do not account for most marketplaces. However, this allows for greater flexibility in the products or services demanded or sold. The listings have to be correctly categorised. Forums are more versatile than e-commerce-based services, although they lack their counterparts' simplicity and ease of use.

The e-shop-based services are considerably more user-friendly for vendors and customers alike. They provide a familiar environment to their users and define an easy-to-understand management interface for the shop. Hosting and managing such services should be considerably easier than running a forum-based community. There are two main branches to the e-shop-based services:

1. *vendor shops*, where the operators of such services usually sell their own goods directly without any external vendors present;
2. *marketplaces* whose operators aim to provide a reliable platform for other vendors to sell their goods at (under a commission).

In summary, marketplaces may take many forms, but, ultimately, they are the places where illicit online trades occur.

2.2 Monetising Models

The wallet-less marketplaces, such as Monopoly Market, cannot force users to move their funds into their web account wallet (and thus into the hands of service operators) before making a purchase. This reduces the risk of fund loss for any customer as they completely control their funds until the product payment itself. When the purchase is handled in a direct deal mode (shown in Fig. 2), this risk is even further reduced since the funds go from the customer directly to the vendor and not to the marketplace itself.

An alternative mode is an escrow deal, shown in Fig. 3. This happens when the customer pays for their order through the marketplace. This, in turn, gives the money to the vendor later, depending on whether the delivery is confirmed or disputed by the customer.

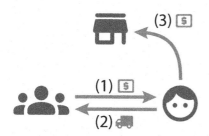 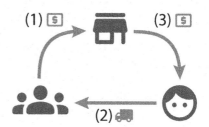

Fig. 2. Direct Deal Payment. (1) First, the user sends their funds directly to the vendor wallet. (2) After the order is paid, the vendor ships the order. (3) Finally, the marketplace receives a commission.

Fig. 3. Escrow Payment. (1) First, the user sends their funds to the marketplace escrow wallet. (2) After the order is paid, the vendor ships the order. (3) Finally, the vendor receives their portion of the payment.

3   Dataset

Existing datasets generally focus on complete snapshots of multiple websites, mainly dark marketplaces, IRCs, and forums. Snapshots include HTML, CSS, JavaScript files, images, fonts, and more.

Our dataset targets only a single darknet market website, namely Monopoly Market. It does not contain full web page snapshots but specific and structured data already extracted from the web page source code. The main feature is the temporal dimension of the data. Data have been periodically extracted, approximately every 15 min for over 10 months, from the website with a focus on information on available products and purchase detection.

This level of temporal resolution provides a unique opportunity to examine and analyse dark marketplace operations in unprecedented detail. Product purchase detection can be used to cross-correlate with public cryptocurrency blockchains or any other relevant open-source or network intelligence.

The structure and content of the dataset are described in detail in Sect. 3.1. Section 3.2 quantitatively describes the features of this dataset. Various visualisation analysis demonstrations are shown in Sect. 4.

3.1   Content Description

The collection of source data focused mainly on the detection of product purchases. However, it also contains additional information from the marketplace:

- **vendor usernames** and their:
  - corresponding **PGP key history** with pre-extracted **key metadata** (such as user-provided name, email, or time of creation),
  - **open order limit** history,
  - **open order count** history,
- **product categories** and their tree structure,
- published **product listings** and their metadata of:
  - **country of origin,**
  - allowed **shipping destinations,**
  - listing **view count,**
  - **time of creation,**
  - and its **age,**
- product listing **sold-count** and **stock-count deltas** between scrapes,
- and historical marketplace-provided USD, BTC and XMR **exchange rates.**

The data are separated into various tables; relationships between the tables can be seen in Fig. 4 (page 9). The complete schema diagram of the database can be found in Fig. 11 on page 16. The tables included in the dataset are as follows:

`pgp__items` Contains unique PGP public keys, their fingerprints, and the time of the first scraping encounter.

`pgp__meta` Contains extracted public PGP key metadata, such as exact time of creation, user name, user mail, and subkey data.

`product__items` Contains basic information on unique products: their category, name, and vendor.

`product__categories` Contains unique product categories. Defines a tree structure with parent and subcategories.

`product__variant__items` Contains all unique variants that can be purchased for each advertised product, a combination of the amount of the product and the shipping options.

`product__variant__prices` Contains historical prices of all variants of products in USD, BTC, and XMR.

`service__items` Contains records of monitored services, in case of this dataset only Monopoly Market.

`service__urls` Contains recorded and used `.onion` URLs belonging to services.

`vendor__items` Contains basic information on unique vendor accounts: their name and time of the first scraping encounter.

`vendor__keys` Contains links between vendor accounts and the public PGP keys used by them.

The dataset itself is available in CSV format, where the contents of each table are located in a single CSV file under the name of the source table. Furthermore, the schema of the database tables can be created using prepared PL/pgSQL scripts, which are also part of the provided archive. For access conditions and download instructions, see Sect. 5.

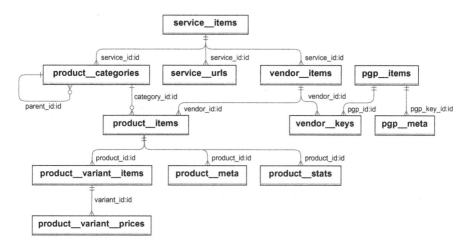

Fig. 4. Simplified Entity Relationship Diagram. This UML diagram displays relationships (foreign keys in relational databases) between tables from the source database.

3.2   Metrics

The first record in the dataset is from 25th February 2021, about a year and a half into the existence of the marketplace. The dataset ends with the last record from 28th December 2021 at 07:54 UTC. The median timestamp between scrapes of all available product pages is 15 min and 44 s.

Although the objective was always to be as consistent in web scraping as possible, it proved very difficult. The counts of product pages visited each day can be seen in Fig. 5 (page 10). A decreasing trend in visit/scrape counts can be clearly seen almost throughout the entire dataset. This is due to the active efforts of marketplace operators to mitigate this kind of user behaviour. Time intervals without scraping count data were caused by downtime of the marketplace website or the scraping framework itself.

Empty data intervals (where no web scraping was done) can also be found. Multiple reasons may be responsible for these events, such as internal software bugs, service availability issues, deployment problems, or active access prevention and security updates by marketplace operators. The most significant events are denoted in Table 1 (page 10). There are 64 of 307 days (20.8%) of scraping with complete outages. During these days, we do not have any monitoring data available.

The marketplace website has been monitored for 307 days. During that time, 211 different verified and active vendors were detected. Customers could browse a selection of more than 2, 200 unique products related to controlled substances from all over the world. Almost 10, 000, 000 product page snapshots have been taken using web-scraping software. The corresponding and other counts of database table records can be found in Table 2 (page 11).

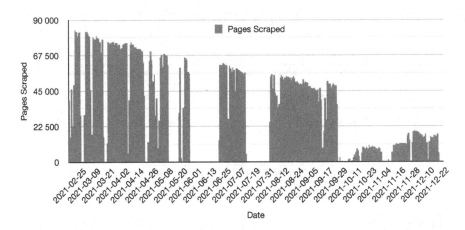

Fig. 5. Website Page Visits per Day. The Y-axis displays the total number of pages scraped daily (shown on the X-axis). A decreasing trend can be seen in the graph – this is due to the active efforts of marketplace operators to limit the amount of web scraping. A rapid drop can also be seen around 2021-09-29 – this signifies the time, when new anti-scraping prevention has been deployed on the marketplace.

Table 1. Data Acquisition Outages. This table displays various timespans during which there were issues with the web-scraping process. There are no monitoring data available in the dataset during these times.

From	To	Days	Reason
2021-03-08	2021-03-09	2	Development and deployment issues
2021-03-27	2021-03-28	2	Deployment issues
2021-04-30	2021-05-01	2	Development and deployment issues
2021-05-19	2021-05-26	8	Major SW optimisations and fixes, monitoring rework
2021-05-30	2021-05-30	1	Deployment issues
2021-06-06	2021-06-28	23	Major SW changes, automation and stability fixes
2021-07-23	2021-08-09	18	Major SW changes, automation and stability fixes
2021-10-06	2021-10-13	7	Implementation of new protection workaround
2021-10-24	2021-10-24	1	Deployment issues
Summary		64	Accounts for 20.8% of the dataset

Table 2. Database Table Sizes. This table shows the final disk usage of dataset tables in the database.

Table Name	Row Count	Data Size	Index Size	Total Size
product__variant__prices	78 949 534	6 045,4 MB	8 154,4 MB	14 200,1 MB
product__meta	61 973 933	4 462,5 MB	8 466,6 MB	12 929,4 MB
product__stats	9 865 452	756,9 MB	1 024,5 MB	1 781,8 MB
product__variant__items	26 187	3,3 MB	1,2 MB	4,5 MB
pgp__items	217	0,2 MB	0,0 MB	1,0 MB
pgp__meta	2 058	0,3 MB	0,2 MB	0,5 MB
product__items	2 231	0,4 MB	0,1 MB	0,5 MB
vendor__keys	217	0,1 MB	0,0 MB	0,1 MB
vendor__items	211	0,1 MB	0,0 MB	0,1 MB
product__categories	51	0,0 MB	0,0 MB	0,1 MB
service__items	1	0,0 MB	0,0 MB	0,1 MB
service__urls	31	0,0 MB	0,0 MB	0,1 MB

4 Evaluation

This section aims to demonstrate the analytic possibilities provided by this dataset and its unique temporal properties. First, various simple aggregation queries yield interesting counts and other analytics. There are records of 77, 316 individual orders in more than 2, 200 distinct products. These orders correspond to total minimum revenue (calculated from the price of the cheapest variant of the product) of 4, 229, 736 USD generated by the vendors; 5% of which (211, 486.8 USD) is the commission of the market service (plus a bonus in the form of all funds in the escrow wallets after the shutdown of the marketplace). All the aforementioned statistics are calculated within the context of the whole dataset.

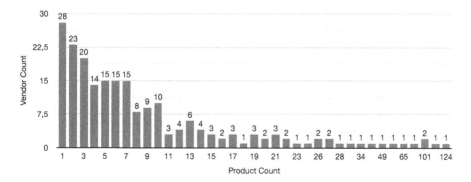

Fig. 6. Advertised product count by the number of advertising vendors. This chart shows how many products (X-axis) were advertised by how many vendors (Y-axis). It can be seen the graph follows the reciprocal distribution.

Figure 6 (page 11) shows how many products are advertised by how many vendors. It tells us that the upper 5% of the vendors (11) with the highest number of advertised products represents 35% of all available products (780) on the entire marketplace. As can be seen, there was a real mix of vendors active on this marketplace – some selling only a handful of products and some offering over a 100 distinct products.

Another possible analysis: show the number of purchases summarised by the country of origin of the corresponding product. The relevant visualisation can be seen in Fig. 7 (page 12). The chart shows us the most prominent countries featured on the marketplace. This strategic information is of interest to local governments and LEAs.

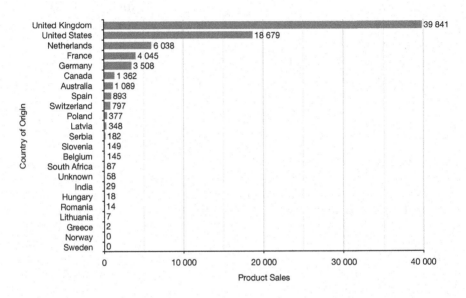

Fig. 7. Sales by a product's country of origin. This chart show a complete summary of all detected purchases by the corresponding product's country of origin.

Another analysis relates to vendors active on the marketplace website. Figure 8 (page 13) shows a weekly total count of verified and active vendors along with weekly change. The extent of information available about new vendors that become active can be closely related to their potential success on the website, the public opinion of the marketplace as a whole, and other significant events on the dark web, as shown and discussed by Nicolas Christin [4].

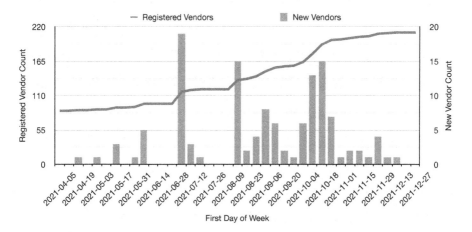

Fig. 8. Weekly count of verified and active marketplace vendors. This chart shows the number of verified and active vendors on Monopoly Market in the given week. A weekly change is also displayed as a separate series in green. (Color figure online)

Finally, plotting high-level trends among product categories can show deviations in the popularity of specific product categories in favour of others. This graph can be seen in Fig. 9 (page 14). Thanks to the temporal resolution of the dataset, these changes can also be detected on a scale of days/hours.

Visualisations leveraging the high-resolution temporal dimension of the data can provide unprecedented analysis of user activity on the marketplace. Figure 10 (page 14) shows the number of purchases detected during a given time interval, on the X-axis, in each day over a period of approximately 6 weeks (from 12th August to 22nd September), on the Y-axis. Such data can reveal information about the primary demographics of customers on the marketplace, assuming people buy in between their regular day-to-day routine and not, for example, during the night when they would usually sleep.

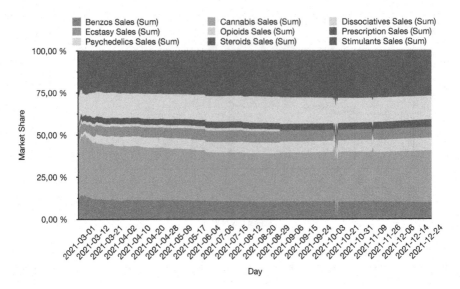

Fig. 9. Product category market shares over time. Displays purchase count share (in percentages) of product categories over the monitored timespan. *Note*: some days have been filtered out to prevent gaps and false values in the chart.

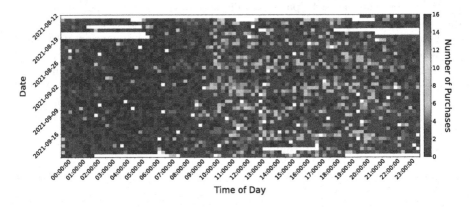

Fig. 10. Counts of detected individual product purchases over time. Visualises the number of individual product purchases detected by the automated scraping in a given time-of-day intervals (X-axis) of a given day (Y-axis). *Note:* white intervals represent that no records were collected during that time. Possible reasons include service outages, connection problems, CAPTCHA challenges or internal program issues.

5   Conclusion

This paper makes two significant contributions to anyone interested in dark web monitoring. First, we gathered and documented a unique dataset that observed activities in the significant dark marketplace during a year of its existence. This dataset is made available to fellow researchers and LEA representatives, who authenticate themselves by email using address from a verifiable domain owned by an academic or government institution. Please contact the leading author at their faculty email in order to receive your copy of the dataset. The results reproduction is available at the paper's webpage[4]. Secondly, we have shown the potential of such temporal data to corroborate evidence for both short- and long-term investigations involving dark marketplaces and their users.

As we have shown, this dataset has witnessed more than 77,000 drug trades by people from all over the world with unprecedented timescale detail. The most successful Monopoly Market vendor, NextGeneration, with more than 19,000 product sales, managed to generate an absolute minimum of 763,463 USD in revenue.

We plan to publish the dataset acquisition process. This would include comprehensive information on the automation of a) parallel access to the web pages; b) authentication, authorisation, and aliveness check bypassing; c) decoding and parsing of the web page content; and d) post-processing and archiving of extracted information. Our web scraping platform allowed us to monitor Monopoly Market so that we could use these data and correlate purchases with corresponding cryptocurrency transactions. As a next step, we would like to receive a peer review of this method and tooling.

The publication of this paper was possible thanks to the support from the Czech national research grant BAZAR (identifier VJ01030004, more information about the project is available at the project's website[5]) funded by the Ministry of Interior of the Czech Republic during 2021 and 2022.

Thanks also to the Brno University of Technology project FIT-S-20-6293 for allowing us to publish and present this paper in person at ICDF2C 2022 in Boston.

---

[4] https://gitlab.nesad.fit.vutbr.cz/papers/icdf2c22-shedding-light-on-monopoly.

[5] https://bazar.fit.vutbr.cz/.

A   Figures

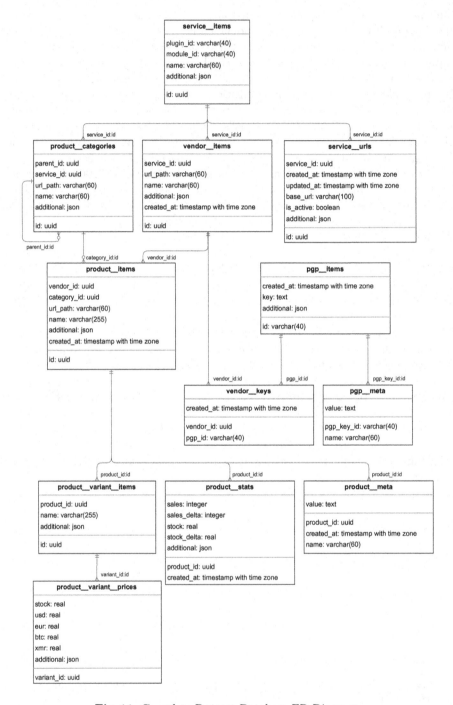

Fig. 11. Complete Dataset Database ER Diagram

References

1. von Ahn, L., Blum, M., Hopper, N.J., Langford, J.: CAPTCHA: using hard AI problems for security. In: Biham, E. (ed.) EUROCRYPT 2003. LNCS, vol. 2656, pp. 294–311. Springer, Heidelberg (2003). https://doi.org/10.1007/3-540-39200-9_18
2. Barratt, M.J., et al.: Exploring televend, an innovative combination of cryptomarket and messaging app technologies for trading prohibited drugs. Drug Alcohol Depend. **231**, 109243 (2022)
3. Branwen, G., et al.: Dark net market archives, 2011–2015 (2015). https://www.gwern.net/DNM-archives. Accessed 27 June 2022
4. Christin, N.: Traveling the silk road: a measurement analysis of a large anonymous online marketplace. In: Proceedings of the 22nd International Conference on World Wide Web, pp. 213–224 (2013)
5. Darknetlive: Market announcement: Monopoly is open for business (2019). https://darknetlive.com/post/market-announcement-monopoly-is-open-for-business/. Accessed 29 June 2022
6. Darknetlive: PSA: White house market is retiring (2021). https://darknetlive.com/post/psa-white-house-market-is-retiring/. Accessed 29 June 2022
7. Darknetlive: Monopoly market and cartel market are gone (2022). https://darknetlive.com/post/monopoly-market-and-cartel-market-are-gone/. Accessed 29 June 2022
8. Darknetpages: Monopoly market and cartel market disappeared (2022). https://darknetpages.com/monopoly-market-and-cartel-market-disappeared/. Accessed 29 June 2022
9. Décary-Hétu, D., Giommoni, L.: Do police crackdowns disrupt drug cryptomarkets? A longitudinal analysis of the effects of operation onymous. Crime Law Soc. Chang. **67**(1), 55–75 (2017)
10. Du, P.Y., et al.: Identifying, collecting, and presenting hacker community data: forums, IRC, carding shops, and DNMs. In: 2018 IEEE International Conference on Intelligence and Security Informatics (ISI), pp. 70–75 (2018)
11. EMCDDA, E.: Drugs and the darknet: perspectives for enforcement, research and policy (2017)
12. May, T.: The crypto anarchist manifesto. High Noon on the Electronic Frontier: Conceptual Issues in Cyberspace (1992)
13. Molnar, D., Egelman, S., Christin, N.: This is your data on drugs: lessons computer security can learn from the drug war. In: Proceedings of the 2010 New Security Paradigms Workshop, NSPW 2010, pp. 143–149. Association for Computing Machinery, New York (2010)
14. Soska, K., Christin, N.: Measuring the longitudinal evolution of the online anonymous marketplace ecosystem. In: 24th USENIX Security Symposium (USENIX Security 2015), pp. 33–48 (2015)
15. Tai, X.H., Soska, K., Christin, N.: Adversarial matching of dark net market vendor accounts. In: Proceedings of the 25th ACM SIGKDD International Conference on Knowledge Discovery & Data Mining, pp. 1871–1880 (2019)
16. United Nations Office on Drugs and Crimes: United States of America v. Alexandre Cazes aka "ALPHA02" aka "ADMIN" (2017). https://web.archive.org/web/20220702065615/https://sherloc.unodc.org/cld/en/case-law-doc/cybercrimecrimetype/usa/2017/united_states_of_america_v._alexandre_cazes_aka_alpha02_aka_admin.html. Accessed 07 July 2022

17. United Nations Office on Drugs and Crimes: United States of America v. Ross William Ulbricht, No. 15-1815-cr (2d Cir. May 31, 2017) (2017). https:// web.archive.org/web/20220702065806/https://sherloc.unodc.org/cld/en/case-law-doc/cybercrimecrimetype/usa/2017/united_states_of_america_v._ross_ william_ulbricht_no._15-1815-cr_2d_cir._may_31_2017.html. Accessed 01 July 2022
18. Van Buskirk, J., et al.: The recovery of online drug markets following law enforcement and other disruptions. Drug Alcohol Depend. **173**, 159–162 (2017)
19. Van Buskirk, J., Naicker, S., Roxburgh, A., Bruno, R., Burns, L.: Who sells what? Country specific differences in substance availability on the agora cryptomarket. Int. J. Drug Policy **35**, 16–23 (2016)
20. Wehinger, F.: The dark net: self-regulation dynamics of illegal online markets for identities and related services. In: 2011 European Intelligence and Security Informatics Conference, pp. 209–213. IEEE (2011)

Extracting Spread-Spectrum Hidden Data Based on Better Lattice Decoding

Fan Yang, Hao Cheng, and Shanxiang Lyu[(✉)]

College of Cyber Security, Jinan University, Guangzhou 510632, China
lsx07@jnu.edu.cn

Abstract. This paper considers the blind extraction of hidden data embedded by the multi-carrier spread-spectrum scheme. Since the conventional multi-carrier iterative generalize least-squares (M-IGLS) scheme suffers from performance degradation when the carriers lack sufficient orthogonality, we develop a novel blind extraction scheme called multi-carrier iterative successive interference cancellation (M-ISIC). M-ISIC is formulated from the perspective of lattices, and it employs a successive interference cancellation subroutine to solve the lattice decoding problem. We show that M-ISIC outperforms M-IGLS by both theoretical justification and numerical simulations.

Keywords: blind extraction · spread spectrum · lattices · successive interference cancellation

1 Introduction

Steganography describes the act of secretly embedding messages into various forms of multimedia (also called the cover data) [7,9,19,20]. It has a close connection to data hiding and watermarking, as they all resemble the variants of communication with side information [5]. Their research goals include reducing the amount of distortion to the cover data so as to get unnoticeable, improving the amount of embedded bits, and rising the security level of the embedding scheme.

Many Steganography/data-hiding schemes have been developed in the past three decades (see, e.g., [1,4,6,12,14]), in which the spread-spectrum (SS) scheme and its variants are among the most popular ones. By using a similar principle as in spread-spectrum communication, the SS method was originally introduced by Cox et al. [3]. In SS, the message is dispersed into many frequency bins contained in the host signal, which makes the energy in each one extremely

This work was supported in part by the National Natural Science Foundation of China under Grants 61902149 and 62032009, the Natural Science Foundation of Guangdong Province under Grant 2020A1515010393, and the Major Program of Guangdong Basic and Applied Research under Grant 2019B030302008.

S. Goel et al. (Eds.): ICDF2C 2022, LNICST 508, pp. 169–182, 2023.
https://doi.org/10.1007/978-3-031-36574-4_10

small and certainly undetectable. SS has been improved in many aspects. E.g, using the technique of minimum-mean-square error to reduce the interference caused by the host itself [15], improving signature design to reduce the decoding error rate [1], and using multi-carriers instead of a single carrier to improve the number of payloads [10, 11].

In recent years, the steganalysis of SS has drawn more attention, especially from the perspective of "Watermarked Only Attack" (WOA). In WOA neither the original host nor the embedding carriers (i.e., the spreading sequences) are assumed known, as its goal is to fully extract the embedded data. To crack the single-carrier SS method, an iterative generalize least squares (IGLS) was proposed in [8], which shows remarkable recovery performance and low complexity. Since an embedder may favor multi-carrier SS transform-domain embedding to increase security/payload, its corresponding steganalysis seems more important. As the underlying mathematical problem is akin to blind source separation (BSS) in speech signal processing, celebrated BSS algorithms such as independent component analysis (ICA) [2] and Joint Approximate Diagonalization of Eigenmatrix (JADE) [18] may be utilized to extract the hidden data. Nevertheless, these BSS algorithms are far from being effective as the multi-carrier SS problem exhibits correlated signal interference [10]. In this regard, Li Ming et al. [10] developed an improved IGLS scheme referred to as multi-carrier iterative generalized least-squares (M-IGLS), whose recovery error probability is close to those of non-blind extraction algorithms.

What motivates this work is that we notice the problem of cracking multi-carrier SS parallels lattice decoding in part. Lattice decoding asks to find the closest lattice vector to a given query vector, in which the message space is the integer set. Multi-carrier SS only involves a special case of lattice decoding where the message space is $\{\pm 1\}$. In addition, since the extraction performance of M-IGLS hinges on a simple lattice decoding algorithm referred to as zero-forcing (ZF), M-IGLS can exhibit satisfactory performance only when the carriers/signatures show sufficient orthogonality. For instance, the simulation of M-IGLS [10] only consider the case of embedding (and extracting) 4 data streams by modifying 63 host coefficients. If the multi-carrier SS has a larger number of embedded data streams within the same number host coefficients, then more sophisticated lattice decoding algorithms become beneficial. By addressing the above issues, the contributions of this work are summarized as follows:

- First, we formulate the problem of cracking multi-carrier SS as a lattice decoding problem. To be concise, the problem can be regarded as the blind extraction of integer sources under the noisy setting, which asks to find the mixing matrix and the integer messages. In an alternating minimization principle, the extraction algorithm should estimate the mixing matrix and the integer messages iteratively. Then with the availability of the mixing matrix, estimating the integer messages is exactly what lattice decoding favors. The term "Least Square" in IGLS and M-IGLS originates from detection design of using no prior information on the source messages, this makes them naturally suboptimal as the prior information for integer sources ($\{\pm 1\}$) has been omitted.

In addition, the part of "Least Square" in M-IGLS is conceived as the ZF algorithm in lattice decoding.

– Second, we propose a new hidden data extraction referred to as multi-carrier iterative successive interference cancellation (M-ISIC). We show that M-ISIC outperforms M-IGLS by both theoretical justification and numerical simulations, where the performance improvement is due to a better lattice algorithm used in the subroutine. Thanks to the lattice-based formulation, the proposed algorithm can also address the scenario when the number of signatures is unknown.

The rest of this paper is organized as follows. In Sect. 2, preliminaries on SS embedding and blind extraction are briefly introduced. In Sect. 3, the proposed algorithm is introduced and comparisons are made. Simulation results are shown in Sect. 4 and Sect. 5 concludes this paper.

The following notation is used throughout the paper. Boldface upper-case and lower-case letters represent matrices and column vectors, respectively. $\mathbb{R}$ denotes the set of real numbers, while $\mathbf{I}$ denotes an identity matrix. $(\cdot)^{\top}$ is the matrix transpose operator, and $|| \cdot ||$, $|| \cdot ||_F$ denote vector norm, and matrix Frobenius norm, respectively. $\text{sign}(\cdot)$ represents a quantization function with respect to $\{-1, 1\}$.

2 Preliminaries

2.1 SS Embedding and Legitimate Extraction

Without loss of generality, we consider a gray-scale host image $\mathbf{H} \in \mathcal{M}^{N_1 \times N_2}$, where $\mathcal{M}$ denotes the image alphabet and $N_1 \times N_2$ denotes the size of the image. Then $\mathbf{H}$ is partitioned into M non-overlapping blocks $\mathbf{H}_1, ..., \mathbf{H}_M$ (of size $\frac{N_1 \times N_2}{M}$). By performing DCT transformation and zig-zag scanning for each block, the cover object in each block can be generated as $\mathbf{x}(m) \in \mathbb{R}^L$, $m = 1, ..., M$. By excluding the DC coefficient, L can be set as $1 \leq L \leq \frac{N_1 \times N_2}{M}$.

In multi-carrier SS, it employs K distinct carriers (signatures) $\mathbf{s}_1, ..., \mathbf{s}_K$ to embed K bits of messages $b_1, ..., b_K \in \{\pm 1\}$ to each $\mathbf{x}(m)$. In general $K \leq L$ such that these signature vectors can exhibit sufficient mutual orthogonality in the L dimensional space. Subsequently, the modified cover (stego) is generated by

$$\mathbf{y}(m) = \sum_{k=1}^{K} A_k b_k(m) \mathbf{s}_k + \mathbf{x}(m) + \mathbf{n}(m), \ m = 1, 2, ..., M, \quad (1)$$

where A_k denotes the embedding amplitude of $\mathbf{s}_k$, $b_k(m)$ denotes the messages of the mth block, and $\mathbf{n}(m)$ represents the additive white Gaussian noise vector of mean $\mathbf{0}$ and covariance $\sigma_n^2 \mathbf{I}_L$. By taking expectation over the randomness of $\mathbf{s}_k$, the embedding distortion due to $A_k b_k(m) \mathbf{s}_k$ is

$$D_k = \mathbb{E}\{||A_k b_k(m) \mathbf{s}_k||^2\} = A_k^2, \ k = 1, 2, ..., K. \quad (2)$$

Algorithm 1: The M-IGLS data extraction algorithm.

Input: $\mathbf{Y}, \mathbf{R_y}$.
Output: $\hat{\mathbf{V}} = \mathbf{V}^{(d)}, \hat{\mathbf{B}} = \mathbf{B}^{(d)}$.

1 $d = 0, \mathbf{B}^{(0)} \sim \{\pm 1\}^{K \times M}$;
2 **while** *a stopping criterion has not been reached* **do**
3    $\quad d \leftarrow d + 1$;
4    $\quad \mathbf{V}^{(d)} \leftarrow \mathbf{Y}(\mathbf{B}^{(d-1)})^{\mathrm{T}}[\mathbf{B}^{(d-1)}(\mathbf{B}^{(d-1)})^{\mathrm{T}}]^{-1}$;
5    $\quad \mathbf{B}^{(d)} \leftarrow \mathrm{sign}\left\{\left((\mathbf{V}^{(d)})^{\mathrm{T}}\mathbf{R_y}^{-1}\mathbf{V}^{(d)}\right)^{-1}(\mathbf{V}^{(d)})^{\mathrm{T}}\mathbf{R_y}^{-1}\mathbf{Y}\right\}$; ▷ Approximate lattice
       decoding via GLS/ZF.

Based on the statistical independence of signatures $\mathbf{s}_k$, the averaged total distortion per block is defined as $D = \sum_{k=1}^{K} D_k = \sum_{k=1}^{K} A_k^2$.

In the receivers' side, legitimate users can employ the pre-shared secrets/signatures $\mathbf{s}_k$ to generate high-quality estimates of messages $b_k(m)$. Define the auto-correlation matrix of $\mathbf{y}(m)$ from that of the host auto-correlation $\mathbf{R_x}$ and noise auto-correlation as:

$$\mathbf{R_y} = \mathbf{R_x} + \sum_{k=1}^{K} A_k^2 \mathbf{s}_k \mathbf{s}_k^{\top} + \sigma_n^2 \mathbf{I}_L. \tag{3}$$

Then the minimum-mean-square-error (MMSE) estimation of the messages is given by

$$\hat{b}_k(m) = \mathrm{sign}\{\mathbf{s}_k^{\top} \mathbf{R_y}^{-1} \mathbf{y}(m)\}. \tag{4}$$

2.2 Blind SS Extraction

The observation Eq. (1) can be written in the form of matrices:

$$\mathbf{Y} = \mathbf{VB} + \mathbf{Z} \tag{5}$$

where $\mathbf{Y} \triangleq [\mathbf{y}(1), ..., \mathbf{y}(M)] \in \mathbb{R}^{L \times M}$, $\mathbf{B} \triangleq [\mathbf{b}(1), ..., \mathbf{b}(M)] \in \{\pm 1\}^{K \times M}$, $\mathbf{V} \triangleq [A_1 \mathbf{s}_1, ..., A_M \mathbf{s}_M] \in \mathbb{R}^{L \times K}$, $\mathbf{Z} \triangleq [\mathbf{x}(1) + \mathbf{n}(1), ..., \mathbf{x}(M) + \mathbf{n}(M)] \in \mathbb{R}^{L \times M}$.

The difference between legitimate extraction and blind extraction lies in the availability of $\mathbf{V}$. The task of a blind extraction requires estimating both $\mathbf{V}$ and $\mathbf{B}$ from the observation $\mathbf{Y}$, which is known as the noisy BSS problem:

$$\mathcal{P}_1 : \min_{\substack{\mathbf{B} \in \{\pm 1\}^{K \times M} \\ \mathbf{V} \in \mathbb{R}^{L \times K}}} \|\mathbf{R_z}^{-\frac{1}{2}}(\mathbf{Y} - \mathbf{VB})\|_F^2, \tag{6}$$

where $\mathbf{R_z} \triangleq \mathbf{R_x} + \sigma_n^2 \mathbf{I}_L$ denotes the pre-whitening matrix. Nevertheless, enumerating all the feasible candidates of $\mathbf{V}$ and $\mathbf{B}$ is infeasible as it incurs exponential complexity.

The M-IGLS proposed by Li et al. can approximately solve (6) efficiently. The pseudo-code of M-IGLS is shown in Algorithm 1. Specifically, M-IGLS estimates $\mathbf{V}$ and $\mathbf{B}$ iteratively by using an MMSE criterion: by either fixing $\mathbf{B}^{(d)}$ or $\mathbf{V}^{(d)}$ and using convex optimization, the formulas for $\mathbf{B}^{(d)}$ or $\mathbf{V}^{(d)}$ are derived.

2.3   Lattice Decoding

To inspect M-IGLS, we review some basic knowledge of lattices as follows. Lattices are discrete additive subgroups. Given K linearly independent vectors $\mathbf{g}_1, ..., \mathbf{g}_K \in \mathbb{R}^L$ with $L \geq K$, they can define a lattice as

$$\mathcal{L}(\mathbf{G}) = \left\{ \sum_{k=1}^{K} x_k \mathbf{g}_k \mid x_k \in \mathbb{Z} \right\} \tag{7}$$

where $\mathbf{G} \triangleq [\mathbf{g}_1, ..., \mathbf{g}_K]$ is called lattice basis.

Many computationally hard problems can be defined over lattices. The one related to this work is called the closest vector problem (CVP) [16]: given a query vector $\mathbf{t}$, it asks to find the closest vector to $\mathbf{t}$ from the set of lattice vectors $\mathcal{L}(\mathbf{G})$. Let the closest vector be $\mathbf{G}\mathbf{x}$, $\mathbf{x} \in \mathbb{Z}^K$, then we have

$$\|\mathbf{G}\mathbf{x} - \mathbf{t}\| \leq \|\mathbf{G}\tilde{\mathbf{x}} - \mathbf{t}\|, \forall \tilde{\mathbf{x}} \in \mathbb{Z}^K. \tag{8}$$

After the detour, consider the step of estimating $\mathbf{B}^{(d)}$ in Algorithm 1, which asks to solve the following problem:

$$\mathcal{P}_2 : \min_{\mathbf{B} \in \{\pm 1\}^{K \times M}} \|\mathbf{R}_{\mathbf{z}}^{-\frac{1}{2}} \mathbf{Y} - \mathbf{R}_{\mathbf{z}}^{-\frac{1}{2}} \mathbf{V}\mathbf{B}\|_F^2. \tag{9}$$

Since $\{\pm 1\}^{K \times M} \in \mathbb{Z}^{K \times M}$, $\mathcal{P}_2$ is a special case of CVP, which asks to find M closest lattice vectors to $\mathbf{R}_{\mathbf{z}}^{-\frac{1}{2}} \mathbf{Y}$, and the lattice is defined by basis $\mathbf{R}_{\mathbf{z}}^{-\frac{1}{2}} \mathbf{V}$.

In general solving CVP for a random lattice basis incurs exponential computational complexity in the order of $\mathcal{O}(2^K)$, but for lattice basis whose $\mathbf{g}_1, ..., \mathbf{g}_K$ are close to being orthogonal, fast low-complexity algorithm can approximately achieve the performance of maximum likelihood decoding. One of such algorithm is called ZF [13]. Considering $\mathcal{P}_2$, define the set of query vectors as $\overline{\mathbf{Y}} \triangleq \mathbf{R}_{\mathbf{z}}^{-\frac{1}{2}} \mathbf{Y}$, and the lattice basis as $\overline{\mathbf{V}} \triangleq \mathbf{R}_{\mathbf{z}}^{-\frac{1}{2}} \mathbf{V}$, then the ZF estimator is

$$\hat{\mathbf{B}}_{\mathrm{ZF}} = \overline{\mathbf{V}}^\dagger \overline{\mathbf{Y}}^{\mathrm{T}}$$
$$= (\overline{\mathbf{V}}^{\mathrm{T}} \overline{\mathbf{V}})^{-1} \overline{\mathbf{V}}^{\mathrm{T}} \overline{\mathbf{Y}}^{\mathrm{T}}. \tag{10}$$

In Appendix A, we show that the geometric least square (GLS) step in line 5 of M-IGLS is the same as ZF. The ZF estimator is linear, which behaves like a linear filter and separates the data streams and thereafter independently decodes each stream. The drawback of ZF is the effect of noise amplification when the lattice basis $\overline{\mathbf{V}}$ is not orthogonal.

3   The Proposed Method

From the viewpoint of lattices, we can improve the ZF detector in M-IGLS by using other lattice decoding algorithms. Based on this idea, a novel hidden data extraction algorithm is proposed. In the following subsections, we will present our scheme and analyze its performance.

3.1   M-ISIC

By using decision feedback in the decoding process, the nonlinear Successive Interference Cancellation (SIC) detector has better performance than ZF. Recall that for $\mathcal{P}_2$, the lattice basis is $\overline{\mathbf{V}}$, and the set of query vectors are $\overline{\mathbf{Y}}$. The SIC algorithm consists of the following steps:

Step i) Use QR decomposition to factorize $\overline{\mathbf{V}}$: $\overline{\mathbf{V}} = \mathbf{Q}\mathbf{R}^1$, where $\mathbf{Q} \in \mathbb{R}^{L \times L}$ denotes a unitary matrix and $\mathbf{R} \in \mathbb{R}^{L \times K}$ is an upper triangular matrix of the form:

$$\mathbf{R} = \begin{bmatrix} R_{1,1} & R_{1,2} & \cdots & R_{1,K} \\ 0 & R_{2,2} & \cdots & R_{2,K} \\ \vdots & \vdots & \ddots & \vdots \\ 0 & 0 & \cdots & R_{K,K} \\ 0 & 0 & \cdots & 0 \\ \vdots & \vdots & \ddots & \vdots \\ 0 & 0 & \cdots & 0 \end{bmatrix}. \tag{11}$$

Step ii) Construct $\mathbf{Y}' = \mathbf{Q}^\top \overline{\mathbf{Y}} \in \mathbb{R}^{L \times M}$, which consists of vectors $\mathbf{y}'(1), ..., \mathbf{y}'(M)$.

Step iii) For $m = 1, ..., M$, generate the estimation as

$$\hat{b}_K(m) = \text{sign}\left(\frac{y'_K(m)}{R_{K,K}}\right), \tag{12}$$

$$\hat{b}_k(m) = \text{sign}\left(\frac{y'_k(m) - \sum_{l=k+1}^{K} R_{k,l}\hat{b}_l(m)}{R_{k,k}}\right), \tag{13}$$

where $k = K - 1, K - 2, ..., 1$, and $y'_k(m)$ denotes the kth component of $\mathbf{y}'(m)$.

By substituting the Step 5 in Algorithm 1 with the SIC steps, we obtain a new algorithm referred to as multi-carrier iterative successive interference cancellation (M-ISIC). Its pseudo-codes are presented in Algorithm 2. Notably, $\mathbf{V}^{(d)}$ is estimated in the same way as that of M-IGLS, and the performance improvements rely on SIC decoding. The stopping criterion can be set as when $\|\mathbf{B}^{(d)} - \mathbf{B}^{(d-1)}\|_F^2 < 10^{-5}$.

Remark 1. The rationale of SIC is explained as follows. When detecting multiple symbols, if one of them can be estimated first, the interference caused by the already decoded can be eliminated when solving another, so as to reduce the effective noise of the symbol to be solved and to improve the bit error rate performance. To be concise, denote the observation equation corresponding to $\mathcal{P}_2$ as

$$\overline{\mathbf{Y}} = \overline{\mathbf{V}}\mathbf{B} + \overline{\mathbf{Z}}, \tag{14}$$

---

[1] For better performance, this paper adopts a sorted version of QR decomposition, where the column vectors in $\overline{\mathbf{V}}$ are sorted from short to long.

Algorithm 2: The M-ISIC data extraction algorithm.

Input: $\mathbf{Y}, \mathbf{R_z}$.
Output: $\hat{\mathbf{V}} = \mathbf{V}^{(d)}, \hat{\mathbf{B}} = \mathbf{B}^{(d)}$.

1 $d = 0, \mathbf{B}^{(0)} \sim \{\pm 1\}^{K \times M}$;

2 **while** *a stopping criterion has not been reached* **do**

3     $d \leftarrow d + 1$;

4     $\mathbf{V}^{(d)} \leftarrow \mathbf{Y}(\mathbf{B}^{(d-1)})^{\mathrm{T}}[\mathbf{B}^{(d-1)}(\mathbf{B}^{(d-1)})^{\mathrm{T}}]^{-1}$;

5   Employ Steps i)-iii) of SIC to estimate $\mathbf{B}^{(d)}$ ▷ Approximate lattice decoding via SIC.

---

with $\overline{\mathbf{Z}}$ being the effective noise. Then the multiplication of $\mathbf{Q}^{\top}$ to (14) is simply a rotation, which maintain the Frobenius norm of the objective function:

$$||\overline{\mathbf{Y}} - \overline{\mathbf{V}}\mathbf{B}||_F^2 = ||\overline{\mathbf{Z}}||_F^2 \tag{15}$$

$$= ||\mathbf{Q}^{\top}\overline{\mathbf{Z}}||_F^2 \tag{16}$$

$$= ||\mathbf{Q}^{\top}\overline{\mathbf{Y}} - \mathbf{R}\mathbf{B}||_F^2. \tag{17}$$

Regarding Step iii), $\hat{b}_K(m), ..., \hat{b}_1(m)$ are estimated in descending order because the interference caused by these symbols can be canceled. Moreover, the divisions of $R_{K,K}, ..., R_{1,1}$ in Eqs. (12) (13) imply that the effective noise level hinges on the quality of $R_{K,K}, ..., R_{1,1}$.

3.2 Performance Analysis

We argue that M-ISIC theoretically outperforms M-IGLS, as SIC has better decoding performance than ZF when approximately solving $\mathcal{P}_2$. With a slight abuse of notations, $\mathcal{P}_2$ can be simplified as M instances of the following observation:

$$\mathbf{y} = \mathbf{R}'\mathbf{b}^* + \mathbf{z} \tag{18}$$

where $\mathbf{y} \in \mathbb{R}^K$, $\mathbf{b}^* \in \{\pm 1\}^K$ is the transmitted message, $\mathbf{R}' \in \mathbb{R}^{K \times K}$ includes only the first K rows of (11), and we assume that $\mathbf{z}$ also admits a Gaussian distribution with mean $\mathbf{0}$ and covariance $\sigma_n^2\mathbf{I}_K$. Then the lattice decoding task becomes

$$\mathcal{P}_3 : \min_{\mathbf{b} \in \{\pm 1\}^K} ||\mathbf{y} - \mathbf{R}\mathbf{b}||^2. \tag{19}$$

It has been shown in the literature [13,21] that SIC outperforms ZF if the constraint of $\mathbf{b}$ in $\mathcal{P}_3$ is an integer set $\mathbb{Z}^K$ and a box-constrained (truncated continuous integer) set $\mathcal{B}$. Therefore, we employ a model reduction technique to show that SIC has higher success probability when decoding $\mathcal{P}_3$.

Proposition 1. *Let the SIC and ZF estimates of $\mathcal{P}_3$ be $\mathbf{b}^{\mathrm{SIC}}$ and $\mathbf{b}^{\mathrm{ZF}}$, respectively. Then the averaged decoding success probability of SIC is higher than that of ZF:*

$$\mathbb{E}_{\mathbf{b}^*}\{\Pr(\mathbf{b}^{\mathrm{SIC}} = \mathbf{b}^*)\} \geq \mathbb{E}_{\mathbf{b}^*}\{\Pr(\mathbf{b}^{\mathrm{ZF}} = \mathbf{b}^*)\}, \tag{20}$$

where the expectation is taken over uniform random $\mathbf{b}^* \in \{\pm 1\}^K$.

Proof. Firstly, Eq. (18) is rewritten as

$$(\mathbf{y} + \mathbf{R} \times \mathbf{1})/2 = \mathbf{R}(\mathbf{b}^* + \mathbf{1})/2 + \mathbf{z}/2. \tag{21}$$

By updating the query vector $\mathbf{y}$ as $\mathbf{y}' \triangleq (\mathbf{y} + \mathbf{R} \times \mathbf{1})/2$, the bipolar constraint model $\mathcal{P}_3$ is transformed to the following box-constrained model $\mathcal{P}_4$:

$$\mathcal{P}_4 : \min_{\mathbf{b} \in \mathcal{B}} ||\mathbf{y}' - \mathbf{R}\mathbf{b}||^2, \tag{22}$$

where the constraint of the variable is $\mathcal{B} = \{0, 1\}^K$. Since [21][Thm. 9] has shown that Eq. (20) holds in this type of box-constrained model, the proposition is proved.

If $\overline{\mathbf{V}}$ is close to being an orthogonal matrix, then ZF and SIC detection can both achieve maximum likelihood estimation. The reason is that they are all solving a much simpler quantization problem $\min_{\mathbf{b} \in \{\pm 1\}^K} ||\mathbf{y} - \mathbf{I}_K\mathbf{b}||^2$. In general, the performance gap between ZF and SIC depends on the degree of orthogonality of the lattice basis $\overline{\mathbf{V}}$. To quantify this parameter, we introduce the normalized orthogonality defect of a matrix as

$$\delta(\overline{\mathbf{V}}) = \left(\frac{\prod_{k=1}^K ||\overline{\mathbf{v}}_k||}{\sqrt{\det(\overline{\mathbf{V}}^\top \overline{\mathbf{V}})}} \right)^{1/K}, \tag{23}$$

where the column vectors of $\overline{\mathbf{V}} = [\overline{\mathbf{v}}_1, ..., \overline{\mathbf{v}}_K]$ are linear independent. From Hardamard's inequality, $\delta(\overline{\mathbf{V}})$ is always larger than or equal to 1, with equality if and only if the columns are orthogonal to each other. Summarizing the above, SIC performs better than ZF in general, and their performance gap decreases as $\delta(\overline{\mathbf{V}}) \to 1$.

3.3   Unknown Number of Signatures

In real-world scenarios it may be more reasonable to assume that the number of carriers/signatures (i.e., K) is unknown. Fortunately, our lattice-based formulation can incorporate this setting in a straightforward manner. The observation equation can still be written as Eq. (5), but the constraints are changed to

$$\mathbf{V} \in \mathbb{R}^{L \times L}, \mathbf{B} \in \{-1, 0, 1\}^{L \times M}. \tag{24}$$

Then the objective function becomes

$$\mathcal{P}_5 : \min_{\substack{\mathbf{B} \in \{-1,0,1\}^{L \times M} \\ \mathbf{V} \in \mathbb{R}^{L \times L}}} ||\mathbf{R}_z^{-\frac{1}{2}}(\mathbf{Y} - \mathbf{V}\mathbf{B})||_F^2, \tag{25}$$

Here $\mathbf{R}_z$ can be set as an identity matrix if it cannot be available. By solving $\mathcal{P}_5$, the non-zero messages indicate the number of signatures. For instance, when $\hat{b}_k(m) = 0$, it implies that the kth column of $\mathbf{V}$ is redundant and inactivated.

Both M-ISIC and M-IGLS can be slightly modified to address $\mathcal{P}_5$, where the needed modification is to change the quantization function from the binary quantization sign$(\cdot)$ to a ternary quantization $\mathcal{Q}_{\{-1,0,1\}}(\cdot)$. In the same vein, Proposition 1 also holds when the number of signatures is unknown.

3.4 Computational Complexity

To compare with M-IGLS and exiting schemes, we give the computational complexity of M-ISIC based on the following conditions:

- The complexity of the multiplication of two matrices $\mathbf{A} \in \mathbb{R}^{M \times N}$ and $\mathbf{B} \in \mathbb{R}^{N \times K}$ is $\mathcal{O}(MNK)$.
- The complexity of an inversion over the square matrix $\mathbf{A} \in \mathbb{R}^{N \times N}$ is $\mathcal{O}(N^3)$.
- The complexity of performing QR decomposition on matrix $\mathbf{A} \in \mathbb{R}^{M \times N}$, $M > N$, is $\mathcal{O}(2MN^2)$.

Notice that $\mathbf{Y} \in \mathbb{R}^{L \times M}$, $\mathbf{V} \in \mathbb{R}^{L \times K}$ and $\mathbf{B} \in \mathbb{R}^{K \times M}$, the computational complexity of Step 4 in M-ISIC is

$$\mathcal{O}(K^3 + K^2(L + M) + LMK).$$

The computational complexity of Step 5 is dominated by the QR decomposition, which is

$$\mathcal{O}\left(K^2 L + M(LK + K)\right).$$

The computational complexity of each iteration of the algorithm is summarized as

$$\mathcal{O}\left(K^3 + 2LMK + K^2(3L + M) + KM\right).$$

With a total of T iterations, the overall complexity is

$$\mathcal{O}\left(T(K^3 + 2LMK + K^2(3L + M) + KM)\right).$$

4 Experimental Studies

This section performs numerical simulations to verify the effectiveness and accuracy of our scheme. Benchmark algorithms include: i) M-IGLS [10], ii) sample-matrix-inversion minimum mean square error (SMI-MMSE) [10], iii) ideal minimum mean square error (ideal MMSE) [10], iv) JADE [18]. The following experiments are run on Matlab R2018b. To ensure fair comparisons, M-IGLS and M-ISIC are initialized with the same $\mathbf{B}^{(0)}$.

Without loss of generality, the carrier images are taken from the BOWS-2 database [17], composed of $10,000$ grey-level images, with different statistical properties. Some typical images are displayed in Fig. 1. We employ 8×8 blockwise DCT transform on the original images and select all bins except the DC value to embed message sequences. The simulations investigate the scenarios with known and unknown number of carriers separately. The normalized orthogonality defect of the simulated carriers are shown in Table 1. The entries in the matrix $\overline{\mathbf{V}}$ are taken from standard Gaussian distribution, and by varying the size of $L \times K$, the carriers exhibit different $\delta(\overline{\mathbf{V}})$.

The bit-error-rate (BER), as a common performance index, is employed to measure the decoding performance. The noise power is fixed as $\sigma_n^2 = 1$ and the signal-to-noise ratio is controlled by varying the distortion D.

(a)	(b)	(c)	(d)	(e)
(f)	(g)	(h)	(i)	(j)
(k)	(l)	(m)	(n)	(o)

Fig. 1. Some representative images in the BOWS-2 database.

Table 1. The normalized orthogonality defect of the simulated carriers.

Knowledge of K	Known			Unknown	
$L \times K$	8×8	32×28	32×20	20×8	16×4
$\delta(\overline{\mathbf{V}})$	2.2123	1.4420	1.2297	1.1171	1.0582

4.1 Known Number of Carriers

In the following, we consider the cases with $\delta(\overline{\mathbf{V}}) = 2.2123, 1.4420, 1.2297$ for the sake of exploring the influence of the lattice bases.

In the first example, we consider the case with $L = 8$, $K = 8$, $\delta(\overline{\mathbf{V}}) = 2.2123$. The BER versus distortion performance of different algorithms are plotted in Fig. 2. With the exact carriers' information, the SMI-MMSE and Ideal-MMSE algorithms serve as the performance upper bounds. The BSS approach, JADE fails to exhibit satisfactory performance. Moreover, M-ISIC outperforms M-IGLS in the whole distortion range of 24–38 dB, over which the improvement can be as large as 4 dB.

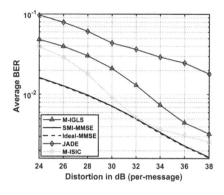

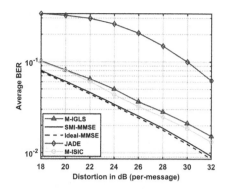

Fig. 2. BER versus distortion ($L = 8$, $K = 8$, $\delta(\overline{\mathbf{V}}) = 2.2123$).

Fig. 3. BER versus distortion ($L = 32$, $K = 28$, $\delta(\overline{\mathbf{V}}) = 1.4420$).

The second example examines the case with $L = 32$, $K = 28$, $\delta(\overline{\mathbf{V}}) = 1.4420$. As depicted in Fig. 3, when the carriers become more orthogonal, both M-IGLS and M-ISIC get closer to SMI-MMSE and Ideal-MMSE. The performance gap between M-IGLS and M-ISIC has become smaller, in which the improvement is about 1 dB. Similar results can be replicated when we further reduce the normalized orthogonality defect. We post one of such figures in Fig. 4 without further comments.

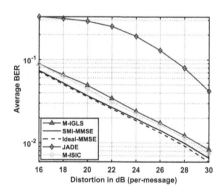

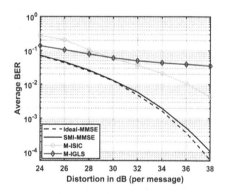

Fig. 4. BER versus distortion ($L = 32$, $K = 20$, $\delta(\overline{\mathbf{V}}) = 1.2297$).

Fig. 5. BER versus distortion ($L = 20$, $K = 8$ is unknown, $\delta(\overline{\mathbf{V}}) = 1.1171$).

From the above, we observe that the performance of M-ISIC is generally not worse than that of M-IGLS. When the carriers $\overline{\mathbf{V}}$ represents a bad lattice basis, M-ISIC apparently outperforms M-IGLS. On the other hand, when the carriers are highly orthogonal, the decision regions of M-IGLS and M-ISIC become similar in shape, then the performance of the two algorithms tends to be the same.

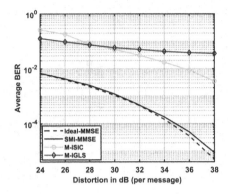

Fig. 6. BER versus distortion ($L = 16$, $K = 4$ is unknown, $\delta(\overline{\mathbf{V}}) = 1.0582$).

4.2 Unknown Number of Carriers

Hereby we investigate the performance of different algorithms for the more realistic scenario with K being unknown. As mentioned in Sect. 3.3, the setting of M-ISIC and M-IGLS are as follows. Initialize $\mathbf{V}$ and $\mathbf{B}$ as matrices with size $L \times L$ and $L \times M$ respectively, and then calculate $\mathbf{B}$ in the same way, except that the quantization function is slightly modified. Here $\mathbf{R}_z$ is replaced by an identity matrix for performance enhancement.

Figures 5 and 6 plot the BER figures with $\delta(\overline{\mathbf{V}}) = 1.1171$ and 1.0582. It turns out that our method still outperforms M-IGLS in most of the distortion range. Since K and the carriers' information are known for ideal-MMSE and SMI-MMSE, they significantly outperform M-IGLS and M-ISIC. As the constraint of the lattice decoding algorithms has increased from binary alphabets to ternary alphabets, the performance degradation of M-ISIC and M-IGLS are reasonable. Nevertheless, sine M-ISIC can generally achieve a small BER of about 10^{-2}, it justifies that multi-carrier SS can be cracked even when K is unknown.

5   Conclusions

This paper explores the issue of extracting spread-spectrum hidden data from digital media and proposes an accurate and more general algorithm based on better lattice decoding. To verify the superiority of our algorithm, M-ISIC is compared with M-IGLS and other non-blind algorithms. The experimental results demonstrate that M-ISIC enjoys better decoding performance especially when the normalized orthogonality defect of the carriers becomes large.

A   The Equivalence of GLS and ZF

Assuming $\mathbf{V}$ is known, the least-squares estimation [10] of $\mathbf{B}$ used in Step 5 of Algorithm 1 is:

$$
\begin{aligned}
\hat{\mathbf{B}}_{\mathrm{GLS}} &= \left(\mathbf{V}^{\mathrm{T}}\mathbf{R}_{\mathbf{y}}^{-1}\mathbf{V}\right)^{-1}\mathbf{V}^{\mathrm{T}}\mathbf{R}_{\mathbf{y}}^{-1}\mathbf{Y} \\
&= \left(\left(\mathbf{V}^{\mathrm{T}}\mathbf{R}_{\mathbf{z}}^{-1}\mathbf{V}\right)^{-1}+\mathbf{I}\right)\mathbf{V}^{\mathrm{T}} \\
&\quad \times \left(\mathbf{R}_{\mathbf{z}}^{-1}-\mathbf{R}_{\mathbf{z}}^{-1}\mathbf{V}\left(\mathbf{V}^{\mathrm{T}}\mathbf{R}_{\mathbf{z}}^{-1}\mathbf{V}+\mathbf{I}\right)^{-1}\mathbf{V}^{\mathrm{T}}\mathbf{R}_{\mathbf{z}}^{-1}\right) \\
&= \left(\mathbf{V}^{\mathrm{T}}\mathbf{R}_{\mathbf{z}}^{-1}\mathbf{V}\right)^{-1}\mathbf{V}^{\mathrm{T}}\mathbf{R}_{\mathbf{z}}^{-1}\mathbf{Y} \\
&= \left(\mathbf{V}^{\mathrm{T}}\mathbf{R}_{\mathbf{z}}^{-\frac{1}{2}}\mathbf{R}_{\mathbf{z}}^{-\frac{1}{2}}\mathbf{V}\right)^{-1}\mathbf{V}^{\mathrm{T}}\mathbf{R}_{\mathbf{z}}^{-\frac{1}{2}}\mathbf{R}_{\mathbf{z}}^{-\frac{1}{2}}\mathbf{Y} \\
&= \left[(\mathbf{R}_{\mathbf{z}}^{-\frac{1}{2}}\mathbf{V})^{\mathrm{T}}(\mathbf{R}_{\mathbf{z}}^{-\frac{1}{2}}\mathbf{V})\right]^{-1}(\mathbf{R}_{\mathbf{z}}^{-\frac{1}{2}}\mathbf{V})^{\mathrm{T}}(\mathbf{R}_{\mathbf{z}}^{-\frac{1}{2}}\mathbf{Y}). \qquad (26)
\end{aligned}
$$

In the language of ZF, recall that $\overline{\mathbf{Y}} = \mathbf{R}_{\mathbf{z}}^{-\frac{1}{2}}\mathbf{Y}$, and $\overline{\mathbf{V}} = \mathbf{R}_{\mathbf{z}}^{-\frac{1}{2}}\mathbf{V}$. Thus Eq. (26) equals to $(\overline{\mathbf{V}}^{\mathrm{T}}\overline{\mathbf{V}})^{-1}\overline{\mathbf{V}}^{\mathrm{T}}\overline{\mathbf{Y}}^{\mathrm{T}}$, which justifies $\hat{\mathbf{B}}_{\mathrm{GLS}} = \hat{\mathbf{B}}_{\mathrm{ZF}}$.

References

1. Bailey, C.P., Chamadia, S., Pados, D.A.: An alternative signature design using L1 principal components for spread-spectrum steganography. In: IEEE International Conference on Acoustics, Speech and Signal Processing, ICASSP 2020, Barcelona, Spain, pp. 2693–2696. IEEE (2020)
2. Bingham, E., Hyvärinen, A.: A fast fixed-point algorithm for independent component analysis of complex valued signals. Int. J. Neural Syst. **10**(1), 1–8 (2000)
3. Cox, I.J., Kilian, J., Leighton, F.T., Shamoon, T.: Secure spread spectrum watermarking for multimedia. IEEE Trans. Image Process. **6**(12), 1673–1687 (1997)
4. Cox, I.J., Miller, M.L., Bloom, J.A., Honsinger, C.: Digital Watermarking, vol. 53. Springer, Cham (2002)
5. Cox, I.J., Miller, M.L., McKellips, A.L.: Watermarking as communications with side information. Proc. IEEE **87**(7), 1127–1141 (1999)
6. Du, Y., Yin, Z., Zhang, X.: High capacity lossless data hiding in JPEG bitstream based on general VLC mapping. IEEE Trans. Dependable Secur. Comput. **19**(2), 1420–1433 (2022)
7. Fridrich, J.: Steganography in Digital Media: Principles, Algorithms, and Applications. Cambridge University Press, Cambridge (2009)
8. Gkizeli, M., Pados, D.A., Batalama, S.N., Medley, M.J.: Blind iterative recovery of spread-spectrum steganographic messages. In: Proceedings of the 2005 International Conference on Image Processing, ICIP 2005, Genoa, Italy, pp. 1098–1100. IEEE (2005)
9. Huang, J., Shi, Y.Q.: Reliable information bit hiding. IEEE Trans. Circuits Syst. Video Technol. **12**(10), 916–920 (2002)
10. Li, M., Kulhandjian, M., Pados, D.A., Batalama, S.N., Medley, M.J.: Extracting spread-spectrum hidden data from digital media. IEEE Trans. Inf. Forensics Secur. **8**(7), 1201–1210 (2013)

11. Li, M., Liu, Q.: Steganalysis of SS steganography: hidden data identification and extraction. Circuits Syst. Signal Process. **34**(10), 3305–3324 (2015)
12. Lin, J., Qin, J., Lyu, S., Feng, B., Wang, J.: Lattice-based minimum-distortion data hiding. IEEE Commun. Lett. **25**(9), 2839–2843 (2021)
13. Ling, C.: On the proximity factors of lattice reduction-aided decoding. IEEE Trans. Signal Process. **59**(6), 2795–2808 (2011)
14. Lu, W., Zhang, J., Zhao, X., Zhang, W., Huang, J.: Secure robust JPEG steganography based on autoencoder with adaptive BCH encoding. IEEE Trans. Circuits Syst. Video Technol. **31**(7), 2909–2922 (2021)
15. Malvar, H.S., Florêncio, D.A.: Improved spread spectrum: a new modulation technique for robust watermarking. IEEE Trans. Signal Process. **51**(4), 898–905 (2003)
16. Micciancio, D., Goldwasser, S.: Complexity of Lattice Problems. Springer, Boston (2002)
17. Bas, P., Furon, T.: Image database of bows-2. https://bows2.ec-lille.fr/
18. Sheinvald, J.: On blind beamforming for multiple non-Gaussian signals and the constant-modulus algorithm. IEEE Trans. Signal Process. **46**(7), 1878–1885 (1998)
19. Simmons, G.J.: The Prisoners' problem and the subliminal channel. In: Chaum, D. (ed.) Advances in Cryptology, pp. 51–67. Springer, Boston (1984). https://doi.org/10.1007/978-1-4684-4730-9_5
20. Tao, J., Li, S., Zhang, X., Wang, Z.: Towards robust image steganography. IEEE Trans. Circuits Syst. Video Technol. **29**(2), 594–600 (2019)
21. Wen, J., Chang, X.: On the success probability of three detectors for the box-constrained integer linear model. IEEE Trans. Commun. **69**(11), 7180–7191 (2021)

Traffic Analysis and Monitoring

MQTT Traffic Collection and Forensic Analysis Framework

Raymond Chan[1(✉)], Wye Kaye Yan[1], Jung Man Ma[1], Kai Mun Loh[1],
Greger Chen Zhi En[1], Malcolm Low[1], Habib Rehman[2], and Thong Chee Phua[2]

[1] Singapore Institute of Technology, Singapore, Singapore
{Raymond.Chan,Wyekaye.Yan,Jungman.Ma,Malcolm.Low}@singaporetech.edu.sg,
{2100817,2100641}@sit.singaporetech.edu.sg
[2] Firefish Communications, Singapore, Singapore
{habib,thongchee}@firefishcomms.com

Abstract. Message Queue Telemetry Transport (MQTT) is a common protocol used for Internet-of-Things (IoT) devices communication. In recent years, IoT devices are deployed in Operational Technology (OT) systems such as building management system (BMS). It enables the capability to control the infrastructure within a building, and can be considered a miniature industrial control system. With the increased use of these devices to further enhance the functionality of such systems, there is also an increased risk of vulnerabilities that come with these devices. Cyber-security must be one of the top priorities to be taken into the consideration at the various stages when designing the BMS to achieve operational reliability. In this paper, we proposed a real-time MQTT logging and abnormal detection framework with push notifications. It can be used to collect digital evidence for forensic investigation and monitor cyber-attacks.

Keywords: Building management system · forensic analysis · MQTT · Internet of Things

1 Introduction

The use of IoT devices is increasing every year, and is considered one of the key factors that contributes to the huge volume of data exchanged in Information and Communication Technology (ICT) networks [1]. The MQTT protocol is commonly used within an IoT environment, and is designed to be a lightweight, machine to machine (M2M) network protocol, which at its core, uses a publish and subscribe communication model. The protocol functions on a server-client model, where the client publishes messages and the server, also known as the broker, will receive those messages filtering them by topic before relaying the messages to the subscribers. MQTT protocol is making significant gains into industrial automation and is also widely used in other applications and areas

© ICST Institute for Computer Sciences, Social Informatics and Telecommunications Engineering 2023
Published by Springer Nature Switzerland AG 2023. All Rights Reserved
S. Goel et al. (Eds.): ICDF2C 2022, LNICST 508, pp. 185–202, 2023.
https://doi.org/10.1007/978-3-031-36574-4_11

such as ECG monitoring system for healthcare [2], smart home automation [3], push notification system for smartphone applications [4], weather monitoring and smart farming for agriculture sector [5].

Compared to other protocols like HTTP, MQTT protocol has the ability to transfer data at a much faster rate [6]. Therefore, it is more ideal for resource constraint environments. However, although there are many advantages in using MQTT protocol, there are security risks involved with the increasing complexity of the IoT model, security flaws and vulnerabilities are highly common today in IoT devices, and there are a wider variety of attacks than in the past [7]. The security mechanism of MQTT protocol required further improvement and development [8] as many existing MQTT systems currently in use are still lacking basic security controls [9]. In [9], the authors performed Man-in-the-middle (MITM) attack on MQTT-based IoT devices. They concluded that their designed attack scheme had successfully avoided commonly used classification-based anomaly detection models. The security of the MQTT protocol was further investigated in [10] which the authors identified the weakness of the MQTT protocol to a slow denial of service attack. The configuration of the KeepAlive parameter and MQTT packets were two specific MQTT flaws that the authors exploited to launch a cyberattack against the MQTT broker. The results have shown that the attacks were successful and the vulnerability can be used to execute a denial of service against the IoT network by maintaining the connection for a very long time.

In a BMS setup that has IoT devices within the network, the devices are connected to a MQTT server and subscribe or publish to a topic. The messages are small in size, hence the popularity for its uses in IoT. Therefore, to safeguard the MQTT protocol from security risk, the proposed solution will consist of two parts: a network-based detection component for traffic collection and a methodology to analyze the traffic for anomaly detection, and a notification component for the front-end to alert users of the anomaly detected.

2   Related Work

There are several approaches to detect cyber threats and attacks on MQTT protocols. Budiana introduced a method to use a fuzzy logic algorithm embedded in a node to detect Denial of Service (DoS) in the MQTT protocol with feature selection nodes. The SUBSCRIBE and SUBACK traffic was monitored, and it provided the information to fuzzy input nodes to detect DoS attacks [11].

Another proposed way is to develop classification models that can use for an Intrusion Detection System (IDS), utilizing a specific dataset with particular attacks for the MQTT protocols. In their case study, machine learning techniques were used to classify the frames that an IDS can assign as attack or normal traffic [12]. In [13], the authors introduced ARTEMIS, an IDS for IoT that analyzes data from IoT devices using machine learning to detect changes from the system's typical behavior and sends alarms in the event of abnormalities. Hindy [14] discussed the effectiveness of six machine learning techniques to detect MQTT-based attacks. A MQTT simulated dataset is produced for the training and evaluation processes. The authors concluded that the results highlighted how crucial it is to distinguish between MQTT-based attacks and legitimate traffic using flow-based features, whereas packet-based features are sufficient to identify traditional networking attacks.

In recent years, machine learning techniques have been utilised to detect cyber-attacks on networks and infrastructure. There are a number of research studies applying machine learning for MQTT attack detection. Vaccari presented MQTTset, a dataset that combines the legitimate dataset with cyber-attacks against the MQTT network [1]. The authors evaluated and validated the dataset by implementing and comparing it to different machine learning algorithms widely adopted in the cyber-security field. They concluded that MQTTset can be used for a possible detection system related to the MQTT protocol.

Through intrusion and DoS attacks on publicly available MQTT test brokers, Chunduri analysed the availability of MQTT network traffic and obtained sensitive information and validated its security implications [15]. The purpose of their research is to demonstrate the negative impact of security measures on MQTT by attacking the MQTT brokers. Similarly, Anthraper provided an overview of the security and privacy concerns of the IoT by analysing MQTT protocol [16]. Afterward, the paper discussed IoT forensics and concluded by highlighting the security challenges related to IoT. In [17], the author introduced a method Value-to-Keyed-Hash Message Authentication Code (Value-to-HMAC) mapping to ensure the confidentiality and integrity of information in MQTT.

Research studies in MQTT data analysis and attack detection areas are still considered very limited and insufficient. In order to fill this gap, we proposed a framework for traffic analysis based on MQTT traffic collected from an IoT-enabled BMS. Moreover, a push notification is created based on the proposed analysis framework to provide attack detection alerts to the users. The notification component alerts users in the event of unauthorised subscription, denial of service attack, brute force attack, and inactivity of Zigbee devices. Though device inactivity is uncommon, there are devices by default that are designed to operate in idle or inactive until a specific function call activates it. Also, though exploitable, MQTT has a KeepAlive feature that by nature is used to verify the device's connectivity with the system. However, there are scenarios like bridging Zigbee to MQTT and Modbus to MQTT where it does not have a KeepAlive feature or a function with a similar feature by default. The team has recognised it as a security risk due to the increasing complexity of the IoT model that compromises the integrity of the Confidentiality, Integrity, and Availability (CIA) triad and the Authentication, Authorization, and Accounting (AAA) security framework.

3   MQTT Traffic Collection and Analysis Methodology

3.1   Testbed Implementation

By leveraging on an existing IoT integrated BMS, various devices within the setup have been selected for traffic collection and analysis. As illustrated in

Fig. 1, these devices can be classified into two categories: MQTT devices such as a people counting radar and an elevator control system, and non MQTT devices that have been bridged to the MQTT protocol such as Zigbee-enabled smart light bulbs, smart air quality sensors, and smart locks.

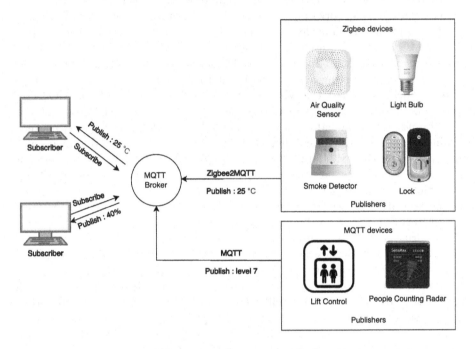

Fig. 1. Architecture of testbed

3.2 MQTT Protocol Implementation

As mentioned above, the selected devices are connected, controlled and monitored using a central control system called Home Assistant (HA). A locally integrated MQTT protocol is available in HA, it runs on a 3.1.1 specification by default and falls back to version 3.1 if the chosen server does not support it. For this experiment, Eclipse Mosquitto broker which supports MQTT version 3.1.1 is used. The Mosquitto broker acts as an intermediary between clients, in this case, between the devices selected. These clients will publish messages to other clients which have subscriptions established. As illustrated in Fig. 2, the description of the MQTT parties and their functions in the protocol are as follows:

- Broker (Centralised Server): Receives, filters, and distributes relevant messages to clients that are subscribed
- Publisher: Publishers send a message to a topic, which is sent via the broker. Subscribers will then be notified of the message

– Subscriber: Clients send a SUBSCRIBE message to the broker to receive messages on specific topic(s) of interest '

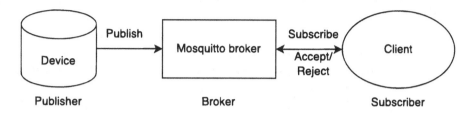

Fig. 2. MQTT subscriber and publisher model

3.3 MQTT Network-Based Forensic Framework

MQTT Traffic Collection. It is done through a containerised docker custom-made to run on HA that will leverage the current functionalities and Application Programming Interfaces (API) provided by HA. The docker container runs in a unique Alpine Linux environment and has controlled access to the HA host environment using the Bashio shell library and API. Each add-on is isolated from one another and can only communicate through the HA host or shared file system volumes. Within the docker container is the proposed network-based detection component, to streamline the support for MQTT with the Mosquitto broker, a MQTT client developed by Eclipse is used. The Paho Python client supports the same MQTT versions as the Mosquitto broker, and Python versions 2.7 and 3.x. Furthermore, Scapy, a packet manipulation tool written in Python that supports MQTT is included in the docker container and used to collect and analyse the traffic.

Similar to the research conducted by Husnain [18], a detection model that monitors the network for anything MQTT related protocols and MQTT Control packets is done through Scapy. There are 13 MQTT Control packet sub-layers that Scapy monitors:

– **MQTT**
– **MQTTConnack:** Connection acknowledgement from Server to Client
– **MQTTConnect:** Request to connect from Client to Server
– **MQTTDisconnect:** A disconnect message from Client to Server
– **MQTTPuback:** Publish acknowledgement (QoS 1 Response) from Client to Server and vice versa
– **MQTTPubcomp:** Publish complete (Last part of the QoS 2) from Client to Server and vice versa
– **MQTTPublish:** Publish message from Client to Server and vice versa
– **MQTTPubrec:** Publish received (First part of QoS 2) from Client to Server and vice versa

- **MQTTPubrel:** Publish released (Second part of QoS 2) from Client to Server and vice versa
- **MQTTSubscribe:** Request to subscribe from Client to Server
- **MQTTUnsuback:** Unsubscribe acknowledgement from Client to Server
- **MQTTUnsubscribe:** Request to unsubscribe from Client to Server

Out of the 13 MQTT Control packet sub-layers that Scapy monitors, only 4 signals from the packets are used by clients. Those signals are Publish, Subscribe, Unsubscribe, and Connect. The other signals are part of the server-client model protocol functions that MQTT makes use of through the use of the publish and subscribe communication model.

MQTT Forensic Analysis Methodology. is conducted by employing two methods: a log-based analysis method to analyse MQTT topics, and a rule-based engine for MQTT traffic analysis. In the log-based analysis method, there are two types of logs that are generated from the Mosquitto broker, namely System Status, and Information and Debugging logs. By default, the log types that are log are Error, Information, Notice, and Warning events. However, as Mosquitto broker allows its users to configure its logging for all log types, by doing so, all types of events for activities such as debugging can be monitored. These logs are generated into a log file. To leverage the contents in the log for anomaly detection, it has been configured for remote monitoring by routing the logs to the $SYS topic.

For the design and structure of the rule-based engine definitions, it is similar to Snort rules, which is a common method used in IDS and intrusion prevention system (IPS). This makes the rule definitions flexible and relatively simple to configure to detect threats on a case-by-case basis by defining the parameters. The rule definition structure consists of 4 rule options: Header, Name, Priority, and Additional options. Within each rule option are configurable parameters as illustrated in Fig. 3, description of the configurable parameters in the rule options are as follows:

Header	Name	Priority	Additional options
mqtt $EXTERNAL_NET -> $SELF src;	name: External access to local-only topic (Zigbee2MQTT);	priority: 3;	cooldown: 0; msg_type: publish, subscribe; topics: zigbee2mqtt/#

Fig. 3. Rule options parameters

- Header: In the Header, the user decides which protocol to analyse, from a source, to a destination, and the target to be identified as the threat actor.
  Protocol: TCP/MQTT
  Source: Source IP/$ALIAS
  Destination: Destination IP/$ALIAS
  Target: Source/Destination

– Name: Declares a rule name which will be included in the notification payload
– Priority: Classifies the priority of the threat.
  Priority 4: Critical
  Priority 3: High
  Priority 2: Medium
  Priority 1: Low
  Priority 0: Informational
– Additional: There are two types of additional parameters that can be configured to fine-tune the detection.
  General options: Threshold/Interval/Cooldown
  MQTT options: msg_type/QoS/Retcode/topics.

3.4 Attack Detection

This component that is part of the proposed solution is designed to complement the MQTT traffic collection and analysis framework. The purpose of the push notifications is to provide real-time alerts to the users about the abnormalities detected. These real-time alerts are essential for preventing possible attacks made on the system thus, WebSocket which is a low-latency bi-directional communication protocol between server and client is used.

Furthermore, by leveraging on WebSocket protocol, Socket.io which is a library based on WebSocket protocol that enables real-time, event-based bi-directional communication will be employed in the solution. As compared to pure WebSocket protocol, it provides extra features that reduce the complexity of producing WebSocket applications [19] thus, making it suitable for this setup.

Figure 4 illustrates the communication flow between the MQTT broker and front-end notifications. MQTT communications have a persistent connection with the back-end of the Notification component which is written in JavaScript running on Node.js. For the purpose of this experiment, SQLite3 database is chosen for the persistent structured data storage as the package is lightweight and relatively performant for this setup. At the front, web technologies written in HyperText Markup Language (HTML), Cascading Style Sheets (CSS), and JavaScript ES6 provide visualisation for the alerts panel.

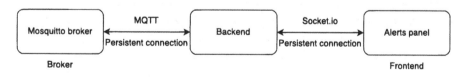

Fig. 4. Communication flow

3.5 Technology Stack

The architecture for the proposed solution leverages on an existing IoT integrated BMS as part of the testbed. With the use of a central control system, HA, a custom docker container that is designed for MQTT traffic collection and analysis works as a client with a locally installed Mosquitto broker in HA. Results from the traffic collection and analysis are pushed to the front-end alerts panel for easy visualisation. This is done so through a persistent connection from MQTT to the back-end of the notification component which has a database to store the persistent structured data before pushing the alerts to a web front-end through a persistent connection using Socket.io (Fig. 5).

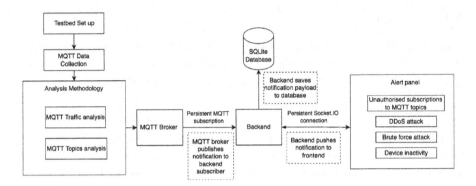

Fig. 5. MQTT traffic capture architecture

4   Experiment

In this section, we discussed the MQTT common vulnerabilities and further analysed the effectiveness of the proposed solution for detecting MQTT vulnerabilities in MQTT and Zigbee devices. With the proposed methodology, we are able to provide a front-end notifications component to alert users about abnormal detection. Our notifications component includes the following four vulnerability detection: Unauthorised Subscription Detection, Denial-of-Service Attack Detection, Brute Force Attack Detection and Zigbee2MQTT Devices Inactivity Detection. The detection methods are further explained in the following subsections.

4.1 Unauthorised Subscription Detection

In general, MQTT topics are created by subscribers or publishers, and the brokers use the topic of a message to decide which client receives which message. Apart from the typical topics, there is a special topic that contains information about the broker itself, which is $SYS topics. Topics of this type are unique meta topics that allow the broker to communicate details about the broker and the MQTT client session.

An example of $SYS topics is $SYS/broker/clients/connected, this topic provides information about the total number of currently connected clients. $SYS topics also contain MQTT logs that reveal information such as broker version, IP addresses, client names, and subscriptions that should not be made known to any unauthorised users. $SYS topics are often used for developing and debugging MQTT applications. However, attackers can take advantage of this feature and exploit $SYS topics to expose internal information and lead to data breaches.

An access control list (ACL) can be built within the broker to make sure that all access is allowed in order to prevent unauthorised subscription of $SYS topics. The default ACL is intended to restrict the client's permissions on the system topic $SYS/# and all wildcard topics. The ACL, however, is insufficient to guarantee privacy when using devices that communicate using the MQTT protocol. This is because ACL is a useful security measure against attacks that target user credentials, but the attacker's aim isn't always the user's credentials [20]. In addition, if the attackers are able to bypass ACL, the confidentiality of the system will be compromised. Therefore, it's crucial to have an additional layer of security features in place that provides quick and effective detection for unauthorised subscriptions.

In our proposed solution, unauthorised subscription to $SYS topics detection is done by checking subscriptions to the $SYS and any subtopics of $SYS. The '$SYS/broker/log/M/subscribe' topic is subscribed in order to keep track of which clients are subscribed to which $SYS topics. This would help link the source of the client to any of the $SYS topics that it is subscribed to. There is a list of whitelisted IP addresses that are permitted to subscribe to any $SYS topics or a specified topic. Therefore, if an IP address that does not belong to the list of allowed IP addresses is detected to be subscribing to any of the $SYS topics, it is considered as an unauthorised subscription. The Fig. 6 shows how a notification for an unauthorised user subscribing to any $SYS topics or access to protected topics will appear in the dashboard, if it is detected every 30 s. As long as the IP is not whitelisted, it would be considered as unauthorised subscription. As shown in Fig. 7 and 8, the metadata of the unauthorised subscription will be shown in JSON format under the raw details section.

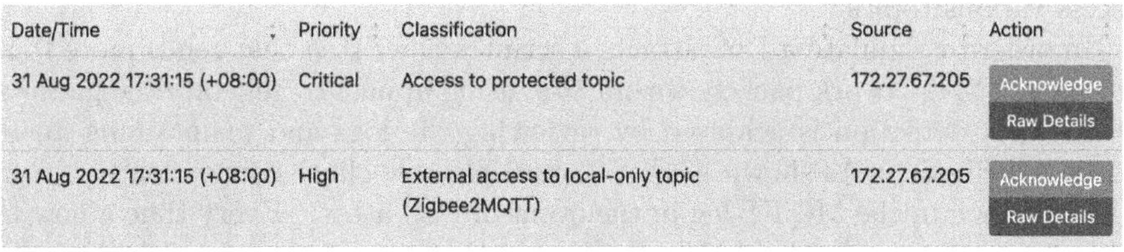

Date/Time	Priority	Classification	Source	Action
31 Aug 2022 17:31:15 (+08:00)	Critical	Access to protected topic	172.27.67.205	Acknowledge / Raw Details
31 Aug 2022 17:31:15 (+08:00)	High	External access to local-only topic (Zigbee2MQTT)	172.27.67.205	Acknowledge / Raw Details

Fig. 6. Unauthorised subscription alert

```
{
  "uuid": "f3c6641a6ac54b7683f3a57d46a5e7eb",
  "datetime": "2022-08-31T17:31:15.639841+08:00",
  "classification": "Access to protected topic",
  "priority": "Critical",
  "src": "172.27.67.205",
  "rule_raw": "mqtt $EXTERNAL_NET -> $SELF src; name: Access to protected topic; priority: 4;
      cooldown: 0; msg_type: publish, subscribe; topics: $SYS/#, is2/mqtt_attack_notifications",
  "metadata": {
    "first_violation": "2022-08-31T17:31:15.639841+08:00",
    "total_violation": 1,
    "mqtt": {
      "client_id": [
        "mqtt-explorer-ddf55658"
      ],
      "auth": {
        "username": [
          "mqtt-user"
        ],
        "password": []
      },
      "topics": {
        "publish": {},
        "subscribe": {
          "# (QOS: 0)": 1
        },
        "unsubscribe": {}
      }
    }
  }
}
```

Fig. 7. Access to protected topic metadata

4.2 Denial of Service Attack Detection

DoS attacks aim to overload server resources and prevent legitimate clients from accessing the services. A massive volume of publishing, subscribing, and connecting messages that eventually exhaust node resources and prevent the node from delivering normal services is referred to as a DoS attack against MQTT [7].

In MQTT, DoS attacks can be performed in several ways depending on the control packet type and access level. The most common method is to flood the targeted MQTT broker with a large volume of CONNECT packets to overwhelm the broker with the processing of authentication requests. Another common method is by embedding a will payload on a CONNECT packet so the packet size increases. As a result, both the bandwidth and CPU resources of the victim server will be consumed, preventing new connections from being processed [21]. Additionally, it is also possible for an attacker to flood the broker with invalid subscriptions even with valid credentials but are not authorised to access various topics.

In order to simulate a DoS attack, a script was written that sends more than 100 TCP SYN network packets within 10 s, using hping3 to generate the packets. DoS attack detection is achieved by reviewing the logs and maintaining an IP address dictionary. As shown in Fig. 9, multiple new client connection messages will be shown in the MQTT log in the event of DoS attack. Every time a new IP address is discovered, it will be added to the dictionary as a key with the value of 1. Subsequently, if the IP address already exists in the dictionary as a key, its value will be incremented by 1. In Fig. 10, a notification alert will be triggered as a DoS if the total violation value is higher than the threshold of 100. Moreover,

```
{
  "uuid": "9a591f127ba347fe81f15206f19aaefe",
  "datetime": "2022-08-31T17:31:15.639841+08:00",
  "classification": "External access to local-only topic (Zigbee2MQTT)",
  "priority": "High",
  "src": "172.27.67.205",
  "rule_raw": "mqtt $EXTERNAL_NET -> $SELF src; name:
   External access to local-only topic (Zigbee2MQTT); priority: 3; cooldown: 0;
   msg_type: publish, subscribe; topics: zigbee2mqtt/#",
  "metadata": {
  "first_violation": "2022-08-31T17:31:15.639841+08:00",
  "total_violation": 1,
  "mqtt": {
    "client_id": [
      "mqtt-explorer-ddf55658"
    ],
    "auth": {
     "username": [
       "mqtt-user"
     ],
     "password": []
    },
    "topics": {
     "publish": {},
     "subscribe": {
       "# (QOS: 0)": 1
     },
     "unsubscribe": {}
    }
   }
  }
}
```

Fig. 8. External access to local-only topic metadata

monitoring and detection are not only focused on client connections but also on excessive MQTT messages being published to the broker. As shown in Fig. 12, the notification is triggered as excessive MQTT message publish activity if the total violation value is more than 20 within 5 s. As DoS attacks in MQTT can also be launched by flooding the broker with high QoS messages on the most subscribed topic. Therefore, it is important to monitor the number of messages being published to the brokers.

4.3   Brute Force Attack Detection

Brute force attacks usually consist of attempts to gain access to a system by employing a guessing technique for the authentication token, i.e. password, username, one-time token, etc. Attacks of this nature will be challenging to detect and investigate due to the high number of client devices. Furthermore, such attacks are extremely common in MQTT as the MQTT built-in authentication mechanism is very weak [22] and most users still use weak credentials that can be guessed easily [23]. It is therefore important to detect brute force attacks as early as possible to protect the system from security threats.

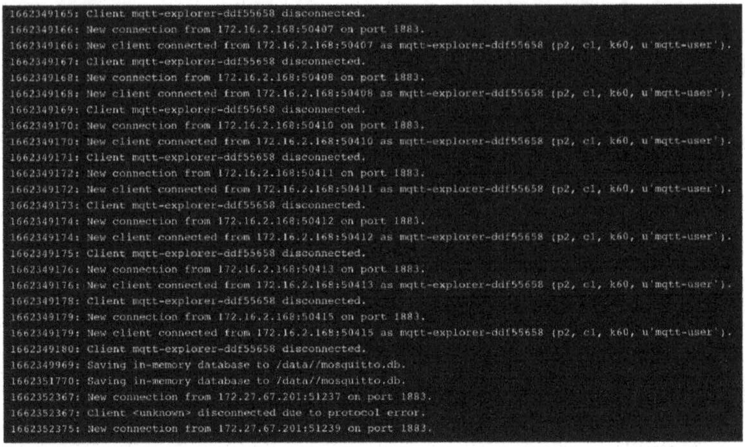

Fig. 9. Denial of service alert

Date/Time	Priority	Classification	Source	Action
05 Sep 2022 15:24:27 (+08:00)	High	Denial of Service	172.27.67.201	Acknowledge Raw Details

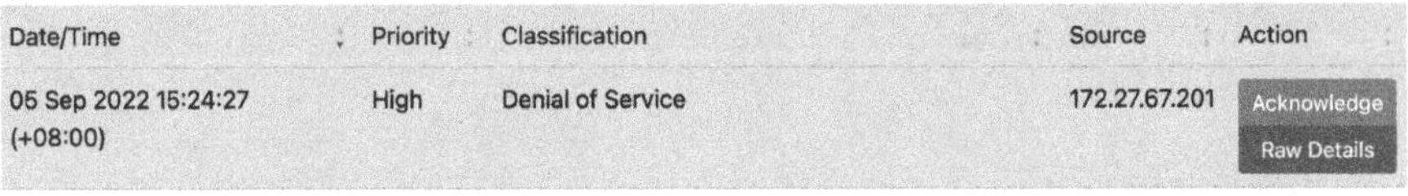

Fig. 10. Denial of service alert

A brute force attack was simulated using MQTT explorer, in which unauthorised connection attempts were made five times within 30 s. The detection method is by looking for a specific "client unknown" string in the logs. In Fig. 14, this message is shown after an unsuccessful connection to the broker due to invalid credentials. As these connections do not meet the broker's authentication requirements, they are deemed as unauthorised connections. As a result, if the broker receives a continuous stream of unauthorised connections, this might be a sign that an attacker is trying to brute force the password and username. A brute force attack notification will be flagged in the dashboard, as shown in Fig. 15, if more than 5 connection failures are detected in the logs within 60 s.

4.4   Zigbee2MQTT Devices Inactivity Detection

Device inactivity refers to when a device stops communicating or producing updates to a MQTT broker and the device status is unknown. The possible reasons for device inactivity could be due to devices that are operating in idle or inactive mode until a specific function call activates them, or devices that are actually disconnected from the broker due to connectivity issues with the Zigbee dongle, or even faulty devices. Usually, in such situations, MQTT devices have a default keep-alive feature that ensures the connection between the broker and the MQTT device is still connected by sending PINGREQ and PINGRESP packets.

```
{
  "uuid": "f6fa88b6ae6946cc9de8aaf999a62c6f",
  "datetime": "2022-09-05T15:24:27.194538+08:00",
  "classification": "Denial of Service",
  "priority": "High",
  "src": "172.27.67.201",
  "rule_raw": "tcp any -> $SELF src; name: Denial of Service; priority: 3;
   threshold: 100; interval: 10; cooldown: 10",
  "metadata": {
   "first_violation": "2022-09-05T15:24:17.271353+08:00",
   "total_violation": 433,
   "mqtt": {
    "client_id": [
     "mqtt-explorer-ddf55658"
    ],
    "auth": {
     "username": [
      "mqtt-user"
     ],
     "password": []
    },
    "topics": {
     "publish": {},
     "subscribe": {},
     "unsubscribe": {}
    }
   }
  }
}
```

Fig. 11. Denial of service metadata

Fig. 12. Excessive MQTT publish activity alert

However, in Zigbee2MQTT devices, the default functionality does not include a keep-alive feature. Instead, Zigbee2MQTT devices use their own availability feature checks to identify between idle devices and disconnected devices (Figs. 11, 13, 16).

```
{
  "uuid": "2397b1fa00754031ac68cc3a5ae51170",
  "datetime": "2022-08-11T02:44:14.036049+08:00",
  "classification": "Excessive MQTT PUBLISH activity",
  "priority": "Medium",
  "src": "172.16.2.82",
  "rule_raw": "mqtt any -> $SELF src; name: Excessive MQTT PUBLISH activity;
   priority: 2; threshold: 20; interval: 5; msg_type: publish",
  "metadata": {
   "first_violation": "2022-08-11T02:44:10.176617+08:00",
   "total_violation": 20,
   "mqtt": {
    "client_id": [
     "ESP32_99C490"
    ],
    "auth": {
     "username": [
      "mqtt-user"
     ],
     "password": []
    },
    "topics": {
     "publish": {
      "smx/device/051001006/single_ts/20220812/151001006Z1 (QOS: 2)": 2,
      "smx/device/051001006/position (QOS: 2)": 9,
      "\"dst\":false, (QOS: 2)": 5,
      "smx/device/051001006/sync_list (QOS: 2)": 4,
      "smx/device/051001006/single_ts/20220812/251001006Z1 (QOS: 2)": 2
     },
     "subscribe": {},
     "unsubscribe": {}
    }
   }
  }
}
```

Fig. 13. Excessive MQTT publish activity metadata

```
1662361168: Client mqtt-explorer-ddf55658 disconnected.
1662362576: Saving in-memory database to /data//mosquitto.db.
1662363001: New connection from 172.27.67.201:54772 on port 1883.
error: received null username or password for unpwd check
1662363001: Client <unknown> disconnected, not authorised.
1662363004: New connection from 172.27.67.201:54773 on port 1883.
error: received null username or password for unpwd check
1662363004: Client <unknown> disconnected, not authorised.
1662363004: New connection from 172.27.67.201:54774 on port 1883.
error: received null username or password for unpwd check
1662363004: Client <unknown> disconnected, not authorised.
1662363005: New connection from 172.27.67.201:54775 on port 1883.
error: received null username or password for unpwd check
1662363005: Client <unknown> disconnected, not authorised.
1662363006: New connection from 172.27.67.201:54776 on port 1883.
error: received null username or password for unpwd check
1662363006: Client <unknown> disconnected, not authorised.
1662363006: New connection from 172.27.67.201:54777 on port 1883.
error: received null username or password for unpwd check
1662363006: Client <unknown> disconnected, not authorised.
1662363007: New connection from 172.27.67.201:54778 on port 1883.
error: received null username or password for unpwd check
```

Fig. 14. Unauthorised connection requests in MQTT log

Date/Time	.	Priority	Classification	.	Source	Action
05 Sep 2022 15:30:06 (+08:00)		High	Brute Force (Auth)		172.27.67.201	Acknowledge Raw Details

Fig. 15. Brute force attack alert

```
{
  "uuid": "1572b51303214dd4bf30d3b2499a366c",
  "datetime": "2022-09-05T15:30:06.250113+08:00",
  "classification": "Brute Force (Auth)",
  "priority": "High",
  "src": "172.27.67.201",
  "rule_raw": "mqtt $SELF -> any dst; name: Brute Force (Auth);
   priority: 3; threshold: 5; interval: 60; msg_type: connack; retcode: 5",
  "metadata": {
   "first_violation": "2022-09-05T15:30:01.958344+08:00",
   "total_violation": 5,
   "mqtt": {
    "client_id": [
     "mqtt-explorer-ddf55658",
     "mqttx_88f6220f"
    ],
    "auth": {
     "username": [
      "mqtt-user"
     ],
     "password": []
    },
    "topics": {
     "publish": {},
     "subscribe": {},
     "unsubscribe": {}
    }
   }
  }
}
```

Fig. 16. Metadata of brute force attack

The detection is done by leveraging the availability feature of Zigbee2MQTT and monitoring the MQTT topic used by the device to communicate with Zig-bee2MQTT as a fallback. A list of connected devices and their information is retrieved by subscribing to the topic "[zigbee2mqtt]/bridge/devices". In Zig-bee2MQTT, the availability feature checks for a response when reading "zclVer-sion" from the "genBasic" cluster. A fallback mechanism is used if the availability feature is disabled, by subscribing to the device's MQTT topic and monitoring its last publish activity and the device is considered inactive if the topic remains quiet after a set period of time. As shown in Fig. 17, the Zigbee2MQTT device inactivity notification is triggered if the device does not respond to ping and no MQTT activity detected in the last 600 s (Fig. 18).

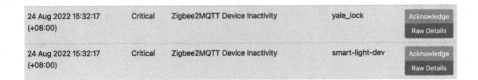

| 24 Aug 2022 15:32:17 (+08:00) | Critical | Zigbee2MQTT Device Inactivity | yale_lock | Acknowledge / Raw Details |
| 24 Aug 2022 15:32:17 (+08:00) | Critical | Zigbee2MQTT Device Inactivity | smart-light-dev | Acknowledge / Raw Details |

Fig. 17. Device inactivity detection

```
{
  "uuid": "55f62c9aa36a40d584a225e8ea6d8bb5",
  "datetime": "2022-08-24T15:32:17.261909+08:00",
  "classification": "Zigbee2MQTT Device Inactivity",
  "priority": "Critical",
  "src": "yale_lock",
  "rule_raw": "Device not responding to Zigbee2MQTT ping and
              no MQTT activity detected in the last 600 second(s)",
  "metadata": {
    "zigbee2mqtt_device_topic": "zigbee2mqtt/yale_lock",
    "friendly_name": "yale_lock",
    "ieee_address": "0x000d6f0010c9a6bc",
    "definition": {
      "description": "Assure lock",
      "model": "YRD226HA2619",
      "supports_ota": false,
      "vendor": "Yale"
    },
    "last_mqtt_activity": "2022-08-24T15:22:16.486078+08:00",
    "last_ping_activity": null
  }
}
```

Fig. 18. Metadata of device inactivity

4.5 Real-Time Detection Experiment

As per the mentioned experiments conducted above, this experiment for the real-time notification was conducted to benchmark if the proposed framework is reliable for use from the point of attack detection to notification of attacks in the alerts panel by utilizing a standardised benchmark suite to evaluate the experiment. The results are summarized as the following Table 1:

Table 1. Attack detection experiment results

Experiment results				
Attack type	Shortest delay timing	Longest delay timing	Mean delay timing	Number of attempts
Unauthorised Subscription Detection	1 ms	12 ms	6.1 ms	20
Denial-of-Service Attack Detection	1 ms	7 ms	2.85 ms	20
Brute Force Attack Detection	1 ms	9 ms	3.75 ms	20

5 Conclusion and Future Work

To conclude, this paper proposes a possible way to collect MQTT traffic for forensic investigation and analysis. We utilized the existing building management infrastructure and collected real-life MQTT communication for forensic analysis and analysis. Our experiment shows that it is possible to find out cyber-attacks from both MQTT traffic and MQTT logs.

For future work, we are planning to train a machine learning model for cyber-attacks detection. Hence we are going to collect a large MQTT communication dataset for further studies. Since the dataset contains actual BMS traffic, it is valuable to other researchers who would like to study the behavior of BMS communication. We are planning to release the BMS MQTT communication dataset in the coming future.

References

1. Vaccari, I., Chiola, G., Aiello, M., Mongelli, M., Cambiaso, E.: MQTTset, a new dataset for machine learning techniques on MQTT. Sensors **20**(22), 6578 (2020)
2. Yang, Z., Zhou, Q., Lei, L., Zheng, K., Xiang, W.: An IoT-cloud based wearable ECG monitoring system for smart healthcare. J. Med. Syst. **40**(12), 1–11 (2016)
3. Cornel-Cristian, A., Gabriel, T., Arhip-Calin, M., Zamfirescu, A.: Smart home automation with MQTT. In: 2019 54th International Universities Power Engineering Conference (UPEC), pp. 1–5. IEEE (2019)
4. Tang, K., Wang, Y., Liu, H., Sheng, Y., Wang, X., Wei, Z.: Design and implementation of push notification system based on the MQTT protocol. In: 2013 International Conference on Information Science and Computer Applications (ISCA 2013), pp. 116–119. Atlantis Press (2013)
5. Pooja, S., Uday, D., Nagesh, U., Talekar, S.G.: Application of MQTT protocol for real time weather monitoring and precision farming. In: 2017 International Conference on Electrical, Electronics, Communication, Computer, and Optimization Techniques (ICEECCOT), pp. 1–6. IEEE (2017)
6. Atmoko, R., Riantini, R., Hasin, M.: IoT real time data acquisition using MQTT protocol. J. Phys.: Conf. Ser. **853**(1), 012003 (2017)
7. Chen, F., Huo, Y., Zhu, J., Fan, D.: A review on the study on MQTT security challenge. In: 2020 IEEE International Conference on Smart Cloud (SmartCloud), pp. 128–133. IEEE (2020)
8. Andy, S., Rahardjo, B., Hanindhito, B.: Attack scenarios and security analysis of MQTT communication protocol in IoT system. In: 2017 4th International Conference on Electrical Engineering, Computer Science and Informatics (EECSI), pp. 1–6. IEEE (2017)
9. Wong, H., Luo, T.: Man-in-the-middle attacks on MQTT-based IoT using BERT based adversarial message generation. In: KDD 2020 AIoT Workshop (2020)
10. Vaccari, I., Aiello, M., Cambiaso, E.: SlowTT: a slow denial of service against IoT networks. Information **11**(9), 452 (2020)
11. Budiana, M.S., Negara, R.M., Irawan, A.I., Larasati, H.T.: Advanced detection denial of service attack in the internet of things network based on MQTT protocol using fuzzy logic. Register: J. Ilmiah Teknol. Sist. Inform. **7**(2), 95–106 (2021)

12. Alaiz-Moreton, H., Aveleira-Mata, J., Ondicol-Garcia, J., Muñoz-Castañeda, A.L., García, I., Benavides, C.: Multiclass classification procedure for detecting attacks on MQTT-IoT protocol. Complexity **2019** (2019)
13. Ciklabakkal, E., Donmez, A., Erdemir, M., Suren, E., Yilmaz, M.K., Angin, P.: Artemis: an intrusion detection system for MQTT attacks in internet of things. In: 2019 38th Symposium on Reliable Distributed Systems (SRDS), pp. 369–3692. IEEE (2019)
14. Hindy, H., Bayne, E., Bures, M., Atkinson, R., Tachtatzis, C., Bellekens, X.: Machine learning based IoT intrusion detection system: an MQTT case study (MQTT-IoT-IDS2020 dataset). In: Ghita, B., Shiaeles, S. (eds.) INC 2020. LNNS, vol. 180, pp. 73–84. Springer, Cham (2021). https://doi.org/10.1007/978-3-030-64758-2_6
15. Chunduri, N.V.H., Mohan, A.K.: A forensic analysis on the availability of MQTT network traffic. In: Thampi, S.M., Wang, G., Rawat, D.B., Ko, R., Fan, C.-I. (eds.) SSCC 2020. CCIS, vol. 1364, pp. 262–274. Springer, Singapore (2021). https://doi.org/10.1007/978-981-16-0422-5_19
16. Anthraper, J.J., Kotak, J.: Security, privacy and forensic concern of MQTT protocol. In: Proceedings of International Conference on Sustainable Computing in Science, Technology and Management (SUSCOM). Amity University Rajasthan, Jaipur (2019)
17. Dinculeană, D., Cheng, X.: Vulnerabilities and limitations of MQTT protocol used between IoT devices. Appl. Sci. **9**(5), 848 (2019)
18. Husnain, M., et al.: Preventing MQTT vulnerabilities using IoT-enabled intrusion detection system. Sensors **22**(2), 567 (2022)
19. Introduction | Socket. IO. https://socket.io/docs/v4/
20. Yara, A.: Preventing vulnerabilities and MitigatingAttacks on the MQTT protocol (2020)
21. Syed, N.F., Baig, Z., Ibrahim, A., Valli, C.: Denial of service attack detection through machine learning for the IoT. J. Inf. Telecommun. **4**(4), 482–503 (2020)
22. Buccafurri, F., De Angelis, V., Nardone, R.: Securing MQTT by blockchain-based OTP authentication. Sensors **20**(7), 2002 (2020)
23. Agazzi, A.E.: Smart home, security concerns of IoT. arXiv preprint arXiv:2007.02628 (2020)

IoT Malicious Traffic Detection Based on FSKDE and Federated DIOT-Pysyft

Ke Zhang[1] , Guanghua Zhang[1(✉)] , Zhenguo Chen[2] , and Xiaojun Zuo[3]

[1] School of Information Science and Engineering, Hebei University of Science and Technology, Shijiazhuang 050018, China
zhanggh@hebust.edu.cn

[2] Hebei IoT Monitoring Engineering Technology Research Center, North China Institute of Science and Technology, Langfang 065201, China

[3] State Grid Hebei Electric Power Research Institute, Shijiazhuang 050021, China

Abstract. In order to solve the limitations of existing malicious traffic detection methods in the Internet of Things (IoT) environment, such as resources, heterogeneous devices, scarce traffic, and dynamic threats, this paper proposes the Feature Selection based on Kernel Density Estimation (FSKDE) and the federated learning method Detection Internet of Things based on Pysyft (DIOT-Pysyft). First, IoT devices perform data preprocessing operations on the collected network traffic data; Second, the FSKDE is used to calculate the probability density of each column of features and selects features according to a preset abnormal threshold; Third, the DIOT-Pysyft is build. It initializes the server that the federated convolutional neural network (CNN) is sent to the IoT devices. The IoT devices use the processed data to train the federated CNN and send them to server secretly. After that, the improved FedAvg algorithm is used to average the gradient of the federated CNN model, which for training and transmitting the encrypted and averaged gradient to the server to build a new global model to participate in the next round of training. Finally, this paper uses the UNSW-NB15 dataset to verify the proposed method for detecting malicious traffic in the IoT environment. The experimental results show that the identification accuracy of the IoT malicious traffic detection based on FSKDE and federated DIOT-Pysyft reaches 91.78%, which can detect potential malicious traffic in the IoT environment. The improved FedAvg method further protects the privacy and security of IoT data and ensures the accuracy while protecting the data.

Keywords: IoT · FSKDE · Federated Learning · DIOT-Pysyft · Malicious Traffic Detection

1 Introduction

With the continuous emergence of application scenarios such as smart homes, smart medical care, smart transportation, and smart cities, Internet of Things (IoT) devices and their technologies have brought convenience to human life. However, a large number of IoT devices and cloud servers are directly exposed to the Internet at present. If

S. Goel et al. (Eds.): ICDF2C 2022, LNICST 508, pp. 203–221, 2023.
https://doi.org/10.1007/978-3-031-36574-4_12

it is exploited, it will lead to security risks such as equipment loss of control, user privacy leakage, cloud server data theft, etc., and even have a serious impact on the basic communication network. The security challenges of the IoT have not been considered in-depth, resulting that the IoT environment has always been the hardest hit area for various vulnerability attacks [1]. Various security threats in the IoT emerge in an endless stream. The botnet malware controlled 100,000 IoT devices to launch Distributed Denial of Service (DDoS) attacks on the domain name servers managed by Dyn, which directly caused the complete paralysis of most of the Internet in the United States [2]. The existence of 250 vulnerabilities in IoT devices, including open ports, outdated firmware, and unencrypted transmission of sensitive data [3, 4] results in the lack of key security functions of IoT. Once the IoT devices with vulnerabilities enter the network, which can be easily exploited by attackers to launch Denial of Service (DoS) attacks. Therefore, malicious traffic detection for attack behaviors generated by IoT devices can mitigate network security risks.

Most of the detection methods based on malicious traffic are designed for servers or personal computers with sufficient resources. There are relatively few abnormal traffic detection methods and technologies for the characteristics of the IoT. Compared with the traditional Internet, the IoT has the following characteristics [5]: 1) Resources are limited. The functions of IoT devices are limited, so the available memory and computing resources are insufficient. 2) The devices are heterogeneous. There are many IoT devices, the behaviors of different IoT devices are very diverse, the traffic patterns in different time periods are quite different, so the attacks on different devices are also different. 3) Communication traffic is scarce. Compared to the Internet, some IoT devices generate less traffic which often triggered by infrequent user interactions. 4) Dynamic threats increase. New IoT devices are released every day with security vulnerabilities, and attackers develop attacks against these devices at the same high rate. Threats targeting IoT devices are increasing dynamically. The above characteristics of IoT devices make traditional Internet-based intrusion detection methods not directly applicable to the IoT, which makes IoT terminal devices more vulnerable to malware attacks.

Considering the above problems, this paper proposes the Feature Selection based on Kernel Density Estimation (FSKDE) and federated learning method Detection Internet of Things based on Pysyft (DIOT-Pysyft) to detect IoT malicious traffic. The main contributions of this method are:

– A feature selection method based on FSKDE is proposed. This method considers the problem of limited memory and computing resources when the model is calculated in IoT devices, so a feature selection method based on FSKDE is proposed to select the optimal subset of features. The algorithm uses the Gaussian kernel density estimation method without the need for the distribution of the data samples to be assumed in advance. The features that contribute more to the classification are initially screened.
– A traffic detection method based on federated DIOT-Pysyft is proposed, which utilizes the characteristics of federated learning and secure multi-party computation, uses the dataset of IoT devices to train the local federated convolutional neural network (CNN) model, and encrypts the gradient of the model during training with the improved FedAvg algorithm after the aggregation is averaged, it is uploaded to the server to

update the model, and it participates in the next round of training. This method realizes the detection of malicious traffic and protects the privacy of user data.

– Combined with the feature selection method based on FSKDE and the traffic detection method based on federated DIOT-Pysyft, the UNSW-NB15 dataset is multi-classified for malicious traffic, the federated CNN method is used for model training, and the performance and time of different algorithms is compared. The method proposed in this paper are evaluated.

2 Related Work

Most of the detection methods currently don't take into account the characteristics of the IoT. Literature [6] used different Back Propagation (BP) neural networks on the gateway to establish different anomaly detection models for different types of IoT devices, but this strategy increased the calculation and storage of the gateway. It was not suitable for the application environment of the home IoT; Literature [7] proposed a lightweight detection method for DDoS malicious traffic, which effectively solved the problem of limited resources of IoT devices, but did not consider the heterogeneity between devices; In addition, most of the current experiments use public network traffic data sets, and some of the data are collected in the Internet environment, so the amount of traffic is huge. But the problem of the small amount of actual IoT traffic is not considered. Signature-based detection methods match specific patterns or strings in known attacks or threats to detect malicious traffic. By building a knowledge base to identify known threats in the network environment, unknown attacks and potential threats cannot be detected.

In recent years, Machine Learning (ML) and Deep Learning (DL) technologies have been widely used in IoT scenarios to mitigate malicious attacks, and related research has also proposed various improved algorithms to improve the detection ability of Intrusion Detection Systems (IDS). The experiments show that ML and DL have great advantages in enhancing the accuracy of IDS. Reference [8] proposed a mirai botnet attack detection method based on a bidirectional long memory Recurrent Neural Network (RNN). Simulation experiments showed that it had achieved good experimental results, but the model was too complex and was not suitable for the IoT network environment with insufficient computing and storage resources. Reference [7] deployed the abnormal traffic detection model on the IoT gateway, which can prevent network attacks to the greatest extent. Reference [9] proposed an IoT anomaly detection algorithm, which was effective and sensitive against DoS. It can quickly detect high-traffic situations, and it can also handle abnormal problems caused by system failures and human operations, but this method relied on serial communication protocols and the network attacks detected were relatively simple. Reference [10] proposed a security scheme by analyzing the architecture of the IoT layer and proposed a security measure against the vulnerabilities existing in other network layers.

Although ML and DL can improve the detection performance of IDS, the training of the model needs to upload the data from the client to the server. The data is managed centrally. It is difficult to apply to distributed network traffic data from different devices through a single entity. In the IoT environment, this entity can access the communication data and network traffic of different devices participating in the training process, which may have the problem of privacy leakage [11]. Therefore, this paper adopts a more secure data management scheme, federated learning, to alleviate the problems caused by malicious traffic in the IoT environment.

Federated learning (FL) was proposed in 2016 [12]. In federated learning, the client does not share its data, but jointly trains the model under the coordination of the central server. The client only needs to transmit encrypted gradient-related data, and use multi-source data to collaborate and train a unified model [13], which can keep the training data decentralized. In recent years, the development of federated learning-based intrusion detection systems in IoT scenarios has attracted more and more researchers' interest [14–16]. Reference [17] proposed a federated learning-based framework that covered Multilayer Perceptron (MLP) and Auto-Encoders (AE) to detect network attacks affecting IoT devices in a way that protected data privacy, but it can only perform binary classification, dividing traffic into normal traffic and malicious traffic, while there was no further distinction between the types of malicious traffic. Reference [18] proposed a cloud intrusion detection scheme based on blockchain federated learning. The proposed method was based on unrealistic data distribution, inappropriate datasets, and unsuitable settings among the various parties. Reference [19] discussed the challenges and future development directions of federated learning-based intrusion detection systems but did not provide experiments and evaluation results to support their contributions.

This paper proposes an IoT malicious traffic detection method based on FSKDE and federated DIOT-Pysyft. First, a feature selection method based on FSKDE is proposed to reduce redundant features on IoT devices, find optimal feature subsets, and reduce the impact of IoT resource consumption and irrelevant features on malicious traffic detection performance during model training. The traffic detection based on federated DIOT-Pysyft enables IoT devices to use local datasets to train models separately, and use the improved FedAvg algorithm to encrypt and aggregate the federated gradients generated during training. Then, the gradient is uploaded to the server to update the model which can be added to the next round of training. When the model converges, the training end. The method alleviates the problem of inaccurate identification caused by insufficient traffic of some IoT devices and realizes multi-classification by combining the knowledge learned from each IoT device. Finally, combining the FSKDE-based feature selection method and the federated DIOT-Pysyft-based traffic detection method, the experiments are carried out on the UNSW-NB15 dataset. The experimental results show that the proposed method not only guarantees accuracy but also pays attention to protecting the privacy of user data. In addition, it can alleviate the problems existing in traditional methods such as device heterogeneity, and less communication traffic, and can effectively detect unknown attacks.

3 The IoT Malicious Traffic Detection Based on FSKDE and Federated DIOT-Pysyft

FSKDE is a feature selection algorithm based on gaussian kernel density estimation, and DIOT-Pysyft is a federated learning-based IoT malicious traffic detection method, as shown in Fig. 1. First, IoT devices perform data preprocessing operations on their respective network traffic data. Then, FSKDE is used to calculate the probability density of each column of features, and feature selection is performed according to a pre-set anomaly threshold to reduce computing and communication resources in federated learning training. Second, build the central server as a model aggregator, the IoT devices receive the federated CNN model transferred by the server, train the model by using the federated CNN and local data, encrypt the parameter weights of the trained model, and transmit them to the server. The aggregator uses the FedAvg aggregation algorithm to combine all parameter weights to build a new global model to participate in the next round of training. Finally, this paper uses the UNSW-NB15 dataset to perform the IoT malicious traffic detection based on FSKDE and federated DIOT-Pysyft. The method is verified to realize the identification of various malicious traffic in the IoT environment and protect the privacy of users.

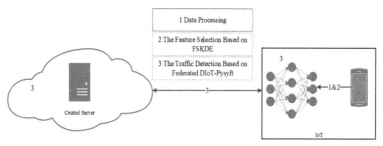

Fig. 1. The framework of IoT malicious traffic detection based on FSKDE and federated DIOT-Pysyft

The system architecture used in this solution is divided into two subsystems: the central server-side and the IoT client side.

Each client contains multiple IoT devices. For simplicity, only one smart device is used for the architecture and experiments. The client is responsible for collecting traffic data from IoT devices, which uses port mirroring through the switch connecting the IoT devices, as described in [20]. Firstly, because the collected data is unstructured, it cannot be used directly, and the data needs to be structured; secondly, in the data preprocessing part, missing values and data normalization need to be processed. Then, considering the practical problem of insufficient malicious traffic resources in the IoT environment, a feature selection algorithm based on gaussian kernel density estimation (Feature Selection Based on Kernel Density Estimation, FSKDE) is proposed. In the network traffic data, the features that contribute prominently to malicious traffic detection are screened out according to the FSKDE, and the optimal subset is selected to reduce the dimension of the sample features.

On the central server-side, the traffic detection method based on federated DIOT-Pysyft transmits the federated CNN model to the client to be trained on the server-side. After the client receives the model, it's trained for one or more rounds using local standardized data. Then, the encrypted model gradients upload to the server after training. The server aggregates the model gradients from each client using improved FedAvg to update the model parameters, which completes an iterative process of the model. Finally, When obtaining the optimal model parameters after several iterations, the server sends the optimized model to the client for final malicious traffic detection. The local training method of this method can speed up the detection time. In addition, because the optimized model aggregates the parameters of all training data from multiple IoT devices, knowledge sharing is realized. The devices participating in the training can detect the malicious traffic categories owned by different participants in a private way.

3.1 Data Preprocessing

The quality of the data determines the prediction and generalization ability of the model, as does the actual network traffic data. The UNSW-NB15 dataset used in this paper contains missing values, invalid values, categorical and numerical features. The quantitative units are also different. In order to ensure that the accuracy of the model is not affected, this paper preprocesses the data before training.

(1) **Handling of missing and invalid values:** The UNSW-NB15 dataset contains a small amount of missing data (e.g. np.nan). For a small number of missing values, the strategy of directly deleting the row of data is adopted. For the categorical type of the 'service' column, the data contains 57% of invalid data '-'. The method of mode filling will make the data out of reality and the method of predicting using the correlation between each feature will increase computational cost. Therefore, this paper directly deletes the column data containing '-'.

(2) **Data normalization:** The advantage of data normalization is that it can eliminate the differences between data of different dimensions and make the data of different dimensions comparable after normalization. Each feature in the UNSW-NB15 dataset has different value ranges. To ensure the reliability of the training results, each feature must be normalized to the [0, 1] range. This paper uses the Min-Max Normalization method to normalize the data, as shown in Eq. (1).

$$x'_{ij} = \frac{x_{ij} - x_{\min}}{x_{\max} - x_{\min}} \tag{1}$$

Among them, x_{ij} is the original data, $x_{\min}$ is the minimum value of the eigenvalues of the column, $x_{\max}$ is the maximum value of the eigenvalues of the column, and x'_{ij} is the normalized result.

(3) **Categorical feature processing:** For the 'state' feature in the UNSW-NB15 dataset, its value is limited to ['FIN', 'INT', 'CON', 'REQ', 'ACC', 'CLO', 'RST'], this paper adopts the form of one-hot encoding. For the 'proto' feature, the corresponding value of its variables is too much, this paper adopts the weight of evidence. This method considers the relationship between the independent variable and the target, which is the natural logarithm of the odds ratio in mathematics. By calculating the WOE value of 'proto', the 'proto' column can be replaced by the WOE.

3.2 The Feature Selection Based on FSKDE

Considering the limited computing and communication resources of IoT devices, this paper proposes a feature selection method based on FSKDE. Kernel density estimation (KDE), as a non-parametric estimation method in statistics, is very suitable for estimating the probability of unknown sample sets. Compared with parameter estimation, the advantage of the KDE method is that it does not need to assume the distribution model of the data samples in advance. The test sample set is used for density estimation of unknown probabilities.

Assuming that there are n samples independently distributed in the data sample set $\{X \mid x_1, x_2, \cdots, x_n\}$, and the probability density function of sample $x_i \in X$ is $f(x_i)$, the kernel density estimation formula is shown in Eq. (2):

$$f_h(x_i) = \frac{1}{n} \sum_{j=1}^{n} K_h(x_i - x_j) = \frac{1}{nh} \sum_{j=1}^{n} K\left(\frac{x_i - x_j}{h}\right) \tag{2}$$

Among them, $K(\cdot)$ is the kernel function, which usually has symmetry and satisfies $\int K(x_i)dx = 1$; the parameter h is the bandwidth of the kernel function, which is used to balance the deviation and variance of the kernel density estimation. This paper uses the kernel parameter estimation method proposed in the literature [20] to estimate h. In addition, there are many options for the kernel function. In theory, all smooth peak functions can be used as the kernel function for kernel density estimation. This paper uses the gaussian function as the kernel function.

Assuming that the set of normal traffic samples in the training set is $R^{n_1 \times m}$, n_1 is the number of samples, m is the sample dimension. The sample $x_i \in R^{n_1 \times m}$ represents the $i - th$ sample of $R^{n_1 \times m}$, let $x_i = \{x_i^1, x_i^2, \cdots, x_i^d, \cdots, x_i^m\}$, then x_i^d represents the value of the $d - th$ dimension feature x_i, $a^d = \{x_1^d, x_2^d, \cdots, x_{n_1}^d\}$ denotes the all feature of the $d - th$ dimension, then the set of all eigenvalues can be expressed as $A = \{a^1, a^2, \cdots, a^d, \cdots, a^m\}$. When $a^d \in A$, using the gaussian kernel density estimation method to train, the probability density function f^d corresponding to the eigenvalues of the $d - th$ dimension features of all samples in $R^{n_1 \times m}$ can be obtained, and the probability density function corresponding to the eigenvalues of the $d - th$ dimension features in the sample $x_i \in R^{n_1 \times m}$ is $f^d(x_i^d)$. The value $f^d(x_i^d)$ is larger, the more it can show that x_i^d is more in line with the eigenvalue distribution of the $d - th$ dimension feature in normal traffic samples. Based on the above research, this paper proposes the following feature selection method based on FSKDE, and its pseudocode is shown in Algorithm 1.

Algorithm 1. The feature selection based on FSKDE-normal traffic sample set

Input:

   $R^{n_1 \times m}$: Normal traffic sample sets

Output:

   F : The probability density function of all normal traffic sample features is saved in F

   $F(A)$: Save the probability density of all normal sample eigenvalues in $F(A)$

1: $A \leftarrow (R^{n_1 \times m})^T$ // Each row in A represents a feature

2: **For** a^d in A **do**

3:     Use Eq. (1) to calculate f^d // Calculate the probability density function corresponding to the d-dimensional eigenvalue

4:     $F \leftarrow f^d$

5: **End For**

6: **For** a^d in A **do**

7:     **For** x_i^d in a^d **do**

8:         $f^d(a^d) \leftarrow f^d(x_i^d)$

9:     **End For**

10:     $F(A) \leftarrow f^d(a^d)$

11: **End For**

12: **Return** F , $F(A)$

The more features of the sample, the greater the amount of computation required, which will increase the computational overhead of IoT devices. In addition, not all features contribute to malicious traffic detection, so this paper adopts the FSKDE method for feature selection. First, according to the kernel density estimation formula, each feature column is traversed. we calculate the probability density function of the feature F, bring the eigenvalues belonging to the feature in turn, and calculate the probability density $f^d(x_i^d)$ of the eigenvalues of each feature. The probability density set $f^d(a^d)$ of the feature is obtained. Then, this paper sorts the results $F(A)$ obtained by Algorithm 1 in ascending order, and the sorting result is recorded as $sort(f^d(a^d))$. Pick the value t^d at a percentage of τ locations from $sort(f^d(a^d))$ as the filter threshold for the $d - th$ dimension feature. τ is an empirical parameter, which is usually taken $\tau = 0.1\%$. When the eigenvalue probability density of the $d - th$ dimensional feature of the sample x_j is $f^d(x_j^d) < t^d$, it means that the eigenvalues of the $d - th$ dimensional feature don't match the eigenvalue distribution of normal traffic samples, and the more likely it is malicious traffic data. Therefore, the screening threshold of all features is set as T, and the set is expressed as $T = \{t^1, t^2, \cdots, t^d, \cdots, t^m\}$.

Finally, the eigenvalues of each dimension feature of all samples in the malicious sample set $R'^{n_2 \times m}$ in the training set are brought into F for probability density calculation to obtain $f^d(x_i^d)$, the number of $f^d(x_i^d) < t^d$ in the $d - th$ dimension is counted as z^d. z^d represents the number of abnormal data detected by the feature value of the $d - th$ dimension feature. The number of abnormal data of m dimensional eigenvalues is recorded as $Z = \{z^1, z^2, \cdots, z^d, \cdots z^m\}$. Assuming that the number of malicious samples in the training set is n_2, when $\frac{z^d}{n_2} \geq \alpha$, it means that the $d - th$ dimension feature

feature_d is added to the selected feature subset. All features are traversed, where α is the set threshold, usually 0.8. Its pseudocode is shown in Algorithm 2.

Algorithm 2. The feature selection based on FSKDE-malicious traffic sample set

Input:

F : The probability density function of all normal traffic sample features is saved in F

$F(A)$: Save the probability density of all normal sample eigenvalues in $F(A)$

$R^{'n_2 \times m}$: Normal traffic sample sets

Output:

S : Feature subsets using FSKDE

1: **For** $f^d(a^d)$ in $F(A)$ **do** // Calculate the filter threshold for each dimension of data

2:   $t^d \leftarrow \tau \times sort(f^d(a^d))$

3: **End For**

4: $A' \leftarrow (R^{'n_2 \times m})^T$

5: $Z = [0,0,\cdots,0]_{1\times m}$

6: **For** $a^{'d}$ in A' **do**

7:   **For** x_i^d in $a^{'d}$ **do**

8:     **If** $f^d(x_i^d) < t^d$ **then**

9:       $z^d = z^d + 1$

10:    **End If**

11:   **End For**

12: **End For**

13: **For** z^d in Z **do** //select features

14:   **If** $\dfrac{z^d}{n_2} \geq \alpha$ **then**

15:     $S \leftarrow feature_d$

16:   **End If**

17: **End For**

18: **Return** S

3.3 The Traffic Detection Based on Federated DIOT-Pysyft

With the rapid growth of IoT-connected devices, traditional malicious traffic detection methods are prone to introduce a single point of failure and compromise data privacy, which has a negative impact on the development of new industries such as smart homes and smart healthcare. Considering the resource, communication, and privacy security issues of IoT devices, this paper proposes an IoT traffic detection method based on federated DIOT-Pysyft. The method performs local training on the detection model to maintain data privacy. At the same time, the trained gradient encryption is uploaded to the server to update the model, and the improved detection model is shared with the participating devices, which can benefit from the knowledge of the participants. The architecture of this solution is shown in Fig. 2 below, which describes the architecture of the client and the interaction with the server after data collection. IoT data preprocessing, FSKDE-based feature selection, and model training and evaluation are all done on the client-side, and the server participates in model gradient aggregation and model update, acting as a model aggregator.

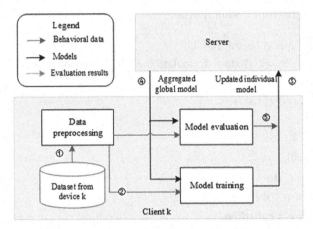

Fig. 2. Detailed view of client architecture in training evaluation

The DIOT-Pysyft Model Training

This solution consists of a federated DIOT-Pysyft learning system composed of a server and N IoT devices, and uses the FedAvg algorithm to jointly train a global model. Considering that the existing federated learning has many participants and is widely distributed, the federated learning scheme discussed in this paper is limited to the IoT network scenario. Assuming that each IoT device client $k \in N$ has a local dataset D_k, for any data sample $\{x_k, y_k\}$, x_k represents the input of the model, the learning task of the device is to find a model parameter w to describe y_k, and minimize the loss function $f_k(w)$ of the model. The loss function is used to evaluate the gap between the model prediction results and the real situation. The smaller the gap, the better the model. This paper uses $|D_i|$ to denote the dataset size of the $i - th$ device and defines the total size of the data involved in learning by $D = \sum_{i=1}^{N} D_i$. Therefore, the loss function of the $i - th$ terminal device on its dataset is defined as Eq. (3):

$$F_i(w) = \frac{1}{|D_i|} \sum_{j \in D_i} f_j(w) \tag{3}$$

According to the FedAvg algorithm, the server's global loss function can be defined as Eq. (4):

$$F(w) = \sum_{i=1}^{N} \frac{D_i}{D} F_i(w) \tag{4}$$

When DIOT-Pysyft starts training, the server initializes a global model parameter, and the terminal device optimizes this parameter. The convergence of the loss function is achieved after T global iterations. Similarly, the terminal device i needs to find the best model parameters through multiple rounds of local training on its local dataset D_i in each global iteration process, as shown in Eq. (5):

$$w_i^{(t)} = \arg \min F(w) \tag{5}$$

Due to the inherent complexity of most machine learning models, formula (5) is usually solved using Stochastic Gradient Descent (SGD) [21]. The optimal local update parameters $w_i^{(t)}$ trained on the local dataset by these terminal devices need to be uploaded to the server to participate in global aggregation. According to the FedAvg algorithm, the global aggregation process can be expressed as Eq. (6):

$$w^{(t+1)} = \sum_{i=1}^{N} \frac{D_i}{D} w_i^{(t)} \tag{6}$$

The goal of global aggregation is to minimize the loss function in formula (4), and then the server broadcasts $w^{(t+1)}$ to all end devices as the global model parameters for the next iteration. After many global iterations, the global model converges and a stable global model accuracy is finally obtained.

Encrypted Transmission of Gradients
During federated learning with DIOT-Pysyft, the server-side aggregates the gradients of the models of multiple clients, then updates the global model, and sends it to these clients. This process iterates again until the model converges to some extent. The gradient of the model update is essentially a function, which is calculated based on the initial model and local data. So this function is related to the local data to a certain extent. Although it is difficult to calculate the local data through the gradient, for the training model is a simple model, such as logistic regression. The relationship between the gradient and the local data is closely related, the local data can be obtained by solving the equations to solve the unknowns. For complex models, the optimization method of machine learning can be used to reverse, an approximate solution can be obtained from the optimization. An accurate result may not be obtained, but a roughly similar result can be obtained. In essence, the original data can still be inferred. Therefore, this paper proposes to use secure Multi-Party Computation (SMPC) to improve the FedAvg gradient aggregation algorithm to protect this gradient.

The core of SMPC is to realize the collaborative completion of model training and prediction by exchanging information on the premise of protecting that multiple client data doesn't leave the local area. Therefore, this paper uses SMPC to improve the aggregation algorithm FedAvg method to implement secure transfer of gradients.

SMPC does not use public key and private key to encrypt gradient variables, but it splits each value into multiple parts, as shown in Fig. 3, which describes the process of obtaining the average gradient of the gradient data encryption transmission of 3 IoT clients that do not trust each other. The model gradients obtained by training the model according to the local data are W_1, W_2 and W_3. Each IoT device is set with two additional random numbers respectively, and the intermediate data is calculated by the remainder operation of the two random numbers. Each IoT device has only a fraction of the gradient-related data, the corresponding value can only be obtained when the three data participate in the operation at the same time. The final required gradient sum cannot be obtained only through a part of the gradient. Each part of the data operates like a

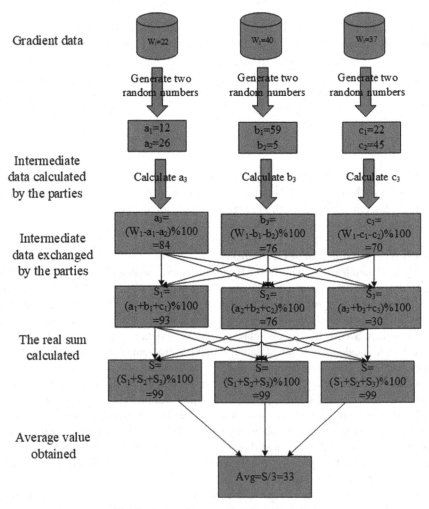

Fig. 3. Encryption process of gradient data

private key, S_1, S_2 and S_3 is the encrypted data of the three devices. SMPC can perform operations on the encrypted data. The operation results are also encrypted values, and the corresponding real values can be obtained by decrypting the operation results.

The SMPC is used to improve FedAvg aggregation algorithm to realize the encryption operation of the gradient in this paper. It does not require a trusted third party to collect the original data from all participating nodes, but only needs to exchange data which is encrypted between each participating IoT device. It is guaranteed that other participating devices cannot reverse the original plaintext data after obtaining the encrypted data, which ensures the privacy of the data of each participating IoT device.

4 Experiment and Result Analysis

4.1 Experimental Design

This paper designs and implements an IoT malicious traffic detection method based on FSKDE and federated DIOT-Pysyft, uses the public dataset UNSW-NB15 [22], which contains 9 malicious traffic generated by attacks and 1 normal traffic. The malicious attack traffic includes Fuzzers, Analysis, Backdoors, DoS, Exploits, Generic, Reconnaissance, Shellcode and Worms. The dataset has a total of 49 features, and the training set and test set have been divided. There are 175,341 records in the training set and 82,332 records in the test set. This paper selects 40% of the data set as the experimental data.

Data loading, processing, training and testing are all done in a virtual machine. The virtual machine uses a Centos7 system with 60G storage space and 4G memory, and the processor is Intel(R) Core(TM) i5-6300HQ CPU @ 2.30 GHz 2.30 GHz, the experiment is implemented based on python3.9 programming, combined with keras, pytorch, pysyft and other libraries, the programming software used is Jupyter Notebook.

4.2 Evaluation Metrics

To evaluate the classification performance of IoT malicious traffic detection based on FSKDE and federated DIOT-Pysyft, four evaluation indicators such as accuracy are defined.

$$Accuracy = \frac{TP + TN}{TP + TN + FP + FN} \tag{7}$$

$$Recall = \frac{TP}{TP + FN} \tag{8}$$

$$Pr\,ecision = \frac{TP}{TP + FP} \tag{9}$$

$$F1 - Score = \frac{2 * Pr\,ecision * Recall}{Pr\,ecision + Recall} \tag{10}$$

where True Positive (TP) represents the number of correctly identified positive samples, True Negative (TN) represents the number of correctly identified negative samples, False

Positive (*FP*) denotes the number of wrongly identified positive samples, False Negative (*FN*) denotes the number of wrongly identified negative samples. The accuracy rate is the percentage of correct prediction results in the total samples; the recall rate is the probability of being predicted to be malicious traffic samples among the samples that are actually malicious traffic; the precision rate is the percentage of all samples that are predicted to be malicious traffic samples that are actually malicious traffic samples; The *F*1 − *Score* considers both the precision rate and the recall rate, so that the two can reach the highest at the same time and achieve a balance.

4.3 Experimental Evaluation

Effectiveness of Feature Selection Method Based on FSKDE

In the first experiment. We evaluate the effectiveness of the feature selection algorithm based on FSKDE proposed in this paper, the performance and time of malicious traffic detection using the FSKDE feature selection method and the feature selection algorithm without FSKDE (noFSKDE) on the CNN model and the MLP model are analyzed for comparison in this paper. As shown in Figs. 4 and 5, the four detection models are the CNN detection model without the FSKDE feature selection algorithm (noFSKDE_CNN), the MLP detection model without the FSKDE feature selection algorithm (noFSKDE_MLP), The CNN detection model (FSKDE_CNN) with the FSKDE feature selection algorithm and the MLP detection model with the FSKDE feature selection algorithm (FSKDE_MLP). The performance comparison is shown in Fig. 4, and the time comparison is shown in Fig. 5:

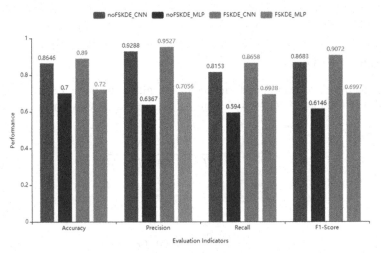

Fig. 4. Performance effectiveness for FSKDE

In terms of performance, the accuracy, precision, recall and F1-score of the noFSKDE_CNN model are 0.8646, 0.9288, 0.8153, and 0.9072 respectively, which are 0.1646, 0.2921, 0.2213, 0.2537 higher than the detection efficiency of the noF-SKDE_MLP model in terms of accuracy, precision, recall, and F1-score respectively. Therefore, this paper concludes that CNN has more advantages than MLP in detecting malicious traffic on the Internet of Things. Compared with the noFSKDE_CNN model, the FSKDE_CNN model has better accuracy, precision, and recall rate. And F1-scores. It improves 0.0254, 0.0239,0.0505, and 0.0389 than noFSKDE_CNN model, while FSKDE_MLP compared with noFSKDE_MLP improves 0.0200, 0.0689, 0.0998, and 0.0851 in accuracy, precision, recall, and F1-score, the results show that the model based on the FSKDE feature selection method proposed in this paper can remove redundant features in the dataset, find the optimal feature subset, and improve the detection indicators of the model.

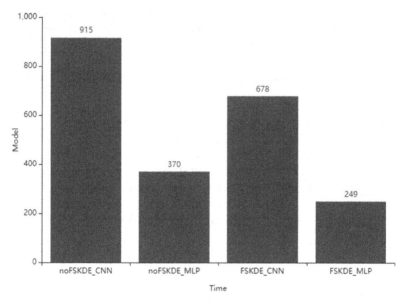

Fig. 5. Time effectiveness for FSKDE

In terms of time, as shown in Fig. 5 above, the FSKDE_CNN model saves 237s in time compared with the noFSKDE_CNN model, and the FSKDE_MLP saves 121s compared to the noFSKDE_MLP. This result shows that the FSKDE-based feature selection method proposed in this paper can reduce the running time of the model. When detecting malicious traffic, it can quickly identify malicious traffic to take effective defense measures. This method reduces the feature dimension, retains important features for malicious traffic detection, and reduces the difficulty of model learning tasks, so the running time is reduced.

In the second experiment, we compare our proposed feature selection approach with other feature selection ones. Table 1 shows the detection accuracy using the FSKDE and other proposed methods such as the greedy algorithm [23] and the CFS-DE [24]. The greedy algorithm makes use of all features and computes the detection accuracy as the initial detection accuracy, then one feature is deleted at each stage as the decremental

Table 1. The detection accuracy of the FSKDE and other feature selection methods

Method	Accuracy
The FSKDE	**0.8900**
The Greedy Algorithm [23]	0.7040
The CFS-DE [24]	0.8730

learning, and the detection accuracy is calculated for each feature removed. Table 1 shows that our proposed feature selection method can obtain 0.0890 accuracy, and the greedy algorithm just reaches to 0.7040, which is 0.186 lower than the FSKDE. The CFS-DE method calculates the variance of each feature and removes features with variance below a threshold to reduce the dimension of the features and search for the best feature subset. This method is usually used for feature selection, but it isn't created for IDS. We can get the accuracy 0.8730, which is lower than our proposed method FSKDE. The results show that the FSKDE method has stronger ability to capture malicious features in the IDS field.

Effectiveness of Traffic Detection Based on Federated DIOT-Pysyft

In order to verify the effectiveness of traffic detection based on federated DIOT-Pysyft, This paper uses federated DIoT_CNN (CNN model with DIOT-Pysyft) algorithm and federated DIoT_DNN (DNN model with DIOT-Pysyft) algorithm to conduct experiments under the federated DIOT-Pysyft system architecture. As shown in Fig. 6 below, the two detection models use the FSKDE feature selection. The experiment uses the federated DIoT_CNN algorithm with FSKDE and uses the federated DIoT_DNN algorithm with FSKDE.

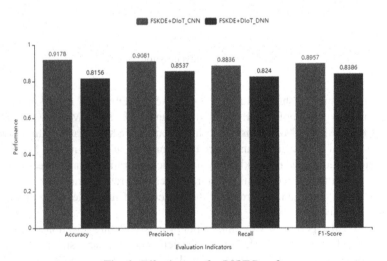

Fig. 6. Effectiveness for DIOT-Pysyft

As can be seen from Fig. 6 above, the accuracy rate of the FSKDE+DIoT_CNN algorithm is 0.9178, the precision rate is 0.9081, the recall rate is 0.8836, and the F1-score is 0.8957. Compared with the federated DIoT_DNN under the DIOT-Pysyft system architecture, the accuracy, precision, recall and F1-score are 0.1022, 0.0544, 0.0596 and 0.0564 higher respectively. The federated DIoT_CNN algorithm has more advantages than the federated DIoT_DNN in detecting malicious traffic and can learn traffic data more accurately. Therefore, this paper selects the federated DIoT_CNN as the malicious traffic detection algorithm under the DIOT-Pysyft framework.

Table 2. The performance of FSKDE+DIoT_CNN and FSKDE+CNN

Method	Accuracy	Precision	Recall	F1-Score	Time
FSKDE+CNN	0.8900	0.9527	0.8658	0.9072	678 s
FSKDE+DIoT_CNN	**0.9178**	**0.9081**	**0.8836**	**0.8957**	**247 s**

From Table 2, it can be concluded that compared with deep learning CNN, the accuracy, precision, recall rate and F1-score of federated DIoT_CNN have been improved to a certain extent when detecting malicious traffic in the IoT. Different from centralized model training, DIoT_CNN uses the respective data to train on their own devices, and each IoT device is trained in parallel. The training time is determined by the longest training time. Compared with FSKDE+CNN, the training time of FSKDE+DIoT_CNN is about 1/3 of it. we can infer that the method can achieve effective detection of malicious traffic, and reduce the model training time. Therefore, we combine FSKDE and DIoT_CNN as our final model of the federated DIOT-Pysyft system architecture.

Table 3. The detection accuracy of the DIOT-Pysyft and other federated learning approaches

Method	Accuracy
DIOT-Pysyft	**0.9178**
FILCNN [25]	0.8685
FL [26]	0.9026

Table 3 shows that the experimental results of our proposed DIOT-Pysyft approach, FILCNN [25], and FL [26] proposed by other papers are analyzed and compared to verify the advantages of the algorithm. The final experimental results show that DIOT-Pysyft has higher detection accuracy than FILCNN and FL. The detection accuracy is respectively 0.9178, 0.8685, and 0.9026. Our proposed method has more advantages in detecting malicious traffic. Besides, the improved FedAvg algorithm with SMPC further protects user privacy.

5   Conclusion

In view of the existing problems in the current Internet of Things malicious traffic detection technology, including insufficient computing power due to resource constraints, differences in attack types due to heterogeneous equipment, inaccurate detection due to less communication traffic, and insufficient data privacy protection, a malicious traffic detection method based on FSKDE and federated DIOT-Pysyft is proposed, this method combines the feature selection algorithm based on FSKDE and the traffic detection based on federated DIOT-Pysyft. The FSKDE algorithm is used on the IoT device side to filter features, reduces feature redundancy, and makes up for the problem of insufficient computing power of the IoT device. After that, the traffic detection based on federated DIOT-Pysyft algorithm is used to train each IoT device and data on their respective clients, and the gradients were encrypted and transmitted, which is used to protect the data privacy of IoT devices. At the same time, it can detect the attack type of each IoT device and reduces the problem of inaccurate detection caused by insufficient communication traffic. Compared with traditional machine learning algorithms, it has higher accuracy, precision, recall and F1-score. In the future work, each IoT device will be used to resolve the differences in bandwidth and processing speed, and reduce the differences in device performance and time.

References

1. Andrea, I., Chrysostomou, C., Hadjichristofi, G.: Internet of things: security vulnerabilities and challenges. In: 2015 IEEE symposium on computers and communication (ISCC), pp. 180–187. IEEE, Cyprus (2015)
2. Kolias, C., Kambourakis, G., Stavrou, A., et al.: DDoS in the IoT: Mirai and other botnets. Computer 50(7), 80–84 (2017)
3. CALERO. 3 Ways the Internet of Things will Impact Enterprise Security. https://www.calero.com/mobility-service-support/3-ways-the-internet-of-things-will-impact-enterprise-security/. Accessed 17 June 2018/27 Feb 2022
4. Stankovic, J.A.: Research directions for the internet of things. IEEE Internet Things J. 1(1), 3–9 (2014)
5. Nguyen, T.D., Marchal, S., Miettinen, M., et al.: A. DÏoT: a crowdsourced self-learning approach for detecting compromised IoT devices. ArXiv, abs/1804.07474 (2018)
6. Yang, W.C., Guo, Y.B., Zhong, Y., et al.: Anomaly detection of internet of things traffic based on device model classification and BP neural network. Inf. Netw. Secur. 11(12) (2019)
7. Mendonça, G., Santos, G.H., e Silva, E.D.S., Leao, R.M., Menasché, D.S., Towsley, D.: An extremely lightweight approach for DDOS detection at home gateways. In: 2019 IEEE International Conference on Big Data (Big Data), pp. 5012–5021. IEEE, USA (2019)
8. McDermott, C.D., Majdani, F., Petrovski, A.V.: Botnet detection in the internet of things using deep learning approaches. In: 2018 International Joint Conference on Neural Networks (IJCNN), pp. 1–8. IEEE, Brazil (2018)
9. Elkhadir, Z., Mohammed, B.: A cyber network attack detection based on GM Median Nearest Neighbors LDA. Comput. Secur. 86, 63–74 (2019)
10. Palmieri, F.: Network anomaly detection based on logistic regression of nonlinear chaotic invariants. J. Netw. Comput. Appl. 148, 102460 (2019)
11. Ding, W., Jing, X., Yan, Z., et al.: A survey on data fusion in internet of things: towards secure and privacy-preserving fusion. Inf. Fusion 51, 129–144 (2019)

12. McMahan, B., Moore, E., Ramage, D., Hampson, S., y Arcas, B. A.: Communication-efficient learning of deep networks from decentralized data. In: Artificial Intelligence and Statistics, pp. 1273–1282. PMLR (2017)
13. Konečný, J., McMahan, H.B., Yu, F.X., Richtárik, P., Suresh, A.T., Bacon, D.: Federated learning: strategies for improving communication efficiency. arXiv preprint arXiv:1610.05492 (2016)
14. Nguyen, T.D., Marchal, S., Miettinen, M., Fereidooni, H., Asokan, N., Sadeghi, A.R.: DÏoT: a federated self-learning anomaly detection system for IoT. In: 2019 IEEE 39th International Conference on Distributed Computing Systems (ICDCS), pp. 756–767. IEEE, Dallas (2019)
15. Al-Marri, N.A.A.A., Ciftler, B.S., Abdallah, M.M.: Federated mimic learning for privacy preserving intrusion detection. In: 2020 IEEE International Black Sea Conference on Communications and Networking (BlackSeaCom), pp. 1–6. IEEE (2020)
16. Huong, T.T., et al.: Lockedge: Low-complexity cyberattack detection in IoT edge computing. IEEE Access **9**, 29696–29710 (2021)
17. Rey, V., Sánchez, P.M.S., Celdrán, A.H., Bovet, G.: Federated learning for malware detection in IoT devices. Comput. Netw. **204**, 108693 (2022)
18. Hei, X., Yin, X., Wang, Y., Ren, J., Zhu, L.: A trusted feature aggregator federated learning for distributed malicious attack detection. Comput. Secur. **99**, 102033 (2020)
19. Agrawal, S., Sarkar S, Aouedi O, et al.: Federated learning for intrusion detection system: concepts, challenges and future directions. Comput. Commun. (2022). https://doi.org/10.48550/arXiv.2106.09527
20. Meidan, Y., Bohadana, M., Mathov, Y., et al.: N-BaIoT—network-based detection of IoT botnet attacks using deep autoencoders. IEEE Pervasive Comput. **17**(3), 12–22 (2018)
21. Wang, S., Tuor, T., Salonidis, T., et al.: When edge meets learning: adaptive control for resource-constrained distributed machine learning. In: IEEE INFOCOM 2018-IEEE Conference on Computer Communications, pp. 63–71. IEEE, USA (2018)
22. Moustafa, N., Slay, J.: UNSW-NB15: a comprehensive data set for network intrusion detection systems (UNSW-NB15 network data set). In: 2015 military Communications and Information Systems Conference (MilCIS), pp. 1–6. IEEE, Australia (2015)
23. Qin, Y., Masaaki, K.: Federated learning-based network intrusion detection with a feature selection approach. In: 2021 International Conference on Electrical, Communication, and Computer Engineering (ICECCE), pp.1–6. IEEE, Kuala Lumpur (2021). https://doi.org/10.1109/ICECCE52056.2021.9514222
24. Zhao, R., Mu, Y., Zou, L.: A hybrid intrusion detection system based on feature selection and weighted stacking classifier. IEEE Access **10**, 71414–71426 (2022). https://doi.org/10.1109/ACCESS.2022.3186975
25. Ji, X., Zhang, H., Ma, X.: A novel method of intrusion detection based on federated transfer learning and convolutional neural network. In: 2022 IEEE 10th Joint International Information Technology and Artificial Intelligence Conference (ITAIC), vol. 10, pp. 338–343. IEEE, Chongqing (2022). https://doi.org/10.1109/ITAIC54216.2022.9836871
26. Mothukuri, V., Khare, P., Parizi, R.M., Pouriyeh, S., Dehghantanha, A., Srivastava, G.: Federated-learning-based anomaly detection for IoT security attacks. IEEE Internet Things J. **9**(4), 2545–2554 (2021). https://doi.org/10.1109/JIOT.2021.3077803

Crime and Incident Watch for Smart Cities: A Sensor-Based Approach

Francis N. Nwebonyi[✉], Xiaoyu Du, and Pavel Gladyshev

Digital Forensics Investigation Research Laboratory, School of Computer Science, University College Dublin, Dublin, Ireland
{francis.nwebonyi,xiaoyu.du,pavel.gladyshev}@ucd.ie
http://dfire.ucd.ie/

Abstract. Beyond the many advantages which Smart City brings, the issue of security and privacy remain very important concerns. As things get more interconnected, cyber orchestrated crimes such as cyberterrorism may become more prevalent. For example, an autonomous vehicle or drone may be used to commit acts of terrorism, such as driving or flying into a crowd. Responses to such incidents need to be swift and likewise smart. Law enforcement needs to be equipped with the necessary tools to respond speedily and even automatically, equally taking advantage of the Internet of Things (IoT). We propose a Sensor-Based Crime and Incident Watch for Smart Cities (SBCI-Watch), leveraging Human Activity Recognition (HAR). SBCI-Watch may be used to automatically detect and possibly report occurrences of public disturbances (likely caused by acts of terrorism or similar crimes) to foster swift response. Slightly similar reports exist, but they are focused on different topics, such as helping law enforcement to pick suitable officers to respond to crime scenes based on proximity, but without attempting to automatically detect crimes. We are using the sensor-based approach; it is less privacy intrusive compared to the vision-based method, which is dominant in the public surveillance area but also more privacy intrusive and more expensive. To the best of our knowledge, our work is the first to address the problem in this fashion, and the results illustrate the viability of the SBCI-Watch.

Keywords: Smart City · Human Activity Recognition (HAR) · Incident watch · Crime watch · Privacy

1 Introduction

We can tell the behaviour of an entity or object by observing its movement pattern. By looking at the variation of the speed of cars, for instance, we can get an idea of the traffic pattern. Significantly high variation may mean that the vehicle slows down frequently after picking up some speed, and that can give us some information about the traffic situation. A smoother transition and less variation may suggest a smoother traffic condition.

© ICST Institute for Computer Sciences, Social Informatics and Telecommunications Engineering 2023
Published by Springer Nature Switzerland AG 2023. All Rights Reserved
S. Goel et al. (Eds.): ICDF2C 2022, LNICST 508, pp. 222–238, 2023.
https://doi.org/10.1007/978-3-031-36574-4_13

It can also be applied at the pedestrian level to predict people's activities in public spaces by observing their movement patterns. The literature documents these diverse applications, including the application in the area of transportation systems [5], traffic-anomaly-detection; that is, observing when there are traffic obstructions due to large events, protests, etc. [6], predicting or sensing people's activities such as shopping, working, in a meeting or at home [7], and detecting abnormal activities in social events [8].

The obvious and popular method for observing activities that are indicative of criminal acts such as acts of terrorism and similar emergencies in the public space is video surveillance, using CCTV cameras and similar devices. Although such surveillance devices may be common, it can be very expensive to hire people with the right skill-sets to analyse the videos. This has led to the popularity of real-time analysis methods, to better detect the activities and thus deter and/or respond accordingly. Many video-based algorithms for detecting abnormal behaviours in the crowd have therefore been proposed in recent years to improve the detection of such abnormal behaviours in the crowd; each method attempting to address a particular challenge associated with the process. These challenges range from crowd occlusion to illumination challenges, especially in a dense crowd [4]. There are other issues with the visual method of surveillance as we shall discuss shortly.

In this work, we have adopted a different approach, by extending the non-video-based behaviour observation methods, which have been applied in other areas, towards improving public safety by using it as a kind of a surveillance system, particularly in the context of a smart city, and not with the goal of replacing the video-based surveillance but rather to complement and extend its reach. We shall now briefly discuss the concept of Human Activity Recognition (HAR) which is the umbrella concept for this topic; we will also further highlight the relevance of our approach. The remainder of the paper discusses HAR as part of Sect. 1 and literature review in Sect. 2. The Proposed Approach and Methods are enumerated in Sect. 3, before experiment and results in Sect. 3.2, and conclusion and future work in Sect. 4.

Human Activity Recognition (HAR): This concept has gained popularity due to its application in various aspects of the society, including event analysis, Ambient Assisted Living (AAL), Intelligent Video surveillance systems, and anomaly detection, among others. We can detect anomalies in human activities by identifying non-regular or non-conforming patterns in a given data; the more distinctive the activity is, the more easily detectable it may be. Motion orientation and magnitude are among the common attributes that are often used.

There are two main approaches to HAR; vision-based, and sensor-based [27]. The vision-based approach uses RGB video cameras, as well as depth cameras to capture human actions and skeletal data. On the other hand, the sensor-based approach uses sensors such as body-worn devices, ambient, mobile phone sensors, etc. The vision-based is also popularly categorized as single-person, and multiple-person or crowd, and then applied based on need. For instance, single-person techniques like silhouette have been applied in the area of elderly healthcare to observe falling, fainting, chest pain, headache, etc. Despite being popular, the silhouette has also been reported to have a high cost of implementation, and unsuitable for long-term real-time analyses [1,2].

Multiple-person HAR or simply Crowd Activity Analysis is focused on identifying human activities in the crowd, e.g. riots and acts of terrorism. The first step under this method is usually to identify patterns of group activities, in order to recognize when a given activity becomes abnormal. And the second step is often to represent behaviours of individuals in the crowd using trajectory-based and shape-based techniques, among others.

In general, the vision-based HAR raises very high privacy concerns, way more than the sensor-based methods. However, there is a third method which is also beginning to gain popularity and is considered even less intrusive than sensor-based approach; the WiFi-based method. The bases for the WiFi-based method is that a human activity can generate multi-path reflections of wireless signals from a transmitter (TX) to a receiver (RX), which can be uniquely used to identify such activity. The Receiver Signal Strength (RSS) and the Chanel State Information (CSI) are the two popular WiFi-based HAR approaches. Although the CSI may withstand more environmental variations compared to RSS (which is single-valued), WiFi-based HAR is generally more suitable for well-controlled and fixed environments, e.g. indoors. For this reason, it may not be suitable for the proposed system, which is why we have opted for a sensor-based approach [3].

The real-world surveillance system is dominated by the vision-based HAR. But apart from the earlier mentioned privacy concerns, there are two more key problems with this method; (i) Cost of installation and upgrading of video capturing devices: There are millions of surveillance cameras all across Europe, for example, but they still do not cover every part because it may not be financially efficient to do so. Additionally, upgrading the equipment to keep up with the advancements in technology can also be very expensive. Currently, there are many older surveillance systems that are of very low resolution and are in need of upgrade. (ii) The footage of the crowd in public places is often self-occluding, and as a result, it can be difficult to accurately describe captured individuals and their actions [4]. Sensor-based devices such as the mobile phone may help us to overcome these challenges since individuals own their phones and smart devices, thereby flattening the curve on the cost of purchasing hardware surveillance equipment. The issue of self-occluding is also resolved; since there are no videos involved.

2   Related Work

The traffic system that we currently have is a result of huge research efforts dating back to 1970 and earlier. At that time, traditional means such as surveys, slow motion pictures, trial and error experimentation were used for the research and studies in this area, as demonstrated by Fruin JJ. in his thesis [10]. But modern monitoring systems have since emerged, and are being adopted, including surveillance cameras, Bluetooth, WiFi, and Sensor based techniques.

Yang et al. [11] studied the movement characteristics of pedestrians in stair-case, and found that their speed differs considerably under normal and emergency situations, while Wang et al. and others have worked on identifying abnormal behaviours in the crowd [12–14], albeit using the vision-based approach. In this work, however, we shall be focusing on the application of sensor-based HAR in related areas.

Application of Sensor-Based HAR in Museums, and for Crowd Management: Understanding the visitors' dynamics in the Museums can help the management to make better plans. For instance, peak periods and art pieces which attract higher attention can be identified for appropriate planning. Centorrino et al. used Bluetooth beacons for this purpose. Visitors are given the beacons upon entrance, while stationed receivers capture the trajectory of the visitors (can also be called pedestrians) as they move within the museum [15]. Similar techniques are also used in large events to keep track of visitors or recognize returning ones, and monitor passengers' movements in a train station [16,19].

WiFi Access points are also used to gather location-related information in similar environments. For instance, Danalet et al. used this technique to gather data and model the choice of catering locations on a campus. As people login to use the WiFi, anonymized data were gathered and processed [17]. A similar method was used by Gioia et al. to monitor dynamic crowds and to gather information that may be relevant for planning, such as number of people in attendance as well as their spatiotemporal distribution [18].

Organizing large events can be tedious, and as crowds move within a 'confined' space, there may be a risk of a stampede in cases where appropriate plans are not made. To help event planners and crowd managers, Blanke et al. [21] leveraged HAR by using the GPS traces from mobile phones to monitor (or predict) crowd movement in a big event, focusing on schedules and attraction locations within the crowd mobility. Also based on GPS traces and still in the concept of crowd management, Duives et al. [22] proposed a model for forecasting the movement of people in a crowd, leveraging Recurrent Neural Networks. The area of crowd management and mobility has received significant attention, and information from mobile phones and other sensors have been leveraged to address concerns in this area [8,23,24].

Application of Sensor-Based HAR on Traffic Management and City Centre Planning: To observe and investigate the movement and experience of pedestrians in a city centre, Van in his work distributed GPS tracking devices to visitors in a city, at strategic locations such as parking lots. The devices were returned by the volunteers after moving about with it, and the gathered information was further analysed [20]. The goal of this project was to help the city managers to improve the physical condition and experience of visitors in their city centres. It was intended to help them in the areas of beautification and landscaping, among others.

The sensor-based HAR has also been featured considerably in the area of traffic management. The authors of [5, 6, 25, 26] have utilized the trajectory information, gathered while using taxis as sensors, to monitor the traffic behaviours and (when possible) suggest alternative routes to drivers. By recognizing the information that is related to the vehicles as they travel along different routes, researchers are able to predict or suggest safer routes to users or volunteers. It is also possible to fish out a malicious taxi operator who would rather take passengers through an unusually long route to a destination that has a clearly shorter route, perhaps to charge a higher fare.

And for indoor or in-campus navigation, Jackermeier et al. [28] worked on being able to recognize when a pedestrian is performing activities like walking straight, walking through a door by pushing or pulling it, turning right, left, standing still or just looking around. Similarly, Faye et al. [7] used the GPS and accelerator sensors in mobile phones and smartwatches to understand the activities of volunteers, such as when they are at work, shopping, etc. The information provided by the sensor allowed the researchers to determine if the participants are sitting, running, walking or in a vehicle. Such information was then correlated with activities such as shopping, working at the office and similar others.

Public Safety and Policing the Smart City: Joh has postulated that as cities become smarter, they also embed policing within themselves in an increasing way [29]. Smart city features (eg. HAR as we have seen here) can improve service delivery in several areas such as traffic management, event management, parking space, among others. Joh argues that if it can improve services in those areas, then it can also enhance even a more important service which is the public safety and policing. There may be a few laws limiting data collection for use by law enforcement, but Josh has noted that in the case of the United States, for instance, data collection about persons and activities in public spaces is not against the first Amendment. And if the law enforcement retrieves data from third-party companies, then not many restrictions would apply under the current American law, according to Joh. This may suggest that the use of the SBCI-Watch would be in line with existing laws in America and other western countries. Nonetheless, we assume that the responsibility of ensuring the fulfillment of every legal or regulatory requirement for data use will rest upon a trusted third party. Regulatory matters are therefore out of scope here. The data which we have used for experiment was collected under full consent and was anonymized.

Applying sensor-based HAR for crime watch or policing-related goals are emerging and there are no much work in the literature at the moment. A somewhat related work is reported by Welsh and Roy [30]; using sensors that are built into smartphones, they worked on recognizing gunshots, and their model achieved an average accuracy of 86.6% on gunshot classification. But as mentioned earlier, the focus of this and similar reports are different. Our work focuses on utilizing non-vision-based HAR to detect public disturbances or serious crimes such as acts of terrorism, so that appropriate authorities may be promptly notified, leading to prompt response. We utilize common sensors built into smartphones and Apps which people already use, to address this. To the best of our knowledge, we are the first to address this problem using the mentioned approach.

3 The Proposed Approach and Methods

In this section, the concept and overview of the SBCI-Watch are presented, as well as the data collection method and the modeling approach.

3.1 The Concept of SBCI-Watch

As highlighted in Sect. 2, although the smart city may present novel security challenges when rolled out at a bigger and more detailed scale, it also comes equipped with resources that may help to bring about the solution to that problem - mainly the advanced interconnectedness and data pool. The proposed system aims at taking advantage of these resources to better secure the city. We consider it important to focus on utilizing the readily available resources that are already embedded in the city to bring about the needed solution. Because this would make data management, as well as the adoption of the proposed solution, easier. Popular Apps and smart devices are part of the rich resources of smart cities.

Figure 1 illustrates the SBCI-Watch concept. It starts with the gathering of anonymous information from consenting individuals using a mobile App. The information is then passed onto a deep learning model which is able to predict the movement pattern of people in a given location (or venue, eg. Museum) at a given time. The idea is that if a reasonably large number of people within a location or venue (in a smart city) at a given time suddenly start running in an unusual and chaotic way, clearly different from the average known pattern of that particular area or location (see Fig. 3), then perhaps something may be going on and some attention may need to be called to it. An example could be if there is an active shooter or armed rubber at a location and many people suddenly start running for their lives away from the dangerous spot, towards different other directions. Having information about past patterns for that location or venue, and at a similar time/season can help in determining such sudden chaotic scene.

In addition to understanding the movement pattern, other factors, such as analysing whether or not there has been shooting, car accidents, collusion, etc. in the area can provide further verification steps and more confidence in the conclusion which the model may arrive at. Information about firearms has been incorporated into SBCI-Watch as part of the verification step (also see Fig. 5).

Once such information has been gathered, the next step, as also portrayed in Fig. 1, is to pass the data through our deep learning model (which will be residing with a trusted authority) for analysis. The model uses the information which can be retrieved from the data to determine whether there is a suspected occurrence of acts of public disturbance or a related crime, and if that is the

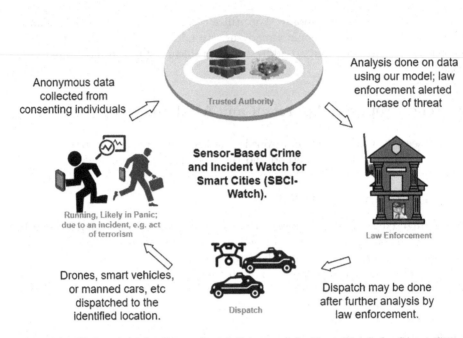

Fig. 1. An Illustration of a Sensor-Based Crime and Incident Watch for Smart Cities (SBCI-Watch)

case, the appropriate authorities (e.g. the law enforcement) can be alerted to further scrutinize the report and dispatch response if it is deemed appropriate. Some of the key steps which we take to reach a tentative conclusion regarding whether there is an incident or not is illustrated in Fig. 2, while the analysis and verification part is further illustrated in Fig. 5 and discussed in Sect. 3.2.

The Long Short-Term Memory (LSTM) has been used to train our model because information about past events needs to be factored in, in order to determine if there has been a public disturbance that is worth being flagged. For instance, while analysing the state of a location or venue at a given time, we need to also take into account what the situation of that area has been prior to the time of the suspected incident. LSTM is known to be very good at this kind of tasks, ensuring that while making analysis at time t, the occurrences at t-1, t-2, etc. are not ignored, because they help to determine unusual patterns.

3.2 Experiment and Results

As earlier mentioned, vision-based HAR is the predominant approach in this area, traditionally involving CCTV cameras and similar other devices, which are more privacy intrusive and expensive to install, maintain and upgrade. But we can also detect public disturbances and crime in public spaces by understanding people's reactions and movement patterns, in addition to other information, which can all be gathered with common sensors that are present in mobile phones

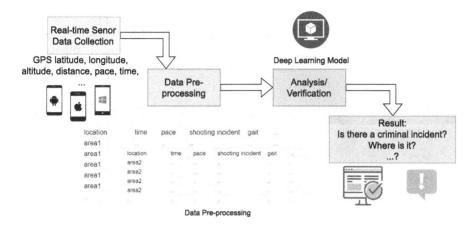

Fig. 2. Data Analysis Steps.

Fig. 3. People running in a chaotic fashion, away from a suspected incident or crime.

and other smart devices; this is the focus of our work. Nonetheless, due to the difference in focus between our work and earlier reports of HAR in the literature, the existing dataset is not suitable for the SBIC-Watch use case, which is why we assembled a fresh dataset. We shall however incorporate features from a firearm dataset [33] into the model as an added verification layer.

Generating the Data Set: In line with our idea of using already available resources, we used an App that is already available at the Play Store and Appstore, called GPS Logger. The interface and settings are shown in Fig. 4. Some of its features include background logging (GPS latitude, longitude, altitude, distance, speed) which is more power-friendly compared to Apps that require active recording. The GPS Logger also allows files to be exported in different file formats including CVS which makes it almost ready for instant pre-processing.

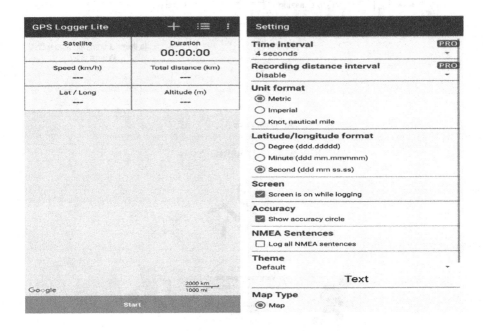

Fig. 4. GPS Logger and settings

A total of seven people participated in the data collection exercise, and it was mainly collected in 2 days involving many sessions. First with 3 volunteers and then with six volunteers on the second day. Two of the volunteers participated on both exercises. Varieties of phone models were used but they were all either Android or iOS; they include iPhone 11 Pro Max, OnePlus 6T, iPhone 7 Plus, Samsung Galaxy A51, Infinix 8, and Samsung Galaxy J5. Participants walked at their normal paces from different directions, heading towards a location. And before they were to reach a common location, they were "startled" with a loud sound as a way of simulating a sudden chaotic situation. On hearing that sound they ran (as they would in a panic situation) in different directions. This way, the area or spot where an attack or public disturbance has occurred maybe predictable.

The experimental process was explained to the participants, including the use of a sound to simulate a situation of panic. The App which was installed on the phones were turned on before each session. The process was repeated many times, and we recorded information about the time, location (latitude/longitude), altitude, pace/speed (km/h), and total distance (km). Data was generally captured every 4 s, and was processed at a central location (an on-site machine at University College Dublin). Future versions of SBCI-Watch will likely feature edge computing architecture, after the privacy implications of such architecture on the use case has been ascertained.

After data pre-processing, we realized over 2000 captures. Based on the information which we gathered from the literature [7] and based on the observed ground truth, we capped the chaotic runs at 15 km/h while walking/stationary under calm situations were capped at about 7 km/h; outliers were removed based on this. The data was also labelled and reshaped accordingly.

Choice of Deep Learning and Hierarchical HAR Approach: Traditional Machine Learning methods are generally being overtaken by deep learning methods in many areas. The success of Recurrent Neural Networks (RNNs), and the LSTM in particular, in handling input data that has temporal patterns is well documented in the literature [28]. Accordingly, LSTM has been used for our model; the loss generally drops after relatively few iterations and the predictions are in line with the ground truth which was observed in the field by the researcher. LSTM ensures that data is not simply classified, it helps our model to account for circumstances within the area being monitored, prior to the time of monitoring; without such consideration, the analysis will not make much sense.

Furthermore, we adopted the hierarchical (HAR) approach which has also been reported to have improved performance [34]. The main idea behind this concept is to have heterogeneous and hierarchical layers or classifiers that deal with specific use-cases using more relevant or impactful features, and then similarly moving on to applicable sub-categories, leading to a more precise result. The downside of this approach is a possibility of higher computational load, but it has also been shown that this is not a big issue in practice [28]. And in the case of LSTM, the number of layers for each sub-category can be carefully chosen to better conserve resources.

As illustrated in Fig. 5, Our model first uses generic information such as movement pattern, time, and previous state (location is also a factor here) to determine whether there is a case of public disturbance in a public place, for instance a museum or a given location in a smart city street. If there is a significant reason to suspect that a serious act of public disturbance has occurred or is currently taking place, then a further verification step is taken in a sublayer of the hierarchy, combining the earlier output with additional more specific data, which in this case is the feature that was extracted from a shooting detection dataset, published by Khan et al. [33]. This combination is fed back into the model and further processed for a better precision. Basically, the sub-layer seeks to know if there are specific serious crimes that have also been detected in the area at about the same time. This may help law enforcement, for instance, to decide whether an action is necessary as well as the kind of response that may be needed. Such details may not be available with a traditional nonhierarchical approach. To calculate the resultant energy (E) from the x, y, and z axis of the accelerometer data, we used the same formula that was used in [33]:

$E = \sum_{i=0}^{l} = (x^2 + y^2 + z^2)$, where l represents the window length. We used l = 5, to correspond to the 20 s time steps which the model uses. Recall that our dataset was recorded per 4 s, during the data collection. Khan et al. [33] uses this energy to select gunshot related frames, we refer readers to their work for more on this.

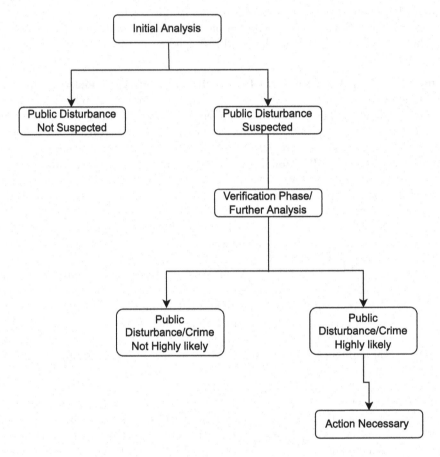

Fig. 5. The Hierarchical HAR Approach used in SBCI-Watch

Results and Discussion: The data set was split for training (90%) and testing (10%). The split was done sequentially because using the traditional train_test_split to do it (randomly) would be unsuitable. We need to keep note of prior events, and splitting the data randomly would make it disorderly. LSTM was used because of its documented success with this kind of data.

The model converges smoothly with an accuracy of about 98.5%. Accuracy ranges between 97.3 and 99.8% were also recorded. Our result is generally better than the results of most HAR-related reports which may be considered to be in the same domain as our work, including 95.21% which was achieved by Yang et al. [31], 98% by zhou et al. [32], and 97.2% recorded by Jackermeie and Ludwig [28]. Jackermeie and Ludwig also recorded performances that ranged from 62.6% to 98.7%, but our model is still within their best recorded performance.

Our goal is to be able to identify when people start 'running for their lives' at a location or venue within a smart city, e.g. Museum. Figure 6 illustrates how the model performed in the task. People walk/run at different paces and for different reasons, there were also other factors considered, such as the timing and location, among others. Chaos or public disturbance may be suspected if there is a clear deviation from the normal state of pedestrian traffic in an area, and people appear to be running in large numbers in different directions and seemingly deserting (or fleeing from) an area, as shown in Fig. 3. The deserted area(s) could be the points of attack, and with close to real-time information processing, the law enforcement may be able to respond swifter, for instance, by deploying drones and personnel quickly to the scene.

In general, our model was able to reconcile the differences; identifying ideal and panic situations with a good level of accuracy, in line with the ground truth. The data was reshaped accordingly, and the model steps back every 20 s. This enables it to make predictions regarding the likely current situation of a location. There is no particular reason for choosing the 20 s interval, it is merely for illustration purposes. The best fit (interval) may be subject to the peculiarities of a location being monitored and available resources. That is, a threshold that may be considered high enough to trigger an alarm can be set at the decision-making level, considering possible peculiar security needs of a given area or location.

The unexpected spike which can be noticed in Fig. 7 may be due to the fact that the model does not have an earlier reference point, since it was still at an 'initialization' stage when the spike occurred. Nonetheless, decision making based on this model, particularly with regard to the considered scenario, would be relatively accurate because it was able to predict the occurrences in line with the ground truth. It is however important to understand that more data regarding a given venue (considering different scenarios) may need to be gathered over a period of time, and fed into the model, in order to determine the day-to-day situation of that venue, and to allow for higher confidence in the outcome, particularly in a production environment. This work is therefore a proof of concept at this stage.

The presented results capture several sessions which were used in the testing phase. As earlier explained, during each session, all the participants perform two main acts; walking normally (or/and other normal activities including staying idle), and running as if they were in panic. Data were then gathered and labelled according to the ground truth. Figure 7 illustrates the sessions.

Figure 8 represents the result of the additional verification step which the hierarchical approach has allowed us to do. Results from the previous step were combined with the firearm data which were earlier described, in order to ascer-

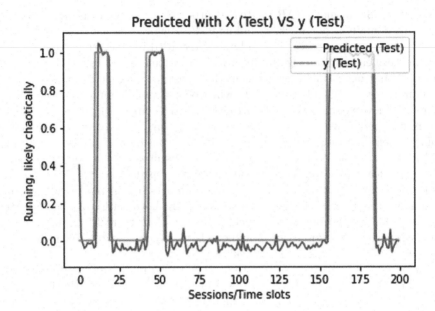

Fig. 6. Sessions of simulated panic running. People walk and run at different paces among other features, but the model is able to identify the panic sessions.

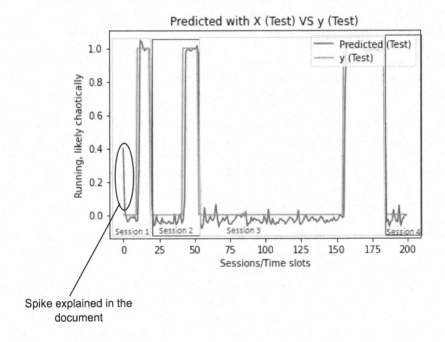

Fig. 7. Showing different sessions, and a slight anomaly

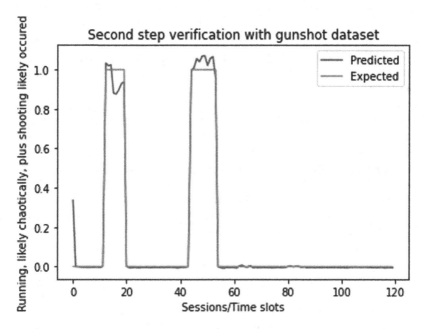

Fig. 8. Further verification step, using firearm data-set. This kind of verification will help to minimise false alarms.

tain if there was also an indication of shooting, in addition to the suspected scene of public disturbance. This would add to the weight and confidence in the recommendation being made. Like in the previous results, the clearly high spikes or peaks indicate cases of suspected public disturbance, incident, or a related crime at the location being considered. The clearly low ones represent normal activity, while the not-so-high spike at the beginning, which was also recorded in the previous results, can be ignored for the same reason which was earlier stated. We would like to state that the two datasets (the one generated by us, and the one from literature) were obviously not collected at the same time and location, therefore such information (about time and location) was abstracted out, particularly in the second step.

4   Conclusion and Future Work

Various aspects of our cities and homes are becoming smarter. In some cities, drones and some kinds of robots are already able to deliver packages to the right addresses. We can warm up our homes even without being physically there, and many people are now familiar with the idea of autonomous cars. But this is just a tip of the iceberg. Different components of the cities are expected to continue to evolve along this line, including crime watch, policing, and response to distress.

   This work has explored the prospects of a sensor-based surveillance system for a smart city, focusing on a particular location. We have demonstrated that common sensors which are available on devices that we use daily, such as smartphones and smartwatches can be used to gain insight into the movement patterns of individuals in a location or venue such as a Museum. And that based on such information and other relevant data, which can also be gathered through the sensors (such as gunshot information), it is possible to predict incidents of public disturbances or crime automatically, so that appropriate authorities can be likewise alerted for swift intervention. This sensor-based approach can be an alternative, or a compliment, to the vision-based approach which can be more expensive and more privacy intrusive.

We have focused on using readily available Apps and devices of various types to make adoption easy for any entity that may consider adopting SBCI-Watch, when it is fully developed. The data which may be collected from consenting individuals is almost or exactly the same data that they are already willing to share while using their regular Apps. The custodian of such data is expected to remain the same, to ensure necessary compliance. For example, many Museums already have Apps which they use - if they were to adopt SBCI-Watch, it will not take control or responsibility over the data away from them; they would still be in-charge.

Results suggest that the solution is viable and we believe that it can help to tackle terrorism and other serious crimes in the public spaces (of a smart city). It would help appropriate authorities to get information and respond swifter to incidents within the public spaces. It is also cost-effective, since most of the resources needed to make it work are embedded into the city.

Future Work: We shall be expanding the scope of the project, having ascertained its viability through this work. We shall seek to collaborate with the managers and other individuals within Museums and similar public spaces around Ireland and Europe to bring about a bigger scope. This shall be done with full compliance to applicable regulations related to data and a keen adherence to data privacy good practices.

Acknowledgement. This project has received funding from the European Union's Horizon 2020 Research and Innovation Programme under Grant Agreement No. 883596. The content of the publication herein is the sole responsibility of the publishers and it does not necessarily represent the views expressed by the European Commission or its services.

References

1. Dhiman, C., Vishwakarma, D.K.: A review of state-of-the-art techniques for abnormal human activity recognition. Eng. Appl. Artif. Intell. 1(77), 21–45 (2019)
2. Fereidoonian, F., Firouzi, F., Farahani, B.: Human activity recognition: from sensors to applications. In: 2020 International Conference on Omni-layer Intelligent Systems (COINS), pp. 1–8. IEEE (2020)
3. Zhang, L., Cui, W., Li, B., Chen, Z., Wu, M., Gee, T.S.: Privacy-preserving cross-environment human activity recognition. IEEE Trans. Cybern. (2021)

4. Song, B., Sheng, R.: Crowd counting and abnormal behavior detection via multi-scale GAN network combined with deep optical flow. Math. Probl. Eng. **16**, 2020 (2020)

5. Pang, L.X., Chawla, S., Liu, W., Zheng, Y.: On detection of emerging anomalous traffic patterns using GPS data. Data Knowl. Eng. **1**(87), 357–373 (2013)

6. Pan, B., Zheng, Y., Wilkie, D., Shahabi, C.: Crowd sensing of traffic anomalies based on human mobility and social media. In: Proceedings of the 21st ACM SIGSPATIAL International Conference on Advances in Geographic Information Systems, pp. 344–353 (2013)

7. Faye, S., Frank, R., Engel, T.: Adaptive activity and context recognition using multimodal sensors in smart devices. In: Sigg, S., Nurmi, P., Salim, F. (eds.) Mobi-CASE 2015. LNICST, vol. 162, pp. 33–50. Springer, Cham (2015). https://doi.org/10.1007/978-3-319-29003-4_3

8. Irfan, M., Tokarchuk, L., Marcenaro, L., Regazzoni, C.: Anomaly detection in crowds using multi sensory information. In: 2018 15th IEEE International Conference on Advanced Video and Signal Based Surveillance (AVSS), pp. 1–6. IEEE (2018)

9. Hoogendoorn, S.P., Bovy, P.H.: Pedestrian route-choice and activity scheduling theory and models. Transp. Res. Part B: Methodol. **38**(2), 169–190 (2004)

10. Fruin, J.J.: Designing for pedestrians a level of service concept. Polytechnic University (1970)

11. Yang, L., Rao, P., Zhu, K., Liu, S., Zhan, X.: Observation study of pedestrian flow on staircases with different dimensions under normal and emergency conditions. Saf. Sci. **50**(5), 1173–1179 (2012)

12. Wang, B., Ye, M., Li, X., Zhao, F., Ding, J.: Abnormal crowd behavior detection using high-frequency and spatio-temporal features. Mach. Vis. Appl. **23**(3), 501–511 (2012)

13. Favaretto, R.M., Dihl, L.L., Musse, S.R.: Detecting crowd features in video sequences. In: 2016 29th SIBGRAPI Conference on Graphics, Patterns and Images (SIBGRAPI), pp. 201–208. IEEE (2016)

14. Duives, D.C.: Analysis and modelling of pedestrian movement dynamics at large-scale events. Doctoral dissertation, Delft University of Technology (2016)

15. Centorrino, P., Corbetta, A., Cristiani, E., Onofri, E.: Measurement and analysis of visitors' trajectories in crowded museums. arXiv preprint arXiv:1912.02744 (2019)

16. Versichele, M., Neutens, T., Delafontaine, M., Van de Weghe, N.: The use of Bluetooth for analysing spatiotemporal dynamics of human movement at mass events: a case study of the Ghent Festivities. Appl. Geogr. **32**(2), 208–220 (2012)

17. Danalet, A., Tinguely, L., de Lapparent, M., Bierlaire, M.: Location choice with longitudinal WiFi data. J. Choice Modell. **1**(18), 1–7 (2016)

18. Gioia, C., Sermi, F., Tarchi, D., Vespe, M.: On cleaning strategies for WiFi positioning to monitor dynamic crowds. Appl. Geom. **11**(4), 381–399 (2019)

19. Ton, D., van den Heuvel, J., Daamen, W., Hoogendoorn, S.: Route and activity location choice behaviour of departing passengers in train stations. In: hEART (European Association for Research in Transportation) 2015 Conference. Copenhagen, Denmark, pp. 9–11 (2015)

20. van der Spek, S.: Spatial metro: tracking pedestrians in historic city centres. Res. Urban. Ser. **1**(1), 77–97 (2008)

21. Blanke, U., Tröster, G., Franke, T., Lukowicz, P.: Capturing crowd dynamics at large scale events using participatory GPS-localization. In: 2014 IEEE Ninth International Conference on Intelligent Sensors, Sensor Networks and Information Processing (ISSNIP), pp. 1–7. IEEE (2014)

22. Duives, D.C., Wang, G., Kim, J.: Forecasting pedestrian movements using recurrent neural networks: an application of crowd monitoring data. Sensors **19**(2), 382 (2019)
23. Zhang, K., Wang, M., Wei, B., Sun, D.: Identification and prediction of large pedestrian flow in urban areas based on a hybrid detection approach. Sustainability **9**(1), 36 (2016)
24. Yang, Y., Heppenstall, A., Turner, A., Comber, A.: Who, where, why and when? Using smart card and social media data to understand urban mobility. ISPRS Int. J. Geo Inf. **8**(6), 271 (2019)
25. Hoseinzadeh, N., Arvin, R., Khattak, A.J., Han, L.D.: Integrating safety and mobility for pathfinding using big data generated by connected vehicles. J. Intell. Transp. Syst. **24**(4), 404–420 (2020)
26. Chen, C., Zhang, D., Samuel Castro, P., Li, N., Sun, L., Li, S.: Real-time detection of anomalous taxi trajectories from GPS traces. In: Puiatti, A., Gu, T. (eds.) MobiQuitous 2011. LNICST, vol. 104, pp. 63–74. Springer, Heidelberg (2012). https://doi.org/10.1007/978-3-642-30973-1_6
27. Jung, I.Y.: A review of privacy-preserving human and human activity recognition. Int. J. Smart Sens. Intell. Syst. **13**(1), 1–3 (2020)
28. Jackermeier, R., Ludwig, B.: Smartphone-based activity recognition in a pedestrian navigation context. Sensors **21**(9), 3243 (2021)
29. Joh, E.E.: Policing the smart city. Int. J. Law Context **15**(2), 177–182 (2019)
30. Welsh, D., Roy, N.: Smartphone-based mobile gunshot detection. In: 2017 IEEE International Conference on Pervasive Computing and Communications Workshops (PerCom Workshops), pp. 244–249. IEEE (2017)
31. Yang, J., Cheng, K., Chen, J., Zhou, B., Li, Q.: Smartphones based online activity recognition for indoor localization using deep convolutional neural network. In: 2018 Ubiquitous Positioning, Indoor Navigation and Location-Based Services (UPINLBS), pp. 1–7. IEEE (2018)
32. Zhou, B., Yang, J., Li, Q.: Smartphone-based activity recognition for indoor localization using a convolutional neural network. Sensors **19**(3), 621 (2019)
33. Khan, M.A., Welsh, D., Roy, N.: Firearm detection using wrist worn tri-axis accelerometer signals. In: 2018 IEEE International Conference on Pervasive Computing and Communications Workshops (PerCom Workshops), pp. 221–226. IEEE (2018)
34. Ashqar, H.I., Almannaa, M.H., Elhenawy, M., Rakha, H.A., House, L.: Smartphone transportation mode recognition using a hierarchical machine learning classifier and pooled features from time and frequency domains. IEEE Trans. Intell. Transp. Syst. **20**(1), 244–252 (2018)

Malware Analysis

The Lightweight Botnet Detection Model Based on the Improved UNet

Chengjie Li[1,2], Yunchun Zhang[1,2], Zixuan Li[1,2], Fan Feng[1,2], Zikun Liao[1,2], and Xiaohui Cui[2,3(✉)]

[1] School of Software, Yunnan University, Kunming, China
yczhang@ynu.edu.cn, zixuanli@mail.ynu.edu.cn
[2] Research Center of Cyberspace, Yunnan University, Kunming, China
[3] School of Cyber Science and Engineering, Wuhan University, Wuhan, China
xcui@whu.edu.cn

Abstract. Botnet detection tasks in many network devices require deployment of a large number of detection models. Deep learning-based Botnet detection models are big and resource-intensive. Besides, the UNet is primarily used for two-dimensional inputs but with higher complexity. This paper presents a One-Dimensional UNet (1D-UNet) based on one-dimensional feature vectors generated to design a lightweight detection engine. Second, we propose a One-Dimensional Lightweight UNet (1DL-UNet) by combining the 1D-UNet with depthwise separable convolution to reduce the model's complexity. Finally, we reduce the number of packets for Botnet detection based on our observation that the first packet with an effective payload in a network session plays the most important role in detection. The experiments show that the 1DL-UNet outperforms other models with 99.66% accuracy and is 12 times smaller than one-dimensional MobileNet. Meanwhile, the designed 1DL-UNet is 4 times smaller than the 1D-UNet. Furthermore, it is observed that 4 packets are enough to achieve satisfactory Botnet detection while only 1 packet with effective payload is possible with 99.26% accuracy in the 1DL-UNet.

Keywords: Botnet detection · Convolutional neural networks · One-dimensional convolution · UNet

1 Introduction

The deployment of network devices is remarkably increased in the areas of industry, health care, smart home, and smart city. The number of devices integrated into the Internet has sharply increased and it is estimated that there will be 75.44 billion of IoT devices by 2025 [1]. IoT device is mainly composed of low-cost devices with limited resources by combining physical devices with digital intelligent networks. The whole network is highly heterogeneous and dynamic. The nature of limited resource on a end device and the large volume of network

© ICST Institute for Computer Sciences, Social Informatics and Telecommunications Engineering 2023
Published by Springer Nature Switzerland AG 2023. All Rights Reserved
S. Goel et al. (Eds.): ICDF2C 2022, LNICST 508, pp. 241–255, 2023.
https://doi.org/10.1007/978-3-031-36574-4_14

traffic among inter-connected devices on the Internet makes those devices fail to implement highly complex security tasks. Meanwhile, many vulnerabilities are born in nature within a network and are used for launching illegal activities to control, subvert and destroy network devices. A typical attack scenario is Botnet where attackers can manipulate some devices to launch DDoS (Distributed Denial-of-Service) attack. In a typical Botnet attack, once a end device is controlled by an attacker, the attacker will then enlarge its attacking speed and target more devices by using Command-and-Control ($C\&C$) communications. The attacking effect can be greatly enhanced then. Meanwhile, many Botnets are using BaaS (Botnet as a Service) to provide network services. This greatly helps the botmaster to control and manipulate attacks while hiding from being detected. Therefore, Botnets are flourishing on the Internet and the scale of attacks is increasingly large, such as that in Mirai [2]. In Mirai, a large number of network devices are manipulated to launch DDoS against the provider's DNS (Domain Name Server).

Deep neural networks are trained and deployed for Botnet detection recently [3]. But the trained neural networks are usually computing-intensive and resource-intensive. To solve the Botnet detection problem on the Internet with the aim of both improving the detection accuracy and simplifying the data processing procedure, this paper makes the following contributions.

(1) Based on the combination of the network packet transmission state and transmission contents, we improved the UNet [4] for Botnet detection based on network traffic. By converting the network traffic into bytes streams and used as inputs, the One-Dimensional UNet (1D-UNet) convolutional neural network is proposed. This 1D-UNet achieves 0.42% improvement on accuracy than the best model in [5].

(2) As network devices are usually power limited, we improve 1D-UNet and propose the One-dimensional Lightweight UNet (1DL-UNet) based on the design methodology and mechanism in MobileNet [6]. The experimental results show that the 1DL-UNet achieves comparable detection accuracy while reducing its parameter volumes to 8% of the 1D-MobileNet and reducing the computational cost to 22% of the 1D-MobileNet. The 1DL-UNet is also applicable for Botnet detection on end devices on the Internet.

(3) We propose a method to reduce the number of network packets required to detect the Botnet with comparable performance. The proposed method relies on the extraction of the first network packet with effective payloads. The experiments show that only one network packet within a session is enough for effective Botnet detection. Two critical factors that have a direct impact on the detection performance are also analyzed, including the number of packets selected and the length of packets extracted (in bytes).

2   Related Works

Botnets are quickly evolved with more powerful destruction against both the Internet and IoT. In recent years, deep learning-based detection models are popular for Botnet detection by modeling it as an anomaly detection problem. The anomaly detection-based methods are primarily based on the observations of communication patterns from the network traffic [7]. BotHunter [8] achieves Botnet detection based on the sequential communication traffic in the periods of bot broadcasting and infection. BotMiner [9] and BotSniffer [10] are mainly based on measuring the similarity of their behavior. Other features extracted based on the TCP connection and network traffic logs are also applicable for anomaly detection [11,12].

The deep learning-based Botnet detection methods are more effective than anomaly detection-based models. Many deep neural networks are trained based on network traffic data, such as RNN (Recurrent Neural Network) [13], Bi-LSTM (Bi-directional Long Short-Term Memory) [14], deep auto-encoder [15], etc. Some benchmark datasets for Botnet detection are proposed and ISCX Botnet [16] is the most popular one. To enhance the detection performance, Hosseini et al. [17] addressed the problem of weak correlation of statistical features of network traffic by using a two-stage feature fusion method. The proposed solution uses CNN for spatial logical correlation of statistical features in the first stage and LSTM for temporal logical correlation of the proposed features in the second stage to ensure a high detection accuracy even when using statistical features with weak correlation. The BotCathcer [18] proposed a detection method of byte sequences and statistical features as combined features. Both imaged byte sequences and statistical features are input into CNN and LSTM respectively. Then, the output nodes of the two networks combine the features for subsequent feature input. As some botnet samples are small, Zou et al. [5] investigated the application of GAN (Generative Adversarial Network) in image recognition and proposed a DCGAN-based botnet detection model. The proposed method can effectively expand the number of samples and improve the detection capability of the model while achieving the highest detection accuracy of 99.23%.

Although deep learning models are featured by their efficient automatic feature extraction and satisfactory performance for Botnet detection, most of them are computation-intensive and unsuitable for end devices in IoT especially for micro devices based on Micro-Controller Units (MCU) [19]. For deployment into low-energy environments, the authors in [20] combine the BNN (Binarized Neural Network) with federated learning for Botnet detection, but the accuracy is only 94.5%. Thus, designing a lightweight neural network for Botnet detection is challenging. This paper aims to design a lightweight model that is not only energy-saving but also comparable to the previous methods on all performance metrics.

3 Methodology

Many state-of-the-art Botnet detection models, especially deep neural network-based, are applicable on the Internet. But a typical deep neural network is too big to apply on devices with limited resources. A successful Botnet detection model for IoT devices should be small in size. To design a lightweight detection

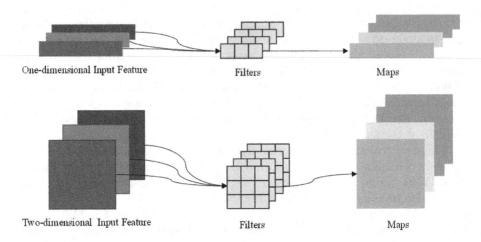

Fig. 1. The differences between the one-dimensional and two-dimensional Convolutional Neural Networks.

engine in Internet, this paper optimizes the existing method from two sides: model optimization and inputs reduction.

3.1 1D-UNet for Botnet Detection

Deep learning models are widely deployed for botnet detection based on traffic gray-scale images. Gray-scale images generated from either traffic flow byte sequence or features extracted from the network traffic flows are two-dimensional. Thus, Two-Dimensional Convolutional Neural Networks (2D-CNN) are introduced for Botnet detection because those models are commonly used for image classification and segmentation. The 2D-CNN is good at extracting spatial structure patterns and analyzing the space logic within a two-dimensional space. On the contrary, One-Dimensional CNN (1D-CNN) is good at extracting useful features from a short or fixed-length segment. The filter in a 1D-CNN usually slides in a unidirectional way and the convolutional operation is considered as a feature distillation process without any feature ordering or feature selection. All in all, the differences between 1D-CNN and 2D-CNN are shown in Fig. 1.

Based on the basic configurations of network and the requirement of training a lightweight Botnet detection model on end devices, this paper designed a small convolutional neural network, called One-Dimensional UNet (1D-UNet). The designed model is based on the improvements to UNet [4] that featured with its high performance on two-dimensional inputs and is commonly used for image classification and segmentation. While Botnet attacks are usually with a high volume of network packets, the designed 1D-UNet uses network packets, including packet header and packet payload, as inputs.

We define a series of network packets as a **Network flow**, abbreviated as *NetFlow*. A *NetFlow* is defined as a logical unit of packets denoted by a five

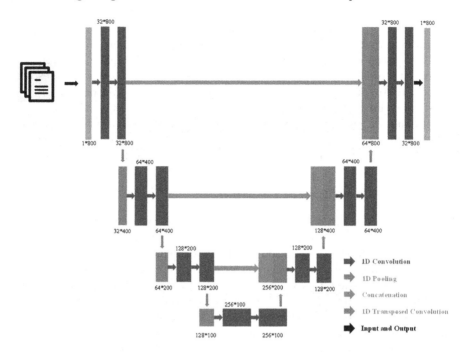

Fig. 2. The system architecture of the 1D-UNet for Botnet detection.

elements tuple as $<SrcIP, SrcPort, DstIP, DstPort, Protocol>$, where Src and Dst means the source node and the destination node, respectively. The $NetFlow$, as a uni-directional processing method of packets, is highly effective for network anomaly detection. However, Botnet is highly characterized by its bi-directional communications. We combine two $NetFlows$ with the same IP and $Port$ into a single $session$. By extracting a segment of the $session$ as input x, the designed UNet is defined as $y_i = F_\theta(x_i)$, where $y_i \in \{0, 1\}$ which means the given input is classified as Botnet when $y_i = 1$. Each input x_i is extracted from X^d where d means the length of the extracted segment in bytes. Once trained and optimized, the 1D-UNet is with the best parameter value θ. The whole process from input x into the 1D-UNet to output $\hat{y} \in \{0, 1\}$ is denoted as a mapping by $f : x \to \hat{y}$. While inputs are bytes extracted from the $NetFlow$, the whole mapping process aims at minimizing the loss function $\mathcal{L}(\theta, x, y)$ where we choose binary cross-entropy and define the objective function as:

$$\mathcal{L}(\Theta, x, y) = -\frac{1}{N} \sum_{i=1}^{N} (y_i \cdot log(p(y_i)) + (1 - y_i) \cdot log(1 - p(y_i))) \qquad (1)$$

where, N means the total numbers of predicted classes and $N = 2$ in this paper as a typical binary classification problem.

The designed 1D-UNet is mainly composed of a U-type structure with encoding and decoding. The encoding focuses on feature extraction from input byte sequences based on convolutional operations and down-sampling. By applying up-sampling to the inputs from the encoding component, the decoding restores a feature to its original size. Then, the last fully connected layer output the predicted labels for Botnet detection. As the byte sequences used in this paper are discrete and differ from two-dimensional images, the designed 1D-UNet is configured with less convolutional layers for efficient processing of byte sequences. The network architecture of the 1D-UNet is shown in Fig. 2.

3.2   1DL-UNet for Botnet Detection

The 1D-UNet uses multiple convolutional blocks with twice one-dimensional convolutional operations. The classification accuracy is enhanced but the number of parameters and the computation cost increased simultaneously. To reduce the number of parameters to a reasonable level, the Depthwise Separable Convolution (DSC) in MobileNet [6] is introduced. We then propose a One-Dimensional Lightweight UNet (1DL-UNet) for Botnet detection in Internet.

The 1DL-UNet optimizes the original 1D-Unet from two sides. First, the one-dimensional convolutional operations in the original convolution block are substituted for one-dimensional depthwise separable convolution (1D-DSC). Second, the stride of the convolutional operations in the process of the second depthwise separable convolution block is enlarged from 1 to 2, replacing the original max pooling by reducing the dimension during feature learning. Based on the above improvements, the architecture of the 1DL-UNet is shown in Fig. 3.

The 1D-DSC, as a decomposed form of the standard one-dimensional convolutional operation, is composed of depthwise convolution and pointwise convolution as shown in Fig. 4. The standard one-dimensional convolution takes $D_{in} \times M$ as the input feature mapping F and output $D_{out} \times N$ as the output feature mapping G, where D_{in} represents the size of the input feature vector. M means the number of channels of the input feature vector. D_{out} represents the width and height of the output features. N means the number of channels of the output feature vector. Then, the one-dimensional convolutional kernel K is defined as:

$$K = D_k \times M \times N \tag{2}$$

where, D_k means the dimension on features by convolutional kernel. If we set both the stride and padding as 1, the output feature mapping is computed by the standard convolution as:

$$G_{k,n} = \sum_{i,m} K_{i,m,n} \cdot F_{k+i-1,m}. \tag{3}$$

where, m and n represent the input and output channel, k represents the size of the convolution kernel, and i represents the beginning position of the convolution operation on the input vector.

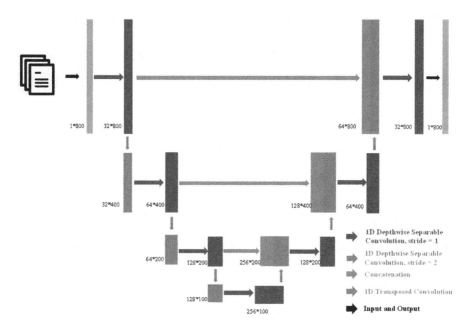

Fig. 3. The architecture of the 1DL-UNet for Botnet detection.

Then, the number of parameters $Params_{Conv}$ and the computational cost $FLOPs_{Conv}$ in floating point operations can be computed as:

$$Params_{Conv} = D_k \cdot M \cdot N \tag{4}$$

$$FLOPs_{Conv} = D_k \cdot M \cdot D_{out} \cdot N \tag{5}$$

As shown in Eq. (4) and (5), the computation cost is determined by the number of input and output channels, kernel size, and feature mappings. To reduce the cost to a reasonable level, the designed 1DL-UNet decomposes the standard convolutional operations based on diminishing the dependence between the output channels and the size of the convolutional kernel. We substitute the filter and combination operations in the standard convolution process with depthwise convolution and pointwise combination in 1DL-UNet, respectively. The one-dimensional depthwise convolution applies a filter on each input channel as:

$$G'_{k,m} = \sum_i K'_{k,m} \cdot F_{k+i-1,m} \tag{6}$$

where, K' is a depthwise convolutional kernel with $D_K \times D_K \times M$ in size. The m-th filter in K' is applied on the m-th channel in F to generate the m-th channel on the output feature mapping in G'. The depthwise convolution is designed as shown in Fig. 5.

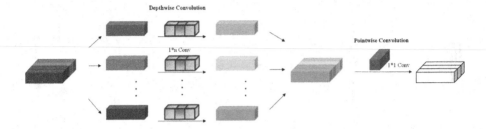

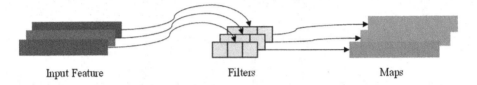

Fig. 4. The one-dimensional (1D) depthwise separable convolution.

Input Feature   Filters   Maps

Fig. 5. The detailed implementation of the depthwise convolution.

Based on the above analysis, the number of parameters $Params_{DC}$ and the computation cost $FLOPs_{DC}$ in the depthwise convolution are computed as:

$$Params_{DC} = D_K \cdot M \tag{7}$$

$$FLOPs_{DC} = D_K \cdot M \cdot D_{out} \tag{8}$$

As the depthwise convolution only achieves filtering operations to the input feature mappings, it fails to combine all filtered feature maps into an integrated output. To solve this issue, we introduce an additional linear combination with 1×1 convolutional operation in a pointwise convolutional layer, as shown in Fig. 6.

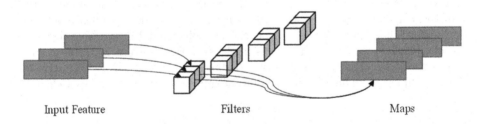

Input Feature   Filters   Maps

Fig. 6. The detailed implementation of the pointwise convolution.

Based on the above design, the number of parameters $Params_{PC}$ and the computation cost $FLOPs_{PC}$ in the pointwise convolution are computed as:

$$Params_{PC} = M \cdot N \tag{9}$$

$$FLOPs_{PC} = M \cdot D_{out} \cdot N \tag{10}$$

By combining the depthwise convolution with pointwise convolution, the overall parameter volume and computation cost in the 1D-DSC are computed as:

$$Params_{DSC} = D_k \cdot M + M \cdot N \tag{11}$$

$$FLOPs_{DSC} = D_K \cdot M \cdot D_{out} + M \cdot D_{out} \cdot N \tag{12}$$

Finally, the ratio of both the number of parameters $Params_{ratio}$ and the cost computation $FLOPs_{ratio}$ between the depthwise separable convolution and the standard convolution are computed as:

$$Params_{ratio} = \frac{D_K \cdot M + M \cdot N}{D_K \cdot M \cdot N} = \frac{1}{N} + \frac{1}{D_K} \tag{13}$$

$$FLOPs_{ratio} = \frac{D_K \cdot M \cdot D_{out} + M \cdot D_{out} \cdot N}{D_K \cdot M \cdot D_{out} \cdot N} = \frac{1}{N} + \frac{1}{D_K} \tag{14}$$

The degree of reduction in the number of parameters and computations contained in depthwise separable convolution and the number of output channels and convolution during convolution operations are as shown in Eqs. (13) and (14). The kernel size is related. When the output channel and the convolution kernel are large, the content of parameters and computation in the depthwise separable convolution is more different from the original standard convolution. The deep neural network model obtained by introducing the depthwise separable convolution meets the goal of botnet detection on the Internet based on network traffic data.

4 Experiments and Result Analysis

4.1 Configurations, Data Processing and Evaluation Metrics

All models trained in this paper are running on Ubuntu with 32GB memory, Intel(R) Xeon(R) CPU E5-2680 v4 @ 2.40 GHz, and TITAN XP. All models are written by Pytorch and accelerated with Adam. We set $batch\_size = 64$, $epoch = 40$ and $learning\_rate = 0.001$.

The benchmark ISCX Botnet dataset [16] is chosen. This dataset contains 16 types of botnet attacks and benign traffic. The original data are stored in .pcap files. We organized the network traffic into *NetFlow* with $P = p_1, p_2, ..., p_n$ while $p_i = (f_i, s_i, t_i)$, where f_i represents the *NetFlow* information extracted, s_i means the size of this network flow and t_i means the beginning time when communication happens. When *NetFlow* differentiate the communications in directions, we combine them into a network session defined as $Session_j = p_1, p_2, ..., p_k$ and all flows are organized sequentially according to their happening times where $t_1 < t_2 < \cdots < t_k$.

To reduce the number of packets for Botnet detection with both 1D-UNet and 1DL-UNet, two strategies denoted as *Exp*1 and *Exp*2 are applied. We extract the first packet in a session for analysis in $Exp1$. In $Exp2$, if a session contains effective payloads, we choose the first packet with an effective payload as the starting point to extract a given length of bytes for later analysis. Otherwise, starting with the first packet of the session. When the number or length of the data packets is insufficient, we use $0x00$ for padding. Finally, all samples extracted are randomly partitioned into the training set, validation set, and testing set with $3 : 1 : 1$ in ratio.

All models are compared under the same performance metrics, including accuracy, precision, recall and F1-score, as shown in Eqs. (15)–(18).

$$Accuracy = \frac{TP + TN}{TP + FP + FN + TN} \tag{15}$$

$$Precision = \frac{TP}{TP + FP} \tag{16}$$

$$Recall = \frac{TP}{TP + FN} \tag{17}$$

$$F1\text{-}score = 2 \cdot \frac{Precision \cdot Recall}{Precision + Recall} \tag{18}$$

where $TP(TruePositive)$ represents the number of Botnet traffic that can be correctly detected, $TN(TrueNegative)$ represents the number of benign traffic that can be correctly detected, $FP(FalsePositive)$ represents the number of benign traffic that mistakenly classified as Botnet, and $FN(FalseNegative)$ represents the number of Botnet traffic that mistakenly classified as benign.

4.2 Results and Analysis

4.2.1 Number of Packets and Performance

The number of packets and the size of each packet varied remarkably among different network communication sessions. The statistical features of packets in the ISCX dataset are summarized in Table 1. As shown in Table 1, the number of packets in a session varies greatly. In our experiments, we set the size of the extracted data as 100. Considering the median value for the number of packets is 6, we tested whether the number of packets will seriously affect the final performance and set different values for this parameter. The results under both the 1D-UNet and the 1DL-UNet are shown in Table 2 and 3.

Based on the performance results under both the 1D-UNet and 1DL-UNet as shown in Table 2 and 3, we made the following observations.

(1) Under the $Exp1$ where we extract packets from the beginning of a network session for analysis, both 1D-UNet and 1DL-UNet achieve the best detection accuracy with 99.65% and 99.66% when 8 packets are extracted for analysis. When more than 4 packets are used, the detection accuracy keeps stable under both 1D-UNet and 1DL-UNet with minor fluctuations as 0.08% and 0.10%.

Table 1. Basic statistical patterns in the ISCX Botnet dataset

Statistical Indicators	Quantity
Total number of sessions	373,107
Average number of packets in a session	36
Maximum number of packets in a session	944,228
Minimum number of packets in a session	1
Mode of packets for sessions	6
Median of packets for sessions	6

Table 2. The performance of two models under different settings with the number of packets extracted for learning on $Exp1$.

No. of packets	1D-UNet				1DL-UNet			
	Accuracy	Precision	Recall	F1-score	Accuracy	Precision	Recall	F1-score
1	96.81	95.64	96.89	96.26	96.75	96.65	95.82	96.23
2	99.28	99.11	99.22	99.16	99.26	99.30	98.98	99.14
4	99.58	99.54	99.49	99.51	99.63	99.61	99.52	99.56
6	99.59	**99.59**	99.47	99.53	99.61	99.52	99.58	99.55
8	**99.65**	99.50	**99.67**	**99.59**	**99.66**	99.54	**99.68**	99.61
10	99.61	99.49	99.59	99.54	99.62	99.54	99.58	99.56
12	99.63	99.49	99.65	99.57	99.57	99.59	99.40	99.50
14	99.59	99.47	99.59	99.53	99.56	99.49	99.49	99.49
16	99.57	99.51	99.49	99.50	99.61	**99.62**	99.48	**99.69**

(2) Under the $Exp2$ where we extract packets from the first packets with effective payload in a network session for analysis, both 1D-UNet and 1DL-UNet achieve the best detection accuracy with 99.62% and 99.63% when 8 packets are extract for analysis. There is minor performance degradation with 0.03% on average when compared with that under the $Exp1$. The main reason is that some Botnet attacks are mainly DDoS attacks without sending any effective payload.

(3) When both models are tested under two data extraction methods, including $Exp1$ and $Exp2$, it is shown that the detection accuracy under $Exp2$ achieves the best performance than $Exp1$ with 2.69% improvements when using 1 packet for analysis. When more than 2 packets are used, the detection performance quickly converges and remains stable.

(4) When applied on end devices with limited resources and computing power, both 1D-UNet and 1DL-UNet are applicable for Botnet detection with only 4 packets for analysis. Under some critical situations, a satisfactory detection accuracy with only 1 or 2 packets for analysis is possible. Therefore, the designed 1D-UNet and 1DL-UNet are not only lightweight but also effective for Botnet detection on the Internet and IoT.

Table 3. The performance of two models under different settings with the number of packets extracted for learning on *Exp2*.

No. of packets	1D-UNet				1DL-UNet			
	Accuracy	Precision	Recall	F1-score	Accuracy	Precision	Recall	F1-score
1	99.19	98.92	99.18	99.05	99.26	98.92	99.35	99.14
2	99.34	99.14	99.32	99.23	99.38	99.31	99.24	99.27
4	99.54	99.49	99.44	99.47	99.58	99.46	99.55	99.50
6	99.61	**99.59**	99.49	99.54	99.57	99.54	99.46	99.50
8	**99.62**	99.51	**99.59**	**99.55**	**99.63**	99.51	**99.63**	**99.57**
10	99.47	99.41	99.36	99.38	99.56	99.47	99.50	99.48
12	99.58	99.55	99.46	99.51	99.63	**99.56**	99.58	99.57
14	99.49	99.33	99.49	99.41	99.62	99.56	99.56	99.56
16	99.56	99.53	99.46	99.49	99.61	99.50	99.59	99.55

4.2.2 Number of Parameters and Computation Cost

The top goal of our design is a compressed neural network with satisfactory performance on Botnet detection on the Internet. When configured with the best parameter as shown in the former section, we compared our models with the One-Dimensional Mobile (1D-MobileNet) based on the MobileNet [6]. All three models are compared under two different settings, including *Exp1* with 8 packets and *Exp2* with 1 packet, as shown in Table 4 and 5, respectively. Based on the results in Table 4 and 5, we made the following observations.

Table 4. Performance comparison among three models under *Exp1* with 8 packets for analysis.

Method	Accuracy	Precision	Recall	F1-score	Params(M)	FLOPs(G)
1D-UNet	99.65	99.50	99.67	99.59	0.716	0.141
1DL-UNet	99.66	99.54	**99.68**	99.61	**0.245**	**0.056**
1D-MobileNet	**99.68**	**99.59**	99.65	**99.62**	3.178	0.258

Table 5. Performance comparison among three models under *Exp2* with 1 packet for analysis.

Method	Accuracy	Precision	Recall	F1-score	Params(M)	FLOPs(G)
1D-UNet	99.22	**98.94**	99.23	99.08	0.715	0.025
1DL-UNet	99.26	98.92	99.35	99.14	**0.243**	**0.007**
1D-MobileNet	**99.28**	98.94	**99.38**	**99.16**	2.434	0.046

(1) All models achieve satisfactory performance on accuracy as higher as 99.6%. When using only 1 packet for analysis, the detection accuracy shows 0.4% degradation when compared with the setting under *Exp1* with 8 packets. However, the number of packets extracted is greatly reduced and thus more

suitable for end devices in Internet. The computation cost under the 1DL-UNet with $Exp2$ is only 12.5% of that under the 1D-UNet with $Exp1$ on 8 packets.

(2) The number of parameters can be greatly compressed. As a lightweight model, the 1D-MobileNet is smaller than MobileNet [6]. However, the 1D-MobileNet is 4 times bigger than 1D-UNet and 12 times bigger than 1DL-UNet in the number of parameters. Meanwhile, the computation cost of the 1D-MobileNet is 1.5 and 4 times higher than that of the 1D-UNet and 1DL-UNet, respectively.

4.2.3   Performance for Botnet Detection

The designed 1DL-UNet is then compared with other models for Botnet detection on the Internet, including ResNet-DCGAN [5], BiLSTM-GAN [5], Rule Induction [12], BNN [20] and LSTM-CNN [17]. The results are shown in Table 6. Based on the results, we made the following observations.

Table 6. Performance comparison with similar models for Botnet detection.

Method	Accuracy	Precision	Recall	F1-score
ResNet+DCGAN [5]	99.23	99.46	99.29	99.37
BiLSTM+GAN [5]	85.51	91.55	82.38	86.72
Rule Induction [12]	98.8	98.7	98.8	99.4
BNN [20]	94.5	94.5	76.6	84
LSTM-CNN [17]	99	98	**100**	–
1DL-UNet+Exp1(8 packets)	**99.66**	**99.54**	99.68	**99.61**
1DL-UNet+Exp2(1 packet)	99.26	98.92	99.35	99.14

(1) The 1DL-UNet achieves the best performance on all metrics when compared with other models. Even when tested under $Exp2$ with one packet for analysis, the 1DL-UNet is 0.03% better than ResNet-DCGAN [5] on accuracy. The ResNet-DCGAN takes the beginning 1,024 bytes from the network flows for analysis by converting them into images. The generated images are usually failed to preserve the typical communication logic relations. When compared with the ResNet-DCGAN, the 1DL-UNet is not only smaller but also good at extracting network communication logic based on the combination of both network communication states and contents included.

(2) Four models, including BiLSTM-GAN [5], Rule Induction [12], BNN [20] and LSTM-CNN [17], are mainly based on a separated statistical feature extraction process on network packets. Therefore, the detection performance is highly affected by the quality of the feature processing method. As the majority of the feature extraction works are done manually, the performance of the trained model is thus seriously damaged. Thus, the 1DL-UNet outperforms others on the whole. More importantly, the byte sequences extracted

from the raw network packet are effective for Botnet detection instead of using discrete statistical features.

(3) When compared with BNN [20] that mainly deployed on the end device in Internet, the 1DL-UNet achieves 4.76% higher detection accuracy while introducing lower parameters and computation cost. Above all, the 1DL-UNet is applicable on either Internet servers or end devices with limited resources.

5   Conclusions

Designing a high-performance intrusion detection system is challenging because of the tedious configurations and heterogeneous devices on the Internet. Some state-of-the-art solutions are mainly server-oriented and expose the end device to attackers. The Botnet, as a popular attack dominated on the Internet and the Internet-of-Things, is hard to defend without all devices' cooperation in the whole network. Therefore, this paper presents a deep learning-powered Botnet detection model applicable for both servers and end devices. Two models, including 1D-UNet and 1DL-UNet, are demonstrated to be effective on Botnet detection with limited resources.

Based on our work, future research works are possible in the following directions. First, it is possible to distribute a compressed model from the server to the end device instead of training a lightweight model on the end device. But both the distribution process and the compressed model are vulnerable against adversarial attackers. Second, most of the existing solutions are demonstrated to be effective in detecting Botnet except the source tracing especially when DDoS involves. Third, both lightweight models and compressed models are vulnerable to adversarial attacks. Thus, all Botnet detection models should be secured and enhanced.

References

1. Nobakht, M., Sivaraman, V., Boreli, R.: A host-based intrusion detection and mitigation framework for smart home IoT using OpenFlow. In: 11th International Conference on Availability. Reliability and Security (ARES), pp. 147–156. IEEE, Salzburg (2016)
2. Antonakakis, M., et al.: Understanding the mirai botnet. In: 26th USENIX Security Symposium, pp. 1093–1110. USENIX Association, Vancouver (2017)
3. Vinayakumar, R., Alazab, M., Srinivasan, S., Pham, Q.V., Padannayil, S.K., Simran, K.: A visualized botnet detection system based deep learning for the Internet of Things networks of smart cities. IEEE Trans. Ind. Appl. **56**(4), 4436–4456 (2020)
4. Ronneberger, O., Fischer, P., Brox, T.: U-net: convolutional networks for biomedical image segmentation. In: Navab, N., Hornegger, J., Wells, W.M., Frangi, A.F. (eds.) MICCAI 2015. LNCS, vol. 9351, pp. 234–241. Springer, Cham (2015). https://doi.org/10.1007/978-3-319-24574-4_28
5. Zou, F., Tan, Y., Wang, L., Jiang, Y.: Botnet detection based on generative adversarial network. J. Commun. **42**(7), 95–106 (2021)

6. Howard, A.G., Zhu, M., Chen, B.: MobilenEts: efficient convolutional neural networks for mobile vision applications. arXiv preprint arXiv:1704.04861 (2017)
7. Zhao, D., Traore, I., Sayed, B., Lu, W., Saad, S.: Botnet detection based on traffic behavior analysis and flow intervals. Comput. Secur. **39**, 2–16 (2013)
8. Gu, G., Porras, P.A., Yegneswaran, V., Fong, M., Lee, W.: BotHunter: detecting malware infection through IDS-driven dialog correlation. In: 16th USENIX Security Symposium, vol. 7, pp. 167–182. USENIX Association, Boston (2007)
9. Gu, G., Perdisci, R., Zhang, J., Lee, W.: BotMiner: clustering analysis of network traffic for protocol-and structure-independent botnet detection. In: 17th USENIX Security Symposium, pp. 139–154. USENIX Association, San Jose (2008)
10. Gu, G., Zhang, J., Lee, W.: BotSniffer: detecting botnet command and control channels in network traffic. In: Proceedings of the Network and Distributed System Security Symposium (NDSS), San Diego, pp. 1–19 (2008)
11. L. Bernaille, R. Teixeira, K. Salamatian: early application identification. In: ACM CoNEXT Conference, Lisbon, pp. 1–12 (2006)
12. Mahardhika, Y.M., Amang, S., Barakbah, A.R.: An implementation of Botnet dataset to predict accuracy based on network flow model. In: 6th International Electronics Symposium on Knowledge Creation and Intelligent Computing (IES-KCIC), pp. 33–39. IEEE, Surabaya (2017)
13. Torres, P., Catania, C., Garcia, S., Garino, C.G.: an analysis of recurrent neural networks for botnet detection behavior. In: 2016 IEEE Biennial Congress of Argentina (ARGENCON), pp. 1–6. IEEE, Buenos Aires (2016)
14. McDermott, C.D., Majdani, F., Petrovski, A.V.: Botnet detection in the internet of things using deep learning approaches. In: 2018 International Joint Conference on Neural Networks (IJCNN), pp. 1–8. IEEE, Rio de Janeiro (2018)
15. Meidan, Y., Bohadana, M., Mathov, Y., Shabtai, A., Breitenbacher, D., Elovici, Y.: N-BaIoT: network-based detection of IoT botnet attacks using deep autoencoders. IEEE Pervasive Comput. **17**(3), 12–22 (2018)
16. Beigi, E.B., Jazi, H.H., Stakhanova, N., Ghorbani, A.A.: Towards effective feature selection in machine learning-based botnet detection approaches. In: 2014 IEEE Conference on Communications and Network Security (CNS), pp. 247–255. IEEE, San Francisco (2014)
17. Hosseini, S., Nezhad, A.E., Seilani, H.: Botnet detection using negative selection algorithm, convolution neural network and classification methods. Springer Sci. Bus. Media Deutschland GmbH **13**(1), 101–115 (2018)
18. Wu, D., Fang, B., Cui, X., Liu, X.: BotCatcher: botnet detection system based on deep learning. J. Commun. **39**(8), 18–28 (2018)
19. Lin, J., Chen, W.M., Lin, Y., Cohn, J., Gan, C., Han, S.: MCUNet: tiny deep learning on IoT devices. In: 34th Conference on Neural Information Processing Systems (NeurIPS), vol. 33, pp. 11711–11722. Curran Associates Inc., Vancouver (2020)
20. Qin, Q., Poularakis, K., Leung, K.K., Tassiulas, L.: Line-speed and scalable intrusion detection at the network edge via federated learning. In: 2020 IFIP Networking Conference and Workshops, pp. 352–360. IEEE, Paris (2017)

On the Application of Active Learning to Handle Data Evolution in Android Malware Detection

Alejandro Guerra-Manzanares$^{(\boxtimes)}$ and Hayretdin Bahsi

Tallinn University of Technology, Tallinn, Estonia
{alejandro.guerra,hayretdin.bahsi}@taltech.ee

Abstract. Mobile malware detection remains a significant challenge in the rapidly evolving cyber threat landscape. Although the research about the application of machine learning methods to this problem has provided promising results, still, maintaining continued success at detecting malware in operational environments depends on holistically solving challenges regarding the feature variations of malware apps that occur over time and the high costs associated with data labeling. The present study explores the adaptation of the active learning approach for inducing detection models in a non-stationary setting and shows that this approach provides high detection performance with a minimal set of labeled data for a long time when the uncertainty-based sampling strategy is applied. The models that are induced using dynamic, static and hybrid features of mobile malware are compared against baseline approaches. Although active learning has been adapted to many problem domains, it has not been explored in mobile malware detection extensively, especially for non-stationary settings.

Keywords: mobile malware · Android · malware detection · active learning · concept drift · data evolution

1 Introduction

Mobile devices play a significant role in our personal and professional lives. Malicious actors target these devices for various purposes ranging from pursuing economic benefits to collecting information for espionage activities. Mobile malware is one of the greatest cyber threats in this digital ecosystem. Android is the most targeted mobile operating system (OS) by attackers; its share in the threat landscape constitutes 98% of the mobile cyber attacks [10]. The security efforts of Google and device vendors in this regard [4,16] have not been able to put a stop to the increasing trend of this type of cyber attack. Machine learning methods have been proposed to detect malware [20] as these techniques may discriminate behavioral patterns of mobile apps to identify new malicious applications.

© ICST Institute for Computer Sciences, Social Informatics and Telecommunications Engineering 2023
Published by Springer Nature Switzerland AG 2023. All Rights Reserved
S. Goel et al. (Eds.): ICDF2C 2022, LNICST 508, pp. 256–273, 2023.
https://doi.org/10.1007/978-3-031-36574-4_15

The research studies that apply machine learning methods to cyber security problems, in general, and mobile malware detection, in particular, usually validate their results on static data sets belonging to specific time frames (e.g., Drebin [2]). However, the threat landscape is subject to constant evolution due to the inherent attack-defense confrontation between the malicious actors and the security experts in the domain. Relevant dynamic and static features of mobile malware have been proved to continuously change (i.e., legitimate apps are also prone to change to some extent) so that the discrimination capabilities of the learning models diminish over time [9]. Thus, handling the non-stationary property of the data should be one of the building blocks of an operational system to maintain continuous high detection performance for malware detection purposes. This denotes that the learning model should be retrained when a significant data distribution shift is detected. Based on the resources available, one option would be to perform periodic retraining of the model to guarantee an updated model regardless of the variations in the data.

Finding labeled data is always a significant challenge in the cyber security domain due to the lack of human resources or confidentiality concerns that eliminate the possibility of data sharing between different organizations. Although one-class models, which are trained on only legitimate samples, provide a solution to some extent, their performance is usually lower when compared to supervised models and they do not enable the induction of multi-class models which may be highly beneficial to identify malware families. Additionally, they require additional mechanisms to prove that legitimate samples are free from any malicious content, which refers to another form of labeling. Similar to all settings, the effectiveness of non-stationary ones also hugely depends on feeding the training sets with recent samples which are correctly labeled. Therefore, the design considerations of such operational detection systems should holistically address labeling and retraining aspects.

On the other side, despite the aforementioned problems, it does not mean that the cyber security vendors (i.e., companies providing mobile malware scanners or protection products in our case) cannot assign any resources for labeling. A typical vendor has teams of malware analysts that work on a daily basis to investigate the new malware samples. Therefore, we contemplate that both data labeling and model retraining can be achieved by adapting active learning to a non-stationary environment. Active learning approaches create an interactive channel between experts and models so that the models themselves select the most informative samples from an unlabeled data pool, ask the class label from the experts and incorporate their answers into the model. Active learning approaches aim to minimize the labeling efforts to achieve the highest model performance possible. These approaches are very instrumental in cases where obtaining unlabeled data is easy and cheap, but labeling is expensive, which reflects the needs of our target problem [17].

In this study, we adapted a pool-based active learning approach that uses the uncertainty sampling strategy to a non-stationary setting and demonstrated its effectiveness in terms of detection performance and the required labeling effort for mobile malware detection in Android devices. We utilized the Android malware data set *KronoDroid* [6] which suits well for non-stationary model experiments as it has timestamped malware and *goodware* samples encompassing the whole Android historical timeline. Dynamic and static features of Android apps, more specifically, system calls and permissions, are used for inducing the models separately or in hybrid mode. We compared our results with two baseline models: (1) a *batch retraining* strategy that uses all the previous labeled samples for inducing a model for the next time period, and (2) an iterative learning strategy that randomly selects a sample from the unlabeled data pool without using any informativeness criteria. Our results show that the uncertainty sampling method achieves over 91% F_1 score, on average, throughout a 7-year-long period while enormously minimizing the required labeling effort (i.e., 2–3% of the labeled samples are enough for high detection performance when compared to the batch retraining strategy).

The performance of active learning in non-stationary settings, subject to concept drift issues, has not been demonstrated comprehensively for mobile malware detection. Therefore, this study provides a solid contribution by proposing active learning for addressing the problems of such detection systems in operational settings.

It is important to note that although this study presents experimental results of a solution that covers both data labeling and model retraining, our focus was to elaborate on the trade-off between the labeling effort and its impact on model performance. We assumed that the model is retrained in fixed intervals. It is evident that the detection performance and labeling resource consumption may be also enhanced by different retraining approaches or intervals which can be coupled with various concept drift detectors. However, the detailed analysis of retraining options is out of scope in the present paper.

This paper is structured as follows. Section 2 provides background information and a summary of the related literature. Section 3 provides the methodology while Sect. 4 reports and discusses the main results. Section 5 concludes the study.

2   Background Information and Literature Review

2.1   Background Information

Active Learning. A form of *semi-supervised learning* based on the assumption that a machine learning (ML) algorithm can yield better performance with fewer training iterations (i.e., less data) if it is allowed to select the data from which it learns [18]. For this purpose, a supervised model is trained with a small quantity of data (i.e., *active learner*) and enabled to submit *queries* for selected unlabeled data samples to a labeling *oracle* (i.e., a human expert). The main aim is to achieve high performance using as few labeled samples as possible, thus minimizing the cost of the data labeling process.

The selection of the specific instance for labeling (i.e., query instance) at each training iteration is based on an *informativeness* assessment of the whole set of unlabeled instances performed by the active learner using a specific query strategy [19]. The pool-based framework, described graphically in Fig. 1, is the most common active learning approach. This approach assumes the existence of a small labeled data set and the availability of a large *pool* of unlabeled data [18]. Query instances are selected from the unlabeled pool for expert annotation. The labeled data sample is then incorporated into the labeled training set which is used to update the knowledge of the ML model (i.e., retraining).

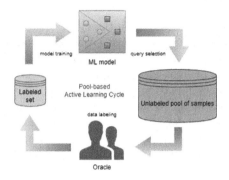

Fig. 1. Pool-based active learning framework

Various query strategies can be used to choose the *most informative* instance [19]. The most commonly used approach is *uncertainty sampling*, where the query instance is selected based on how certain is the learner about the class of the samples. In the *classification uncertainty* scoring strategy, the learner selects the instance (x) for which it is least certain about how to label (i.e., greatest uncertainty). More precisely, the strategy is based on the *least confidence* score (U) computed as:

$$U(x) = 1 - P(y^*|x) \tag{1}$$

where x is a specific instance and y^* is the most likely prediction for that instance.

Concept Drift. Most machine learning models are built on the assumption of *stationary* data, so the testing data attributes are assumed to be similar to the training data attributes, not changing over time. However, in some problem domains, this assumption does not hold as the incoming data features distribution may change over time, thus affecting the *generalization* of the model against new data and, consequently, harming the effectiveness of the detection model over time, a phenomenon called *concept drift* [12]. More precisely, concept drift is observed when the underlying data distribution changes over time (i.e., $P_t(X) \neq P_{t+1}(X)$, where t and $t + 1$ indicate consecutive non-overlapping periods) and affects the decision boundary of the classifier which impacts the target class estimation (i.e., $P_t(y|X) \neq P_{t+1}(y|X)$) and results in a decay of performance over time. The appearance of any type of concept drift requires the update of the knowledge of the learning model to the new data distribution to keep high-performance metrics [12].

As a result of the constant evolution of the threat landscape (e.g., new malware) and the inherent evolution of the Android framework (e.g., system updates), Android malware detection systems are prone to concept drift issues. Therefore, an effective malware detection system must update its knowledge to sustain high detection performance over time.

2.2   Literature Review

The first active learning applications in the cyber security domain were carried out for network intrusion detection using the widely-known KDD Cup 1999 data set [1,11]. Uncertainty sampling strategy achieved the reduction of required labeled data by a factor of eight when compared to the baseline strategy, random sampling, [1] whereas confidence measures identified by transductive reliability estimation reduced this factor to the fifth of the same baseline model [11].

Malicious *doc* files were detected by an active learning solution that yielded a high-performance model with 14% of the labeled samples used by the passive learning model [13]. The directory paths that are retrieved from the hierarchical structure of office documents constitute the features of the detection model in the corresponding study. Uncertainty sampling is complemented by a rare-class detection that is applied in the form of multi-class formulation to annotate malware families [3]. The main idea is to include representative samples from all families while selecting the samples from the pool. The proposed approach was applied to two problems, detection of malicious pdf files and network attacks.

A few Android research studies have concentrated on concept drift handling and none of them used the active learning approach in their method. MaMaDroid [14] and DroidEvolver [21] used API calls and traditional ML and online algorithms, respectively, to handle concept drift, whereas [7,8] used system calls and a data stream methodology to tackle the issue. [5] employed the same approach to address concept drift in the permissions feature space.

[15] draws the attention to experimental biases in malware detection research including the temporal bias and demonstrates how validation designs with such biases influence the results obtained. Although it also demonstrates some results regarding the active learning application in non-stationary settings, the purpose is to underline the biases rather than elaborating on an active learning approach. In our study, we investigate the impact of feature types (i.e., dynamic, static, or both) and data balancing strategies on the detection results. We used a data set that encompasses a longer time frame (i.e., our experimentation covers a period of seven years, whereas [15] covers two years of Android data). Our benchmark includes a comparison with random sampling to show the effectiveness of the uncertainty sampling strategy in our problem formulation.

Similarly, active learning is used as one of the methods for maintaining the detection stability of a mobile malware detection model over time in [22]. Although this period encompasses a long period, five years, this study concentrates on the representation of the feature space rather than the comprehensive evaluation of the active learning approach. More specifically, this study proposes an abstract representation of API call features to grasp better semantic similarities between different malware samples, thus, the model induced using those features can detect the malware evolution better.

3   Methodology

The following sections describe the data set used in our experimental setup, the methodological workflow and the tested scenarios to handle concept drift for Android malware detection using active learning techniques.

3.1   Data Set and Data Features

The data set used in this research is *KronoDroid* [6], a hybrid-featured, labeled, and fully timestamped Android data set, which makes it the most suitable data set for Android concept drift exploration among the available data sets for the purpose of Android malware detection. The *real device* data set was used due to its larger size (i.e., 41,382 malware samples, and 36,755 benign apps). For this study, system calls and permissions features were used as models' input features, along with the *first seen* timestamp and the class labels, which were used to order the samples along the Android historical timeline and class identification, respectively. The *first seen* timestamp, retrieved from *VirusTotal*, provides information about when the sample was received for the first time (i.e., user submission) by the detection system. The usage of this timestamp enabled us to simulate the constant data stream of Android data samples as a realistic scenario for a malware scanner company dealing with an Android malware detection system subject to concept drift issues. For model induction, three sets of input features were used to describe the apps, namely, static (permissions), dynamic (system calls), and hybrid (system calls and permissions) with lengths 166, 288, and 454, respectively, and composed of different variable types. Table 1 summarizes the data set used in this study.

Table 1. Data set summary

Data	Size	Description
Benign samples	36755	Time frame: 2008–2020
Malware samples	41382	Time frame: 2008–2020
Permissions	166	Binary features
System calls	288	Numeric features
Hybrid (perms + syscalls)	454	Binary and numeric features

3.2   Workflow and Scenarios

To explore the application of active learning for concept drift handling and adaptation, the data set was divided into consecutive data chunks, simulating a data stream covering the Android historical timeline. The samples were ordered and grouped in data chunks, according to their timestamp. Additionally, maximum data chunk size and time constraints were used to ensure the existence of sufficient data (i.e., over 100 samples) for every chunk in the whole time frame analyzed. The same classifier algorithm was used in all scenarios and was retrained using different concept drift-handling strategies.

The test scenarios for concept drift handling are described as follows:

- *Batch retraining*: This strategy updates the detection model by retraining the classifier using the whole amount of data available in each specific chunk, and the retrained model is used to forecast the labels for each subsequent period. Therefore, at time t all data from previous time periods (i.e., $s_0, .., s_{t-1}$, where s identifies a data set belonging to a specific time period, t) was used to update the model, and forecast the labels of s_{t+1}. Next, the whole data set belonging to $t+1$ was used to update the model (i.e., retraining) and forecast labels for s_{t+2}. This cycle was repeated for each data chunk until the end of the analysis period. This batch-retraining approach is the frequent solution utilized for concept drift adaptation. It was used as a baseline in our experimentation.
- *Active learning*: This strategy updated the detection model by selecting the *most informative* instances for each data chunk, one at a time, until a predefined performance threshold was reached. The *classification uncertainty* score, as described in Sect. 2.1, was used to rank and select one instance at a time from the unlabeled pool of instances (i.e., whole data chunk). The selected instance was labeled by the *oracle* and used to retrain the model. The rest of the data chunk was used to evaluate the performance increase/decrease after the single retraining step. The training cycle, as depicted in Fig. 1, was repeated until a performance score threshold was achieved. The remaining data, not used in the iterative training steps, were discarded and the trained model was used to forecast all the samples for the next period, as in *batch retraining*. If the performance retrieved processing all the data chunk was lower than the established threshold, the model was rolled back to its best performer configuration and used to forecast the subsequent period data.
- *Random sample selection retraining*: This strategy uses the same iterative training steps as the active learning approach but, in this case, no score is used to select the most informative instances from the unlabeled pool (i.e., whole data chunk). Instead, random sample selection is used. This strategy enabled us to simulate the scenario where a bunch of unlabeled data is available, but no specific criterion is used to select the instances. Thus, samples are selected at random. This model provides the baseline to assess the effectiveness of the sample selection strategy in terms of data labeling minimization.

All the testing scenarios were performed using the same classification algorithm, induced separately using the three feature sets (i.e., static, dynamic, and hybrid). The performance of the induced models, using the different sets of features for all the strategies, was retrieved and compared. In all cases, the model trained using data from period $t - 1$ was used to forecast the labels of the data belonging to the subsequent period, s_t. The main difference among the approaches lies in the training data used and, more specifically, in the strategy used to select the samples for model updating (i.e., all data, random selection or uncertainty score).

The performance of the detection models using the described retraining strategies to handle concept drift was evaluated using two relevant binary classification performance metrics: *accuracy* and F_1 *score* metrics. These metrics were retrieved for each data chunk (i.e., period).

The accuracy metric reports the number of correctly predicted data points out of all the test data points, whereas the F_1 *score* metric is the harmonic mean of *precision* and *recall*. The *precision* of a classification model informs about the fraction of true positive (i.e., malware) data points that the model correctly classified as positive (i.e., malware), while *recall* reports the fraction of samples classified as positive among the total number of positive samples in the testing set.

4   Results and Discussion

The three concept drift-handling retraining strategies described were evaluated using the same base classifier, a Random Forest instance trained using the same initial data set and the default values of Python's *scikit-learn* library. The initial training data set encompassed the months of July and August 2011. This period was selected as it provided enough data to generate a good initial base classification model. Despite that, as the initial training data set was not balanced, a data balancing technique was applied. Two data balancing methods were used (i.e., *random undersampling* and *random oversampling*) and their impact was evaluated. As explained, the remaining data, ordered by their timestamp, were split into consecutive data chunks using temporal and size constraints. Based on experimental tests, the maximum temporal constraint or time window was set at 60 days (i.e., ≈2 months) and the maximum data pool size set to 4000. Therefore, the maximum data chunk size was composed of 4000 data samples, spanning a maximum of 60 days of data per chunk. The time period analyzed ranges from the initial time frame (i.e., July-August 2011) to May-June 2018. Posterior time frames did not provide enough quantity of data to continue our experimentation (e.g., chunks with less than 50 samples), so the experimentation time frame and the provided results encompass 7 years of the Android history.

The active learning query strategy was implemented using Python's *modal* library, while the balancing techniques used the *imblearn* library. Given the inherent randomness of some of the strategies (i.e., random selection) and techniques used (i.e., random under/oversampling) each of the evaluated scenarios was repeated 30 times and the average values were reported. The performance threshold to stop processing data for the active learning approaches was set at

0.95 F_1 score. Therefore, if after processing n samples, an F_1 performance of 0.95 (out of 1) or higher was obtained, no more data was labeled in that quarter and the resulting model was used to forecast the labels for the next period data. When the performance threshold was not achieved, the highest F_1 performer model was used.

Table 2 provides the obtained results using all the described concept drift-handling approaches. More specifically, the column *feature set* describes the input features used by each specific model tested and the *balancing method* column reports the technique used to balance the initial data set, in the case of the two query strategies used (i.e., random and uncertainty), as well as all data chunks for the batch approach (i.e., to avoid that the imbalanced data chunks generated biased RF models). For each combination of the feature sets and balancing methods, three strategies to handle concept drift were evaluated, described in Sect. 3.2, and referenced in the *query strategy* column. The remaining columns in Table 2 report the performance metrics that enabled us to analyze and compare all the evaluated approaches. The *labeled samples* column informs about the average number of samples processed by each model (i.e., $\bar{x}$), that is, the number of instances labeled, to reach the performance threshold, $F_1 \geq 95\%$. The columns F_1 *score* and *accuracy* provide the average performance of the trained models in all time windows in the analyzed time frame (e.g., 45 data chunks spanning between September/October 2011 and May/June 2018). The reported values for labeled samples and the performance metrics are the average values of the 30 tests performed for each specific scenario. The standard deviation (i.e., s) is reported to contextualize better the mean value as a data descriptor. Additionally, for the *labeled samples*, the proportion of the average number of labeled samples reported in relation to the total data available in the analyzed period is reflected by the % column.

As can be observed in Table 2, when the permissions features are used, the active learning approach (i.e., uncertainty) provides similar performance as the baseline model (i.e., batch, using all data), but requires the smallest number of data samples among the tested strategies. The uncertainty-based active learning approach minimizes the data labeling needed to achieve similar performance as the other two approaches using either of the balancing techniques. More precisely, the batch approach, which requires the labeling of all the data samples, shows slightly better performance than the active learning approaches, but these show significantly lower data labeling requirements. In this regard, the uncertainty-based active learning approach outperforms the random selection approach by using less than 18% of the total data in both cases. Even though both single query-based retraining approaches show benefits over the batch approach, the active learning approach requires three times fewer data than the random instance selection to achieve the same performance metrics. This fact evidences that, in the permissions case, the single query-based gradual modification of the classifier decision boundary shows benefits when it is compared to the baseline model, which uses batch processing (all data). The random approach shows slightly lower performance than the baseline model, but with less data labeling

Table 2. Testing scenarios results

Feature set	Balancing method	Query strategy	Labeled samples			F_1 score		Accuracy	
			$\overline{x}$	s	%	$\overline{x}$	s	$\overline{x}$	s
Permissions	Oversampling	Batch	67068	0	100	91.2	0.4	92.5	0.4
		Random	30100.4	129.8	44.9	89.4	1.0	90.3	1.0
		Uncertainty	11845.6	41.7	17.7	89.4	0.6	90.4	0.6
	Undersampling	Batch	67068	0	100	90.9	0.8	92.4	0.8
		Random	29409.9	113.5	43.9	89.5	1.1	90.3	1.1
		Uncertainty	9281.4	35.5	13.8	89.6	0.7	90.5	0.6
Syscalls	Oversampling	Batch	67068	0	100	85.1	0.8	86.1	0.7
		Random	45028.9	127.8	67.1	84.1	0.9	84.9	0.9
		Uncertainty	13098.8	38.6	19.5	84.5	0.9	85.3	0.8
	Undersampling	Batch	67068	0	100	82.7	1.2	83.3	1.2
		Random	45378.7	118.5	67.7	84.5	0.9	85.0	1.0
		Uncertainty	12748.3	52.3	19.0	85.1	1.0	85.5	1.0
Hybrid	Oversampling	Batch	67068	0	100	92.8	0.5	93.5	0.4
		Random	22057.2	121.5	32.9	90.9	1.0	91.2	1.0
		Uncertainty	1991.9	8.9	3.0	91.6	1.2	91.9	1.2
	Undersampling	Batch	67068	0	100	92.5	0.6	93.1	0.6
		Random	20978.4	116.1	31.3	91.0	1.1	91.1	1.1
		Uncertainty	1459.4	6.3	2.2	91.7	1.4	91.9	1.4

needs, evidencing that more data might not be necessary to handle concept drift effectively but that, more importantly, the instance-based gradual retraining of the model may be more beneficial to handle concept drift effectively. There are no major differences in performance in any cases when both balancing methods are compared. However, the *undersampling* approach provides similar performance metrics to the *oversampling* method with significantly fewer data in the *active learning* case (i.e., 28% more data is needed, on average, for the oversampling case than for the undersampling scenario). In conclusion, the best results in terms of both performance and minimization of data labeling needs, when the permissions feature set is used, are obtained using the undersampling balancing strategy combined with the uncertainty-based active learning query approach.

Comparatively, the system calls feature set produced the worst performance models among all tested models in both evaluated metrics, the number of labeled samples needed and performance achieved. More precisely, the batch strategy using undersampling provides average performance metrics below 85%, which are slightly better when oversampling is used. These performance metrics are the worst across all models and feature sets, as none of the tests using the permissions or the hybrid feature sets go lower than 89.4% F_1 and 90.3% accuracy. However, the system calls-based model performance is significantly improved when a single query strategy is implemented, and, more specifically, when the uncertainty-based active learning approach is used, reaching similar performance as the baseline model, as in the permissions case, and even outperforming when undersampling is used. Despite that, the labeling needs for the uncertainty-based active learning, which, again, minimizes the labeling cost, is superior to the permissions case for both sampling techniques (i.e., a minimum of 19% of the data has to be labeled by the oracle). It is worth noting that random selection reaches similar performance as the uncertainty-based strategy but requires, in both cases, over 66.7% of the whole data to be labeled. Thus, again, the single query approach shows advantages over batch processing to handle concept drift effectively, especially when the uncertainty-based active learning approach is applied.

The hybrid feature sets, which combine the permissions and system calls sets for model induction, provide the best overall models, in all cases. The active learning approach using the uncertainty criterion reaches a slightly lower performance than the baseline performance implementing the batch approach. However, in this case, the benefits of the active learning approach are especially evident for both balancing techniques. The labeling needs are significantly lowered, not over-passing 9% of the whole data set. As a result, they provide the best performance-labeling trade-off results among all the test scenarios. In this regard, the best model of all the tested scenarios is obtained using the active learning approach combined with undersampling, yielding an average 91.7% F_1 score and 91.6% accuracy using, on average, only 1460 samples (i.e., $\approx$2.2% of the total data) to provide effective detection in the seven-year-long study period. Comparatively, the uncertainty-based active learning approach for the hybrid-featured models requires 10–15 times fewer data than the random query approach to achieve better performance results and 50 times fewer data to reach similar detection performance than the baseline models. These results show that the hybrid feature set generates better discriminatory models which benefit notably from the active learning approach, being able to handle concept drift with a significantly reduced quantity of labeled data belonging to specific time frames along a seven-year-long time period (i.e., from September-October 2011 to May-June 2018).

To further explore the results, the summary values reported in Table 2 are provided in more fine-grained detail on the analyzed historical timeline of Android in Fig. 2, 3, 4, and 5. More specifically, in these figures, the X-axis reports the time frame of the specific data chunk, encompassing, at maximum, two months of data. The axis labels provide the year and month separated by a slash (e.g., 2011/9–10 reports data comprised between September and October 2011). The left Y-axis reports the number of samples included in every data chunk (i.e., grey color), thus composing the unlabeled pool of samples for the active learning approaches, that were actually labeled by the oracle (i.e., blue color). Given the degree of randomness of the approaches used, the reported values for the number of labeled samples (i.e., blue area on the bars) are mean values with the confidence interval of the mean estimation reported by the white whiskers that extend over and below the mean (i.e., confidence level 95%). The average performance scores obtained on each data chunk are reported by the yellow (i.e., accuracy) and blue (i.e., F_1 score) lines placed on top of the bar chart, and ranging from 0 to 1 (i.e., right Y-axis). The standard deviation of these performance metrics is provided by the colored ribbons surrounding the average lines. Figure 2 provides the average results for the uncertainty-based active learning approach when undersampling and the permissions set were used. Figure 3 reports the same information when the system calls set is used while Fig. 4 provides the hybrid feature set-related information. These figures enable us to compare the impact of the feature set under the same conditions (i.e., uncertainty-based active learning approach using undersampling). Lastly, Fig. 5 enables the comparison between the best active learning model (i.e., hybrid feature set, undersampling using uncertainty score, as depicted in Fig. 4) and the random query strategy for the same feature set and sampling approach configuration.

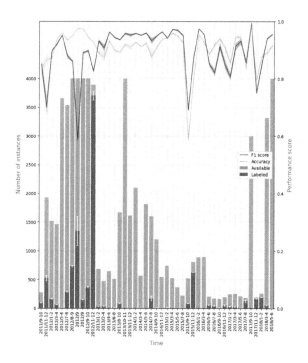

Fig. 2. Permissions, undersampling, and uncertainty-based model results

As can be observed, in Fig. 2, the permissions feature set enabled the handling of concept drift using significantly less labeled data than the system calls feature set, depicted in Fig. 3. With some minor exceptions (e.g., 11–12/2012), the permissions feature set required fewer labeled data per chunk to sustain the training target of 95% F_1 score, over-passing this score in many chunks, thus no data was labeled for training purposes (e.g., 10–11/2013, 11–12/2013, 1–2/2014,

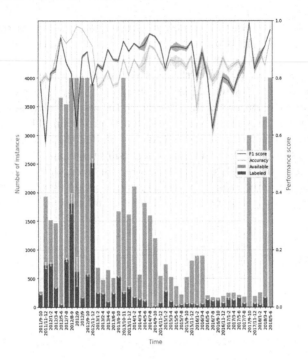

Fig. 3. System calls, undersampling, and uncertainty-based model results

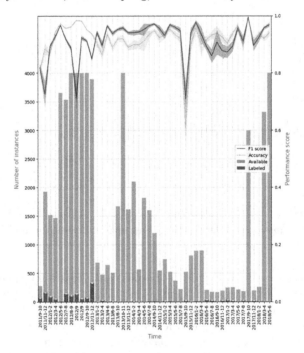

Fig. 4. Hybrid, undersampling, and uncertainty-based model results

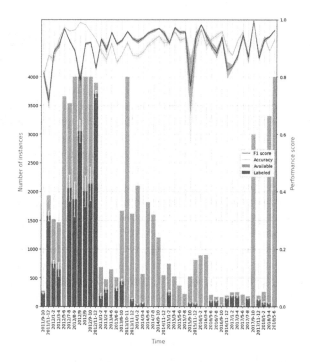

Fig. 5. Hybrid, undersampling, and random selection model results

3–4/2014, and 5–6/2014). Despite the goodness shown by the permissions feature set to handle concept drift using the active learning approach, these results are significantly outperformed by the hybrid feature set, which combines the system calls and permissions feature set. In this case, a reduced proportion of the chunk data is labeled in every chunk to achieve high-performance metrics (e.g., 9–10/2011, 11–12/2011) with extended periods of almost no training data needs (e.g., from 4–6/2013 to 7–8/2015). Therefore, the high-dimensional feature space generated by the joint usage of both feature sets enabled the handling of concept drifts better than any other approach, keeping high-performance metrics with just a few samples labeled per chunk. Even though this feature set reduces the data needs in all approaches and strategies, the uncertainty-based query strategy shows significant improvement concerning random query selection, as can be seen in Fig. 5. The random query strategy requires significantly more labeled data per data chunk to sustain performance and address concept drift, evidencing the superiority of the uncertainty-based selection over random query selection.

The obtained results show that the active learning approach, in its most basic form (i.e., uncertainty sampling) can be effectively used to handle concept drift, keeping high-performance metrics while minimizing the data labeling efforts (i.e., the amount of labeled data needed to keep high performance). As a result, active learning might be an efficient and effective solution to handle concept drift in environments where a large quantity of unlabeled data is available but with high labeling costs. It allows focusing the labeling effort on the *relevant* data to improve the model and discard the *irrelevant* data samples that may not provide benefit to the model. Despite that, uncertainty sampling may yield *biased* classifiers and sub-optimal models if the initial data set is too small or not representative as the model *certainty* is used to rank the *informativeness* or relevancy of the samples. To avoid that, other query strategies could be used such as query by committee or ranked batch-mode [18]. In our case, the initial data set has been proved reliable and large enough to overcome this issue and the performance obtained by the models does not change significantly (i.e., standard deviation values are not large). The exploration of the benefits of other approaches constitutes part of our future work.

The comparative performance metrics provided in this study show that the gradual modification of the decision boundary caused by the addition of a single relevant sample in the training data set provides high-performance models using significantly less data than the batch retraining approach. Random instance selection improves the labeling needs concerning the batch retraining approach, but they are both outperformed significantly by the active learning approach. Random selection requires consistently more data to achieve roughly the same (but not better) performance metrics than the uncertainty sampling approach. This fact evidences the goodness of the active learning approach to induce great performance models with significantly fewer data needs.

To address imbalance issues, two balancing techniques were explored. Random oversampling balances the data by generating artificial but similar data points for the underrepresented class, whereas random oversampling selects a random sample from the overrepresented class to match the number of samples in the underrepresented class. Even though both approaches worked similarly for random and batch strategies, the undersampling approach provided distinctive benefits using the active learning approach for the permissions and hybrid feature sets. This technique minimized the data labeling efforts significantly while producing great discriminatory results. The exploration of more complex balancing approaches is part of our future work.

This paper explores the application of *active learning* as an alternative approach to deal with concept drift in Android malware detection. The related methods in the literature [14, 15, 21, 22] propose the usage of more complex algorithmic solutions that require extensive data labeling efforts and intensive computational resources. The active learning approach, due to its focus on data labeling minimization, reduces the computational load and resources needed to deal effectively with concept drift issues, as demonstrated in this paper. More specifically, the comparison of the results obtained in this study with related works [5, 7, 14, 15, 21, 22] evidences the goodness of the active learning approach to maximize detection performance metrics while minimizing labeling needs and, consequently, computational resources. Most of these proposed solutions assume the labeling of the whole data set at each training step thus they are analogous to the batch retraining approach, which was used as a baseline in our study. Besides, the detection solutions in the literature are more computationally intensive due to their algorithmic complexity. For instance, some methods combine the output of a pool of classifiers [7,21] or use complex adaptive pipelines [14] that increase the burden of system maintenance and the overall resources needed to operate and update the detection system. In our benchmarking, a single classifier model, based on a traditional machine learning algorithm (i.e., Random Forest), using the *active learning* query strategy was capable of providing high detection performance for a long period (i.e., from 2011 to 2018) with few data updates over time and many time frames with zero labeling needs. The performance results are similar to the ones proposed by [7] and the baseline approach (i.e., batch retraining), but use a less complex system, which is easier to maintain and requires less computational and labeling resources. It also outperforms the rest of the concept drift-handling methods in the related literature, which manifest significant performance decay over time [14,21].

5 Conclusions

The active learning approach is built on the assumption that a machine learning model can learn faster (i.e., in fewer training steps) and with less data if the model is allowed to select the data from which it learns. This approach combines the knowledge of an *oracle* and instance selection by the supervised model to enhance performance and minimize data needs. To the best of our knowledge, this is the first study that leverages *active learning* to handle concept drift in Android malware detection. Our results show that the active learning approach, in its most basic form, allows effective concept drift handling in Android malware detection and, more interestingly, minimizes the data labeling needs. Consequently, it becomes an option worth considering for enhancing the ML-based detection systems in cyber security environments (e.g., malware protection companies, security operations centres dealing with Android malware detection), where a large body of unlabeled data is constantly available but the high labeling cost associated makes the task infeasible and prohibitive, thus affecting the detection capabilities of the system.

Acknowledgments. This work is partially funded by the European Union's Horizon 2020 Research and Innovation Programme through ECHO (https://echonetwork.eu/) project under Grant Agreement No. 830943.

References

1. Almgren, M., Jonsson, E.: Using active learning in intrusion detection. In: 2004 Proceedings of the 17th IEEE Computer Security Foundations Workshop, pp. 88–98. IEEE (2004)
2. Arp, D., Spreitzenbarth, M., Hubner, M., Gascon, H., Rieck, K., Siemens, C.: Drebin: effective and explainable detection of android malware in your pocket. In: NDSS, vol. 14, pp. 23–26 (2014)

3. Beaugnon, A., Chifflier, P., Bach, F.: ILAB: an interactive labelling strategy for intrusion detection. In: Dacier, M., Bailey, M., Polychronakis, M., Antonakakis, M. (eds.) RAID 2017. LNCS, vol. 10453, pp. 120–140. Springer, Cham (2017). https://doi.org/10.1007/978-3-319-66332-6_6

4. Google: Google play protect (2021). https://developers.google.com/android/play-protect

5. Guerra-Manzanares, A., Bahsi, H., Luckner, M.: Leveraging the first line of defense: a study on the evolution and usage of android security permissions for enhanced android malware detection. J. Comput. Virol. Hacking Tech. **19**, 1–32 (2022)

6. Guerra-Manzanares, A., Bahsi, H., Nõmm, S.: KronoDroid: time-based hybrid-featured dataset for effective android malware detection and characterization. Comput. Secur. **110**, 102399 (2021)

7. Guerra-Manzanares, A., Luckner, M., Bahsi, H.: Android malware concept drift using system calls: detection, characterization and challenges. Expert Syst. Appl. 117200 (2022). https://doi.org/10.1016/j.eswa.2022.117200

8. Guerra-Manzanares, A., Luckner, M., Bahsi, H.: Concept drift and cross-device behavior: challenges and implications for effective android malware detection. Comput. Secur. **120**, 102757 (2022). https://doi.org/10.1016/j.cose.2022.102757

9. Guerra-Manzanares, A., Nomm, S., Bahsi, H.: In-depth feature selection and ranking for automated detection of mobile malware. In: ICISSP, pp. 274–283 (2019)

10. Kaspersky: Mobile security: Android vs ios - which one is safer? (2020). https://www.kaspersky.com/resource-center/threats/android-vs-iphone-mobile-security

11. Li, Y., Guo, L.: An active learning based TCM-KNN algorithm for supervised network intrusion detection. Comput. Secur. **26**(7–8), 459–467 (2007)

12. Lu, J., Liu, A., Dong, F., Gu, F., Gama, J., Zhang, G.: Learning under concept drift: a review. IEEE Trans. Knowl. Data Eng. **31**(12), 2346–2363 (2018)

13. Nissim, N., Cohen, A., Elovici, Y.: ALDOCX: detection of unknown malicious Microsoft office documents using designated active learning methods based on new structural feature extraction methodology. IEEE Trans. Inf. Forensics Secur. **12**(3), 631–646 (2016)

14. Onwuzurike, L., Mariconti, E., Andriotis, P., Cristofaro, E.D., Ross, G., Stringhini, G.: MaMaDroid: detecting android malware by building Markov chains of behavioral models (extended version). ACM Trans. Priv. Secur. **22**(2) (2019). https://doi.org/10.1145/3313391

15. Pendlebury, F., Pierazzi, F., Jordaney, R., Kinder, J., Cavallaro, L.: {TESSERACT}: eliminating experimental bias in malware classification across space and time. In: 28th USENIX Security Symposium (USENIX Security 2019), pp. 729–746 (2019)

16. Samsung: About knox (2021). https://www.samsungknox.com/en/about-knox

17. Schütze, H., Velipasaoglu, E., Pedersen, J.O.: Performance thresholding in practical text classification. In: Proceedings of the 15th ACM International Conference on Information and Knowledge Management, pp. 662–671 (2006)

18. Settles, B.: Active learning literature survey (2009)

19. Settles, B., Craven, M.: An analysis of active learning strategies for sequence labeling tasks. In: proceedings of the 2008 Conference on Empirical Methods in Natural Language Processing, pp. 1070–1079 (2008)

20. Sharma, T., Rattan, D.: Malicious application detection in android - a systematic literature review. Comput. Sci. Rev. **40**, 100373 (2021)
21. Xu, K., Li, Y., Deng, R., Chen, K., Xu, J.: DroidEvolver: self-evolving android malware detection system. In: 2019 IEEE European Symposium on Security and Privacy (EuroS P), pp. 47–62 (2019). https://doi.org/10.1109/EuroSP.2019.00014
22. Zhang, X., et al.: Enhancing state-of-the-art classifiers with API semantics to detect evolved android malware. In: Proceedings of the 2020 ACM SIGSAC Conference on Computer and Communications Security, pp. 757–770 (2020)

Volatility Custom Profiling for Automated Hybrid ELF Malware Detection

Rahul Varshney, Nitesh Kumar, Anand Handa[✉], and Sandeep Kumar Shukla

C3i Center, Department of CSE, Indian Institute of Technology, Kanpur, Kanpur,
India
{rvarshney20,niteshkr,ahanda,sandeeps}@cse.iitk.ac.in

Abstract. The increasing prevalence of Linux malware poses a severe
threat to private data and expensive computer resources. Hence, there
is a dire need to detect Linux malware automatically to comprehend its
capabilities and behavior. In our work, we attempt to analyze the ELF
binary files before, during, and after execution (or postmortem inspection) using open-source tools. We analyze the ELF binaries in a controlled sandboxed space and monitor the activities of these binaries and
their child processes to assess their capabilities and behaviors. We set up
INetSim, and simulate the fake internet services to increase the chances
of malware behaving as intended. We also generate a custom OS profile
of Ubuntu 16.04. The Volatility tool employs this profile to analyze the
memory dump and extract the artifacts. We modify the Limon sandbox
to use only specific volatility plugins, which reduces the time for report
generation. We extract features from these behavior reports and reports
from memory forensics and combine them with features extracted using
static analysis to build a hybrid model for ELF malware detection. Our
trained hybrid model offers a good accuracy of 99.2% on a recent dataset
of benign and malware samples and with a minimal false-positive rate
of 0.9%. To the best of our knowledge, no one in the literature has performed the memory analysis of ELF malware using the Volatility profile
customization for efficient ELF malware detection.

Keywords: ELF malware · Malware detection · Memory forensics ·
Machine learning · Volatility · Limon sandbox

1 Introduction

Due to the proliferation of Internet usage in the past few years, the quantity of
malware has exploded. Therefore, the computer user community requires automated malware detection strategies that are effective and efficient. Linux, a
UNIX resembling OS has garnered global adoption. This is because of its open-
source nature and widespread popularity on desktop and server systems. Due

© ICST Institute for Computer Sciences, Social Informatics and Telecommunications Engineering 2023
Published by Springer Nature Switzerland AG 2023. All Rights Reserved
S. Goel et al. (Eds.): ICDF2C 2022, LNICST 508, pp. 274–291, 2023.
https://doi.org/10.1007/978-3-031-36574-4_16

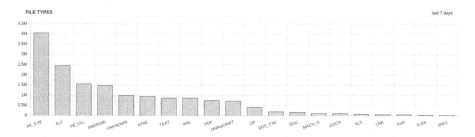

Fig. 1. Samples submitted to VirusTotal [3] in last 7 days

to Linux's extensive use in mobile and server machines, makes it a viable target for malware developers. The quantity of ELF samples reported to VirusTotal [3] in the last week of May 2022 is comparable to that of Windows PE binaries as shown in Fig. 1.

In 2008, a sudden surge in Linux-targeting malware was detected. "Shane Coursen, a senior technical consultant at Kaspersky Lab, stated, The surge of Linux malware is simply attributable to Linux's rising popularity, particularly as a desktop operating system" [7]. Malware (short for "malicious software") is a code chunk or an executable file, typically transmitted over a network, that infects, steals, investigates, or does practically any activity an attacker desires. Malware can be divided into numerous categories based on its behaviours. Some of them are – backdoor, trojan, virus, cryptojackers, etc.

There exist a few approaches to detect malware which are signature based and anomaly based. Signature based technique uses the pre-programmed list of known threats developed by the antivirus companies. This list generally contains signatures of the known threats that uniquely identifies that specific malware and the antivirus keeps on updating the list. In the past, this technique provided adequate protection until the malware authors became more advanced and developed methods like polymorphism to evade such signature based detection. An anomaly-based detection system employs machine learning models to teach the system to estimate a normalised baseline, as opposed to looking through a pre-programmed list to detect known threats. One of the advantages of using anomaly-based systems is that they have the potential to discover unknown threats. However, these systems are easily susceptible to a high number of false detection. This technique was particularly designed to detect suspicious characteristics that can be present in unknown and modified versions of existing known malware samples. "Malware authors are constantly developing new threats, and the anomaly-based approach is the only way to deal with this volume of malware emerging daily [9]." This strategy is one of the few that can combat polymorphic malware which undergoes continual changes and adapts to the environment. This method employs several different techniques such as static, dynamic, and memory analysis.

In static analysis, only static characteristics of a binary file are used. All the analysis should be complete without executing the binary, only using the contents of the ELF header, embedded strings, and other statically extracted information. This analysis is rapid as we are not executing the binary, but along with its benefits, it has some limitations. Static analysis does not perform well for polymorphic and packed malware. In dynamic analysis, a binary executable is allowed to execute inside a secure and isolated environment. This environment is preferably a controlled virtual machine which is recoverable to a known safe state. This analysis requires the examination of the behaviour of binary under execution to classify it as malware or benign. It has the advantage of remaining unaffected by run-time packing and code obfuscation. Therefore this analysis overcomes the problem of polymorphic and packed malware. Besides these benefits, it has some limitations as well; some of them are – code coverage, anti-VM techniques, etc. Memory analysis can uncover unorthodox malware, such as memory-resident and fileless malware. Memory Analysis is the process of obtaining information about the status of a computer, the processes running on it, network connectivity, and other digital artifacts by analysing a memory image. Analysing the memory after malware execution provides a postmortem perspective and facilitates the extraction of forensics artifacts. Memory analysis also has some limitations like damaged/corrupted memory dump, unsupported memory structure, etc.

A memory image is simply the snapshot of the system's component and the current state of the main memory at a particular instant of time. Memory Image is basically like a photocopy of the main memory, which is helpful in the later examination. The generated image is saved in a format suitable for forensic examination, "Forensic image format namely .vmem, .mem, .dmp, .dump, .crash, .dat and many others". Some of these formats can differentiate between the main memory image and a secondary disk image. For instance, the image of physical memory will have some inaccessible sections as these were used in memory-mapped I/O, while the disk image does not. Various tools can be used to image and analyse the main memory of the machine. The procedure for accessing the main memory is different for different operating systems. After the memory is imaged, it is submitted for memory analysis to determine the system's current state and extract network information and other useful artifacts.

In the current scenario, there is a vast range of malware used to steal personal information, commit financial fraud, and attack vital infrastructures. Top multinational corporations and government organisations are currently investing large sums of money to be protected against these malicious activities. Either these enterprises attempt to rely on antivirus vendors, or they develop their own malware detection systems. Typically, these systems employ signature-based or anomaly-based detection approaches. We seek to construct a model that extracts information before, during and after execution of Linux binaries which is free from shortcomings of signature and anomaly based systems. We attempt to blend all three approaches, as one assists the others in overcoming their limitations. However, avoiding one analysis makes the executable susceptible to others. For instance, packaging and obfuscation prevent the executable from being analysed statically. As the executable file must do additional activities for execution, it is easily traceable utilising system calls and additional process creation in dynamic and memory analysis. Consequently, it is considerably more difficult for malware programmers to circumvent all techniques simultaneously. Hence, we develop a model that combines characteristics from all of them with a minimum number of false positives and high detection accuracy. In our work, we have faced the following challenges –

- We have faced the challenge of exact memory image creation for the extraction of memory artifacts from the memory dump. One cannot be 100% sure that the formed memory image represents the correct state of **running** system.
- Even after memory image creation, the volatility framework [6] does not able to extract the artifacts from that memory dump because it does not support the kernel version of Ubuntu 16.04 or higher.

The major contributions of our work are as follows –

- To avoid the problem of damaged or corrupted memory image, we have used the **VMWare Workstation** which provides us the exact memory image of the guest OS by first saving and suspending the guest virtual machine.
- To avoid the problem of unsupported memory structure, we have built a specific OS profile [22] for Ubuntu 16.04 using **dwarfdump** tool. This profile is used by the volatility framework to parse the memory dump and provide the relevant information using a variety of volatility plugins.
- We have also customised the Limon sandbox to use specific volatility plugins for Linux OS such as **linux_pslist**, **linux_pstree**, **linux_psxview**, **linux_psaux**, **linux_malfind**, **linux_netscan**, etc. Only these plugins are providing some output for memory image of used Linux OS.
- We have extracted the distinctive features before, during and after the execution of ELF. We have also built a machine learning model that uses an aggregate of extracted features from static, dynamic, and memory analysis and performs automatic malware detection on a significant count of binary executable files without the need for manual intervention.

The rest of the paper is organized as – Sect. 1 discusses the various approaches to detect malware, challenges faced in our work and the contributions. We addressed some prior work in the realm of Linux malware detection employing static, dynamic, and memory analysis in Sect. 2. Section 3 explains the design methodology. The experimental results and the dataset description is described in Sect. 4. Section 5 concludes the work with subjective future directions.

2   Related Work

This section examines some of the researches in the field of Linux malware detection. They are discussed as follows –

Static Detection Approaches. Shalaginov Andrii [21] proposed a methodology for the classification of Linux malware into various families using Deep

Neural Network (DNN). Their approach overcomes the limitation of the shallow neural network used for Windows PE files classification. Their dataset includes 10574 ELF files labelled by Microsoft following the naming convention of malware standardised by CARO (Computer Anti-Virus Research Organization). The authors have extracted 30 features from ELF format and VirusTotal for classification and achieved an accuracy of 71% for classification among 19 different malware categories with a concise model of 10 layers. However, adding features from the behavioural analysis may result in an improvement in accuracy.

Jinrong Bai et al. [11] introduced a new technique for detecting malware in which system calls were extracted from the executable's symbol table. They chose 100 of these extracted system calls as features out of the numerous available options. Their dataset collection includes 756 benign ELF executables extracted from Linux systems binaries and 763 malicious ELF executables downloaded from the VX heavens. Their approach achieved a detection rate of 98% for malware.

The writers of ELF-Miner [19], Shahzad F. analysed executable and linkable format (ELF). They have retrieved 383 features from the ELF header. Information gain has been employed as the algorithm for feature selection. For categorisation, they used the well-known algorithms of supervised learning, namely decision tree J48, PART (Partial Decision Tree), RIPPER (Repeated Incremental Pruning to Produce Error Reduction), and C4.5 Rules. Their dataset collection included 709 benign ELF executables scraped from the Linux system binaries and 709 malicious ELF executables scraped from VX heavens and offensive computing. Their approach recorded a detection rate of approximately 99% with less than 0.1% false alarms.

Static Analysis techniques can have less detection time as the binary is not allowed to execute, but it can be easily thwarted by malware authors using packing and obfuscation techniques. Due to the packing of executables, one can not extract much helpful information without allowing it to execute in a system.

Dynamic Detection Approaches. Zhang Zhaoqi [23] proposed a novel low-cost feature extraction approach from dynamic analysis of Windows malware and an effective deep neural network (DNN) architecture for quick malware detection. They have represented API call arguments in the hashed form to keep distinct features. DNN architecture initially transforms those extracted features using Gated-CNNs (convolutional neural network), and these transformed features are further passed through bidirectional LSTM (long short term memory network) to understand the correlation among API calls. They have used a dataset of 27287 malicious and 33400 benign PE samples obtained from SecureAge Technology of Singapore. After various experiments on the count of gated CNNs and bi-LSTM layers, their final configuration achieved an accuracy of 98.80%. They have not mentioned using anything to evade the sandbox detection before the generation of execution logs.

K. A. Ashmita [10] proposed a method depending on the use of system call characteristics. They employ 'strace' to monitor all the system calls made by executables operating in a contained environment. They have classified the system calls into four classes: union, intersection, and distinctive features for benign and malware files. They have used correlation-based feature reduction in two steps. In order to rank the features, they evaluated feature-class correlation using entropy change and information gain before calculating feature-feature correlation to eliminate redundant features. For the classification of Linux malware, they employed three popular algorithms of supervised learning namely decision tree J48, Random Forest, and AdaBoost, and their feature set had 27 features. The dataset employed by the authors of this work contains 668 files, 442 of which are benign and 226 of which are malware. From this strategy, they achieved a 99.40% accuracy.

Shahzad, F., and Shahzad M. [20] have presented the idea of a genetic footprint that mines the information from the kernel's Process Control Block (PCB) of ELFs and uses that information to determine the behaviour of a process at runtime. In their method, the authors have selected 16 from a total of 118 available "task_struct" parameters for each operational process. The writers claim to have conducted forensics research to determine which factors to use. According to the authors, the selected parameters will describe the semantics and behaviour of the executing process. They have compiled a system call dump containing these parameters collected over 15 s with a 100-ms resolution. In the WEKA environment, all benign and malicious sample processes are classified by employing multiple algorithms, namely the J48 decision tree, SVM, a propositional rule learner (J-Rip), and RBF-Network. They have analysed their results and identified J-48 J-Rip classifiers with the least amount of class noise. The dataset employed by the authors consists of 219 samples, 105 of which are benign processes and 114 newly gathered malicious processes. From this strategy, they achieved a 96% accuracy and 0% false positive rate within less than 100 ms of the onset of malicious operation.

Dynamic analysis can provide a better understanding of malware behaviour than static analysis, but some precautions should be taken to avoid potential security risks. Moreover, dynamic analysis is more expensive both in terms of time and resources used for malware detection. As the malware analyst does not manually interact with the binary during execution, multiple paths for execution remain unexplored.

Memory Based Detection. "Memory analysis has been demonstrated to be a potent analysis tool that can effectively examine the activities of malware" [18]. Memory analysis draws malware experts because it provides a full examination of malware by examining malicious hooks and code outside the regular scope of a function. It analyses information about executing processes and the general overview of the system using stored memory image.

Sihwail Rami [17] presented a novel approach for classification and detection of Windows malware, which retrieves memory-based characteristics from images utilising memory forensic procedures. Those characteristics may reveal the malware's true behaviour, such as demanding elevated rights to carry out particular tasks, interaction with the operating system, connecting with the command and control server, and DLL and process injection. Their dataset collection consists of 966 benign and 2502 malicious executables retrieved from VirusTotal. Their approach represents malicious behaviour by six feature types, namely API calls, the process handles, network, DLLs, code injection, and privileges resulting in a total feature count of 8898 features. The authors claim to do feature selection using Information gain and correlation as well, but it results in degradation of accuracy. Using the SVM classifier, their method achieved a detection accuracy of 98.5% for malware with a false positive rate of as low as 1.24%. Due to a vast number of features, their approach suffers in time complexity, thereby taking much longer to train and test the model.

Mosli Rayan [15] employs difference in 'the use of handles' by benign and malware executables. They have extracted and exploited this usage difference to classify the executables into two categories (malware and benign). The authors have used the cuckoo sandbox for automating malware execution and generation of memory dumps. They have also used the volatility framework for extracting the handles information from the memory dump. Their dataset consists of 3130 malware samples and 1157 benign samples, which are divided in the ratio of 80:20 for training and testing, respectively. They have trained three classifiers, namely KNN, Random Forest, and SVM. Random Forest surpassed the other two methods and achieved an accuracy of 91.4% with precision and recall of 89.8% and 91.1%, respectively. Their approach primarily focuses only on handles information and neglects the other artifacts present in the memory.

Using only the memory analysis technique for malware detection suffers from a drawback that it can only be employed after the system gets infected, thereby making it the second layer of defence against malware detection.

3   Design and Implementation

The complete overview of our proposed framework for malware detection is shown in Fig. 2. We first filter the samples using ssdeep to eliminate polymorphic samples and acquire the actual labels for ELFs using VirusTotal API [5]. We use tools like readelf [4], strings to extract features from various headers of ELF. Our framework submits the ELF executable to the Limon sandbox for their safe execution inside a guest virtual machine. The framework starts INetSim [1] to simulate all the fake internet services and their simulation to decrease the chances of sandbox detection by the malware. We execute the samples for 30 s. During this time frame, our framework monitors all the activities such as – system calls, files or directories accessed, IPs contacted, etc. After execution, volatility processes the guest machine's memory dump for extraction of memory forensics artifacts. We then perform feature reduction and classification for malware detection.

For dynamic analysis, we setup Limon Sandbox. Currently, Limon supports Python 2 only. We install some tools on the host OS, some on the guest OS and some tools on both. Some of these tools are preinstalled on recent Linux distributions. The following tools are required to be installed for the proper functioning of the Limon sandbox which is explained as follows:

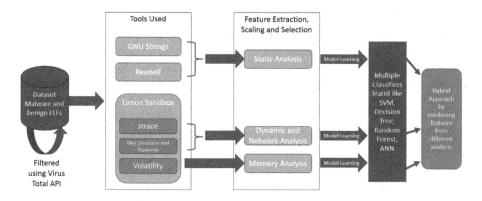

Fig. 2. General Architecture for Linux malware detection

Host System Configurations. We use the host system with specific configurations. The OS on the host machine is Ubuntu 18.04.6 LTS with Intel Core i7 CPU, 1 TB hard drive space, and 16 GB RAM. We install VMWare Workstation 16.1.2 on the host machine. It is used to create a guest virtual machine and to generate a consistent memory image for analysis. Next, we set up the ssdeep on the system because Limon uses it to filter the samples using the fuzzy hashing technique, GNU strings utility to extract meaningful strings from executables, and readelf to extract header data from ELFs. To detect the packed executables, we install YARA-Python on the host. INetSim is installed on the host machine to simulate the fake internet services. Lastly, we configure the Volatility Framework to analyze the memory dump provided by the VMWare workstation. We build a custom profile for Ubuntu 16.04 (guest machine) to ensure the proper functioning of the volatility framework. The profile for Linux is a zip file with information about the kernel's data structures and debug information. We built the profile using the tool known as dwarfdump, which requires the exact kernel version.

Guest System Configurations. On the VMWare workstation, we install a guest OS with the specifications – Ubuntu 16.04 LTS OS with Intel i7 CPU, 4 GB RAM and 60 GB hard drive space. This guest machine is used by the Limon for the execution of samples and generation of reports. We set the 'root' password of the guest OS and enable the root login using the graphical user interface to execute the malware as root. We install strace to collect the system call traces and for execution of 32-bit samples on the 64-bit OS, we add i386 architecture. We also install a few library packages namely libc6:i386, libstdc++6:i386, and libncurses5:i386. Lastly, we allocate a static IP to the guest machine, clear up the bash history, and capture a snapshot of the guest machine. We name this snapshot as cleansnapshot, and it is used as a checkpoint to revert the guest machine to a non-infected state before the execution of the next ELF binary file.

Once the host and guest machine setup is completed, we configure the Limon sandbox's configuration file – `conf.py`. The configuration file includes various settings like the guest machine static IP, directory for sample transfer to the guest machine, root login details of the guest machine, directory for saving final report on the host machine, path for memory dump of the guest machine, path for `tcpdump` to sniff the network activity of the guest machine, path for `strace`, `VirusTotal Public API` to get detection results from antivirus engines, etc. The proposed methodology includes – data generation, feature extraction, feature selection, and classification which are explained further.

3.1 Data Generation

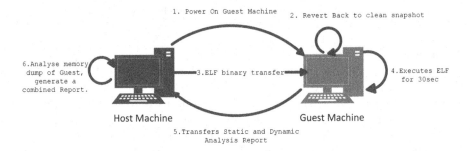

Fig. 3. Process of Report generation

Figure 3 shows the overall setup which is used for data generation for an ELF file. We modify the Limon sandbox source code to extract the output for a specific volatility plugin running on a dump of a particular Linux kernel of Ubuntu 16.04. We submit the sample to the guest machine after the machine gets restored to the uninfected state to ensure that one ELF's effects do not affect others' reports. We start the execution of the ELF binary for 30 s. After this, we stopped the monitoring processes and suspended the guest virtual machine. Next, we acquire the main memory image of the guest machine formed by the VMWare worksta-tion. We analyze the acquired memory image using the Volatility framework 2.6.1 for extracting the list of processes running, list of hidden processes, list of open and closed IP ports, etc. Lastly, we store the complete report, network cap-ture file, and malicious artifacts for further analysis. We repeat this process for all the available ELFs and store their respective reports for feature extraction.

3.2 Feature Engineering

In this section, we discuss the various features extracted from static, dynamic, and memory analysis. We use different tools for the feature extraction in these categories of analysis. The various categories of features are as follows:

Static Features. We extract features from various parts of the ELF structure. These structures are available with the help of two tools; GNU strings and

Table 1. ELF header comparison Benign vs Malware

Features	Mean for Benign	Mean for Malware
Number of section headers	30.609	248.171
Size of ELF header	69.178	52.425
Number of program headers	9.211	4.024
Start of section headers	287014.754	6884126.476
Start of program headers	70.629	5037.257
Section header string table index	28.591	246.143
Size of program headers	58.391	32.977
Size of section headers	67.163	40.804

readelf. Using various arguments to these tools, one can obtain a specific part of the ELF structure. Some of these parts are listed are as follows –

ELF Header: One can extract the ELF header using the 'readelf -h [elf_file]' command. This header gives us information about the organisation of the ELF File. Mean comparison of the features extracted from the ELF header for benign and malware samples is listed in Table 1.

Program Header Table: One can extract the program header table using the 'readelf -l [elf_file]' command. We use segment type (LOAD, PHDR, INTERP, NOTE, DYNAMIC) in the feature set as a binary feature.

Section Header Table: One can extract the section header table using the 'readelf -S [elf_file]' command. We use section name (like .bss, .comment, .data, .dynamic, .rodata, .strtab etc.) and section type (like NOBITS, DYNAMIC, SYMTAB, HASH, RELA, PROGBITS, NULL etc.) as features. We use both section names and section types as binary feature.

Symbol Table: One can extract the symbol table using the 'readelf -s [elf_file]' command. The symbol table contains considerable data required for linking and debugging files. We use the count of .dynsym entries, count of .symtab entries, type of .dynsym entries, and type of .symtab entries as features.

Dynamic Section: One can extract the dynamic section of the ELF file using the 'readelf -d [elf_file]' command. The runtime linker uses this segment to find all the necessary information needed for dynamic linking and relocation. The number of entries in the dynamic section is not fixed. We use the entries (like FINI, NULL, INIT_ARRAY, FINI_ARRAY, HASH etc.) in the feature list as binary feature.

Strings: We use the 'strings' tool from GNU Binutils to extract the printable character sequences that are at least four characters long and follow an unprintable character. The output of strings tools lists HTTP GET request to a website as shown in Fig. 4.

Fig. 4. Portion of **strings** output for ELF

Dynamic Features. The runtime behavior-based characteristics are extracted from the reports of the files provided by Limon. The complete Limon sandbox report is a text file containing system call traces and network activity (captured using Wireshark). The system call describes the operations a process performs, which is referred to as its runtime behavior. Limon sandbox uses "strace" to obtain a comprehensive system call trace of a process and its child processes. In this work, we use the system calls, system call arguments, and TCP packet information as a feature set. Also, we extract the directories and files supplied as arguments to these calls as a feature. Our feature set includes the top 20 directories or files accessed and the generated system calls. Some important features are – **open, close, read, write, connect, clone, /dev, /usr, /proc, etc.**

Memory Artifacts. The Volatility tool uses the snapshot of the main memory and the Volatility profile for the underlying OS. The variety of Volatility plugins provides the information from the memory dump as an output which is further formulated as a feature. Some extracted features are the count of running processes, multiple processes started by an ELF, child processes count, hidden processes count, the number of TCP packets shared with a specific IP, number of IPs contacted, count of distinct IPs contacted, and whether an IP is contacted via multiple ports. Features retrieved using the Volatility tool are listed as follows:

– Using the linux_pslist command, we can determine whether multiple processes are created, or multiple instances of the same process are created. All of these processes are *marked* using PID for further feature extraction.
– There are some processes that are not listed using linux_pslist but visible using linux_psxview, all these process are *marked* as hidden processes.
– Count of IPs contacted with single or multiple ports. Count of ports, count of distinct IPs contacted, etc. are used in the feature set.

- We extract the count of malicious processes which contains injected or statically hidden code using the 'linux_malfind' plugin.
- We extract all the network connections made by processes using the 'linux_netstat' plugin. Extraction of connection information (whether the connection is open or closed) for any *marked* process is used in the feature set.
- We also extract the output of other volatility plugins like 'linux_ifconfig', 'linux_check_tty' but they does not provide any distinct data and some plugins like 'linux_bash' currently does not return any output for the version of Ubuntu 16.04 and higher versions.

After feature generation from the report, we attempt to reduce the features using Principal Component Analysis (PCA) [14]. Initially, we have extracted 87 static features, 328 dynamic features, and 26 memory features. However, all the extracted features are not necessary while training the classifiers. Therefore, we apply PCA to reduce the dimensionality of the feature vector. The final feature vector contains 60 static features, 40 dynamic features, and 21 memory features.

3.3 Classification

We use machine learning classifiers such as – Decision Tree [13], Random Forest [12], and SVM [16] for ELF malware detection. To train and test the models, we use Python's `sklearn` library, and ten-fold-cross validation is used for model evaluation on unseen data. In our work, we use stratified k-fold cross-validation. The reason to use cross-validation is that it results in less biased and less promising outcomes. In our work, we utilize the default value of the number of trees as 100 in the case of the Random Forest classifier. Similarly, we use the default parametric values for the rest of the classifiers – SVM and Decision Tree.

4 Experimentation and Results

4.1 Dataset

We collect the ELF malware samples from a publicly available repository VirusShare [8]. We filter the samples using the `ssdeep` utility to remove more than 80% of identical polymorphic samples. To double-check the labels for malware files, we use VirusTotal API to obtain the detection results from various antivirus engines. We label a sample as malware if any sample is marked as malware by more than four antivirus engines. The final dataset (referred as `Dataset-1`) contains 5,772 ELF files, of which 2,268 are benign executables collected from the Linux directories such as /usr/bin, /usr/sbin, etc., and 3,504 are malicious. Apart from these samples, we gather a few recent malware samples from Virussamples [2]. We mix the collected recent malware samples with a few benign executables, which are not part of `Dataset-1`. This mixed dataset is referred to as `Dataset-2`, containing 888 samples with 413 benign and 475 malicious samples. We use `Dataset-2` to test the robustness of our model. Table 2 presents the exact details of both the datasets.

Table 2. Dataset Description

Sample Type	Dataset Name	
	Dataset-2	Dataset-1
Benign	413	2268
Malware	475	3504

4.2   Evaluation Metrics

To evaluate our work, we use the following evaluation metrics:

- **True Positive(TP):** Benign Samples predicted correctly.
- **False Positive(FP):** Malicious Samples predicted as benign.
- **False Negative(FN):** Benign Samples predicted as malicious.
- **True Negative(TN):** Malicious Samples predicted correctly.

- **Accuracy:** It is defined as the proportion of times the classifier makes accurate predictions.

$$Accuracy(Acc) = \frac{TP + TN}{TP + FP + TN + FN}$$

- **Precision:** It is defined as the proportion of times the classifier predicts true which are actually true.

$$Precision(Pr) = \frac{TP}{TP + FP}$$

- **True Positive Rate:** It is defined as the proportion of samples classifier predicts true to actual true samples. It is also called as Recall (Re).

$$TPR = \frac{TP}{TP + FN}$$

- **False Positive Rate:** It is defined as the proportion of samples classifier predicts true to actual false samples.

$$FPR = \frac{FP}{FP + TN}$$

4.3   Results

This section presents the results of various classifiers on a different combination of features extracted from static, dynamic, and memory analysis. We perform feature scaling before we train the classifiers and split the Dataset-1 in the ratio of 80:20 for training and testing the classifiers. We test the robustness of our models, which are trained on Dataset-1 using recent samples of Dataset-2. Table 3 presents the values of different evaluation matrices obtained using the

Table 3. Results for Static Analysis using multiple classifiers

Classifier	Dataset-1				Dataset-2			
	Acc(%)	Pr(%)	TPR(%)	FPR(%)	Acc(%)	Pr(%)	TPR(%)	FPR(%)
SVM	97.9	97.2	99.6	4.9	92	97.4	87.4	2.7
Decision Tree	97.8	97.9	98.6	3.5	97.7	98.7	96.2	1.5
Random Forest	98.6	98.4	99.4	2.8	97.4	95.5	99.1	4.4

static feature set. It is evident from Table 3 that all three classifiers provide almost similar test accuracy on `Dataset-1`. When we test our trained models on samples from `Dataset-2`, the accuracy and TPR of the SVM classifier reduced significantly. In comparison, there is only a slight decrease for the other two classifiers.

Similarly Table 4 and Table 5 presents the results using dynamic and memory-based feature sets. Here, the accuracy and TPR on `Dataset-2` for the SVM classifier is less than the values for other classifiers. Due to fewer samples in the `Dataset-2`, the precision and FPR have not changed significantly. One can infer from the tables that out of all three classifiers, Random Forest outperforms the other two classifiers for both `Dataset-1` and `Dataset-2`. It is also clear from the tables that classifiers on static features set perform slightly better than dynamic and memory-based features set.

Table 4. Results for Dynamic Analysis using multiple classifiers

Classifier	Dataset-1				Dataset-2			
	Acc(%)	Pr(%)	TPR(%)	FPR(%)	Acc(%)	Pr(%)	TPR(%)	FPR(%)
SVM	91.6	91.0	95.9	15.0	85.0	96.7	74.5	2.9
Decision Tree	93.4	95.8	93.3	6.5	90.4	98.0	82.5	1.9
Random Forest	94.5	96.5	94.4	5.4	91.2	98.5	84.0	1.4

Table 5. Results for Memory Analysis using multiple classifiers

Classifier	Dataset-1				Dataset-2			
	Acc(%)	Pr(%)	TPR(%)	FPR(%)	Acc(%)	Pr(%)	TPR(%)	FPR(%)
SVM	83.3	92.9	77.9	8.7	73.3	86.9	58.9	10.1
Decision Tree	89.1	93.5	87.8	9.0	82.4	96.9	68.0	2.4
Random Forest	90.7	95.3	88.8	6.4	85.3	97.7	73.5	1.9

Next, we reduce the features using PCA based on the correlation among features for better generalization. Feature reduction results in a slight decrease in accuracy for the Random Forest classifier on static, dynamic, and memory feature sets, whereas we see an improvement in the results for the Decision

Table 6. Results for Static Analysis after Dimensionality Reduction

Classifier	Dataset-1				Dataset-2			
	Acc(%)	Pr(%)	TPR(%)	FPR(%)	Acc(%)	Pr(%)	TPR(%)	FPR(%)
SVM	97.9	97.2	99.5	4.9	94.1	97.5	91.3	2.7
Decision Tree	98.4	98.5	98.8	2.6	96.9	98.6	94.3	1.5
Random Forest	98.6	97.9	99.8	3.5	98.9	99.1	97.9	1.0

Tree and SVM classifiers. Table 6 shows the results for all three classifiers after dimensionality reduction for the static features set.

Table 7 and Table 8 show the result for the reduced dynamic and memory-based feature set with dimensions 40 and 21, respectively. In the case of the dynamic-based feature set, all three classifiers have similar accuracy on Dataset-1, but the Random Forest has the least FPR (which also results in less TPR). Random Forest shows the minimum reduction in accuracy when testing Dataset-2, while all three classifiers show a significant decrease in TPR.

Table 7. Results for Dynamic Analysis after Dimensionality Reduction

Classifier	Dataset-1				Dataset-2			
	Acc(%)	Pr(%)	TPR(%)	FPR(%)	Acc(%)	Pr(%)	TPR(%)	FPR(%)
SVM	93.1	95.3	93.2	6.8	83.6	95.5	73.0	3.8
Decision Tree	93.2	95.8	92.8	6.0	86.8	96.3	77.0	3.4
Random Forest	93.2	95.9	92.6	5.8	88.9	98.4	79.9	1.5

Table 8. Results for Memory Analysis after Dimensionality Reduction

Classifier	Dataset-1				Dataset-2			
	Acc(%)	Pr(%)	TPR(%)	FPR(%)	Acc(%)	Pr(%)	TPR(%)	FPR(%)
SVM	83.1	92.3	78.2	9.7	74.1	87.4	60.2	9.9
Decision Tree	90.0	95.7	87.2	5.7	83.4	97.0	69.8	2.4
Random Forest	90.0	94.9	87.9	6.8	85.0	97.7	72.8	1.9

We combine all three categories of features and form a hybrid feature set for detection result improvement on Dataset-2. We observe from static, dynamic, and memory analysis that the Random Forest classifier performs the best among all the classifiers in terms of all the evaluation metrics. Therefore, we choose to utilize Random Forest with 100 trees to train various combinations of hybrid classification models. Till now, we have observed that the detection results for ELF malware are not promising. Even though the static analysis performs well compared to dynamic and memory analysis methods, the single feature category results are not enough to detect ELF malware. Hence, we evaluate our model using different combinations of static, dynamic, and memory features as shown

Table 9. Results of Random Forest on Hybrid Features

Feature Set	Dataset-1				Dataset-2			
	Acc(%)	Pr(%)	TPR(%)	FPR(%)	Acc(%)	Pr(%)	TPR(%)	FPR(%)
Static + Dynamic	98.6	98.8	98.8	1.7	97.1	95.9	98.9	4.8
Dynamic + Memory	96.6	98.0	96.2	2.7	93.4	99.7	87.8	2.0
Static + Memory	98.5	98.3	99.2	2.5	97.7	98.3	97.4	1.9
Static + Dynamic + Memory	99.4	99.5	99.5	0.7	99.2	99.1	99.4	0.9

in Table 9. We train the Random Forest classifier using these combinations of features on 80% of the samples from `Dataset-1`, and the remaining 20% are used to test the model. To check the efficacy of our model, we test our trained model using recent samples from `Dataset-2`. Table 9 shows that the combination of dynamic and memory-based features gives the least accuracy among other combinations. The combination of static, dynamic, and memory-based features achieves the best accuracy and least FPR on both the datasets – `Dataset-1` and `Dataset-2`. Also, this combined feature set detects malware with high TPR without predicting much benign as malware (low FPR) which explains the high precision value of the model.

5   Conclusion and Future Work

In this work, we perform analysis on ELF executables using static, dynamic, and memory analysis approaches. We utilize different tools to extract features from all the analysis techniques. We use `readelf` and `strings` tools to retrieve the static features. The Limon sandbox is set up in VMWare to extract the behavioral logs for dynamic analysis. We also customize the Volatility profile for successfully creating and analyzing memory dump for memory forensics using various Volatility plugins, which is one of the key contributions of our work. The experiments are performed using two different datasets: one dataset is used to train and test the model, and the second dataset contains recent samples to test the robustness of the model. We also utilize feature reduction using PCA for faster prediction. After performing the feature engineering, we build three classification models; two of them are tree-based classifiers – Decision Tree and Random Forest, and one is a support vector machine. Our experimental results include the analysis using features obtained from individual approaches and the various combination of all the features from different approaches. We achieve the best result using hybrid features having static, dynamic, and memory analysis features with the Random Forest classifier, which is 99.47% for `Dataset-1` and 99.21% for `Dataset-2`. The results prove that our work can detect unseen malware which is not part of the training and testing dataset with low false positives. The data and codes are available on request.

Currently, our work primarily focuses on the ELF file format. However, there are threats to the Linux OS using other file formats, such as Python scripts, shell scripts, PERL scripts, PDF files, etc. One can add the support for these file formats after adding respective features and training the model on a significant dataset.

References

1. Inetsim: Internet services simulation suite. https://www.inetsim.org/downloads. html
2. Malware and virus samples. https://www.virussamples.com/
3. Malware statistics by virustotal. https://www.virustotal.com/gui/stats
4. readelf: A tool for accessing elf headers. https://sourceware.org/binutils/docs/ binutils/readelf.html
5. Virustotal api responses. https://developers.virustotal.com/v2.0/reference/api-responses
6. The volatility foundation - open source memory forensics. https://www. volatilityfoundation.org/#%21releases/component_7140
7. Linux malware (2022). https://en.wikipedia.org/wiki/Linux_malware#cite_note-Yeargin-2
8. Virusshare (2022). https://virusshare.com/
9. Andrade, C.A.B.D., Mello, C.G.D., Duarte, J.C.: Malware automatic analysis. In: 2013 BRICS Congress on Computational Intelligence and 11th Brazilian Congress on Computational Intelligence, pp. 681–686 (2013). https://doi.org/10. 1109/BRICS-CCI-CBIC.2013.119
10. Asmitha, K.A., Vinod, P.: Linux malware detection using non-parametric statistical methods. In: 2014 International Conference on Advances in Computing, Communications and Informatics (ICACCI), pp. 356–361 (2014). https://doi.org/10. 1109/ICACCI.2014.6968611
11. Bai, J., Yang, Y., Mu, S.G., Ma, Y.: Malware detection through mining symbol table of Linux executables. Inf. Technol. J. **12**, 380–384 (2013)
12. Dogru, N., Subasi, A.: Traffic accident detection using random forest classifier. In: 2018 15th Learning and Technology Conference (L&T), pp. 40–45. IEEE (2018)
13. Gunnarsdottir, K.M., Gamaldo, C.E., Salas, R.M., Ewen, J.B., Allen, R.P., Sarma, S.V.: A novel sleep stage scoring system: Combining expert-based rules with a decision tree classifier. In: 2018 40th Annual International Conference of the IEEE Engineering in Medicine and Biology Society (EMBC), pp. 3240–3243. IEEE (2018)
14. Maćkiewicz, A., Ratajczak, W.: Principal components analysis (PCA). Comput. Geosci. **19**(3), 303–342 (1993)
15. Mosli, R., Li, R., Yuan, B., Pan, Y.: A behavior-based approach for malware detection. In: Peterson, G., Shenoi, S. (eds.) Advances in Digital Forensics XIII, pp. 187–201. Springer International Publishing, Cham (2017). https://doi.org/10. 1007/978-3-319-67208-3_11
16. Noble, W.S.: What is a support vector machine? Nat. Biotechnol. **24**(12), 1565–1567 (2006)
17. Sihwail, R., Omar, K., Arifin, K.A.Z.: An effective memory analysis for malware detection and classification. Comput. Materi. Continua **67**(2), 2301–2320 (2021). https://doi.org/10.32604/cmc.2021.014510, http://www.techscience.com/ cmc/v67n2/41330
18. Rathnayaka, C., Jamdagni, A.: An efficient approach for advanced malware analysis using memory forensic technique. In: 2017 IEEE Trustcom/BigDataSE/ICESS, pp. 1145–1150 (2017)
19. Shahzad, F., Farooq, M.: Elf-miner: using structural knowledge and data mining for detecting Linux malicious executables. Knowl. Inf. Syst. **30**, 589–612 (2012)
20. Shahzad, F., Shahzad, M., Farooq, M.: In-execution dynamic malware analysis and detection by mining information in process control blocks of Linux OS. Inf.

Sci. **231**, 45–63 (2013). https://doi.org/10.1016/j.ins.2011.09.016, https://www.sciencedirect.com/science/article/pii/S0020025511004737

21. Shalaginov, A., Øverlier, L.: A novel study on multinomial classification of x86/x64 Linux elf malware types and families through deep neural networks. In: Malware Analysis using Artificial Intelligence and Deep Learning (2020)

22. Volatilityfoundation: Creation of linux volatility profile. https://github.com/volatilityfoundation/volatility/wiki/Linux#creating-a-new-profile

23. Zhang, Z., Qi, P., Wang, W.: Dynamic malware analysis with feature engineering and feature learning (2019). https://doi.org/10.48550/ARXIV.1907.07352, https://arxiv.org/abs/1907.07352

Security Risk Management

The Need for Biometric Anti-spoofing Policies: The Case of Etsy

Mohsen Jozani[1], Gianluca Zanella[2], Maxium Khanov[3], Gokila Dorai[1(✉)], and Esra Akbas[4]

[1] Augusta University, Augusta, USA
{mjozani,gdorai}@augusta.edu
[2] University of Texas at San Antonio, San Antonio, USA
gianluca.zanella@utsa.edu
[3] University of Wisconsin Madison, Madison, USA
mkhanov@wisc.edu
[4] Georgia State University, Atlanta, USA
eakbas1@gsu.edu

Abstract. Effective, safe, and fast identity recognition is crucial in today's rapidly growing society. As a convenient and reliable alternative to traditional identification methods, biometric technologies are increasingly adopted for security applications, such as the verification of ID cards or passports and the authentication of computer and mobile devices. However, if spoofed, such technologies can create serious privacy and security risks, and the proliferation of high quality multimedia content on social media platforms facilitates such spoofing attacks. Unfortunately, many users are unaware of the risks of posting their biometric information online and social media companies are not taking appropriate action to protect them. In this paper, we make the case for biometric anti-spoofing policies by examining the social media enabled marketplace of Etsy. We demonstrate that biometric information can be collected from social media users and that the level of privacy concerns is not a predictor of a user's biometric information sharing behavior.

Keywords: Privacy in Social-media · Digital multimedia forensics · Biometrics

1 Introduction

The term "Biometry" has been used to refer to the field of statistical methods applicable to a wide range of topics in biology. Recently the term Biometrics has also been used to refer to the emerging field of the automated recognition of people based on intrinsic physical or behavioral traits, such as those based on retina-scans, iris-patterns, fingerprints, or face recognition. Facing a steady growth of the population and a "digitalization" of services, many countries around the world have already started making efforts to establish biometric

© ICST Institute for Computer Sciences, Social Informatics and Telecommunications Engineering 2023
Published by Springer Nature Switzerland AG 2023. All Rights Reserved
S. Goel et al. (Eds.): ICDF2C 2022, LNICST 508, pp. 295–306, 2023.
https://doi.org/10.1007/978-3-031-36574-4_17

identity of their citizens. On the other side, an increasing number of private organizations are leveraging biometric identification for applications like employee
attendance, door security and logical access. Manufacturers are integrating biometric technologies into mobile and computer devices for fingerprint, face, and
iris recognition.

Biometric technologies are becoming widely popular and are replacing the
traditional identification methods in our daily computing devices. Entering
passwords and PINs, or swiping patterns (which may take several frustrating
attempts), are being replaced by fingerprint scanning or using Face ID as a
user picks up their phone from the table and looks at their screen. The major
advantages of biometric technologies over their traditional counterparts are their
convenience, portability, and presumed safety, as they cannot be circumvented
by hacked passwords or duplicate ID cards.

However, while the public may perceive biometric identification as a safe and
fraud-proof process, biometric technologies such as finger and facial scanning
have been shown to be susceptible to spoofing attacks [1]. In fact, it is relatively
easy to spoof an off-the-shelf face recognition system using a picture downloaded
from social media [2], and a fingerprint replica made of wood glue and printed
out with special ink that mimics the conductive properties of human skin can be
used to unlock fingerprint-protected devices [3]. These spoofing attacks are often
successful, and they are listed as medium level threats in the National Vulnerability Database of the National Institute of Standards and Technology (NIST)
in the United States. The fact that leaked biometric information can potentially
threaten not just our information security, but also our physical security [4]
warrants further study.

Popular online social networks (OSN) constantly encourage users to share
content from their daily lives. As a result, photos, voice recordings, details
about individuals' jobs, social/family lives, hobbies, and their geolocation data
can often be collected from their profiles and triangulated across platforms to
reveal sensitive information about them. Besides, there is a growing amount of
biometric data and personally identifiable information (PII) present on online
platforms [5].

While most users understand the privacy risks associated with posting sensitive textual data, many are not aware of the security threats of posting nontex-
tual data, such as pictures and videos. Such content can be manipulated [6] or
misused to impersonate legitimate users [2,4]. On average, users interact with
about 7 social media platforms [7], and many think their multiple accounts are
not related to each other, without realizing how much sensitive information can
be obtained by connecting a single user's profiles across different platforms and
merging data from multiple sources. Since each OSN may focus on a specialized
need such as socializing, health issues, and professional or academic network,
merging data from several sources can provide an accurate presentation of a
given user. Moreover, users can be aware of privacy risks associated with their
sharing habits without realizing the potential security risks. For example, privacy concerned users may disregard the risks connected to sharing a close-up

picture of their hand because it does not create a privacy threat, but the picture may be used to collect their fingerprints, thus enabling identity theft and other security-related risks. From a theoretical point of view, it would be interesting to test the interplay of privacy-based and security-related behavioral aspects of social media users. It must be established if users that are cautious about exposing their private information on online platforms will still reveal a wide amount of biometric data across their accounts, mainly sharing pictures and videos. Unfortunately, past studies have only focused on leveraging metadata to expose privacy and security potential threats [8].

In this study, we explore the potential threat of collecting biometric information and PII from OSN user profiles. This exploratory research focuses on social media influencers and sellers because they generally post many videos, pictures, and text materials on specific platforms, such as online marketplaces. We argue that the availability of such data may allow malicious actors to collect and merge biometric and other PII data which, in turn, can pose serious privacy and security threats. The goal of this study is to understand whether privacy concerned users are cautious about posting multimedia content that may contain PII and if their proactive behavior is successful in preventing security threats.

We focus on the social media enabled e-commerce website, Etsy, and collect data from each Etsy store, the seller profile associated with the store, and the images and text data of each item sold at the store. Then, we calculate a privacy risk score for each seller and develop a machine learning (ML) based image recognition approach to identify biometric data shared by each seller in the data set.

This research examines the interplay of privacy and security and sheds light on the largely ignored security issue around the multimedia content shared on OSNs. The rest of the paper will present a brief theoretical introduction, the design of this study, the results, and a brief discussion and conclusion section.

2   Theoretical Background

2.1   Privacy

Privacy and privacy concerns play a crucial role on user's online behavior. Active participation in online social communities and networks satisfies people's fundamental needs, such as the need for social relationships [9], social support, self-presentation [10], emotional connection and entertainment [11], identity construction [12], and social capital [13,14]. The perceived benefits of sharing information within a social collective often outweighs the perceived privacy concerns [15]. The decision of sharing information on online platforms is the result of an exchange paradigm process in which the perceived rewards are evaluated against the potential threats to the user's privacy [16]. The result of the (privacy) calculus is often in favor of the leak of private information on online platforms that rewards with social benefits, even in presence of serious threats to the individual privacy. Unfortunately, the body of literature that concerns online privacy does not take into account security or, to some extent, assumes security as a concept that overlaps privacy.

The definition of privacy refers to the ability of "claiming full control on when, how, and to what extent information about them is communicated to others" [17] while security is referred to as the technological guarantees that ensure that the personal information is transmitted and stored in such a way that third parties are not able to access or tamper with it [18]. Ordinary users often fail to distinguish between security and privacy because they focus exclusively on protecting the availability of personal data on online platforms [19]. This, in turn, prevents users from enacting mitigating strategies for security threats. For example, influencers and sellers on online marketplaces post multimedia content that can trigger online conversations about the brands they endorse [20] that, in turn, increase sales and create product awareness. Given that visual communication is more effective in marketing a product or service, influencer posts often include close-up pictures. These pictures, both face and hands, are the potential source of biometric information that can be then connected to PII information gathered from multiple sources of data.

The technological innovations of the past few years have changed the breadth and depth of potential exposure of private information, mainly because of the increased number of third parties involved in the provision of mobile-enabled services [21]. The growing perception of these risks is reflected in people's increasing concerns about their privacy and the collection and use of their personal information [22]. However, despite of the great concerns about the risks related to privacy leaks, users still expose a great amount of sensitive information across multiple platforms. There are various explanations for this apparent paradox, all based on a mixture of rational and non-rational factor in the human decision-making process. On top of rational cognitive processing, innate limitations such as information asymmetry can make difficult to estimate the potential of the privacy risk. This can be the case of the risks connected to multiple OSN accounts, that are not easily recognized by regular users. Other psychological factors, such as optimism or temporal construal [16] can contribute to over valuate the social rewards from online data leaks of personal data and, at the same time, under valuate the potential risks. This is especially true when the rewards are not only social but also economic, such in the case of social media influencers. These theories explain why people fail to protect personal information even if they are concerned for their privacy. Indeed, past studies find that privacy concerns negatively affect, but do not prevent, online privacy leaks or data exposure. To make things worse, new technologies are creating opportunities to expose biometric information that can be used to access digital and physical private spaces.

2.2   Biometric Identification

Biometrics is a multidisciplinary field concerned with measuring specific biological traits that can be used as an individualized code for recognition. The need and the complexity of identity recognition is increasing because of the population growth and increased mobility. Biometrics is considered as an indispensable tool to overcome these challenges. While passwords or badges can be easily stolen and used by an intruder, biometric measures have the unique advantage to truly verify that a person is in fact who he claims to be. However, there is an inevitable dilemma in accepting biometrics as private. It is almost impossible to claim that our facial images are private whilst they are captured by surveillance cameras or even shared on social media platforms. Our voices are recorded by most phone-based services or shared through TikTok videos. Therefore, the concern of identity theft prevents the adoption of biometrics as mainstream form of identification in high-security applications [23]. Contrary to password-protected systems, biometric information is widely available and extremely easy to retrieve from websites such as Flickr or Facebook. On the other hand, it can be argued that fingerprint biometrics are more private, in the sense that we don't explicitly share them on social media platforms. In addition, forensic experts have shown limited ability to detect forgeries in the case of fingerprints that are fabricated carefully with well-chosen and processed materials. In fact, spoofing attacks on fingerprint sensors using artificial fingerprint films are successful 80% of the times [3]. As in case of the privacy in social media, the perceived benefits of biometric-based security identification are countered by related risks. Indeed, the perceived security of our fingerprints as authentication method does not trigger as many concerns as other methods do. The perceived security emerges as a critical factor to build user's trust on technology that, in turn, affects the intention to use it and the frequency of usage. However, the assumption of intrinsic security of our fingerprints may prove wrong.

3   Methodology

3.1   Data Collection

To build the dataset for this study, we searched for small handmade items that sellers often photograph holding in their hands. As the pictures of these items are more susceptible to contain fingerprint data. After careful examination of the platform, we decided to focus on five keywords: *flower, keychain, lanyard, pin, and ring.* We built a Python web scraper that first searches for Etsy stores associated with the above keywords and retrieves store-level data such as name, description, location, rating, and the number of items available in each store. Next, since each store is linked to a seller's personal Etsy page, our script collects the seller's name, profile picture, biographic information, location, number of followers, number of following, and items they liked. Finally, the script collects item-level data, including item description, price, shipping method, and all the item pictures posted by the seller. Our dataset contains the data for over 200,000 items sold in 6636 stores.

3.2   Privacy Risk Score

Like users of any other social media platform, Etsy sellers have different tolerance levels for privacy risks and use privacy controls to adjust the type and extent of information they disclose about themselves [24]. Although some cautious sellers use a nickname (for example, flowergirl79) or their store name on their profile, others use a phrase that includes their first name (for example, Amy's store), and some even disclose their full name on their profile page. Besides, they may decide to post no profile photo, a photo that represents their business (such as a logo or a product portfolio), or a personal picture of themselves. They may also vary in disclosing their location, biographic information, and social and platform interactions.

To understand sellers' privacy preferences, we first use a BERT-based named entity recognition model to examine if they disclose their first and last names [25]. Then, we use a machine learning approach by OpenCV [26] to determine if the seller has posted an identifiable photo of themselves on their profile page. Overall, we extract seven privacy items from each seller's profile page: *first_name, last_name, location, like, follow, picture, biography*.

Based on these items, we compute a total privacy risk score for each seller following Liu and Terzi [27] naïve privacy score computation framework. For N number of sellers and n number of privacy items, we define a matrix with size $N \times n$ where the range of items i is $1 \leq i \leq n$ and the range of sellers j is $1 \leq j \leq N$.

Every item for each seller takes a binary label (0 or 1). If seller j disclosed information regarding item i, that item takes the response value of 1 $(R_{i,j} = 1)$. Otherwise, if the seller did not disclose or made that information private, $(R_{i,j} = 0)$.

Privacy risk score is measured using the two dimensions of sensitivity and visibility of information.

(a) **Sensitivity**
Sensitivity is measured across all users for each privacy item and describes the general likelihood of publicly sharing a specific piece of information. That is:

$$S_i = \frac{N - R_i}{N} \tag{1}$$

where R_i is the sum of all (non-zero) instances of i. Some items are naturally more sensitive than others (such as follow, biography, and picture) and therefore, sellers are less likely to disclose them. Table 1 shows the sensitivity scores calculated for all seven privacy items.

(b) **Visibility**
Visibility of a privacy item i depends on its value across the entire sample, as well as the perception and valuation of user j. It is computed as:

$$V_{i,j} = \frac{R_i}{N} \times \frac{R_j}{n} \tag{2}$$

The higher the value of V_i, the less sensitive is the item.

Table 1. Sensitivity scores

No	Item	Sensitivity Score
1	Follow	0.707
2	Biography	0.657
3	Picture	0.649
4	Last Name	0.603
5	Like	0.469
6	Location	0.257
7	First Name	0.248

The total privacy risk score for user j is, therefore, the sum of the product of j's sensitivity and visibility scores for each privacy item i:

$$PR\_Score_j = \sum_i S_i \times V_{i,j} \tag{3}$$

Figure 1 shows privacy risk score distribution for all sellers. The minimum value of zero represents sellers who disclosed none of the privacy items and the highest disclosure (privacy leak) value for sellers who disclosed all seven items is 1.31. The sample has a normal distribution with mean and median values of 0.67 and 0.65, respectively.

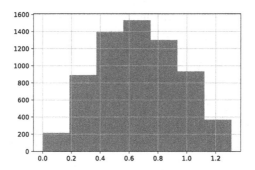

Fig. 1. Distribution of Privacy risk scores

3.3 Extracting Fingerprint Data

To find images containing fingers in the collected dataset, we employ a hierarchical finger detection algorithm including 2 steps: hand detection(1) and finger detection (2). In the hand detection step, our primary goal is to eliminate images without hands efficiently. We use a neural network model as a machine learning algorithm for this goal. We utilize the YOLO (V3) - based NN model designed by Alam et al. [28]. The architecture of this model consists of 106 convolutional

True positives

False positives

Fig. 2. Examples of Good and Bad Finger Identification

layers. The first 53 convolutional layers form a base neural network called Darknet. Darknet was pre-trained on the image net dataset and served as a feature extractor for the network. The subsequent 53 convolutional layers detect the object in the image; in our case, just the part that detects the hand is used. The initial data reduction step runs efficiently with an average speed of 330 images per second. After eliminating many images without a hand, we apply pre-trained Google's MediaPipe framework [29], as a more robust hand and finger detection model but computationally more expensive model. It identifies each hand and joint more accurately with an average speed of 116 images per second. The Mediapipe hand detection framework crops the hands and runs a joint detection model, which consists of a feature extractor that generates all the hand joint positions.

The entire work of extracting fingerprint data is done without using GPUs. Instead, we employ the Ray Python library to parallelize the data analysis. In the first step, the confidence threshold for the hand detection model is intentionally set low to reduce the number of false negatives to preserve the most data. The MediaPipe model used in the second step performs poorly with images like the following: (a) with partially occluded hands; (b) the hand covered the whole image; (c) images that are not related to our case, like toys with fingers, as shown in Fig. 2. Using our hierarchical model, we can flag 2% of the images as containing fingers. We then process the finger data to determine whether any of the sellers had any fingers in their listings.

4   Findings

We performed simple statistical analyses to examine the role of privacy risk on disclosing fingerprint data. From 6,492 seller profiles we examined, 46% posted at least one photo with visible fingerprints. Moreover, we created a binary variable based on the median of privacy risk score ($Q2 = 0.65$) and compared LOW_PR vs $HIGH\_PR$ sellers in terms of fingerprint data leak. While the probability of fingerprint leak for $HIGH\_PR$ sellers is 48%, LOW_PR sellers have 52% probability of leaking their fingerprint data. We also performed logistic regression to examine if privacy risk score can predict fingerprint data leakage. Our finding suggests that privacy risk is not a significant predictor of disclosing fingerprint data ($\beta = -0.0108$, $p = 0.74$).

Our findings suggest that regardless of privacy risk level, people on social media are likely to post their sensitive biometric data and it is up to the platforms to take appropriate measures to protect the security and privacy of social media users.

5   Discussion and Conclusion

This paper focuses on the divide between user protective strategies to mitigate privacy-related risks and security threats. By analyzing data from Etsy users' feeds, we demonstrate that the level of users' privacy concerns does not predict the amount of biometric information they may inadvertently disclose in their social media posts. While privacy concerned users may take strategies such as using nicknames or removing profile photos to mitigate privacy-related risks, they may still inadvertently disclose their biometric information in the images and videos they share. A possible takeaway is that users may not be aware of the potential security threats of posting their biometrics. Perhaps, given the fast pace of technological innovation, it is not reasonable to ask users to be competent and up-to-date in cyber-focused technicalities. Policies and regulations should be in place to require social media platforms to restrict and protect posts with users' PII as they already do with offensive or indecent content. Indeed, our paper joins the many calls for privacy policies that take into account the real dispersion and depth of sensitive information [30].

5.1   Research Implications

This research contributes to the growing body of research on the ethical implications of the use of biometrics for identifying and authenticating people. On one hand, the use of biometrics raises difficult questions regarding data protection. More directly theoretical questions concern the conceptualisation of persons as a "machine-readable body" [31], as well as the role of biometrics in various sociopolitical and economic settings [32]. A part of the ethical issue that biometrics information changes overtime in aging individuals [33], biometrics poses a serious threat to individual security because it falls outside the radar of an individual's privacy concerns. This calls for the evolution of the concepts of privacy as a multi-factor or multi-domain concept that should include also security-related components.

5.2   Practical Considerations

It can be observed that users are increasingly dissatisfied with the policies of online social media companies. At the same time, policymakers are trailing behind technical innovation, with regulations that are not applicable to up-to-date technologies. The European general data protection regulation (GDPR) is considered a milestone in this sense, because it leaves flexibility for technological advancements [34]. The GDPR specifically recognizes biometric data as a subset of sensitive personal data deemed a "sensitive category of personal data." Still, it does not explicitly consider the case of biometric data casually embedded in shared pictures. Until the legal ramifications of this gray area are clarified, the first approach is to call social media companies into action. As companies tag posts as "not verified" or offensive, they should alert the users when a post may contain biometric data. Offering this feature will improve not only the user's security, but will also contribute in building trust between customers and companies, which will benefit both.

References

1. Ratha, N.K., Connell, J.H., Bolle, R.M.: Enhancing security and privacy in biometrics-based authentication systems. IBM Syst. J. **40**(3), 614–634 (2001)
2. Wen, D., Han, H., Jain, A.K.: Face spoof detection with image distortion analysis. IEEE Trans. Inf. Forensics Secur. **10**(4), 746–761 (2015)
3. Mott, N.: Hacking fingerprints is actually pretty easy-and cheap, November 2021
4. Alnabhi, H., Al-naamani, Y., Al-madhehagi, M., Alhamzi, M.: Enhanced security methods of door locking based fingerprint. Int. J. Innov. Technol. Explor. Eng. **9**(03), 1173–1178 (2020)
5. Girelli, C.M.A., et al.: Application of a standard procedure to avoid errors when comparing fingerprints with their reversals in fake documents. J. Forensic Sci. Med. **2**(1), 60 (2016)
6. Boididou, C., et al.: Verifying information with multimedia content on twitter. Multimed. Tools Appl. **77**(12), 15545–15571 (2018)
7. Dean, B.: Social network usage & growth statistics: how many people use social media in 2021, vol. 2, p. 2021 (2021). Accessed July 2021
8. Gouert, C., Tsoutsos, N.G.: Dirty metadata: understanding a threat to online privacy. IEEE Secur. Priv. **01**, 2–9 (2022)
9. Krämer, N.C., Schäwel, J.: Mastering the challenge of balancing self-disclosure and privacy in social media. Curr. Opin. Psychol. **31**, 67–71 (2020)
10. Kim, J., Tussyadiah, I.P.: Social networking and social support in tourism experience: the moderating role of online self-presentation strategies. J. Travel Tour. Mark. **30**(1–2), 78–92 (2013)

11. Sheth, S., Kim, J.: Social media marketing: the effect of information sharing, entertainment, emotional connection and peer pressure on the attitude and purchase intentions. GSTF J. Bus. Rev. (GBR) **5**(1) (2017)
12. Berger, C.R., Calabrese, R.J.: Some explorations in initial interaction and beyond: toward a developmental theory of interpersonal communication. Hum. Commun. Res. **1**(2), 99–112 (1974)
13. Ellison, N.B., Steinfield, C., Lampe, C.: The benefits of Facebook "friends:" social capital and college students' use of online social network sites. J. Comput.-Mediat. Commun. **12**(4), 1143–1168 (2007)
14. Ellison, N.B., Steinfield, C., Lampe, C.: Connection strategies: social capital implications of Facebook-enabled communication practices. New Media Soc. **13**(6), 873–892 (2011)
15. Kokolakis, S.: Privacy attitudes and privacy behaviour: a review of current research on the privacy paradox phenomenon. Comput. Secur. **64**, 122–134 (2017)
16. Hallam, C., Zanella, G.: Online self-disclosure: the privacy paradox explained as a temporally discounted balance between concerns and rewards. Comput. Hum. Behav. **68**, 217–227 (2017)
17. Westin, A.F.: Privacy and freedom. Wash. Lee Law Rev. **25**(1), 166 (1968)
18. Mekovec, R., Hutinski, Ž.: The role of perceived privacy and perceived security in online market. In: 2012 Proceedings of the 35th International Convention MIPRO, pp. 1549–1554. IEEE (2012)
19. Flavián, C., Guinalíu, M.: Consumer trust, perceived security and privacy policy: three basic elements of loyalty to a web site. Ind. Manag. Data Syst. (2006)
20. De Veirman, M., Cauberghe, V., Hudders, L.: Marketing through instagram influencers: the impact of number of followers and product divergence on brand attitude. Int. J. Advert. **36**(5), 798–828 (2017)
21. Jozani, M., Ayaburi, E., Ko, M., Choo, K.-K.R.: Privacy concerns and benefits of engagement with social media-enabled apps: a privacy calculus perspective. Comput. Hum. Behav. **107**, 106260 (2020)
22. Madden, M.: Public perceptions of privacy and security in the post-snowden era, (2014)
23. Schuckers, S.A.: Spoofing and anti-spoofing measures. Inf. Secur. Tech. Rep. **7**(4), 56–62 (2002)
24. Cavusoglu, H., Phan, T.Q., Cavusoglu, H., Airoldi, E.M.: Assessing the impact of granular privacy controls on content sharing and disclosure on Facebook. Inf. Syst. Res. **27**(4), 848–879 (2016)
25. Devlin, J., Chang, M.-W., Lee, K., Toutanova, K.,: Bert: pre-training of deep bidirectional transformers for language understanding, arXiv preprint arXiv:1810.04805 (2018)
26. Bradski, G., Kaehler, A.: Opencv. Dr. Dobb's J. Softw. Tools **3**, 2 (2000)
27. Liu, K., Terzi, E.: A framework for computing the privacy scores of users in online social networks. ACM Trans. Knowl. Discov. Data (TKDD) **5**(1), 1–30 (2010)
28. Alam, M.M., Islam, M.T., Rahman, S.M.: Unified learning approach for egocentric hand gesture recognition and fingertip detection. Pattern Recogn. **121**, 108200 (2022)
29. Lugaresi, C., et al. : Mediapipe: a framework for perceiving and processing reality. In: Third Workshop on Computer Vision for AR/VR at IEEE Computer Vision and Pattern Recognition (CVPR) 2019 (2019)
30. Patsakis, C., Zigomitros, A., Papageorgiou, A., Galván-López, E.: Distributing privacy policies over multimedia content across multiple online social networks. Comput. Netw. **75**, 531–543 (2014)

31. Ploeg, I.V.D., Lyon, D.: Biometrics and the body as information: normative issues of the socio-technical coding of the body. Surveillance as Social Sorting: Privacy, Risk, and Digital Discrimination. Londres e Nova Iorque, Routledge, pp. 57–73 (2002)
32. Agamben, G., Murray, S.J.: No to biopolitical tattooing. Commun. Crit. Cult. Stud. **5**(2), 201–202 (2008)
33. Rebera, A.P., Mordini, E.: Biometrics and ageing: social and ethical considerations. Age Factors Biom. Process. 37–58 (2013)
34. Goddard, M.: The EU general data protection regulation (GDPR): European regulation that has a global impact. Int. J. Mark. Res. **59**(6), 703–705 (2017)

VPnet: A Vulnerability Prioritization Approach Using Pointer Network and Deep Reinforcement Learning

Zhoushi Sheng, Bo Yu$^{(\boxtimes)}$, Chen Liang, and Yongyi Zhang

National University of Defense Technology, ChangSha, China
{shengzhoushi12,yubo0615,liangchen16,zhangyongyi}@nudt.edu.cn

Abstract. Vulnerability prioritization is becoming increasingly prominent in vulnerability management. The contradiction between mountains of vulnerability scan results and limited remediation resources is so stark that using severity scores and crude heuristics to prioritize vulnerabilities is overwhelmed. To implement better vulnerability management, this paper proposes a vulnerability prioritization approach using a pointer network and deep reinforcement learning, called VPnet. In VPnet, the objective of vulnerability prioritization is maximizing the total risk reduction in the target environment under limited resources. First, we transform vulnerability scan reports into a matrix. Each item in the matrix consists of a vulnerability risk and cost value. The former is quantified by combining severity, threat, impact, and asset criticality factors, and the latter is an estimate of the time required to patch a vulnerability. Then, we construct a pointer network that takes the matrix and a constraint value as inputs to output a priority vulnerability remediation plan. Furthermore, we use deep reinforcement learning to train the pointer network model parameter, since obtaining pointer network labels is computationally expensive. A novel method integrating imitation learning and autonomous learning is also devised to speed up the training process and produce a better model. The proposed approach VPnet is evaluated by generating simulated scenarios. Results show that our approach develops nearly optimal solutions in seconds under different scale scenarios and constraints, and achieves a 22.8% performance improvement in a practical example, indicating that our approach is effective while exhibiting flexibility and efficiency.

Keywords: vulnerability prioritization · vulnerability management · risk · pointer network · deep reinforcement learning

1 Introduction

With the rapid development of information technology, the number of vulnerabilities is growing explosively, and tens of thousands of vulnerabilities are discovered and disclosed to the public every year. As a result, a steady stream of

Supported by the Natural Science Foundation of China (61902416, 61902412).

S. Goel et al. (Eds.): ICDF2C 2022, LNICST 508, pp. 307–325, 2023.
https://doi.org/10.1007/978-3-031-36574-4_18

security alerts is generated when firms scan systems with vulnerability detection software, and it is impractical to fix all vulnerabilities due to limited processing capacity. Hence, considering vulnerability remediation priorities in the practice of vulnerability management is critical.

The Common Vulnerability Scoring System (CVSS) has long been a de facto standard in the community when prioritizing vulnerabilities [15]. However, the CVSS aims to measure the severity levels of vulnerabilities, not the risks that people truly care about. According to Tenable Research [10], 75% of vulnerabilities with CVSS scores of 7 or higher have never been exploited, which means that vulnerabilities with high severity scores are not necessarily high-risk vulnerabilities. When the CVSS is used alone to prioritize remediation efforts, a great number of resources are wasted on patching nonhigh-risk vulnerabilities; meanwhile, massive potential risks still exist in the target network.

Increasing research has been invested in ranking and prioritizing vulnerabilities to change the status quo ([1,8,15,19,20]). Particularly, there are many methods that have been proposed to measure risk factors in addition to severity, such as threat forecasting and context impact estimation. As people's perceptions of risk are maturing, security vendors cannot wait to release various risk-based vulnerability management products, such as vulnerability prioritization rating(VPR) [23] and Vulnerability Management Services(VMS) [7], which undergo continuous improvement.

However, these products are far from satisfying customer expectations. There are two challenges that this paper seeks to address. On the one hand, the risk calculation methods of these products are opaque, poorly interpretable, and require powerful real-time data-driven, which is difficult for ordinary enterprises to implement. On the other hand, vulnerability prioritization directly on the risk score of individual vulnerabilities is not sufficient, the optimal allocation of resources should also be addressed due to limited resources. As we know, the available resources in the process of vulnerability remediation are limited. For instance, enterprises limit the total vulnerability remediation time during a vulnerability remediation campaign to ensure that other businesses are not affected. Because the time costs required for patching various vulnerabilities are different, the developed vulnerability remediation priority strategy is likely suboptimal when optimal allocation is not considered.

In this paper, we formulate the vulnerability prioritization problem as a combinatorial optimization problem, that is maximizing the total risk reduction of the target network given limited resources. The problem is NP-hard [17]. In order to address this problem efficiently, we propose a vulnerability prioritization approach using a pointer network and deep reinforcement learning, called VPnet. First, we transform vulnerability scan reports into a matrix. Each item in the matrix consists of a vulnerability risk and cost value. The former is quantified by combining severity, threat, impact, and asset criticality factors, and the latter is an estimate of the time required to patch a vulnerability. Then, we construct a pointer network that takes the matrix and a constraint value as inputs to output a priority vulnerability remediation plan. Furthermore, we use deep reinforcement learning to train the pointer network model parameter.

The main contributions of this paper are summarized as follows:

- VPnet, a new approach for vulnerability prioritization, is proposed; VPnet uses a pointer network and deep reinforcement learning to develop a optimal vulnerability prioritization plan.
- A simple to implement and interpretable risk quantification formula is proposed; we quantify risk score by considering severity, threat, impact, and asset criticality factors.
- A novel method that integrates imitation learning and autonomous learning to improve the performance of model training is proposed.
- Our approach is validated by experiments over various scenarios to demonstrate the effectiveness of VPnet.

2   Related Literature

Various vulnerability prioritization methods have recently been proposed both in academia and industry.

In academics, [20] presented a testable stakeholder-specific vulnerability categorization (SSVC) method that avoids some problems faced by the CVSS. SSVC takes the form of decision trees for different vulnerability management communities. [9] produced the first open, data-driven framework for predicting the probability that a vulnerability will be exploited within 12 months following public disclosure; this framework is called the exploit prediction scoring system (EPSS). This system adopts a logistic regression technique that is transparent, intuitive, and easily implemented, and the output score provides useful assessments of the threat of a given vulnerability. [1] proposed an automated context-aware vulnerability risk management (AC-VRM) methodology to prioritize vulnerabilities for remediation based on organizational context rather than severity only. The proposed solution considers multiple vulnerability databases to attain great coverage of known vulnerabilities and to determine vulnerability rankings.

In industry, IBM Security X-Force Red Vulnerability Management Services (VMS) [7] prioritize the most critical vulnerabilities exposing those systems and remediate those vulnerabilities in a systematic, "light lifting" fashion. Prioritization Scan results are inputted into X-Force Red's hacker-built automated ranking engine, which enriches and prioritizes findings based on weaponized exploits and key risk factors. Tenable has authored a new research technology called the Vulnerability prioritization Rating (VPR) [23]. The VPR aims to help prioritize mitigation efforts and help the organization understand the likelihood a given vulnerability will be exploited by using a combination of machine learning and threat intelligence. Delve Security develops and provides a vulnerability management solution leveraging machine learning to automate vulnerability management scanning and prioritization [5], a key element is machine-learning Contextual Prioritization, which evaluates 40-plus factors for each vulnerability on an enterprise network.

It can be seen from the above that the current research trend is to properly measure risks. [3] recognized that risk is a combination of the"threat" faced by the target system (the ability and intention of the threat actor), the "vulnerability" (weakness or exposure) of the system, and the "impact" (consequence or destruction) of a successful exploiting of vulnerability on the organization. Guided by [3], this paper quantifies risk by combining recent works on threats and the CVSS standard. However, considering the risks of vulnerabilities alone is not sufficient for vulnerability prioritization. Some vulnerabilities present high risks, but their repair costs are higher, and it is not cost-effective to repair such vulnerabilities. To minimize the total risk with limited resources, the cost factor should be considered, and the vulnerability prioritization problem is formulated as a combinatorial optimization problem as follows:

$$G = \max_{x_i \in \{0,1\}} \sum_{i=1}^{I} r_i * x_i \quad \text{subject to} \sum_{i=1}^{I} c_i * x_i \leq C \tag{1}$$

where i is the vulnerability instance (VI) index, $1 \leq i \leq I$, I is the total number of VIs in the scan. x_i is a binary 0-1 indicator variable with value 1 if the corresponding VI is selected for remediation and 0 otherwise. r_i and c_i are the risk and cost score of VI i.

Nonetheless, the problem is NP-hard [17]. With the scale of the problem increasing, the time and space complexity grow rapidly,it cannot be efficiently solved with a traditional algorithm ([12,14]), such as a dynamic program algorithm [14]. Motivated by recent advancements in deep learning techniques, neural combinatorial optimization was proposed to address combinatorial optimization problems [2], this approach can effectively adapt to different scale scenarios. Therefore, we take advantage of the recent progress regarding neural combinatorial optimization and develop a vulnerability prioritization approach.

3   Materials and Methods

3.1   Overall Framework of VPnet

The overall framework is designed as shown in Fig 1. The framework mainly consists of two core modules: a data pre-processing module and a remediation plan generation module. In the data pre-processing module, we quantify the risk and cost of each VI from the original scanner reports, and generate an input matrix for a point network. Specifically, the risk score is a combination of four factors: severity, threat, impact, and asset criticality, while the cost score is based on the repair suggestions. The remediation plan generation module consists of offline training and online deployment. Its main task is to train a pointer network model offline by using deep reinforcement learning, and testing or applying the model online. This trained pointer network model can output an optimal priority vulnerability remediation plan given the input.

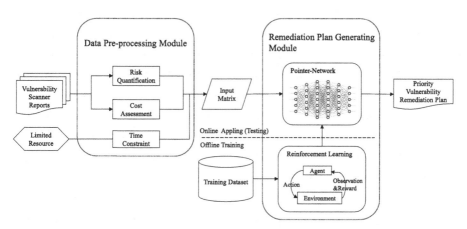

Fig. 1. The overall framework of VPnet

3.2   Data Pre-processing Module

Collecting Raw Data. We use a Nessus tool to scan the enterprise network, comprehensively collecting raw vulnerability scanner reports. Table 1 displays a sample of what the vulnerability scanner data obtained via Nessus look like, the actual IP is replaced by the host number to protect privacy and some unnecessary columns are ignored, such as port. Each vulnerability instance is measured as a unique tuple $< v, h, p >$. such as the first item in Table 1, which can be measured as <CVE-2019-0708, Host1, Windows_xp> .

Computation of Risk Score. The risk score is a fundamental concept in VPnet, It is a quantitative value that offers security teams the ability to focus their efforts on the greatest risk vulnerabilities. However, no unified standard is available for the computation of risk scores, as this task is still undergoing continuous research. Many security vendors have diverse risk calculation methods that are not transparent, such as Kenna Security Vulnerability Risk Score [11] and Rapid7's Real Risk Score [18]. Guided by the literature [3], we propose a feasible risk calculation method that is a combination of severity, threat, impact, and asset criticality factors, which is easy to implement. It can be formulated as:

$$r_i = q_i * (\alpha * S_i + \beta * T_i + \gamma * I_i) \tag{2}$$

-i is the VI index, which match a unique VI tuple $< v, h, a >$.

-S_i is the severity score of the VI obtained from the base CVSS score. The base CVSS score reflects the severity of a vulnerability by capturing its intrinsic characteristics, ranging from 1 to 10, where 1 represents the least severe score and 10 represents the most severe score. S_i is normalized to a scale between 0 and 1, and the normalization formula is $S_i = baseScore/10$.

-T_i is the threat score of the VI obtained from the EPSS. The EPSS characterizes the probability that a software vulnerability will be exploited in the

Table 1. Example of data collected via scan tool

HOST	Program	CVE	Description	Solution
Host1	Windows_xp	CVE-2019-0708	A remote code execution vulnerability exists in Remote Desktop Services when an unauthenticated visitor connects to the target system using RDP and sends specially crafted requests.	Disable Remote Desktop Services if they are not required.
Host2	Apache-httpserver	CVE-2017-7679	In Apache httpd 2.2.x, mod_mime can read one byte past the end of a buffer when sending a malicious Content-Type response header	Oracle strongly recommends that customers apply CPU fixes as soon as possible

wild in the next 30 days and produces a probability score between 0 and 1. The higher the score is, the greater the vulnerability threat. The EPSS score can be obtained via an online API(https://www.first.org/epss/api).

-I_i is the impact score of the VI obtained from the CVSS impact score. The CVSS impact score reflects the actual outcome of exploiting the vulnerability, and its value ranges from 1 to 10. I_i is normalized to a scale between 0 and 1, and the normalization formula is $I_i = impactScore/10$.

-q_i is the asset criticality score specified by the system operators. An asset criticality assessment(ACA) identifies and ranks the most critical assets in the target network, helping security teams focus efforts where they are most needed. In practice business, the score can be obtained through an ACA tool, usually ranging from 0 to 1, and the higher the value, the higher the criticality. In our experiment, we classify the criticality of assets into three levels: general, medium, and critical, corresponding to the values of 0.5, 0.75, and 1, respectively.

-α, β, and γ are manually assigned weight values, which are determined by the actual enterprise needs. In our experiments, we assigned the same 1/3 value to these three parameters, in the absence of specific background knowledge.

Assessing Vulnerability Remediation Cost. Accurately valuating the resource consumption of each vulnerability is difficult due to the various practical factors that should be considered. Fortunately, time cost of remediating a vulnerability is relatively easy to quantify, while a vulnerability remediation activity possesses a total time constraint. This paper draws on the research in [6] and assesses the vulnerability remediation cost according to the time factor.

We first divide the cost values into three categories based on the difficulty of remediation: 1 to 3 h, 3 to 6 h, and 6 to 9 h. If the solution description provided by Nessus contains keywords such as "default password," "configuration changes," "weak cipher," or "password update", it indicates that the remediation is relatively simple; therefore, the cost value falls into the first category. If a version upgrade is required in the solution, it is classified into the second category. If a system update is needed, it is classified into the third category. Next, the exact cost value is randomly generated from the corresponding period and normalized to a scale between 0 and 1. In addition, if no solution is available for the vulnerability, we set a far greater cost value than those described above because such vulnerabilities are too costly for ordinary enterprises to patch.

Constructing the Input Matrix. After the calculation of the risk and cost value, a vulnerability instance can be represented by the node (r_i, c_i), for instance, VI_1 can be represented by $(0.422058, 0.1)$. Thus, we can construct a matrix M by combining all the scanned VI nodes. M belongs to $R^{N \times 2}$ where N is the total number of VIs in the scan. Together with a constraint value C, M is used as the input of the pointer network, where the final input belongs to $R^{(N+1) \times 2}$. Specifically, the last node is the constraint value while carrying a duplicate redundant value, and before is the M (Table 2).

Table 2. Data pre-processing

VI_ID	Host	Program	CVE_ID	Risk	Cost
1	Host1	Windows_xp	CVE-2019-0708	0.422058	0.1
2	Host2	Apache_httpserver	CVE-2016-2161	0.290605	0.3

3.3   Remediation Plan Generating Module

Pointer Network. The essence of vulnerability prioritization is to select and determine the remediation of order vulnerabilities from all the scanned VIs, and this can be formalized as a combinatorial optimization problem. Motivated by [24], we design a pointer network to solve this problem. Figure 2 presents the architecture of the pointer network. This network comprises two sub-network modules, called encoder and decoder.

The encoder network first utilizes a d-dimensional embedding layer to process the input matrix generated by data preprocessing, and each VI node is converted to a d-dimensional vector φ^T. Here, the role of the embedding layer is to embed 2-dimensional VIs into a continuous d-dimensional vector, so as to better train the pointer network model and ensure the model is inductive. Second, a recurrent neural network that consists of long short-term memory (LSTM) cells reads the embedded sequence, one node at a time, and the i-th time step outputs a latent memory state e_i, where $e_i \in R^d$. In addition, the total constraint cost value C is transferred to the decoder network for further judgment.

The decoder network also adopts LSTM cells to construct a recurrent neural network and maintains the latent memory state d_i at each step i, where $d_i \in R^d$. G is a d-dimensional vector, which is the input of the first decoding step and is treated as a trainable parameter of the neural network. Then, the decoder iteratively selects VIs for remediation until the total cost exceeds the constraint C. A pointing mechanism is the core for selecting VIs; at each step i, it produces a probability distribution over the VIs, and we can select a VI to patch under the probability of each node. A selected VI is taken as the input of the next

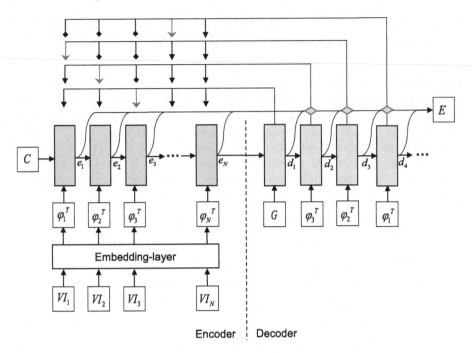

Fig. 2. Proposed pointer network for vulnerability prioritization. A tan-colored arrow suggests that the pointing node has the highest probability of being selected, and a rhombus arrow suggests that the pointing node has been selected before.

decoder step, and it will never be selected in all subsequent decoding steps. The probability distribution p is calculated by the following formulas:

$$u^i_j = v^T \tanh(W_1 e_j + W_2 d_i) \qquad j \in (1, ..., N) \tag{3a}$$

$$p = \text{softmax}(u^i) \qquad u^i = \{u^i{}_1, ..., u^i{}_N\} \tag{3b}$$

Where v, W_1, and W_2 are learnable parameters, e_j and d_i are latent memory states, and the softmax function is a function that turns u^i into a vector of N real values that sum to 1, which can represent the probability distribution. In addition, the probability of a VI is set to $-\infty$ if this VI has been selected before.

The pointer network design is very suitable for dealing with the vulnerability prioritization problem. Due to its pointing mechanism, we can apply a neural network model trained on small-size training data to larger scenarios, which is beyond the reach of other network structures. For example, the sequence-to-sequence model [21], which is highly popular in AI, needs to train a separate model for each N, which makes deployment difficult. More details will be shown in the following chapter.

Deep Reinforcement Learning. This paper follows the deep reinforcement learning (DRL) paradigm to train the pointer network model parameters based on full research ([2,13,16]). While supervised learning seems to be a more common way to train a neural network [4], it is not suitable for the vulnerability prioritization problem. On the one hand, obtaining optimal labels via a problem solver is expensive because the problem is NP-hard, on the other hand, the problem may be revised with a deepening understanding of vulnerability prioritization, while constructing a new problem solver is very difficult. However, it is relatively easy to find feasible solutions under resource constraints, and we can provide a reward function for verifying the quality of a set of feasible solutions. Hence, we follow the DRL paradigm to tackle the above problem, precisely speaking, we adopt a Monte Carlo policy gradient approach to solve the problem [22].

Reward Function. If there is no reward function incentive, the vulnerability priority solution output through the untrained pointer network is random rather than optimal, then what kind of solution is optimal? Obviously, our goal is to first patch the most serious vulnerabilities to minimize the overall system security risk under limited resources. Given an input matrix $S = \{VI_i\}_{i=1}^{N}$ and contraint value C, where each $VI_i = (r_i, c_i)$, we are concerned with finding a vulnerability remediation solution π that patches the vulnerabilities in sequence until the constraints are exceeded and has the best effect in reducing risk. Therefore, we design a reward function as follows:

$$L(\pi \,|\, S, C) = \sum_{i=0}^{n-1} \gamma^i r_{\pi(i)} \tag{4}$$

where γ is a discount factor that is normally set to a value in the range $[0.9, 1]$, and n is the total numbers of vulnerabilities in solution π. The practical significance of this design is not only to minimize the total risk but also to give priority to repairing higher-risk vulnerabilities. Eventually, driven by this reward function and using reinforcement learning to continuously optimize the parameters of the pointer network, the pointer network model can output the optimal vulnerability prioritization solution instead of a random one.

Optimization the Pointer Network Parameter with Policy Gradients. We adopt a Monte Carlo policy gradient approach to optimize the parameters of a pointer network denoted by θ. Our training goal is to maximize the expected return given an input matrix S and contraint value C, which is defined as:

$$J(\theta \,|\, S, C) = E_{\pi \sim p_\theta(.|s)} L(\pi \,|\, S, C) \tag{5}$$

The gradient of the above objective function can be formulated as follows:

$$\nabla_\theta J(\theta \,|\, S, C) = \mathbb{E}_{\pi \sim \, p_\theta(.|s)} \left[(L(\pi \,|\, S, C) - b(S, C)) \nabla_\theta \log p_\theta(\pi \,|\, S, C) \right] \tag{6}$$

where $b(S, C)$ is a baseline function which is important for training, we will discuss it further in the following paragraph, and $p_\theta(\pi \,|\, S, C)$ is a stochastic policy that assigns high probabilities to high-quality solutions. It can be calculated by a chain rule:

$$p_\theta(\pi | S, C) = \prod_{i=1}^{n} p_\theta(\pi(i) | \pi(< i), S, C) \tag{7}$$

During the training phase, by sampling cases $(s_1, c_1), (s_2, c_2), ..., (s_B, c_B)$ from the training data D and a solution $\pi_i | s_i, c_i$ per case, the gradient (6) can be approximated with Monte Carlo sampling as follows, and it can be trained with an Adam optimizer [12].

$$\nabla_\theta J(\theta) = \frac{1}{B} \sum_{i=1}^{B} (L(\pi | s_i, c_i) - b(s_i, c_i)) \nabla_\theta \log p_\theta(\pi | s_i, c_i) \tag{8}$$

Baseline Function. Constructing a good baseline function $b(s_i, c_i)$ is significant for the policy gradients. Adding a baseline function does not change the expectation of the objective function, but it can effectively reduce the variance and improve the stability of the training process. On the other hand, not all solutions can be sampled due to the presence of a large number of feasible solutions. Some low-quality solutions will receive positive rewards once sampled, while some high-quality solutions will receive zero rewards if they are not sampled. As a result, the neural network cannot learn good strategies. Adding a baseline function that makes the rewards both positive and negative values can prevent this problem, and bad solutions are gradually phased out. Currently, two popular baseline functions are available, and they are described as follows.

(1) Exponential Moving Average. A simple baseline $b(s_i, c_i)$ is an exponential moving average (EMA) of the rewards, reflecting the fact that the given policy improves with training over time. The EMA is calculated by the formula below:

$$EMA_t = \begin{cases} reward_0 & t = 0 \\ reward_t * (\frac{\xi}{1+t}) + reward_{t-1} * (1 - \frac{\xi}{1+t}) & t > 0 \end{cases} \tag{9}$$

where t represents the number of training time steps. $reward_i$ is the average reward value of the i-th training step. ξ is a smoothing factor, and the most common choice is $\xi = 2$. If the smoothing factor is increased, more recent observations have more influence on the EMA.

(2) Actor-Critic Training. Another popular choice for the baseline function is to construct an auxiliary neural network called the critic network. This neural network parameterized by θ_v aims to learn the expected reward values $E_{\pi \sim p_\theta(.|s)} L(\pi | s)$. Given an input (s_i, c_i), the objective of the critic network is to minimize the loss between its prediction $b_{\theta_v}(s_i, c_i)$ and the actual reward $L(\pi | s_i, c_i)$; therefore, the loss function is formulated as:

$$\mathcal{L}(\theta_v) = \frac{1}{B} \sum_{i=1}^{B} \| b_{\theta_v}(s_i, c_i) - L(\pi_i | s_i, c_i) \|_2^2 \tag{10}$$

Besides, the actor network is the pointer network parameterized by θ, the complete algorithm is shown in Algorithm 1.

Algorithm 1: Actor-Critic Training

Data: training data D, total number of training steps T, and batch size B

Result: θ, θ_v

1 Initialize the pointer network params θ, the critic network params θ_v, training step $t = 0$

2 **while** $t < T$ **do**

3   Sample instance $(s_i, c_i) \sim D$ for $i \in (1, ..., B)$

4   Sample solution $\pi_i \sim p_\theta(.|s_i, c_i)$ for $i \in (1, ..., B)$

5   Calculate $b_i = b_{\theta_v}(s_i, c_i)$ for $i \in (1, ..., B)$ with Critic

6   Calculate $\nabla_\theta J(\theta) = \frac{1}{B} \sum_{i=1}^{B} (L(\pi|s_i, c_i) - b(s_i, c_i)) \nabla_\theta \log p_\theta(\pi|s_i, c_i)$

7   Calculate $\mathcal{L}(\theta_v) = \frac{1}{B} \sum_{i=1}^{B} \|b_{\theta_v}(s_i, c_i) - L(\pi_i|s_i, c_i)\|_2^2$

8   Update $\theta \leftarrow Adam(\nabla_\theta J(\theta))$

9   Update $\theta_v \leftarrow Adam(\mathcal{L}(\theta_v))$

10   Update $t \leftarrow t + 1$

11 **end**

However, these two options for the baseline function perform not well in experiments, and the possible reasons for this will be analyzed in Sect. 4. To achieve improved performance, we propose a novel method that is a combination of a strong heuristic and the actor-critic algorithm, which the former is like imitation learning, while the latter is similar to autonomous learning.

(3) Our Method. Intuitively, if a vulnerability presents a high risk but is easy to repair, it should be remediated first because of cost performance, so we can find an easy yet strong heuristic algorithm. The algorithm takes the VIs ordered by their risk-to-cost ratios until the total cost exceeds the imposed constraint C. We believe that a strong heuristic algorithm can hasten the learning process of the neural network, and a novel method is proposed in this paper based on the above cognition. Our method first takes the reward of a solution provided by the strong heuristic as the baseline so that the pointer network can quickly learn good strategies and then applies the actor-critic algorithm to better conduct autonomous learning. The details is shown in algorithm 2.

Algorithm 2: Our Method

Data: training data D, number of training steps for phase1 T_1, total
number of training steps T, and batch size B

Result: θ, θ_v

1 Initialize the pointer network params θ, the critic network params θ_v,
   training step $t = 0$

2 **Phase1: Imitation learning**

3 **while** $t < T_1$ **do**

4   Sample instance $(s_i, c_i) \sim D$ for $i \in (1, ..., B)$

5   Sample solution $\pi_i \sim p_\theta(.|s_i, c_i)$ for $i \in (1, ..., B)$

6   Generate solution $\pi_{Si} \sim Strong\_Heuristic(s_i, c_i)$

7   Calculate $b_i = L(\pi_{Si}|s_i, c_i)$ for $i \in (1, ..., B)$

8   Calculate $\nabla_\theta J(\theta) = \frac{1}{B} \sum_{i=1}^{B} (L(\pi_i|s_i, c_i) - b_i) \nabla_\theta \log p_\theta(\pi_i|s_i, c_i)$

9   Update $\theta \leftarrow Adam(\nabla_\theta J(\theta))$

10   Update $t \leftarrow t + 1$

11 **end**

12 **Phase2: Autonomous Learning**

13 Update $\theta_v \leftarrow \theta$

14 **while** $t < T$ **do**

15   Update $\theta_v, \theta \leftarrow Actor\_Critic(\theta_v, \theta)$

16   Update $t \leftarrow t + 1$

17 **end**

Sampling on trained model. After the training process of the pointer network model is completed, we apply this model to output a solution, that is, a priority vulnerability remediation plan. However, the process of constructing a solution is stochastic; it requires iteratively selecting VIs to patch under the probability of each VI, which is given by the trained policy $p_\theta(\pi|S, C)$. Therefore, we sample solutions given an input case to develop a final solution, and the two sampling strategies detailed below are considered in this paper.

(1) Repeat Sampling. Our first strategy is simply to repeat an input case many times. Multiple candidate solutions are produced when given repeated input cases using the pointer network model, and we choose the final solution with the greatest reward.

(2) Shuffle Sampling. Consider the fact that if we shuffle the input sequence without changing the feature value of each VI, the optimal solutions should be

the same. At the same time, we deem that the shuffling procedure increases exploration and improves the possibility of finding an optimal procedure. Therefore, our second strategy randomly shuffles the input sequence many times, and we choose the best sequence from the multiple candidate solutions.

In addition, a temperature hyperparameter T_{softmax} plays an important role when choosing a VI in the decoding phase and influences the sampling procedure. The temperature parameter controls the softness of the probability distribution. This is realized by rewriting formula(3b) as $p = \text{softmax}(u^i/T_{\text{softmax}})$. When $T_{\text{softmax}} > 1$, the probability distribution is smoother, leading to the candidates being more divergent. The optimal temperature parameter value is determined by experimentation.

4   Experiments

Before starting the experiments, we list the table comparing VPnet with other works. From the Table 3, we see that our work is an extension of works such as CVSS [15] and EPSS [9], ensuring measuring risk is comprehensive. Some commercial tools such as VPR [23] and VMS [7] measuring risk may be more comprehensive due to richer data sources, but they are not transparent, so it is difficult to set up experimental comparisons, at the same time, these tools do not consider combination optimization problems (COP) which is important for vulnerability prioritization, and we think that is our advantage. The most comparable work is VULCON [6], which also abstracts the vulnerability prioritization problem into a combinatorial optimization problem, but it takes a traditional mixed-integer programming method that spent 3 min to complete a task, and such efficiency obviously cannot support real-time requirements, since continuous scanning makes the recommended solution to constant change. Our work shifts the computational burden to the offline training phase, while in the applying phase, we adapt to real-time requirements by a well-trained solver that can output solutions in seconds.

Table 3. Comparison of different vulnerability prioritization works

Works	Quantitative	Risk measure	Transparent	Use AI	COP
CVSS3.0 [15]	Yes	Part(Severity)	No	No	No
EPSS [9]	Yes	Part(Theats)	Yes	No	No
SVCC [20]	No(Decsion)	No	Yes	No	No
AC-VRM [1]	Yes	Part(Context-aware)	No	No	No
VMS [7]	Yes	Comprehensive	No	Yes	No
VPR [23]	Yes	Comprehensive	No	Yes	No
VULCON [6]	Yes	Comprehensive	Yes	No	Yes
VPNET	Yes	Comprehensive	Yes	Yes	Yes

In order to prove the effectiveness of VPnet, there are two main aspects to consider, on the one hand, whether the VPnet can train a good pointer network solver, the evaluation criterion is the effectiveness of reinforcement learning in the training phase, if the reward value in the training iteration can increase and finally stabilize at the highest value or near the highest value, then it means that my model is effective. On the other hand, how well the trained pointer network solver performs, and the main concerns are how much the time is spent, whether the optimal solution can be obtained, and how scalable it is. Guide by the above reasons,we conduct experiments to investigate the behavior of VPnet.

4.1   Experimental Details

Experimental Environment Configuration. The software and hardware configuration of the experimental environment is shown in Table 4.

Table 4. Experimental environment configuration

Experimental environment	Experimental parameters
OS	Windows 10
CPU	Intel(R) Core(TM) i7-10510U
GPU	NVIDIA GeForce MX250 @ 2 GB
RAM	16 GB
Programming tool	Python3.7
Deep learning framework	Pytorch1.10.1+cu102

Experimental Datasets. During the training phase, we randomly generate three training datasets, VP30, VP50 and VP100, consisting of ten thousand instances with items' risks and costs drawn uniformly at random from $[0, 1]$, and a constraint value is generated randomly in $[0, sum(c_i)]$ for each instance, such as VP30, it belongs to $R^{B \times 31 \times 2}$, where B is the instances number. During the testing phase, we use the vulnerability scan reports drawn from scenarios of different sizes as raw data, and we preprocess the raw data and set different constraint values as final inputs for our model.

Experimental Setup. In order to obtain a well-trained model of a pointer network and verify the performance of our approach. We first train the pointer network models as vulnerability prioritization solvers using different methods. Next, we compare two sampling strategies and test the impact on the sampling process of a sensitive parameter T_{softmax}. Then, we test the performance of our solver by setting different numbers of VIs and various constraint values. Finally, we demonstrate the vulnerability prioritization plan provided by VPnet through a practical example.

4.2 Results

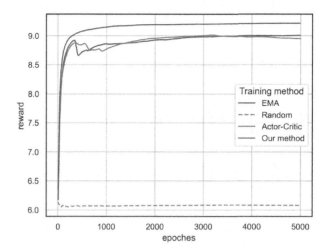

Fig. 3. The results obtained with different training methods.

The Results of Training Models. We first train VP30 solvers with two popular policy gradient algorithms, the EMA and actor-critic algorithm; however, the performances of such solvers are not satisfactory when we test them. After conducting an in-depth analysis, we think the main reason for this is that the number of feasible solutions satisfying the constraint is countless, so it is difficult to learn an optimal by strategy starting from a random state, and the objective function is likely to fall into local optima when updating the gradient. To overcome this situation, we propose a new method, which is detailed in Algorithm 2, and the result is presented in Fig 3. We can see from Fig 3 that the red curve is very steep in the early stage and quickly stabilizes at a higher reward value than those of the other two curves, indicating that our method speeds up the training process and trains better policy parameters.

The Results of the Sampling Solutions. After a well-trained model provides a policy for vulnerability prioritization, we also need to perform sampling to develop a final solution. In Fig 4(a), we construct five test cases to verify the performance of the two strategies. From the figure, we can see that among all the test cases, the result of sampling by shuffling the input is closer to the optimal result than that of repeated sampling, where the optimal result is calculated by a dynamic programming algorithm. In Fig 4(b), we test the sensitivity of the parameter T_{softmax} to inputs with different scales, and the result shows that the best-performing value for the parameter T_{softmax} may be related to the sizes of the inputs. In addition, the number of samples has a certain impact on the results; the more samples there are, the better the results. However, as the number of samples increases, the performance improvement becomes slight, while the computational cost grows linearly, so we compromise to form a balance between obtaining better results and incurring fewer costs. The number of samples is generally set to 64 in our paper.

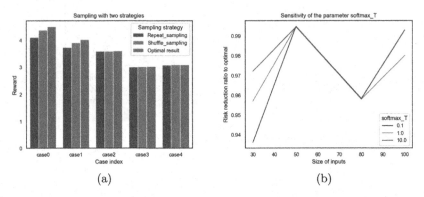

Fig. 4. The results of sampling solutions.

The Performance of Our Solver. In Fig. 5, we use a solver trained by the VP30 dataset and a shuffling sampling strategy to develop a final vulnerability prioritization plan, and we use the risk reduction ratio to optimal indicator to evaluate the performance of VPnet, the indicator value is between 0 and 1, with larger values indicating that our method is closer to the optimal solution. As displayed in Fig 5(a), near-optimal solutions are obtained by a VP30 solver with different size inputs, and even the worst performance reaches 95.8% ratio to the optimal, while the time consumption is within a few seconds. In Fig 5(b), we assign different constraint values to a simulate instance, results show that the risk reduction ratio to the optimal all exceeded 99% while the time consumption is relatively constant at about 1 s. Both pictures indicate that our model that is trained by small-size data can be applied to the scenarios of different scales, and our approach is effective with the advantage of flexibility and efficiency.

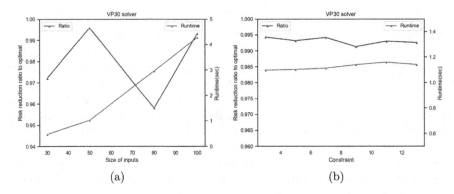

Fig. 5. The performance of our solver.

Showing Results Through a Practical Example. We test VPnet in a practical scenario. In the scenario, 53 vulnerability instances are scanned using the Nessus tool, the risk and cost value of each VI are obtained by the data preprocessing module, and the total given patch time is 30 h, corresponding to a constraint value of 3. As a result, VPnet recommends that 9 of the 53 vulnerabilities should be patched first, as shown in Table 5. These results are relatively consistent with expert perceptions, and the top-ranked vulnerabilities are recognized as the riskiest vulnerabilities by the public. For example, CVE-2019-0708, which is also known as "BlueKeep", is very popular in the hacking community. In Table 6, we show some key indicators. The baseline is the reward for a vulnerability remediation plan, which is ranked directly based on the observed risk without considering the cost. The results show that our approach achieves a 22.8% performance improvement and takes only 1.2 s.

Table 5. The priority vulnerability remediation plan provided by VPnet

Rank	Host	Program	CVE_ID
1	Host9	ProFTPD 1.3.5	CVE-2015-3306
2	Host1	Windows_xp	CVE-2019-0708
3	Host6	Apache Log4j2	CVE-2021-44228
4	Host4	Quest NetVault	CVE-2017-17653
5	Host4	Parse-server	CVE-2022-24760
6	Host7	Novell	CVE-2011-3176
7	Host7	Redis	CVE-2021-41099
8	Host0	Windows_7	CVE-2017-0143

Table 6. Key indicators

VPnet reward	Baseline	Improvement ratio	Runtime(Sec)
4.575062	3.723954	0.228549	1.257781

5   Limitations and Discussion

We concede that our current work has some limitations.

From an internal perspective of VPnet, there is no ground truth to compare in the vulnerability prioritization, and different ways of measuring risk bias the results. In addition, it is sometimes inappropriate for us to treat each vulnerability as an isolated instance. Some vulnerabilities that exist in the same software may be patched together through software updates. Such vulnerabilities should be combined into one instance to be fixed.

From a broader perspective, the actual situation is more complex than we currently consider since stakeholders in vulnerability management scenarios are diverse, and enterprises also have different practical needs. Vulnerability prioritization may be a multiobjective optimization problem when enterprises consider a combination of economic concerns, business requirements, security, and other impacts, and research on vulnerability prioritization still needs to go deeper.

However, we believe that our approach will be inspiring to both enterprises and researchers. This paper applies a pointer network to vulnerability prioritization for the first time and demonstrates its great potential through experiments. Until now, the pointer network has achieved great success in the fields of combinatorial optimization and nature language processing (NLP) since it was first proposed. In particular, it outperforms many other neural networks in performing the summarization task of NLP. Seeing the essences of these problems through phenomena, the common denominator of these problems in different fields is ranking and choosing the most important options from the candidate nodes; this is also the heart of the pointer network. Although this problem may be revised with an evolving understanding of vulnerability prioritization and the fact that enterprises' practices for estimating risk vary to suit specific needs, we can still use a pointer network to develop a priority vulnerability remediation plan, as long as we properly redesign the input format and reward function. Therefore, we believe that using pointer networks for vulnerability prioritization is a large step in the right direction, and we will continue to augment and improve VPnet in future work.

6   Conclusion

This paper deeply discusses various factors regarding vulnerability prioritization and recognizes that the essence of vulnerability prioritization is a combinatorial optimization problem. Based on the above understanding, we present VPnet, a vulnerability prioritization approach using a pointer network and deep reinforcement learning. We evaluate VPnet through experiments, results show that our approach develops nearly optimal solutions in seconds under different scale scenarios and constraints, and achieves a 22.8% performance improvement in a practical example. We also present a new training method that integrates imitation learning and autonomous learning to improve model training performance. Additionally, we implement an easy-to-implement vulnerability risk calculation formula, which combines severity, threat, impact, and asset criticality factors.

References

1. Ahmadi, V., Arlos, P., Casalicchio, E.: Normalization of severity rating for automated context-aware vulnerability risk management. In: 2020 IEEE International Conference on Autonomic Computing and Self-Organizing Systems Companion (ACSOS-C), pp. 200–205. IEEE (2020)
2. Bello, I., Pham, H., Le, Q.V., Norouzi, M., Bengio, S.: Neural combinatorial optimization with reinforcement learning. arXiv preprint arXiv:1611.09940 (2016)
3. Blank, R.M.: Guide for conducting risk assessments (2011)

4. Caruana, R., Niculescu-Mizil, A.: An empirical comparison of supervised learning algorithms. In: Proceedings of the 23rd International Conference on Machine Learning, pp. 161–168 (2006)

5. Delve Security: Ai-driven vulnerability management solution (2020). https://www.secureworks.com/products/taegis/vdr. Accessed 07 Jul 2020

6. Farris, K.A., Shah, A., Cybenko, G., Ganesan, R., Jajodia, S.: Vulcon: a system for vulnerability prioritization, mitigation, and management. ACM Trans. Priv. Secur. (TOPS) **21**(4), 1–28 (2018)

7. IBM: X-force red vulnerability management services (2021). https://www.ibm.com/security/services/vulnerability-management. Accessed 14 Aug 2021

8. Jacobs, J., Romanosky, S., Adjerid, I., Baker, W.: Improving vulnerability remediation through better exploit prediction. J. Cybersecur. **6**(1), tyaa015 (2020)

9. Jacobs, J., Romanosky, S., Edwards, B., Adjerid, I., Roytman, M.: Exploit prediction scoring system (EPSS). Digit. Threats Res. Pract. **2**(3), 1–17 (2021)

10. Aboud, J.: Why you need to stop using CVSS for vulnerability prioritization (2020). https://www.tenable.com/research. Accessed 27 Apr 2020

11. Kenna Security: Vulnerability scores and risk scores (2021). https://www.kennasecurity.com/blog/vulnerability-scores-and-risk-scores. Accessed 16 Oct 2021

12. Kingma, D.P., Ba, J.: Adam: a method for stochastic optimization. arXiv preprint arXiv:1412.6980 (2014)

13. Li, Y.: Deep reinforcement learning: an overview. arXiv preprint arXiv:1701.07274 (2017)

14. Martello, S., Pisinger, D., Toth, P.: Dynamic programming and strong bounds for the 0–1 knapsack problem. Manag. Sci. **45**(3), 414–424 (1999)

15. Mell, P., Scarfone, K., Romanosky, S.: Common vulnerability scoring system. IEEE Secur. Priv. **4**(6), 85–89 (2006)

16. Mnih, V., et al.: Asynchronous methods for deep reinforcement learning. In: International Conference on Machine Learning, pp. 1928–1937. PMLR (2016)

17. Papadimitriou, C.H.: On the complexity of integer programming. J. ACM (JACM) **28**(4), 765–768 (1981)

18. Rapid7: Quantifying risk with insightvm (2020). https://www.rapid7.com/products/insightvm/features/real-risk-prioritization/. Accessed 20 Sep 2020

19. Sharma, R., Sibal, R., Sabharwal, S.: Software vulnerability prioritization using vulnerability description. Int. J. Syst. Assur. Eng. Manag. **12**(1), 58–64 (2021)

20. Spring, J.M., Hatleback, E., Householder, A., Manion, A., Shick, D.: Prioritizing vulnerability response: a stakeholder specific vulnerability categorization. Technical report, CARNEGIE-MELLON UNIV PITTSBURGH PA PITTSBURGH United States (2019)

21. Sutskever, I., Vinyals, O., Le, Q.V.: Sequence to sequence learning with neural networks. Adv. Neural Inf. Process. Syst. **27** (2014)

22. Sutton, R.S., McAllester, D., Singh, S., Mansour, Y.: Policy gradient methods for reinforcement learning with function approximation. Adv. Neural Inf. Process. Syst. **12** (1999)

23. Tenable: Vulnerability prioritization rating (2019). https://www.tenable.com/sc-dashboards/vulnerability-priority-rating-vpr-summary. Accessed 11 Feb 2019

24. Vinyals, O., Fortunato, M., Jaitly, N.: Pointer networks. Adv. Neural Inf. Process. Syst. **28** (2015)

Are External Auditors Capable of Dealing with Cybersecurity Risks?

Yueqi Li$^{(\boxtimes)}$ ⓘ, Sanjay Goel ⓘ, and Kevin Williams ⓘ

State University of New York at Albany, Albany, NY 12222, USA
yli69@albany.edu

Abstract. Cyber risk presents a significant threat to financial reporting systems and capital markets, regulatory authorities expect external auditors to obtain the competence necessary to deal with cyber risk. As an exploratory study, we aim to address the urgent question that whether current external financial auditors can deal with cybersecurity-related tasks, as well as what drives their performance in these emerging tasks related to cybersecurity. Based on the survey data of external auditors from accounting firms located in Shanghai, China, we found that these auditors did not consistently understand fundamental concepts related to cyber risk. Using partial least squares based structural equation modeling, results indicate that the personality trait of openness to experiences positively, while operating stress negatively impact auditor performance in cybersecurity. Auditors' risk attitudes did not show significant influence on their cybersecurity performance. These findings can be used as a new source for regulators, researchers, and practitioners in their efforts of identifying audit quality drivers in the changing environments.

Keywords: External Auditor · Cybersecurity Performance · Personality · Operating Stress · Risk Attitudes

1 Introduction

In recent years, cyberattacks have become unprecedented, and cybersecurity has become critical to the success of businesses. According to China's National Internet Emergency Center, there were 23.07 million malicious programs, 13, 083 security breaches, over 13, 000 spoofing websites during the first half year of 2021 (National Internet Emergency Center 2021). A Chinese technology risk expert at Deloitte, China suggested seven hidden costs of a cyberattack, including disruption or damage to business operations, loss of customers, loss of contract revenue and the added value, devaluation of the trademark, reputation damage, intellectual property damage, and potential cybersecurity insurance costs (Xue 2017). External auditors, who provide assurance over companies' financial reporting, has been expected to consider cybersecurity risks in their operations.

Today, accounting regulators and standards-setters are concerned about whether companies and auditors are paying enough attention to cyber risks and related disclosures (International Organization of Securities Commissions (IOSCO) 2016; Li et al. 2020;

S. Goel et al. (Eds.): ICDF2C 2022, LNICST 508, pp. 326–340, 2023.
https://doi.org/10.1007/978-3-031-36574-4_19

PCAOB 2014; Securities and Exchange Commission (SEC), 2014, 2018). According to AICPA 2021 exam blueprints, CPAs should be able to identify the risks associated with protecting sensitive and critical information within information systems (AICPA, 2021). In the Chinese Institute of Certified Public Accountants (CICPA)'s CPA Industry Informatization Construction Plan 2021–2025, CICPA highlighted the importance and necessity of implementing cybersecurity education in the CPA profession (CICPA 2021). To address regulatory concerns, auditors have increased their audit risk awareness and put adequate procedures in place to deal with the consequences of cybersecurity incidents (Rosati et al. 2019), and accounting firms have established cybersecurity service lines. However, these classically trained auditors may not be adequately equipped to perform cybersecurity-related tasks. Whether auditors can deal with cybersecurity-related tasks remains a critical and urgent question.

This current study aims to understand how skilled auditors are in dealing with cyber risk and what affects their capability of conducting cybersecurity-related tasks. External auditors who work in accounting firms and perform auditing services for their clients are increasingly expected to assess cybersecurity risk and its impact on financial reporting. We use a sample of Chinese external auditors to assess external auditors' performance in cybersecurity related tasks and explores factors that affect their performance in cybersecurity performance. We found that these traditional financial auditors did not consistently understand cybersecurity basics, which call for extended and systematic cybersecurity training in the audit profession. The personality of openness to experience and operating stress both significantly affect auditors' cybersecurity performance. These findings will inform audit leaders in their efforts of personnel management, as well as audit regulators in their efforts of identifying audit quality drivers.

2 Background

2.1 Cybersecurity Regulations in Accounting

As cyber risk presents a growing threat to the financial reporting system and capital markets, many accounting regulatory authorities have addressed concerns and developed frameworks regarding cyber risk. The SEC emphasized the responsibilities of management and boards regarding cybersecurity and provide guidance in assisting public companies to prepare for their disclosures about cybersecurity risks and incidents in its *Commission Statement and Guidance on Public Company Cybersecurity Disclosures* (SEC 2018). The PCAOB specifically alerts external auditors to consider how cyber incidents might affect a firm's internal control over financial reporting (ICFR) (PCAOB 2010). In April 2017, the American Institute of Certified Public Accountants (AICPA) introduced a market-driven, flexible, and voluntary cybersecurity risk management reporting framework that highlights the importance of security/cybersecurity attestation in organizations (AICPA 2017a). The AICPA has also developed guidance for certified public accountants (CPAs) to help manufacturers and distributors better understand cybersecurity risks in their supply chains (AICPA 2018). The Financial Industry Regulatory Authority (FINRA) offered two studies on best practices for cybersecurity—FINRA (2015) covers overall cybersecurity issues; FINRA (2018) is targeted to particularly significant concerns and specifically addresses cybersecurity controls. The

Committee on Payments and Market Infrastructures and the Board of the IOSCO released the *Guidance on Cyber Resilience for Financial Market Infrastructures,* which is the first internationally agreed-upon guidance on cybersecurity targeting the financial industry (IOSCO, 2016).

China released *Cybersecurity Law of the People's Republic of China (2016 CSL, with effect from 1 June 2017)* in 2016 to promote cybersecurity and maintain cyberspace in the nation (Cybersecurity Law of the People's Republic of China, 2016). In the Chinese Institute of Certified Public Accountants (CICPA)'s *CPA Industry Informatization Construction Plan 2021–2025,* CICPA highlighted the importance and necessity of implementing cybersecurity education in the CPA profession (CICPA 2021). Researchers at the National Audit Office in China proposed that the cybersecurity audits should include the assessment of the cybersecurity risks faced by the organization and the assessment of whether their cybersecurity protection measures can effectively address the cybersecurity risks (Chen and Sui 2019), their work focuses on the cybersecurity audits for government agencies. Cyberspace Administration of China (CAC) released *Regulations on Network Data Security Management (Draft fort Comments)* in 2021, which first proposed a data security audit system (No. 58). The system provides two types of data security audits: 1) the self-audit requires the data processor to hire the data security audit professionals to carry out regular compliance audits on their personal data handling; 2) the examination audit requires managers and supervisory departments to carry out audits on important data processing activities (CAC 2021).

2.2 Auditors' Role in Cyber Risk

According to the CICPA, auditors work as independent third parties to express an opinion on financial statements being audited. To fulfill their roles, auditors shall comply with the code of professional ethics, plan and perform audits according to the requirements of auditing standards, obtain sufficient and appropriate evidence, and draw a reasonable audit conclusion based on the audit evidence obtained (CICPA 2006). Over the last two decades, auditing markets in China are dominated by "Big Four" accounting firms. The nature of the external audit services and the definition of audit quality does not vary between China and foreign countries (Zhou and Lv 2007).

Many accounting regulatory authorities and academic research have defined individual auditors' and audit firms' role with respect to cybersecurity. Their expected auditors' responsibilities in regard to cybersecurity have been summarized as follows:

Auditors are expected to:

- Consider cybersecurity risk in their operations (CAQ 2018);
- Identify cybersecurity risks associated with protecting critical and sensitive information within information systems (AICPA 2021; CICPA 2021);
- Focus on the information technology (IT) that a public company uses to prepare its financial statements and automated controls around financial reporting (PCAOB 2010);
- Evaluate whether financial statements are presented fairly under the applicable accounting principles as a whole and if the financial statements reflect cybersecurity-related incidents (PCAOB 2009; Knechel 2021);

- Review clients' cybersecurity disclosures and other cybersecurity related information in financial reports (CAQ 2018; Calderon and Gao 2020; Knechel 2021);
- Understand the controls in place and the methods used to prevent and detect cyber incidents that may materially affect a company's financial reporting (Hamm 2019);
- Understand management's approach to cybersecurity risk management (CAQ 2018);
- Assist boards of directors in their oversight of cybersecurity risk management (CAQ, 2018);
- Audit firms are expected to perform cybersecurity-related advisory, assurance, and audit services (Eaton et al. 2019).

To date, external auditors' ability of dealing with cybersecurity-related tasks is not well understood and evaluated in the current state of research. There has been no clear description on external financial auditors' responsibility relating to cybersecurity. In this study, we specifically focus on external auditors' performance in understanding and identifying cybersecurity risks, which is fundamental to their roles surrounding cybersecurity subject matter. The dependent variable in this study is external auditors' performance in cybersecurity. Consistent with the latest AICPA and CICPA's exam requirements for CPA candidates, we define auditors' performance in cybersecurity as their performance in identifying cybersecurity risks associated with protecting sensitive and critical information (AICPA 2021; CICPA 2021).

3 Hypotheses

3.1 Personality of Openness

The extant cybersecurity and auditing literature has examined the personality character-istics of external auditors (Dewi and Dewi 2018; Samagaio and Felício 2022). Barrick and Mount (1991) found that the openness trait has a positive effect on performance. Openness to information, experience, or being open to new things is a personality dimen-sion that categorizes people based on their interest in new things, creativity, imagination, and high intelligence (Kumar and Bhakshi 2010). As one of the five personality traits within Big Five Personality Model (BFM) (Cherry 2021; Robbins and Judge, 2008), the openness captures one's attitudes towards emerging subjects. Cybersecurity-related tasks are relatively new to traditional financial auditors. The current external auditors of financial statements are mostly experts of financial accounting and auditing with few backgrounds of cybersecurity, which makes cybersecurity-related tasks challenging to traditional external auditors. Rustiarini (2013) found that external auditors with a high openness personality can overcome problems in a short time, with limited information, and under high uncertainty, which leads auditors to perform better on the tasks they are unfamiliar with, like cybersecurity-related tasks. Therefore, auditor with higher open-ness characteristic is likely to be associated with a higher level of professional skepticism employed in an emerging task, which leads to improvement in their cybersecurity per-formance. To date, how openness affects external auditors' performance in dealing with emerging tasks, such as cybersecurity-related tasks, have not been studied.

Therefore, it is hypothesized that higher openness personality is correlated with better auditors' performance in assessing cyber risk.

H1: Openness to experience significantly and positively predicts an auditor's performance in cybersecurity.

3.2 Risk Attitudes

Auditors' attitudes constitute components of their feelings and beliefs about risk (Nolder and Kadous 2018). Risk attitudes, which are described as a "chosen state of mind with regard to those uncertainties that could have a positive or negative effect on objectives" (Hillson and Murray-Webster 2006, p. 4), are an important aspect of external auditors' attitudes in risk assessment tasks. Clarke (1987) showed that significant systematic differences exist among auditors regarding individual risk attitudes and perception biases and that auditors' risk attitudes affect their decisions of the audit scope. Risk attitudes also refer to risk appetite (i.e., risk-averse, risk-neutral, or risk-prone) (Farmer 1993), or risk capacity (Hindson 2013). People who are classified as risk-averse have a lower risk tolerance and are likely to see an event as risky. The majority of audit firms agree that Big Four firms are more risk-averse with respect to the reputation damage from public scandals and/or audit failures (Sawan and Alsaqqa 2013). Research findings also suggest that audit partners that are more risk-prone conduct lower quality audits; the clients of more risk-prone partners are more likely to misstate, pay lower audit fees, and less timely recognize loss (Pittman et al. 2019). In terms of individual auditors, auditors who are risk-averse tend to express a more severe audit opinion (Breesch and Branson 2009). Auditors who are detailed processors that read all of the available information tend to process more risk cues before making their final judgment and be more aware of the dangers implied by these cues, which leads to more risk-averse judgments (Goldhaber and deTurck 1988). These dangers, which are cyber risks, are more likely to be identified and evaluated by risk-averse auditors. Therefore, a higher level of risk aversion can lead to a higher level of susceptibility to cyber risks.

H2: The level of risk aversion significantly and positively predicts an auditor's performance in cybersecurity.

3.3 Operating Stress

Auditors and cybersecurity professionals are operating under great pressure, given the complex and difficult nature of their tasks (Gaertner and Ruhe 1981). DeZoort and Lord (1997) (p. 33) defined auditors' job stress as "the stress caused by his or her self-perceived inability to perform well in an ongoing auditing work environment". Stress is generally recognized as being negatively associated with cognitive abilities, task effectiveness, and general well-being (Linden et al. 2005). While stress could to some extent lead to a higher work efficiency (DeZoort and Lord 1997; McDaniel 1990), the potential of pressure-induced dysfunctional behavior could lead to impaired auditors' job performance (DeZoort and Lord 1997; Smith et al. 2007). Given the high-risk and mission-critical nature of audit tasks, stress can be harmful to auditors in their daily operations. The excessive workload and mental stress could eventually prevent current auditors to commit themselves in emerging tasks, such as tasks related to cybersecurity domain. This current study applied the fatigue level (physical tiredness) and frustration level (mental tiredness) to represent operating stress in the context of auditors' cybersecurity performance. Fatigue and frustration were proposed by Dykstra and Paul's (2018) Cyber Operation Stress Survey (COSS) as indicators of operating stress of cybersecurity professionals. When financial auditors experience a great workload and harsh work conditions, their fatigue levels tend to increase, which is likely to cause errors and lead to decreased performance (Li et al. 2013). Many factors that potentially lead to worker frustration include a lack of means and materials, inadequate work environments, deficits in human resource management, and opaque and unfair training opportunities (Mathauer and Imhoff 2006). This frustration demotivates workers from realizing their highest potential. Using fatigue and frustration to indicate both physical and mental tiredness would open up new approaches for job stress studies in the audit literature.

H3: Operating stress, indicated by fatigue level and frustration level, significantly and negatively predicts an auditor's performance in cybersecurity.

4 Research Methods

4.1 Sample

The sample for this research was composed of external auditors from accounting firms located in Shanghai, China[1]. The sampling was anonymous, and the researchers determined the admission of participants from the applicant pool using the following goals: auditors who work at public accounting firms or who have worked as auditors in public accounting firms within the past six months.

4.2 Data Collection

This study used primary data, which were collected by emailing anonymous survey links to the respondents. To recruit Chinese auditor participants, the snowball sampling technique was used in which research participants are asked to identify additional potential subjects for the research. The recruiting advertisement was sent to the group of auditor alumni via social media in Shanghai, and then the auditor alumni participated in the survey voluntarily and circulated the recruiting information among their auditor colleagues. These auditors are from 10 accounting firms, including both big accounting firms and local accounting firms. Most of them are from Big 4 accounting firms, including EY (34.5%) and KPMG (17.3%).

The questionnaire was translated by the author of this current study and validated by a Chinese faculty member who works in a prestigious U.S. educational institution and a Chinese audit professional who is proficient in English. Eligible auditors who applied to participate in this study were sent an anonymous link to the survey via email.

The total number of recorded responses is 69, with 37 of which are incomplete. The incomplete responses either did not approve the written information consent or left the cyber risk task unanswered. These incomplete responses are not paid, we only provided payments to people who answered all the required questions in the survey, and

---

[1] IRB exemption has been granted by the Institutional Review Board at the State University of New York (Study number: 20X242; date of approval: October 15, 2020).

we expect participants to be engaged while they participate in the survey. Finally, 32 out of 69 recorded questionnaires were considered complete and usable (see Table 1 for details). To calculate an acceptable sample size, we use parameter values of anticipated effect size of 0.35 (we anticipate a large effect), desired statistical power level of 0.8 and probability level of 0.05. The effect sizes that we obtained from regression analyses confirm that the predictors have a fairly large effect. In this study, we have total of four predictors, with two of which were retained after stepwise regression. Therefore, the acceptable sample size for the regression with four predictors is 39, the acceptable sample size for the regression with two predictors is 31. Therefore, our sample size is acceptable for our analyses.

Table 1. Details of Distribution and Recorded Questionnaires

Explanation	Amount	Percentage (%)
Recorded questionnaires	69	100.0
Canceled questionnaires (incomplete filling)	37	53.6
Used questionnaires	32	46.4
Valid response rate = 32/69 * 100% = 46.4%		

As an exploratory study, we mainly focus on addressing the current auditors' performance in the emerging cybersecurity-related tasks. Dealing with cybersecurity-related tasks poses some challenges for all the participating auditors, auditors in China generally have very busy schedule, both of which make it difficult to recruit them in the survey. However, we argue that understanding current auditors' performance in cybersecurity-related tasks is of great importance and urgence given the regulatory emphasis and the concerns from key stakeholders. We acknowledge that the respondents of convenience may not wholly represent the population of interest, which are current external auditors, but we eliminated bias as much as possible in the process of sampling and data collection. We anticipate this work to serve as a guiding resource for future studies both in China and internationally.

4.3 Measurement of Independent Variables

The personality trait of openness was tested following Goldberg's (1992) Big Five personality markers, which uses a publicly available source of the 50-item IPIP version of the Big Five Markers score the five personality traits. For this study, we only extracted the ten questions testing openness trait. For each question, participants rated their level of agreement from 1 to 5 (1 = strongly disagree, 5 = strongly agree). The level of risk aversion was used to represent risk attitudes. The Passive Risk-Taking Scale (Keinan and Bereby-Meyer, 2012) was used, in which 25 Likert questions are included (1 = strongly disagree, 7 = strongly agree).

Fatigue and frustration were tested using the question suggested in the Cyber Operations Stress Survey (COSS). To test fatigue and frustration level, auditors were given seven progressive stages and asked to identify the stage that best fits their actual condition right before doing the cybersecurity task (Dykstra and Paul 2018, p. 8). Fatigue level is rated from "fully alert, wide awake" to "exhausted, unable to function effectively", while frustration level is rated from "very low" to "very high" on the question about "how insecure, discouraged, irritated, and annoyed are you right now." Both fatigue and frustration were tested immediately before and immediately after the cybersecurity task.

4.4 Measurement of Dependent Variable – Auditors' Performance in Cybersecurity

The dependent variable in this study is referred to as external auditors' performance in cybersecurity. To test the dependent variable, we used a case scenario task extracted from a cyber risk assessment case study developed by Ayo et al. (2018). Consistent with the latest CPA exam blueprint's requirement on future CPA's skills in identifying cybersecurity risks associated with protecting sensitive and critical information, we asked respondents to examine the case scenario and identify all the threats, vulnerabilities, and risks they perceive. Auditor performance is the action or execution of auditing tasks completed by an auditor within a certain period (Trisnaningsih, 2007). The measurement of an auditor's performance in the case scenario task was done according to an executive rubric developed by the authors of this current study and modified by an external cybersecurity risk assessment expert. The external cybersecurity expert also graded a few responses as sample gradings. Based on the rubric and the sample gradings, auditor performance was evaluated independently by two Ph.D. students with both CPA and cybersecurity backgrounds. They reached a consensus on each response and assign a final score for each response. Each auditor's performance in cybersecurity was scored numerically on a scale from 0 to 100, where 0 meant no relevant answers were provided, and 100 meant the performance was as good as the performance of a cybersecurity expert. All the instruments can be found in the Appendix.

The Ayo et al. (2018) case study is to provide a full cybersecurity risk assessment on an African company called "SparTax Collection Agency" based on some background scenario of the agency. To examine students' performance in cybersecurity, we extracted the background scenario of the agency, including its recent cybersecurity breach history in Africa, the major business that the agency does (i.e., to contracted by the Finance Authority of local governments to collect revenue in the form of taxes), implemented technologies and third-party contracted information systems, security policies, personnel, and organizational structure. We asked students to identify cybersecurity threats, vulnerabilities, and risks, should they exist. As CPA candidates and future accounting professionals, we expect them to 1) systematically distinguish the basic cybersecurity concepts (i.e., threats, vulnerabilities, and risks); 2) sufficiently identify cybersecurity threats, vulnerabilities, and risks that may exist for the agency; 3) look into cybersecurity issues from different aspects (e.g., cybersecurity risks emerged from security policies, personnel management, third parties, etc.); 4) and clarify the impact of each identified cybersecurity issues.

4.5 Analysis

The hypothesis testing in this research was done through partial least squares (PLS) based structural equation modeling (SEM). Previous studies have showed evidence for the validity of using PLS-based SEM for small sample sizes (Henseler et al. 2016; Reinartz et al. 2009; Rigdon 2016; Sarstedt et al. 2016). We employed partial least squares (PLS) based Structural Equation Modeling (SEM) to explore both the measurement model of operating stress and the structural model of cybersecurity performance.

5   Results

5.1 Descriptive Statistics

Among all the 32 participants, the average age was 24.5, and 16 *(50%)* of them are male. Participants have averagely been trained for cybersecurity for 19.66 h during the last year (2019–2020). 22 of the 32 participants *(68.8%)* have the highest educational degree as bachelor's, while the rest 10 of the 32 participants *(31.3%)* have a master's degree. Participants' experiences in the field of auditing run from a few months to 9 years, with a mean of 14.63 months. Therefore, our Chinese auditor sample consists of relatively newer auditors.

Overall, the respondents' openness level *(M = 24.38, SD = 4.95)* and risk aversion level *(M = 87.84, SD = 18.21)* are about the moderate level. On average, the respondents were between "very responsive, but not at the peak" and "okay, somewhat fresh" in terms of fatigue level and slightly low on frustration level *(M = 2.91, SD = 1.35)* immediately before the cybersecurity task. After completing the cybersecurity task, participants' fatigue level *(MD = 0.66, p < .01)* and frustration level *(MD = 0.44, p < .05)* both significantly increased. The average performance score was not high *(M = 40.34, SD = 19.65)*. On average, auditors were able to identify 5.47 items related to cybersecurity issues, while there were 24 significant possible cybersecurity threats and 24 significant vulnerabilities exist in the scenario (see Ayo et al. 2018). Most auditors were able to find cybersecurity issues related disgruntled employees, outdated security policies, insufficient security training for employees, and third-party risks, and cloud security. However, very few students explained why such cybersecurity issues may exist or illustrated the negative impacts. They were also not able to identify specific cybersecurity threats (e.g., SQL injections, social engineering, etc.) that are likely to occur for the agency.

The internal consistency reliability was acceptable for all scales (Cronbach's alpha was above 0.8) (Lance et al. 2006). None of the control variables was significantly correlated with performance or was sufficiently significant to enter the regression model at a significance level of .05, leading us to exclude them in both the correlation and regression analyses.

5.2 PLS-Based SEM Analyses

We used PLS-based structural equation modeling (SEM) to model the effects of openness personality, risk aversion, and operating stress indicators of fatigue and frustration on

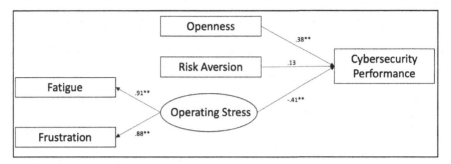

Fig. 1. PLS-based SEM Results

auditors' cybersecurity performance. The PLS-based SEM results are reflected in Fig. 1. The assumption of noncollinearity was met.

PLS-SEM requires a two-step approach in analyzing and interpreting a research model (Hair et al. 2017), including the measurement model and the structural model. The assessment of the measurement model requires the inspection of convergent validity and reliability (Hair et al. 2017, 2019). Convergent validity was analyzed using the standardized loadings of the indicators and the average variance extracted (AVE). We found fatigue and frustration both showed high standardized factor loadings (above 0.8), the average variance extracted (AVE) was above 0.8, indicating the model has convergent validity. Composite reliability (CR) was above the threshold of 0.70 (Hair et al. 2017), suggesting that all constructs have good reliability.

For the structural model, the personality of openness positively $(B = .38, p < .01)$, while operating stress negatively $(B = -.41, p < .01)$ affect auditors' cybersecurity performance. The adjusted R-square is 0.423, indicating 42.3% variances in cybersecurity performance could be explained by the presented SEM-PLS model, showing high model predictive accuracy. The insignificant effect of risk aversion is consistent with our findings in stepwise regression analyses. We also run the effect size (f^2) to measure the effect of each performance driver. Using Cohen (1988) threshold, we found both openness $(f^2 = 0.245)$ and operating stress $(f^2 = 0.270)$ to have small to medium effects.

6 Discussion

6.1 Discussion of Findings

This study explores external auditors' performance in cybersecurity and how personality, risk attitudes, and operating stress affect such performance. According to the responses from the research participants, we can conclude that the auditors did not consistently understand the differences among the concepts of cybersecurity threats, vulnerabilities, and risks. Understanding the basic concepts of cybersecurity and cyber risk is fundamental when dealing with cybersecurity-related tasks in daily operations. The results show that the auditors lacked fundamental competence in identifying cyber risk. In addition, auditors' responses to cybersecurity tasks indicate that they are able to identify cybersecurity issues with personnel management, such as insufficient security training and disgruntled employees, while few of them could extend their scope of assessment to governance structures, mission/business processes, enterprise architecture, information security architecture, facilities, equipment, system development life cycle processes, supply chain activities, and external service providers (National Institute of Standards and Technology (NIST), 2012).

Personality traits have long been ignored in the security and IT audit literature. We found openness significantly improves auditors' performance in assessing cyber risks, which lends support to Neuman et al.' s (1999) and Rustiarini's (2013) findings on openness and performance in auditing tasks. Openness is a typical trait of professionals in technology fields, especially cybersecurity (Freed 2014). Our findings support that openness is also an important trait that auditors should have to perform well in cybersecurity-related tasks. The personality trait of openness also tends to mitigate the level of frustration, according to the correlation analysis. An open and curious attitude enables individuals to more competently deal with emotion-eliciting situations, which contributes to their general capability of dealing with daily challenges effectively (van der Kaap-Deeder et al. 2021), which could explain the negative correlation between openness and frustration.

The findings suggest that operational stress, represented by fatigue and frustration, negatively affects auditor performance in cybersecurity. The findings are in line with Linden et al. (2005)'s finding that stress diminishes one's performance. Hopstaken et al. (2015) argues that fatigue reduces motivation for effortful activity and impairs task performance. Therefore, the severe negative impact of fatigue on auditor performance in cybersecurity may be due to fewer auditing efforts that auditors have employed during a task. The utilization of fatigue and frustration to indicate the personal tiredness at both physical and mental levels will open up new approaches for future studies of auditors' job stress. While the risk aversion did not significantly affect cybersecurity performance, this could be a result that auditors did not systematically understand the definition of cybersecurity basics. Hence, they fail to identify cybersecurity threats, vulnerabilities, and risks even though they are sensitive to risks in general.

6.2   Implications

The results of this study have implications for academics and practitioners. First, this paper enriches the existing literature uniquely by exploring factors personality of openness, risk aversion, and operating stress that affect auditors' performance in cybersecurity. This is a critical step toward improving auditors' performance in cybersecurity related tasks. The problem that current auditors are not capable of identifying cybersecurity risks and potentially other cybersecurity-related tasks calls for comprehensive training in the auditing profession and academics. Future research should consider how training can be appropriately designed and effectively implemented to facilitate auditors' adaption to cybersecurity-related tasks, especially for younger and entry-level auditors. While factors of operating stress can be managed through effective staffing and planning, it is obvious that personality cannot easily be changed. Fortunately, American colleges and accounting firms can use the resources from this study to discover students and professionals to fit their educational/recruiting objective or distribute cybersecurity related tasks within the audit team more appropriately (Aufman and Wang 2019). Third, the operating stress indicators derived from cybersecurity performance literature opens up new approaches for future studies on auditors' job stress. Future research could continue to use fatigue and frustration levels in measuring audit professionals' operating stress. Fourth, these factors could be used as part of a quality control program to conduct post-audit reviews, which could improve external audit quality when cybersecurity-related tasks are involved (Stoel et al. 2012). Finally, regulators and policymakers can incorporate these factors into ongoing or new frameworks of audit quality drivers.

6.3 Limitations

While this study contributes to both academia and practice, it also has limitations. First, the small sample size and the use of convenience sample may introduce additional biases. Given a smaller number of predictors used in this study, and a larger effect size anticipated, we believe using of a small sample size will produce credible results. As an exploratory study, we mainly focus on addressing the urgent question regarding current auditors' performance in the emerging cybersecurity-related tasks. Dealing with cybersecurity-related tasks poses some challenges for all the participating auditors, auditors in China generally have very busy schedule, both of which have made it difficult to recruit current auditors in the survey. However, we argue that understanding current auditors' performance in cybersecurity-related tasks is of great interest to regulators, business leaders, accounting firms, and other key stakeholders. We have eliminated biases as much as possible in the process of sampling and data collection. We encourage future studies to use this study as a guiding resource and further explore how personality traits, attitudes, and operational stress affect external auditors' performance in emerging tasks related to cybersecurity, such as cyber risk identification, with a larger and random auditor sample. Second, it only focused on external auditors from accounting firms in China. Future studies may consider how these identified factors contribute to U.S. and other foreign external auditors' success in identifying cyber risks. Third, this study only measured the individual characteristics of external auditors; factors at the process, firm, and environmental levels should be further studied. In addition, the sample was comprised of relatively young auditors (see, e.g., Christensen et al. 2016); future studies should look at how these factors also work for the older population.

References

1. American Institute of Certified Public Accountants (AICPA): Description criteria for management's description of the entity's cybersecurity risk management program (2017a)
2. American Institute of Certified Public Accountants (AICPA): Enhancing audit quality. American Institute of Certified Public Accountants, New York, NY (2017b)
3. American Institute of Certified Public Accountants (AICPA): Information for entity management (2018)
4. American Institute of Certified Public Accountants (AICPA): Uniform CPA Examination® Blueprints (2021)
5. Aufman, S., Wang, P.: Discovering student interest and talent in graduate cybersecurity education. Adv. Intell. Syst. Comput. **800** Part F1 (2019)

6. Ayo, S.C., Ngala, B., Amzat, O., Khoshi, R.L., Madusanka, S.I.: Information security risks assessment: A case study. Cornell University (2018)
7. Barrick, M.R., Mount, M.K.: The Big Five personality dimensions and job performance: a meta-analysis. Pers. Psychol. **44**(1), 1–26 (1991)
8. Breesch, D., Branson, J.: The effects of auditor gender on audit quality. IUP J. Account. Res. Audit Pract. **8** (3/4) (2009)
9. Calderon, T.G., Gao, L.: Cybersecurity risks disclosure and implied audit risks: evidence from audit fees. Int. J. Audit. **25**(1), 24–39 (2020)
10. Chen, Y., Sui, X.: Research on Chinese government cybersecurity protection and auditing methods (2019)
11. CICPA: Objectives and general principles of the audit of financial statements (2006). https://www.cicpa.org.cn/news/newsaffix/7699_2006817_21.pdf. Accessed 15 Aug 2022
12. CICPA: Construction of cybersecurity ensures data security and business continuity. China Accounting News (2021). https://www.cicpa.org.cn/xxfb/Media_Fax/202106/t20210617_62435.html. Accessed 15 Aug 2022
13. Clarke, D.: An Examination of the Impact of Individual Risk Attitudes and Perceptions on Audit Risk Assessment. ProQuest Dissertations Publishing (1987)
14. Cohen, J.: Statistical Power Analysis for the Behavioral Science. Lawrence Erlbaum, Mahwah (1988)
15. Cyberspace Administration of China: Cybersecurity Law of the People's Republic of China (2016). http://www.cac.gov.cn/2016-11/07/c_1119867116.htm. Accessed 15 Aug 2022
16. Cyberspace Administration of China: Regulations on Network Data Security Management (Draft fort Comments), Pub. L. No. 58 (2021). http://www.cac.gov.cn/2021-11/14/c_1638501991577898.htm. Accessed 15 Aug 2022
17. Deloitte LLP: Advancing quality through transparency. Deloitte LLP Inaugural Report (2010)
18. Dewi, I.G.A.A.P., Dewi, P.P.: Big five personality, ethical sensitivity, and performance of auditors. Int. Res. J. Manage. IT Soc. Sci. **5**(2), 195–209 (2018)
19. DeZoort, F.T., Lord, A.T.: A review and synthesis of pressure effects research in accounting. J. Account. Lit. **16**, 28 (1997)
20. Dykstra, J., Paul, C.L.: Cyber operations stress survey (COSS): studying fatigue, frustration, and cognitive workload in cybersecurity operations (2018)
21. Eaton, T.V., Grenier, J.H., Layman, D.: Accounting and cybersecurity risk management. Current Issues in Auditing (2019)
22. Farmer, T.A.: Testing the effect of risk attitude on auditor judgments using multiattribute utility theory. J. Acc. Audit. Financ. **8**(1), 91–110 (1993)
23. Financial Industry Regulatory Authority (FINRA): Report on Cybersecurity Practices, Cybersecurity Investor Alert (2015). http://bit.ly/2W3B 1N1. Accessed 15 Aug 2022
24. Financial Industry Regulatory Authority (FINRA): Report on Selected Cybersecurity Practices (2018). http://bit.ly/2MuW9MK. Accessed 15 Aug 2022
25. Gaertner, J.F., Ruhe, J.A.: Job-related stress in public accounting: CPAs who are under the most stress and suggestions on how to cope. J. Account. **151**(June), 68–74 (1981)
26. Goldberg, L.R.: The development of markers for the Big-Five factor structure. Psychol. Assess. **4**, 26–42 (1992)
27. Goldhaber, G.M., deTurck, M.A.: Effectiveness of warning signs: gender and familiarity effects. J. Prod. Liability, **11**(3) (1988)
28. Hair, J., Hult, T., Ringle, C., Sarstedt, M.: A Primer on Partial Least Squares Structural Equation Modeling (PLS-SEM), 2nd edn. Sage Publication, California (2017)
29. Hair, J.F., Risher, J.J., Sarstedt, M., Ringle, C.M.: When to use and how to report the results of PLS-SEM. Eur. Bus. Rev. **31**(1), 2–24 (2019)

30. Hamm, K.M.: Cybersecurity: Where we Are; What more can be done? A call for auditors to lean in. Baruch College 18th Annual Financial Reporting Conference. Public Company Accounting Oversight Board (2019). https://pcaobus.org/news-events/speeches/speech-detail/cybersecurity-where-we-are-what-more-can-be-done-a-call-for-auditors-to-lean-in_700#_ednref26. Accessed 15 Aug 2022

31. Henseler, J., Hubona, G.S., Ray, P.A.: Using PLS path modeling in new technology research: updated guidelines. Ind. Manag. Data Syst. **116**(1), 1–19 (2016)

32. Hillson, D. Murray-Webster, R.: Managing risk attitude using emotional literacy. In: PMI® Global Congress 2006—EMEA, Madrid, Spain. Project Management Institute, Newtown Square (2006)

33. Hindson, A.: Risk appetite & tolerance guidance paper. The Institute of Risk Management (2013)

34. Hopstaken, J., Linden, D., Bakker, A., Kompier, M.: A multifaceted investigation of the link between mental fatigue and task disengagement. Psychophysiology **52**(3), 305–315 (2015)

35. International Organization of Securities Commissions (IOSCO): Cyber Security in Securities Markets – An International Perspective Report on IOSCO's cyber risk coordination efforts (2016)

36. Keinan, R., Bereby-Meyer, Y.: "Leaving it to chance"—Passive risk taking in everyday life. Judgm. Decis. Mak. **7**(6), 705–715 (2012)

37. Knechel, W.R.: The future of assurance in capital markets: reclaiming the economic imperative of the auditing profession. Account. Horiz. **35**(1), 133–151 (2021)

38. Kumar, K., Bakhshi, A.: The five factor model of personality: is there any relationship? Humanities Soc. Sci. J. **5**(1), 25–34 (2010)

39. Lance, C.E., Butts, M.M., Michels, L.C.: What did they really say? Organ. Res. Methods **9**(2), 202–220 (2006)

40. Harris, D. (ed.): EPCE 2013. LNCS (LNAI), vol. 8020. Springer, Heidelberg (2013). https://doi.org/10.1007/978-3-642-39354-9

41. Li, H., No, W.G., Boritz, J.E.: Are external auditors concerned about cyber incidents? Evidence from audit fees. Audit.: J. Pract. Theory **39** (1), 151–171 (2020)

42. Linden, D., Keijsers, G., Eling, P., Schaijk, R.: Work stress and attentional difficulties: An initial study on burnout and cognitive failures. Work Stress. **19**(1), 23–36 (2005)

43. Mathauer, I., Imhoff, I.: Health worker motivation in Africa: the role of non-financial incentives and human resource management tools. Hum. Res. Health **4**, 1–17 (2006)

44. McDaniel, L.S.: The effects of time pressure and audit program structure on audit performance. J. Account. Res. **28**(2), 267–285 (1990)

45. National Institute of Standards and Technology (NIST): Guide for conducting risk assessments. NIST Special Publication 800–30 Revision 1 (2012)

46. National Internet Emergency Center: China's network security report in the first half year of 2021 (2021). https://www.cert.org.cn/publish/main/46/index.html. Accessed 15 Aug 2022

47. Neuman, G.A., Wagner, S.H., Christiansen, N.D.: The relationship between work-team personality composition and the job performance of teams. Group Org. Manage. **24**(1), 28–45 (1999)

48. Nolder, C.J., Kadous, K.: Grounding the professional skepticism construct in mindset and attitude theory: A way forward. Acc. Organ. Soc. **67**, 1–14 (2018)

49. Pittman, J.A., Stein, S.E., Valentine, D.F.: Audit partners' risk tolerance and the impact on audit quality. SSRN Electr. J. (2019)

50. Possible Questionnaire Format for Administering the 50-Item Set of IPIP Big-Five Factor Markers. International Personality Item Pool (2019). https://ipip.ori.org/new_ipip-50-item-scale.htm. Accessed 15 Aug 2022

51. Public Company Accounting Oversight Board (PCAOB): Other information in documents containing audited financial statements. Auditing Standards (AS) 2710 (2009). https://pca obus.org/oversight/standards/auditing-standards/details/AS2710. Accessed 15 Aug 2022

52. Public Company Accounting Oversight Board (PCAOB): Identifying and assessing risks of material misstatement. Auditing Standards (AS) 2110 (2010). https://pcaobus.org/oversight/standards/auditing-standards/details/AS2110. Accessed 15 Aug 2022

53. Public Company Accounting Oversight Board (PCAOB): Standing Advisory Group Meeting: Cybersecurity (2014)

54. Reinartz, W.J., Haenlein, M., Henseler, J.: An empirical comparison of the efficacy of covariance-based and variance-based SEM. Int. J. Res. Mark. **26**(4), 332–344 (2009)

55. Rigdon, E.E.: Choosing PLS path modeling as analytical method in European management research: a realist perspective. Eur. Manag. J. **34**(6), 598–605 (2016)

56. Robbins, S.P., Judge, T.A.: Essential Organizational Behavior. Pearson Education Inc, Upper Saddle River (2008)

57. Rosati, P., Gogolin, F., Lynn, T.: Audit firm assessments of cyber-security risk: evidence from audit fees and SEC comment letters. Int. J. Account. **54**(03), 1950013 (2019)

58. Rustiarini, N.: Pengaruh karakteristik auditor, opini audit, audit tenure, pergantian auditor pada audit delay. Jurnal Ilmiah Akuntansi dan Humanika, **2**(2) (2013)

59. Samagaio, A., Felício, T.: The influence of the auditor's personality in audit quality. J. Bus. Res. **141**, 794–807 (2022)

60. Sarstedt, M., Diamantopoulos, A., Salzberger, T., Baumgartner, P.: Selecting single items to measure doubly-concrete constructs: a cautionary tale. J. Bus. Res. **69**(8), 3159–3167 (2016)

61. Securities and Exchange Commission (SEC): Cybersecurity Roundtable (2014). https://www.sec.gov/spotlight/cybersecurity-roundtable.shtml. Accessed 15 Aug 2022

62. Securities and Exchange Commission (SEC): Commission Statement and Guidance on Public Company Cybersecurity Disclosures (2018). https://www.sec.gov/rules/interp/2018/33-10459.pdf. Accessed 15 Aug 2022

63. Smith, K.J., Davy, J.A., Everly, G.S.: An assessment of the contribution of stress arousal to the beyond the role stress model. Adv. Acc. Behav. Res. **10**, 127–158 (2007)

64. Stoel, D., Havelka, D., Merhout, J.: An analysis of attributes that impact information technology audit quality: a study of IT and financial audit practitioners. Int. J. Account. Inf. Syst. **13**, 60–69 (2012)

65. Sawan, N., Alsaqqa, I.: Audit firm size and quality: does audit firm size influence audit quality in the Libyan oil industry?. Afr. J. Bus. Manage. **7**(3) (2013)

66. The Center for Audit Quality (CAQ): Cybersecurity risk management oversight: A tool for board members (2018). https://www.thecaq.org/wp-content/uploads/2019/03/caq_cybersecurity_risk_management_oversight_tool_2018-04.pdf. Accessed 15 Aug 2022

67. Trisnaningsih, S.: Independensi auditor dan komitmen organisasi sebagai mediasi pengaruh pemahaman good governance, gaya kepemimpinan dan budaya organisasi terhadap kinerja auditor. Jurnal Simposium Akuntasi Nasional, UNHAS Makasar (2007)

68. van der Kaap-Deeder, J., Brenning, K., Neyrinck, B.: Emotion regulation and borderline personality features: the mediating role of basic psychological need frustration. Personality Individ. Differ. **168**, 110365 (2021)

69. Xue, Z.: China CFO insights - Seven hidden costs of a cyberattack (2017). https://www2.deloitte.com/content/dam/Deloitte/cn/Documents/finance/deloitte-cn-cfo-insights-seven-hidden-costs-cyberattack-zh-170403.pdf. Accessed 15 Aug 2022

70. Zhou, H., Lv, C.: Does accounting firm size change investors' perception of audit quality? Chin. Account. Financ. Rev. **9**(3) (2007)

Deep Learning-Based Detection of Cyberattacks in Software-Defined Networks

Seyed Mohammad Hadi Mirsadeghi[1(✉)], Hayretdin Bahsi[1], and Wissem Inbouli[2]

[1] Department of Software Science, Tallinn University of Technology, Tallinn, Estonia
semirs@teltech.ee, hayretdin.bahsi@taltech.ee
[2] University of Lorraine, LORIA, Nancy, France
wissem.inbouli@loria.fr

Abstract. This paper presents deep learning models for binary and multiclass intrusion classification problems in Software-defined-networks (SDN). The induced models are evaluated by the state-of-the-art dataset, InSDN. We applied Convolutional Autoencoder (CNN-AE) for high-level feature extraction, and Multi-Layer Perceptron (MLP) for classification that delivers high-performance metrics of F1-score, accuracy and recall compared to similar studies. Highly imbalanced datasets such as InSDN underperform in detecting the instances belonging to the minority class. We use Synthetic Minority Oversampling Technique (SMOTE) to address dataset imbalance and observe a significant detection enhancement in the detection of minority classes.

Keywords: Software-Defined Network · Intrusion Detection · Deep Learning · Dataset Balancing

1 Introduction

Software-Defined Networking (SDN) has revolutionized network management through the physical separation of the control plane from forwarding devices. Through the decoupling of control and data planes in the SDN paradigm, all network intelligence and control logic is migrated from network devices to a logically centralized software-based entity known as the network controller. Thus, SDN provides network-wide visibility, centralized network intelligence, and network programmability. However, these features and the SDN architecture itself introduce new security risks and attack vectors that are not present in conventional network deployments. The new attack surface introduced by SDN is due to the inherent alterations to network components and the relationships between them. For example, centralized architecture brings about a single point of failure (SPOF). In other words, if the network controller is compromised by an adversary, the entire network may be in jeopardy. Moreover, SDN elements themselves may be used as reflectors in Amplification DDoS attacks.

S. Goel et al. (Eds.): ICDF2C 2022, LNICST 508, pp. 341–354, 2023.
https://doi.org/10.1007/978-3-031-36574-4_20

Intrusion detection is a critical detective security function for identifying cyber attacks usually in near real-time and initiating the relevant course of action. The common solutions depend on attack signatures, meaning that such intrusion detection systems (IDSs) have a limitation to detect future variations or enhancements of the existing attack types. Machine learning-based approaches promise to detect new attack types, eliminating the need for signature generation tasks. Instead, they learn from the data. In an SDN architecture, security functions such as intrusion detection can be embedded as a software application on top of the controller or it can be deployed as an independent system component. Thus, a machine learning-based detection function can be applied in various ways.

In this paper, we introduce deep learning-based models for detecting intrusions in software-defined networks. More specifically, we have developed two binary classification models, one of them focusing on DDoS detection and the other one discriminating all intrusions from normal traffic. We also created a detection system for identifying intrusion types, which is achieved by a model that performs multi-class classification. We observed very low detection rates for minority classes. Thus, we applied balancing strategy to boost the performance. We used a relatively new dataset [8] that is generated in an SDN network. There exist some studies (e.g., [2]) that apply deep learning models without a dataset balancing strategy. This study demonstrates that balancing is a significant enabler for better performance.

The structure of this paper is as follows: Sect. 2 gives background information about the subject and reviews the literature. The machine learning workflow and the applied methods are introduced in Sect. 3. The results are given and discussed in Sect. 4. Section 5 concludes the paper.

2   Related Work

The industry is exploring ways to exchange information among trusted parties to improve network security. A collaborative concept called DDoS eXchange Points (DXP) has been proposed [20] based on combining information from multiple sources across the network. Recent studies [14] suggest combining ML and SDN to construct a scalable and accurate bot-detection framework. Such a framework leverages centralized learning with distributed detection to achieve better accuracy. In 2016, a bot detection scheme in SDNs was proposed [16] by gathering centralized network flow statistics and applying a decision tree that depends on a supervised machine learning classification algorithm which achieved an 80% detection rate over a publicly available real-world botnet dataset. In 2017, a flow-based approach to detecting botnets in software-defined networks was proposed [17] using ML algorithms without the need for reading packet payload which achieved a 90% accuracy testing their method on publicly available CTU-13 botnet datasets and ISOT botnet datasets. In 2018, an SDN framework for detection of defense against DDoS attacks was proposed [21]. This framework consists of a traffic collection module, flow table delivery module as well as DDoS attack detection module that was built using the SVM model. This experiment was conducted using the KDD99 dataset demonstrating a high accuracy rate of 99.8%. Even though the KDD99 dataset has been widely used for testing and training network intrusion detection datasets, it does not resonate with Software-defined networks and may pose compatibility issues.

Deep Learning-based approaches have outperformed existing machine learning techniques when applied to various classification problems in SDN networks [11]. CNN-based models for Intrusion detection in Software-defined Networks have been presented [7]. Hybrid CNN-LSTM Model for anomaly detection has been presented [1] by training a model on the InSDN dataset both in space and time. Moreover, a Gated Recurrent Unit Recurrent Neural Network (GRU-RNN) was proposed for intrusion detection systems in SDN [15] which was only tested on classical intrusion dataset NSL-KDD. It is apparant that the research community can benefit from more intrinsic SDN data.

3 Method

3.1 Dataset

Even though SDN is increasingly deployed in cloud computing infrastructure and globally deployed in WANs, the technology is still under development. While classical intrusion detection datasets such as KDD'99 [6] and NSL-KDD [18] provide us with cases of various attacks vs normal traffic, they do not reflect the characteristics of SDN. Actual traffic data captured from data centers and globally deployed WANs such as Google B4 [9] and Espresso [22] can shed a light on the specifics of DDoS detection in SDN but they are not publicly available. Even though helpful in understanding how to detect attacks in traditional networks, using a non-specific SDN dataset may cause compatibility problems as attack vectors would not resonate with the SDN architecture.

For our study, we leverage InSDN [8], a recent specific attack dataset obtained from an SDN environment. InSDN dataset contains a total number of 343,939 network flow traces where normal traffic brings 68,424 instances and attack traffic is split into seven different attack classes. DDoS and Probe attacks are represented by 121,942 and 98,129 instances, respectively [8]. The remaining one per cent of attack traffic consists of 53616 DoS, 1405 BFA, 192 web attack, 164 botnet and only 17 U2R instances, indicating an outstanding imbalance in the dataset. It is common to describe the imbalance of classes in terms of a ratio of a class with respect to the largest class. For instance, the imbalance ratio of U2R compared to DDoS is 1:7173.

This dataset provides flow-level features such as flow duration, inter-arrival time, number of packets, and number of bytes. The dataset also includes statistical features such as the maximum, minimum, mean, or standard deviation of the flow-level features. These features can be directly extracted from the SDN controller through API queries or by extracting from the flow data.

3.2 Overview of the Classification Tasks

Deep learning models learn the data representation with multiple levels of abstraction. These methods have dramatically improved the model performances in speech recognition or visual object recognition among others [3]. In this study, we seek to design, implement and evaluate deep learning architectures that learn the structures of the dataset for three different supervised classification problems: (1) A binary classifier that discriminates DDoS instances from the normal ones (DDoS classification), (2) A binary classifier that recognizes whether an instance is an intrusion (i.e., not limited to DDoS) or not (Intrusion classification), (3) Multi-class classifier that identifies the exact type of intrusion (Intrusion Type classification).

The experiments were carried out using Python and the Pytorch [12] library. The computing resource has a processor with 2199.998 MHz, 13G memory and 56320K L3 cache.

3.3   Binary Classification

We induced three separate deep-learning models for DDoS and intrusion classification problems:

(1) A deep learning architecture composed of various neural network layers for the raw features (Basic Architecture),
(2) A similar deep learning architecture but obtains high-level features from an autoencoder architecture (Autoencoder Architecture),
(3) A simple ensemble model that combines the decision of results obtained from (1) and (2) (Simple Ensemble Architecture).

For the basic architecture, we included a 7-layer neural network with 52, 128, 512, 512, 128, 64, and 16 nodes respectively. The rectified linear activation function (ReLU) has been used at each layer to increase the non-linearity degree and set all negative values in the feature set by zero. Finally, the output layer incorporates the Sigmoid function to represent the probability of each input flow belonging to either class. We use the Adam optimization algorithm for stochastic gradient descent where the learning rate is set to 0.0001 and train the deep learning model. At each backpropagation step during the training process, we calculate the reconstruction loss using Binary Cross Entropy criterion (Fig. 1).

Autoencoder, generally deployed as a generative model, is proficient at extracting high-level features from data by transforming it into a latent space by an architecture composed of an encoder, bottleneck and decoder. The latent space representation of data lies at the bottleneck layer of Autoencoder, which is later used to generate new data instances by mapping the original instances to the new space. Convolutional Autoencoders have proven to be excellent at denoising data. Thus, for the second model, we design a Convolutional Autoencoder and train it over the InSDN dataset. Then the bottleneck representation of the dataset is fed to a deep learning framework.

The architecture of the convolutional autoencoder is composed of three convolutional layers taking in flow-level values through one input channel and expanding it first to 8 and next to 16 and 32 channels. Each channel corresponds to a different filter applied throughout the convolution process. The output of

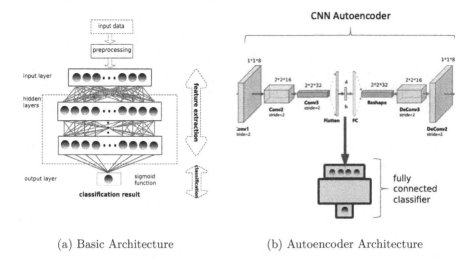

(a) Basic Architecture   (b) Autoencoder Architecture

Fig. 1. Deep Learning models

convolutional layers is then flattened and linearly transformed into the bottle-neck space dimension of [1,4]. The decoder has the same architecture as the encoder except in reverse order. Throughout the training process, the decoder reconstructs training data instances with the aim of minimizing the loss between the original and reconstructed ones.

As a first pre-processing step, we reshape each flow instance of dimensions [1,52] into an image-like structure of shape [8,8]. This transformation is carried out to suit the input dimensions of the convolutional autoencoder using a linear function (52,64) which then is unflattened to shape [8,8]. Convolutional autoen-coder is trained over a train set for 200 epochs leaving us with a latent space representation view of network traffic data. In this fashion, we can extract 4 high-level features out of 52 features. As depicted in Andrew's curve for high-level features (Fig. 2a), we observe more linearity in feature space as the curves for normal and DDoS behavior are definitively less tangled and more easily sep-arable for DDoS classification than the original features (Fig. 2b).

We insert the 4-dimensional output from the bottleneck of the Convolu-tional Autoencoder into a deep learning classifier with the architecture of a fully-connected classifier consisting of six linear layers going from 4 to 16, 32, 32, 16, and 1 node at each layer. We use rectified linear unit activation function at each layer.

The third one, the basic ensemble model, combines the classification results of the first and second models. Aggregation of information from the two models may result in decisions that are superior to those made by either single model. We combine the proposed classification models in such a fashion that they share their decisions on each flow instance. If either model decided that a flow belongs to an attack category, then it is considered an attack. In the case that both models agree on a flow instance being normal, then it is considered normal.

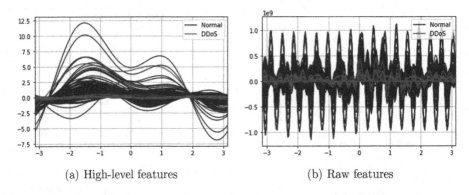

(a) High-level features   (b) Raw features

Fig. 2. Comparison of Andrew's Curves for raw and high-level features

3.4   Multiclass Classification and Dataset Balancing

For the intrusion type classification problem, we propose a 10-layer fully connected neural network with 52, 128, 512, 1024, 1024, 512, 512, 128, 64, 16, and 8 nodes in each layer. The architecture takes 52 features, gradually expands across the data space, obtains high-level abstractions of training data and ultimately measures class probabilities at the output nodes.

The intrusion class of the InSDN dataset has 7 distinct intrusion types which are listed with their instance numbers in Table 1. The majority of traffic flows belong to DDoS, DoS and Probe attack classes with the remaining classes making up about 1% of the dataset (e.g., an imbalance ratio of 1:7173 between U2R and DDoS). Thus, the model may not effectively learn the decision boundary in the case of minority classes which are also important to identify.

We use Synthetic Minority Over-sampling Technique (SMOTE) to address the imbalance issue of InSDN Intrusion dataset. In this technique, minority classes are over-sampled by creating synthetic examples rather than by over-sampling with replacement. In this fashion, minority classes are over-sampled by taking each minority class sample and introducing synthetic examples along the line segments joining any/all of the k minority class nearest neighbors. Depending on the amount of over-sampling required, neighbors from the k nearest neighbors are randomly chosen [5].

A dataset is imbalanced if its classes are not approximately equally represented. Imbalance on the order of 100 to 1 is prevalent in fraud detection and imbalance of up to 100,000 to 1 has been reported in other applications [13]. Deep learning models trained with imbalanced cybersecurity data cannot recognize minority classes effectively. One way to address this issue is to use resampling in an attempt to adjust the ratio between different classes to obtain a balanced dataset.

The research community has addressed the notion of class imbalance mainly in two ways. One approach is to assign distinct costs to training examples [10].

The other angle is to re-sample the original dataset, either by over-sampling the minority class and/or under-sampling the majority class [4].

Table 1. The number of instances in the dataset before and after data augmentation

Intrusion Type	Number of instances in Original Source	Number of instances after data augmentation
BFA	1405	50181
U2R	17	48793
Probe	98129	146905
DoS	53616	78004
DDoS	121942	121942
Web-Attack	192	48968
Botnet	164	48940
Normal	68424	79127

Authors of SMOTE [5] suggest combining the Synthetic Oversampling Technique with random undersampling of the majority class. Therefore, we intend to first oversample the minority class to have as many more examples as 25 per cent of the number of majority class, then use random undersampling to reduce the number of examples in the majority class by 75 per cent of the minority class. The balanced intrusion dataset includes 636545 samples in total. Table 1 reports dataset statistics before and after the data augmentation.

We conducted separate experiments by training our 10-layer fully connected neural network with original and balanced datasets for a total of 200 epochs. Both experiments were carried out using the same test set obtained before balancing.

3.5   Evaluation Criteria

To evaluate the performance of our classifiers, we use classification accuracy, precision, recall, and F1 score as performance metrics. In addition, we calculate the confusion matrix where:

- `True Positive (TP)` indicates attack traffic correctly classified as malicious(DDoS).
- `True Negative (TN)` indicates normal traffic correctly classified as benign.
- `False Positive (FP)` indicates normal traffic incorrectly classified as malicious.
- `False Negative (FN)` indicates attack traffic incorrectly classified as normal.

4   Results and Discussion

4.1   Data Pre-processing

Socket information such as Source IP, Destination IP, and flow ID is removed to avoid the over-fitting problem given that these features can be changed from network to network. The original dataset includes 77 features [8]. InSDN dataset also includes as many as 8 zero variation features that do not contain any information useful for classification purposes. These features (**Fwd Byts/b Avg'**, **'Fwd Pkts/b Avg'**, **'Fwd Blk Rate Avg'**, **'Bwd Byts/b Avg'**, etc.) along with TCP flags are removed, leaving us with a total of 52 numerical features. Finally, features have different ranges, so they need to be standardized to restrict the scale of values.

We split more than 189000 network flow traces provided by the InSDN dataset (i.e., DDos and normal instances)for DDoS traffic classification into training and test sets with an 80% train, 20% test ratio.

4.2   Explotary Data Analysis

Our feature set includes basic features such as the duration of a flow and flow Inter-arrival time as well as statistical features such as min, max, and standard deviation of the basic features. First, we use the Pearson correlation coefficient to compute the pair-wise correlation matrix for all features. We conducted this analysis for the intrusion classification problem. This matrix reveals that time-related features such as Flow Duration, Flow Inter-Arrival Time, and Idle Std seem to be correlated. Next, we reduce the dimensionality of the feature space by applying a principle component analysis (PCA). A PCA decomposition can be used to project a high-dimensional space to a lower-dimensional space by relying on the initial principal components. In effect, it converts a set of values of M possibly correlated variables into a set of K uncorrelated variables, the PCAs. We find that a significant number of the features are correlated since the first 8 PCAs explain more than 70% of the variance and the first 15 about 90% as shown in Fig. 3a. In 3b, it is observed that the first and second PCA vectors provide relatively distinguishable feature space projection for the intrusion classification task.

4.3   Experimental Results: Binary Classification

DDoS classifier with Basic Architecture is trained over the train set in the course of 200 epochs and demonstrates a remarkable accuracy of 99.72%.

In the context of DDoS detection, a false negative means an attack instance was missed. While our basic architecture performs remarkably for DDoS classification, there are 6 false negatives in the confusion matrix (Fig. 4a). We also observe 99 normal flow instances that were classified as DDoS instances by this architecture.

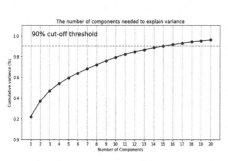 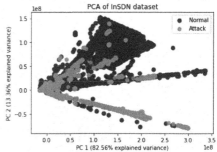

(a) Cumulative Explained Variance by Principal Components

(b) Benign vs. Malicious: projection of feature space to 2 Principle Components.

Fig. 3. PCA Results of Intrusion Classification

Table 2. Binary Classification Results

Model	DDoS Classification				Intrusion Classification			
	Accuracy	Precision	Recall	F1-Score	Accuracy	Precision	Recall	F1-Score
Basic	**99.72**	**99.59**	99.97	99.78	99.67	99.64	99.94	99.79
Autoencoder	99.08	98.90	99.67	99.28	91.53	95.04	94.35	94.69
Simple Ensem.	99.14	98.70	**99.98**	99.33	**99.71**	**99.66**	**99.97**	**99.81**

Autoencoder architecture is trained with the same train dataset for a total of 4000 epochs. Although autoencoder enabled us to represent the whole feature space by only 4 features, the performance of this architecture has slightly less than the basic one in all metrics as shown in Table 2 for DDoS classification. The confusion matrix given in Fig. 4b depicts that false positives and false negatives increase in this model type. However, a simple ensemble model that merges the results of the other two models provided a better recall value, decreasing the false negative samples (see Fig. 4c). Still, the basic architecture is better in other metrics, accuracy, precision and F1-score due to the lower false positive number.

Our experiments regarding the intrusion classification indicate similar results to the case of DDoS classification except the simple ensemble model is slightly better than all other models in all metrics as shown in Table 2. Still, the autoencoder model has the worst performance when it is individually evaluated. However, this model contributes to the simple ensemble model positively and slightly boosts its performance when used with basic architecture in tandem. The number of false negative instances obtained from a simple ensemble decreases to 13 from 28 when compared to the basic architecture (see Fig. 5).

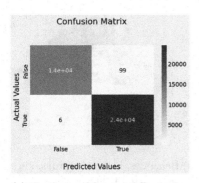

(a) Confusion Matrix of Basic Architecture

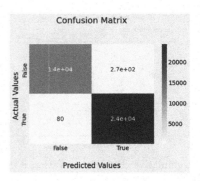

(b) Confusion Matrix of Autoencoder Architecture

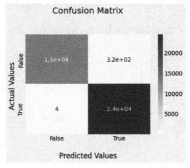

(c) Confusion Matrix of Simple Ensemble Architecture

Fig. 4. Confusion Matrices for DDoS Classification

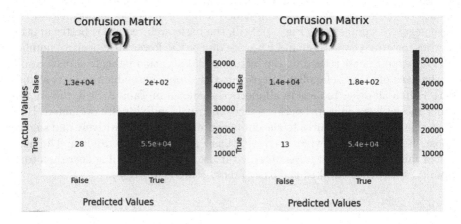

Fig. 5. Confusion Matrices of intrusion classification: (a) Basic Architecture (b) Simple Ensemble Architecture

4.4   Results of Intrusion Type Classification and Data Balancing

The unbalanced nature of a dataset may have implications on the multiclass classification setting as minority classes may not be identified by the model due to their limited representation in the training datasets. We observed this limitation in our experimental results regarding the intrusion type classification. As demonstrated in Table 3, despite very accurate results for the intrusion types, DDoS, DoS and Probe, the detection rates of BFA, Web-Attack and botnet are lower. In a more extreme case, any instance belonging to the intrusion type, U2R, has not been identified in the test dataset.

When the model is trained with a balanced dataset (i.e., recall that we use SMOTE as a balancing method in this study), we obtain a remarkable increase in detection rates of minority classes. As shown in Table 3, the new model is able to detect approximately 67% of the U2R attacks. We also observed significant increases in the detection rates of Botnet, Web-Attack and BFA.

Table 3. F1 Performance of Multi-class Classification over balanced dataset

Class	BFA	Botnet	DDoS	DoS	Normal	Proble	U2R	Web-Attack
balanced dataset	95.72	100	99.99	99.81	99.74	99.05	66.66	100
unbalanced dataset	82.43	57.57	99.98	99.90	99.92	99.79	0	44.73

The study, [2], proposes multiple deep-learning models for detecting Denial-of-Service attacks in the InSDN dataset. Their models induced by RNN, LSTM, and GRU models [2] proposed to take in 48 features from InSDN dataset and perform adequately by measures of precision, recall, and F1-scores. V-NKDE, an ensemble model that incorporates Voting -Naive Bayes, K Nearest Neighbors, Decision Tree, and Extra Trees has been proposed by [19]. The concept behind the voting classifier is to merge various machine learning classifiers conceptually and use a majority vote to predict class labels. Both of these studies provide multiclass classification models for the same dataset that we used in this study.

As demonstrated in Table 4, our model for the balanced dataset achieves the highest detection rates for BFA, Botnet, Web-Attack and U2R. Despite the fact that [2] uses relatively advanced models for grasping the temporal aspect of the dataset and [19] uses a well-developed ensemble method, our results for DDoS, DoS and Probe are very close to their performances and we obtained higher detection rates for minority classes. These results indicate that balancing the dataset in this problem domain would be essential for better performance regardless of the complexity of the utilized ML algorithm.

Table 4. Comparison of Multiclass Classification Results

Type Detection	per-class F1-score (%)						
Model	BFA	Botnet	DDoS	DoS	Probe	U2R	Web-Attack
RNN[2]	75.6	79.51	99.93	98.82	98.60	21.05	12.78
LSTM[2]	80.50	82.50	99.94	97.87	98.18	12.90	13.80
GRU[2]	80.33	53.65	99.94	98.11	98.48	36.36	12.84
V-NKDE[19]	92.7	95.7	100	99.9	99.9	not mentioned	69.3
Our Balanced Model	95.72	100	99.99	99.81	99.05	66.66	100

5   Conclusion

InSDN dataset paves the way for the research community to develop machine learning models for detecting intrusions in SDNs. In this study, we propose deep learning-based models for binary and multiclass classification problems by using this dataset. We developed two distinct binary models, one for discriminating DDoS from normal traffic and one for detecting any type of intrusion. The multiclass model identifies the type of intrusion among 8 different classes that also include the normal class.

We investigated whether low-dimensional vectors obtained from Convolutional Encoders improve the performance of a basic deep-learning model composed of various neural network layers. We found that utilizing such vectors for model building slightly reduces the number of false negatives but creates many false positives. A simple ensemble that combines the outputs of two models, one created with raw features and one with vectors of autoencoder layer slightly increases performance, indicating that still, weaker models enhance detection when they contribute to the ensemble rather than acting as a standalone model.

We applied a balancing strategy, SMOTE, in the context of multiclass classification and achieved better results in identifying the minority intrusion types which can create significant harm to their targets. When we compared our results with the findings of studies that address the same dataset, we deduced that the application of a balancing strategy would be more instrumental than the complexity of the machine learning algorithm.

Acknowledgement. This work is partially funded by the European Union's Horizon 2020 Research and Innovation Programme through ECHO (https://echonetwork.eu/) project under Grant Agreement No. 830943.

References

1. Abdallah, M., An Le Khac, N., Jahromi, H., Delia Jurcut, A.: A hybrid CNN-LSTM based approach for anomaly detection systems in SDNs. In: The 16th International Conference on Availability, Reliability and Security, pp. 1–7 (2021)
2. Alshra'a, A.S., Farhat, A., Seitz, J.: Deep learning algorithms for detecting denial of service attacks in software-defined networks. Procedia Comput. Sci. **191**, 254–263 (2021)

3. Bengio, Y., LeCun, Y., et al.: Scaling learning algorithms towards AI. Large-scale Kernel Mach. **34**(5), 1–41 (2007)
4. Chawla, N.V.: Data mining for imbalanced datasets: an overview. In: Maimon, O., Rokach, L. (eds.) Data Mining and Knowledge Discovery Handbook, pp. 875–886. Springer, Boston (2009). https://doi.org/10.1007/978-0-387-09823-4_45
5. Chawla, N.V., Bowyer, K.W., Hall, L.O., Kegelmeyer, W.P.: Smote: synthetic minority over-sampling technique. J. Artif. Intell. Res. **16**, 321–357 (2002)
6. Divekar, A., Parekh, M., Savla, V., Mishra, R., Shirole, M.: Benchmarking datasets for anomaly-based network intrusion detection: KDD CUP 99 alternatives. In: 2018 IEEE 3rd International Conference on Computing, Communication and Security (ICCCS), pp. 1–8. IEEE (2018)
7. Elsayed, M.S., Jahromi, H.Z., Nazir, M.M., Jurcut, A.D.: The role of CNN for intrusion detection systems: an improved CNN learning approach for SDNs. In: Perakovic, D., Knapcikova, L. (eds.) FABULOUS 2021. LNICST, vol. 382, pp. 91–104. Springer, Cham (2021). https://doi.org/10.1007/978-3-030-78459-1_7
8. Elsayed, M.S., Le-Khac, N.A., Jurcut, A.D.: InSDN: A novel SDN intrusion dataset. IEEE Access **8**, 165263–165284 (2020)
9. Jain, S., et al.: B4: experience with a globally-deployed software defined wan. ACM SIGCOMM Comput. Commun. Rev. **43**(4), 3–14 (2013)
10. Margineantu, D.: Building ensembles of classifiers for loss minimization. Comput. Sci. Stat., 190–194 (1999)
11. Niyaz, Q., Sun, W., Javaid, A.Y.: A deep learning based DDoS detection system in software-defined networking (SDN). arXiv preprint arXiv:1611.07400 (2016)
12. Paszke, A., et al.: Pytorch: an imperative style, high-performance deep learning library. In: Wallach, H., Larochelle, H., Beygelzimer, A., d' Alché-Buc, F., Fox, E., Garnett, R. (eds.) Advances in Neural Information Processing Systems, vol. 32, pp. 8024–8035. Curran Associates, Inc. (2019). http://papers.neurips.cc/paper/9015-pytorch-an-imperative-style-high-performance-deep-learning-library.pdf
13. Provost, F., Fawcett, T.: Robust classification for imprecise environments. Mach. Learn. **42**(3), 203–231 (2001)
14. Shinan, K., Alsubhi, K., Alzahrani, A., Ashraf, M.U.: Machine learning-based botnet detection in software-defined network: a systematic review. Symmetry **13**(5) (2021). https://doi.org/10.3390/sym13050866. https://www.mdpi.com/2073-8994/13/5/866
15. Tang, T.A., Mhamdi, L., McLernon, D., Zaidi, S.A.R., Ghogho, M.: Deep recurrent neural network for intrusion detection in SDN-based networks. In: 2018 4th IEEE Conference on Network Softwarization and Workshops (NetSoft), pp. 202–206. IEEE (2018)
16. Tariq, F., Baig, S.: Botnet classification using centralized collection of network flow counters in software defined networks. Int. J. Comput. Sci. Inf. Secur. **14**(8), 1075 (2016)
17. Tariq, F., Baig, S.: Machine learning based botnet detection in software defined networks. Int. J. Secur. Appl **11**(11), 1–12 (2017)
18. Tavallaee, M., Bagheri, E., Lu, W., Ghorbani, A.A.: A detailed analysis of the KDD CUP 99 data set. In: 2009 IEEE Symposium on Computational Intelligence for Security and Defense Applications, pp. 1–6. IEEE (2009)
19. Tayfour, O.E., Marsono, M.N.: Collaborative detection and mitigation of DDoS in software-defined networks. J. Supercomput. **77**(11), 13166–13190 (2021)
20. Wagner, D., et al.: United we stand: collaborative detection and mitigation of amplification DDoS attacks at scale. In: Proceedings of the 2021 ACM SIGSAC Conference on Computer and Communications Security, pp. 970–987 (2021)

21. Yang, L., Zhao, H.: DDoS attack identification and defense using SDN based on machine learning method. In: 2018 15th International Symposium on Pervasive Systems, Algorithms and Networks (I-SPAN), pp. 174–178. IEEE (2018)
22. Yap, K.K., et al.: Taking the edge off with espresso: scale, reliability and programmability for global internet peering. In: Proceedings of the Conference of the ACM Special Interest Group on Data Communication, pp. 432–445 (2017)

Deep Learning Based Network Intrusion Detection System for Resource-Constrained Environments

Syed Rizvi[1], Mark Scanlon[2], Jimmy McGibney[1], and John Sheppard[1]([✉])

[1] South East Technological University, Waterford, Ireland
Syed.Rizvi@postgrad.wit.ie, {Jimmy.McGibney,John.Sheppard}@setu.ie
[2] School of Computer Science, University College Dublin, Dublin D04 V1W8, Ireland
mark.scanlon@ucd.ie

Abstract. Network intrusion detection systems (IDS) examine network packets and alert system administrators and investigators to low-level security violations. In large networks, these reports become unmanageable. To create flexible and effective intrusion detection systems for unpredictable attacks, there are several challenges to overcome. Much work has been done on the use of deep learning techniques in IDS; however, substantial computational resources and processing time are often required. In this paper, a 1D-Dilated Causal Neural Network (1D-DCNN) based IDS for binary classification is employed. The dilated convolution with a dilation rate of 2 is introduced to compensate the max pooling layer, preventing the information loss imposed by pooling and downsampling. The dilated convolution can also expand its receptive field to gather additional contextual data. To assess the efficacy of the suggested solution, experiments were conducted on two popular publicly available datasets, namely CIC-IDS2017 and CSE-CIC-IDS2018. Simulation outcomes show that the 1D-DCNN based method outperforms some existing deep learning approaches in terms of accuracy. The proposed model attained a high precision with malicious attack detection rate accuracy of 99.7% for CIC-IDS2017 and 99.98% for CSE-CIC-IDS2018.

Keywords: Intrusion Detection Systems · Dilated Causal Neural Network · Network Investigation

1 Introduction

Communication and networking systems are vulnerable to numerous intrusion threats due to the number of applications that operate on modern networks and their increasing size, complexity, and vulnerability. The investigation of modern networks results in massive volumes of information to be analyzed and classified by investigators [27], and this volume is set to be further compounded by the growing prevalence of Internet of Things (IoT) devices. To address these growing vulnerabilities, modern network systems must be capable of detecting and investigating network breaches in a more intelligent and effective way [10].

© ICST Institute for Computer Sciences, Social Informatics and Telecommunications Engineering 2023
Published by Springer Nature Switzerland AG 2023. All Rights Reserved
S. Goel et al. (Eds.): ICDF2C 2022, LNICST 508, pp. 355–367, 2023.
https://doi.org/10.1007/978-3-031-36574-4_21

Network-based intrusion detection systems (IDS) are an attack detection method that offers protection by continuously scanning network traffic for illegal and suspicious activity [15]. Network IDSs can be considered in two categories:

1. *Signature-based approach* – identifies attacks based on known signatures.
2. *Anomaly-based approach* – detects anomalous attacks based on artificial intelligence (AI) techniques.

Anomaly detection offers the benefit of detecting unknown attacks rather than relying on the signature profiles of known attacks. For this reason, much effort has been devoted to the development of anomaly detection IDSs based on machine learning and deep learning algorithms [17,28].

Machine learning techniques have relatively straightforward structures, whereas deep learning relies on an artificial neural network (ANN). Deep learning outperforms typical machine learning techniques when engaging with large sets of data [7]. Moreover, machine learning algorithms require human involvement for feature extraction to achieve better results. Manual feature engineering is unrealistic with multidimensional and large-scale data due to the fast growth in transmitted traffic [6]. Deep learning algorithms can acquire feature representations from datasets without human interaction to generate more effective results. Traditional machine learning models are often referred to as shallow models, due to their simple structure. Deep structure, which has numerous hidden layers, is one distinguishing feature of deep learning. However, due to the complex architecture, multi-layer deep learning models require a significant amount of computation and processing time [7].

To overcome this limitation, lightweight algorithms with minimal computational costs that can effectively address complex problems are being developed for resource-constrained environments. Lightweight deep learning techniques, such as 1D-Dilated Causal Neural Network (1D-DCNN), have been demonstrated to be effective for both classification and regression problems [19,22].

1.1 Contribution of This Work

In this paper, a 1D-DCNN based intrusion detection model has been employed to perform binary classification on two popular datasets used in the literature, namely, CIC-IDS2017 [23] and CSE-CIC-IDS2018 [4]. To the best of the authors' knowledge, this work is the first time that a 1D-DCNN model has been applied to network intrusion detection. The suggested approach identifies attacks with high accuracy through less complex architecture. Furthermore, numerous experiments have been performed to evaluate the behavior of our proposed model on recent datasets. The suggested model achieved 99.7% and 99.98% accuracy on the CIC-IDS2017 and CSE-CIC-IDS2018 datasets respectively.

2   Related Work

Deep learning has been used in network intrusion detection due to its scalability and automated feature development [7]. It has the capacity to extract better representations from data and to analyze sophisticated traffic patterns from massive amounts of network traffic data.

Convolutional Neural Network (CNN) and Long Short-Term Memory (LSTM) were employed to extract features and classify network data on CIC-IDS2017 by [24]. LSTM was used to find temporal information, while a CNN was employed to extract spatial characteristics. The authors additionally optimized weights on the training dataset to address the class imbalance problem. Compared to other machine learning methods, 1D-CNN is growing in popularity because of its superior feature extraction skills. The authors of [3] used a 1D-CNN on time-series data with 42 features for supervised learning. To reduce computational complexity, increase feature count, and improve output size, a max pooling layer is combined with the CNN layer. The performance of the proposed 1D-CNN is compared against Support Vector Machine (SVM), Random Forest (RF), and the hybrid architecture of 1D-CNN and LSTM for both balanced and unbalanced training datasets. Random oversampling was employed to solve the problem of imbalanced data after a comprehensive analysis were carried out utilizing the publicly available dataset.

Kim et al. [14], presented a CNN model for the CSE-CIC-IDS2018, by transforming data into images and evaluating its effectiveness with a Recurrent Neural Network (RNN) model. The experimental outcomes illustrate that CNN outperforms the RNN model on CSE-CIC-IDS2018. Lin et al. [16], suggested a method to increase network efficiency for anomaly detection by merging LSTM with Attention Mechanism (AM). The presented model was developed using the CSE-CIC-IDS2018 dataset, and analysis revealed that accuracy was 96.22%, detection rate was 15%, and recall rate was 96%. Kim et al. [14] compared the efficacy of a CNN model to an RNN model on the CSE-CIC-IDS2018 dataset. The experimental results show that CNN outperforms the RNN model.

3 Methodology

3.1 Dilated Causal Neural Network Architecture

Dilated convolutions, also known as atrous convolutions, are convolutions in which the filter is applied across a region that is longer than its length by omitting input values at a specific phase. By diluting the original filter with zeros, it becomes comparable to a convolution with a bigger filter, and in spite of this fact, it is far more effective. The architecture for dilated convolution is shown in Fig. 1. Using x[n] as the input, D as the dilation factor, N as the length, and p_k as the parameters, a dilated causal convolution is performed. y[n] is the resulting receptive field, that is:

$$y[n] = \sum_{k=0}^{N-1} p_k \cdot x[n - D \cdot k] \tag{1}$$

Even though y has only N parameters, it has a size of D (N1) + 1. Higher receptive fields require a minimal number of parameters while retaining causality,

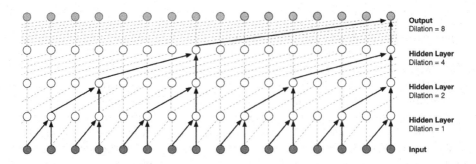

Fig. 1. Visualization of Dilated Causal Neural Network (Figure by [20]).

sampling rate, and using all inputs by stacking dilated causal convolutions with increasing dilation factors [11].

The manner by which causal convolution operates preserves the input's time sequence order, such that the model's projected outcomes are independent of upcoming time steps. Every convolutional layer in the dilated convolution has a set number of steps – where part of input values are skipped. The primary characteristic is that the network's receptive field does not require excessively large filters or convolutional layers, which significantly, or often exponentially, decrease the network's size.

Training such a model has the objective of minimizing the cost function by determining the weights at each layer of the network. Based on the error function, the optimizer progressively changes the weights. The output form of each layer's convolution is created by utilizing an activation function, which enables the model to identify a non-linear representation of the data.

3.2   Dataset Description

CIC-IDS2017. The Canadian Institute for Cybersecurity created the CIC-IDS2017 dataset in 2017 [23]. An experimental setup with malicious activity and victim networks was put up in order to construct the dataset. The dataset was collected over a 5-day period (Monday to Friday) using real-world data and is supplied as packet captures files and CSV files, with each row including generic information paired with characteristics derived by CICFlowMeter. An agent based on the `java-B-profile` system was built, which produced 80.32% benign traffic. Furthermore, several different types of network attacks are contained in the dataset including Heartbleed, botnet, SSH brute-forcing, web login brute-forcing, denial of service (DoS), distributed denial of service (DDoS), SQL injection, infiltration, and cross-site scripting. Through the experiment, more than 80 characteristics and 15 classes were recorded. It distinguishes from other network datasets in that it generates ultra-realistic network data and attack data based on actual users using distinct network profiles. This makes the CIC-IDS2017 a contemporary solution for supplementing intrusion detection systems. However, class imbalance is one of the dataset's major drawbacks.

CSE-CIC-IDS2018. The Canadian Communications Security Establishment (CSE) and CIC collaborated on an IDS dataset in 2018, the CSE-CIC-IDS2018 dataset [4]. The data set includes system logs and network traffic. It comprises 10 days of sub-datasets acquired on different days through executing 16 distinct sorts of attacks. The CICFlowMeter-V3 utility was utilized to build this dataset, which comprises around 80 different types of characteristics. This dataset contains numerous attack profiles that may be applied to network topologies and protocols in a comprehensive way in the field of intelligent security. The attacker's infrastructure consists of 50 computers, as opposed to the victim organization, which has 5 departments, 420 machines, and 30 servers. This dataset contains seven separate attack scenarios, including brute-force, DoS, DDoS, Heartbleed, botnet, web attacks, and penetrating an organization from within.

4   Experiments and Results

4.1   Experiments

Simulation Environment. The simulation environment was based on the Windows operating system. Its components comprised of an Intel Core i7-1165G7 with 8GB RAM. Python 3.9.7 was used for the development of the proposed DC-CNN model together with Keras, Tensorflow, and scikit-learn and data preprocessing was achieved with the `pandas` library.

Exploratory Data Analysis. Firstly, different days from the datasets have been concatenated to perform Exploratory Data Analysis (EDA). EDA is an essential process to achieve the desired output from an AI model. The dataset consists of 80 features, out of which 7 different irrelevant features, i.e., "Dst Port, Timestamp, FwdPSH Flags, Bwd PSH Flags, Fwd URG Flags, Bwd URG Flags, Flow Byts/s, Flow Pkts/s", have been removed to train our proposed model. The dataset required some pre-processing to deal with missing and duplicate values and to convert the labels to binary form (benign as 0 and attacks as 1), which could be utilized to perform binary classification. The outcomes of EDA on the CIC-IDS2017 and CSE-CIC-IDS2018 datasets are shown in Figs. 2a and 2b. After EDA, the datasets were split into the same ratio to train the model and evaluate the results.

Dilated Causal Neural Network. 1D-DCNN is capable of identifying and learning proper characteristics from a dataset. The proposed model is based on an input layer, hidden layers, and an output layer, each with its own set of parameters. Initially, investigation with number of filters: 8, 16, 64, and 128 with filter size: 4 and 8 along with incremental dilation rates with padding causal has been executed, but the results were insignificant. Other hyperparameters, including but not limited to activation functions, optimizer, and loss function, were crucial to achieving significant improvement. Initial experiments show that the number

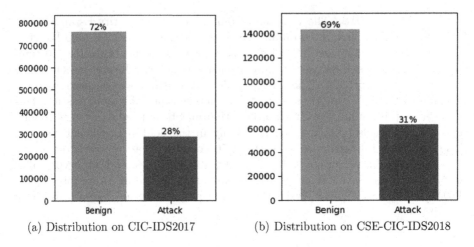

(a) Distribution on CIC-IDS2017   (b) Distribution on CSE-CIC-IDS2018

Fig. 2. Benign and Attacks Distribution for Model Training.

```
Model: "sequential"

_____
 Layer (type)                Output Shape              Param #
=================================================================
 conv1d (Conv1D)             (None, 103294, 64)        19264

 conv1d_1 (Conv1D)           (None, 103294, 64)        16448

 conv1d_2 (Conv1D)           (None, 103294, 64)        16448

 conv1d_3 (Conv1D)           (None, 103294, 64)        16448

 conv1d_4 (Conv1D)           (None, 103294, 64)        16448

 conv1d_5 (Conv1D)           (None, 103294, 64)        16448

 conv1d_6 (Conv1D)           (None, 103294, 64)        16448

 dropout (Dropout)           (None, 103294, 64)        0

 dense (Dense)               (None, 103294, 1)         65

=================================================================
Total params: 118,017
Trainable params: 118,017
Non-trainable params: 0
_____
```

Fig. 3. 1D-dilated casual neural network model summary.

of filters > 64 leads to lower accuracy and longer training time. Our optimum convolution operation parameters are: number of filters = 64, filter size = 4, and batch size = 32 using a blend of two distinct activation functions, namely *tanh* and *selu*. The model summary is shown in Fig. 3. The summary is descriptive and provides details about the model's layers and their arrangement: each layer's output form and number of parameters (weights) and the total number of model parameters (weights). The dense layer with activation functions *sigmoid* has been utilized with a dropout value of 0.1. The performance of the model was also examined with several optimizers such as Adam, Stochastic Gradient Descent (SGD), and RMSProp along with different loss functions at distinct learning rates of 0.01, 0.001, and 0.0001. The learning curve was reviewed intensely during training to determine the hyperparameters of the optimizer. *Binary cross entropy* has been selected as the loss function. Besides, to identify the optimal performance, various momentum values for SGD have been evaluated.

Following experimentation with tuning various hyperparameters, the following parameters have been set to achieve the best performance: number of filters set to 64, filter size set to 4, and SGD as an optimizer with a learning rate of 0.01, momentum = 0.9, loss function = binary cross entropy with epochs set to 1800. The 1D-DCNN IDS model has been evaluated using the two datasets CIC-IDS2017 and CSE-CIC-ISD2018. It has been employed for binary classification to distinguish between attacks and normal traffic. All benign traffic was considered as 0, whereas all types of attacks are counted as 1. In the training phase, an early stopping technique was employed. After specific iterations, if the validation accuracy did not increase, model training was terminated and the hyperparameters were modified. This procedure persisted until the model training hyperparameters were all established.

4.2   Experimental Results

It was noticed that the proposed 1D-DCNN model performed considerably better on both datasets in terms of accuracy and that the model's training time is reasonably low – in the 1,000 to 1,800 epoch range. The outcomes of some extensive experiments using different hyperparameters are represented in Table 1. According to the results, the proposed model performed best with a combination of two different activation functions, namely *selu* and *tanh*, along with a specific number of filters and filter sizes, whereas the dilation rate was incremental in each experiment. The highest accuracy score achieved during the experiment on the CSE-CIC-IDS2018 dataset was 99.98%, as shown in Fig. 4.

Moreover, the performance of our proposed model on another IDS dataset, CIC-IDS2017, is shown in Fig. 5. The model achieved 99.7% accuracy on this dataset. Table 2 shows the comparison between the proposed 1D-DCNN based IDS and other existing work in terms of accuracy.

4.3   Discussion

Deep learning models have been a challenge to use on resource-constrained IoT devices because they require significant computational resources including memory, processor, and storage. As IoT devices are often easier to infiltrate than traditional computing systems, they are increasingly being targeted by malware-based attackers. This is caused by a variety of factors, including but not limited

Table 1. Results of hyperparameters tuning of the proposed model

Exp No	No of filters	Filter size	Activation function	Loss	Accuracy	Wall Time
1	8	4	relu	0.305	66.91	6 min 35 s
2	16	4	relu	0.307	69.27	9 min 9 s
3	32	4	relu	0.307	69.36	15 min 56 s
4	64	4	relu	0.307	69.27	39 min 7 s
5	8	8	relu	0.32	68.90	7 min 55 s
6	16	8	relu	0.307	69.45	6 min 29 s
7	32	8	relu	0.306	69.26	12 min 3 s
8	64	8	relu	0.307	69.27	26 min 37 s
9	16	4	relu/selu	0.307	69.28	5 min 21 s
10	32	4	relu/selu	0.306	69.40	16 min 40 s
11	64	4	relu/selu	0.307	69.28	18 min 32 s
12	16	8	relu/selu	0.307	69.27	7 min 9 s
13	32	8	relu/selu	0.307	69.27	12 min 20 s
14	8	4	tanh/selu	0.305	69.50	4 min 48 s
15	16	4	tanh/selu	0.075	93.76	6 min 54 s
16	32	4	tanh/selu	0.073	94.02	16 min 48 s
17	64	4	tanh/selu	0.067	94.25	29 min 48 s
18	16	8	tanh/selu	0.303	69.72	11 min 48 s
19	32	8	tanh/selu	0.297	70.38	20 min 50 s
20	64	8	tanh/selu	0.109	92.61	39 min 24 s

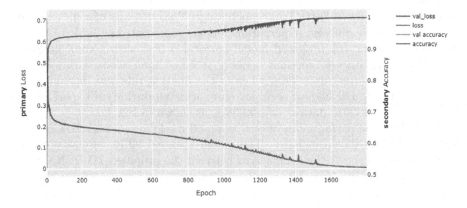

Fig. 4. Accuracy Progression During Learning on CSE-CIC-IDS2018 dataset

to the presence of legacy devices with no security upgrades, a low emphasis assigned to security throughout the development cycle, and insufficient login credentials (Table 3).

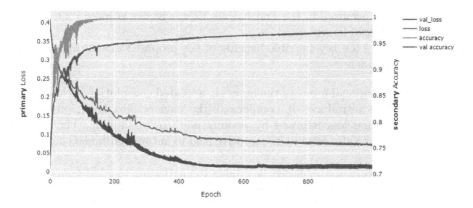

Fig. 5. Accuracy Progression During Learning on CIC-IDS2017 dataset

Table 2. Comparison of our proposed model with existing approaches

Dataset	Reference	Accuracy
CSE-CIC-IDS2018	Farhan et al. [9]	90.25%
	Peng et al. [26]	95%
	Lin et al. [16]	95%
	Kim et al. [14]	96%
	Khan [12]	97.75%
	Emeç and Özcanhan [8]	98.78%
	Our model	99.98%
CIC-IDS2017	Kim et al. [13]	93%
	Varanasi and Razia [25]	99%
	Asad et al. [2]	98%
	Pekta and Acarman [21]	99.09%
	Ma et al. [18]	99.62%
	Alsyaibani et al. [1]	98.34%
	Our model	99.70%

Table 3. Confusion Matrix: 1D-DCNN on CSE-CIC-IDS2018

	Predicted Normal	Predicted Attack
Actual Normal	71,550	0
Actual Attack	16	31,728

IoT devices are interesting to attackers for a myriad of reasons such as creating a botnet for DDoS attacks, mining cryptocurrencies, stealing private information, sabotage, or as a springboard for potential attacks and lateral movement through the network. According to a Kaspersky report [5], over 1.5 billion IoT device breaches occurred in the first half of 2021, which was more than double the equivalent 2020 figure.

The following are key tangible benefits of the proposed model over existing classification models:

- In the convolutional layers of the network, a dilated convolution with dilation rate of 2 was introduced to compensate the max pooling layer, preventing the information loss imposed by pooling and down-sampling. The dilated convolution can also expand its receptive field to gather additional contextual data.
- The architecture of 1D-DCNN facilitates the gathering of additional contextual data, which helps to reduce the false alarm rate.
- The depthwise separable convolution used to decrease computational complexity and increase computational efficiency, allowing the model to successfully learn the representative features of datasets.
- 1D-DCNN are often more efficient and less costly to train compared to RNN and CNN models.

The approach outlined as part of this paper also has some limitations:

- The suggested IDS approach only investigated binary classification, i.e., normal and attack traffic.
- The lower threshold of computational power needed to successfully run the developed models on resource constrained environments has not yet been evaluated.
- The 1D convolutional network, without dilated convolutions, is a natural predictor. The prediction should not be dismissed with a peek into the future that occurs when convolutions are not causal. Measuring the proposed models' applicability and effectiveness versus other novel techniques is outside the scope of this paper.

While considering the above benefits and limitations, the application of the proposed technique still has significant merit due to its lightweight nature for resource constrained environments. As a result of these benefits, the lightweight 1D-DCNN outlined as part of this paper can be deployed on IoT/edge devices for intrusion detection with higher accuracy and precision.

5   Conclusion

This paper introduces an IDS model based on a 1D-dilated convolutional neural network approach for network attack detection and investigation. A dilated convolution, as compared to standard convolution, can enhance the receptive field without changing network parameters or reducing network capacity. 1D-DCNN has already proven its effectiveness in other application areas. The CIC-IDS2017 and CSE-CIC-IDS2018 datasets were used to train and test the suggested approach. The effectiveness of DCNNs to extract discriminative and efficient features from the data has been demonstrated through experimental studies. The method suggested here is more reliable for IDS when compared to other state-of-the-art techniques. The depthwise separable convolution was used to decrease computational complexity and increase computational efficiency, allowing the model to successfully learn the representative features of the datasets.

The increasing prevalence of attackers targeting IoT/edge devices and networks is correlated with the increasing adoption of this new technology. The lightweight nature of 1D-DCNN facilitates its deployment on IoT/edge devices. Enabling the devices themselves to categorize their network traffic locally can contribute to the protection of IoT networks from sophisticated attacks.

5.1 Future Work

Our experiments achieved promising outcomes on both the CIC-IDS2017 and CSE-CIC-IDS2018 datasets in terms of accuracy, i.e., 99.70% and 99.98% respectively, with high precision. However, there is potential for improvement. The effectiveness of the model in terms of computational cost and performance needs to be compared with other state-of-the-art deep learning approaches, such as CNN and RNN, and with traditional machine learning algorithms such as Random Forest (RF) and Support Vector Machine (SVM). Hyperparameter tuning combined with dimensionality reduction and/or attention mechanism techniques may be able to further improve results and is worthy of future exploration. The model also needs to explore multi-classification, to investigate the detection rate of different attacks instead of the detection of anomalies. Moreover, other commonly used datasets in the literature, e.g., NSL-KDD and UNSW-NB15, can also be considered to further assess the performance of the proposed model against the state-of-the-art.

References

1. Alsyaibani, O.M.A., Utami, E., Hartanto, A.D.: An intrusion detection system model based on bidirectional LSTM. In: 2021 3rd International Conference on Cybernetics and Intelligent System (ICORIS), pp. 1–6 (2021). https://doi.org/10.1109/ICORIS52787.2021.9649612
2. Asad, M., Asim, M., Javed, T., Beg, M.O., Mujtaba, H., Abbas, S.: DeepDetect: detection of distributed denial of service attacks using deep learning. Comput. J. **63**(7), 983–994 (2020)
3. Azizjon, M., Jumabek, A., Kim, W.: 1D CNN based network intrusion detection with normalization on imbalanced data. In: 2020 International Conference on Artificial Intelligence in Information and Communication (ICAIIC), pp. 218–224 (2020). https://doi.org/10.1109/ICAIIC48513.2020.9064976
4. Canadian Institute for Cybersecurity: A Realistic Cyber Defense Dataset (CSE-CIC-IDS2018). https://registry.opendata.aws/cse-cic-ids2018/. Accessed 02 June 2022
5. Cyrus, C.: IoT cyberattacks escalate in 2021, according to Kaspersky (2021). https://www.iotworldtoday.com/2021/09/17/iot-cyberattacks-escalate-in-2021-according-to-kaspersky/

6. Dib, M., Torabi, S., Bou-Harb, E., Assi, C.: A multi-dimensional deep learning framework for IoT malware classification and family attribution. IEEE Trans. Netw. Serv. Manage. **18**(2), 1165–1177 (2021)
7. Du, X., et al.: SoK: exploring the state of the art and the future potential of artificial intelligence in digital forensic investigation. In: Proceedings of the 15th International Conference on Availability, Reliability and Security. ARES 2020, Association for Computing Machinery, New York, NY, USA (2020). https://doi.org/10.1145/3407023.3407068
8. Emeç, M., Özcanhan, M.H.: A hybrid deep learning approach for intrusion detection in IoT networks. Adv. Electr. Comput. Eng. **22**(1), 3–12 (2022)
9. Farhan, R.I., Maolood, A.T., Hassan, N.F.: Optimized deep learning with binary PSO for intrusion detection on CSE-CIC-IDS2018 dataset. J. Al-Qadisiyah Comput. Sci. Math. **12**(3), 16 (2020)
10. Friday, K., Bou-Harb, E., Crichigno, J., Scanlon, M., Beebe, N.: On Offloading Network Forensic Analytics to Programmable Data Plane Switches. World Scientific Publishing, Singapore (2021)
11. Harell, A., Makonin, S., Bajić, I.V.: Wavenilm: a causal neural network for power disaggregation from the complex power signal. In: ICASSP 2019–2019 IEEE International Conference on Acoustics, Speech and Signal Processing (ICASSP), pp. 8335–8339 (2019). https://doi.org/10.1109/ICASSP.2019.8682543
12. Khan, M.A.: HCRNNIDS: hybrid convolutional recurrent neural network-based network intrusion detection system. Processes **9**(5), 834 (2021)
13. Kim, A., Park, M., Lee, D.H.: AI-IDS: application of deep learning to real-time web intrusion detection. IEEE Access **8**, 70245–70261 (2020). https://doi.org/10.1109/ACCESS.2020.2986882
14. Kim, J., Shin, Y., Choi, E.: An intrusion detection model based on a convolutional neural network. J. Multimed. Inf. Syst. **6**(4), 165–172 (2019)
15. Li, J., Qu, Y., Chao, F., Shum, H.P., Ho, E.S., Yang, L.: Machine learning algorithms for network intrusion detection. AI in Cybersecur., 151–179 (2019)
16. Lin, P., Ye, K., Xu, C.-Z.: Dynamic network anomaly detection system by using deep learning techniques. In: Da Silva, D., Wang, Q., Zhang, L.-J. (eds.) CLOUD 2019. LNCS, vol. 11513, pp. 161–176. Springer, Cham (2019). https://doi.org/10.1007/978-3-030-23502-4_12
17. Liu, H., Lang, B.: Machine learning and deep learning methods for intrusion detection systems: a survey. Appl. Sci. **9**(20), 4396 (2019). https://doi.org/10.3390/app9204396
18. Ma, C., Du, X., Cao, L.: Analysis of multi-types of flow features based on hybrid neural network for improving network anomaly detection. IEEE Access **7**, 148363–148380 (2019). https://doi.org/10.1109/ACCESS.2019.2946708
19. Ma, H., Chen, C., Zhu, Q., Yuan, H., Chen, L., Shu, M.: An ECG signal classification method based on dilated causal convolution. Comput. Math. Methods Med. (2021)
20. van den Oord, A., et al.: WaveNet: a generative model for raw audio. In: Arxiv (2016). https://arxiv.org/abs/1609.03499
21. Pektaş, A., Acarman, T.: A deep learning method to detect network intrusion through flow-based features. Int. J. Netw. Manage. **29**(3), e2050 (2019) https://doi.org/10.1002/nem.2050. https://onlinelibrary.wiley.com/doi/abs/10.1002/nem.2050
22. Rizvi, S.M., Syed, T., Qureshi, J.: Real-time forecasting of petrol retail using dilated causal CNNs. J. Ambient Intell. Humanized Comput. **13**(2), 989–1000 (2022)

23. Sharafaldin, I., Lashkari, A.H., Ghorbani, A.A.: Toward generating a new intrusion detection dataset and intrusion traffic characterization. In: Proceedings of the 4th International Conference on Information Systems Security and Privacy (ICISSP 2018), vol. 1, pp. 108–116 (2018). https://doi.org/10.5220/0006639801080116

24. Sun, P., et al.: DL-IDS: extracting features using CNN-LSTM hybrid network for intrusion detection system. Secur. Commun. Netw. (2020)

25. Varanasi, V.R., Razia, S.: CNN implementation for IDS. In: 2021 3rd International Conference on Advances in Computing, Communication Control and Networking (ICAC3N), pp. 970–975 (2021). https://doi.org/10.1109/ICAC3N53548.2021.9725426

26. Wei, P., Li, Y., Zhang, Z., Hu, T., Li, Z., Liu, D.: An optimization method for intrusion detection classification model based on deep belief network. IEEE Access 7, 87593–87605 (2019). https://doi.org/10.1109/ACCESS.2019.2925828

27. van de Wiel, E., Scanlon, M., Le-Khac, N.A.: Enabling non-expert analysis of large volumes of intercepted network traffic. In: Peterson, G., Shenoi, S. (eds.) Advances in Digital Forensics XIV, pp. 183–197. Springer International Publishing, Cham (2018). https://doi.org/10.1007/978-3-319-99277-8_11

28. Xin, Y., Kong, L., Liu, Z., Chen, Y., Li, Y., Zhu, H., Gao, M., Hou, H., Wang, C.: Machine learning and deep learning methods for cybersecurity. IEEE Access 6, 35365–35381 (2018)

Poisoning-Attack Detection Using an Auto-encoder for Deep Learning Models

El Moadine Anass[1,2], Coatrieux Gouenou[1,2], and Bellafqira Reda[1,2(✉)]

[1] IMT Atlantique; Technopole Brest-Iroise, CS 83818, 29238, Cedex 3 Brest, France
{anass.el-moadine,gouenou.coatrieux,reda.bellafqira}@imt-atlantique.fr
[2] Unit INSERM 1101 Latim, 29238 Brest Cedex, France

Abstract. Modern Deep Learning *DL* models can be trained in various ways, including incremental learning. The idea is that a user whose model has been trained on his own data will perform better on new data. The model owner can share its model with other users, who can then train it on their data and return it to the model owner. However, these users can perform poisoning attacks *PA* by modifying the model's behavior in the attacker's favor. In the context of incremental learning, we are interested in detecting a *DL* model for image classification that has undergone a poisoning attack. To perform such attacks, an attacker can, for example, modify the labels of some training data, which is then used to fine-tune the model in such a way that the attacked model will incorrectly classify images similar to the attacked images, while maintaining good classification performance on other images. As a countermeasure, we propose a poisoned model detector that is capable of detecting various types of *PA* attacks. This technique exploits the reconstruction error of a machine learning-based auto-encoder *AE* trained to model the distribution of the activation maps from the second-to-last layer of the model to protect. By analyzing *AE* reconstruction errors for some given inputs, we demonstrate that a *PA* can be distinguished from a fine-tuning operation that can be used to improve classification performance. We demonstrate the performance of our method on a variety of architectures and in the context of a *DL* model for mass cancer detection in mammography images.

Keywords: Deep Learning Model · Poisoning Attack · Anomaly Detection · Auto-Encoder · Flipping Attack · Pattern Addition Attack

1 Introduction

Deep learning is an expanding field of study with applications in all activity sectors. This is particularly true in the field of healthcare, where it offers new

This work was partly supported by the Joint Laboratory SePEMeD, ANR-13-LAB2-0006-01, and the French ANR via the European program "Preservation of *R&D* employment in the framework of the French recovery plan" under the reference ANR-21-PRRD-0027-01.

S. Goel et al. (Eds.): ICDF2C 2022, LNICST 508, pp. 368–384, 2023.
https://doi.org/10.1007/978-3-031-36574-4_22

perspectives by providing algorithms for making decisions to improve the quality of care, disease prevention, personalized treatment, and so on.

As the industry rapidly integrates machine learning (*ML*) into products and customers make decisions based on these systems, security experts warn of the security risks associated with these models [1,22], namely the potential of "Poisoning Attacks" (*PA*) [4]. *PA* was designed to maliciously degrade the performance of this technology. For instance, in crowd-sourced platforms, an attacker can cause massive damages without direct access to the system, but rather by poisoning the collected data from it [14]. Some other examples are autonomous driving cars [7], health systems [15], online review systems [18] and malware/spam detection systems [16]. *PA* attacks are usually executed during the re-training of the model based on newly collected data. The objective is to contaminate the model by gradually injecting bad examples into the training data that compromise its output to the benefit of the attacker.

Modern poisoning attack detection solutions rely on auto-encoder *AE* based anomaly detection [3,5,11,12,17]. Its basic idea is to train an *AE* model to reconstruct normal data (data without anomalies) or, equivalently, to learn their representations, and then use the *AE* reconstruction error to detect anomalies by assuming that normal samples have a small reconstruction error. In contrast, a large reconstruction error will identify anomalous samples. Those solutions can be divided into two categories: Methods from the first class [3,12,17] use *AE*s directly on suspicious data with as purpose to find poisoned data in the training set. The second kind of solution operates in the context of federated learning (*FL*). *FL* allows several participants to train a model without sharing their training data. The basic idea of *FL* is that each owner trains locally on its own model on its data and then communicates its parameters to a central server, a trusted entity also called an aggregator, to build the shared model. To detect if a participant is training its model on poisoned, the detection algorithms proposed in [5,11], are based on training a Variational *AE* (VAE) or a conditional VAE (CVAE), respectively, on a subset of the shared models' parameters trained on normal data. In each *FL* round, the server calculates the reconstruction error of the parameters of the models received from the participants and discards from the aggregation step models with too large an error.

In this work, we are more interested in the context of what is called "online or incremental learning" [2]. The owner of a trained model, Alice, shares it with another user, Bob, in order to improve the model's performance. Alice's model is fine-tuned by Bob, who adds his own data and sends it back to Alice. We've come up with a way to figure out if the model Bob fine-tuned is poisoned or not without being able to look at the training data set he used. Notice that the approach from [3,12,17] is not suitable for our framework since it requires access to the fine-tuning data set. The solutions of [5,11] are not suitable either because their detectors are based on the knowledge of several fine-tuned models, at least two or more. A second main originality of our proposal is that it applies *AE* based anomaly detection on the *ML* model activation maps (*AM*) for some given inputs, unlike [5,11] which use a subset of the fine-tuned model parameters. Our main idea is that for *ML* model devoted to classification purposes, a *PA* attack will merely impact the AM distribution to make possible the miss-classification of data. So, the system we propose simply consists of training an AE on model activation maps and conducting an anomaly detection analysis.

The rest of the paper is organized as follows. In Section 2, we first introduce the threat model we considered before describing the attacks we focus on: the flipping attack (FA) and the pattern addition attack (PAA). Section 3 details the detection system we propose. In Sect. 4 we evaluate its performance through various experiments over different databases, model architectures (CNN, ResNet18, ResNet152, VGG19, WideResnet), as well as in the context of a real medical application for mass cancer detection in mammography images.

2   Threat Model and Attacks

Herein, we introduce the threat model and the vulnerabilities that a deep learning model can deal with and the attacks that we are particularly interested in.

2.1   Threat Model

Threat modeling allows for identifying and quantifying a given system's security requirements and potential vulnerabilities. As summarized in (see Fig. 1), the threat model of a poisoning attack on a ML model depends on the attacker's knowledge, goal, strategy, and ability to influence training data.

Attacker's Knowledge. One can distinguish different contexts of attack depending on the knowledge the attacker has about the target ML model classifier:

– *White-box context*: it is equivalent to the perfect-knowledge framework, where the adversary has complete knowledge of the target system, including training data, feature representation set, learning method, training parameters, and so on. It is the worst-case scenario for the target system.
– *Gray-box context*: where the attacker has limited information about the target system, including the surrogate training data sampled from a similar distribution, the feature representation set, the learning algorithm, and the parameters trained by the surrogate classifier. This setting allows attackers to replicate a more realistic scenario involving the target system.
– *Black-box context*: this is the equivalent to the zero-knowledge scenario in which the attacker can only query the target system to discover its backsides. In comparison to the white-box and gray-box options, the black-box configuration presents an extreme difficulty for the attacker.

Attacker's Goal. The objective of the attacker is to get the DL model outputs he wants by training it with poisoned data. According to [23], the attacker's goal can be characterized as follows:

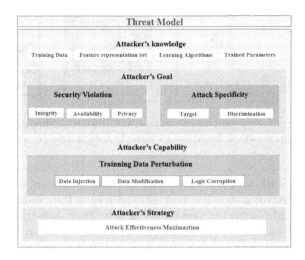

Fig. 1. Threat modeling of poisoning attacks

- Security violations can be classified as: *i)- integrity violations*, when poisoning attacks are successfully implemented without affecting other normal system operations, *ii)- availability violations*, when normal system performance are impacted, or *iii)- privacy violations*, when confidential training data or private user information is obtained.
- Specificity can be divided into two parts: a targeted attack, which tries to make the *DL* model output falls into a specific target category for a given input; and an indiscriminate attack, which uses any feature samples to maximize the model's prediction error or make the *DM*'s functionality unavailable.

The Attacker's Capability and Strategy. The attacker's capability corresponds to his or her ability and strategy to manipulate the training data obtained from devices in various intelligent networks; the amount of malicious data added or updated; and the portion of training data influenced by these later. A "strong attacker" usually has a lot more information about the training data than a "weak attacker," who usually only gets a small amount of the information fed to the model during training. Since ill-posed work is more likely to happen when the poisoning rate is high, existing attacks usually only control a small subset of the training data. They do this by data injection, data modification, or logic corruption. Regarding the former manipulation, the attacker can: corrupt the target model by injecting poisoned data into the training set; alter training data or the *DL* model. We will talk about data modification when the attacker adjusts training data attribute values or labels. Finally, logic corruption refers to an attacker's ability to change the *DL* model (e.g., its parameters or its architecture). Therefore, designing countermeasures against such attacks is not a simple task.

Fig. 2. Poisoning attack examples in the case of CIFAR10 - Flipping attack: (a) and (b) - Pattern addition attack based on a white square pattern: (c) and (d).

The attacker's strategy is to change the training samples in a way that makes the attack as effective as possible and gets the results they want. Specifically, it specifies how to adjust the training data characteristics, how to change the class label, and which portion of the training data has the greatest influence on the *ML* model.

2.2   Considered *PA* attacks

In general, a data poisoning attack is an adversarial *ML* attack that occurs when an attacker carefully creates input feature samples and injects them into the training dataset to cause the target to deviate during the training phase. In this work, we consider the white-box mode where the attacker accesses the model parameters and investigate *PA* against supervised classifier methods with the strategy of not degrading the model's performance. We study two types of poisoning attacks:

- *Flipping Attack(FA)* - A flipping attack, also known as a label-flipping attack, is a specific type of data poisoning attack where the adversary can only change the training labels (see Fig. 2 (a) and (b)). The classifier is then trained on the corrupted training set with no knowledge of which samples have been changed. For example, an adversary could mislabel images presenting a cancer cell (mass) as benign cells or images presenting horses as frogs.
- *Pattern Addition Attack (PAA)* - In this attack, the attacker generates a fixed pattern, like a white square, as shown in Fig. 2 (c) and (d), that is next added to some training samples so that the target model classifies images with such a pattern into a specific class.

2.3   Fine-Tuning

In general, a *DL* model is fine-tuned for different reasons and in different ways [26]. Fine-tuning is by far the dominant strategy for transfer learning [24] and for making a model more performant. In our context, we will consider the second reason. In practice, fine-tuning can be done as follows:

1. Remove the final layer from the target network and replace it with a new *SoftMax* layer that is relevant to a particular issue. For example, a target model trained on ImageNet to classify 1000-classes can be turned into 10-classes by replacing the 100 class *SoftMax* layer with a new 10 *SoftMax* layer.
2. Retrain the network at a lower learning rate. Since it is expected the target model weights are already quite good, the idea here is to refine the minimum local of the model. Making the initial learning rate 10 times smaller than the one used for training is a common approach.
3. Freeze the weights of the first few layers of the target model. Because these ones usually capture universal features; like curves and edges in images, that are relevant to the classification problem, freezing is thus a way to keep those weights intact while making the network focus on learning data-set-specific features in the subsequent layers.

Fine-tuning a model also depends on the data used. Two situations may occur:

- The operation is conducted on the same training dataset as the target model with the objective of better adjusting the performance of the model while staying around the target model's minimum local.
- The fine-tuning process is applied to another but similar dataset. Since there is more data, the risk of the model overfitting is reduced.

In our experiments, we consider that a target model can be fine-tuned with the purpose of increasing its accuracy, i.e., with the objective of finding a new local minimum that preserves or increases the model's accuracy. This operation will be done with a small variation of the learning rate value to stay close to the original model's local minimal. Reducing the learning rate allows the model to continue to converge towards a local minimum when the model stagnates at the previous learning rate. In doing so, we consider that a huge change in this minimum corresponds to a non-authorized modification of the target model, or equivalently, that the integrity of its work is endangered.

3 Auto-encoder Solution for Detecting Model Poisoning Attack

As stated previously, in the context of image classification, the basic idea of our proposal detects that a *DL* model has been poisoned by analyzing the activation maps of some of its layers, the second to last layer in particular, depending on some given input data. Since the goal of the flipping and pattern addition attacks is to make the target model misclassify data, they should have an effect on how the activation maps are distributed statistically. Detecting such a change can be formulated as an anomaly detection problem. Here, we propose to treat it with an auto-encoder neural network that we trained to reconstruct the activation maps and use the reconstruction error in a hypothesis test to decide if the target model has been poisoned or not.

3.1   Auto-encoder Based Anomaly Detection

A dimension reduction-based method for finding anomalies looks for an optimized subspace in which normal and unusual data look very different from each other. Let us assume that the normal training set made up of $\{x_1, x_2, ..., x_n\}$, where each of which is a d-dimensional vector $(x_i \in \mathbb{R}^d)$. In its training phase, that is unsupervised, the auto-encoder *(AE)* model learns to project training data into a lower dimensional subspace (a latent space) and, from this subspace, to output the data $\{x'_1, x'_2, ..., x'_n\}$ with $x'_i \in \mathbb{R}^d$ such that x'_i is as close as possible to x_i (i.e. $x'_i \sim x_i$). Therefore, an *AE* aims to get the optimal subspace that minimizes the reconstruction error (e.g., mean square error (MSE) as loss function):

$$E(x_i, x'_i) = \sum_{j=1}^{d} \frac{1}{n}(x_i - x'_i)^2 \tag{1}$$

Notice that by doing so, with *AE*, one can delete redundancies and noise from input data. Briefly, the architecture of a very basic *AE* model consists of two neural networks: an encoder and a decoder. The encoder compresses input data onto m neurons, the latent space, such as $m < d$ for dimension reduction. The decoder allows the reconstruction of data from the latent space. The activation of the neuron i in the $l + 1^{th}$ hidden layer is given by:

$$h_i^{l+1} = f(\sum_{j=1}^{d} W_{ij}^l h_j^l + b_i^l) \tag{2}$$

where: h_j^l is the output of the jth neuron from the layer l; W_i^l and b_i^l are the vector weights and the bias of the ith neuron of layer l, respectively; and, f is the activation function (e.g. Relu, Sigmoid).

As an *AE* model aims at reconstructing its input with the best fidelity possible, it usually well captures the main characteristics of the distribution of the input data. This is the reason why *AE* is widely used for anomaly detection. The subjacent idea is that since the normal input meets the normal data profile learned in the training phase, the corresponding reconstruction error should be rather small, whereas an anomalous input will have a relatively high reconstruction error [13]. As a result, by thresholding such error, one can differentiate anomalous from normal data, that is to say:

$$c(x_i) = \begin{cases} normal & \epsilon_i = E(x_i, x'_i) \leq Tr \\ anomalous & \epsilon_i = E(x_i, x'_i) > Tr \end{cases} \tag{3}$$

where Tr is the decision threshold. Our proposal follows the same strategy.

3.2   Proposed Method

The main difference between our proposal and existing approaches [5,11] is that it works with the model activation maps rather than with the model parameters.

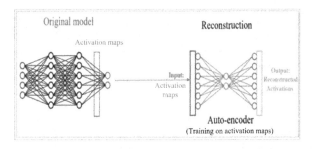

Fig. 3. Protection process of a target model

Consider a target model M dedicated to a classification application, as well as a subset of the training set called the trigger set T_s. Let us also define M_a a suspicious version of M derived from a fine-tuned process over poisoned data or not. To protect M we train an auto-encoder AE_M as follows:

1. Select a trigger set T_s of N samples. T_s could be a subset of the training or testing data set but should be built to be representative of the input data distribution.
2. For each sample t_i of T_s compute the activation map of the second to last layer of the target model M, or more clearly the output $g_M(t_i)$ of this layer. The set $T_{ae} = g_M(t_i)_{i=1..N}$ will constitute the training set of our AE model.
3. Train AE_M using T_{ae} so as to minimize the mean square error *(MSE)*.

This procedure is summarized in Fig. 3. The key idea behind this process is to capture the distribution of the second to last activation maps, which carry the most important pieces of information about the inputs, their class labels, and the parameters of the model. An attempt to make the model miss-classifying some inputs may deeply change the activation maps distribution, assigning the characteristics of these inputs to different classes (e.g. flipping attack) or change the contribution of some characteristics in the classification decision (e.g., pattern addition attack). The detection stage of our proposal works as follows(see Fig. 3):

1. Select a T_s^d trigger set with N^d samples. T_s^d and T_s can be the same. The most important point is that T_s^d, like T_s, represents the input data distribution.
2. For each sample t_i of T_s^d calculate the activation map of the second to last layer of the suspicious model $M_a : g_{M_a}(t_i)$.
3. With the auto-encoder AE_M compute the reconstruction errors e_{M_a} $(g_{M_a}(t_i))_{i=1..N}$ for all activation maps.
4. Compute the mean of all reconstruction errors, that is to say, the mean square error E_{MSE} of AE_M over the trigger set.
5. Compare E_{MSE} to the threshold T_r to decide whether the suspicious model has been poisoned or not.

There are many ways to compute T_r. As we will see in Sect. 3, since the distribution of the reconstruction error is Gaussian, we decided to follow a common strategy [13] defining the anomaly threshold T_r such as:

$$T_r = \overline{(e(g_{M_f}(t_i)))} + \sigma_{e(g_{M_f}(t_i))} \qquad (4)$$

where: "$\overline{(.)}$" is the mean operator; σ the standard deviation; and, M_f a fine-tuned version of M with normal data. Such a threshold gives the possibility for one user to make some updates on the target model in each margin.

4   Experimental Results

In this section, we evaluate the performance of our system against the flipping and pattern addition attacks while considering several classical DL model architectures, as well as a model dedicated to mass cancer detection from mammography images, [25].

4.1   Datasets and Target Models

Our proposal has been tested on well-known public image data sets: *CIFAR10* [9] and *DDSM- CBIS* (Digital Database for Screening Mammography) [10]: (i) **CIFAR10** - This dataset consists of 32×32 color images organized into 10 classes. It has $50,000$ training samples and $10,000$ testing samples. For training, the pixel values of images were re-scaled to the range $[0, 1]$. (ii) **DDSM-CBIS** - It contains approximately 2500 mammograms, including normal, benign, and malignant cases with verified pathology information and coarse ground truth manual delineations. In this work, we selected 586 pairs of CC/MLO mammograms, that is to say, 1172 images. This dataset has 2 classes: the presence or absence of a mass cancer in the image.

We trained different well-known DL models of different complexity to classify CIFAR10 images : convolutional neural network (CNN), ResNet18, ResNet152 [6], Wide-ResNet (WRN) [27] and VGG19 [20]. The architecture of CNN that we used is very simple. It consists of $32C(3) - 32C(3) - MP2(2) - 64C(3) - 64C(3) - MP2(2) - 512FC - 10FC$ where : $32C(3)$ indicates a convolutional layer with 32 output channels and 3×3 filters applied with a stride of 1; $MP2(1)$ denotes a max-pooling layer over regions of size 2×2 and stride of 1; and, $10FC$ is a fully-connected layer with 10 output neurons. Regarding the medical image dataset, we use the model $VGG - 16 - YY$ proposed in [25]. This system is a multi-view mass detection system in mammography, the architecture of which is given in Fig. 4 and which is in part based on the VGG16. This system is based on two steps. The first step is to provide patches of the two views of the same breast with a positive or negative score for the presence or absence of a mass, while the second decides if the two patches presented as input to it match or not, and if they contain a mass in order to reduce the false positive rate. As we will see later, it is VGG16 that will be poisoned.

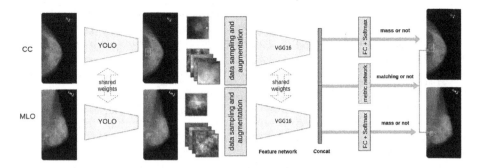

Fig. 4. Architecture of the multi-view mass detection system proposed in [25].

In the following experiments, we use the same optimizer settings for training these neural networks except that the learning rate is reduced by a factor of 10 to prevent an accuracy drop in the prediction of legitimate input data. Note another exception for Wide-ResNet for which we used 50 and 100 epochs to reach good accuracy, mainly because of its huge number of parameters.

4.2   Experimentations

For each of the models CNN, ResNet18, ResNet152, Wide-ResNet, and VGG19, we trained an auto-encoder on the activation maps of their second to last layer using the complete testing data set as a trigger set T_s (see Sect. 3). For each model, the detection threshold T_r was computed as given in Eq. 4 by fine-tuning the model on the whole training data set with 25 or 50 epochs and, we used the same learning rate as in the final phase of DL model training, considering the fact that if another user attempts to fine-tune the underlying DL model with a high learning rate, the DL model accuracy will suffer significantly. We give in Table 1 the accuracies of the models CNN, ResNet18, ResNet152, VGG19 and Wide-ResNet trained on CIFAR10 and of Vgg-16-YY trained on DDSM CBIS as well as of their fined-tuned versions.

These models were then attacked by applying FA or PAA. To conduct these attacks, we use an image attack set extracted from a target class to attack (i.e. images the label of which was flipped to another class - FA, or to which a pattern was added - PAA). This attack set corresponds to a percentage of images equal to 50% of the target class. Regarding the PAA, this one corresponds to a white square of 5×5 pixels positioned randomly in the target image (see Fig. 2). Attacked models result from the fine-tuning of these attack sets of the genuine or target model after 25 epochs or 50 epochs. We give in Tab 1, the accuracies of the resulting attacked models in the case the attack set corresponds to 50% of the target class, and we also provide in Table 2 the miss-classification rates of the FA and PAA attacks for the same conditions. Indeed, an attacker may not fully achieve his objective even though he increases his number of epochs as he has to preserve the accuracy reached by the genuine model. In the case of FA,

Table 1. Accuracy of the different genuine models, models after honest fine-tuning, and models after a flipping attack (*FA*) and pattern addition attack (*PAA*) applied with different epochs. "-" indicates that the attack degrades drastically the accuracy of the model.

Dataset	Architecture	Accuracy					
		Normal	Fine-tuned	*FA*		*PAA*	
				Number of epoch		Number of epoch	
				25	50	50	50
Cifar10	ResNet18	90.85 %	84.6%	86.4%	85.9%	90.2%	89.0 %
	ResNet152	93.49 %	93.3%	91.3%	91.5%	93.3 %	93.2 %
	CNN	87.15 %	87.1%	82.6%	83.9%	86.6 %	86.7 %
	Wide-ResNet	95.45 %	95.9 %	92.8	92.3%	93.4 %	93.6 %
	VGG19	93.90 %	93.8 %	93.4%	92.8%	93.4%	93.6%
DDSM-CBIS	Vgg-16-YY	88.70 %	88.8%	82.03 %	81.68 %	-	-

where attacked images correspond to images whose labels have been changed, the miss-classification rate corresponds to the number of attacked images well miss-classified over the total number of attacked images for a given number of epochs. Similarly, for *PAA*, where the attacked model should classify images with a given pattern in a specific class, the miss-classification rate corresponds to the number of images with a pattern correctly miss-classified over the total number of patterned images used to train the attacked model. One can see that *PAA* preserves well the accuracy of the target model while *FA* somewhat reduces or at least achieves the same performance. Beyond, both attacks are efficient in terms of miss-classification.

To demonstrate the discrimination power of an auto-encoder working with the second to last layer activation maps, we computed the histograms of the auto-encoder reconstruction error (i.e. MSE see Eq. 4) for the genuine, fined tuned, and attacked ResNet18, ResNet152, WRN, VGG19 and CNN models on the detection trigger set T_s^d which, in the following experiments, corresponds to the testing set. Let us recall that, as given in Table 1, both original and honestly fine-tuned models get an accuracy greater than 90% for the models ResNet18, ResNet152, WRN, VGG19 and that *PAA* preserves such accuracies, while *FA* somewhat impact them, especially after 50 epochs. As it can be seen from Fig. 5, AE MSE histograms of attacked models can be clearly discriminated against the genuine and fine-tuned models. In general, the average MSE for attacked models is much higher than for fine-tuned and genuine ones. Also note that the more epochs the attack is conducted with, the more *AE* will detect the attack. Regarding CNN, as shown in Fig. 5, we cannot detect the *PAA* with our threshold given by the *AE*. One explanation of this detection failure stands on the CNN architecture we designed which is quite simple with poor accuracy (80% see Table 1).

In our last experimentation with ResNet18, to examine how our proposal responds when fine-tuning a protected model on new data, we trained a ResNet18 on 80% of the CIFAR10 training set. We next fine-tuned with 100% of the

Table 2. Efficiency of flipping attack (*FA*) and pattern addition attack (*PAA*) expressed in terms of successful miss-classification rate for different deep learning model architectures. "-" indicates results not yet obtained.

Architecture	FA		PAA	
	Percentage of the attack		Percentage of the attack	
	50%		50%	
	25 epoch	50 epoch	25 epoch	50 epoch
ResNet18	48.20%	74.36%	89.00 %	90.20 %
ResNet152	27.28%	33.0%	99.44 %	98.92 %
CNN	36.08%	48.60%	96.44%	97.56 %
Wide-ResNet	23.08 %	41.56 %	99.20 %	99.52 %
VGG19	1.68 %	4.64 %	97.60 %	99.04 %

training data set in order to increase its accuracy from 84.60% to 87.93% with 50 epochs. Figure 6 provides the corresponding histograms of *AE* MSE of the genuine, fine-tuned and *FA*, *PAA* attacks. One can observe that when fine-tuning increases the performance of the ResNet18 model, the *AE* reconstruction error decreases for the fine-tuned model while the same error increases with the attacked models. We can expect that fine-tuning a model on new data to improve it will make our detector more performant. The proposed solution was also tested on the multi-view mass detection system in mammography depicted in Sect. 4. The attack we conducted consists of disrupting the operation of its second, which relies on a VGG16, by applying a flipping attack to it. This one consists of changing 50% of the label of the class *mass present* to the class *mass absent* and fine-tuning the VGG16 with these data. As shown in Fig. 7, one can well differentiate the genuine, fine-tuned and *FA* attacked models from the mean of their respective *AE* MSE histogram. Noting that the precision of *PAA* in VGG16 was so poor and the attacked model lost its accuracy, we chose not to present it in this paper.

To complete these experiments, we give in Table 3 the detection results of the system we proposed when applying our complete detection procedure along with the detection trigger set T_s^d equals to the testing set and the decision threshold T_r computed as given in Eq. 4. As it can be seen, all the above *FA* and *PAA* attacks with an attack set corresponding to 50% of a target class for a different number of epochs (25 and 50 epochs), applied to more or less complex and performant architectures, are detected.

4.3   Evaluation

In this section, we present a comparison with existing papers on the detection of poisoning attacks. Unlike the solutions in the literature, we use activation maps, and we show that it is possible to detect the change in behavior of the model using a simple auto-encoder. We present in Table 4 that:

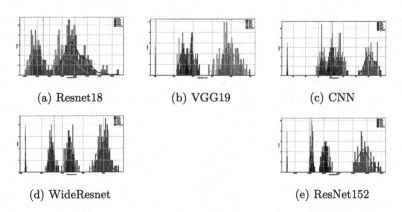

(a) Resnet18	(b) VGG19	(c) CNN

(d) WideResnet	(e) ResNet152

Fig. 5. Distribution of AE reconstruction error (i.e. MSE) for the genuine (green), honestly fine-tuned after 50 epochs (blue), FA with 25 epochs (red) and 50 epochs (black) ; PAA with 25 epochs (yellow) and 50 epochs (mauve), considering the testing set as detection trigger set T_s^d. The red dash-line presents the detection threshold.

Table 3. Detection of FA and PAA poisoning attacks with our proposal, means that the attacked model was detected while "-" indicates that the attack degrades the accuracy of the model.

Dataset	Architecture	\multicolumn{4}{c} Attack
		\multicolumn{2}{c} FA	\multicolumn{2}{c} PAA
		25	50	25	50
Cifar10	Resnet18	✓	✓	✓	✓
	ResNet152	✓	✓	✓	✓
	CNN	✓	✓	✗	✓
	Wide-ResNet28	✓	✓	✓	✓
	VGG19	✓	✓	✓	✓
DDSM-CBIS	VGG16-YY	✓	✓	-	-

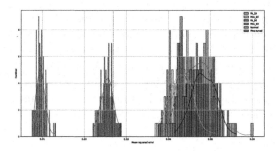

Fig. 6. Result of experimentation with FA and PAA attacks in comparison with a fine-tuning operation with 20% of new data.

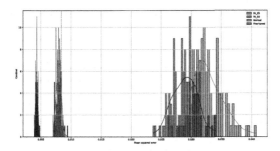

Fig. 7. Experimentation results applying flipping and pattern addition attacks on VGG16-YY from the multi-view mass detection system proposed in [25].

- The application context of the state of the art is not the same as for our method (Federated $\neq$ centralized/incremental).
- In the case of federated learning, poisoning attacks are detected during training, which is not the case for us.
- Concerning attacks, those whose objective is to degrade performance or prevent learning (Byzantine Attacks/Optimal Attacks) of the global model are not applicable in our context. As explained in our paper, we can easily detect this type of attack thanks to the "testing set".
- Another difference is that for us, we already have a trained model, so we can use it for detection, unlike in the Federated case.
- The most suitable attack for our scenario is the PAA, because it does not degrade the performance of the model by adding a pattern into some samples of the training set. Unlike other existing papers, which do not consider this attack.

On the basis of the points that were mentioned earlier, we have come to the conclusion that the federated methods cannot be projected in the case of incremental learning because that requires: i) Multiple models to detect the poisoned ones. ii) The notion of "round" which is used in the training of Conditional Variational AE (CVAE) in [5]. To the best of our knowledge, we are the first that detect the poisoning model attacks in the context of incremental learning. Our solution allows an auto-encoder to learn the activation distribution representation of a model trained on unpoisoned data. If this model is shared with other users in order to improve its performance, our auto-encoder is able to detect whether it is fine-tuned on poisoned data or not. As shown in Fig 5, fine-tuning a model on poisoned data changes significantly the distribution of activation maps. In Table 3, we present the performance of our proposed method on different architectures and against several attacks.

Table 4. Comparison of our proposed method with the state of the art

Learning		Centralized		Federated	
Methods		Razmi [17]	Ours	Li [11]	Gu [5]
Architectures		SVM	CNN, ResNet18/152 VGG16/19, Wide-ResNet	CNN, RNN, Logistic Regression	SVM, MLP
Datasets	Cifar10	✓	✓	-	-
	MNIST	✓	-	✓	✓
	Fashion-MNIST	✓	-	✓	-
	FMNIST	-	-	-	✓
	Others	-	DDSM	Sentiment 140	Vehicle [21] Synthetic [19]
Attacks	FA	✓	✓	✓	✓
	PAA	-	✓	-	-
	Optimal	✓	-	-	-
	Semi-Optimal	✓	-	-	-
	Sign-flipping	-	-	✓	✓
	Add-noise	-	-	✓	✓
	Same value	-	-	-	✓
	Model replacement	-	-	✓	✓
Evaluation of Detection		F1-Score	See Table 3, Backdooring, Testing accuracy	F1-Score, Testing accuracy	Backdooring, Testing accuracy
AE metric		L_p	MSE	Divergence K-L [8]	Divergence K-L
AE Architecture		CAE	AE	VAE	CVAE
Attacks	AE-inputs	Images	Activation maps	Weight update	Weight update
	Threshold	Gaussian Mixture Model	Threshold T_r	reconstruction error mean value /round	reconstruction error mean value/round

5   Conclusion and Perspectives

In this work, we proposed a new system for detecting whether a *DL* model dedicated to a classification task has been poisoned or not by a flipping attack or a pattern addition attack. Its main originality stands on using the reconstruction error of an auto-encoder trained to model the distribution of the activation maps of the second to last layer of the target model. In doing so, our system is not only able to detect a poisoned model but also to differentiate it from a fine-tuned one. Unlike the state of the art, it is not necessary to access the poisoned data for detection. Our scheme has been successfully tested on *FA* and *PAA* attacks of different strengths, on architectures of various complexity and performance (ResNet18, ResNet152, VGG19, Wide-ResNet28) as well as on a mammography mass cancer detection system. Being based on very classical auto-encoders, one can expect to improve the performance of our system with *AE* of architecture more complex, such as variational auto-encoders (VAEs), and generalize it to other poisoning attacks, in addition, we will test our work in a federated environment. This is part of our future work.

References

1. Bellafqira, R., Coatrieux, G., Genin, E., Cozic, M.: Secure multilayer perceptron based on homomorphic encryption. In: Yoo, C.D., Shi, Y.-Q., Kim, H.J., Piva, A., Kim, G. (eds.) IWDW 2018. LNCS, vol. 11378, pp. 322–336. Springer, Cham (2019). https://doi.org/10.1007/978-3-030-11389-6_24
2. Castro, F.M., Marín-Jiménez, M.J., Guil, N., Schmid, C., Alahari, K.: End-to-end incremental learning. In: Proceedings of the European Conference on Computer Vision (ECCV), pp. 233–248 (2018)
3. Chen, J., Zhang, X., Zhang, R., Wang, C., Liu, L.: De-pois: an attack-agnostic defense against data poisoning attacks. IEEE Trans. Inf. Forensics Secur. **16**, 3412–3425 (2021)
4. Cinà, A.E., Grosse, K., Demontis, A., Biggio, B., Roli, F., Pelillo, M.: Machine learning security against data poisoning: are we there yet? arXiv preprint arXiv:2204.05986 (2022)
5. Gu, Z., Yang, Y.: Detecting malicious model updates from federated learning on conditional variational autoencoder. In: 2021 IEEE International Parallel and Distributed Processing Symposium (IPDPS), pp. 671–680. IEEE (2021)
6. He, K., Zhang, X., Ren, S., Sun, J.: Deep residual learning for image recognition. In: Proceedings of the IEEE Conference on Computer Vision and Pattern Recognition, pp. 770–778 (2016)
7. Jiang, W., Li, H., Liu, S., Luo, X., Lu, R.: Poisoning and evasion attacks against deep learning algorithms in autonomous vehicles. IEEE Trans. Veh. Technol. **69**(4), 4439–4449 (2020)
8. Joyce, J.M.: Kullback-leibler divergence. In: Lovric, M. (ed.) International Encyclopedia of Statistical Science, pp. 720–722. Springer, Heidelberg (2011). https://doi.org/10.1007/978-3-642-04898-2_327
9. Krizhevsky, A., Hinton, G., et al.: Learning multiple layers of features from tiny images. Technical report (2009)
10. Lee, R.S., Gimenez, F., Hoogi, A., Miyake, K.K., Gorovoy, M., Rubin, D.L.: A curated mammography data set for use in computer-aided detection and diagnosis research. Scientific data **4**(1), 1–9 (2017)
11. Li, S., Cheng, Y., Wang, W., Liu, Y., Chen, T.: Learning to detect malicious clients for robust federated learning. arXiv preprint arXiv:2002.00211 (2020)
12. Madani, P., Vlajic, N.: Robustness of deep autoencoder in intrusion detection under adversarial contamination. In: Proceedings of the 5th Annual Symposium and Bootcamp on Hot Topics in the Science of Security, pp. 1–8 (2018)
13. Meidan, Y., et al.: N-baiot-network-based detection of IoT botnet attacks using deep autoencoders. IEEE Pervasive Comput. **17**(3), 12–22 (2018)
14. Miller, D.J., Xiang, Z., Kesidis, G.: Adversarial learning targeting deep neural network classification: a comprehensive review of defenses against attacks. Proc. IEEE **108**(3), 402–433 (2020)

15. Mozaffari-Kermani, M., Sur-Kolay, S., Raghunathan, A., Jha, N.K.: Systematic poisoning attacks on and defenses for machine learning in healthcare. IEEE J. Biomed. Health Inform. **19**(6), 1893–1905 (2014)
16. Muñoz-González, L., et al.: Towards poisoning of deep learning algorithms with back-gradient optimization. In: Proceedings of the 10th ACM Workshop on Artificial Intelligence and Security, pp. 27–38 (2017)
17. Razmi, F., Xiong, L.: Classification auto-encoder based detector against diverse data poisoning attacks. arXiv preprint arXiv:2108.04206 (2021)
18. Shafahi, A., et al.: Poison frogs! targeted clean-label poisoning attacks on neural networks. In: Advances in Neural Information Processing Systems, vol. 31 (2018)
19. Shamir, O., Srebro, N., Zhang, T.: Communication-efficient distributed optimization using an approximate newton-type method. In: International Conference on Machine Learning, pp. 1000–1008. PMLR (2014)
20. Simonyan, K., Zisserman, A.: Very deep convolutional networks for large-scale image recognition. arXiv preprint arXiv:1409.1556 (2014)
21. Smith, V., Chiang, C.K., Sanjabi, M., Talwalkar, A.S.: Federated multi-task learning. In: Advances in Neural Information Processing Systems, vol. 30 (2017)
22. Soni, R., Paliya, S., Gupta, L.: Security threats to machine learning systems. In: 2022 IEEE International Students' Conference on Electrical, Electronics and Computer Science (SCEECS), pp. 1–3. IEEE (2022)
23. Wang, C., Chen, J., Yang, Y., Ma, X., Liu, J.: Poisoning attacks and countermeasures in intelligent networks: Status quo and prospects. Digital Commun. Netw. **8**, 225–234 (2021)
24. Wang, Y.X., Ramanan, D., Hebert, M.: Growing a brain: fine-tuning by increasing model capacity. In: Proceedings of the IEEE Conference on Computer Vision and Pattern Recognition, pp. 2471–2480 (2017)
25. Yan, Y., Conze, P.H., Lamard, M., Quellec, G., Cochener, B., Coatrieux, G.: Towards improved breast mass detection using dual-view mammogram matching. Med. Image Anal. **71**, 102083 (2021)
26. Yu, F.: A comprehensive guide to fine-tuning deep learning models in keras (part i). Felix Yu (2020)
27. Zagoruyko, S., Komodakis, N.: Wide residual networks. arXiv preprint arXiv:1605.07146 (2016)

Privacy and Security

Attribute-Based Proxy Re-encryption with Privacy Protection for Message Dissemination in VANET

Qiuming Liu, Zhexin Yao, Zhen Wu[✉], and Zeyao Xu

Jiangxi University of Science and Technology, School of Software Engineering, Nanchang, China
{liuqiuming,zxyao,6720200926}@jxust.edu.cn, wuzhen35@163.com

Abstract. Message dissemination between the infrastructures and vehicles is the most common operation in the vehicular ad hoc network (VANET). However, only some specific vehicles can access the disseminated message with keys. When other vehicles do need to access this message, they have to send requests to the infrastructures like the trusted authority (TA). TA negotiates with this vehicles and may produce many encryption redundancies for the same message, which costs extra communication and computation overhead. Thus, the proposed scheme adopts attribute-based proxy re-encryption (ABPRE) with privacy protection, which is suitable for one-to-many communication mode in VANET. By shifting the re-encryption work to roadside units (RSUs) and cloud servers, the computation overhead of the trusted authority (TA) is significant reduced. Besides, pseudonym and batch verification are introduced in authentication work to ensure the security. The security analysis shows that our scheme meets the secure requirements of VANET. The simulation evaluates the cost of each phase, which demonstrated that the scheme has a low computation cost and reduces the redundancy work.

Keywords: Vehicular ad hoc network (VANET) · Attribute-based proxy re-encryption (ABPRE) · Pseudonym · Message dissemination

1 Introduction

Vehicular ad hoc network (VANET) technology has been adopted in the modern transport system to improve traffic security and driving experience effectively [1]. VANET consists of vehicles and infrastructures like roadside units (RSUs) and trusted authority (TA). Vehicles are equipped with the onboard unit (OBU) plays the role of information generator and message transmitter. Message may include traffic information, road situation, and vehicle's status. Meanwhile, the

Supported by Natural Science Foundation of Jiangxi Province (Grant No. 20202BAB212003), Science and technology project of Jiangxi Provincial Department of Education(GJJ210853).

S. Goel et al. (Eds.): ICDF2C 2022, LNICST 508, pp. 387–402, 2023.
https://doi.org/10.1007/978-3-031-36574-4_23

vehicle can receive messages from other vehicles and infrastructures [2]. With real-time data sharing, the transport agency can predict some potential traffic accidents and vehicles can get the latest surrounding traffic situation.

As we all know, vehicles have the feature of high mobility and the communication among vehicles is conducted in the open wireless network [3]. Hence, security and efficiency must be ensured during message exchange. The security of VANET means the validity and privacy of participating entities must be protected. Besides, due to the mobility of vehicles, VANET must realize efficient data sharing. There have been many schemes proposed to improve the security and efficiency of VANET in message dissemination [4].

The communication modes in VANET can be divided into three kinds: one-to-one, one-to-many, and many-to-many. However, in the reality, one-to-many and many-to-many are formed by one-to-one mode [5]. Under one-to-one mode, the same message may has been encrypted for many times to match the different receivers. The computation and communication cost is quite unworthy and should be avoided. To solve this problem, Chen et al. [6] proposed a scheme that broadcasts ciphertext with a shared key to achieving one-to-many communication. Unfortunately, the encryption of ciphertext is based on bilinear maps, which causes a huge computation cost. Cui et al. [7] applied group key encryption with the method of self-healing key distribution in the scheme. Though the scheme using the elliptic curve cryptosystem to improve authentication efficiency, the risk of sharing the same group key in the same area shouldn't be ignored.

Ciphertext-policy attribute-based encryption (CP-ABE) can realize one-to-many encryption. CP-ABE has been applied for secure authentication and efficient communication in many VANET schemes. With CP-ABE, the data owner encrypts messages by access policy, and only receivers whose attributes satisfy the policy can get the plaintext. Liu et al. [8] proposed a message dissemination scheme in VANET with CP-ABE, which realizes secure and efficient communication. Based on that, Li et al. [9] proposed a VANET scheme adopting ABE to ensure security and privacy. Besides, the scheme outsources encryption and decryption to cloud servers to reduce computation overhead. Similarly, Horng et al. [10] proposed a CP-ABE data sharing scheme which also outsources encryption and decryption to third party.Furthermore, the scheme adopted identity revocation to keep secure authentication.

Above all, attribute-based encryption with fine-grained access control can be well applied with data dissemination in VANET. But the schemes mentioned above didn't consider the situation of ciphertext re-encryption.Consider this scenario (see Fig. 1): Vehicle A uploads a traffic message encrypted by access policy ('RSU1' and 'Jiefang Avenue') or ('RSU2' and 'Renmin Road'), which indicates vehicles in RSU1's area on the Jiefang Avenue or in RSU2's area on the Renmin Road can access the message. Vehicle B with attributes ('RSU2', 'Nanjing Road'), who will pass by Renmin Road, can't decrypt the ciphertext. But if the ciphertext includes the traffic accident information happened in Renmin Road, transport agency do need to disseminate the message to surrounding vehicles including vehicles. Otherwise, vehicles like B knowing nothing will drive into the Renmin Road normally, causing the traffic situation more serious. To avoid that, the trivial solution is that transport agency request data owner A decrypts the original ciphertext and re-encrypts with designed access policy for vehicles like B. However, in this method, with the number of vehicles growing, the re-encryption phase would cost huge computation and the ciphertext would be encrypted redundantly.

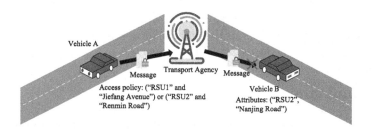

Fig. 1. Example of data sharing in VANET with ABE.

To improve efficiency, proxy re-encryption is introduced during data sharing. Ciphertext can be converted by proxy re-encryption. Zhong et al. [11] proposed a broadcast re-encryption scheme, which realizes the transformation from identity-based broadcast encryption (IBBE) to identity-based encryption (IBE). However, the design of the whole system sharing the same secret parameters r_1 and r_2 makes the privacy feeble. Liu et al. [12] proposed an attribute-based proxy re-encryption (ABPRE) scheme with multi-RSU, which achieves an efficient seamless handover and ciphertext conversion. However, this scheme ignores message verification and privacy protection. Furthermore, Ge et al. [13] proposed a verifiable and fair ABPRE scheme, which focuses on ciphertext verification during re-encryption, while this scheme ignores the message authentication during the uploading process.

Therefore, a scheme that adopts attribute-based proxy re-encryption (ABPRE) with privacy protection is proposed. In VANET, numbers of RSUs are distributed along the road in the coverage of TA. The proposed scheme makes RSUs and cloud servers conduct re-encryption work to reduce the computation overhead of TA. RSU also plays the role of attribute management in its coverage. Besides, to ensure privacy protection and security, pseudonyms and batch verification are adopted. The primary contributions of this paper are summarized as follows:

- To present an efficient and secure communication mode, a scheme that adopts attribute-based proxy re-encryption with privacy protection is proposed. Besides, batch verification is introduced during the message verification to improve working efficiency further.
- The detailed structure of the proposed scheme is introduced with the operation procedure. The security analysis proves that the scheme is confidential, privacy-preserving, and traceable.

– Through the performance evaluation and comparison, it is remarkable that the proposed scheme can achieve efficient one-to-many communication with privacy protection.

The rest structure of this paper is shown below. Section 2 introduces the preliminary knowledge, components' functions and security requirements. The detailed communication procedures are introduced in Sect. 3. Section 4 demonstrates the comprehensive security analysis of the proposed scheme. The comparison of different schemes and the simulation results are described in Sect. 5. Finally, Sect. 6 gives the summary of this paper.

2   Preliminaries

This section first introduces the mathematical knowledge adopted in this paper: linear secret sharing scheme, attribute-based proxy re-encryption. Then, the communication model is proposed with the description of the entities. Meanwhile, the security requirements are listed according to the communication model.

2.1   Linear Secret Sharing Schemes

A linear secret sharing scheme (LSSS) Π over a set of parties $\mathcal{P}$ (over $\mathbf{Z}_p$) is linear if:

– The share of each party is a vector over $\mathbf{Z}_p$.
– There exists a $l \times n$ matrix m and a function ρ, where $\rho(j) \in \mathcal{P}$ denotes jth row of M , $j \in \{1, 2, \cdots l\}$. Let r be a secret number and random numbers $r_2, r_3, \cdots, r_n \in \mathbf{Z}_p$. Construct a vector $\vec{v} = (r, r_2, \cdots, r_n)$, then $M \cdot \vec{v}$ is a vector of l shares of r according to Π and $M_j \cdot \vec{v}$ is a share belonging to $\rho(j)$.

Suppose that A is an authorized attribute set and J is a constant set that $J = \{j : \rho(j) \in A\} \subset \{1, 2, \cdots l\}$. The linear reconstruction of LSSS states that there exists a vector $\vec{\theta}$, such that $\{M_j\}_{j \in J} \cdot \vec{\theta} = (1, 0, \cdots, 0)^T$, $\vec{v} \cdot \{M_j\}_{j \in J} \cdot \vec{\theta} = r$.

2.2   Attribute-Based Proxy Re-encryption

Attribute-based proxy re-encryption (ABPRE) is an algorithm that combined CP-ABE and proxy encryption, which can achieve flexible access control and efficient ciphertext conversion [13]. The proposed scheme utilizes ABPRE in VANET for secure traffic information transmission.

– *Setup*(λ, U): It takes the security parameter λ and the attribute universe U as input. Algorithm *Setup* generates system public parameter pp and master secret key msk.
– *Key_Gen*(msk, A): It takes the master secret key msk and attribute set A as input. Then, it outputs secret key sk based on A for requesters.

- $Enc(m, (\boldsymbol{M}, \rho))$: It takes message m and access policy $(\boldsymbol{M}, \rho)$ as input and generates ciphertext CT based on $(\boldsymbol{M}, \rho)$.
- $Re\_Key\_Gen(sk, (\boldsymbol{M}', \rho'))$: This step inputs sk based on attribute and another access policy $(\boldsymbol{M}', \rho')$. Then, it generates a re-encrypted key rk to re-encrypt original ciphertext.
- $Re\_Enc(rk, CT)$: Based on re-encrypted key rk, it coverts the original ciphertext CT to re-encrypted ciphertext CT' without revealing plaintext.
- $Dec1(CT, sk)/Dec2(CT', sk)$: This step decrypts original ciphertext or re-encrypted ciphertext with attribute-based key sk and outputs message m.

2.3   Communication Model

The proposed vehicular network contains four entities including trusted authority (TA), roadside units (RSUs), cloud servers (CS), and vehicles carried with the on-board unit (OBU), where vehicles connected to other vehicles or RSUs by the dedicated short-range communication protocol (DSRC). Figure 2 illustrates the communication framework and the details of entities are described as follows.

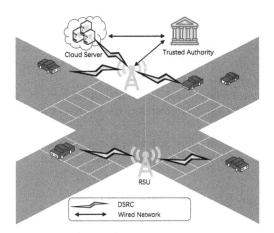

Fig. 2. Data sharing model in VANET

- TA: TA is considered a trusted traffic center with sufficient computing power and storage space. TA initiates the system by generating global parameters and takes charge of vehicle's registration. TA generates pseudonyms and secret keys for vehicles. Besides, TA can trace the real identities of vehicles for partial anonymity.
- RSU: RSUs are distributed along the road. RSU is also a gateway between vehicles and upper entities in the system. RSU takes charge of traffic message collection and dissemination in its coverage. In the network, RSU also plays the role of generating attribute-based key and re-encryption key for vehicles.

- CS: CS is a semi-trusted third party and equipped with sufficient computing power and huge storage space. In the proposed scheme, CS is also considered as a proxy server, which achieves ciphertext conversion without disclosing plaintext by re-encryption key from RSU.
- Vehicle: Each vehicle equips with an OBU to collect surrounding traffic information and transfer it to neighboring RSUs and other vehicles by DSRC. In the proposed scheme, vehicles carry a set of attributes and other private data, e.g., secret keys, pseudonyms.

2.4   Security Requirement

Security and privacy are two basic preconditions in a stable VANET. Besides, the proposed scheme should also meet other requirements listed below.

- Message Confidentiality: The message OBU collected may contain some sensitive information. Thus, the message must keep confidential during the communication.
- Message Authentication and Integrity: Receivers must verify the validity of the message transmitted in the VANET. On the one hand, the source of the message must be authenticated to ensure the validity. On the other hand, it is important to ensure the integrity of the message to prevent forgery.
- Identity Protection: Vehicles would transmit message with identity information in the public channel continuously. To protect identity privacy, the vehicle uses pseudonym instead of real identity.
- Traceability: Vehicles broadcast message and requests in VANET. But if the vehicle exists some malicious behavior, the real identity of the vehicle should be designed to traceable.
- Other Common Attacks: The scheme should also have the ability to resist some common attacks, such as replay attacks, simulation attacks and so on.

3   The Proposed Scheme

In this section, the procedures of the proposed scheme are described. TA plays the role of manager in the whole communication system. To reduce the computation pressure, TA's management area is divided into multiple pieces by RSUs. RSU takes charge of message authentication and assists re-encryption working in its coverage. Vehicle as the traffic information collector and receiver must register with TA and RSU to get further communication service. For secure and efficient message dissemination, traffic information is encrypted by ABE before uploading. And then during the dissemination, if the receiver's attribute set doesn't satisfy the designed access policy, it couldn't access the ciphertext. To deal with that, the proposed scheme adopts proxy re-encryption, where RSU generates re-encrypted key and CS utilizes the key for ciphertext re-encryption. The notations utilized in the proposed scheme are listed in in the Table 1.

Table 1. List of notations

Notations	Definition	Notations	Definition
G, G_T	Multiplicative group	key_{TA}	Private key of TA
r_1, r_2	Master private key	key_{id}	Identity-based key of vehicle
g	A generator of group G	key_{att}	Attribute-based key of vehicle
p	Large prime number	key_{re}	Key for re-encryption
Q_1, Q_2	Random generator in G	t_1, t_2	time stamp
$h(\cdot)$	One-way hash function	A, S	Attribute set
CT	Original ciphertext	CT'	Re-encrypted ciphertext

3.1   System Initialization

TA initializes the system by generating system public parameter pp and master secret key key_{TA} based on security number λ and attribute universe U.

- TA generates two multiplicative groups G and G_T with the same prime order p, where g is a generator of G. These two groups satisfy the bilinear map $e : G \times G \to G_T$.
- TA picks two secret numbers $r_1, r_2 \in Z_p$, $r_1 \neq r_2$ and computes auxiliary parameters $pub_1 = g^{r_1}$, $pub_2 = g^{r_2}$. Then, TA stores master secret key as $key_{TA} = (r_1, r_2)$.
- TA chooses two random generators $Q_1, Q_2 \in G$ and five cryptographic hash functions: $h_1 : G \to \{0,1\}^*$, $h_2, h_3 : \{0,1\}^* \to Z_p$, $h_4 : G_T \to \{0,1\}^*$ and $h_5 : G_T \to Z_p$.
- For each attribute x of U, TA chooses a number $h_x \in Z_p$ and computes $H_x = g^{h_x}$. Then, TA publishes $pp = (e, g, p, pub_1, pub_2, Q_1, Q_2, \{H_x\}_{\forall x \in U}, h_i(\cdot), \Delta t)$ to all entities, where Δt means the expected delay.

After the initialization of TA, RSU generates secret key key_{RSU} and publish its parameter rpp in its coverage.

- RSU chooses two random exponents $\alpha, a \in Z_p$, and sets its secret key as $key_{RSU} = g^\alpha$.
- RSU computes $e(g, g)^\alpha$, g^a, and publishes parameter $rpp = (e(g, g)^\alpha, g^a)$.

3.2   Key Generation

Before joining the communication system, vehicle must register with TA. Vehicle v sends its unique real identity rid to TA. Then, based on the vehicle's identity, TA generates corresponding pseudo identity pid and identity-based private key key_{id}.

- TA picks a random number $k \in Z_p$ and computes $pid_1 = g^k$, $pid_2 = rid \oplus h_1(pub_1^k)$. Set pseudo identity as $pid = (pid_1, pid_2, vp)$, where vp is the valid period of pid.

- Based on the pid, TA computes $sk_1 = pid_1^{r_1}$, $sk_2 = Q_1^{r_2 h_2(pid_1 \| pid_2 \| vp)}$. $Q_2^{h_3(pid_1)}$. Set identity-based private key as $key_{id} = (sk_1, sk_2)$ for vehicle v.
- TA transmits tuple (pid, key_{id}) to vehicle in a secure channel and vehicle stores it in tamper-proof devices.

When vehicle v enters an RSU coverage, it picks a valid pid from identity pool. Then, v sends pid and its attribute set A to the RSU to request for attribute-based key key_{att}.

- RSU maintain a list of vehicles' pseudonyms and attribute sets. Receiving the key request from the vehicle, RSU first checks the validity of pid. Then, RSU checks whether pid and attribute set A already existing in the list. If not, RSU continues the next procedure.
- RSU picks a random number $b \in Z_p$ and computes attribute-based key as $key_{att} = (A, K_1 = g^\alpha g^{ab}, K_2 = g^b, \forall x \in A, K_x = H_x^b)$.
- RSU sends key_{att} to the vehicle in a secure channel.

3.3 Message Encryption

To ensure confidentiality and integrity, the message must be encrypted and signed. Vehicle encrypts message by CP-ABE and signs the message with Algorithm 1.

Algorithm 1. Signature Algorithm $Sign()$

Input: Ciphertext CT; Identity based key $key_{id} = (sk_1, sk_2)$; Timestamp t_1;
Output: Signature σ;
1: compute hash value $w = h_3(CT \| t_1)$;
2: compute signature $\sigma = sk_1 \cdot sk_2^w$;
3: **return** σ;

- v defines access policy (M, ρ), where M is a $l \times n$ matrix and ρ is a function associate each row of matrix to an attribute.
- v chooses a vector $\vec{u} = (r, y_2, \cdots, y_n)^T \in Z_p$, where r is the main security number. Then, vehicle computes $\vec{\lambda} = M \cdot \vec{u} = \{M_j\} \cdot \vec{u} = (\lambda_1, \lambda_2, \cdots, \lambda_l)^T$, in which M_j represents jth row of matrix, $j \in [1, l]$.
- v randomly selects $b_j \in Z_p$ for each M_j, $j \in [1, l]$, and computes ciphertext as $CT = ((M, \rho), C = m \oplus H(e(g, g)^{\alpha r}), C_1 = g^r, C_{2,j} = g^{a\lambda_j} H_{\rho(j)}^{-b_j}, C_{3,j} = g^{b_j}, j \in [1, l])$.
- v picks a valid pid and corresponding key_{id}, then signs ciphertext with Algorithm 1 generating signature σ. Vehicle sends (CT, σ, pid, t_1) to local RSU, where t_1 is timestamp to against replay attack.

3.4 Message Verification

RSU receives (CT, σ, pid, t_1) from vehicle v. First, RSU checks the validity of timestamp t_1. If $t_r - t_1 < \Delta t$, where t_r is the time the message arriving, RSU continues next verification steps; or, RSU would reject the message. Then, RSU check the validity of pseudo identity with vp. To keep efficient operation and reduce computation overhead, RSU introduces batch verification technology. Assume that RSU receives messages as $\{CT_i, \sigma_i, pid_i, t_{i,1}\}_{i=1}^n$ and verifies these messages by Algorithm 2. If the result of verification is true, RSU transmits messages to CS to store. Otherwise, invalid signature search algorithm [14] is adopted.

Algorithm 2. Verification Algorithm $Verify()$

Input: messages $\{CT_i, \sigma_i, pid_i, t_{i,1}\}_{i=1}^n$; parameters (Q_1, Q_2, pub_1, pub_2);
Output: $True$ or $False$;

1: choose a vector $\vec{a} = (a_1, a_2, \cdots, a_k)^T$, $a_i \in [1, 2^d]$;
2: check whether equation

$$e(\sum_{i=1}^n (a_i)^2 \sigma_i, g) = e(\sum_{i=1}^n (a_i)^2 (sk_{i,1} \cdot sk_{i,2}^{w_i}), g)$$

$$= e(\sum_{i=1}^n a_i pid_{i,1} Q_2^{h_3(CT_i \| t_{i,1}) h_2(pid_{i,1})}, pub_1) \qquad (1)$$

$$\cdot e(\sum_{i=1}^n a_i Q_1^{h_3(CT_i \| t_{i,1}) h_3(pid_{i,1} \| pid_{i,2} \| vp_i)}, pub_2)$$

holds or not;
3: **return** $True$ or $False$;

3.5 Message Re-encryption

Vehicle sends its message request to RSU. If the vehicle's attributes don't satisfy the ciphertext's access policy, RSU then generates re-encryption key for the vehicle.

- RSU defines another access policy (M', ρ') which satisfies vehicle's attribute-based key $key_{att} = (A, K_1 = g^\alpha g^{ab}, K_2 = g^b, \forall x \in A, K_x = H_x^b)$.
- RSU randomly chooses $O \in G_T$ and encrypts O with policy (M', ρ'). The encryption procedure is the same as message encryption in Sect. 3.3. Set the ciphertext of O as C_0.
- RSU computes $\varphi = h_5(O)$ and sets re-encryption key as $key_{re} = (S, RK_1 = K_1^\varphi, RK_2 = K_2^\varphi, \forall x \in S, RK_x = K_x^\varphi, C_0)$, where S is the attribute set of RSU, and then RSU sends key_{re} to CS.

Once receiving re-encryption key key_{re}, CS re-encrypts the requested ciphertext. After a conversion without disclosing the plaintext, the re-encrypted ciphertext could be decrypted by initial requester.

- CS picks the original ciphertext CT in database. Let $J = \{j | \rho(j) \in S\} \subset \{1, \cdots, l\}$ be a constant set which denotes attribute satisfies access policy. Then, there exists a vector $\vec{\theta} = (\theta_1, \theta_2, \ldots, \theta_j)^T$, $j \in J$, $\theta_j \in Z_p$, which satisfies $\sum_{j \in J} M_j \vec{\theta} = (1, 0, \dots, 0)^T$. CS computes

$$
\begin{aligned}
C_p &= \frac{e(C_1, RK_1)}{\prod_{j \in J} \left(e(C_{2,j}, RK_2) e(C_{3,j}, RK_x) \right)^{\theta_j}} \\
&= \frac{e(g^r, (g^\alpha g^{ab})^\varphi)}{\prod_{j \in J} \left(e(g^{a\lambda_j} H_{\rho(j)}^{-b_j}, g^{b\varphi}) e(g^{b_j}, H_x^{b\varphi}) \right)^{\theta_j}} \\
&= e(g, g)^{\alpha r \varphi}.
\end{aligned}
\tag{2}
$$

- Set $C' = C$, $C_1' = C_1$ and construct re-encrypted ciphertext as $CT' = ((M', \rho'), C', C_1', C_0, C_p)$.
- CS utilizes Algorithm 1 to generate signature σ' of CT' and disseminates the re-encrypted message (CT', σ', pid, t_2) to the vehicles.

The re-encryption procedure can be summarized as Algorithm 3 describing the calculation and transmission details.

Algorithm 3. Ciphertext Re-encryption Algorithm

Input: Vehicles key_{att}; RSU attribute set S; Ciphertext CT;
Output: Re-encrypted ciphertext CT';

1: **if** $R(A, (M, \rho)) = 0$ **then**
2:     $//R(A, (M, \rho)) = 0$ means A doesnt meet access policy (M, ρ).
3:     Define another policy (M', ρ');
4: **else**
5:     Attributes satisfy access policy, stop re-encryption!
6: **end if**
7: **if** $R(A, (M', \rho')) = 1$ **then**
8:     Randomly choose $O \in G_T$; $Enc(O, (M', \rho')) \rightarrow C_0$;
9:     Compute $\varphi = h_5(O), RK_1 = K_1^\varphi, RK_2 = K_2^\varphi, RK_x = K_x^\varphi$;
10:     Set $key_{re} = (S, RK_1, RK_2, \forall x \in S, RK_x, C_0)$;
11: **end if**$//$Re-encryption key generation finished.
12: $//$ Then, RSU transmits re-encryption key to CS.
13: **if** $R(S, (M, \rho)) = 1$ **then**
14:     Find $J = \{j | \rho(j) \in S\} \subset \{1, \cdots, l\}$;
15:     Compute $\sum_{j \in J} M_j \vec{\theta} = (1, 0, \dots, 0)^T \rightarrow \vec{\theta}$;
16:     Compute $C_p = \frac{e(C_1, RK_1)}{\prod_{j \in J} (e(C_{2,j}, RK_2) e(C_{3,j}, RK_x))^{\theta_j}}$;
17: **end if**
18: Set $C' = C, C_1' = C_1$;
19: **return** $CT' = ((M', \rho'), C', C_1', C_0, C_p)$;

3.6 Message Decryption

In order to describing the decryption more specifically, the proposed scheme divides this procedure into two types, the decryption of original ciphertext and the decryption of re-encrypted ciphertext.

1) Vehicle receives original ciphertext (CT, σ, pid, t_1) from CS. Suppose that vehicle's attribute-based key is $key_{att} = (\boldsymbol{A}, K_1, K_2, \forall x \in \boldsymbol{A}, K_x)$ and attribute set $\boldsymbol{A}$ meets the access policy $(\boldsymbol{M}, \rho)$.

   – Vehicle verifies the integrity of the message by Algorithm 2 proposed in Sect. 3.4 and if the result is true, carries out the next procedure.

   – Let $J = \{j | \rho(j) \in \boldsymbol{A}\} \subset \{1, \cdots, l\}$ be a constant set which denotes attribute satisfies access policy. Then, find a vector $\vec{\boldsymbol{\theta}} = (\theta_1, \theta_2, \ldots, \theta_j)^T$, $j \in \boldsymbol{J}, \theta_j \in \boldsymbol{Z}_p$, which satisfies $\sum_{j \in J} \boldsymbol{M}_j \vec{\boldsymbol{\theta}} = (1, 0, \ldots, 0)^T$.

   – Due to $(\vec{\boldsymbol{\lambda}})^T \cdot \vec{\boldsymbol{\theta}} = r$, Vehicle computes

$$\Theta = \frac{e(C_1, K_1)}{\prod\limits_{j \in J} (e(K_2, C_{2,j}) e(K_{\rho(j)}, C_{3,j}))^{\theta_j}}$$
$$= \frac{e(g^r, g^\alpha g^{ab})}{\prod\limits_{j \in J} (e(g^{a\lambda_j} H_{\rho(j)}^{-b_j}, g^b) e(g^{b_j}, H_x^b))^{\theta_j}} \qquad (3)$$
$$= e(g, g)^{\alpha r}$$

   and gets the original content by $m = C \oplus h_4(\Theta)$.

2) Vehicle receives re-encrypted message (CT', σ', pid, t_2) and checks the integrity of the message by Algorithm 2 first. Then, vehicle decrypts CT' by following steps.

   – Vehicle utilizes key_{att} to decrypt ciphertext C_0 and gets the result of decryption O. The decryption procedure is the same as the description above.

   – Then vehicle computes $\varphi = h_5(O)$ and $\Theta = (C_p)^{\frac{1}{\varphi}}$. After that, the original plaintext is $m = C' \oplus h_4(\Theta)$.

4   Security Analysis

In this section, the security analysis is presented. Based on the security requirement proposed in Sect. 2.4, the analysis shows the realization of security in the proposed scheme. Let's first introduce Computational Diffie-Hellman problem (CDHP) on Definition 1 and Discrete Logarithm assumption (DLA) on Definition 2.

Definition 1. *Given a cyclic group $\boldsymbol{G}$ with the order p and generator g. For $g, g^a, g^b \in \boldsymbol{G}$, the goal of CDHP is to find $g^{ab} \in \boldsymbol{G}$. The CDHP holds in $\boldsymbol{G}$, if there is no algorithm $\mathcal{B}$ who can output g^{ab} in a probabilistic polynomial time (PPT) with probability at least ε as: $Pr[g^{ab} \leftarrow \mathcal{B}(g, g^a, g^b) : a, b \in \boldsymbol{Z}_p] \geq \varepsilon$.*

Definition 2. *Based on a bilinear tuple $(e, \boldsymbol{G}, \boldsymbol{G}_T, g, g^\beta, p)$, $\beta \in \boldsymbol{Z}_p$, the DLA means that the time for an adversary $\mathcal{A}$ to find the integer β with the advantage of a probabilistic polynomial time (PPT) is negligible. Formally, the advantage of a PPT adversary $Adv_{DLA} = Pr(\mathcal{A}(e, \boldsymbol{G}, \boldsymbol{G}_T, p, g, g^\beta) = \beta)$ is negligible.*

- Message confidentiality: Messages are transmitted as the form of ciphertexts CT, where original text m is encrypted as $C = m \oplus H(e(g,g)^{\alpha r})$. Through the method of LSSS, plaintext is encrypted by the access policy $(\boldsymbol{M}, \rho)$ with the secret number r, which is CCA secure proved in [15]. Due to the DLA, even the adversary obtains the ciphertext, without r, the plaintext couldn't be disclosed.
- Message authentication and integrity: In the proposed scheme, only the registered vehicle can transmit message. Each message has the signature $\sigma = sk_1 \cdot sk_2^{h_3(CT\|t_1)}$. The signature is produced by pseudonym pid, identity-based key key_{id} and ciphertext CT to ensure the authentication and integrity. After receiving the message, RSUs or vehicle could verify whether the signature satisfies the Equation $e(\sigma, g) = e(pid_1 Q_2^{h_3(CT\|t_1)h_2(pid_1)}, pub_1) \cdot e(Q_1^{h_3(CT\|t_1)h_3(pid_1\|pid_2\|vp)}, pub_2)$. According to [16], there is no adversary can solve the CDHP in polynomial time. Thus, if the message get forged, the equation would not hold. After the re-encryption, the message (CT', σ', pid, t_2) could also utilize the equation to check the integrity.
- Identity protection: In the proposed scheme, each message is transmitted with the pseudonym to protect the identity privacy. Pseudonym is designed as $pid = (pid_1 = g^k, pid_2 = rid \oplus h_1(pub_1^k))$. Due to the DLA, though the parameters like g and pub_1 is public, it is hard to compute secret number k from $pid_1 = g^k$. Without knowing k, the adversary couldn't disclose the real identity from $pid_2 = rid \oplus h_1(pub_1^k)$.
- Traceability: If there exists some malicious vehicles, the system should have the ability to trace the real identities. In the proposed scheme, pseudonym $pid_1 = g^k$ and $pid_2 = rid \oplus h_1(pub_1^k)$, where secret number k is randomly selected and stored in TA. Thus, TA has the ability to trace the real identity by $pid_2 = rid \oplus h_1(pub_1^k)$. But other entities in the scheme can't reveal the real identity of vehicles due to the DLA.
- Replay attack: The message (CT, σ, pid, t_1) contains valid time period vp of pid and time stamp t_1. Thus, the receivers could check vp timestamp t_1 to resist replay attacks.
- Simulation attack: The adversaries conduct simulation attacks by signature forgery. The signature is consisted by $sk_1 = pid_1^{r_1}$ and $sk_2 = Q_1^{r_2 h_2(pid_1\|pid_2\|vp)} \cdot Q_2^{h_3(pid_1)}$ and secret numbers r_1 and r_2 are stored in TA. Thus, the adversaries can't obtain the secret numbers, so the signature wouldn't be forged.

5   Performance Evaluation and Comparison

In this section, we conduct a series of comparisons with three related schemes [6, 11, 13] introduced in the Sect. 2 and evaluate the performance of these schemes. Different from these three schemes, the proposed scheme also contains the phases of vehicle registration and message authentication, which are designed to ensure the security of data sharing. Hence, the performance evaluation mainly focuses on the message encryption phase, re-encryption phase and decryption phase.

Table 2. Execution Time of Three Operation

Notations	Description	Time(ms)
T_{bp}	The execution time of bilinear pairing	4.512
T_{eo}	The execution time of exponential operation	0.564
T_{smo}	The scale multiplication operation	0.313

First, the bilinear pairing algorithm $e : G \times G \to G_T$ and the elliptic curve algorithm $E : Y^2 = X^3 + X$ are built with the same security level of 128 *bits*. Then, the group order is set as 160 *bits*. The simulation is operated on a laptop of 2.9 GHZ i5-10400 with the MIRACL library, 8 GB memory, Windows 10 operating system. The running time of the three phases are listed in Table 2.

5.1 Functionality Comparison

Table 3. Functionality comparison with [6,11] and [13]

Schemes	Mode	Encryption	Authentication	Re-encryption	Access control
Chen et al. [6]	One-to-many	IBE	×	×	×
Zhong et al. [11]	One-to-many	IBE	✓	✓	×
Ge et al. [13]	One-to-many	ABE	×	✓	✓
Ours	One-to-many	ABE	✓	✓	✓

Here, a functionality comparison of the proposed scheme and schemes [6,11,13] is demonstrated. As is shown in the Table 3, these four schemes are all proposed for one-to-many communication mode. To keep confidentiality, schemes [6,11] adopt identity-based encryption (IBE), while our scheme and scheme [13] utilize attribute-based encryption (ABE). Compare with IBE, ABE has the advantage of flexible access control for ciphertext. Moreover, the computation cost of is not related to the number of vehicles. Different with scheme [13], our scheme also considers message authentication while communication.

5.2 Computation Cost Evaluation

Here, the corresponding computation cost evaluation in encryption step, re-encryption step and decryption step of each scheme is presented. The total computation cost is listed in the Table 4, where n represents the number of the vehicle and l represents the size of attribute set. In the scheme [6], the broadcaster has to calculate each receivers' personalized key K_i with exponentiation operation during encryption phase. So the computation cost is $(3n+3)T_{eo}+2nT_{smo}$. When decrypting ciphertext Hdr, receiver utilizes bilinear pairing with key K_i' and the cost here is $T_{bp} + 6T_{eo} + 4T_{smo}$. In the scheme of [11], the sender owns master

Table 4. Computation cost comparison with [6,11] and [13]

Schemes	Encryption	Re-encryption	Decryption
Chen et al. [6]	$(3n+3)T_{eo} + 2nT_{smo}$	×	$T_{bp} + 6T_{eo} + 4T_{smo}$
Zhong et al. [11]	$3T_{eo} + T_{bp}$	$4T_{bp} + (n+3)T_{eo}$	$2T_{bp} + nT_{eo}$
Ge et al. [13]	$(3l+5)T_{eo}$	$(3l+8)T_{eo} + (2l+3)T_{bp}$	$(2l+1)T_{bp}$
Ours	$(3l+2)T_{eo}$	$(4l+4)T_{eo} + (2l+1)T_{bp}$	$(2l+1)T_{bp}$

private key β, so the sender can directly calculate ciphertext and the computation cost is $3T_{eo} + T_{bp}$. During the re-encryption phase, the authenticated vehicle and cloud server take over the computation cost. The re-encryption cost related to the size of authenticated group S is $4T_{bp} + (n+3)T_{eo}$. In the decryption phase, receiver has to compute ciphertext with public parameters and the cost is $2T_{bp} + nT_{eo}$. Different with scheme [13], our scheme improves the re-encryption phase and the cost is lower.

Considering the realistic situation in VANET, the simulation sets the number of vehicles from 10 to 100. Besides, we set each vehicle with the size of attribute set as 5. During the encryption phase, as is shown in Fig. 3, the computation cost of Chen et al. [6] increases rapidly with the number of vehicles grow while the other three has no influence. Figure 4 shows that when the number of vehicles is small, the re-encryption cost of Zhong et al. [11] is least. However, the proposed scheme performs better while the number of vehicles is over 80. In Fig. 5, the decryption cost of Chen et al. [6] is the least among these schemes. Finally, the Fig. 6 shows the total cost of all cryptographic phases. As it shows, when the number of vehicles is below 20, the scheme of Chen et al. [6] performs best. When the number of vehicles is over 80, our scheme has the lowest computation cost. Above all, we can see if the number of the vehicle keeps small-scale, the scheme based on identity has less cost, while with the number of vehicle increasing, the advantage of attribute-based algorithm is more obvious.

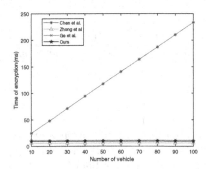

Fig. 3. Comparison of encryption cost

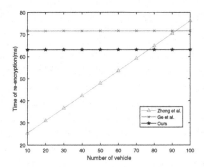

Fig. 4. Comparison of re-encryption cost

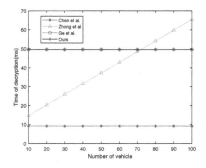
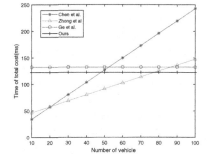

Fig. 5. Comparison of decryption cost   **Fig. 6.** Comparison of total cost

6 Conclusion

In daily VANET, the number of vehicle increasing rapidly and more traffic problems are following. Thus, it is urgent to adopt efficient and secure message dissemination in VANET to improve transport system. To solve the existing encryption redundancy problem, the proposed scheme utilizes ABPRE method for this one-to-many communication mode. Combined with proxy re-encryption, the proposed scheme reduces the computation cost of re-encryption significantly. To meet the secure requirements, pseudonyms and batch verification are applied in communication. Furthermore, in the future, we will try more efficient and lightweight technology and construct a more secure scheme for VANET.

References

1. Lieira, D.D., Quessada, M.S., Cristiani, A.L., De Grande, R.E., Meneguette, R.I.: Mechanism for optimizing resource allocation in VANETs based on the PSO bioinspired algorithm. In: 2022 18th International Conference on Distributed Computing in Sensor Systems (DCOSS), pp. 283–290 (2022)
2. Goudarzi, S., et al.: A privacy-preserving authentication scheme based on elliptic curve cryptography and using quotient filter in fog-enabled vanet. Ad Hoc Netw. **128**, 102782 (2022)
3. Zhong, H., Han, S., Cui, J., Zhang, J., Xu, Y.: Privacy-preserving authentication scheme with full aggregation in VANET. Inf. Sci. **476**, 211–221 (2019)
4. Shafiq, M., Tian, Z., Bashir, A.K., Du, X., Guizani, M.: IoT malicious traffic identification using wrapper-based feature selection mechanisms. Comput. Secur. **94**, 101863 (2020)
5. Shafiq, M., Tian, Z., Bashir, A.K., Du, X., Guizani, M.: CorrAUC: a malicious bot-IoT traffic detection method in IoT network using machine-learning techniques. IEEE Internet Things J. **8**(5), 3242–3254 (2020)
6. Chen, L., Li, J., Zhang, Y.: Anonymous certificate-based broadcast encryption with personalized messages. IEEE Trans. Broadcast. **66**(4), 867–881 (2020)

7. Cui, J., Wu, D., Zhang, J., Xu, Y., Zhong, H.: An efficient authentication scheme based on semi-trusted authority in VANETs. IEEE Trans. Veh. Technol. **68**(3), 2972–2986 (2019)

8. Liu, X., Xia, Y., Chen, W., Xiang, Y., Hassan, M.M., Alelaiwi, A.: SEMD: secure and efficient message dissemination with policy enforcement in VANET. J. Comput. Syst. Sci. **82**(8), 1316–1328 (2016)

9. Huang, Q., Li, N., Zhang, Z., Yang, Y.: Secure and privacy-preserving warning message dissemination in cloud-assisted internet of vehicles. In: 2019 IEEE Conference on Communications and Network Security (CNS), pp. 1–8 (2019)

10. Horng, S.J., Lu, C.C., Zhou, W.: An identity-based and revocable data-sharing scheme in VANETs. IEEE Trans. Veh. Technol. **69**(12), 15933–15946 (2020)

11. Zhong, H., Zhang, S., Cui, J., Wei, L., Liu, L.: Broadcast encryption scheme for v2i communication in VANETs. IEEE Trans. Veh. Technol. **71**(3), 2749–2760 (2021)

12. Liu, X., Chen, W., Xia, Y.: Security-aware information dissemination with fine-grained access control in cooperative multi-RSU of VANETs. IEEE Trans. Intell. Transp. Syst. **23**, 2170–2179 (2020)

13. Ge, C., Susilo, W., Baek, J., Liu, Z., Xia, J., Fang, L.: A verifiable and fair attribute-based proxy re-encryption scheme for data sharing in clouds. IEEE Trans. Dependable Secure Comput. **19**, 2907–2919 (2021)

14. Huang, J.L., Yeh, L.Y., Chien, H.Y.: ABAKA: an anonymous batch authenticated and key agreement scheme for value-added services in vehicular ad hoc networks. IEEE Trans. Veh. Technol. **60**(1), 248–262 (2011)

15. Lewko, A., Okamoto, T., Sahai, A., Takashima, K., Waters, B.: Fully secure functional encryption: attribute-based encryption and (hierarchical) inner product encryption. In: Gilbert, H. (ed.) EUROCRYPT 2010. LNCS, vol. 6110, pp. 62–91. Springer, Heidelberg (2010). https://doi.org/10.1007/978-3-642-13190-5_4

16. Jianhong, Z., Min, X., Liying, L.: On the security of a secure batch verification with group testing for VANET. Int. J. Netw. Secur. **16**(5), 351–358 (2014)

PBPAFL: A Federated Learning Framework with Hybrid Privacy Protection for Sensitive Data

Ruichu Yao[1], Kunsheng Tang[1,2], Yongshi Zhu[1], Bingbing Fan[1(✉)], Tian Luo[1], and Yide Song[1]

[1] South China Normal University, Guangzhou 510631, Guangdong, China
fanbb1962@qq.com, {luotian,yide.song}@m.scnu.edu.cn
[2] University of Science and Technology of China, Hefei 230026, Anhui, China

Abstract. Due to the difficulties of exchanging data securely, data silos have become a critical issue in the era of big data. Federated learning provides an advantageous approach by enabling data holders to train a model collaboratively without sharing local data. However, multiple known inference attacks have made it impossible for a purely federated learning approach to protect privacy well enough. We present a PBPAFL algorithm that combines differential privacy with homomorphic encryption based on federated learning with an assessment module that enables the privacy budget parameters to be flexible in response to varying training requirements. The models trained using our proposed PBPAFL algorithm are capable of preventing inference assaults without a severe loss of precision. To demonstrate the efficacy of our proposed framework, we employ the PBPAFL algorithm to train a collection of face image-sensitive data. The experimental results show that our approach can improve the privacy protection of the model while maintaining precision.

Keywords: Federated Learning · Privacy Budget Parameter Adaptive · Differential Privacy · Homomorphic Encryption

1 Introduction

With the growing adoption of cloud computing, there has been a significant rise in the focus on big data. Data may be an essential and valuable commodity, and the value of big data can be used to improve life and serve society through the precise analysis of massive volumes of data using machine learning (ML) techniques. Although these services may appear appealing, it is challenging to ensure that sharing specific data will not violate privacy regulations. For instance, in May 2018, the European Union (EU) enacted the General Data Protection Regulation (GDPR) bill, which stipulates that any information connected to an individual is personal data and that the use of such data must be expressly permitted by users [1]. With the growing emphasis on data security and the adoption of privacy protection regulations, "data silos" must be resolved. Data silos relate to the inability of disparate companies or corporate divisions to share and interact with data.

S. Goel et al. (Eds.): ICDF2C 2022, LNICST 508, pp. 403–416, 2023.
https://doi.org/10.1007/978-3-031-36574-4_24

For machine learning (ML) and deep learning (DL) to deliver the intended outcomes, the quantity and quality of training data have a substantial impact on the results. Accordingly, there is an increasing demand to enhance the quantity of data through sharing [2]. To better use data, increase its value, and enable artificial intelligence (AI) for the benefit of human civilization, data silos must be eliminated. Google was the first organization to introduce the notion of Federated Learning (FL) [3] and apply it for mobile input prediction in order to overcome the issue of data leakage, therefore fulfilling the aim of data sharing and overcoming the data silo conundrum. FL enables data holders interested in training to execute machine learning (ML) algorithms locally and train a model jointly by communicating just model parameters, which will be aggregated by the server. Thus, the possibility of data leaking as a result of leaving the local region is eliminated. Nonetheless, this method does not yet provide enough privacy protection for training data. On the basis of the parameters communicated during the FL process, it is feasible to establish not only whether certain samples belong to a certain node [4], but also to invert some training data [5]. Consequently, the local data still presents some security problems.

We provide the PBPAFL, a framework that extends FL with privacy-preserving approaches like differential privacy (DP) and homomorphic encryption, which can protect model parameters from two main threatening attacks. The issue of low accuracy due to the incorporation of DP noise is resolved. The framework's algorithm, which we name the PBPAFL, constantly changes the amount of noise injected during training to meet different needs, reaching a balance between practicality and privacy protection. The primary results from this study are as follows:

- We propose a protection approach that combines differential privacy and homomorphic encryption to inject noise and encrypt the gradient throughout the training process in order to defend against gradient leak attacks that may be faced in FL and enhance its privacy protection capacity. This resolves the remaining data security concerns within the FL procedure.
- We describe a privacy budget parameter adaptive algorithm, PBPAFL, that can change the amount of noise injected during training to tackle the problem of excessive noise diminishing accuracy and maintaining the model's utility while safeguarding data privacy.
- We verify our approach using the accessible face dataset LFW, and experimental findings demonstrate that our algorithm can control the accuracy loss (ACL) within 3% while maintaining privacy. Our method is relevant to more picture categorization issues.
- We investigate the generalizability of the technique to data that does not follow the ideal IID distribution. In comparison to FL methods trained on IID data, those trained on non-IID data provide less effective models. The results show that our technique is effective even when used with Non-IID data.

2   Methodology

2.1   Overview

In conventional machine learning setups, training datasets are centralized on the server where the algorithm is executed. It will lead to an unavoidable problem where data is out of control when it leaves the local area. Even if all participants can be trusted, we would still like a mechanism to avoid revealing local data to others, particularly when this data contains sensitive personal information such as face images. Federated learning overcomes these restrictions by permitting all participants to train locally and sending only trained parameters to collectively train the same model. But Florida is not absolutely safe either. We also need to look into the possibility of getting back to the original data by changing the parameters.

In this research, we propose a PBPAFL algorithm that upgrades FL to resist eaves-dropping attacks by adding noise and homomorphic encryption to the parameters. In addition, our algorithm is adaptive and may dynamically alter the quantity of noise to preserve the model's effect. Our algorithm comprises the steps listed below: 1) add noise to the parameters, which is obtained by local training on the client side; 2) evaluate model effects and re-add noise to modify parameters (if needed); and 3) homomorphic encryption of the noise-added parameters. It can adjust the privacy budget parameters to provide appropriate privacy protection based on the needs of different situations and lower the amount of noise through homomorphic encryption to balance the accuracy of the model. Experiments reveal that the concept of limiting the amount of noise added by altering the privacy budget settings in order to finally guarantee model performance is viable. And the final accuracy loss of our method can be managed to within 3%.

This paper is structured as follows: In Sect. 2, we define FL and detail the fundamental components of our proposed method, including the noise mechanism, homomorphic encryption, and privacy budget parameter adaptive FL algorithm. Section 3 describes the dataset portion and the experimental details. In Sect. 4, we summarize the outcomes of the experiment. In Sect. 5, we explore a few issues that arose during the tests. Finally, we conclude by summarizing the experiment and drawing conclusions.

2.2   Federated Learning

Federated learning is a machine learning approach in which multiple individuals can train a model cooperatively without trading or combining data. The following is a general description of FL.

Assuming that a FL system consists of 1 server and N clients, and the full training data is D. The i-th client has the training data as D_i, where $i \in \{1, 2, \ldots, N\}$, then $\sum_{i=1}^{N} D_i = D$. During the training phase, each client trains the model with its local data in order to find a vector w_i that minimizes a specific loss function. The server side needs to aggregate the parameters w_i received from each client, i.e.,

$$w = \sum_{i=1}^{N} p_i w_i, \tag{1}$$

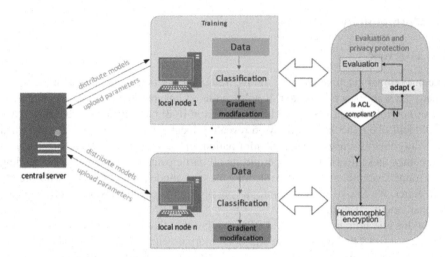

Fig. 1. A privacy budget parameters adaptive framework based on FL.

where p_i indicates the weight of the i-th client, then $p_i = \frac{D_i}{D}$ and $\sum_{i=1}^{N} p_i = 1$. We define the loss function for the i-th client as $F_i()$, then we can state the optimization problem as

$$w^* = \operatorname*{argmin}_{w} \sum_{i=1}^{N} p_i F_i(D_i, w) \tag{2}$$

Through federated learning, more data can be utilized to train a model collectively, tackling the problem of low model accuracy resulting from insufficient data volume. At the same time, the training data stays in the local area, so data leakage is successfully avoided.

Despite the fact that FL provides a novel solution to the problem of local data leakage in the conventional data-centralized ML model, there are still certain security risks involved. The most significant aspect is the transmission parameters for eavesdropping, which may lead to privacy leakage.

2.3 Privacy-Preserving Mechanisms in Federated Learning

Generally speaking, privacy-preserving approaches for distributed learning systems serve two primary objectives: 1) safeguarding the confidentiality of the training data and 2) safeguarding the confidentiality of model parameters shared by the local client and the server. Differential privacy approaches proposed by Zhang et al. [6], data anonymization techniques proposed by Bayardo et al. [7], and homomorphic encryption techniques proposed by Gentry [8] are mainstream privacy-preserving strategies in the field of FL. Following is a detailed description of the differential privacy and homomorphic encryption algorithms utilized by the proposed framework.

Differential Privacy. Differential privacy is primarily the alteration of the original data by introducing noise that fulfills mostly Laplace and Gaussian distributions, such that it differs to some extent from the actual data. It prevents attackers from accessing sensitive information via the published datasets or the given service interface. Zhang et al. [6] define differential privacy as follows:

Definition 2.1 (ϵ - differential privacy (ϵ-DP)). If there are m users, then each user will have their own record. If the function F satisfies the following inequality, then for every two input records m_0, m_1 ($m_0, m_1 \in D_F$), the same output m_* ($m_* \in R_F$) is attained.

$$pr[F(m_0) = m_*] \leq e^{\epsilon} \times pr[F(m_1) = m_*] \tag{3}$$

Then it is claimed that the function F satisfies ϵ- differential privacy, where ϵ is the privacy budget. The above D_F, R_F represent the function F's definition and value domains, respectively. This mechanism's noise satisfies the Laplace distribution.

However, using only differential privacy to protect privacy cannot completely prevent an attacker from gaining access to sensitive information, such as data source and data distribution, from supplied settings. Consequently, we must additionally consider the possibility of data leakage as a result of inference-based attacks on the output.

Homomorphic Encryption. Using homomorphic encryption techniques is another method for protecting data privacy and security in machine learning, particularly in centralized systems such as cloud servers where data is collected for collaborative training without disclosing the original information. Homomorphic encryption makes it possible to execute computations on encrypted forms of data without requiring a decryption key [9]. The result of the computation is delivered in an encrypted format that can only be decrypted by the requester. In addition, homomorphic encryption ensures that the decrypted output is identical to the original output computed on the unencrypted data set.

Homomorphic encryption can be categorized as slightly homomorphic encryption (SWHE) and fully homomorphic encryption (FHE) [10], based on the encryption technique and the class of computational operations that can be performed on the encrypted form. Some conventional cryptographic approaches, such as FHE developed by Gentry et al. in [9], can conduct any arbitrary action on the cipher text (and hence achieve any desired functionality) in order to create encrypted outputs. Using the decryption function, original data or ciphertext calculations may be conveyed mathematically in FHE without conflict. Paillier is the most prevalent homomorphic encryption algorithm in the FL situation. Paillier is defined as

$$\mathrm{Enc}(m_1) + \mathrm{Enc}(m_2) = \mathrm{Enc}(m_1 + m_2) \tag{4}$$

However, performing calculation operations on ciphertexts is computationally intensive. Therefore, the application of homomorphic encryption to large-scale data training remains impracticable.

Our Research Work. Both differential privacy and homomorphic encryption can only guarantee privacy in FL from a single viewpoint, which limits their privacy-preserving impact and model performance. With equal privacy-preserving guarantees, 1) due to differential privacy's susceptibility to output inference attacks that compromise data, this approach requires more noise to achieve the same level of privacy as the method employing a single application of differential privacy. Additionally, more noise leads to a decrease in model prediction accuracy; 2) if only homomorphic encryption is used, it may produce a greater level of model prediction accuracy while maintaining the same level of privacy, since it does not involve direct interference with the original data, hence improving data availability. But there is still a chance that this method could leave sensitive information open to inference attacks.

In this research, we present a hybrid privacy protection mechanism that combines homomorphic encryption and differential privacy approaches to secure privacy in FL from several dimensions and obtain higher privacy guarantees with high accuracy. We add differential privacy noise to the gradient parameters, and then encrypt the noise-added parameters using homomorphic encryption to further enhance privacy protection. Since homomorphic encryption already provides some level of privacy protection, a modest quantity of noise is sufficient to achieve enhanced privacy protection, reducing the necessary privacy budget and achieving enhanced privacy protection while enhancing accuracy.

2.4 Privacy Budget Parameter Adaptive Federated Learning

FL provides a function for the local data privacy concern within the multi-party ML paradigm, hence enabling federated data silos. There is nevertheless a danger of data leaking from the local client in the event of an external attack during the FL process. We consider both adding noise and homomorphic encryption to solve this problem. However, we must also consider the applicability of the model, so we propose a Privacy Budget Parameter Adaptive Federated Learning (PBPAFL) algorithm that can dynamically modify the amount of noise added during each FL round to guarantee the final model's accuracy meets expectations. As illustrated in Fig. 1, our architecture is made up of three parts.

Part 1. Federated Learning. We'll assume the system has one central server and n local clients. The central server launches the training task, picks the local clients that will participate in the training, and selects a model to be trained based on the task while initializing the model. FL enables the use of data from different clients to train a model cooperatively, extending the number of training sets while guaranteeing that the data does not leave the local region.

Part 2. Parameters Protection. Combining differential privacy and homomorphic encryption, two ways to protect privacy, is used to change the gradient and encrypt it. This step is intended to increase the security of data.

Part 3. Privacy Budget Parameters Adaptive FL. The model is checked after noise is added, and the privacy budget parameters are dynamically changed to find a balance between protecting privacy and making the model effective.

Algorithm 1:PBPAFL

Initialization

for each epoch i = 1,2,$\cdots$,t do

    Distribute w_i

    for each client c_k,k=1,2,$\cdots$,n do

        Update the local gradients:

        $w_i^k \leftarrow w_i - \eta \nabla F(w_i, d_k)$

        Add noise:

        $g_i^k \leftarrow w_i^k + Gaussion(\epsilon_k)$

        Evaluation:

        if $acc_{g_i^k} \leq (1 - x\%) * acc_{w_i^k}$

        $\epsilon_k' \leftarrow \epsilon_k$

        $g_i^k \leftarrow w_i^k + Gaussion(\epsilon_k')$

        Homomorphic encryption:

        $\hat{g}_i^k \leftarrow g_i^k$

        return $\hat{g}_i^k$ to server

    Aggregation:

    $w_{i+1} = \sum_{k=1}^n \lambda_k \hat{g}_i^k$

    (return w_{i+1})

After the setup is complete, the iteration begins, and in the i-th round, the central server sends the initial model parameters w_i to each client c_k, $k \in (1, n)$. After training with its local data d_k, each local client obtains the model parameters w_i^k. The local client will choose the privacy budget parameter ϵ_k and add the corresponding noise to it. The parameter after adding noise is noted as g_i^k. Next, the noise-added model is evaluated and the result will be compared to those models without adding noise. If the expected requirement is not met (assuming the desired accuracy loss rate is $x\%$), ϵ_k must be selected again until it passes. After finding ϵ_k, all local clients will use homomorphically encrypt to ensure that the parameters can successfully withstand eavesdropping attacks, and then provide the encrypted parameters $\hat{g}_i^k$ to the central server.

The central server aggregates all received parameters to update the global model and sends the new parameter w_{i+1} to each local client. Then the next round of training will begin. Due to the twofold security provided by noise perturbation and homomorphic encryption, it has become almost unfeasible for eavesdropping attempts to revert the original data. In the meanwhile, we may dynamically modify the quantity of noise during model training to preserve its accuracy. Algorithm 1 describes the execution flow of our framework.

To address the issue of data privacy in FL, we provide a PBPAFL algorithm to deal with the risk of local training data leakage produced by eavesdropping attacks. Furthermore, since adding noise affects accuracy, we analyze the accuracy loss rate in each round in order to dynamically alter the amount of noise added. We will next illustrate the viability of our methodology through experiments.

3 Experimental Setup

In this section, we will first discuss the dataset utilized for the experiments as well as the data preparation portion. Then, we present the experimental framework in this study, including the face recognition algorithms, the privacy budget parameter setup, and the evaluation criteria. Finally, we describe the experimental procedures. We are interested in finding answers to the following questions via our experiments:

Q1. Why are noise and homomorphic encryption necessary?

Q2. What are the advantages of including noise in the parameter as opposed to the dataset?

Q3. How does adaptation reflect?

3.1 Experimental Dataset

In this research, the Labeled Faces in the Wild (LFW) dataset is utilized to validate the feasibility of our experiment. The LFW dataset is widely used for face recognition in uncontrolled scenarios, with a total of 13233 distinct face images, 5749 identity labels (virtual names), and 1680 individuals having two or more face shots. Each image is a jpeg with a resolution of 250×250. We exclude items that have more than 40 face images. Then we chose the remaining portion of items with close to 40 images and augmented them such that the final size of our experimental dataset is 30 individuals with 60 images each, for a total of 1800 face images.

We split the dataset into two portions of 80% and 20%, respectively, as training data for the local clients and a test set to evaluate the performance of the final model when training has been completed. In our research, we treat the independent identical distribution (IID) and the non-independent identical distribution (Non-IID) of training data as two distinct training sets. In the IID case, the training set data is distributed equally among the number of local clients. In the Non-IID case, we split the training data ratio into two categories, 4:3:1 and 4:3:2.

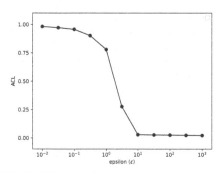

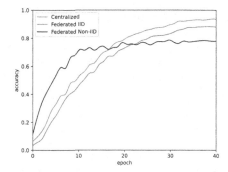

Fig. 2. The correspondence between ACL and ϵ

Fig. 3. Accuracy comparison of three cases without DP noise.

3.2 Model Evaluation Metrics

The objective of machine learning is to learn the characteristics of training data in order to predict the labels of input examples not included in training. To assess the efficacy of the training model, predictions are made on the test set (which was not utilized for training) and then compared to the actual labels. The accuracy of the training model is defined as the ratio of the set of predictions whose outcomes are consistent with the true labels ($n_{correct}$) to the set of true label holdouts ($n_{holdout}$) (ACC).

$$ACC = \frac{n_{correct}}{n_{holdout}} \tag{5}$$

Accuracy is a straightforward indicator of ML prediction performance. Other prevalent measures are AUC, precision, recall, and F-Score. Also, new criteria like model fairness and reducing the amount of work that needs to be done [11] may be needed to evaluate FL performance.

What we focus on is accuracy loss (ACL), which is measured as the performance loss when our privacy-preserving mechanism is applied to the FL process (m) in comparison to a ML model trained without applying the privacy mechanism ($\epsilon = inf$).

$$Accuracy\ Loss(ACL) = 1 - \frac{ACC(m, \epsilon)}{ACC(m, \epsilon = inf)} \tag{6}$$

3.3 Convolutional Neural Network

In this paper, we use a convolutional neural network (CNN) for training and apply the approach to the problem of face image classification. Convolutional neural networks are multilayer neural networks that consist of overlapping convolutional layers for the purpose of feature extraction and sampling layers for the purpose of feature processing. Face images in our training data are the input of CNN. After a number of "convolution" and "sampling" steps, a fully connected layer network is used to map the output to the target. The output is the result of classification after recognition.

In our experiments, the CNN model contains two convolutional (CONV) layers, ReLU, Softmax of 30 classes, and stochastic gradient descent (SGD) as the optimizer. Additionally, we use a cross-entropy loss function. The default settings of CNN used in this paper's experiments are listed in Table 1. We set the following parameters: learning rate = 0.0001, batch size = 64, epoch = 40, weight decay = 0.001, total number of images = 1800, and number of labels = 30.

Table 1. Default parameters for CNN.

Parameter	Default value	Description
learning rate	0.0001	step size for updating the weight matrix
batch size	64	number of samples in each epoch
epoch	40	training rounds
weight decay	0.001	adjust the effect of model complexity on the loss function

3.4 Privacy Budget Parameters and Evaluation Methodology

Privacy Budget Parameters. To avoid the model's accuracy severely degrading owing to excessive noise addition, we manage the amount of noise added by altering the privacy budget parameter. The privacy budget for adding noise is set as

$$\epsilon \in \{0.01, 0.05, 0.1, 0.5, 1, 5, 10, 50, 100, 500, 1000\}$$

We believe that the actual accuracy needed will vary depending on the situation. When the accuracy threshold value of a situation's requirement changes, the quantity of added noise has a direct impact on the final ACL. To solve this problem, local clients compare the value after adding noise to the value without noise in all rounds. If the result does not meet the requirement this time, local clients should adjust the amount of added noise until the requirement is met.

Evaluation Methodology. The training data will be duplicated k times. Perform k rounds of iterations, with k-1 subsets in each iteration serving as the training set and the remaining 1 subset serving as the validation set. Also, make sure that each subset is used as the validation set. We assess the appropriateness of the quantity of noise added by ACL. In each round, we write down the model's ACL values, and then we take the average of these k ACLs to get our final evaluative criterion.

3.5 Experimental Procedure

Our experimental procedure consists of six steps: 1) data preprocessing; 2) model initialization and training; 3) privacy budget selection and noise addition; 4) assessment and dynamic adjustment of; 5) homomorphic encryption of the parameters; and 6) aggregation of the encrypted parameters. First, we need to preprocess the LFW dataset and divide the face data into local clients according to the planned proportions. When the training is launched, the server delivers the training model to local clients. After training, local clients will add noise and evaluate the ACL. Depending on the evaluation results, local clients dynamically alter the chosen privacy budget. Then the modified parameters will be sent to the server after homomorphic encryption. The server gets all of the encrypted parameters, performs aggregation, and sends the updated model to the local clients so that the next round can begin.

When training is finished, the ACL of the final model will be evaluated on the test set. We set up several sets of comparison experiments to verify the effectiveness of our methodology. Moreover, we also performed experiments in the Non-IID case.

Remark

1) We utilize face image data for our research, which is a representative type of sensitive data. Face data is commonly dispersed across several organizations and difficult to integrate, presenting the problem of "data silos".
2) Our methodology primarily analyzes external eavesdropping threats and protects local clients' data from leaking. But we can't protect against every possible threat, like attacks that come from inside the system.
3) With Non-IID data, the final model generally performs badly. So we perform experiments for these cases and discuss the findings in Sect. 4.

4 Experimental Results

Our experiments are conducted on IID and Non-IID data to compare the proposed methodology to traditional data-centralized ML and FL. This section will explain the results of our experiments and answer the questions asked in Sect. 3.

4.1 Performance Analysis

We propose a strategy for controlling noise by modifying the value of ϵ to suit the real feasible demand (ACL value) without compromising privacy protection. Figure 2 shows the effect of our approach on face recognition, where the ACL depends on the value of ϵ. We notice that as ϵ decreases, the quantity of adding noise increases and the ACL value also rises.

Table 2 shows the related data for ACL- ϵ, demonstrating that the value of ϵ may be adjusted to accommodate different ACL values.

Figure 3 depicts the accuracy performance of the LFW dataset for FL and data-centralized ML, demonstrating that while FL may offer some protection, it still leads to a drop in accuracy. Figure 4 shows how our method performs in both the data-centralized and data-distributed cases. It can be seen that our method protects privacy better and has a lower ACL than data-centralized training.

IID vs Non-IID. Two cases are created in Non-IID for the experiments, with a data volume split of 4:3:1 and 4:3:2, respectively. The results are shown in Fig. 5. Our methodology differs in ACL by just 3% between the data-centralized case and the IID case, which indicates that it is possible to balance privacy protection and ACL. But in Non-IID case,

Table 2. The values corresponding to different ACLs.

ACL	ϵ
0.02	100
0.03	10
0.26	5
0.76	1
0.89	0.5

the ACL is slightly lower than in other cases, which may be attributable to the uneven data distribution.

4.2 Summary of Findings

We propose a method to prevent training data leakage during the FL process. After local clients complete training, noise will be added and homomorphic encryption will be applied. In addition, we propose an assessment process to modify the amount of noise added and maintain the model's ultimate result. In answering the questions raised in Sect. 3, we obtained the following conclusions through experimentation:

1) This methodology enables silo data to participate in the model training to improve model quality while providing better protection for training data, which is also suitable for other sensitive data.
2) Typically, there are three options for adding noise to safeguard data privacy: adding noise to the dataset, adding noise to the parameters (e.g., gradients), or adding noise to the model. By adding noise to the parameters, it can prevent participants in FL from accessing training data. Therefore, this step is effective and necessary in our proposed approach.
3) From the experimental results, it can be seen that the ACL is gradually lowered and eventually becomes stable, which demonstrates the method's adaptability to varying ACL demands. In addition, we conducted experiments to compare our method to available methods, both in the ideal IID setting and the more realistic Non-IID case, with conclusive findings demonstrating the superiority of our approach.

5 Discussion

Despite the unique advantages of FL, it still cannot solve all the data security problems in ML. Whether a model can be trained successfully is dependent on data quality, bias, and standard deviation [12]. Appropriate action is needed to counteract these effects. The heterogeneity of face data is a significant factor affecting the effectiveness of FL models. Face data is particularly diverse—not only because of the diversity of patterns, dimensions, and general features but also because of factors such as acquisition differences and local demographics, even within specific protocols. There are substantial distinctions in the characteristics of these several types of faces.

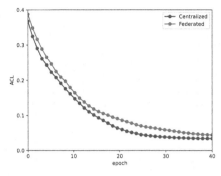
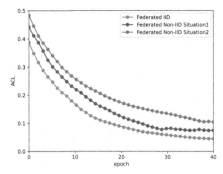

Fig. 4. ACL for FL and data-centralized ML.   **Fig. 5.** ACL of PBPAFL in three data distributed cases.

FL may aid in addressing certain causes of variance by diversifying data sources, but the non-independent identical distribution of data is a challenge for FL algorithms. Recently, a study [13] demonstrated that FL is still achievable even if data is not provided evenly across institutions. However, the effectiveness of the model is drastically reduced compared to that achieved by training with IID data. The results of our experiments demonstrate that our methodology is suitable for Non-IID data as well.

6 Conclusion

Various significant advances in facial recognition technology have been made possible by machine learning. Federated learning is a potential way to generate robust, accurate, and unbiased models since all ML methods considerably benefit from access to close to genuine data distributions.

The primary contribution of this paper is the proposal of a framework based on PBPAFL that balances model performance and privacy protection to effectively tackle problems associated with eavesdropping attacks on sensitive data in FL by making use of combining differential privacy and homomorphic encryption. So, it could make the face recognition industry around the world more effective and secure, and it could also lead to new research on FL.

The future research direction of this paper is to try whether the methodology is applicable in more scenarios. If possible, we will consider whether PBPAFL can be applied to general applications of machine learning.

Acknowledgment. We appreciate the informative remarks made by the anonymous reviewers of this work. This research is supported by the Special Fund for the Key Program of Science and Technology of Guangdong Province, China (Grant No. 2016B030305003).

References

1. Colesky, M., Demetzou, K., Fritsch, L., Herold, S.: Helping software architects familiarize with the general data protection regulation. In: 2019 IEEE International Conference on Software Architecture Companion (ICSA-C), pp. 226–229. IEEE, United States (2019)
2. Kim, J., Ha, H., Chun, B.G., Yoon, S., Cha, S.K.: Collaborative analytics for data silos. In: 2016 IEEE 32nd International Conference on Data Engineering (ICDE), pp. 743–754. IEEE, United States (2016)
3. Ahmed, K.M., Imteaj, A., Amini, M.H.: Federated deep learning for heterogeneous edge computing. In: 2021 20th IEEE International Conference on Machine Learning and Applications (ICMLA), pp. 1146–1152. IEEE, United States (2021)
4. Song, C., Ristenpart, T., Shmatikov, V.: Machine learning models that remember too much. In: Proceedings of the 2017 ACM SIGSAC Conference on computer and communications security, pp. 587–601. ACM, United States (2017)
5. Zhu, L., Liu, Z., Han, S.: Deep leakage from gradients. Ion: Advances in Neural Information Processing Systems, vol. 32. NeurIPS, Vancouver (2019)
6. Dwork, C.: Differential privacy: a survey of results. In: Agrawal, M., Du, D., Duan, Z., Li, A. (eds.) TAMC 2008. LNCS, vol. 4978, pp. 1–19. Springer, Heidelberg (2008). https://doi.org/10.1007/978-3-540-79228-4_1
7. Bayardo, R.J., Agrawal, R.: Data privacy through optimal k-anonymization. In: 21st International Conference on Data Engineering (ICDE 2005), pp. 217–228. IEEE, United States (2005)
8. Gentry, C.: Computing arbitrary functions of encrypted data. Commun. ACM **53**, 97–105 (2010)
9. Gentry, C., Halevi, S.: Implementing gentry's fully-homomorphic encryption scheme. In: Paterson, K.G. (ed.) Advances in Cryptology – EUROCRYPT 2011. EUROCRYPT 2011. Lecture Notes in Computer Science, vol. 6632. Springer, Heidelberg (2011). https://doi.org/10.1007/978-3-642-20465-4_9
10. Acar, A., Aksu, H., Uluagac, A.S., Conti, M.: A survey on homomorphic encryption schemes: theory and implementation. ACM Comput. Surv. (CSUR) **51**(4), 1–35 (2018)
11. Wang, F., Casalino, L.P., Khullar, D.: Deep learning in medicine—promise, progress, and challenges. JAMA Intern. Med. **179**(3), 293–294 (2019)
12. Yaji, S., Bangera, K., Neelima, B.: Privacy preserving in blockchain based on partial homomorphic encryption system for AI applications. In: 2018 IEEE 25th International Conference on High Performance Computing Workshops (HiPCW), pp. 81–85. IEEE, United States (2018)
13. Li, X., Gu, Y., Dvornek, N., Staib, L.H., Ventola, P., Duncan, J.S.: Multi-site fMRI analysis using privacy-preserving federated learning and domain adaptation: ABIDE results. Med. Image Anal. **65**, 101765 (2020)

Cyber Crime Undermines Data Privacy Efforts – On the Balance Between Data Privacy and Security

Michael Mundt[1]([✉])(iD) and Harald Baier[2](iD)

[1] Esri Deutschland GmbH, Bonn, Germany
m.mundt@esri.de
[2] Bundeswehr University - RI CODE Munich, Munich, Germany
harald.baier@unibw.de
https://www.esri.de, https://www.unibw.de/digfor

Abstract. The General Data Protection Regulation (GDPR) was put into effect in the European Union on 25th May 2018. GDPR aims to ensure the protection of personal data from individuals and the free movement of this personal data. Data privacy regulations are also currently being discussed nationwide in the United States of America and other countries. Regular guidelines of the European data protection board (edpb) support the technical GDPR implementation. However, cyber aggressors are increasingly succeeding in penetrating IT systems, e.g., by combining traditional ransomware techniques with data exfiltration. In this paper we address the trade-off between data protection as presumably regulated by the GDPR and the security implications of a hard and fast privacy enforcement. We argue that a too strict interpretation of the rules of data protection in the wrong place can even provoke the very reverse of data protection. The origin of our examination is to classify data in two GDPR relevant categories *personal data* (e.g., personal files of customers and company personal) and *IT operational data* (e.g. log files, IP addresses, NetFlow data), respectively. We then give a plea to strictly protect data of the first category and to handle the GDPR pragmatically with respect to the second one. To support our position we consider sample popular network protocols and show that it is low-threshold to exploit these protocols for data exfiltration, while the defender is only able to detect the attack on base of IT operational data. We hence emphasize the need for a new paradigm of risk assessment.

Keywords: Cyber Threat Intelligence · Data Breach · Regulatory Compliance · Insider Threat Management · Data Security and Privacy

1 Introduction

The objective of the General Data Protection Regulation (GDPR [19, Article 1]) is the protection of natural persons with regard to the processing of personal

S. Goel et al. (Eds.): ICDF2C 2022, LNICST 508, pp. 417–434, 2023.
https://doi.org/10.1007/978-3-031-36574-4_25

data and rules relating to the free movement of data. However, today's cyber criminals stand in the way of these venerable goals, because they intend to smuggle out valuable data and then blackmail the victims by publishing stolen data or simply sell the data on one of the numerous trading platforms, e.g., on the darknet [6]. In order to ensure protection, the GDPR [19, Article 5] requires that processing is minimized to a necessary minimum and that worthy data is deleted immediately after processing. The data must only be processed for a specific purpose and, in general, the data must be stored in a form that allows the data subjects to only be identified as long as necessary for the processing purpose.

Personal data, that is in particular worthy for protection, is defined in a general manner [19, Article 4(1)]. It is defined as "any information relating to an identified or identifiable natural person ('data subject'); an identifiable natural person is one who can be identified, directly or indirectly, in particular by reference to an identifier such as a name, an identification number, location data, an online identifier or to one or more factors specific to the physical, physiological, genetic, mental, economic, cultural or social identity of that natural person". The question arises as to how the term "identifiable" is to be interpreted in concrete terms. Recital 26 attempts to remedy this: "[...] To determine whether a natural person is identifiable, account should be taken of all the means reasonably likely to be used, such as singling out, either by the controller or by another person to identify the natural person directly or indirectly". However, again the phrase "reasonably likely to be used" opens up room for interpretation when considering what is the data to focus protection measures on and when it comes to finding the right way to deal with data as it produced in all Open System Interconnection (OSI) [22] layers of an IT system such as log files and IP addresses.

In this paper we address the trade-off between data protection as presumably regulated by the GDPR and the security implications of a hard and fast privacy enforcement. We argue that a too strict interpretation of the rules of data protection in the wrong place can even provoke the very reverse of data protection. The origin of our examination is to classify data in two GDPR relevant categories *personal data* (e.g., personal files of customers and company personal) and *IT operational data* (e.g. log files, IP addresses, NetFlow data), respectively. While keeping the protection level of the first class of data, our main goal is to find a more balanced risk assessment view on the second data class. To the best of our knowledge such a *balance discussion* has not yet started.

Our use case to demonstrate the trade-off with respect to IT operational data is *data exfiltration*. We are first researching scientific dossiers on its threat landscape and contemporary technologies used for data exfiltration to adopt a first, simple classification scheme to categorize data exfiltration methods. In the next step, we identify relevant articles and considerations of the GDPR, which pursue the goal of protecting personal data. In addition, we evaluate the current guidelines of the European data protection board (edpb) [7] regarding the correct behavior and notification in the event of a data breach. In doing so, we select relevant examples of the policy for our further investigation.

In order to discuss the balanced view on IT operational data, we consider sample widespread network protocols. As baseline of today's attack vectors we make use of the MITRE ATT&CK Framework [9] to exploit conventional network protocols. Our discussion incorporates a sample medium-sized company to determine which network protocols are mostly used on a normal work day. We show the low-threshold potential for misuse of the selected protocols by means of a proof of concept implementation and stress the importance of a more balanced privacy view on IT operational data to defend the attack.

Based on our sample use case we present our recommendations to implement an improved risk assessment for the protection of personal data and to take the security of processing data into account more consciously. The work pursues the concept of concentrating on the highly sensitive personal data and leaving the defender with the database that is necessary to thwart the considered attack vectors in good time.

The rest of the paper is organized as follows: Sect. 2 reviews related work in the scope of privacy and data exfiltration followed by a discussion of relevant articles of the GDPR for our work in Sect. 3. Next we present our sample use case and our practical discussion of the GDPR in the scope of 'data exfiltration' in Sect. 4 followed by our critical reflection of our results in Sect. 5. Section 6 concludes with the summary and an outlook for future efforts.

2   Related Work

In this section we review related work in the scope of our work. We first turn to related work in the context of GDPR in Sect. 2.1 followed by related work of IT operational data in our technical context of a data breach in Sect. 2.2.

2.1   Data Protection Related Work

A similar discussion of data categorization and a balanced view on data protection is sparse, however, a balancing consideration of privacy and security requirements due to Pope et al. [20] is available as preprint. The draft considers the counteracting requirements of privacy and accountability applied to identity management. Thus indicating the existence of an intrinsic tension between IT operations and data protection. Our work looks at this area of tension in greater detail and derives solutions for differentiating sensitive data in the sense of the General Data Protection Regulation during the operation of an IT process. Our work is much broader in scope, considering interactions with known attack vectors. We additionally consider external influences.

The notion of risks, as it is enshrined in the GDPR, is discussed in Gellert's paper [28]. He points out that in particular Art. 35 provides the obligation to carry out data protection impact assessments (DPIAs). However, this need is not yet linked to the attack vectors, i.e. actual cyber procedures. Our work focuses on the needs arising from known cyber attack vectors. We derive a solution approach, based on a comprehensive risk analysis, to classify accruing data of the IT system as *IT operational data* and to treat it separately.

Furthermore some work in the scope of data protection implication assessment is available. For instance Bieker et al. [5] examines the new provisions of GDPR in detail and propose an adaptive process to suit the controller's needs. A balanced view on categories of personal data is not addressed by Bieker's process, though. We are introducing a more differentiated approach to the assessment of implications. Considering the interaction with cyber attack vectors yields important insights in the course of our work. Finally, we introduce the categories *personal data* and *IT operational data*. On this basis, we enable a more differentiated risk analysis and open up new possibilities for handling processed data without violating the requirements of the GDPR.

2.2 Data Exfiltration Related Work

Numerous considerations of technologies used for data exfiltration are available. A wide range of research has already been conducted in this domain in previous elaborations. Protective measures such as the simulation of current methods for data exfiltration are the subject of current work [18]. Here are a few more of the most recent publications. Covert drainage channels are very dangerous, as the victim often does not notice the process immediately. In this example, the exploitation of the properties of the Transmission Control Protocol (TCP) is examined in order to derive code of valuable data via the sequence number that can be deciphered on the receiver side [12]. Covert channels have also been detected between cloud instances in spite of existing countermeasures. The memory bus is exploited. The sender exists in the victim's environment as a trojan or any form of malicious program. The receiver exists in the attacker's environment. Both communicating entities execute without privileges. A rogue transmission channel is established [4, pp. 332,335]. Covert channels have also been demonstrated for Industry Control Systems (ICS). The basic idea is to log authentic ICS network data in normal operations for longer period and to alter this data afterwards with steganographic algorithm; valuable data is so hidden in network traffic by utilizing of various characteristics of network protocols [27]. Finally, a method is used here to exfiltrate sensitive data via the domain name service (DNS). Firewalls are typically configured to allow all packets on User Datagram Protocol (UDP) port 53. DNS is a mission critical service. Valuable data is encoded and hidden in the DNS query. DNS channels may be misused for stealing valuable and sensitive data [27]. It is not enough for us to prove only the abuse potential of individual technical protocols. We go two steps further in our work and put the misuse for data exfiltration into context with the goals of data protection and the currently known attack vectors of advanced cyber attackers. The technical misuse for data theft is part of an attack vector and this counteracts the goals of data protection. From this context, we derive concrete approaches to mitigate the risk for data protection.

Next, some papers are considered that evaluate different approaches to data exfiltration in a specific context. First, the Data Loss Prevention (DLP) System context is considered. Eight different technologies werde tested to determine whether relevant data could be diverted despite a DLP solution in place: Encrypting, compressing, changing file extension, renaming, splitting archives, deleting magic number of the files using Winhex (f.e. jpg starts with hexcode FF D8 FF and ends with FF D9) [15]. The next document tries to make a first classification of methods. For this purpose, a small selection of methods is examined. Three classes are proposed: content-based, header-based, meta-based. This is certainly not a complete classification, but it shows a way to prioritize and help IT experts to bring the issue of data exfiltration to the forefront of cybersecurity planning and actions within business [16, pp. 443,447]. Our work is not about classifying the various technical methods for data exfiltration. Rather, we are pursuing the path of finding a sensible classification for the data processed in an IT-system, so that a differentiated risk analysis and thus a carefully graded handling of the data is made possible.

Looking for more in-depth approaches to classification in the context of data exfiltration, the next paper offers an interesting approach. Data exfiltration countermeasures are classified in three major classes: preventive, detective, investigative. Furthermore, numerous countermeasures are assigned. Package inspection and anomaly based, for example are assigned to the detective class, each further subdivided into individual measures. Known channel inspection here is an example in the package inspection sub-class [1, Chapt. 5.1]. In addition, an attempt is also made here to classify the various methods of data exfiltration. This is more aggregated compared to the previous paper. The "Network" and "Physical" classes are executed and examples are provided for each [1, Chapt. 4.1]. In comparison, the MITRE ATT&CK Framework offers 9 techniques for data exfiltration within the enterprise matrix, i.e. a more differentiated subdivision in order to map them to the different attack vectors [9,10]. This paper concludes by recognizing that data exfiltration is a serious and ongoing issue in the field of information security and that the existence and emergence of such attack vectors make the countermeasures critical for an organisation's security [1, Chapt. 8]. In our work, we take up the quintessence of these works and design a new approach for a better differentiation of the risk and the inclusion of known cyber threats.

Our related work concludes with an extensive study of today's ransomware attacks. Here the trend is expressed that today's ransomware no longer blackmails the users with loss of access to data, but instead with a potential data leak of sensitive data [26, 197:7]. In addition, the ransomware is classified into three classes "detection", "defense", "prevention". This can be mapped to the previously used classification of methods for data exfiltration. This found the connection between ransomware and data exfiltration, which we use to compare the requirements of the GDPR and its corresponding guidelines [26, 197:11]. Our work is highly topical. The use of ransomware is currently a very big risk. Valuable data is being stolen more and more often in combination with ransomware, and we analyze exactly this danger with a view to the objectives of the GDPR.

Ultimately, our solution approach means potentially better protection for data and the freedom of natural persons within the meaning of the GDPR.

3 Relevant Articles of GDPR and Associated Guidelines

We first identify in Sect. 3.1 articles of the GDPR, which are relevant for our categorization of personal and IT operational data, respectively. We then review the edpb guidelines in Sect. 3.2 as a basis for our balanced risk assessment proposal.

3.1 Relevant Articles of GDPR

Arguably the most prominent article on data security in the GDPR is article 32 [19, Article 32]: security of processing. It states that suitable technical and organizational measures must be taken to ensure an appropriate level of protection. Therefore, state of the art technology, cost of implementation, nature, scope purpose of processing have to be taken into account. The risk of varying likelyhood and severity for the rights and freedoms of natural persons is incorporated into the design of the technical and organizational measures. Under the letters (a) to (d), methods such as encryption and pseudonymization as well as the protection goals of confidentiality, integrity, availability and resilience of processing systems and named services are listed. Furthermore, it then reads in article 32 2. that assessing the risk in particular the risk from accidental or unlawful destruction, loss, alteration and unauthorized disclosure shall be taken into account. The definition is directly related to the topic of data exfiltration that we are investigating. The process of data exfiltration results in the condition of unauthorized disclosure.

Recital 49 [19, Recital 49] further describes the measures to ensure security in processing by saying that personal data is processed to the extent strictly necessary and proportionate for the purposes of ensuring network and information security, i.e. the ability of a network or system to resist, at a given level of confidence, accidental events or unlawful or malicious actions that compromise the availability, authenticity, integrity and confidentiality of stored or transmitted personal data.

In principle, article 5 of the GDPR [19, Article 5] requires that personal (sensitive) data is only processed where the processing is necessary, is relevant to the attribution of the processing purpose and is lawful. Particularly interesting is also the requirement of the literal (e) that the identification of the data subject should only be possible for as long as it is necessary for the purposes for which it is processed. A tension is already emerging here. Exactly at the moment when data such as IP addresses or other traffic data are considered personal data, they are to be deleted after processing and are no longer available for analysis of the system or the services in long term. It will need to be considered how this affects data exfiltration countermeasures.

3.2   edpb Guidelines 2021/01 Version 2.0

Article 70 literal (d) [19, Article 70 (d)] enables the European data protection board (edpb) to issue guidelines in order to ensure the consistent application of the GDPR. Following this intention, these guidelines often provide examples explaining the correct implementation of the requirement stemming from the articles of the GDPR. To date, numerous guidelines have been issued. These are made available on the internet on the edpb websites[1]. We consider here the guidelines 01/2021 on examples regarding personal data breach notification. First, version 1.0 [7] of this guidance is considered. In this guideline, the definition of a data breach [19, Article 4 (12)] is first taken up. It is expressly pointed out that the consequences of data breach cannot be reversed perse and that preventive measures have to be taken in order to prevent a data breach [7, p. 6]. Examples are given in the following chapters 2–7. Some of these examples consider data breach due to accidental or intentional leaking of data. Chapter 3 specifically reports data exfiltration attacks.

Table 1. Examples regarding data breach notification with data exfiltration

Case No	Title
04	Ransomware without backup and with exfiltration
05	Exfiltration of job application data from a website
06	Exfiltration of hashed password from a website
07	Credential stuffing attack on a banking website
08	Exfiltration of business data by a former employee
17	Identity Theft
18	E-Mail exfiltration

Table 1 lists all sample cases regarding data exfiltration. We further explore the cases number 4 and number 18 in Table 1. The attacker has penetrated the victim system by abusing well-known protocols or functionality of the victim system. Advisable countermeasures are identified within each case study. For instance the edpb recommends for the case number 04 the forwarding or replicating of all logs to a central log server as one of these countermeasures. The importance of the availability of log files is already recognized at this point

4   Sample Attack Vectors for Balancing GDPR in Case of Data Exfiltration

This section shows for the sample use case of a potential data exfiltration in a small or medium sized company that IT operational data is essential to defend the data breach and hence to protect the actual personal data.

---

[1] https://edpb.europa.eu/our-work-tools/our-documents/publication-type/ guidelines_de.

First, it's important to understand how a skilled attack is executed. For this purpose, we consider the MITRE ATT&CK Framework [9, 10], in whose database the assessments of professional cyber analysts on worldwide incidents are incorporated. Our considerations focus on the enterprise matrix without distinguishing between individual platforms such as Windows, Linux containers, Cloud, etc. The attack vector for an enterprise is broken down into 14 phases (Fig. 1) that occur sequentially [11].

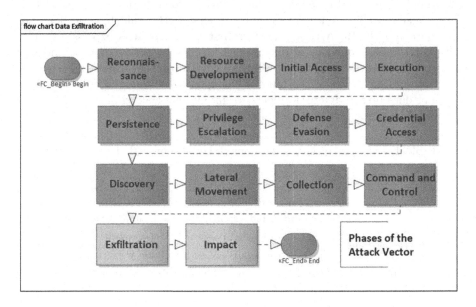

Fig. 1. MITRE ATT&CK Framework Matrix Enterprise

The attack vector is initiated by reconnaissance. Subsequently the attacker prepares himself in the resource development phase. The phase that is intended for initial access to the target system follows. At this point, the attacker is able to penetrate the victim's system. The next two phases, execution and persistence, are used to solidify access to the victim system. Now the attacker strengthen his position, gains rights on the system, disables defenses and gains access to credentials. The phases discovery, lateral movement and collection now serve to get an overview of valuable data and to collect them. Collecting can be understood, for example, as reading out data from information repositories. The attacker is now prepared. The final orders are issued via a command and control infrastructure, often Cobalt Strike, and then the data is exfiltrated. In the last phase, the effect is to be determined. If sensitive data is stolen, this will certainly have serious consequences.

We consider the phase Exfiltration in more detail. Here are two techniques of particular interest: 1) Exfiltration over alternative protocols 2) Exfiltration over web service. Item 1) indicates the abuse of protocols FTP, SMTP, https,

DNS, SMB. Item 2) indicates that websites are being exploited using SSL/TLS encrypted communication. Using the MITRE ATT&CK Framework, the connection between the exploitation of these protocols for data exfiltration and experienced groups (APT) can now be indicated, their attack targets tracked and the threat to one's own company better assessed.

In order to fully understand these possibilities, it is still important to understand the period over which data can be exfiltrated. Sensitive data can be partitioned and exfiltrated in small doses spread over time using one or more of the protocols mentioned. There are statistics on the length of time attackers spend unnoticed in the victim's IT system. Such a statistic for the years 2014 to 2019 can be seen in Fig. 2. The data for the last years 2020–2022 differ greatly.

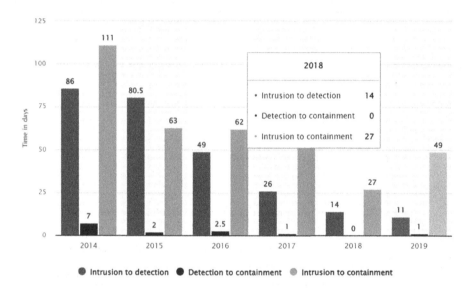

Fig. 2. Median time between intrusion and containment in industry [23]

The statistics were prepared for industrially used IT systems. These systems can be assumed to be well protected. Nevertheless, in 2019 a full 49 d passed before an intruder was detected and contained. Of course, not the entire period is used for dumping data. As previously discussed, the attack vector spans multiple phases. Nevertheless, it must be assumed that there is sufficient time to divert valuable data over days, weeks or even month. In less well-protected systems, the period of time before the attacker is discovered is likely to be much longer. Forbes is writing in 2021: "[...] Industry surveys over the years have shown dwell time ranging from a (sadly rare) best case of a couple of minutes to a worst case of hundreds of days. The average dwell time - depending on region, industry and who is generating the report - has varied widely" [17]. Mandiant, on the other hand, gives the global median dwell time with 21 d for 2022 much shorter then for the following years [21, p. 94].

4.1 Protocol Use Pattern Analysis

In order to get a better understanding of which protocols are used in a normal operation of a company, daily measurements are conducted at a medium-sized company. The results show in an aggregated form the 10 most commonly used network protocols for data transmission from within the company to outside or vice versa. The measurements are conducted on the firewalls of the gateway for the duration of one working day in the period from 10 a.m. to 4 p.m.

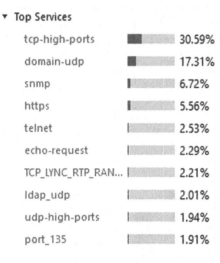

Fig. 3. Top ten ports used during a work day in an enterprise

It can be seen in Fig. 3 that TCP-based protocols in the port range of registered ports between 1014–49151 account for about a third. This is not surprising, since frequently used applications in the cloud, such as Drop Box and others, are located in this port compartment. This is followed by two port areas with domain-udp and snmp, which play an important role in the operation of an IT-network. The utility of the simple network management protocol (snmp) is that it allows information about networked devices to be collected across a variety of hardware and software types in a standardized way. IT-administrators very often utilize this protocol for network management purposes. The other protocol is most likely used to query the Domain Name Service (DNS). Finally the https protocol, which is used to browse websites, follows. Nowadays, websites are mostly accessed via the https protocol. The protocol https establishes a secure and encrypting connection by using the Transport Layer Security (TLS). Most often, the protocol is bound on TCP instead of UDP. The Fig. 3 shows the usage of the https protocol bound on TCP. The predecessor protocol http without encryption is hardly used anymore.

Figure 4 confirms this assessment. The Figure shows which protocols are mostly used by users. Again the top 10 protocols are displayed. The DNS service is requested most frequently, followed by the https protocol for accessing and

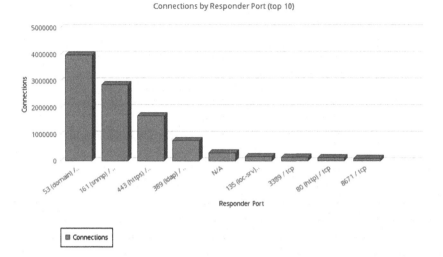

Fig. 4. Top ten services used during a work day in an enterprise

using websites. It's very understandable to see that DNS and https or, a few layer down within the OSI Model, TCP and UDP are used frequently. Most software applications in use today communicate with these protocols. From the perspective of an intruder who wants to exfiltrate data unnoticed, these commonly used protocols offer a good opportunity to hide individual data exfiltration messages in the noise floor.

4.2 Misuse of HTTP/2 Protocol as One Example of Many

The HTTP/2 protocol is the further development of the HTTP protocol. The Internet Engineering Task Force (IETF) [14] is specifying the HTTP/2 protocol. Therefore, the IETF applies the Request for Comments (RFC) procedure [2]. The new protocol brings performance benefits [13]. At the core of the new protocol is a binary framing layer. The HTTP messages are encapsulated in the protocol and then transmitted between client and server. We introduce important HTTP/2 terminology in Table 2.

HTTP/2 is only used for encrypted connections (Transport Layer Security (TLS) 1.2 or higher). The encryption method used employs digital certificates. A connection is established as follows: first of all, the protocol performs the TCP SYN-ACK handshake. Thereupon the TLS handshake follows.

Client and server exchange SSL certificates, cipher suite requirements and randomly generated data for creating session keys [8]. This procedure is shown in Fig. 5. Wireshark software was used to record the individual steps of the protocol. The individual steps are visualized by the software used. In addition, Wireshark offers the functionality to search through each individual entry afterwards in deep detail, up to the hex code analysis. These steps mark the connection

Table 2. HTTP/2 important terminology

Term	Description
Stream	Sequence of frames mapping to a logical request or response message
Frame	Smallest unit in HTTP/2 communication, each containing a frame header which identifies the stream to which the frame belongs to
Message	A complete sequence of frames that map to a logical request or response message

setup between transmitter and receiver. First, the prerequisites for encrypted transmission are created. Having the connection established, client and server exchange binary frames. All frames consist of a common 9-byte header (length of the frame), type, a bit field for flags, and a 31-bit stream identifier. Additionally, a 24-bit length field allows each single frame to carry up bytes of data as frame payload. The protocol is capable of multiplexing. Multiple streams can be transmitted over one connection. For each stream, the HEADERS frame (Fig. 6) is transmitted first, followed by the DATA frames. Various scripting and programming languages provide libraries to use the features and functions of the HTTP/2 protocol. The interpreted, higher-level programming language Python provides various libraries with an implementation of the protocol.

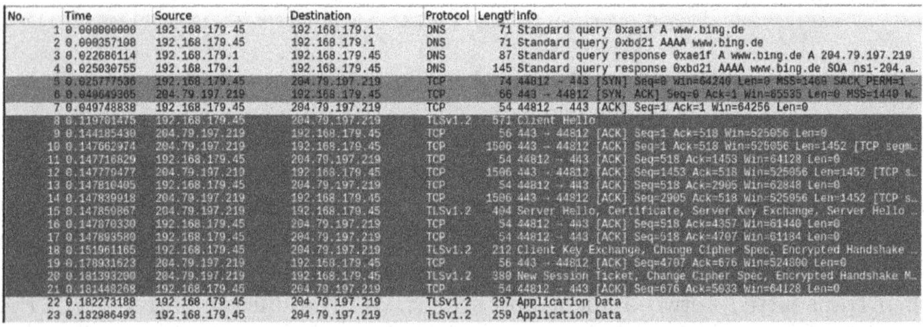

Fig. 5. Wireshark recording from using HTTP/2 protocol

For this we use the "hyper" library [3] to implement an HTTP/2 client. This is just one library among many others that can be used to execute the HTTP/2 protocol. We chose this library because we want to use the Python scripting language and the implementation is comparatively easy using this library. The HTTP/2 client integrates into the Python requests library. The entire connection establishment is carried out via mounting of the HTTP20Adapter to the current session. The data is then send to the server using the POST method of the HTTP/2 protocol. In this case it is not necessary to encrypt the data for exfiltration. This happens anyway via the HTTPS connection between client and server. The defender of the IT victim system cannot inspect this communication due to the encryption.

Bit	+0..7	+8..15	+16..23	+24..31
0	Length			Type
32	Flags			
40	R	Stream Identifier		
...	Frame Payload			

Fig. 6. Nine byte frame header [13]

The wireshark recording in Fig. 7 clearly shows the encrypted transmission of data over the HTTP/2 - HTTPS connection. This transfer does not require higher privileges on the victims system. In this manner we can show that valuable data may be exfiltrated using the HTTP/2 protocol. The excerpts of the Wireshark recording are suitable for deepening our solution. First, we have seen the establishment of the connection and the negotiation of the encryption. We assign this data to the category *IT operational data*. This data contains potentially Personal Identifiable Information (PII) as defined by GDPR. IP and MAC addresses are included. These are declared as PII. More data to come: the connection is established via a process in the IT-system that is executed under a user ID. Data such as the call of the process, the user ID, the time of execution, etc. are inevitably recorded in the IT system. In addition, there are the calls to system functions such as reading data files. This data is also written to log files, mostly managed automatically by the IT system. Sophisticated attackers might use running processes, induce a thread, allocate memory, and copy shellcode into it, which then performs the data exfiltration. Every action leaves digital traces (data) in the IT system. The Wireshark extract offers a first insight into this fact (Fig. 5).

We recommend categorizing this data as *IT operational data* and valuing their particular value for detecting cyber attack vectors in the risk assessment. To explain in more depth the value of this data for detecting attacks, we make an example using the MITRE ATT&CK framework. We pick up a Technique noted in it: Scheduled Transfer[2]. This Technique is used to achieve data exfiltration. To be able to detect the use of this Technique, among other things, the monitoring of network traffic flow[3] and monitoring the creation of network connections[4]

---

[2] https://attack.mitre.org/techniques/T1029/.

[3] https://attack.mitre.org/datasources/DS0029/#Network%20Traffic%20Flow.

[4] https://attack.mitre.org/datasources/DS0029/#Network%20Connection %20Creation.

are proposed. Precisely at this point our approach is strengthened. If the *IT operational data* is deleted too early, this Technique and thus the attack vector can no longer be detected and a complete clarification in retrospect is denied.

No.	Time	Source	Destination	Protocol	Length Info
15	0.147859867	204.79.197.219	192.168.179.45	TLSv1.2	404 Server Hello, Certificate, Server Key Exchange, Server Hello …
16	0.147870330	192.168.179.45	204.79.197.219	TCP	54 44812 → 443 [ACK] Seq=518 Ack=4357 Win=61440 Len=0
17	0.147893580	192.168.179.45	204.79.197.219	TCP	54 44812 → 443 [ACK] Seq=518 Ack=4707 Win=61184 Len=0
18	0.151961165	192.168.179.45	204.79.197.219	TLSv1.2	212 Client Key Exchange, Change Cipher Spec, Encrypted Handshake …
19	0.178931623	204.79.197.219	192.168.179.45	TCP	56 443 → 44812 [ACK] Seq=4707 Ack=676 Win=524800 Len=0
20	0.181393200	204.79.197.219	192.168.179.45	TLSv1.2	380 New Session Ticket, Change Cipher Spec, Encrypted Handshake M…
21	0.181448268	192.168.179.45	204.79.197.219	TCP	54 44812 → 443 [ACK] Seq=676 Ack=5033 Win=64128 Len=0
22	0.182273168	192.168.179.45	204.79.197.219	TLSv1.2	297 Application Data
23	0.182986493	192.168.179.45	204.79.197.219	TLSv1.2	259 Application Data

▸ Frame 22: 297 bytes on wire (2376 bits), 297 bytes captured (2376 bits) on interface wlp3s0, id 0
▸ Ethernet II, Src: LiteonTe_e3:38:12 (74:e5:43:e3:38:12), Dst: AVM_ef:c3:26 (34:31:c4:ef:c3:26)
▸ Internet Protocol Version 4, Src: 192.168.179.45, Dst: 204.79.197.219
▸ Transmission Control Protocol, Src Port: 44812, Dst Port: 443, Seq: 676, Ack: 5033, Len: 243
▸ Transport Layer Security
  ▾ TLSv1.2 Record Layer: Application Data Protocol: http-over-tls
     Content Type: Application Data (23)
     Version: TLS 1.2 (0x0303)
     Length: 238
     Encrypted Application Data: afaebb505f726be50e567b1a79e9f6df8ad3d673931445ef…

Fig. 7. Wireshark recording from encrypted sending of data

Also, the original sensitive data about persons (PII) are processed and are reflected in the Wireshark extract (Fig. 7). At this point, however, this data is already encrypted. This data was previously read from files and encrypted by a process. We recommend that you categorize this original data as *personal data*, protect it as much as possible and delete it as soon as possible. Our categorization in *personal data* and *IT operational data* allows to draw different conclusions in the risk analysis and to manage the data differently without lowering the level of protection of personal data. On the contrary, the level of protection is increased. If PII is stolen and encrypted by cyber-attackers, the guarantee of protection and free flow of information as required by the GDPR can no longer be assured with own strength. Our approach helps to avoid this helpless situation.

4.3 Malicious Reconfiguration of an E-Mail Client

Selected case No. 18 deals with the exfiltration of data via e-mails. Unlike in case No 4 no technical protocols are exploited here. Instead, it is described how e-mail clients used were covertly reconfigured. The configuration happens in such a way that all messages are filtered according to certain criteria and then automatically forwarded to an external e-mail address including any attachments. The attacker can easily acquire knowledge of the configuration via the public support pages of the respective manufacturers [25]. In addition, documentation for all commercial products is openly available online [24]. After the privilege escalation phase of the attack vector, but at latest after the evasion of the defense measures and access to credentials, the attacker is able to carry out these configurations [11]. This procedure can be imagined especially in the case of an insider. The reconfiguration of the e-mail client usually requires higher privileges on the victim's IT system.

In order to be able to track these changes to the configuration afterwards, it is necessary to keep a log file in which each change is saved. Ideally, the system monitors configuration changes of the account in a way, that malicious activities are recognized immediately or at least in case of an investigation. Therefore, the system logs changes of account configuration in date and time. We recommend providing this information to the defense attorney. In order that the information is not deleted immediately after too short a period, we recommend that this data be categorized as *IT operational data.*

5   Balancing GDPR Requirements Against the Hazards

In Sect. 4 we show the exploitation of common IT network protocols for data exfiltration by misusing their technical possibilities. The criminal exfiltration of personal data obviously contradicts the protection goal of the integrity of this data, as formulated in article 5 [19, Article 5 Chap. 1.f.], in article 32 [19, Article 32 Chap. 1.b.], as well as the superior goal of protecting natural persons and their personal data [19, Article 1]. The selection, implementation and regular review of the technical and organizational measures must be checked accordingly in order to contain the threat.

In doing so, it is not sufficient to look isolated at the risk of data exfiltration. The GDPR requires careful risk assessment to ensure a level of security appropriate to the risk [19, Article 32 Chap. 1.]. The entire attack vector must be included in the risk assessment and hence all attack vector tactics must be included in the analysis to meet the threats. The analysis must be performed backwards and forward-looking, over the entire time which might even be longer than a year. Sometimes data theft only becomes known when the personal data concerned is sold on marketplaces on the darknet or confiscated by law enforcement. If the *IT operational data* is already deleted, there will be no way to clarify the incident. The vulnerability used at the time remains undetected.

In the different phases of the attack, digital traces are left behind, which can be reflected in log files, among other data sources. The use of network protocols must be checked at least on a random basis (flow data). Log usage times and patterns need to be analysed for suspicious traces. Log data must be examined to determine whether a mechanical, automated attack on e.g. firewalls or internal services has taken place. In the "Defense Evasion" tactic, the attacker tries to switch off protective measures such as a virus scanner. Here, too, traces are left behind which must now be found as evidence. In the Tactic "Collection" data is collected. Database requests, copying operations or downloads from company core services leave traces here. Repeated access to data sources in the company's core systems should be monitored and critically questioned. Otherwise, it is very likely that the use of these protocols will only be determined retrospectively when the high-quality data has already been dumped.

This has an impact on the consideration of the requirement in article 5 [19, Article 5 Chap. 1.e.] which allows personal data to be kept for as long as it is for statistical purposes in accordance with article 89(1) as subject to implementation of the appropriate technical and organisational measures required by GDPR in order to safeguard the rights and freedoms of the data subject ('storage limitation'). Storage limitations must be carefully considered and not be designed to be shorter than the full duration of the attack vectors. Better longer. This consideration affects data of our category *IT operational data* such as logfiles and IP-addresses within. Early deletion or too excessive anonymisation of data in this category may jeopardise the full assessment of the risk to which the personal data is or has been exposed during processing. It becomes clear that the category of *IT operational data* is essential to combat the identified threats vectors. The data of this category must be available to the defender in sufficient time and detail, even though there is personal data within. Deletion immediately after processing is no longer an option due to the risks. The situation is different with the first category of *personal data*. Anonymization during processing and deletion after processing must be implemented as quickly as possible. Concentrating on this means sustainable data protection through the beneficial interaction with data security.

6   Conclusion and Future Work

In order to achieve the goals of the GDPR a risk assessment must take place for the processing of personal data. The dangers emanating from an attack vector of experienced cyber attackers must be taken into account. The defender must be able to store, to analyze and to document all the *IT operational data* necessary to evaluate traces across all phases of the attack vector and thus recognize intruders as best as possible or even to investigate the case of data theft retroactively. Without sufficient data for evaluation by the defender, a successful attack may result and the exfiltration of important data cannot be prevented in time. At this point, we recommend to focus on the protection of valuable *personal data* and to make the *IT operational data* available to the defense in a way assisting the defense counsel and in this way, to promote the complete clarification and traceability of digital forensics.

In future work, we will drill deeper the investigation on misusing network protocols for criminal data theft. In particular, the cookie technology is disassembled with intent to abuse. In addition, we will investigate how knowledge of the potential for misuse can be used for a simulation in order to gain insights into the effectiveness of protective and mitigating measures.

References

1. Ullah, F., Edwards, M., Ramdhany, R., Chitchyan, R., Babar, M.A., Rashid, A.: Data exfiltration: a review of external attack vectors and countermeasures. J. Netw. Comput. Appl. **101**(2), 18–54 (2017). https://eprints.lancs.ac.uk/id/eprint/88549/1/1_s2.0_S1084804517303569_main.pdf
2. Belshe, M., Peon, R., Thomson, M.: Hypertext transfer protocol version 2 (HTTP/2) (2015). https://datatracker.ietf.org/doc/html/rfc7540. Accessed 07 Mar 2021
3. Cory Benfield. Hyper: HTTP/2 client for python (2015). https://hyper.readthedocs.io/en/latest/. Accessed 13 Mar 2022

4. Semal, B., Markantonakis, K., Mayes, K., Kalbantner, J.: One covert channel to rule them all: a practical approach to data exfiltration in the cloud. In: 2020 IEEE 19th International Conference on Trust, Security and Privacy in Computing and Communications (TrustCom) TRUSTCOM Trust, pp. 328–336 (2020)

5. Bieker, F., Friedewald, M., Hansen, M., Obersteller, H., Rost, M.: A process for data protection impact assessment under the European general data protection regulation. In: Schiffner, S., Serna, J., Ikonomou, D., Rannenberg, K. (eds.) APF 2016. LNCS, vol. 9857, pp. 21–37. Springer, Cham (2016). https://doi.org/10.1007/978-3-319-44760-5_2

6. Darktrace Blog and Dianna Leddy. Double extortion-ransomware (2021). https://www.darktrace.com/de/blog/double-extortion-ransomware/?utm_source=xing&utm_medium=static-awareness-de&utm_campaign=campaign_socialmedia&dclid=CMnvw4O-2vICFdJD4AodzLAPWw. Accessed 22 Oct 2021

7. European Data Protection Board. Guidelines 01/2021 on examples regarding data breach notification, version 2.0 (2021). https://edpb.europa.eu/system/files/2022-01/edpb_guidelines_012021_pdbnotification_adopted_en.pdf. Accessed 06 Mar 2022

8. Cloudflare. What happens in a TLS handshake? — SSL handshake (2022). https://www.cloudflare.com/learning/ssl/what-happens-in-a-tls-handshake/. Accessed 13 Mar 2021

9. MITRE Corporation. MITRE ATT&CK framework (2021). https://attack.mitre.org/. Accessed 04 Mar 2021

10. MITRE Corporation. MITRE ATT&CK navigator (2021). https://mitre-attack.github.io/attack-navigator/. Accessed 04 Mar 2021

11. MITRE Corporation. MITRE ATT&CK navigator - matrix enterprise (2022). https://attack.mitre.org/matrices/enterprise/. Accessed 08 Mar 2022

12. Goverman, J., Tekeoglu, A.: Stealthy data exfiltration via TCP sequence numbers based covert channel. In: 2021 International Conference on Computer Information and Telecommunication Systems, 1–5 Nov 2021. https://ieeexplore.ieee.org/document/9618137

13. Gregorik, I.: High performance browser networking HTTP/2 (2013). https://hpbn.co/http2/. Accessed 13 Mar 2021

14. IETF HTTP Working Group. Http/2 (2015). https://http2.github.io/. Accessed 13 Mar 2022

15. AlKilani, H., Nasereddin, M., Hadi, A., Tedmori, S.: Data exfiltration techniques and data loss prevention system. In: 2019 International Arab Conference on Information Technology (ACIT) Information Technology (ACIT), pp. 124–127 (2019)

16. King, J., Bendiab, G., Savage, N., Shiaeles, S.: Data exfiltration: methods and detection countermeasures. In: 2021 IEEE International Conference on Cyber Security and Resilience (CSR) Cyber Security and Resilience (CSR), pp. 442–447 (2021). https://ieeexplore.ieee.org/stamp/stamp.jsp?tp=&arnumber=9527962

17. Saryu N.: Why the dwell time of cyberattacks has not changed (2021). https://www.forbes.com/sites/forbestechcouncil/2021/05/03/why-the-dwell-time-of-cyberattacks-has-not-changed/?sh=48b387a457d8. Accessed 06 Nov 2022

18. Mundt, M., Baier, H.: Towards mitigation of data exfiltration techniques using the MITRE ATT&CK framework. In: 12th EAI International Conference on Digital Forensics & Cyber Crime (EAI ICDF2C). https://compass.eai.eu/events/detail/242/eai-icdf2c-2021

19. European Parliament. Regulation (EU) 2016/679 of the European parliament and of the council of 27 April 2016 on the protection of natural persons with regard to the processing of personal data and on the free movement of such data, and repealing directive 95/46/EC (general data protection regulation) (2016). https://eur-

lex.europa.eu/legal-content/EN/TXT/PDF/?uri=CELEX:32016R0679. Accessed 06 Mar 2022

20. Pope, N., Goodell, G.: Identification for accountability vs privacy (2022). https://arxiv.org/ftp/arxiv/papers/2201/2201.06971.pdf. Accessed 01 Apr 2022

21. Mandiant Special Report. M-trends 2022 (2022). https://www.mandiant.com/media/15671. Accessed 06 Nov 2022

22. Salvi, M.V., Bapat, M.P.: Mode of data flow in the OSI model. IJIERT - Int. J. Innov. Eng. Res. Technol. **2**(3), 1–7 (2015)

23. Statista. Median time period between intrusion, detection, and containment of industrial cyber attacks worldwide from 2014 to 2019 (2020). https://www.statista.com/statistics/221406/time-between-initial-compromise-and-discovery-of-larger-organizations/. Accessed 07 Mar 2021

24. Microsoft Support. Configure email forwarding in Microsoft 365 (2022). https://docs.microsoft.com/en-us/microsoft-365/admin/email/configure-email-forwarding?view=o365-worldwide. Accessed 11 Mar 2022

25. Microsoft Support. Use rules to automatically forward messages (2022). https://support.microsoft.com/en-us/office/use-rules-to-automatically-forward-messages-45aa9664-4911-4f96-9663-ece42816d746. Accessed 11 Mar 2022

26. McIntosh, T., Kayes, A.S.M., Chen, Y.P.P., Ng, A., Watters, P.: Ransomware mitigation in the modern Era: a comprehensive review, research challenges, and future directions. ACM Comput. Surv. (CSUR). **54**(9), 1–36. ACM, New York, NY (2021)

27. Neubert, T., Vielhauer, C., Kraetzer, C.: Artificial steganographic network data generation concept and evaluation of detection approaches to secure industrial control systems against steganographic attacks. In: The 16th International Conference on Availability, Reliability and Security, pp. 1–9 (2021). https://doi.org/10.1145/3465481.3470073

28. Gellert, R.: Understanding the notion of risk in the general data protection regulation (2016). https://www.sciencedirect.com/science/article/abs/pii/S0267364917302698. Accessed 09 Apr 2022

Automating the Flow of Data Between Digital Forensic Tools Using Apache NiFi

Xiaoyu Du$^{(\boxtimes)}$, Francis N. Nwebonyi, and Pavel Gladyshev

Digital Forensics Investigation Research Laboratory, School of Computer Science, University College Dublin, Dublin, Ireland
{xiaoyu.du,francis.nwebonyi,pavel.gladyshev}@ucd.ie
http://dfire.ucd.ie/

Abstract. In digital forensics, sources of digital evidence range from computer disk drives, memories, mobile phones, network dumps, and all kinds of IoT devices, etc. Therefore, different tools are required for digital evidence collection and analysis from various sources. Even though each tool works automatically, data from one tool to another often need to be prepared manually. This paper introduces a NiFi-based solution that enables automatically moving data between digital forensic tools, reducing manual work in practice. A DataFlow designed in NiFi can monitor and fetch the input data, pre-processing the data and run digital forensic tools for data analytics. Besides, NiFi can also be used for remote evidence acquisition and data sharing between law enforcement agencies (LEAs). This paper also presents a couple of use cases of using NiFi for digital evidence processing: they are 1) file carving, 2) NSRL (National Software Reference Library) hash lookup, 3) categorising files by MIME type, and 4) IoT logs parsing.

Keywords: Digital Forensics · Automated Digital Evidence Processing · Apache NiFi

1 Introduction

The focus of digital forensics gradually has changed from recovering data from storage devices to acquiring and analysing data from mobile devices, tablets, and smart devices. Challenges in digital forensics are widely discussed by researchers in digital forensic field [6,18]. With the prevalence of technology in modern life, the ever-increasing volume of data leads to data collection and analysis taking a longer time. On the other hand, the diverse data formats require various tools for processing, and data from novel devices in new format may not have tools that fit.

With the diverse sources of digital evidence from novel applications and IoT devices raise challenges in digital forensics. For each of types of device like the wearable devices and smart homes, researchers in the field have been working

© ICST Institute for Computer Sciences, Social Informatics and Telecommunications Engineering 2023
Published by Springer Nature Switzerland AG 2023. All Rights Reserved
S. Goel et al. (Eds.): ICDF2C 2022, LNICST 508, pp. 435–452, 2023.
https://doi.org/10.1007/978-3-031-36574-4_26

on analysing what user data are there and how are they preserved [1]. Many forensic tools have been developed to process the various forensic targets. From digital forensic practitioners' perspective, there is a trend that the number of digital forensic tools needed is continually increasing.

Another challenge is digital forensic tools become outdated quickly because, in the age of rapid change in technology, prevalent devices and applications changed over time. For application forensics, different tools are needed as popular applications changes over time. Skype was a popular tool for online calls, research on Skype forensic in 2012 [4]. Since the global pandemic of COVID-19, the video conferencing application Zoom has experienced a surge in its user. Zoom application forensics has become significant as well in 2021 [19]. There are many other tools, TicTok [7], Discord [22], and many more to come in the future.

Currently, in an investigation, to collection and analysis of evidence with multiple tools is very common. Practitioners have to wait for a tool to complete the data collection, and extraction, and then manually prepare the data for analysis. Moreover, as mentioned, due to the ever-increasing volume of data, the processing time takes longer. Even though there are integrated commercial tools, however, in most situations, problems in an investigation can not be solved with a single tool.

This research work explores using Apache NiFi to manage data movement between digital forensic tools. Apache NiFi[1] is a tool for data movement between systems. The NiFi-based solution for digital forensics can automated fetch data from filesystem and database, and run digital forensic tools for data extraction, hash searching and so on. in addition, leveraging NiFi in digital forensics allows to include more analysis modules from excellent open-source projects, like Text Summaries and Sentiment Analysis, which are not forensic tools can also be useful in an investigation. Thereby, only is the cost of developing specialised digital forensics tools saved, but new techniques can be used for digital forensics more quickly.

2   Backgrounds

2.1   Digital Forensic Challenges

Exponential growth in the volume of digital evidence is faced by LEAs around the world. Digital Forensics Laboratories (DFLs) started to face backlogs of 6 months to 1 year as early as 2009 [5], backlogs continue to grow [13], it commonly reached one to two years and even four years in extreme cases in 2016 [18]. It was reported in 2022, police have digital backlogs, 45 police forces across the UK found that a total of 21,022 devices were waiting for examination.

With the constant emergence of new and diverse devices with varied OSs, diverse types of devices and formats of data, there are much more sources of digital evidence. The nature of investigations has changed from simply extracting data, and recovering deleted files to mobile devices forensics, and real-time

---

[1] https://nifi.apache.org/.

network forensics. Digital evidence could be from various devices, and different tools are required for: disk forensics, cloud forensics, memory forensics, and mobile forensics. However, most new innovations take time to develop and can add significant costs to the investigator's toolkit. There is a trend that the number and variety of analytic tools continue to grow [13].

Researchers in the field of digital forensics have proposed solutions aimed at a faster processing, such as data deduplication [9,28], data reduction [25], triage [10,12,20], and other advanced methods. However, there is a gap between research and practice. Additional research is required to address the real-world relevance of the proposed methods and implement practical infrastructural enhancements [21]. The implementation integrates automated collection and examination, heterogeneous evidence process, data visualisation, multi-device evidence and timeline resolution can significantly improve the efficiency of the digital forensic process.

2.2 Digital Forensics: Tools and Techniques

There are many tools/toolkits available for different tasks in investigations [15], such as Autopsy, Encase, Volatility, etc. There are also various techniques such as blockchain [27], machine learning and deep learning [8], which have been constantly employed by researchers in the field to improve the digital forensics process.

Case investigations are various, the evidence collection can be different accordingly. For example, there are different ways of acquisition. Full disk image acquisition preserves all data from a storage device, files from the file system, slack space, and unallocated space which contains deleted data. The forensically sound disk image collection usually takes a very long time for the collection of large data volume. An approach aimed at a faster acquisition has been proposed, named selective acquisition. Selective acquisition only collects data (types of files) which are possibly more relevant to the investigation [26]. *sifting collectors* is an approach proposed in 2015 [11], which images only those regions of a disk with expected forensic value.

Investigators choose the method according to the actual situation. Forensically soundness of the disk image is important when the analysis result is used to prove guilt or innocence in court, the reproducibility of the analysis result is important in this case. Selective imaging should be applied when the case is time-critical, about the life and death of a victim.

In digital forensic examination and analysis, file carving tools are usually applied to the discovery and reconstruction of files in case the system metadata is corrupted, missing, or otherwise unreliable [2]. MIME (multipurpose internet mail extensions) information is usually used in digital forensics for recognising real file types. Because the file extension is for the proper identification of programs that can open and display the correct information, it is easy to be change manually by users. MIME represents file types for messages and files sent over the Internet and is detected using a magic number inside the file [23]. In digital forensics, using the MIME type instead of the file extension to recognise the file type is more reliable.

Hashing is another technique usually used in digital forensics. The hash value is a digital fingerprint of a file, which is used to recognise a file in digital forensics for detecting known illegal files or filtering known benign files. There are forensic corpus data reduction methods proposed by Joseph et al. [16] in 2019, this research proposes an efficient methodology for forensic investigations, that eliminated 49.4 million uninteresting files. NSRL hash databases are freely available over the internet for faster analysis by eliminating tedious files. The NSRL lookup tool developed by Rob Hansen of RedJack Security LLC allows users to extend the hash library in use.

AI-based techniques provide another way for automated analysis in digital forensics [14]. For user files, pictures are important sources of digital evidence. There are a number of tools that can assist in image analysis, such as object detection [24], face detection, age estimation [3]. For text data, different tools could be used determined by the sources (documents, instant messages, and emails) and objectives (clustering, classification, translation).

2.3   Use of Apache NiFi in Research

Apache NiFi is not a digital forensics tool, actually, it is for data management and movement between software systems. It was used and evaluated by some researchers in their work. In a paper by Kim et al. [17], Apache NiFi was applied to deal with different types of spatial information (Geo-IoT sensor, SNS information, unstructured spatial information, etc.). This research reports that NiFi has the advantages: 1) easy to develop DataFlow, 2) real-time data transmission is provided, 3) resource sharing through powerful resource and authority management, 4) data history management, 5) communication between several NiFi systems is available.

2.4   Summary

Digital forensic investigation is complicated as the diverse types of cases, and the investigation focuses can vary. One single tool usually can only solve part of the problem in an investigation. Multiple tools are needed for data collection, extraction and analysis from various devices. It is important for digital forensic tools to accommodate the continued appearance of new devices and formats of data. Besides, removing the research-practice gap is very important for combating the digital forensic backlogs.

3   Methodology

This section presents the what and how NiFi assists to solve challenges and problems in digital forensics.

3.1 Overview

NiFi can be used for processing digital evidence data in many different ways. Firstly, NiFi can be used for data transmission in the digital investigation between investigation phases, different digital forensic tools, as well as different servers. NiFi allows for automatically detecting and fetching data from a system through the configured NiFi processors. Either the data is in the local machine or a remote server, there are corresponding processors for it.

Figure 1 shows that running NiFi in investigators' computers to automatically access services from servers and getting the analysis result back from the server. All these operations can be defined to perform automatically through NiFi: 1) a server preserves data collected, investigators share the collected data in the data storage server; 2) a server runs machine learning models to assist analysis, and investigators send data for analysis to the server and get the analysis result back to local machine; 3) save illegal files found in an investigation into a known file database for sharing between LEAs.

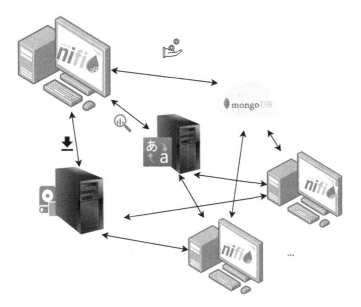

Fig. 1. Use NiFi in Digital Forensics for Data Transmission: NiFi allows to get data/services from different servers and to preserve the result of data processing and analysis of cloud databases, such as MongoDB.

NiFi can also assist to move data between tools in different investigation phases. Figure 2 shows evidence processing in each phase of digital forensics, i.e., collection, extraction, and analysis. NiFi is used to move data from one tool to the next and finally get the processing result to investigators. Even though there are so many tools available, it is not all of them are required for every case investigation. A NiFi DataFlow can be designed to only include the tools which are required by the investigation.

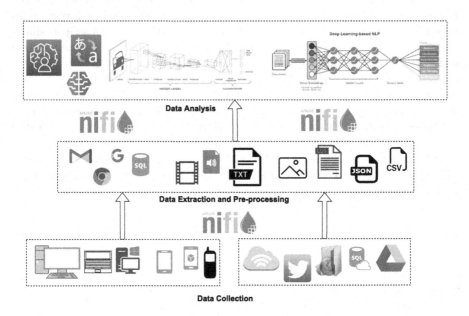

Fig. 2. Use Apache NiFi to automate flow of data between digital forensic tools - 1) run data collection tools within NiFi processors, 2) send the collected data to data extraction tools, 3) send the extracted data to analysis tools.

There are also NiFi processors which can be configured to execute command-line tools and scripts on data for processing and analysing. Thereby, it is convenient to employ open-source tools, and machine learning models (shown in the Fig. 2) for forensic analysis in the NiFi-based digital forensic process.

3.2   Design a NiFi DataFlow for Digital Evidence Data Processing

Apache NiFi is a DataFlow system based on the concepts of flow-based programming. It provides a web-based user interface for design, control, feedback, and monitoring of DataFlows.

A NiFi DataFlow can consist of one or more components. NiFi processor is the most used component in NiFi, various processors are designed to fetch, process and preserve data. When a file is fetched by a processor, the file data in NiFi is in a form called FlowFile. The processors are connected together to process data step by step.

– **Processor**: There are a number of NiFi processors that can fetch data from different sources, and put data to a specified location in a local or remote computer. It is also allowed users to develop a customised NiFi processor. The customised NiFi processor can also be shared with other users.

- **FlowFile**: The FlowFile represents a single piece of data in NiFi. A FlowFile is made up of two components: FlowFile Attributes and FlowFile Content. All kinds of files can be ingested by NiFi processor, disk images, pictures, audios, videos, various log files from systems and applications, as well as file fragments. A FlowFile is created when a file is ingested to the DataFlow. These data can be monitored by a NiFi processor, either they are saved in a folder of the local machine or a remote server, as well as in a cloud data lake.
- **DataFlow**: A NiFi DataFlow consists components for getting data, processing data and preserving data. The process of designing the DataFlow determines how the data will be processed. A DataFlow can be preserved as an XML file for sharing and reusing.

When start the processors in the DataFlow, all operations, fetching data from the source location, transition data, processing data by each digital forensic tool, load data to the destination location, automatically happen.

3.3   NiFi Processors for Auto-Detecting and Fetching Data

There are NiFi processors which can fetch data from different sources locally and remotely. Accordingly, there are processors for load data to destination locations in a local or remote system.

- *GetFile*: Creates FlowFiles from files in a directory.
- *FetchSFTP*: Fetches the content of a file from a remote SFTP server and overwrites the contents of an incoming FlowFile with the content of the remote file.
- *GetMongo*: Creates FlowFiles from documents in MongoDB loaded by a user-specified query.

3.4   NiFi Processors for Auto-Examine and Analysis of Data

There are some other NiFi processors that can be used for data processing for structured data such as JSON, XML, CSV, and records from a SQL/NoSQL database.

- *SplitRecord*: Splits up an input FlowFile that is in a record-oriented data format into multiple smaller FlowFiles
- *QueryRecord*: Evaluates one or more SQL queries against the contents of a FlowFile. The result of the SQL query then becomes the content of the output FlowFile. This can be used, for example, for field-specific filtering, transformation, and row-level filtering. Columns can be renamed, simple calculations and aggregations performed, etc.

It is also possible to run digital forensic tools in a NiFi processor. The tool is configured in a NiFi processor and it starts the process of data automatically when the FlowFile goes down to the processor.

ExecuteStreamCommand is the processor that can be configured to executes an external command. It works on the data of a FlowFile and creates a new FlowFile with the results of the command. For example, the command-line tool *foremost* can be run in this NiFi processor for carving files from a disk image. The output folder can be specified in the processor configuration. It is also possible to run a python script in the NiFi processor.

3.5 Benefits of Using NiFi in Digital Forensics

Even though using script language such as Python could be developed to do the same work as NiFi does - to automatically start to run a digital forensic tool and process data as needed, NiFi provides a web-based user interface and is very easy to use; users only need to drag processors to the canvas and configure the properties.

Figure 3 shows an example of NiFi DataFlow, it monitors a folder in a local machine and fetches data when files are put in this folder the processor fetches it to the DatabFlow, and then data is processed by each processor; the processing includes file carving from a disk image, unzip a file in zip format, know hash library look up, categorising files as their MIME type.

Benefits of using NiFi in digital forensics listed as follows:

– **Easy to use** - After designed and started the DataFlow, users simply need to put the data into the source folder and will get the result in the destination folder.
– **Automate the flow of data between tools** - It allows to automatically send the processing result of one tool to another tool for further analysis, which saves time for manual processing.
– **Remote acquisition and data sharing** - NiFi processors can be configured for dynamic get and transmit data either a remote server or a cloud database. Automate the data movement can be achieved and sharing data between LEAs.
– **Verify the result of a tool** - It can be designed to send the same data to different tools for the same analysis purpose, and compare the analysis results to verify the reliability of the result.

3.6 Summary

This section outlined the key terminologies in the NiFi framework and presented how NiFi can be applied to fit into the digital forensic process model. NiFi can fetch and load data not only from the specified file folder on the local machine, but as well from a remote machine, or cloud database. It is also possible to use NiFi for data processing, splitting, or querying records for structure data.

Fig. 3. An implemented NiFi DataFlow for digital forensic data ingestion and preprocessing: The *GetFile* processor monitors the source folder, and fetches the data put in it; the *RouteonAttribute* processor routes data to different processor groups based on the file type; there are 4 processor groups for unzipping files, carving files from disk images, (the extracted and craved file data are put back to the source folder), single files are compared to NSRL hash library and then categorised as their mime type put to different folders for further analysis.

4   Use Cases

In this section, use cases are presented, showing how NiFi processors are used to performing digital forensic tasks. As it is shown in Fig. 3, firstly, get data from a folder and check the file type. Files then are processed by different process groups based on their types. In the following subsections, process groups for file carving, file system data extraction, NSRL hash lookup and categorising files by MIME types will be introduced.

4.1   File Carving

As it is shown in Fig. 4, a file caving process group consists of 3 NiFi processors. Firstly, the *FetchFile* processor fetches data to the DataFlow. The processor *ReplaceText* replaces the file contents with the filename, because the command-line tool *foremost* is running inside the processor *ExecuteStreamCommand* needs the full path of the file as the input. And then, the *ExecuteStreamCommand* processor executes an external command on the contents of a FlowFile. The file carving tool *Foremost* can be configured to be executed in the processor, so as when a disk image file is in the DataFlow, data can be carved and then put into a specified folder for further processing.

Another argument required by *foremost* is an output folder. In the configuration, to set the output as the source folder, as a result, the carved files will be fetched again and recognised as single files, and then flow to other branches for other analysis operations.

4.2   Data Extraction from Disk Images

Another way that extracting data from disk images based on partition and file system information is also implemented. It works through running a Python

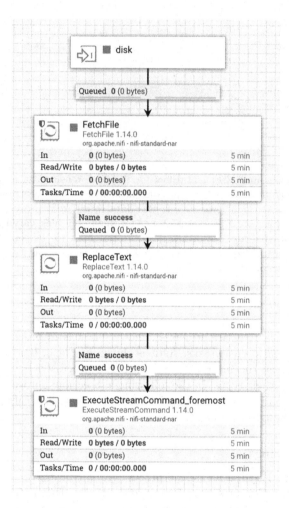

Fig. 4. File Carving from Disk images

script in the processor *ExecuteStreamCommand*. The processor can extract files and data from disk images through configure it to run a Python script.

Figure 5 shows the configuration of the processor for running the script. The Value "pytsk_recursive_extraction.py" for the Property "Command Arguments" specifies the name script file. The python script accesses partitions of an image and extracts file data and metadata from file systems.

The metadata extracted from the disk image is preserved as a CSV file in the result folder for further analysis. The files extracted from the disk image are saved into the source folder, same as the file carving process, the extracted files then are fetched by the DataFlow and processed by other analysis process groups.

Required field

Property		Value
Command Arguments Strategy	❷	Command Arguments Property
Command Arguments	❷	pytsk_recursive_extraction.py
Command Path	❷	**python3**
Ignore STDIN	❷	false
Working Directory	❷	/app
Argument Delimiter	❷	**;**
Output Destination Attribute	❷	No value set
Max Attribute Length	❷	256

Fig. 5. Configure the *ExecuteStreamCommand* Processor: this configuration sets the processor to run the python script for data extraction from disk image

4.3   NSRL Hash Lookup

NSRL lookup tool detects known files. It allows automated filtering out the known benign files and potentially can be applied for eliminating redundant images and videos found across multiple devices. Hash lookup reduces the amount of data an investigator must examine manually.

A process group is created for detecting files by their hash values. NSRL hash sets cover the most common OS installation and application packages and can aid the investigation of data from computer systems. To implement the NSRL filter function, two tools namely *nsrlsvr* and *nsrllookup* are used in this NiFi DataFlow.

As is shown in Fig. 6, the file data is hashed by the processor *HashContent*. Afterwards, the md5 of the file is generated and added to the FlowFile metadata. Other hash algorithms are also available through configuring the property of *HashContent* processor.

The *HashContent* Processor calculates a hash value for the Content of a FlowFile. And then, run the tool *nsrllookup*[2] in the *ExecuteStreamCommand* processor to check if a file existing in the NSRL library. If the file exists, the hash value is returned and if not, no return value.

The file data then is flow to different processors. Files are filtered out directly if they are known by the NSRL library. For files which are not found in the NSRL library, they are moved to the next process group for categorising based on the MEMI type.

4.4   Categorising Files by MIME Type

The *IdentifyMimeType* processor is for identifying the MIME type of a file. As it is shown in Fig. 7, files' MIME are firstly recognised by the IdentifyMimeType

---

[2] http://rjhansen.github.io/nsrllookup/.

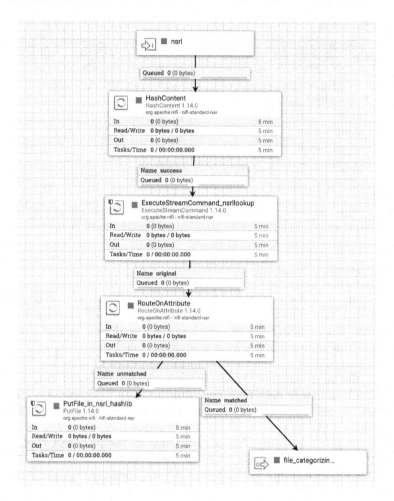

Fig. 6. Example DataFlow: NSRL Lookup

processor and then route to different branches by the RouteonAttribute processor. Finally, as different file types, files are saved to different folders by PutFile processors.

4.5   IoT Sources Ingestion

In the IoT (Internet of Things) domain, interoperability is a problem because different solutions often come with different vendors and file formats, among other differences. To make the advanced processing of IoT data more efficient, it is important to have them in a unified format. Apache NiFi can be used here to unify different file formats from different IoT sources into a common format, to help with further processing or investigation.

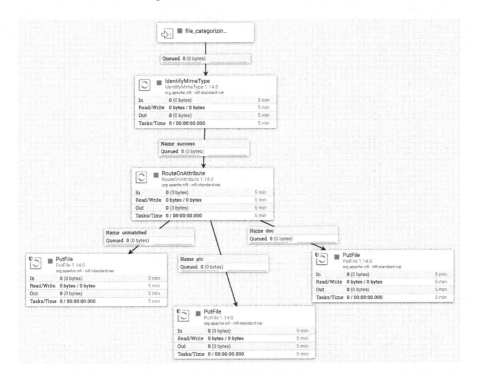

Fig. 7. Example DataFlow: Categorising File by MIME type

To demonstrate this, a DataFlow was built (see Fig. 8) to take in a number of file formats, including Avro, Parquet, and CSV, and convert them to JSON. Several NiFi processors, many of which have been explained, were put together and configured to make this possible. The *ConvertRecord* processor is perhaps worth a mention here. It has properties such as Record Reader and Record Writer which can be configured for reading incoming data and writing out records respectively. Each of these properties can be leveraged to allow the processor to support different file formats. It has some out-of-the-box properties, as well as scripted instances for reading, parsing, and generating records from (and to) FlowFiles, through some of its properties like ScriptedReader and ScriptedRecordSetWriter.

4.6 Summary

This section presented the development of NiFi DataFlow in use for digital forensics tasks, i.e., file carving, NSRL lookup, and MIME categorising. The output data of this DataFlow (files in the destination folders) could be sent to machine learning or deep learning models for further analysis. These output data then can be preserved in a database for further in-depth analysis.

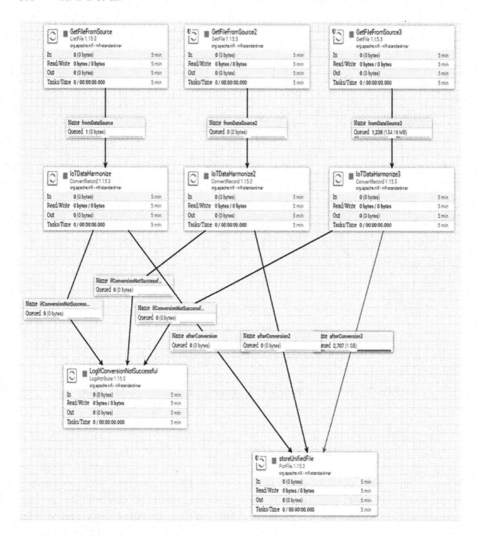

Fig. 8. Harmonizing Several Data Formats (CSV, Avro, and Parquet) into JSON.

5   Experiments and Results

5.1   Test Data

The most common file types in digital forensics are prepared for Experiment to test and verify functions of the NiFi DataFlow. The categories of files for testing are:

- **Raw disk images**, which are generated from VirtualBox, with windows operating system installed.
- **Zip files**, which contain various numbers of files and folders in them;

- **Single Files**, which are documents, Pictures, etc.
- **Data in different formats**, which are JSON, CSV, etc.

5.2 Experiment Environment Setup

Experiments presented in this paper are run in a Docker container, the docker image is from docker hub[3]. Forensic tools (foremost, pytsk, nsrlsvr, nsrllookup) are installed to the docker image.

5.3 Experiments and Results

Firstly, the user needs to start the processors in the web-based user interface. Secondly, the user put test data in the source folder. NiFi fetches the data to the DataFlow and processes it based on the file types of data.

1. **When the input is a zip file:**
   (a) The file was detected in the source folder.
   (b) The file was pulled into the DataFlow.
   (c) The file was recognised as a zip file.
   (d) The file was Route to the unzip process group.
   (e) The file was unzipped by the UnpackContent processor.
   (f) The unpacked files are in the DataFlow.
   (g) The unpacked files (single files) are put back to the source folder.
2. **When the input is a raw disk image file:**
   (a) The file was detected in the source folder.
   (b) The file was pulled into the DataFlow.
   (c) The file was recognised as a raw disk image file.
   (d) The file was Route to the disk image data extraction processor.
   (e) Files on the disk images were extracted by pytsk.
   (f) The extracted files are saved in the source folder.
3. **When the input is a single file** (document, picture, etc.):
   (a) The file was detected in the source folder.
   (b) The file was pulled into the DataFlow.
   (c) The file was a single file and then was Route to NSRL hash Detection process group.
       i. If the file's hash has existed in the hash sets, the file was benign and does not require further processing.
       ii. If the file's hash has not existed in the hash sets, the file was unknown.
   (d) Unknown files are flowing to the next process group - mime type file filter.
   (e) Files are filtered by mime type and put into different destination folders.

After these processing steps, the content of the FlowFiles finally is written to the local file system in the location specified by the *PutFile* processor. If the destination/output folder does not exist, NiFi can dynamically create a folder in the location as specified.

---

[3] https://hub.docker.com/r/apache/nifi.

6   Conclusion

This paper proposed a NiFi-based solution that contributes to the automation of the digital forensics process and reduces manual work in practice. It automatically fetched evidence data, start a digital forensic tool to process (examine or analyse) the data, and load the data to the destination location. Moreover, use cases on processing disk images and documents are presented which preliminary proved the effeteness of the proposed solution. Potentially, NiFi can be applied to process more diverse sources/formats of evidence data.

Another advantage of using NiFi is its browser-based user interface for design, control, feedback, and monitoring enables rapid development and iterative testing. As a result, it is convenient to use it for integrating up-to-date tools and techniques into digital forensic practice.

6.1   Future Work

This research explored using NiFi to run digital forensic tools for digital evidence data processing. Next, further research related to the NiFi-based digital forensics solution will be explored including:

– **Test on larger data sets**: In this paper, the test focuses on verifying the result correctness of the NiFi DataFlow. In the next stage, larger data sets consist of more logs, multimedia files, and disk images to quantify the data processing effectiveness of the approach.
– **NiFi logs analysis**: There are logs generated as the NiFi runs, what data are in the flow and what operations are conducted are recorded by the NiFi logs. To analyse these logs and figure out what are there can be useful for documentation.
– **Multiple sources correlation analysis**: To develop and run multiple NiFi DataFlows for processing data from the same case but different devices and integrate the analysis results from these DataFlows for further in-depth manual analysis.
– **Report generation**: It is also possible to visualise the analysis result and generate a report for non-technical end-users.

Acknowledgment. This project has received funding from the European Union's Horizon 2020 Research and Innovation Programme under Grant Agreement No 883596. The content of the publication herein is the sole responsibility of the publishers and it does not necessarily represent the views expressed by the European Commission or its services.

References

1. Alabdulsalam, S., Schaefer, K., Kechadi, T., Le-Khac, N.-A.: Internet of things forensics – challenges and a case study. In: DigitalForensics 2018. IAICT, vol. 532, pp. 35–48. Springer, Cham (2018). https://doi.org/10.1007/978-3-319-99277-8_3

2. Ali, R.R., Mohamad, K.M., Jamel, S., Khalid, S.K.A.: A review of digital forensics methods for JPEG file carving. J. Theor. Appl. Inf. Technol. **96**(17), 5841–5856 (2018)
3. Anda, F., Lillis, D., Le-Khac, N.A., Scanlon, M.: Evaluating automated facial age estimation techniques for digital forensics. In: 2018 IEEE Security and Privacy Workshops (SPW), pp. 129–139. IEEE (2018)
4. Azab, A., Watters, P., Layton, R.: Characterising network traffic for skype forensics. In: 2012 Third Cybercrime and Trustworthy Computing Workshop, pp. 19–27. IEEE (2012)
5. Casey, E., Ferraro, M., Nguyen, L.: Investigation delayed is justice denied: proposals for expediting forensic examinations of digital evidence. J. Forensic Sci. **54**(6), 1353–1364 (2009)
6. Caviglione, L., Wendzel, S., Mazurczyk, W.: The future of digital forensics: challenges and the road ahead. IEEE Secur. Priv. **15**(6), 12–17 (2017)
7. Domingues, P., Nogueira, R., Francisco, J.C., Frade, M.: Analyzing TikTok from a digital forensics perspective. J. Wirel. Mob. Netw. Ubiquit. Comput. Dependable Appl. (JoWUA) **12**(3), 87–115 (2021)
8. Du, X., et al.: SoK: exploring the state of the art and the future potential of artificial intelligence in digital forensic investigation. In: Proceedings of the 15th International Conference on Availability, Reliability and Security, pp. 1–10 (2020)
9. Du, X., Ledwith, P., Scanlon, M.: Deduplicated disk image evidence acquisition and forensically-sound reconstruction. In: 2018 17th IEEE International Conference On Trust, Security And Privacy In Computing And Communications/12th IEEE International Conference On Big Data Science And Engineering (TrustCom/BigDataSE), pp. 1674–1679. IEEE (2018)
10. Gentry, E., Soltys, M.: SEAKER: a mobile digital forensics triage device. Procedia Comput. Sci. **159**, 1652–1661 (2019)
11. Grier, J., Richard, G.G., III.: Rapid forensic imaging of large disks with sifting collectors. Digit. Investig. **14**, S34–S44 (2015)
12. Horsman, G., Laing, C., Vickers, P.: A case-based reasoning method for locating evidence during digital forensic device triage. Decis. Support Syst. **61**, 69–78 (2014)
13. Hosmer, C.: Python Forensics: A Workbench for Inventing and Sharing Digital Forensic Technology. Elsevier, Amsterdam (2014)
14. Jarrett, A., Choo, K.K.R.: The impact of automation and artificial intelligence on digital forensics. Wiley Interdis. Rev. Forensic Sci. **3**(6), e1418 (2021)
15. Javed, A.R., Ahmed, W., Alazab, M., Jalil, Z., Kifayat, K., Gadekallu, T.R.: A comprehensive survey on computer forensics: state-of-the-art, tools, techniques, challenges, and future directions. IEEE Access **10**, 11065-11089 (2022)
16. Joseph, P., Norman, J.: Forensic corpus data reduction techniques for faster analysis by eliminating tedious files. Inf. Sec. J. A Glob. Perspect. **28**(4–5), 136–147 (2019)
17. Kim, S.S., Lee, W.R., Go, J.H.: A study on utilization of spatial information in heterogeneous system based on apache NiFi. In: 2019 International Conference on Information and Communication Technology Convergence (ICTC), pp. 1117–1119. IEEE (2019)
18. Lillis, D., Becker, B., O'Sullivan, T., Scanlon, M.: Current challenges and future research areas for digital forensic investigation. arXiv preprint arXiv:1604.03850 (2016)
19. Mahr, A., Cichon, M., Mateo, S., Grajeda, C., Baggili, I.: Zooming into the pandemic! a forensic analysis of the zoom application. Forensic Sci. Int. Digit. Invest. **36**, 301107 (2021)

20. Mislan, R.P., Casey, E., Kessler, G.C.: The growing need for on-scene triage of mobile devices. Digit. Investig. **6**(3–4), 112–124 (2010)
21. Montasari, R., Hill, R., Parkinson, S., Peltola, P., Hosseinian-Far, A., Daneshkhah, A.: Digital forensics: challenges and opportunities for future studies. Int. J. Organ. Collective Intell. (IJOCI) **10**(2), 37–53 (2020)
22. Motyliński, M., MacDermott, Á., Iqbal, F., Hussain, M., Aleem, S.: Digital forensic acquisition and analysis of discord applications. In: 2020 International Conference on Communications, Computing, Cybersecurity, and Informatics (CCCI), pp. 1–7. IEEE (2020)
23. Parveen, A., Khan, Z.H., Ahmad, S.N.: Classification and evaluation of digital forensic tools. Telkomnika **18**(6), 3096–3106 (2020)
24. Qadir, S., Noor, B.: Applications of machine learning in digital forensics. In: 2021 International Conference on Digital Futures and Transformative Technologies (ICoDT2), pp. 1–8. IEEE (2021)
25. Quick, D., Choo, K.-K.R.: Big forensic data reduction: digital forensic images and electronic evidence. Clust. Comput. **19**(2), 723–740 (2016). https://doi.org/10.1007/s10586-016-0553-1
26. Quick, D., Choo, K.K.R.: Big Digital Forensic Data: Volume 1: Data Reduction Framework and Selective Imaging. Springer, Berlin (2018)
27. Ryu, J.H., Sharma, P.K., Jo, J.H., Park, J.H.: A blockchain-based decentralized efficient investigation framework for IoT digital forensics. J. Supercomput. **75**(8), 4372–4387 (2019)
28. Scanlon, M.: Battling the digital forensic backlog through data deduplication. In: 2016 Sixth International Conference on Innovative Computing Technology (INTECH), pp. 10–14. IEEE (2016)

Android Mobile Terminal Security Assessment Based on Analytical Hierarchy Process (AHP)

Zhiyuan Hu, Linghang Shi, Huijun Chen, and Jinghui Lu[✉]

vivo Mobile Communication Co., Ltd., Dongguan, China
{huzhiyuan,shilinghang,hj.chen,john.lu}@vivo.com

Abstract. Mobile terminals especially smartphones are changing people's work and life style. For example, mobile payments are experiencing rapid growth as consumers use mobile terminals as part of modern dynamic lifestyles. However, mobile terminal security is a big challenge for mobile application services. In order to mitigate security risks, the mobile terminal security assessment should be performed before accessing the services with high security requirements. A comprehensive approach for security assessment is proposed in this paper by defining security metrics with scores, determining the relative weights of these security metrics based on the analytical hierarchy process (AHP), designing a general system architecture and implementing security assessment system. Until 30 September 2022, around 6 million smartphones support the security assessment solution proposed in this paper. In September 2022, these smartphones had made 77 million online payment transactions, of which 60,000 fraudulent transactions were detected, with the payment fraud rate of about 0.08%.

Keywords: Security Assessment · Security Metric · Relative Weight · Analytical Hierarchy Process (AHP)

1 Introduction

Today, mobile terminals especially smartphones are changing people's work and life style. For example, mobile payments are experiencing rapid growth as consumers use mobile terminals as part of modern dynamic lifestyles; more and more enterprises support employees accessing enterprise services with personal mobile terminals; etc. However, mobile terminal security is a big challenge for these mobile application services. For example, users may unknowingly expose their terminals to malware and put the sensitive data at risk of data breaches. In order to ensure mobile applications and sensitive data's security, it is very important for mobile application services to check if the mobile terminals are secure enough to access the services.

Some solutions were designed for the server to perform mobile terminal security assessment. Wang [1] proposed that the edge server conducts security assessment for mobile intelligent terminals before they access the IoT network. Xi [2] introduced machine learning to evaluate the security of power mobile terminal system. Wu [3]

S. Goel et al. (Eds.): ICDF2C 2022, LNICST 508, pp. 453–471, 2023.
https://doi.org/10.1007/978-3-031-36574-4_27

defined specific evaluation indexes and provided a security evaluation system of smart grid terminals. Ratchford [4] gave a model to conduct BYOD (Bring Your Own Device) security posture assessment with using Euclidian's algorithm to compare a posture among two organizations. Visoottiviseth [5] provided a solution to conduct security assessment for IoT devices by executing penetration testing on targeted IoT devices. Othman [6] discussed the feasibility of information system audit in assessing mobile device security by exploring the risks and vulnerabilities of mobile devices. As for above server-based solutions, the server collects security data from the mobile terminals and conducts security assessment. But the collected security data may include user personal data, which may generate risks to individuals' privacy.

Some solutions were designed for the mobile terminal to conduct security assessment by itself. Cavalcanti [7] and Vecchiato [8] proposed the method to identify and report potentially unsafe settings of Android terminals. Irwan [9] analyzed the latent security vulnerabilities in the applications of the terminals. Khokhlov [10], Raza [11] and Hayran [12] described security assessment for operating system. Khokhlov [13] defined security metrics and provided data security evaluation for mobile devices. Zendehdel [14] proposed a semi-automated framework that can be used to discover both known and unknown vulnerabilities in wearable health monitoring devices. All above terminal-based solutions provided security assessment for the application, operating system and data of mobile terminals, without considering hardware security or communication security of mobile terminals, which is important for some application services. For example, secure element to store sensitive data and confidentiality protection for data in transiting over the networks are important for mobile enterprise services.

So, it is necessary to design a terminal-based comprehensive solution for conducting mobile terminal security assessment, with taking application security, operating system security, hardware security and communication security into account. In this way, mobile application services can determine whether the mobile terminal is secure enough to access the services. Moreover, raw security data for security assessment will neither leave the mobile terminals nor be sent to the mobile application services. Therefore, the risks to individuals' privacy could be reduced and even avoided.

The main contributions of this paper are to define security metrics with scores, to determine relative weights of security metrics based on AHP, to design a general system architecture and to implement security assessment system for Android mobile terminal.

The rest of the paper is organized as follows. In Sect. 2, security metrics with scores are defined. In Sect. 3, Analytical Hierarchy Process (AHP) is introduced to determine the relative weights of security metrics. A general system architecture for Android mobile terminal security assessment is designed in Sect. 4. In Sect. 5, security assessment system is implemented and security assessment is conducted for mobile payment services. Section 6 concludes the paper.

2 Security Metrics and Scoring for Android Mobile Terminals

To reduce security risks, the application service will perform security risk assessment with considering the security assessment of the terminal, network and server before providing the services. This paper only studies the mobile terminal security assessment, which is an important part of security risk assessment for the application services.

To support mobile terminal security assessment, security metrics to be measured should be defined. Based on the technologies GlobalPlatform TEE (Trusted Execution Environment) [15] and ARM TrustZone [16], most Android terminals (e.g., smartphones and tablets) maintain two worlds for all trusted and untrusted applications in REE (Rich Execution Environment) and TEE separately, which is shown in Fig. 1. So, the security metrics related to the mobile terminal could be classified into four categories, i.e., REE security metrics, TEE security metrics, hardware security metrics and communication security metrics. Each security metric category includes a set of sub-metrics, which will be described in the next sections.

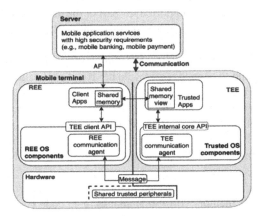

Fig. 1. Framework of Android-based mobile terminal.

2.1 REE Security Metrics and Scoring

REE security metrics mainly include ten sub-metrics which are defined as follows. The scores of each sub-metric are also given.

Mobile application spoofing attack detection in REE (A1) is to identify the attacks in which a malicious mobile application mimics the visual appearance and responses of the genuine one in REE of the terminal. Assigned score could be: 10 - spoofing attack is never detected, 0 - spoofing attack(s) was detected before, but not detected when accessing the services, −10 - spoofing attack(s) is detected when accessing the services.

Virus detection in REE (A2) is to identify the viruses, worms and other types of malwares in REE of the mobile terminal. Assigned score could be: 10 - virus is never detected, 0 - virus(es) was detected before, but not detected when accessing the services, −10 - virus(es) is detected when accessing the services.

Spam protection (A3) is to protect the mobile terminal from spam calls and messages by automatically intercepting suspicious calls and messages. Assigned score could be: 10 - if spam protection is supported, 0 - otherwise.

Malicious activity detection (A4) is to identify the malicious behaviors of the applications, such as inducing internet gambling, bypassing security checks, creating a fraudulent online payment, etc. Assigned score could be: 10 - malicious activity is never detected, 0 - malicious activity was detected before, but not detected when accessing the services, −10 - malicious activity is detected when accessing the services.

Application signature verification (A5) is to assure that an application with a valid signature comes from the expected developers to make sure that: a) the APK (Android Application Package) has not been tampered in the time since it was signed, and b) the application's certificate matches that of the currently installed version. Assigned score could be: 10 - if application signature verification is supported, 0 - otherwise.

Application layer encryption (A6) is to apply the cryptographic protection for the data on application layer to prevent unauthorized disclosure. Assigned score could be: 10 - confidentiality and integrity are supported for all data on the application layer, 5 - confidentiality and integrity are supported for part of the data on the application layer, 0 - neither confidentiality nor integrity is supported for the data on the application layer.

Application integrity protection (A7) is to assure the integrity of the application, which applies IMA (Integrity Measurement Architecture) and extends the chain of trust to the application layer file. Assigned score could be: 10 - if application integrity protection is supported, 0 - otherwise.

REE OS vulnerabilities (A8) include the flaws and weaknesses, such as missing permission check, uninitialized data, buffer overflow, integer overflow, memory corruption, missing pointer check, etc. Assigned score could be: 0 - no well-known vulnerability, −5 - one or two well-known vulnerabilities are discovered, -10 - more than three well-known vulnerabilities are discovered.

Software-based defense mechanisms against memory vulnerabilities (A9) are the methods to prevent the memory corruption attacks (e.g., code injection and code reuse) based on software such as stack canaries, DEP (Data Execution Prevention), ASLR (Address Space Layout Randomization) and CFI (Control Flow Integrity). Assigned score could be: 10 - at least three defense mechanisms are supported, 5 - one or two defense mechanisms are supported, 0 - no defense mechanism is supported.

Verified boot (A10) is to assure the integrity of the software running on mobile terminal. It typically starts with a read-only portion of the terminal hardware which loads code and executes it only after cryptographically verifying that the code is authentic. Assigned score could be: 10 - if verified boot is supported, 0 - otherwise.

2.2   TEE Security Metrics and Scoring

TEE security metrics mainly include nine sub-metrics which are defined as follows. The scores of each sub-metric are also given.

Mobile application spoofing attack detection in TEE (B1) is to identify the attacks in which a malicious mobile application mimics the visual appearance and responses of the genuine one in TEE of the terminal. Assigned score could be: 10 - spoofing attack is never detected, 0 - spoofing attack(s) was detected before, but not detected when accessing the services, -10 - spoofing attack(s) is detected when accessing the services.

Virus detection in TEE (B2) is to identify the viruses, worms and other types of malwares in TEE of the mobile terminal. Assigned score could be: 10 - virus is never detected, 0 - virus(es) was detected before, but not detected when accessing the services, −10 - virus(es) is detected when accessing the services.

Trusted boot (B3) is to perform a measured and verified launch of Linux kernel. In the boot process, a log is maintained with the components that have been loaded and will be audited later. Trusted boot is implemented based on TEE and secure element. Assigned score could be: 10 - if trusted boot is supported, 0 - otherwise.

Trusted user interface (TUI) (B4) is to allow an application to interact directly with the user through the screen, which is controlled by the TEE and isolated from the REE. TUI defends the application against attacks, such as key logger and screen capturing. Assigned score could be: 10 - if TUI is supported, 0 - otherwise.

Biometric authentication (B5) is to verify and identify individuals based on their unique physical traits such as their iris, voice, face or fingerprints. In order to prevent the attacks such as fingerprint-jacking, printed photo and replayed video, biometric authentication is required to be implemented based on TUI. Assigned score could be: 10 - if biometric authentication is implemented based on TUI, 0 - otherwise.

TEE-based secure storage (B6) is to store sensitive data (e.g., user's biometric data, financial accounts, keys, etc.) securely in SE (Secure Element) or RPMB (Replay Protected Memory Block). The secure storage is implemented based on TEE. Assigned score could be: 10 - if data is stored in SE, 8 - if data is stored in RPMB, 0 - otherwise.

TEE-based real-time kernel protection (B7) is to use a security monitor located within TEE in order to provide the required protection, such as preventing kernel data from being directly accessed by user processes and preventing running unauthorized privileged code (i.e., code that has the kernel privilege) on the system. Assigned score could be: 10 - if TEE-based real-time kernel protection is supported, 0 - otherwise.

TEE OS integrity protection (B8) is to assure the integrity of the TEE OS files with establishing the chain of trust based on IMA. Assigned score could be: 10 - if TEE OS integrity protection is supported, 0 - otherwise.

TEE-based kernel integrity protection (B9) is to validate the integrity of the kernel files before they are loaded (and perhaps executed) based on IMA with the support from TEE. It is to help prevent modifications of kernel and driver code. Assigned score could be: 10 - if TEE-based kernel integrity protection is supported, 0 - otherwise.

2.3 Hardware Security Metrics and Scoring

Hardware security metrics mainly include nine sub-metrics which are defined as follows. The scores of each sub-metric are also given.

Hardware root of trust (C1) is to root the identity (e.g., hardware identifier) and cryptographic keys (e.g., root key, hardware unique key) in the hardware of a device in order to ensure the identity and authenticity of silicon devices at an atomic level. Assigned score could be: 10 - if hardware root of trust is supported, 0 - otherwise.

Secure element (SE) (C2) is to store sensitive data (e.g., financial accounts, keys, etc.) and run secure applications (e.g., mobile payment, mobile banking, etc.). Assigned score could be: 10 - if SE is supported, 0 - otherwise.

Hardware-based encryption (C3) is to use dedicated processor physically located on the encrypted drive to perform the task of authentication and encryption. Hardware-based encryption is more secure than software-based encryption because the encryption process is kept separate from the rest of the machine. Assigned score could be: 10 - if hardware-based encryption is supported, 0 - otherwise.

Memory vulnerabilities (C4) include the flaws and weaknesses in the memory such as memory leak, stack overflow, heap overflow, and allocation of memory without limitations. Assigned score could be: 0 - no well-known memory vulnerability, −5 - one or two well-known memory vulnerabilities are discovered, −10 - more than three well-known memory vulnerabilities are discovered.

Hardware-based defense mechanisms against memory vulnerabilities (C5) are the methods to prevent the memory corruption attacks (e.g., code injection and code reuse) based on hardware mechanisms, such as MTE (Memory Tagging Extension), PAC (Pointer Authentication Code) and BTI (Branch Target Identification). Assigned score could be: 10 - at least three defense mechanisms are supported, 5 - one or two defense mechanisms are supported, 0 - no defense mechanism is supported.

Memory encryption (C6) is to implement on-the-fly RAM encryption in order to protect data and code against attackers with physical access to a memory. Assigned score could be: 10 - if memory encryption is supported, 0 - otherwise.

Firmware version (C7) is to check which version of the firmware the terminal has. It is likely that the latest versions of firmware have less vulnerabilities than older ones. Assigned score could be: 10 - the latest firmware version, 0 - previous firmware version, −10 - outdated firmware version.

Protection against side-channel attack (SCA) (C8) is to prevent the attacks that extract secrets from a chip or a system. The countermeasures against side-channel attacks include designing cryptographic code to resist cache attacks, jamming the emitted channel with noise to deter timing attacks, power line conditioning and filtering to deter power-monitoring attacks, etc. Assigned score could be: 10 - at least three countermeasures against SCA are supported, 5 - one or two countermeasures against SCA are supported, 0 - no countermeasure against SCA is supported.

Protection against physical fault injection attack (FIA) (C9) is to prevent the attacks that insert the faults into the executing instructions and critical data. The countermeasures include concurrent error detection procedures as a hardware countermeasure against fault-injection-based cryptanalysis, an information leakage sensor against the laser fault injection attack, etc. Assigned score could be: 10 - at least three countermeasures against FIA are supported, 5 - one or two countermeasures against FIA are supported, 0 - no countermeasure against FIA is supported.

2.4 Communication Security Metrics and Scoring

Communication security metrics mainly include five sub-metrics which are defined as follows. The scores of each sub-metric are also given.

False base station detection (D1) is to check if the cellular base station, to which the terminal is connecting, is a legitimate one or false one. A false base station is employed for malicious and illegal purposes, such as sending scam messages, capturing signaling messages and collecting the terminal information. Assigned score could be: 10 - the terminal is connecting to a legitimate base station, −10 - the terminal is connecting to a false base station.

Security state of Wi-Fi access point (AP) (D2) is to check if the Wi-Fi AP the terminal connecting to is a secure one or rogue one, and also check if the Wi-Fi AP supports WPA2 (Wi-Fi Protected Access II) or WPA3. Assigned score could be: 10 - the terminal is connecting to a secure AP with supporting at least WPA2, -10 - the terminal is connecting to a rogue AP, or the AP does not support WPA2 or WPA3.

Protected communication (D3) is to provide strong cryptographic protection of data transmitted over the networks (e.g., TLS, IPsec) to mitigate unauthorized disclosure or modification. Assigned score could be: 10 - if protected communication is supported, 0 - otherwise.

SMS verification code encryption (D4) is to encrypt the SMS verification code sent to the user from the server, as a kind of two-factor authentication, in order to make mobile application services (e.g., mobile banking, mobile payment) more secure and to reduce fraud. Assigned score could be: 10 - if SMS verification code encryption is supported, 0 - otherwise.

DNS (Domain Name System) encryption (D5) is to encrypt DNS messages and to make snoopers much harder to look into the DNS messages, or to corrupt them in transit. Two mechanisms are available for encrypting DNS, i.e., DoT (DNS over TLS) and DoH (DNS over HTTPS). It will further enhance user privacy. Assigned score could be: 10 - if DNS encryption is supported, 0 - otherwise.

2.5   Summary of Security Metrics and Scoring

33 security metrics with scores are defined for Android mobile terminals in this paper. The score of each security metric is obtained through the security management functional components of the terminal according to the security status of the terminal when accessing services. The metric is based on a scale of -10 to 10, with 10 being a perfect score. Moreover, the security metrics will increase with emerging security threats.

3   Determining Relative Weights of Security Metrics Based on AHP

Security metrics are defined for Android mobile terminal security assessment in Sect. 2. However, it's very difficult to determine the relative weights of these security metrics when conducting security assessment. Decision-makers may assign different weights to the same security metric. In such a problem of identifying relative weights of multiple metrics for security assessment, the most widely used method is analytical hierarchy process (AHP) [17, 18]. For example, He et al. [19] applied AHP to conduct the information security risk assessment. Petrova [20] performed cybersecurity risk assessment based on AHP to conduct cost-benefit analysis, design and optimize cybersecurity in the systems. Attaallah [21], Ahmad [22] and Ma [23] applied AHP to perform security assessment for medical devices which collect, store and process health data.

In order to support overall and comprehensive Android mobile terminal security assessment, the procedure of determining relative weights of security metrics based on AHP is summarized as follows.

1) *Creating hierarchy structure of security metrics.* A hierarchy structure of security metrics is created.
2) *Forming pairwise comparison matrixes.* The pairwise comparison matrixes are constructed by comparing the security metrics of each level in pairs. A Saaty's 9-point scale [17] in Table 1 is used to determine the importance and preference in pairwise

comparisons. Preferences at forming the pairwise comparison matrixes must satisfy the reciprocal and homogeneity conditions.

Table 1. A Saaty's 9-point scale.

Scale (a_{ij})	Meaning (the comparison of two security metrics)
1	the two metrics i and j are of equal importance
3	the metric i is slightly more important than the metric j
5	the metric i is obviously more important than the metric j
7	the metric i is strongly more important than the metric j
9	the metric i is extremely more important than the metric j
2, 4, 6, 8	median of the two adjacent judgements above
1, 1/2, …, 1/9	the importance ratio of the metric i and the metric j is a_{ij}, so the importance ratio of the metric j and metric i is $a_{ji} = 1/a_{ij}$

3) *Calculating local weight of security metric through the matrix.* The local weight of security metric is calculated through each pairwise comparison matrix. The weight vector of the pairwise comparison matrix can be obtained by the method of solving the characteristic root. Furthermore the consistency index (CI) is also obtained. To verify the acceptability of consistency, it is necessary to calculate the consistency ratio (CR), which is performed by dividing the CI of the matrix by the corresponding value of the random index (RI) in Table 2 suggested by Saaty [17, 18]. If the CR is less than 0.1, the pairwise comparison matrix passes the consistency test. So, the eigenvector is the weight vector.

Table 2. RI for different number of the matrix.

Number of Matrix(n)	1	2	3	4	5	6	7	8	9	10	11
RI	0	0	0.52	0.89	1.11	1.25	1.35	1.40	1.45	1.49	1.51

4) *Calculating total weight of security metric.* The total weight of each security metric is equal to the sum of the product of the local weight of the security metric relative to the weight of the corresponding group that the security metric belongs to. The higher the total weight of a security metric, the better its ranking position, the greater influence on mobile application services.

Therefore, the overall security assessment score is obtained based on the equation:

$$Score = \sum\nolimits_{i=1}^{n} Security\_metric\_score_i * Total\_weight_i \qquad (1)$$

where:

- *Security_metric_score$_i$*: the score of the security metric i which is obtained based on the current security status and the corresponding score defined in Sect. 2.
- *Total_weight$_i$*: the total weight of the security metric i which is determined based on AHP.

4 An Architecture for Android Mobile Terminal Security Assessment System

Figure 2 shows a functional architecture for Android mobile terminal security assessment system with four main components in blue, which will be described in Sect. 4.1.

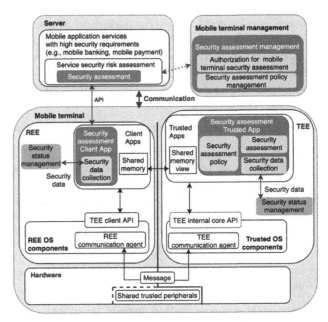

Fig. 2. Functional architecture for Android mobile terminal security assessment system.

4.1 Main Components of Functional Architecture

In Fig. 2, the *Security assessment Client App*, as a part of the mobile terminal software in REE, has the capabilities as follows.

- The *Security assessment Client App* is to receive the security assessment request together with a token from the *Security assessment* of the mobile application services and then send it to *Security assessment Trusted App* in TEE.
- The *Security assessment Client App* is to receive the security assessment reply together with the security level from *Security assessment Trusted App* in TEE and then send it to the *Security assessment* of the mobile application services.

- The *Security assessment Client App* is to collect security data from the Security status management in REE and send it to *Security assessment Trusted App* in TEE.

The *Security assessment Trusted App*, as a part of the mobile terminal software in TEE, has the capabilities as follows.

- The *Security assessment Trusted App* is to receive the security assessment request together with a token from the *Security assessment Client App* in REE.
- The *Security assessment Trusted App* is to validate the security assessment token provided by the *Security assessment* of the mobile application services.
- The *Security assessment Trusted App* is to calculate the overall security assessment score.
- The *Security assessment Trusted App* is to identify the security level based on the obtained overall security assessment score.
- The *Security assessment Trusted App* is to send the security assessment reply together with the security level to the *Security assessment Client App* in REE.
- The *Security assessment Trusted App* is to define security metrics and determine the relative weights of them.
- The *Security assessment Trusted App* is to get security data (e.g., hardware security status, etc.) from the *Security status management* in TEE.

The *Security assessment* of the mobile application services has the capabilities as follows.

- The *Security assessment* is to get the security assessment token from the *Security assessment management* of the mobile terminal management.
- The *Security assessment* is to send the security assessment request together with a token to the *Security assessment Client App* in REE and receive the security assessment reply together with security level from the *Security assessment Client App* in REE.

The *Security assessment management* of the mobile terminal management has the capabilities as follows.

- The *Security assessment management* is to upgrade *Security assessment Client App* in REE and S*ecurity assessment Trusted App* in TEE, including security assessment policy and the rule of security data collection.
- The *Security assessment management* is to generate the security assessment token used by the mobile application services to get the security assessment result.

4.2   Procedure of Mobile Terminal Security Assessment

According to Fig. 2, the procedure of a mobile application service obtaining an overall security assessment result from the mobile terminal is described as follows.

1) The *Security assessment* of a mobile application service sends a security assessment request to the *Security assessment Client App* in REE. The security assessment request includes a token, which is obtained from the *Security assessment management* in mobile terminal management.

2) The *Security assessment Client App* in REE receives the security assessment request and sends it to the *Security assessment Trusted App* in TEE through the communication mechanisms defined in [15]. The *Security assessment Client App* in REE collects security data (e.g., REE security status, communication security status) from time to time and forwards it to the *Security assessment Trusted App*.

3) The *Security assessment Trusted App* in TEE receives the security assessment request and verifies the token, and then calculates the overall security assessment score according to the Eq. (1).

4) The *Security assessment Trusted App* in TEE identifies the security level based on the obtained security assessment score.

5) The *Security assessment Trusted App* in TEE sends the security assessment reply including the security level to the *Security assessment Client App* in REE.

6) The *Security assessment Client App* in REE receives the security assessment reply including the security level and then sends it to the *Security assessment* of the mobile application services.

5   Implementation and Evaluation

According to the system architecture for Android mobile terminal security assessment in Sect. 4, the security assessment system is implemented. Android mobile terminal security assessment is carried out for mobile payment services.

5.1   Conducting Mobile Terminal Security Assessment for Mobile Payment

When implementing security assessment system, the security assessment policies should also be created. Of course, the related security metrics with the corresponding weights, as part of security assessment policies, should be defined.

5.1.1   Defining Security Metrics and Relative Weights

As for mobile payment services, relevant security metrics with the corresponding weights are defined as follows according to the method in Sect. 3.

1) A two-level hierarchy structure of security metrics is created and shown in Fig. 3. The level-2 security metric *C1 (Hardware root of trust)* also contributes to level-1 REE security assessment (A) as level-2 *A11*. In the same way, the level-2 *C2 (Secure element)* and *C3 (Hardware-based encryption)* also contribute to TEE security assessment (B) as level-2 *B10* and *B11* respectively.

2) Based on the two-level hierarchy structure of security metrics in Fig. 3, five pairwise comparison matrixes are constructed by comparing the security metrics of each level in pairs according to the Saaty's 9-point scale in Table 1. These five pairwise comparison matrixes are M_S, M_A, M_B, M_C and M_D, which are constructed for Android mobile terminal security assessment (S), REE security assessment (A), TEE security assessment (B), hardware security assessment (C) and communication security assessment (D) respectively.

In order to construct these five pairwise comparison matrixes, some experts for academic and industry background are consulted. After introducing this project briefly to

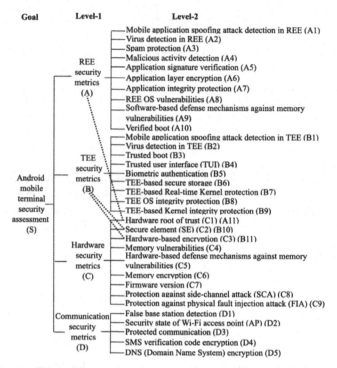

Fig. 3. Two-level hierarchy structure of security metrics.

them, the values of security metrics are provided by them based on their own experience in relevant field. According to their values, five pairwise comparison matrixes are constructed. For example, the pairwise comparison matrix M_S is constructed as the Eq. (2) for mobile payment services.

$$M_S = \begin{bmatrix} & A & B & C & D \\ A & 1 & 5 & 3 & 7 \\ B & 1/5 & 1 & 1/2 & 2 \\ C & 1/3 & 2 & 1 & 4 \\ D & 1/7 & 1/2 & 1/4 & 1 \end{bmatrix} \tag{2}$$

3) The weight vector W_S of the pairwise comparison matrix M_S is obtained as follows.

- *According* to the matrix M_S, the vector $\Phi = (2.3164, 0.4851, 0.9304, 0.2681)^T$ is calculated by normalizing columns and then calculating the sum of the row. By normalizing the vector Φ, the eigenvector $W_S = (0.5791, 0.1213, 0.2325, 0.0670)^T$ is obtained. The largest eigenvalue λ_{max} associated with the matrix M_S is obtained as 4.1185. Furthermore the consistency index (CI) is also obtained as 0.0095.
- To verify the acceptability of consistency, it is necessary to calculate the consistency ratio (CR), which is performed by dividing the CI of matrix M_S by the corresponding value of the random index (RI) in Table 2 suggested by Saaty [17, 18]. As for matrix S, CR = CI/RI = 0.0095/0.89 = 0.011, which is less than 0.1. So, the pairwise

comparison matrix M_S passes the consistency test. What's more, the eigenvector W_S is the weight vector.

- So, the weight of level-1 REE security assessment (A), TEE security assessment (B), Hardware security assessment (C) and Communication security assessment (D) for Android mobile terminal security assessment for mobile payment are 0.5791, 0.1213, 0.2325, 0.0670 respectively.

In the same way, the weight vectors of other four matrixes (i.e., M_A, M_B, M_C and M_D) for mobile payment services are obtained as follows.

$$W_{A1-A11} = (0.0780, 0.0551, 0.0377, 0.2769, 0.2029, 0.1081, 0.1484, 0.0204, 0.0170, 0.0249, 0.0307)^T \quad (3)$$

$$W_{B1-B11} = (0.0197, 0.0197, 0.1432, 0.0258, 0.0258, 0.2039, 0.0564, 0.0789, 0.1088, 0.2784, 0.0393)^T \quad (4)$$

$$W_{C1-C9} = (0.3086, 0.2197, 0.1557, 0.0264, 0.1074, 0.0748, 0.0350, 0.0515, 0.0209)^T \quad (5)$$

$$W_{D1-D5} = (0.0987, 0.0642, 0.2810, 0.5121, 0.0440)^T \quad (6)$$

So, the local weights of the level-2 security metrics are obtained based on the Eqs. (3)–(6), i.e., the weight vectors of the four pairwise comparison matrixes.

4) Table 3 shows the total weight of each security metric for mobile payment services, which is equal to the sum of the product of the local weight of the level-2 security metric relative to each weight of the level-1 security metric. Table 3 also shows the ranking position of each security metric, which is ranked based on its total weight. The higher the total weight of a security metric, the better its ranking position, the greater influence on mobile payment services.

In Table 3, security metrics *malicious activity detection (A4), application signature verification (A5)* and *hardware root of trust (C1)* have a comparatively great proportion of the weight, which shows that they have great influence on the Android mobile terminal security assessment for mobile payment services.

5.1.2 Conducting Security Assessment of Mobile Terminal for Mobile Payment

Based on the system architecture for Android mobile terminal security assessment in Sect. 4, a security assessment system is implemented with Android mobile phone settings as follows.

- OS: Android 12.
- Linux kernel: 5.10.
- CPU: Snapdragon 8 Gen 1.
- Internal memory: RAM: 8G/12G, ROM: 256G/512G.
- TEE: QTEE 5.0.

According to the procedure of security assessment in Sect. 4.2, the mobile payment service receives an overall mobile terminal security assessment result including security level from the Android mobile terminals.

Table 3. Total weight of each security metric for mobile payment.

Factors of Level 1 (metric & weight)	Factors of level 2		Total Weight	Rank
	Security metric	Local weight		
REE security metrics (0.5791)	A1	0.0780	0.0451	7
	A2	0.0551	0.0319	10
	A3	0.0377	0.0219	13
	A4	0.2769	0.1603	1
	A5	0.2029	0.1175	2
	A6	0.1081	0.0626	6
	A7	0.1484	0.0859	4
	A8	0.0204	0.0118	19
	A9	0.0170	0.0099	20
	A10	0.0249	0.0144	17
TEE security metrics (0.1213)	B1	0.0197	0.0024	32
	B2	0.0197	0.0024	32
	B3	0.1432	0.0174	15
	B4	0.0258	0.0031	29
	B5	0.0258	0.0031	29
	B6	0.2039	0.0247	12
	B7	0.0564	0.0068	23
	B8	0.0789	0.0096	21
	B9	0.1088	0.0132	17
Hardware security metrics (0.2325)	C1	0.3086	0.0896[*a]	3
	C2	0.2197	0.0849[*b]	5
	C3	0.1557	0.0410[*c]	8
	C4	0.0264	0.0061	26
	C5	0.1074	0.0250	11
	C6	0.0748	0.0174	15
	C7	0.0350	0.0081	22
	C8	0.0515	0.0120	18
	C9	0.0209	0.0049	27
Communication security metrics (0.0670)	D1	0.0987	0.0066	25

(*continued*)

Table 3. (continued)

Factors of Level 1 (metric & weight)	Factors of level 2		Total Weight	Rank
	Security metric	Local weight		
	D2	0.0642	0.0043	28
	D3	0.2810	0.0188	14
	D4	0.5121	0.0343	9
	D5	0.0440	0.0030	31

[a] sum of C1 (0.0718) and A11 (0.0178)
[b] sum of C2 (0.0511) and B10 (0.0338)
[c] sum of C3 (0.0362) and B11 (0.0048)

The security level is defined based on the obtained security assessment score according to the Eq. (1). Security level is a measure of the security strength that the mobile terminal achieves. It represents the level corresponding to the required effectiveness of countermeasures and inherent security properties of the mobile terminals. For example, security level of mobile terminals can be defined in Table 4. High security level means the security of the mobile terminal is strong enough to access all mobile application services.

Table 4. Security rating scale.

Rating	Security assessment score
High	8.0–10.0
Medium	6.0–7.9
Low	Less than 5.9

It's suggested that only the mobile terminal with high security level (i.e., the security assessment score is higher than 8.0) is allowed to perform mobile payments.

5.2 Evaluation

According to the system architecture in Sect. 4, the security assessment system has already been implemented since June 2022. Figure 4 shows around 6 million smartphones which support the security assessment solution proposed in this paper in Sep. 2022.

As the number of smartphones supporting security assessment increases, so does the volume of payment transactions. Figure 5 shows that the smartphones supporting security assessment made the total online payment transactions per month, of which the fraudulent transactions were detected. Furthley, it's obtained that the payment fraud rate per month is around 0.08%, which is shown in Fig. 6. It's observed that the payment fraud rate in June 2022 is around 0.05%. One of reasons is that it was the first month to

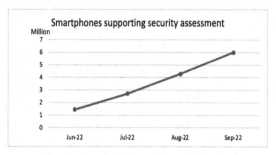

Fig. 4. Smartphones supporting security assessment since June 2022.

implement this security assessment system and the collected payment transaction data may be incomplete. Note: in this paper, security assessment of the mobile terminal is conducted for the mobile payment, which is only triggered by the third-party mobile Apps.

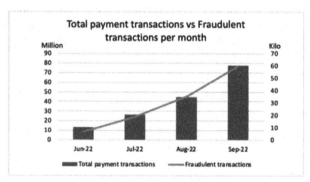

Fig. 5. Smartphones supporting security assessment performed the total payment transactions per month, of which fraudulent transactions were detected.

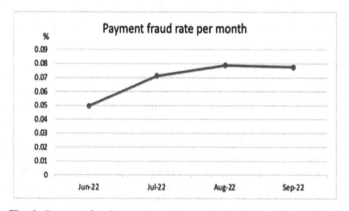

Fig. 6. Payment fraud rate per month was obtained according to Fig. 5.

It's found that top 5 security metrics with great influence on security assessment to support payment security risk assessment are *malicious activity detection (A4), application signature verification (A5), hardware root of trust (C1), application integrity protection (A7),* and *secure element (SE) (C2),* shown in Table 3.

Currently, security assessment of Android mobile terminals is also being tested for mobile enterprise services. Consulting with some experts from academia and industry, the relative weights of security metrics are determined based on AHP. It's found that a security metric has different total weight values for mobile payment and mobile enterprise service, which is shown in Fig. 7.

It's also found that top 5 security metrics with great influence on security assessment to support enterprise service security risk assessment are *secure element (SE) (C2), hardware root of trust (C1), hardware-based encryption (C3), protected communication (D3),* and *TEE-based kernel integrity protection (B9).*

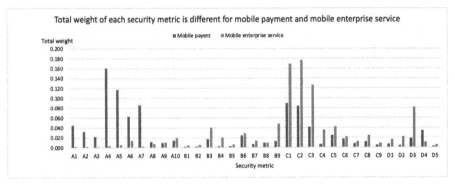

Fig. 7. Total weight of each security metric is different for mobile payment and mobile enterprise service.

5.3 Limitation

In this paper, the proposed approach for security assessment only works for the mobile terminal with Android OS. Moreover, mobile terminal security assessment is only conducted for mobile payment services, which are only triggered by the third-party mobile Apps. Some important security metrics for other mobile application services may not be included in this paper.

With emerging security threats, the security metrics will increase and the relative weights will change accordingly. It's not appropriate to consult experts from time to time to determine the relative weights. So, it is useful for optimizing the current solutions or design new solutions to determine the relative weight of each security metric without involving experts.

In this paper, all possible security metrics are taken into account for security assessment, which may cause computational burden and performance degradation if a lot of mobile application services need to conduct mobile terminal security assessment. In order to simplify the calculation and improve the system performance, it's suggested to take the top security metrics with great influence on security assessment into account for service security risk assessment.

6 Conclusion and Future Work

In order to reduce security risks, mobile terminal security assessment should be performed before accessing the services with high security requirements. To support conducting mobile terminal security assessment, we defined security metrics with scores, determined the relative weights of these security metrics based on AHP and designed a system architecture. Moreover, we implemented a security assessment system and carried out security assessment for mobile payment services. Until 30 September 2022, around 6 million smartphones support the security assessment solution proposed in this paper. In September 2022, these smartphones made 77 million online payment transactions, of which 60,000 fraudulent transactions were detected, with the payment fraud rate of about 0.08%.

We also tried to determine the relative weights of security metrics for mobile enterprise services and found that a security metric has different weight values for different mobile application services.

In the future, we plan to optimize the current solution and consider the top security metrics with great influence on security assessment for service risk assessment in order to improve the system performance. We plan to design new solutions to determine the relative weight of each security metric without involving experts. We also plan to define new security metrics from time to time because new security threats emerge all the time.

References

1. Wang, F., Jiang, D., Wen, H., Song, H.: Adaboost-based security level classification of mobile intelligent terminals. J. Supercomput. **75**(11), 7460–7478 (2019). https://doi.org/10.1007/s11 227-019-02954-y
2. Xi, Z., Chen, L., Chen, M., Dai, Z., Li, Y.: Power mobile terminal security assessment based on weights self-learning. In: 2018 10th International Conference on Communication Software and Networks (ICCSN) (2018). https://doi.org/10.1109/ICCSN.2018.8488313
3. Wu, S., Ma, Y., Jiang, H., Liu, T., Zuo, J., Peng, T.: Smart grid terminal security assessment method based on subjective and objective comprehensive weighting. In: 2021 IEEE Sixth International Conference on Data Science in Cyberspace (DSC) (2021). https://doi.org/10.1109/DSC53577.2021.00102
4. Ratchford, M., Wang, Y.: BYOD-insure: a security assessment model for enterprise BYOD. In: 2019 5th International Conference Mobile Secure Services MOBISECSERV 2019, no. 1, pp. 1–10 (2019). https://doi.org/10.1109/MOBISECSERV.2019.8686551
5. Visoottiviseth, V., Kotarasu, C., Cheunprapanusorn, N., Chamornmarn, T.: A Mobile application for security assessment towards the internet of thing devices. In: 2019 IEEE 6th Asian Conference on Defence Technology (ACDT), Bali, Indonesia, 13–15 November 2019 (2019). https://doi.org/10.1109/ACDT47198.2019.9072921
6. Othman, N.A.A., Norman, A.A., Kiah, M.L.M.: Information system audit for mobile device security assessment. In: 2021 3rd International Cyber Resilience Conference (CRC), Langkawi Island, Malaysia. https://doi.org/10.1109/CRC50527.2021.9392468

7. Cavalcanti, K., Viana, E., Lins, F.: An integrated solution for the improvement of the mobile devices security based on the android platform. IEEE Lat. Am. Trans. **15**(11), 2171–2176 (2017)
8. Vecchiato, D., Vieira, M., Martins, E.: Risk assessment of user-defined security configurations for android devices. In: 2016 IEEE 27th International Symposium on Software Reliability Engineering (ISSRE), Ottawa, ON, Canada (2016). https://doi.org/10.1109/ISSRE.2016.30
9. Asnar, Y., Hendradjaya, B.: Confidentiality and privacy information security risk assessment for Android-based mobile devices. In: 2015 International Conference on Data and Software Engineering, Yogyakarta, Indonesia. Proceedings of the ICoDSE 2015, pp. 1–6 (2015). https://doi.org/10.1109/ICODSE.2015.7436972
10. Khokhlov, I., Reznik, L.: Android system security evaluation. In: 2018 15th IEEE Annual Consumer Communications & Networking Conference (CCNC) (2018). https://doi.org/10.1109/CCNC.2018.8319325
11. Raza, N., Kirit, N.: Security evaluation for android OS using expert systems (2019). https://doi.org/10.13140/RG.2.2.27162.08640
12. Hayran, A., İğdeli, M., Yılmaz, A., Gemci, C.: Security evaluation of IOS and android. Int. J. Appl. Math. Electron. Comput. IJAMEC. **4**(Special Issue), 258–261 (2016). https://doi.org/10.18100/ijamec.270378
13. Khokhlov, I., Reznik, L.: Data security evaluation for mobile android devices. In: 2017 20th Conference of Open Innovations Association (FRUCT) (2017). https://doi.org/10.23919/FRUCT.2017.8071306
14. Zendehdel, G.A., Kaur, R., Chopra, I., Stakhanova, N., Scheme, E.: Automated security assessment framework for wearable BLE-enabled health monitoring devices. ACM Trans. Internet Technol. **22**(1), 1–31 (2022). https://doi.org/10.1145/3448649
15. GlobalPlatform Technology TEE System Architecture Version 1.2. https://globalplatform.org/wp-content/uploads/2017/01/GPD_TEE_SystemArch_v1.2_PublicRelease.pdf
16. ARM TrustZone for AArch64. https://developer.arm.com/documentation/102418/0101/?lang=en
17. Saaty, T.L.: The Analytic Hierarchy Process Mcgraw Hill, New York. Agricultural Economics Review, vol. 70 (1980)
18. Abu Dabous, S., Alkass, S.: Decision support method for multi-criteria selection of bridge rehabilitation strategy. Constr. Manage. Econ. **26**(8), 883–893 (2008). https://doi.org/10.1080/01446190802071190
19. He, M., An, X.: Information security risk assessment based on analytic hierarchy process. Indonesian J. Electr. Eng. Comput. Sci. **1**(3), 656–664 (2016). https://doi.org/10.11591/ijeecs.v1.i3.pp656-664
20. Petrova, V.: A cybersecurity risk assessment. Int. Sci. J. Sci. Tech. Union Mech. Eng. "Ind. 4.0" **6**(1), 37–40 (2021). https://stumejournals.com/journals/i4/2021/1/37
21. Attaallah, A., Ahmad, M., Jamal Ansari, M.T., Pandey, A.K., Kumar, R., Khan, R.A.: Device security assessment of internet of healthcare things. Intell. Autom. Soft Comput. **27**(2), 593–603 (2021). https://doi.org/10.32604/iasc.2021.015092
22. Ahmad, M., Al-Amri, J.F., Subahi, A.F., Khatri, S., Seh, A.H., Nadeem, N., Agrawal, A.: healthcare device security assessment through computational methodology. Comput. Syst. Sci. Eng. **41**(2), 811–828 (2021). https://doi.org/10.32604/csse.2022.020097
23. Ma, P., Wang, Z., Hei, X., Zou, X., Zhang, J., Liu, Q., et al.: A quantitative approach for medical imaging device security assessment. In: 2019 IEEE/IFIP International Conference on Dependable Systems and Networks Supplemental, Portland, OR, USA (2019). https://doi.org/10.1109/DSN-S.2019.00008

A General Steganalysis Method of QR Codes

Jia Chen[1,2], Kunlin Chen[1,2], Yongjie Wang[1,2], Xuehu Yan[1,2(✉)],
and Longlong Li[1,2]

[1] National University of Defense Technology, 460 Huangshan Road,
Shushan District, Hefei 230037, China
publictiger@126.com
[2] Anhui Key Laboratory of Cyberspace Security Situation Awareness
and Evaluation, Hefei 230037, China

Abstract. With the wide application of quick response (QR) codes,
its security has been paid more and more attention. There are many
steganography schemes to embed the secret message into QR codes,
which can be used in terrorist activities, spread viruses, etc. However,
there is currently no effective scheme for detecting stego QR code. This
paper divides the spatial QR code-based steganography schemes into
three categories and then proposes a steganalysis method for QR codes.
The method includes detecting stegao codes and recovering pure QR
codes, which is realized by the code regeneration, module comparison,
and embedded information filtering operations. Our method can per-
fectly distinguish the stego code and block the transmission of embedded information for the spatial QR code-based steganography schemes.
Theoretical analysis and experiments show that the proposed method is
feasible, universal, and robust.

Keywords: QR codes · Steganography · Steganalysis · Code
regeneration · Protection

1 Introduction

The quick response (QR) codes [1] were invented by Japanese company Denso
Wave in 1994 for tracking components in vehicle manufacturing. These barcodes
now are widely applied in location, printing, online advertising, mobile payment
and Internet commerce, etc. With the popularity of smartphones, QR codes
have become a fast and efficient URL connector, known as the "entrance" of the
mobile Internet. They are convenient, easy to convey information. Meanwhile,
smartphones can quickly and easily use built-in cameras or decoders downloaded
from the Internet to decode QR codes.

Supported by the Program of the National University of Defense Technology and the
National Natural Science Foundation of China (Number: 61602491).

S. Goel et al. (Eds.): ICDF2C 2022, LNICST 508, pp. 472–483, 2023.
https://doi.org/10.1007/978-3-031-36574-4_28

With the widespread usage and promotion of QR codes, its security issues have attracted more and more attention. In 2010, Kaspersky Lab captured the first attempt to use malicious QR codes for cybercrime, linking the QR codes to malware for Android (OS) and J2ME (Java). A malicious QR code is usually a malicious link embedded in a normal QR code. When users scan it, they jump to malware or a designated website. Recently, vicious crimes based on QR codes have increased, and the common QR code scam are clickjacking, phishing links, and Trojan horse viruses, etc. [2].

Data hiding [3,4] and secret sharing [5,6] are common data protection techniques. However, steganography can also be used to embed malicious information into a QR code. In recent years, more and more researchers have studied QR code-based steganography schemes. Some redesigned the QR code module to embed the secret message, such as [7–11]. The most common method is to implement steganography based on the error correction capability of the QR code [12–17]. There is also a scheme of embedding secret information into padding bits [18]. These QR code-based steganography schemes may be used for terrorist activities, cybercrime, and so on.

Faced with the security issues of QR codes caused by data hiding technology, a steganalysis scheme for QR codes is urgently needed to identify the stego code. The QR code is not only a typical two-dimensional barcode, but also a standard image. Currently, there are many image steganalysis schemes. Early schemes used statistical features for steganalysis [19,20]. Avcibas et al. [21] proposed a scheme to detect the stego image with the aid of image quality features and multivariate regression analysis. Later, some researchers proposed more complex feature sets with high dimension to improve the detection performance of steganalysis, such as subtractive pixel adjacency model (SPAM) [22], Spatial Rich Models (SRM) [23], and Discrete Cosine Transform Residual (DCTR) [24], etc. Meanwhile, some feature selection algorithms have also been proposed, such as the Genetic Algorithm (GA) [25], Binary Bat Algorithm (BBA) [26] and so on. Recently, many image steganalysis schemes tend to be implemented based on deep learning [27,28]and convolution neural network [29–31].

However, the above steganalysis schemes are not effective when applied to QR codes, and many of them require considerable samples to train the model. Moreover, there is currently no scheme specifically designed to detect stego QR codes. Meanwhile, the special structure of the black and white blocks of the barcode does not have general image statistics and texture features, etc. To solve the increasingly serious security issues of QR codes, and overcome the difficulty that QR code-based steganography schemes are not easy to detect, this paper proposes a general steganalysis method of QR codes. The code regeneration and module comparison operation are used to detect stego codes, and the secret message is filtered to recover pure QR codes. The contributions of this paper are summarized as follows.

1. We review the QR code-based steganography schemes and divide them into three categories according to implementation principles.

2. We design a steganalysis method for QR codes, which contains detecting stegao codes and recovering pure QR codes.
3. Experiments verify the feasibility and robustness of the proposed method, and the robustness is consistent with the robustness of the steganography scheme.

The rest of this paper is organized as follows. In Sect. 2, we briefly introduce the features of the QR code, and review the QR code-based steganography schemes. The proposed method and the theoretical analyses are described in Sect. 3. Section 4 gives experimental results. Finally, conclusions are drawn in Sect. 5.

2   Preliminaries

2.1   QR Code Features

A QR code consists of black and white squares (called modules). Each module represents 1 bit of data, where black (white) modules represent 1 (0), respectively. According to the QR code standard, there are a total of 40 different versions of QR codes. The number of modules in a QR code is determined by the version number v. For a version-v QR code, the number of modules is $(17 + 4v) \times (17 + 4v)$. In addition, the Reed-Solomon code is applied to achieve the error-correction capability of QR codes. Four error-correction levels (L, M, Q, and H) are available, and corresponding error-correction capabilities are about $7\%, 15\%, 25\%$, and 30%, respectively.

Figure 1 shows the structure of a standard version-7 QR code. All modules of a QR code can be divided into two parts: the function pattern and data region. The function pattern contains the quiet zone, finder patterns, separators, timing patterns, and alignment patterns, and is applied to locate and identify the QR code parameters. The data region includes the format information, version information, and data and error-correction codewords. In general, the function pattern of the same version QR code is the same, and the data region determines the essence of the QR code. Through the encoding and decoding phase of the QR code as shown in Algorithm 1, we analyzed that the same content can generate the same QR code with the same version and format information.

2.2   Steganography Based on QR Codes

According to the implementation principles of these schemes and the encoding and decoding characteristics of QR codes, we divide the steganography schemes based on QR codes into three categories:

1. Redesign the modules of the cover QR code to embed secret information [7–11]. A module is a pixel block composed of some pixels. Usually, a module is designed into a 3×3 or 5×5 pixel block. The key pixels remain unchanged, and the secret information is embedded in other pixels.

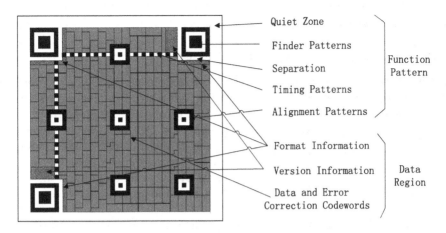

Fig. 1. Structure of a version-7 QR code.

Algorithm 1. The encoding and decoding phase of the QR code.

The encoding phase
Step 1. Analyze the input data stream to determine the type of characters to be encoded. And select the required error correction level.
Step 2. Encode the data into a bitstream with every eight bits as a codeword, and adding padding codewords if necessary.
Step 3. Encode the bitstream with the RS code.
Step 4. Construct the final information and place function patterns in the matrix.
Step 5. Masking the data and error-correction codewords of the symbol.
Step 6. Generate the the format and version information, and then obtain the final matrix.

The encoding phase
Step 1. Identifie all black and white modules.
Step 2. Decode the format and version information.
Step 3. Remove the mask pattern.
Step 4. Recover the data and error correction codewords.
Step 5. Check the error with error-correcting codewords.
Step 6. Decode the data codewords.

2. Utilize error correction mechanism of the QR code [12–17]. The secret information is embedded by modifying the QR code modules within the scope of fault tolerance. During decoding, the RS code can correct data errors and recover the correct information.
3. Take advantage of the redundancy of the QR code. The padding bits are added in each data block if there are insufficient data bits. When constructing the final information, remainder bits are filled if needed. The secret information is embedded utilizing these redundant and meaningless bits [18].

3   The Proposed Method

3.1   The Steganalysis Method for QR Codes

In the proposed method, we first detect the stego code, and then recover the pure QR code. Among the three types of QR code-based steganography schemes summarized above, the embedding method based on the redesigned cover module is easy to see the difference from the standard QR code. So the embedded information is directly filtered to recover the pure QR code. For the remaining two categories, the QR code cannot be determined from the appearance to be abnormal. Therefore, it is necessary to judge the stego code first, and then filter out the embedded information. The flow chart of the proposed method is shown in Fig. 2.

The detailed steps of the proposed method are described in Algorithm 2. Given a cover QR code, first identify whether it is stego code. If the QR code is abnormal in appearance, we directly filter out embedded information by code regeneration. The so-called code regeneration operation, specifically, decodes the QR code to obtain the cover content, version, and format information, and then regenerates a pure QR code (called re-code) based on these information. The original QR code becomes a stego code after embedding secret information. The re-code is the same as the original QR code in the module distribution. As a result, the re-code blocks the transmission of secret information to protect the QR code.

In proposed method, we detect the stego QR codes using the code regeneration and module difference rate (MDR), if the stego code cannot be determined directly. First, perform the code generation operation to obtain the re-code. Then compare the re-code with all modules of the cover code to calculate the MDR. Finally, set the threshold t, and the stego code is distinguished based on MDR and t. If this code is a stego code, output the pure re-code to filter the embedded information. Otherwise, this code can be used directly without security issues.

3.2   Theoretical Analysis

Feasibility. Filtering embedded information is based on code regeneration operation, and the detection process also depends on the code regeneration operation. Therefore, the key to the feasibility of the proposed method lies in whether the code regeneration operation can be realized. According to the encoding and decoding processes of the QR code as shown in Algorithm 1, the generation of QR code is related to cover content, version, error correction capability, and mask. Given the same cover content, then select the same version and error correction capability. Eight kinds of mask patterns are fixed, and an optimal one is selected based on the evaluation. Therefore, when the content, version, and format information are the same, the QR code is unique. Based on the uniqueness of QR codes, we can implement the proposed method.

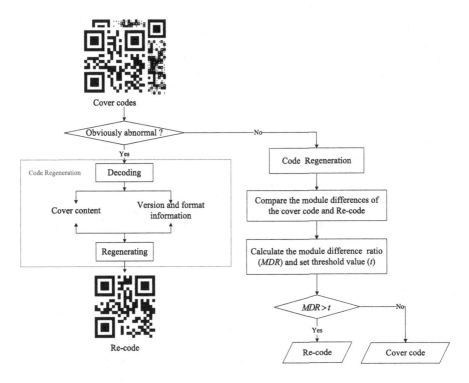

Fig. 2. The flowchart of the protection for QR codes.

Algorithm 2. The process of protection method for QR codes.

Input: A cover QR code.
Output: A secure QR code.

Step 1. Decode the cover QR code to obtain the cover content, version, and format information.
Step 2. Regenerate the re-code based on the decoded information.
Step 3. Determine whether the cover code is a stego code. If it can be determined directly, go to Step 6; otherwise, go to Step 4.
Step 4. Compare the re-code with all modules of the cover code to calculate the MDR, and set the threshold t.
Step 5. If $MDR \geq t$, go to Step 6; otherwise, go to Step 7.
Step 6. Output the re-code.
Step 7. Output the cover QR code.

Universality. The QR code-based steganography schemes are divided into three categories according to the implementation principles. Our proposed method is applicable to all three types of stego QR codes. On the one hand, the code regeneration operation is carried out directly to recover a standard pure QR code for the abnormal code. On the other hand, the detection of the stego code depends on our steganalysis scheme for codes without obvious abnormalities. The embedded secret information will cause changes in QR code module. As long as the module changes, it will be successfully captured by our steganalysis scheme. Therefore, the proposed method can be applied to the protection of all QR codes. In addition, the idea of our proposed method can also be used to protect all barcodes.

Robustness. The robustness of our proposed method depends on the robustness of decoding. As long as a standard decoder can decode a QR code, we can perform steganalysis and protection. Generally, the QR code-based steganography schemes will ensure that the QR code can be decoded normally to reduce the probability of being discovered. So the stego code has good robustness and can resist various noise and other attacks. In our proposed method, the robustness of steganography determines the robustness of steganalysis. As long as the stego code can be decoded normally, our scheme is effective.

Threshold Estimation. Embedding secret information will cause changes to the QR code cover module, but this change will be within the error correction capability to ensure correct decoding. So based on the number of modules used for error correction, we can roughly estimate the upper limit of the threshold t as shown in 1. Where n represents the total number of modules, and ecc denotes each error correction level provides error-correction capabilities ($L \sim 7\%$, $M \sim 15\%$, $H \sim 25\%$, $Q \sim 30\%$).

$$t_h = \frac{\lfloor n \cdot ecc \times 8/2 \rfloor}{(17 + 4v)(17 + 4v)} = \frac{\lfloor 4 \times n \cdot ecc \rfloor}{(17 + 4v)(17 + 4v)} \tag{1}$$

Generally, there are no error modules for electronically printed QR codes. That is, the error rate is 0. In addition, our proposed method adopts the module difference rate instead of the pixel difference rate, which can also overcome the interference caused by noise, blur, printing, etc. Because the change of a pixel will not affect the recognition of the module. Therefore, we set the lower limit of the threshold $t_l = 0.01$. In summary, if $0.01 \le MDR \le \frac{\lfloor 4 \times n \cdot ecc \rfloor}{(17+4v)(17+4v)}$, it means that the QR code is embedded with secret information.

4   Experimental Results and Comparison

In this section, to verify the effectiveness of the proposed method, experiments are given for each type of stego code in Python and executed on a PC with a 3.40 GHz CPU and 16.0 GB of RAM running the Windows 7 operating system. Since some steganographic algorithms based on QR codes are not open source, the test sample codes used in the experiment are screenshots from the corresponding papers.

Figure 3 shows the experimental results of the proposed protection method for stego codes based on module redesign. Figure 3 (*a*) is a nested QR code captured from [9]. The outer QR code encodes the URL "https://www.yzu.edu.tw", and the inner QR code is the URL "https://www.youtube.com/watch?v=9i_UQC4znvu". Figure 3 (*c*) is the re-code based on the outer QR code. Figure 3 (*e*) shows a two-level QR code taken from [10]. Figure 3 (*g*) is the re-code according the public-level message "cover Response Code 1". Figure 3 (*a*) and (*e*) are obviously abnormal QR codes. Figure 3 (*c*) and (*g*) are re-code which remove the embedded content. Figure 3 (*b*), (*d*), (*f*) and (*h*) are the decoding of Fig. 3 (*a*), (*c*), (*e*) and (*g*), respectively. From the decoding result, the re-code and cover code can carry the same information and achieve the same function.

Figure 4 shows the experimental results for stego QR codes based on error correction mechanism and encoding redundancy. Figure 4 (*a*) is a version 1-L stego code based on error correction mechanism captured from [14]. Its public message is the URL "fcu.edu.tw", and the embedded secret is the number "29", which requires a specific decoder to decode it. Figure 4 (*b*) shows a secure QR code generated based on public message. Figure 4 (*c*) shows the different modules marked in red modules between the cover code and re-code, and $MDR = 7.710\%$. Figure 4 (*d*) is a version 40-M QR code embedded with secret message. Its public message is "guofangkejidaxuedianziduikangxueyuan", and the secret message "This the a secret.0000..." is embedded in the padding bits of the QR code. Figure 4 (*e*) shows the re-code. Figure 4 (*f*) displays the different modules with 5.471%.

Experiments for robustness verification were conducted. The cover QR codes of the steganalysis samples are all derived from QR code-based steganography schemes related papers of. Experiments show that our method can accurately distinguish stego codes from all samples, and the embedded messages can be filtered through code regeneration. The robustness of the proposed protection method is consistent with the robustness of the corresponding steganography scheme. As long as the stego QR code can be decoded by a standard decoder, our proposed method can work successfully.

Table 1 compares the properties of classic image steganalysis schemes with our method. The schemes in [21, 23, 27, 29] are classic image steganalysis methods and require many samples to train the model. However, when they are applied to QR code detection, the effect of steganalysis is not ideal. Our scheme adopts code regeneration operation, only one cover QR code is needed to realize real-time protection, and the detection effect is perfect.

480   J. Chen et al.

Fig. 3. The proposed protection method for stego codes based on module redesign. (a) shows the nested code taken from [9]. (b) is the result of decoding (a). (c) is the re-code. (d) presents the decoding result of (c). (e) is the stego code taken from [10]. (f) shows the decoding result of (a). (g) is the re-code. (h) displays the result of decoding (g).

Fig. 4. The proposed protection method for stego codes. (a) − (c) are based on error correction mechanism, and (d) − (f) are based on the padding code. (a) shows the cover code taken from [14]. (b) is the re-code. (c) displays the differences between (a) and (b) with $MDR = 7.710\%$. (d) is the cover code from [18]. (e) is the re-code. (f) shows the differences between (d) and (e) with $MDR = 5.471\%$.

Table 1. Comparisons of the proposed method and classic image steganalysis schemes.

	Based method	Main Detection Object	The steganalysis effect for QR codes	Number of samples required
[21]	Image quality metrics	Image	Not ideal	Many
[23]	Rich models	Image	Not ideal	Many
[27]	Deep learning	Image	Not ideal	Many
[29]	Convolutional Neural Network	Image	Not ideal	Many
Our	Code regeneration	Barcodes	Perfect	One

5   Conclusion

This paper proposes a general steganalysis method of QR codes. We apply the code regeneration and module comparison operation to distinguish the stego QR codes. Furthermore, the embedded message can be filtered out by code regeneration to recover the pure QR code. The proposed method can effectively determine the stego QR code and block the transmission of secret messages. The accuracy of steganalysis is almost 100%, and the proposed method has a perfect effect on QR code protection. In future work, researchers could attempt to extend this method to other barcode protection, design a model to protect all barcodes, and further focus on studying steganalysis methods based on deep learning for QR codes.

References

1. JTC1/SC, I.: Information technology - automatic identification and data capture techniques - QR code 2005 bar code symbology specification (2006)
2. Arntz, P.: QR code scams are making a comeback (2020). https://blog.malwarebytes.com/scams/2020/10/qr-code-scams-are-making-a-comeback/
3. Shi, Y.Q., Li, X., Zhang, X., Wu, H.T., Ma, B.: Reversible data hiding: advances in the past two decades. IEEE Access 4, 3210–3237 (2016). https://doi.org/10.1109/ACCESS.2016.2573308
4. Ma, K., Zhang, W., Zhao, X., Yu, N., Li, F.: Reversible data hiding in encrypted images by reserving room before encryption. Inf. Forensics Secur. IEEE Trans. 8, 553–562 (2013). https://doi.org/10.1109/TIFS.2013.2248725
5. Yan, X., Lu, Y., Yang, C.N., Zhang, X., Wang, S.: A common method of share authentication in image secret sharing. IEEE Trans. Circ. Syst. Video Technol. 31, 2896–2908 (2020)
6. Yan, X., Lu, Y., Liu, L., Song, X.: Reversible image secret sharing. IEEE Trans. Inf. Forensics Secur. 15, 3848–3858 (2020). https://doi.org/10.1109/TIFS.2020.3001735
7. Mohamed Amin, M., Salleh, M., Ibrahim, S., Katmin, M.: Stenography: random LSB insertion using discrete logarithm, pp. 234–238 (2003)

8. Tkachenko, I., Puech, W., Destruel, C., Strauss, O., Gaudin, J.M., Guichard, C.: Two-level QR code for private message sharing and document authentication. IEEE Trans. Inf. Forensics Secur. **11**, 1 (2016). https://doi.org/10.1109/TIFS.2015.2506546

9. Chou, G.J., Wang, R.Z.: The nested QR code. IEEE Sig. Process. Lett. **27**, 1230–1234 (2020). https://doi.org/10.1109/LSP.2020.3006375

10. Cheng, Y., Fu, Z., Yu, B., Shen, G.: A new two-level QR code with visual cryptography scheme. Multimedia Tools Appl. **77**(16), 20629–20649 (2018). https://doi.org/10.1007/s11042-017-5465-4

11. Baharav, Z., Kakarala, R.: Visually significant QR codes: image blending and statistical analysis, pp. 1–6 (2013). https://doi.org/10.1109/ICME.2013.6607571

12. Chiang, Y.J., Lin, P.Y., Wang, R.Z., Chen, Y.H.: Blind QR code steganographic approach based upon error correction capability. KSII Trans. Internet Inf. Syst. **7**, 2527–2543 (2013). https://doi.org/10.3837/tiis.2013.10.012

13. Bui, T., Vu, N., Nguyen, T., Echizen, I., Nguyen, T.: Robust message hiding for QR code, pp. 520–523 (2014). https://doi.org/10.1109/IIH-MSP.2014.135

14. Huang, P.C., Li, Y.H., Chang, C.C., Liu, Y.: Efficient scheme for secret hiding in QR code by improving exploiting modification direction. KSII Trans. Internet Inf. Syst. **12**(5), 2348–2365 (2018)

15. Lin, P.Y., Chen, Y.H.: High payload secret hiding technology for QR codes. EURASIP J. Image Video Process. **2017**(1), 1–8 (2017)

16. Wan, S., Lu, Y., Yan, X., Ding, W., Liu, H.: High capacity embedding methods of QR code error correction, pp. 70–79 (2018). https://doi.org/10.1007/978-3-319-72998-5_8

17. Liu, S., Fu, Z., Yu, B.: A two-level QR code scheme based on polynomial secret sharing. Multimedia Tools Appl. **78**, 21291–21308 (2019). https://doi.org/10.1007/s11042-019-7455-1

18. Tan, L., Lu, Y., Yan, X., Liu, L., Chen, J.: (2, 2) threshold robust visual secret sharing scheme for QR code based on pad codewords. In: Yang, C.-N., Peng, S.-L., Jain, L.C. (eds.) SICBS 2018. AISC, vol. 895, pp. 619–628. Springer, Cham (2020). https://doi.org/10.1007/978-3-030-16946-6_50

19. Luo, X., Liu, F., Lian, S., Yang, C., Gritzalis, S.: On the typical statistic features for image blind steganalysis. IEEE J. Sel. Areas Commun. **29**, 1404–1422 (2011)

20. Li, F., Zhang, X.: Steganalysis for color images based on channel co-occurrence and selective ensemble. J. Image Graph. (2015)

21. Avcibas, I., Memon, N., Sankur, B.: Steganalysis using image quality metrics. IEEE Trans. Image Process. **12**(2), 221–229 (2003). https://doi.org/10.1109/TIP.2002.807363

22. Kodovsky, J., Pevný, T., Fridrich, J.: Modern steganalysis can detect YASS, vol. 7541, p. 754102 (2010). https://doi.org/10.1117/12.838768

23. Fridrich, J., Kodovsky, J.: Rich models for steganalysis of digital images. IEEE Trans. Inf. Forensics Secur. **7**(3), 868–882 (2012). https://doi.org/10.1109/TIFS.2012.2190402

24. Holub, V., Fridrich, J.: Low-complexity features for jpeg steganalysis using undecimated DCT. IEEE Trans. Inf. Forensics Secur. **10**(2), 219–228 (2015). https://doi.org/10.1109/TIFS.2014.2364918

25. Song, S.K., Gorla, N.: A genetic algorithm for vertical fragmentation and access path selection. Comput. J. **43**(1), 81–93 (2000). https://doi.org/10.1093/comjnl/43.1.81

26. Liu, F., Yan, X., Lu, Y.: Feature selection for image steganalysis using binary bat algorithm. IEEE Access **8**, 4244–4249 (2020). https://doi.org/10.1109/ACCESS.2019.2963084
27. Ni, J., Ye, J., YI, Y.: Deep learning hierarchical representations for image steganalysis. IEEE Trans. Inf. Forensics Secur. 12, 2545–2557 (2017). https://doi.org/10.1109/TIFS.2017.2710946
28. Yang, L., Cao, X., He, D., Wang, C., Wang, X., Zhang, W.: Modularity based community detection with deep learning (2016)
29. Wei, L., Gao, P., Jia, L., Liu, M.: Image steganalysis based on convolution neural network. Appl. Res. Comput. **1**, 235–238 (2019)
30. Li, L., Zhang, W., Qin, C., Chen, K., Zhou, W., Yu, N.: Adversarial batch image steganography against CNN-based pooled steganalysis. Sign. Process. **181**, 107920 (2021). https://doi.org/10.1016/j.sigpro.2020.107920
31. Chen, B., Li, H., Luo, W., Huang, J.: Image processing operations identification via convolutional neural network. Sci. Chin. (Inf. Sci.) **63**(03), 275–281 (2020)

Author Index

Printed in the United States
by Baker & Taylor Publisher Services